Routledge Revivals

Handbook of Primary Education in Europe

Published in 1989 in conjunction with the Council of Europe, this book is a major source of reference for those interested in the comparative study of primary education in Europe.

Whilst there is much material available at secondary level, there is little information about the organisation and practice of primary education in different European countries. This book, based on reports and case studies collected by the Council of Europe as part of its five-year project *Innovation in Primary Education in Europe* remedies this providing an essential resource in the area. Divided into six sections, each contributed to by member state of the Council of Europe, this book covers topics including organisation policy and practice, professionalism in primary school teachers and innovation in primary education.

Handbook of Primary Education in Europe

Edited by Maurice Galton and Alan Blyth

Routledge
Taylor & Francis Group

First published in 1989
by David Fulton Publishers

This edition first published in 2018 by Routledge
2 Park Square, Milton Park, Abingdon, Oxon, OX14 4RN
and by Routledge
711 Third Avenue, New York, NY 10017

Routledge is an imprint of the Taylor & Francis Group, an informa business

Publisher's Note
The publisher has gone to great lengths to ensure the quality of this reprint but points out that some imperfections in the original copies may be apparent.

Disclaimer
The publisher has made every effort to trace copyright holders and welcomes correspondence from those they have been unable to contact.

ISBN 13: 978-0-8153-6640-9 (hbk)
ISBN 13: 978-1-351-25888-3 (ebk)
ISBN 13: 978-0-8153-6642-3 (pbk)

COUNCIL OF EUROPE

Founded on 5 May 1949 to achieve greater unity between the European parliamentary democracies, the Council of Europe is the oldest of the European political institutions. Its headquarters is the *Palais de l'Europe* in Strasbourg, France.

Through a flexible system of co-operation between governments, members of parliament and experts, the Council of Europe seeks to protect and develop human rights and democracy and to harmonise the policies of its twenty-three member states in a wide variety of fields including education, culture, social welfare, health, architectural heritage, environment, local government and justice, but excluding defence.

★ ★ ★

The Council of Europe's work on education and culture is run by the Council for Cultural Co-operation (CDCC) in which the Council's twenty-three member states (Austria, Belgium, Cyprus, Denmark, Finland, France, Federal Republic of Germany, Greece, Iceland, Ireland, Italy, Liechtenstein, Luxembourg, Malta, Netherlands, Norway, Portugal, San Marino, Spain, Sweden, Switzerland, Turkey, United Kingdom) are joined by the Holy See and Yugoslavia which have acceded to the European Cultural Convention.

The CDCC works to:

- bring the new ideas, techniques and achievements of each of its members to the notice of all;
- increase contacts and co-operation between European educators;
- take up questions of importance identified by the European Ministers of Education and Culture;
- develop mutual aid among member states;
- make the people of Europe aware of their common heritage.

David Fulton Publishers Ltd
2 Barbon Close, Great Ormond Street, London WC1N 3JX

First published in Great Britain by
David Fulton Publishers 1989

British Library Cataloguing in Publication Data

Handbook of primary education in Europe.
1. Western Europe. Primary education
I. Council of Europe. II. Blyth, W. A. L. (William Alan Lansdell), 1921–
III. Galton, Maurice, 1937–
372.94

ISBN 1-85346-091-5

CONTENTS

List of Contributors

PROFESSOR ALAN BLYTH
Alan Blyth has taught in schools, colleges and universities in England. From 1964 to 1983 he was Professor of Education in the University of Liverpool, where he is now an Honorary Senior Fellow. His writing has mostly been in the field of primary education and the primary curriculum. During the 1970s he directed a curriculum development project in primary humanities and has acted as consultant to a primary social studies project in Singapore. He is at present completing a book on assessment in primary humanities.

DR MATS EKHOLM
Mats Ekholm has directed the Swedish School Leadership Education Programme since 1975. This project, sponsored by the Swedish National Board of Education, is open to all head teachers and deputy head teachers. Dr Ekholm's research interests are in the field of school improvement and school development. His most recent English publication, co-authored with Mathew B. Miles and Roland Vandenberghe, is *Lasting School Improvement: Exploring the Process of Institutionalisation* (1987).

JOSS ELSTGEEST
Joss Elstgeest works at the Regional Pedagogic Centre of Zeeland in the Netherlands, producing teachers' and pupils' materials for primary science. He has worked in Tanzania (1957–73) where he was actively and productively involved in the African Primary Science Program. He has worked on the UNESCO Maths and Science Teacher Education Project at the University of Lesotho (1973–76). As a member of the Committee for the Teaching of Science of the International Council of Scientific Unions (ICSU/CTS) he has taken part in various activities promoting primary science education and teacher training throughout the world.

PROFESSOR MAURICE GALTON
Maurice Galton is Director of the School of Education at Leicester where he has directed a number of large-scale observation studies of teaching and learning in the primary school. His latest book, *Teaching in the Primary School*, is published by David Fulton, also the publisher of this Handbook. Professor Galton was a consultant on the CDCC Project No. 8, 'Innovation in Primary Education'.

PROFESSOR ERIC HOYLE
Eric Hoyle is Professor of Education and Head of the School of Education at

the University of Bristol. He was a school teacher for nine years before becoming a lecturer in a college of education. He was a Senior Lecturer in the Sociology of Education at the University of Manchester before moving to Bristol University in 1971. His major interests are school management, the processes of educational innovation, and aspects of teaching as a profession: status, roles, professionality, careers and professional development. From 1980 to 1986 he was Consulting Editor of the *World Yearbook of Education*, during which period he edited, amongst other volumes, *The Professional Development of Teachers* (1980) and *The Management of Schools* (1986). In 1987 he published *The Politics of School Management*.

DR ROGER HARTLEY
J.R. Hartley has been Director of the Computer Based Learning Unit in the School of Education at Leeds University since 1972. His general research interests concern software design and strategies of using software to support learning. In primary education in mathematics, this work has included both adaptive practice and LOGO-like learning environments. A current project in science is concerned with using some of the techniques of artificial intelligence in software designed to stimulate and assist conceptual change in children's thinking. Among his listed publications are 'Learning from computer band learning' in *Science Journal for Studies in Science Education* (vol. 15, 1980) and 'Question answering and explanation giving in on-line help systems' in J. Self (ed.), *Artificial Intelligence and Human Learning* (1988, pp. 338–60).

MOGENS JANSEN
Mogens Jansen trained as a teacher and then studied psychology at the University of Copenhagen. Since 1967 he has been Director of Research and Development at the Danish Institute for Educational Research and in 1987 he became the Institute's acting Director. He is a leading authority on motor tongue language teaching, particularly beginning reading, and has published extensively in Denmark and also in Germany and the United Kingdom. His best known English writings are *The School is more than Subject Matter* (1976) and two editions of the Book of Reading (1983 and 1989). He is an honorary member of the International Reading Association.

DR DOOK KOPMELS
Dook Kopmels is director of the Regional Pedagogic Centre of Zeeland (RPCZ), a support centre for primary education and special education in Zeeland, one of the twelve provinces of the Netherlands. The centre employs 70 people (50 in full-time jobs including the administrative staff) and assists 277 schools.

Dook Kopmels started his professional life as a primary teacher. After five years he became headmaster of a primary school in one of the big cities in the Netherlands. The school was one with many children from socially deprived families and ethnic minorities.

MARCEL LEURIN

Marcel Leurin studied at the Free University of Brussels and was a primary teacher from 1949 until 1933 when he moved to the Inspectorate. He now has special responsibility for multicultural education and for educational priority areas. He is a consultant to the Free University of Brussels, where he is director of the 'normal' course for special needs education.

DR ROGER MERRY

Roger Merry is head of the primary PGCE course at the School of Education, University of Leicester. He moved into teacher training after having taught for six years. His particular interests are cognitive psychology and special educational needs. Publications include articles in visual imagery and a range of topics in the area of special educational needs, including a section of the Macmillan Teacher Information Pack. He is currently involved in writing a series of books for children and their parents and another series of story books for beginner readers.

PROFESSOR KLAUS SCHLEICHER

Klaus Schleicher is Professor of Comparative and International Education, University of Hamburg. He has been responsible for national and international reports on 'pre-school, family and media education'. His special interests are in human ecology and multicultural education.

Publications include: *Familienbildung. Dringlichkeit–Aufgabe–Möglichkeit* (ed. 1977); *Elternitsprache und Elternbildung* (ed. 1973); *Elternhaus und Schule. Kooperation ohne Erolog?* (ed. 1972); *The Use of Television in Pre-School Education in Sparsely Populated Areas* (1977); and *Sesame Street für Deutschland?* (1972).

JEAN-MICHEL SIVIRINE

Jean-Michel Sivirine studied geography at university and then lectured at teacher-training college. He moved to the local education inspectorate before returning to teacher training as a director of a college. Subsequently he moved to the French Ministry of Education where hs assumed responsibility for educational provision for the children of ethnic minorities. His is currently a regional inspector in the Ministry and was the general *rapporteur* for the CDCC's Project No. 8 'Innovation in Primary Education'.

He is the author of 'Ecole, immigration, dynamisme externe', in *Ecole de la démocratie* (1988).

NORMAN THOMAS

Norman Thomas taught in primary schools for fifteen years, the last five as a head teacher. He joined Her Majesty's Inspectorate of Schools for England and Wales in 1962, retiring as Chief Inspector for Primary Education in 1981. He has since conducted reviews of primary education and in-service training for a number of local authorities and advised a parliamentary select committee for its 1986 report on primary education. He holds honorary professorships at

Warwick and Nottingham universities. He was a member of the national committee which advised on the assessment of children's progress in the National Curriculum.

MONICA GATHER THURLER

Monica Gather Thurler trained as an educational psychologist in Geneva and Tübingen (FRG). She is currently carrying out research with Professor Martin Huberman at the Faculty of Psychology and Education at the University of Geneva while lecturing, part time, at the University of Fribourg in Switzerland. She specialises in assessment, in knowledge dissemination and utilisation and in educational innovation. From 1981 to 1986 she was jointly responsible for the Swiss Primary School Innovation Project (SIPRI) and in this context was her country's representative on Project No. 8.

DR DAVID WINKLEY

David Winkley studied at the Universities of Cambridge and Birmingham and has a doctorate in philosophy of Oxford University. He has published and lectured widely and is the author of a recent book on LEA advisers and management, *Diplomats and Detectives*. He is a member of CATE, head teacher of Grove School, Hansworth, and current Director of the National Primary Centre. He has been Gwilym Gibbon Fellow of Nuffield College, Oxford.

Introduction

The Council of Europe's Council for Cultural Co-operation (CDCC[1]) has maintained, as a part of its regular activities, a series of projects in different spheres including education. During the 1970s, attention was paid to pre-school education (Woodhead 1979) and to the 14–19 age-range, and it was felt that in the 1980s the CDCC should devote a new project (No. 8) to another basic concern of all the member states of the Council, one that falls between the other two, namely primary education. It was, however, felt that this was an age of rapid change in primary education, one that called for and frequently saw planned innovation under way, and so the title decided for the new project was 'Innovation in Primary Education'.

The project was initiated by requests to member states to submit national reports on primary education, which could form a valuable resource for all those concerned with the study, administration and practice of primary education in Europe and beyond. In addition, a conference was held in November 1982 at Vaduz, in Liechtenstein, on the theme *Primary Education in Western Europe: Aims, Problems and Trends* <DECS/EGT [83] 64>.[2] This conference raised a number of interesting and important matters, which were reflected in the national reports as they were being written, and which have continued to concern the CDCC in subsequent years. Guidelines and priorities were suggested for the conduct of Project No. 8 and for the Project Group appointed to supervise it. In addition to the national reports that were to be produced (augmented by one from an associate member of the Council of Europe at that time, Finland), a programme of symposia on particular topics was encouraged, and a network of 'contact schools' was established in various countries to be visited by representatives of the CDCC during the 1980s.

These suggestions were vigorously implemented. Most of the national reports were submitted to Strasbourg in 1984; the programme of seminars and conferences and workshops (see Appendix 2) was sustained; and in 1987, under the guidance of the Project Group, a Final Report was drafted <DECS/EGT [87] 23>. Having magisterially surveyed the current situation in primary schools in their social context and the nature and practicability of innovation, the Report set out 'not only to summarise current thinking and research on the subject [viz. innovation in primary education] but to place them in a dynamic context by means of conclusions and recommendations'. The Report makes stimulating reading, and will be referred to elsewhere in the present volume. Its final suggestion was that the accumulated documentation from Project No. 8 itself should be 'disseminated in a satisfactory manner'.

The present Handbook is one outcome of that recommendation. The CDCC and the Project Group were anxious that the outcome of the project, and in particular the national reports, should be made more widely available. The joint editors, one of whom had been a member of the Project Group, were invited to undertake the task of producing the Handbook on lines proposed by the Secretariat of the CDCC, embodying both the national reports and the wider outcomes of Project No. 8. Thus the Handbook itself constitutes a further step in the process of considering primary education in Europe, and is issued in full recognition that other developments, some foreseen and others unpredictable, will take place before the end of the millennium. Yet it is valuable, a decade before AD 2000, to present to a wider public some impression of primary education in Europe today, not just as an exercise in comparative study, but also as a basis for reflective and constructive approaches to opinion formation and policy making within and between the Council's member states and beyond.

Over the many centuries during which the character of European primary education has been shaped, the education of younger children has been viewed from many perspectives: as an introduction to Christian belief; as a prelude to secondary and higher education in the humanist mould; as a means of establishing national identities; as a phase of life in its own right; and now perhaps as a foundation for particular political ideologies or technological skills. In the member states of the Council of Europe and their historical forerunners, and of course elsewhere too, various combinations of these perspectives have been salient at different times. Yet there are some features that distinguish primary education in non-communist Europe from its counterparts elsewhere. It is not characterised by one dominant ideology. It is not brought from overseas in the wake of colonisation, or blended with ancient cultural traditions developed elsewhere, or designated as a means of creating and sustaining new nations. So, despite its various manifestations and its distortions not so long ago under Nazism and Fascism, it does manifest some unity; and that unity has been reinforced by the growth of European institutions of differing range and scope, and in particular by the Council of Europe itself, now to be augmented by the adherence of San Marino and Finland and by the participation of Yugoslavia in its educational and cultural activities. It is this unity, and its attendant diversity, that this Handbook endeavours to express.

Project No. 8 has no exact forerunners. Because of the autonomy permitted to member states in their participation and in the submission of the national reports, the project does not constitute a rigorously designed piece of research, or even a looser instance of action research, in comparative education. The reports themselves provide a wealth of interesting detail about primary education in the different countries, and convey an impression of innovation, more substantial in some cases than in others; but this detail requires supplementation from official national and international statistics if it is to be used for strict comparisons between countries or times. Perhaps the most original feature of the reports is that they are the outcome of a joint initiative by the member governments of CDCC, rather than of world-wide organisations or of independent research bodies, in the field of primary education.

Although there are no strict precedents for the project, it is useful to set its outcomes alongside some previous and well-established sources of data. Those with the widest base are mostly associated either with UNESCO or with the International Bureau of Education. Both have produced vast banks of statistical data, and both have been linked with the series of Year Books, global in scope, which have been maintained since the Second World War. These Year Books, although each has been devoted to a theme of current importance, do also yield a narrative of change within national systems as well as internationally, and, in this narrative, primary education is fully represented. Both agencies have also sponsored substantial publications, and one UNESCO publication is particularly relevant to Project No. 8, namely Robert Dottrens' world-wide survey of primary curricula three decades ago (Dottrens 1962). Some of the data and interpretations included in that publication do enable some direct comparisons to be made with the project's data. A valuable addition to this repertoire of comprehensive information is the description of 159 national systems of education in a recently published encyclopaedia of comparative education (Postlethwaite 1988).

Some international coverage is also provided by monitoring services such as the *Bulletin signalétique: sciences de l'éducation* (Paris, CNRS). Another agency covering the more developed world countries is the OECD, whose Centre for Educational Research and Innovation (CERI) has fostered a number of corporate studies, one of which, on *Creativity of the school*, has evident relevance to Project No.8, though it was not specifically confined to primary education (CERI 1978).

Smaller-scale studies proliferate at the national level, and figure in some cross-national comparisons in the major comparative journals. In addition, there have been studies in the European Community (e.g. Elvin 1981; Neave 1984). However, the CDCC itself has undertaken the most substantial initiatives in Western Europe. The two earlier projects have already been mentioned, and mention should also be made of Project No. 7, on 'Migrants in Europe', to which reference will be made in subsequent chapters. In addition, there is a substantial series of other publications including conference reports (e.g. Van der Eyken 1982) and expert commentaries (e.g. Benattig 1988). One journal, *Western European Education*, though not itself a Council publication, carries regular reports of CDCC activities. Prior to any of these, the Council gave its approval to a monumental survey of European educational institutions by Schultze (revised edition 1968), which, together with Mallinson's scholarly survey of most of the member states (Mallinson 1980), constitutes a necessary baseline for any serious study of education, including primary education, in this continent.

This array of comparative material is immense, but less so than might at first appear. For on the international scene, including the major comparative journals, studies in European primary education are not very well represented. Maybe there is thought to be more interest and urgency in other matters such as secondary and especially higher education, education of migrants, apprenticeship, pre-school provision, the education of children with special needs, and the daunting problems of education in developing countries, alongside which mainstream primary education in the European context may appear commonplace. As already indicated, the CDCC itself adopted something of this order of priorities in deciding its programme of projects. As for the comparative journals, it is a pleasant surprise to find even an occasional article specifically about primary education in European countries, though relevant data can be abstracted from some of the more general articles.

It is hoped that this Handbook will, by the very fact of its production, go some way towards establishing the legitimacy and importance of this field of study, both nationally and on the comparative plane. That is a purpose that it is equipped to serve, though again with the reservation that the data from the national reports themselves should be cautiously used if they are quoted for comparative purposes.

The origin of the Handbook, and its sponsorship, have to some extent determined its organisation and contents. It does not purport to cover every aspect of primary education, but rather lays emphasis on those aspects that Project No. 8 and the authorities in each country considered of particular importance. Meanwhile, a deliberate attempt has been made to avoid neglecting other elements in the education of younger children, and these are referred to in Section 2 and elsewhere, though not always in specific chapters.

Section 1 is intended to establish something of the aims and context of primary education in Europe. It is followed by the most substantial part of the book, in which the national reports from Project No. 8, in many cases brought up to date since their original submission in 1984, are presented and analysed.

The remaining sections are all concerned with specific issues that Project No. 8 singled out for consideration. In Section 3, on 'The new basics', particular attention is paid to the three subject areas – language, mathematics and science/technology – which have come to be widely regarded as the core of the primary curriculum. Some of the most important cross-curricular issues such as multicultural education, organisational questions, parental participation and school-to-school continuity, which attracted particular attention in Project No.8, are discussed in Section 4. Section 5 recognises the obvious centrality of teachers and teaching, and of the professional education of teachers. It is noteworthy that recent developments in this field have rendered teachers more ready to welcome well-conceived innovations and more willing to consider the relevance of research in relation to innovation, the theme of Section 6. That final section embodies the essence of Project No. 8 itself: Innovation in Primary Education.

The authorship of the various chapters reflects quite substantially the membership of Project No.8 itself, supplemented where necessary by acknowledged experts from among the member states. It has not proved possible to maintain an exact balance in authorship across the various countries, but broad representation has been an important consideration in deciding who should be approached to write chapters. In one or two instances it became necessary to forgo contributions from authors who were unable to find time to write, but other able authors were forthcoming to take their places. A decision was taken to pool the chapter bibliographies at the end of the volume, so that the consolidated bibliography may provide a serviceable collected introduction to source material on aspects of European primary education.

Perhaps that is in itself significant. Students in individual European states have in many cases shown limited awareness of developments elsewhere in their own continent. Indeed, the vast scale and publicity of research and comment in the United States, and elsewhere in the English-speaking world, have militated against pan-European understanding and research in primary education, as indeed elsewhere in the field of education generally. It is a strange reversal of the situation in the previous century, when the ideas of Pestalozzi, Froebel and Herbart were eagerly espoused and developed in the Normal Schools that proliferated during the expansion of the USA. The monitoring of the 'contact schools' in some member states by representatives of others during the currency of Project No.8 may symbolise the intensification of mutual understanding that is desirable. The educational consequences of the 1992 changes in the EEC will provide an additional justification for the extension of a European dimension in primary education. A further reason for maintaining a dialogue about primary education, and other aspects of education, among members of the Council of Europe is the likely extension of contacts with the socialist countries of Eastern Europe, among whom there is substantial recognition of a shared European heritage, together with a curiosity, now capable of more overt expression, about the ways in which that heritage has developed differently in the western part of the continent. For it is becoming widely recognised again that Europe has a long tradition of cultural unity which, despite all its divisions and conflicts, has given rise to so many of the world's unifying concepts, including that of universal primary education itself.

Notes

1. These initials, derived from the French version of the title, are regularly used in English publications.
2. References to unpublished CDCC material will be given throughout in this format. Such material is listed separately in the Bibliography and in Appendix 2.

SECTION 1

PRIMARY EDUCATION IN EUROPE: AIMS AND CONTEXT

Introduction

Alan Blyth

Primary education is a process that takes children as they are, and leads them towards what they can become. It starts from a context and moves towards an aim. There may in fact be a series of contexts and a number of aims, but that basic model of the process of primary education remains the same.

This is recognised in the Handbook, and is in accordance with the intentions of Project No. 8. Section 1, concerned with aims and context, has precedence not only over the more specialised topics considered later, but over the national reports themselves, which must be seen in the light of aims and contexts. In the first chapter, Professor Norman Thomas surveys aims that are common to the European tradition, though differently interpreted in different member states. In doing so he in fact draws upon the national reports as well as on other relevant material. The general context is considered next by M. J.-M. Sivirine, with special reference to demographic, social, cultural and technological changes. These two chapters necessarily touch upon each other's themes, and indeed upon the national reports and much that appears later in the book; but, taken together, they set the scene for what follows, and indicate clearly the ambience within which European primary education takes place.

CHAPTER 1.1

The Aims of Primary Education in Member States of the Council of Europe

Norman Thomas

The definition of educational *aims* used in this chapter is as follows: they are statements about the directions in which one wishes to go. They may be broad or narrow, general or specific. For example, it may be an aim that children should use and develop their powers of communication; or that they should spell in conventional ways. Aims are different from objectives, which identify either a final or an intermediate level of achievement. Aims do not, for instance, propose which or how many words should be spelt conventionally at a given stage of a child's education; but an objective may.

It is tempting to think of primary education as though it were innocent and pure so that it could be conducted in the unsullied interests of children and without being stained by those of the outside world. The temptation should be avoided. If the context within which primary education operates is taken as given, there may be too little critical examination of its effects. Primary education's purposes are conditioned by and, to different degrees, condition both its conduct and its circumstances. To expand on one part of the inter-relationship: the purposes of primary education are constrained by what is feasible, and what is feasible depends upon the talents of the adults and children engaged in it and the support they receive from the community. Furthermore, while primary schools should be regarded as providing a distinct stage of education, their effectiveness also depends upon what is done with children before they are first admitted, upon their experiences outside the school, and on how secondary schools build upon what they have done.

In consequence, this chapter on the aims of primary education is divided into four sections: children as individuals; the requirements and constraints of society; primary education as an educational stage; and some reflections.

1. Children as individuals

Widely held tenets of society in Western Europe in the 1980s include respect for the uniqueness and rights of individuals. It is not surprising that these are reflected in the aims of primary education by member states of the Council of Europe. They are treated in a number of different aspects. In particular, the rights of individual children are recognised in the determination of countries to make primary schools places to which children wish to go. Ways of achieving that goal include: Portugal's intention that children 'discover and develop their interests'; Norway's requirement that children should be participants in their education; Denmark's insistence that daily life in the school must be based on intellectual freedom and democracy; and the trend in a number of countries to involve children in the assessment of their own progress.

At its most idealistic, concern for individuality leads to the view that provision should be made so that each child, though different, can develop to the full. The requirement has led some to question whether more specialist teaching needs to be introduced into primary schools (e.g. Italy: Ghilardi 1988), while others such as Liechtenstein are strengthened in their intention to provide 'more security for the pupils' through improvement of the system of class teachers. We shall come to some restraints on the meaning of 'full' later on, but the general intention has some profound implications for primary education. Most are positive, though there are negative outcomes also, at least potentially, especially if the notion leads to a supposition that there are predetermined limits to learning: a point where the individual is full.

Full can be understood in two senses. It can refer to the range of activities and learning on which a child is engaged, or it can mean that each child should make as much progress as he or she possibly can. We begin with the first.

The range of the educational programme

In most of the countries in the project, the expressed aim is to provide a wide-ranging education at the primary stage, covering children's intellectual, social, moral and spiritual, emotional and physical development. None of the member states excludes any of those as being irrelevant, though the spiritual element may relate to knowing about religious ideas, rather than believing in them, or be chosen to fit with the beliefs of parents, as in Spain. All want children to be informed about their place in history and in today's world, and to acquire knowledge of the natural world. Liechtenstein reports some difference of opinion over whether such an all-pervading ambition as full development is realisable in a small country. Some – including Spain, Cyprus and Belgium – place more emphasis than others on the development of the imagination, aesthetic and artistic appreciation and expression when judged by the papers submitted, and the French paper refers to 'sustained efforts to promote *musical* and *artistic* education'.

The overall aim, then, is to provide an education service that touches all aspects of human development that are capable of being educated. The contributory aims may be stated in broad and in specific terms. For example, it may be thought to be enough to acknowledge the importance of physical development and well-being; or there may be specific reference also to teaching children about a balanced diet. The encouragement of aesthetic response usually includes reference to music as well as to the visual arts, but may or may not include mention of the use of musical instruments. Views about the priority that should be given to some parts of the curriculum as compared with others are sometimes revealed by making some activities compulsory and others voluntary. For example, choral singing is an extra or voluntary activity in Austria. The availability of options may also stem from a view about differences in the talents of children – for example, provision for exceptional interest and skill in playing a musical instrument. Otherwise, differences of detail in the documents may be indications of what was at the front of the mind of a writer rather than a real difference in day-to-day practice in schools.

The balance between first-hand and second-hand sources

Looked at from a child's point of view, the development of breadth implies a curriculum that allows access to and the use of knowledge about what people believe and what they do; about the characteristics of the environment (living and non-living, near and far – in both distance and time); and about the part he or she might play in the circumstances of life. It is difficult to envisage how these aims could be satisfied unless children have opportunities to test out their growing skills and concepts. If the trialling process is to fit such a broad set of aims, it needs to encompass social behaviour and the exercise of social influence. It must also incorporate practical investigations and use of the environment, including the materials and objects of which it is composed. Certainly, the ways in which aims are expressed usually imply that children learn at first hand as well as at second hand, as in Malta's expressed intention to help children acquire an active attitude towards problems; Austria's determination to encourage independent judgement; and Denmark's aim to give children the chance to make independent assessments, evaluations and form personal opinions. Ghilardi (1988) comments on the Italian 1985 Act No. 104, noting that the role of the teacher has 'undergone a deep transformation' in which he or she is 'asked to organise a "learning environment in which each pupil is able to gradually develop his own field of action, of planning and testing, of exploration, of thinking and of individual study" '. But the roots of primary schooling may so bias practice as to make it desirable that the case for a non-sedentary education is made even more strongly.

Literacy and numeracy

The history of compulsory formal education is short – even in countries such as Norway, where compulsory basic education has existed since the eighteenth century. Its traditions everywhere have ensured that special emphasis is, rightly, placed on teaching children to read, write and calculate, skills that are often referred to as *basic*. The purpose has been to widen children's opportunities to learn and to engage in social life, especially but not only in paid employment. The needs of the children and of society have been and remain in tune in these respects as the operations of society have become increasingly complex. In the early years of compulsory education it was plainly absurd to expect illiterate parents to be responsible for teaching their children to be literate. Teaching children to read was a job for the school. Attitudes, once struck, have a way of persisting. For example, in England and Wales it has only been during the last dozen years, and after more than a century of compulsory education, that a significant number of teachers have began to suppose that parents might have a part to play in the process.

The seizure of the words *basic* and *elementary* by the educational establishments for the early stages of reading, writing and arithmetic has been powerful, and generally accepted by the lay public. Yet the usage hardly stands examination if one thinks about the prior requirements of speech, motor control and social interchange, for all of which parents continue to be the informal teachers in the earliest stages.

Social development

The question of when children are ready for school is decided in light of perceptions of their social maturity as well as of their capacity to learn. Contextual questions relating to social aims will be considered in the next section, but there is no escaping the fact that a child entering school – even if he or she has experienced pre-school education – engages in a major shift of social experience and learning. In Switzerland it is recognised that 'during the 1st school year pupils must progress from play to a set activity and submit to a certain discipline'. Teachers of young children must pay a lot of attention to their pupils' need to accommodate to their new circumstances, and there is no shortage of aims reflecting upon children's social attitudes and competencies. The Spanish paper signals the importance of 'developing the ability to coexist', and the Portuguese contribution argues for a balance between school culture and everyday culture; for the development of individual and team work; for the acquisition of positive attitudes, habits and co-operation conducive to good family relationships and thoughtful, responsible involvement with the environment.

Yet one seldom has the impression on visiting schools that this aspect of children's learning is thought of positively as a part of the curriculum. The stress is on persuading children to behave in ways that conform with the requirements of the school. Behaviour is more likely to be discussed with children at length when it is aberrant than for the purpose of making explicit the variety of ways in which co-operation can profitably take place, the kinds of roles that group members may adopt, and the ways in which individual initiative can best contribute.

The common approach, necessary but not sufficient, is that the teaching and learning are *about* social behaviour and organisation through subjects such as the local environment, geography, history, social studies, civics and notions of democracy, at least two of which form part of what is taught in the primary schools of each member state. These are, of course, important routes through which children learn about their cultural heritage, are helped to understand how the past has shaped the present and something of the complexity of the modern world. The learning needs to be linked to daily life inside and outside the school.

Some countries, for example Portugal, require specifically that schools should 'bring about a national awareness of the world situation, from a standpoint based on universalist humanism, solidarity and international understanding'. In many Western European primary schools the actual teaching is more mundanely concerned with bringing the children's attention to the extent to which they rely on the efforts of people in their own country and elsewhere to provide raw materials, including food, and manufactured goods for daily life. The stories of people who behave in commendable fashions provide models of good behaviour. The sympathies of children for others worse off than themselves are often aroused and may lead to positive attempts to compensate, for example through fund-raising for charities or the 'adoption' of a child in a Third World country.

On the other hand, much learning is on an impersonal, even grand scale. Teachers in France are more encouraged than they were to help children to relate their learning to everyday experience. Nevertheless, by the end of the primary stage they are expected to have covered pre-history, pre-Roman Gaul and the Gallo-Roman period, the High Middle Ages, the twelfth- and thirteenth-century renaissance, the Ancien Régime, the French Revolution and the Empire, the changes brought about during the nineteenth century, the two world wars, and the period since 1945 (Lewis 1985).

The place of local and foreign languages

Perhaps it is right to refer under 'social development' to the teaching of two, three or more languages in primary schools. There appear to be three motives.

One is the perpetuation of an indigenous language that is not the main language of the country, or is one of two or more main languages. Examples include Frisian in the Netherlands; Welsh in Wales; Irish and English in Ireland; Gaelic in Scotland; Flemish, Walloon and German in Belgium;

French, German and Italian in Switzerland; French and German as well as Luxemburgish in Luxembourg; Sami or Lapp in Norway and Sweden, and Finnish in Sweden; Catalan in Spain. There can be dissatisfaction that the local language is not given sufficient regard, but the principle that it should be taught where appropriate is widely accepted. To have three languages taught as in Luxembourg - in addition to meeting the language needs of non-nationals - is time consuming and may act as a constraint on other aspects of the curriculum. Luxembourg is considering how far the constraint can be overcome by shortening the lessons and increasing their number.

The second motive is to teach children their home language if it is that of immigrant parents or even grandparents.

The teaching of languages introduced by recent immigrants raises two main considerations. The first concerns integration. It is the experience, for example in the Federal Republic of Germany, that many post-1939 immigrants arrived believing they would stay for a few years and then return to their former homes; and that the intention to return permanently often fades with time. If the in-comers and their children, more and more of them born in the new country, are to become settled, is it not best that they should forget their foreign language and ways and be integrated as soon and as completely as possible? The opposing and prevailing view welcomes the enrichment of the national character the newcomers bring and worries that too large a proportion of immigrants and their families are in lower-paid forms of employment or none, and that their condition is exacerbated by low expectations of them by the indigenous population, and also by low expectations the children may have of themselves. Everything should be done to raise expectations, to acknowledge the worth of the home language and culture, and to make sure that children know of people from their culture who have made significant contributions to mathematics, science, music and art - to learning generally - and who have succeeded in their new countries.

In *Länder* of the Federal Republic of Germany and in the Netherlands, as examples, teaching uses the home language as a medium of instruction. In those Swedish schools where there are 'many immigrant children of the same origin in a school at the junior and the middle level they often form bi-lingual classes'. The practical difficulties of providing home-language teaching in some schools are formidable: there are schools in the United Kingdom where more than ten languages, even more than 40 languages, are spoken by the pupils. Supplementary schools are supported financially, but run by members of the ethnic-minority group. They help children to acquire both literacy in their home language and knowledge of their religion and culture. In some ordinary schools, teachers familiar with both the national and the home languages are members of staff, either full time or on a visiting and advisory basis. There may also be ancillary workers, from the children's language groups, employed to work under the general direction of teachers. They use the national and the home language interchangeably. It is very doubtful whether the practices best suited to these children have yet been fully evolved in any country.

The third motive for teaching more than one language was formalised in the recommendation of the Committee of Ministers of the Council of Europe (Mallinson 1980). It is the wish to introduce children to a second, widely spoken language, the choice often being English because of its use internationally. Some countries, such as Sweden and the Netherlands, have responded more positively than others to the notion that a second, widely spoken language should be introduced. Worry in Italy, shared by others, was that it is difficult for children to learn a second language before they have sufficiently mastered their own (Mallinson 1980), but Law No. 104 of 1985 requires the teaching of a foreign language from 1987. In the United Kingdom, uncertainty stems also from the effort that was made in the 1960s to teach French in primary schools (Burstall 1974). Doubts are less to do with desirability than with practicality, for the indigenous population has not been renowned for learning modern languages other than its own and there may be difficulty in staffing the teaching of a modern foreign language for all even in secondary schools when the national curriculum is introduced.

Other adaptations of the curriculum

It can also be necessary, as in the Sami area of Norway, to make other adaptations to the curriculum and the distribution of school time to allow for local circumstances. Perhaps that is no more than an extreme case of making provision so that the curriculum can be seen to be relevant to local life, even to the point where the characteristics of a school's catchment area influence the choice of content. The matter is dealt with in Denmark by making some parts of the national curriculum compulsory and allowing variety in others.

Physical development

Some aspects of motor control have already been acquired by normal children well before they come to school. They can sit, walk, run, jump. In countries where they begin school at 7, most children can control scissors, a pencil, a paint brush or crayon when they are first admitted. Some can by 5.

Teachers continue to be interested in children's control of tools and equipment. Handwriting is an important skill and the aim may simply be to develop legibility and reasonable speed, though it may extend to settling on a chosen style. Drawing and painting are universal activities that call on the imagination as well as on manual skill. In some countries more than others, children are encouraged to make things because they will be attractive to look at (e.g. figures or pots from clay); or because they might be useful (e.g. a book to write in, a meal to eat or an item of clothing); or because they are part of an investigation being undertaken in the curriculum (e.g. a model of an old house, or working traffic lights to aid the understanding of traffic movement); in places, micro-computers are used to control models.

Opportunities for improving gross motor control continue to be of wide interest in European schools. They are directed at enhancing balance, speed and variety of movement, and the encouragement of climbing, jumping, ball control, and team games. The teaching of swimming is thought of as a school responsibility in some places and not in others.

There is also concern for healthy living in other senses. Sex education is part of the curriculum in some countries and may deal with human sexual relations, or with the study of plants and animals, or both. Diet, road safety and, more recently, the dangers of abusing drugs are of increasing interest.

A child should achieve as much as he or she can

The other sense of fullness relates to the depth of children's achievement and itself has two aspects. One relates to the appropriateness of what children are taught day by day: is what they do taking them into new ground or merely allowing them to exhibit what they already know? The second relates to their long-term achievements and contains a notion of potential, which may have some use when selecting aims but carries a dangerous infection leading to suppositions of ultimate limitation when attached to objectives.

Taking children as far as they can now go

It is obvious that the aims adopted should be appropriate to the children to whom they are applied; it is not always so easy to apply the truism in practice. Teachers have experience of the range of achievements exhibited by children of a given age, yet it is widely thought that teachers' expectations more often underestimate than overestimate children's competence. That might be too simple an interpretation of what researchers observe. Children can sometimes do both more and less than teachers suppose - more if the children have had the background experience and opportunities to examine its implications critically; less if they are asked to interpret events without knowledge of the underlying factors, and are accustomed to remembering standard explanations rather than arguing ideas through on the basis of personal and general experience. The importance of taking account of what children comprehend and can do is undeniable, and acknowledged in references such as that in a paper, submitted by Sweden, that warns of the importance of feeding back to schools the results of experience and research.

Earlier in this chapter it was argued that the emphasis on literacy and numeracy in primary education is partly due to the development of primary schools from basic or elementary schools. The message on the obverse of the coin is that children of primary school age are at a stage in their development when they can make a formal beginning to learning to read, write and calculate: progress in an aim should be realisable as well as desirable. Assumptions vary about exactly when it is best to start teaching children to read and write, and the choice made has an effect on the entry age for formal education. In the United Kingdom, the belief is that most children can make a start by 5 and increasing numbers of children are enrolled at 4 plus. Changes in the Netherlands in recent years have brought together nursery and primary education and have been accompanied by the view that children can achieve literacy earlier than was supposed. Across the member states, the age of admission to primary school and the beginning of the formal teaching of reading ranges in practice from 4 to 8 plus.

The problem is not simply to decide when to begin one aspect of teaching. It is also necessary to form a view about how the different aspects relate to each other. The issue may seem to be more a question of objectives than of aims, using the definitions adopted here, but the issue crops up in papers submitted to the Council of Europe. That from Greece refers to the matter explicitly when it expresses the need for a *harmonious and balanced* development of the intellectual and psycho-physical abilities of pupils, and refers to the importance of developing pupils with integrated personalities. These intentions are highly significant in deciding what to do and when, day by day, in the classroom. At the simplest of levels: should this child be given more practice in measuring to an accuracy of 2 mm, or is the priority to introduce the child to an author whose work will give insight into dealing with conflict in a small group? What differences of perception led the government in the United Kingdom, unusually at the time, to stimulate the use of microcomputers in primary schools; and the *Land* of North-Rhine–Westphalia in the Federal Republic of Germany to argue that 'the principle of teaching "according to age" makes a systematic examination of the new technologies inadvisable at the primary level'. In this case it must surely have been a difference of view about the purposes of introducing children to microcomputers: (a) to aid learning generally, and (b) to teach children how computers work and how to program them. It could hardly have related to real differences in the children.

One's opinion about balance in the curriculum is based on perceptions about what children can do, about what it is now important for them to get better at, and about the resources available and their use. The allocation of time is one means by which balance might be achieved; it does not, in itself, provide a definition of balance. The essential problem is to identify the stages of learning in the various aims and to relate them to one another. The search for balance across the curriculum calls for the description of these stages against which children's achievements can be assessed. Anyone who supposes that can be managed with high precision will be defeated by human nature and the complexity of what must be learnt.

Taking children as far as they can ever go

Another sense of *full* development assumes that there is a limit to what children can be taught, and that the limit should be reached. The work of the Council of Europe on Permanent Education ought to have scotched the notion, but it lingers still in the backs of our minds and is associated with the ideas of potential and general intelligence. Even if true, they are unhelpful in what should be the optimistic process of helping children, day by day, to extend their powers and their perceptions. Perhaps most invidiously, the assumptions currently depress the expectations of too many teachers about what children from materially poor homes may achieve.

There are no known upper limits to what children can eventually do. As the papers from member states indicate, children change over time. Mr Honeth, of the Swedish Ministry of Education, made the point strongly at the Vaduz conference, and the paper from Malta reminds readers that children mature physically earlier now than in past decades. They have more sources of information, through television, video-recording and micro-technology, than earlier generations. By comparison with their predecessors, they are changed by the circumstances in which they live. The changes include the possibility and speed of travel; and the greater mix of religious, cultural and racial groups. The changes must be taken into account by schools, even though one knows that there are also children in every territory, from Ireland in the west to Turkey in the east, who live in communities that are indigenous to the neighbourhood, rarely meet people from any other culture in the flesh, and seldom or never get to the nearest large town.

Individual differences

Expressions of aims in the various countries recognise individual differences. 'Full' is not the same for everyone. Allowances should be made for differences due to children's age, ability and aptitude, in their interests and beliefs, in their preferred techniques and methodologies. These differences should, within limits, be fostered. Differences of language and culture should be provided for; but negative attitudes concerning race, culture and gender should be corrected. The paper from Greece stresses that educational provision has to be available irrespective of a child's sex or social class.

Some children, on grounds of maturity, may be admitted to school in Austria and the Federal Republic of Germany at earlier or later ages than apply to the majority. The decision is taken by the headmaster, on advice from a doctor and in consultation with parents. Parents in any country need to be unusually strong-minded to withstand the combined might of the doctor and the head. Nevertheless, this permitted flexibility of response to individual differences is by no means repeated in all member states, and the starting age may be closely defined and applied.

Even moderate differences between children, well within what may be regarded as a normal range of achievement at a given age, have implications for the organisation of teaching and learning within a primary school. The practice of requiring children to repeat a year is said to be diminishing in some countries where it has long been prevalent. In Austria's report of 1988, 13 per cent of children started school later than most of their age group. In North-Rhine-Westphalia the corresponding figure in 1984/5 was 8.6 per cent (House of Commons 1986), and the age-range in a reception class may be as much as 2 years 6 months; in 1982/3 the percentages of children not moved up at the end of the 2nd, 3rd and 4th years were, respectively, 3.4 per cent, 2.6 per cent and 2.1 per cent.

Where schools arrange children more strictly according to age, there may be special arrangements for teaching some children in small groups by employing a teacher additional to the class teachers. In Sweden, approximately 25 per cent of the state grants are distributed per capita and can be used mainly for two purposes: for extra support to pupils with difficulties; and for teaching small groups of pupils to facilitate individualisation. Whatever organisational solution is adopted, ordinary primary school classes contain children of a wide range of abilities, aptitudes and interests. The aim to provide for them according to individual need puts a considerable burden upon teachers, even in countries such as Luxembourg, which can claim that most primary school classes have fewer than 20 pupils and not many have more than 25.

Unless special support is provided, meeting individual differences is made more complex by the trend, in many countries, to admit to general primary schools some children who would a few years ago have been separated off into special schools for the handicapped. Many member states now share the view that the requirement is not to identify the mental or physical handicap and provide a label for the child accordingly; it is to identify any special educational need and provide for it with as little disruption to a child's ordinary life as possible - preferably in a mainstream school.

The balance between personal need and community membership

Is there no limit to the degree to which children should be taught differently to allow for their unique personalities and competencies? Should each child be taught, probably individually, according to his or her precise stage of learning and experience; or should attending school not also enable children to learn to accommodate the differences between them, give them the chance to work together, and allow them to experience the advantages of co-operation and team work in the classroom, the gymnasium and on the sports field? The papers provided by the member countries leave no doubt that there is wide agreement that it is important to encourage a sense of community and an awareness of how society is organised. The question is: how does one balance the two aims, one of which stresses the servicing of individual differences, and the other of which gives pride of place to membership of a community? The practicalities of teaching may count as much as principle in the chosen solutions.

2. The requirements and constraints of society

The previous section discussed the aims of primary education mainly from the points of view of the teachers and children. In this section, the main consideration will be: what does society require of primary education and its pupils?

The first point to be made is that there is less stress on development to the full, and more on accepting priorities and constraints characteristic of the society that provides the education. This is not reprehensible in principle: one's view in any particular case depends upon one's opinion of the society making the requirement. The principle is illuminated in many of the reports from member states. That from Iceland quotes an Act of Parliament on the needs for co-operation between home and school and for preparation for life in a modern democratic state. The Act requires that schools should 'endeavour to widen the children's horizon and develop their understanding of their environment, social conditions, the characteristics and history of Icelandic society and the obligations of the individual to society'. The already quoted periods of history to be covered in French primary schools have an understandably French bias. The Norwegian Basic School Act of 1969, as amended in 1975, requires the basic schools 'to help give the pupils a Christian and moral upbringing'. The Swedish curriculum 'reflects the view of the democracy on society and man, the implication being that human beings are active and creative and that they both can and must assume responsibility and seek knowledge in order to co-operate with others . . .'. The official aims of primary education in Turkey require schools to 'enable every Turkish child to acquire all the necessary basic knowledge, skills and habits required for effective citizenship and to raise him in a manner commensurate with national ethical concepts'. Children need to know that they must obey the rules of society as well as use them; contribute to social well-being as well as draw from it.

There are complications. No society is static, though some – world-wide – are more stable than others. It is not sufficient simply to act in accord with today's social practices and ambitions: everyone who can should assist in improving the general lot, socially and materially. As seen by the current providers – and there is no intention here to imply that any other stance could reasonably be expected at government level – the changes should be within limits that are acceptable to current society. In the words of the Icelandic Act: 'the school must foster independent thought *and* co-operative attitudes' (emphasis added).

Change may be on an individual or wider scale. The stimuli for change stem from different sources:

(a) The acceptance and promotion of modern scientific and technological developments

It is no accident that the national curriculum introduced in England and Wales in 1989 includes science as well as English and mathematics among its core subjects, and technology among its foundation subjects for primary schools. It is unlikely that science would have been given the same priority or technology have appeared at all for the primary stage even as recently as 20 years ago. Portugal requires schools to keep pupils abreast of new knowledge. Section 9 of the Netherlands Primary Education Act requires that science, including biology, is taught in primary schools, and Mr van Eijndhoven at the Vaduz Conference <DECS/EGT [83] 64> heralded the arrival of micro-computers in Netherlands' primary schools. In Malta, 'it is a fact that innovation . . . was prompted by radical changes in contemporary society and the challenge children have to cope with owing to new discoveries in science and technology'.

(b) Changes in the cultural, racial and religious make-up of the community

The populations of many countries of Western Europe have, in recent years, become far more mixed in culture, race and religion than they were. They contain a substantial number of families who speak languages and, to a marked degree, retain life-habits they brought with them from afar. Some children may speak little or none of the national language of the country when they first enter school. Those children may be concentrated in districts where they form a large part of the school population: almost 100 per cent in a small proportion of schools. In the city of Luxembourg, 55 per cent of school children are foreigners.

The main issues referred to in the aims of primary education in countries experiencing these changes relate, on the one hand, to the indigenous population and, on the other, to the ethnic minority groups. It has to be remembered that many children of once-immigrant families were born in their new country: they are not immigrants. Indeed, many children in primary classes are the grandchildren of immigrants, for their parents also were born in the country of their domicile.

The minimum aim with regard to the indigenous population is, usually, that its members should exercise tolerance towards and understanding of the newcomers. They were, after all, permitted and even encouraged to enter the country to fill gaps in the existing workforce. Better still, the indigenous population should welcome the presence of the minority ethnic groups because of the skills and cultures they bring, not only in music, art and food, but also in richness of language. The presumption is that tolerance will grow as knowledge grows and contact between groups increases.

For the minority groups the issues are often sharper. Maintenance of one's religion, culture and language contributes to one's sense of identity. Acceptance of the principle that home languages should be maintained was discussed earlier, though it is not always realised as well as it should be.

Providing for the home language is not enough. Individuals do not have a full range of opportunities open to them, in either education or employment, unless they can speak and write the national language in its standard form. Generally speaking, provision is made, although there can be difficulties for children who enter the education system late. In Luxembourg, as in a number of other countries, special classes in the local language are set up for new entrants. In the United Kingdom, teachers may be specially funded and employed to assist children who have little or no English. In the Federal Republic of Germany, Turkish supplementary teachers are employed both to help children with their own language and to assist them when German is the language of instruction.

(c) Political change

Where there have been marked changes in the political beliefs underpinning the government of a country, they are reflected in the strength of expression in some educational aims. In Spain and Portugal, recently emerged from authoritarian and nationalistic regimes, there is more than ordinary stress on children as citizens of the world and on the freedom of individuals and their rights, including the right to participate in decisions about their own lives as soon as they are ready.

Variation in the national demand

Some differences within a country are regarded as necessary to the national character and supported through the school system. Notably they include the preservation and development of indigenous languages spoken by a minority of the population and discussed previously. In some countries there is a strong delegation of authority to local levels so that differences among them can be reflected. Reference has already been made to provision for the Sami population of Norway. The *Folkeskoler* in Denmark are encouraged to relate their curricula to local circumstances. In the Netherlands, Denmark and Norway, schools may be established that operate according to the preferred pedagogies of the founding group and be supported financially by the government. For example, a group may establish a school based on principles advocated by one or other of the educational pioneers such as Dalton, Montessori, Peter Peterson or Rudolf Steiner. Indeed, the same variety may be achieved within the different *Länder* in the Federal Republic of Germany. In the United Kingdom, it was the case that schools' curricula were settled locally, almost completely by the wishes of the head and teachers of the school, but that is no longer so since the national curriculum was introduced in 1989, under the Education Act, 1988 (though timetables and methodology will still be decided by schools, as will aspects of the curriculum that fall outside the national requirements, and may be chosen to suit local circumstances).

Many countries have some schools that are sustained by fees charged to parents, or from charitable or other private funds, including voluntary contributions via the church, mosque or synagogue. Schools serving particular religious foundations may also be grant-aided by a state.

Parents make contact with, influence and may take part in the conduct of a school, and in doing so express opinions, offer advice and possibly take part in the appointment of staff. Whatever the precise mechanism – whether through the opinions expressed by an elected parent on a school committee (for example, the combined parent/teacher group that makes up the French school board), or informal discussion between parent and teacher about a missing article of clothing, or the search of the prospective fee-paying parent for a suitable school – schools are open to the influence of adults who are close to them but not members of their staffs. In countries such as Turkey, issues may be discussed by the elementary education councils established in villages.

Some limits to variety

There are practical limits to the notice schools can take of the wishes of individual parents or other interested groups. Not only the content but also the pedagogy has to be reasonably consistent within classes and across a school, though, rarely, examples can occur of a school within a school. In one establishment visited in the Netherlands, some classes were taught by standard methods and others by a Montessori approach. The parents chose which classes their children attended.

The ethos and pedagogy of a school are frequently finely tuned to the needs of the community it serves, but schools must offer an education acceptable to the nation to which they belong. Schools, including primary schools, are tools of the community. Even those financed independently of the state are permitted to exist only in so far as what they do is tolerated by the nation as a whole. The point is clearly made in the Italian paper: 'all schools, state-controlled or otherwise, public or private, must comply with the national legislation . . . with . . . decrees and regulations.'

Schools' conformity to national requirements may be achieved through the establishment of national criteria and inspection. Various systems of inspection operate and, with differences of balance from one country to another, they report (a) on the conduct of individual schools and (b) on the quality of the educational system as a whole. In doing so they may have to concern themselves with schools' role in reducing some regional differences. Children may be taught to use a standard form of the national language rather than the local dialect, as occurs in the German-speaking areas of Switzerland, where an aim is to move children from the spoken dialect to the form of German used in writing. Sometimes the practice is to add the standard form of the language to the child's repertoire rather than to replace the dialect. Perhaps this is a lesson to be learnt from teachers of children whose home language is wholly different from the national language: many have found it beneficial to make explicit their recognition of the high quality of the home language as a means of communication. That is not to disguise the fact that the ability to use the standard form may be vital to a child's social and economic progress.

3. Primary education as an educational stage

Primary education draws strength from the fact that it is the successor of basic or elementary education. Few people doubt that it is essential. It suffers in status (almost but not quite as much as pre-school provision) from the fact that it is dealing with young children who do not require subject specialist teaching to the extent common in the secondary stage. On the other hand, if the children are to be taught well, the work calls for considerable skills of organisation and teaching, knowledge of children and how they learn, and insight into the concepts embedded in subjects.

In particular, teachers need to be able to introduce children to formal education in ways that establish positive attitudes towards learning and create expectations of success. They need to help the children make the transition from the less formal social climate of their home and perhaps the kindergarten or nursery school. They must also teach the children to acquire skills such as handwriting, to read and write as means of communicating, and to use everyday tools and instruments. None of these requirements belongs exclusively to any academic subjects but they are essential to all.

Pre-school to the primary stage

The common aim is to provide a system of education in which children make progress as they move through each stage and as they move from stage to stage. In some countries pre-school provision is regarded firmly as part of the education service, while in others it may, wholly or in part, be the responsibility of the social services or depend upon voluntary effort, for example by the churches; though sometimes voluntary effort may be supported by the state. In the Netherlands, pre-school and primary school provision are now combined, and closer ties are growing in a number of other countries, including Belgium, Finland and Sweden.

The nature of the provision affects the contact and continuity between primary schools and pre-school provision. Sometimes it can be good on a personal level between the head of the receiving school and those responsible for the younger children, especially if the services operate in the same building. It is unusual, except where the provision is firmly within the education service and not always then, to find co-operation effective at the level of continuity and progress in learning.

Continuity within school

It is common practice for schools to keep records of children's achievements so that they may report to parents and to the next teacher. In Italy, a teacher has generally taken the children right through their primary school, and so secured progression and continuity within the school. As with almost all solutions to real problems, there is a cost: the children do not have the chance to meet a range of teachers with different enthusiasms, skills and styles.

From primary to secondary school

In some countries, for example in Finland, Denmark and Norway, the primary stage is part of the full comprehensive school. In Norway, the model plan is that classes remain intact throughout the years of compulsory schooling. In others, such as France, Italy or the Federal Republic of Germany, primary education is provided in separate schools. It is certainly arguable that continuity is easier to achieve within a single school, though those with separate stages of education would probably argue that full-range schools find it more difficult to establish an ethos that is suited to the younger children. The view taken may be more a matter of local perception and custom than of universal natural law.

Whether or not classes remain intact, the organisation of their teaching usually changes over the course of time. The discussion taking place in some countries about whether a class teacher can continue to provide all that is needed was mentioned earlier. In France, a multi-teacher system is introduced at the intermediate level.

Perhaps it is easier to secure continuity and progression where the curriculum is centrally determined, though it takes determination to develop common ground in countries such as Cyprus, where the Department of Primary Education is separate from the Department of Secondary Education. Where that difficulty does not occur, at least there is agreement about the programme to be covered. It may be just as important that there is a common terminology within and between schools. Where those conditions prevail, as in the Federal Republic of Germany, France or Ireland, there seems no current demand that teachers' assessments of pupils shall be calibrated nationally. In England and

Wales, where a national curriculum has been introduced for the first time for many decades, the form rather than the fact of calibration is the issue for political debate.

Not all countries are as determined as Greece and Norway that children should be grouped into classes by age and not by ability. Children may move on from their primary school to a comprehensive school or to one of a number of schools offering different curricula. In the Federal Republic of Germany there is a small number of comprehensive schools, but most children go to the *Hauptschule* or the *Realschule* or the *Gymnasium*, the last providing the most academically challenging course. A somewhat similar range of secondary schools occurs in France and elsewhere. In England, children in most areas transfer from primary to comprehensive secondary schools but, in a smaller number of areas, they go either to an academic, grammar school or to a secondary modern school. The systems of transfer in the multi-type secondary school areas are quite different in some *Länder* in the Federal Republic of Germany as compared with England. Heads of primary schools in the FRG advise parents about which school would suit their child best, but the parent may disregard the head's advice. In England, the matter is virtually always decided as a result of tests in verbal reasoning or English or mathematics or a mixture of these.

4. Some reflections

One should not be surprised that the member states of the Council of Europe agree so closely in their statements of aims for primary education. They have, after all, come together in the Council because they share common interests; they also share interlocking histories. Even more today than formerly, their populations intermingle and have drawn in others from outside. The moral and religious beliefs that underlie the behaviour of their peoples recognise the uniqueness of individuals and that an individual has responsibilities to others. Their populations engage in a mixture of agricultural, industrial and commercial undertakings and require complex organisations of government that call for a literate and numerate population. They are going through a period of rapid change in technology, in their access to information and of material expectations. Some of the activities require a high level of specialist education, for which a primary school foundation is vital.

The differences between them are differences of degree, emphasis and balance. The differences in the primary education received by their children occur not because the aims are different but because they cannot all be applied at once with equal strength. Sometimes the needs of an individual can take priority; sometimes they must give way to the needs of the group; sometimes aims can be held in balance. The Irish paper of 1988 makes a distinction between enabling the child to live a full life as a child, and equipping 'him to avail himself of further education'. While the two aims may be in accord, they may not always seem so to a child practising handwriting on a warm summer day. There are teachers who would seize such an opportunity to walk their pupils by the river, get them to use their eyes and ears and to stretch their tongues; but the handwriting must take priority on enough days if the children are not to be at a disadvantage later.

Some children would be surprised to hear that their teachers and even the government thought they should develop to the full. Why, if so, should anyone stop them playing tricks or fighting for their rights? Full development, not surprisingly, turns out to apply only to those parts of development of which the teacher approves; and here the different levels of tolerance between teachers within a country may be more pronounced than the general differences between nations. Nor is it wise to guess what the level might be from the pedagogical model used.

In a more particular sense, the intention to extend a child's competence in one aspect of learning may have to be set against the search for progress in another. The more time and effort that teacher and children spend singing and playing musical instruments, the less time there is to manipulate paint and clay. So choices have to be made at national, local or school level about time allocations and about how the levels of achievement in different curricular areas match.

But caution is needed. The timetable is a way of organising learning: of bringing together materials, facilities, teachers and children. It may be finely or broadly defined. It is often used also as the single means of prescribing and analysing the curriculum. Unfortunately, that is a practice that encourages the belief that it is possible to establish a taxonomy in which each aspect of the curriculum can be and is dealt with separately in its own periods and, even worse, that these separate parts add up to the whole. Opportunities for reinforcing one strand of learning by connecting it with others are diminished and may even be lost: children need to develop their powers of language, spoken and written, in a wide variety of contexts, whenever they occur during the school day. Where the timetable is used to define the curriculum, proper recognition and prominence are seldom given (to use an earlier example) to teaching children the broader lessons to be drawn from the social changes experienced on entering school. The process of social adjustment seems to get in the way of learning rather than being an opportunity for learning. The effect on teachers' attitudes and probably on children's attitudes to formal education are considerable: the uni-dimensional analysis of the curriculum creates the so-called hidden – and thus unexamined – curriculum.

Opportunities for an idiosyncratic interpretation of aims arises if there is often a confusion between aims and objectives. That leads to aims being end-weighted. But if an aim is a direction, then it is as important to be on course in the early stages as in the later, perhaps more so. More thought given to where one is at the current stage ought to strengthen the chance of achieving the desired improvement over time, and has immediate relevance in judging what is being achieved and what should be done. The confusion is seen at work strongly when it is supposed that children should learn how to perform a skill before they learn how to apply it, as though a toddler should learn the tongue and lip movements and to synchronise its breathing before being allowed to try to communicate through speech. It is not that the processes of acquiring a skill and applying it should be approached the other way round, but that the two go hand in hand, sometimes one predominating and sometimes the other.

There are many reasons why aims may be interpreted differently at the level of states, local communities, schools and classrooms. Not least, they are interpreted differently because individual men and women of singular temperaments and capacities have to apply them minute by minute in the busy circumstances of the classroom. Perhaps it is just as well that the certainty of variety exists, for none of us can be sure what is best for all children and all conditions of society, now and in the years to come.

Note

This chapter is based on the account of the conference on *Primary Education in Western Europe: Aims, Problems and Trends* <DECS/EGT [83] 64> held in Vaduz in 1982, on papers the member states produced later in the lifetime of Project No. 8, on the sources referred to in the Bibliography, and on the writer's personal experience.

Chapter 1.2

The Social Contexts of Primary Education in Europe

Jean-Michel Sivirine

This chapter's function is clearly to attempt to lay a factual and conceptual foundation for the subsequent chapters that, though not the only one possible, is at least homogeneous and convergent. It is important to make two preliminary remarks that are more than simple matters of politeness; they are much more like filters for what follows which the reader ought to assimilate completely and bear constantly in mind. Otherwise he might - and doubtless rightly - take exception to hasty generalisations in some places and to tendentious comparisons in others and, throughout, to a vision that seeks to be synoptic and therefore, given the space available and the mass of information to be dealt with, neglects other facts that are equally true.

The first of these remarks is as follows. Our old states of Europe are highly diverse and sometimes display profound differences in the organisation of their education systems in the broad sense and of compulsory education in particular. Whether one turns one's attention to the levels of organisation (what comparisons can be made between a 'local educational authority' in the United Kingdom and the French Ministry of National Education with its 1.2 million employees) or of decision-making, to the supervision of courses and teachers or to the school careers and guidance of pupils, it is easy to notice changes and differences that are more than mere nuances from one system to another.

Without of course forgetting this differentiated vision of reality, which renders it necessary to make allowances here and there, it seemed more fruitful to direct attention, through examining the 'context of primary education', to what unites the European education systems rather than to what sets them apart. It is a way of looking at things that is admittedly somewhat arbitrary but, because the point of view lies outside the individual school systems (which will form the thread of subsequent chapters) and necessarily leads to big questions about the links and relationships between 'European society' and its school, it is one that is potentially rich and promising for the future.

The second remark is perhaps more technical but leads to similar conclusions. Our society's vision of schooling forces our minds to divide the young into somewhat rigid age-groups: 3/4–6 years old constitutes pre-school (the continued survival of the word 'pre-school' is an interesting point in itself), 6/7–12 years old primary education, 12–16 years lower secondary, etc. Yet nothing proves that these cut-off points today have the same relevance as formerly, at least from the social point of view. The pace of social, family and cultural change, and the emergence of the 'youth society' that is one of its expressions, do not in fact fit well into such a rigid temporal framework for schooling.

It would, for example, be quite wrong to think that only those social and cultural changes directly affecting the 13–18/20 years age-group influence school systems: the over-intensive attention paid to adolescents and to their affirmation as a recognised social group with its particular distinguishing marks and forms of expression (fashion, music, language, etc.) and the feeling of people almost everywhere in Europe that it is on this vulnerable age-group that the major educational challenges of our time depend (democratisation, success for the greatest number, preparation for new technological developments, etc.) lead all too easily to the view that the younger age-groups (and the educational facilities designed for them) are in some way 'sheltered' from upheavals, pressures and radical changes.

Such a hasty conclusion would overlook:

- the fact that, just as the 0–12 age-groups form part of a family, social and cultural continuum, primary education is an integral part of the school system and that, as such, any change affecting one of the other levels of the whole system (lower secondary school, upper secondary school, university) necessarily affects it too, on the rebound;
- that primary education is, very directly, confronted with the first challenges arising from taking into consideration and developing all the child's potential at a time when the basic mechanisms that organise his/her behaviour and thinking are becoming established. It is for example well known, and beyond dispute, that although the effects of different success rates in school (related as the case may be to the head of family's socio-professional category, to the family situation, to the composition of the sibling group, or to the cumulated interplay of these and many other factors) are especially apparent in the sensitive 13–18 age-group, it is almost always at primary school that the first signs of future strengths and weaknesses appear, and that the mechanisms through which they are taken into account or remedied are or are not established.

This second remark, like the first one, naturally leads to the view that the relations between society and the school, complex as they are, can be studied and grasped only in an overall context; to my mind, it is impossible to limit oneself to such relations within the strict framework of an age-group or specific school system alone.

The enormous strength of the links uniting a society to its schools is self-evident. A single example, but not unimportant: we are fully aware of the impact, in the emergence and promotion of the idea of equality in the right to instruction, of the democratic principle of equality between all human beings. Conversely, access to formal education (and hence the establishment of compulsory schooling) is indeed the first step towards achievement of the democratic principle of equal opportunity and equal fulfilment of individual potential.

Should we then regard the school as a 'reflection', as a 'mirror', or rather as the 'seed of the future', the 'agent of change'? These questions, repeatedly debated among specialists, only become truly meaningful in this context to the extent that our European societies are faced with a whole series of profound and rapid transformations which exert their effects on different scales: macro-phenomena, such as the major trends in population or the economic crisis, but also phenomena that are more limited in scope and above all more diffuse, such as the emergence and affirmation of an adolescent and young people's culture or certain big changes in family life. It is important, and probably indispensable, to ask oneself about the consequences of such radical changes for the operation of our primary schools and, more broadly, for the role that the school itself can and should play in such processes of change.

In other words, it is essential to try to elucidate how the school reacts to the new demand upon it, and it is no less essential to make it clear that in any case the school cannot change everything: the networks of social interaction are so complex that we must, from the start, clearly and lucidly restrain the hopes that might be raised by a maximalist stance regarding the possibilities of the school as an agent of change.

We are all aware that a society struggling with the questioning and doubt engendered within it by modifications to its underlying values tends as a matter of course to turn towards its schools to find solutions. But this attitude shows up the fundamental ambiguity that governs the relationship that is influenced by two completely contradictory – at least at first glance – expectations.

The first expectation is that the school will provide the conceptual as well as pragmatic tools to permit the understanding and control of the changes. This corresponds closely to one of the essential roles of the school, which is to develop in its pupils a critical attitude towards the predominant system of social values (whatever the system and the values referred to).

At the same time, however, the school is regarded as a refuge, its task to preserve 'the sound roots of culture' (Brembeck 1966). This concords with the other major role of the school, which is to pass on the cultural heritage of the community – to pass it on, but also to uphold it.

In this context primary education does not appear as a homogeneous and perfectly circumscribed totality of knowledge and practices. It possesses its own internal dynamism that forces it to evolve and change; it now functions within a broader framework of multiform lifelong learning. In a society marked by change and uncertainty as to the future, it is clear that compulsory education can no longer provide young people with the knowledge and qualifications that they will need, immutably, throughout their lives. It must force itself to build in them foundations for the subsequent development of aptitudes and attitudes, always bearing in mind the need for adaptation.

It also appears, increasingly clearly, that the education dispensed by the primary school constitutes but one of the many paths in the overall process of education. It is necessary to take as broad account as possible of all the sources and all the channels, in addition to schooling, through which information reaches children and whose complex influence is doubtless essential to their development.

1. The demographic context

The demographic situation is obviously the most important of the major trends that can affect school systems since on it depend both total enrolments and intake flows, entirely in the case of compulsory education and to a great extent for the system as a whole.

The evolution of the population in European countries is generally comparable, the principal differences deriving from the period at which they entered the process of crisis that characterises that evolution. When we add the fact that any population change (upward or downward) exerts its impact on the educational structures with a considerable delay (5–6 years for primary education, 10–12 years for university), we can observe that, in the decade from 1970 to 1980, the same major phenomenon – the collapse of the birth rate – produced in Europe virtually every possible situation, from school systems already affected by the overall shrinkage in population to those whose enrolment of pupils was still stable, or even increasing (without counting the effects for many countries of the prolongation of compulsory education, with more and more young people staying on at school as a result of increased access to upper secondary and even university studies).

At the threshold of the 1990s, these differences are now no more than a question of nuance. All studies on the ageing of the population agree, and the consequences for the number of children, hence pupils, hence the 'raw material' of the educational systems, are worrying.

The demographic crisis

Everywhere the origin is the same: a trend reversal in birth rates, usually since the mid-1960s. The example of the Federal Republic of Germany is highly enlightening in this respect (Figures 1.2.1a and 1.2.1b). Two figures to back up this notion of 'crisis': between 1964 and 1978, the number of births fell by 46 per cent in the Federal Republic of Germany and by 34 per cent in the United

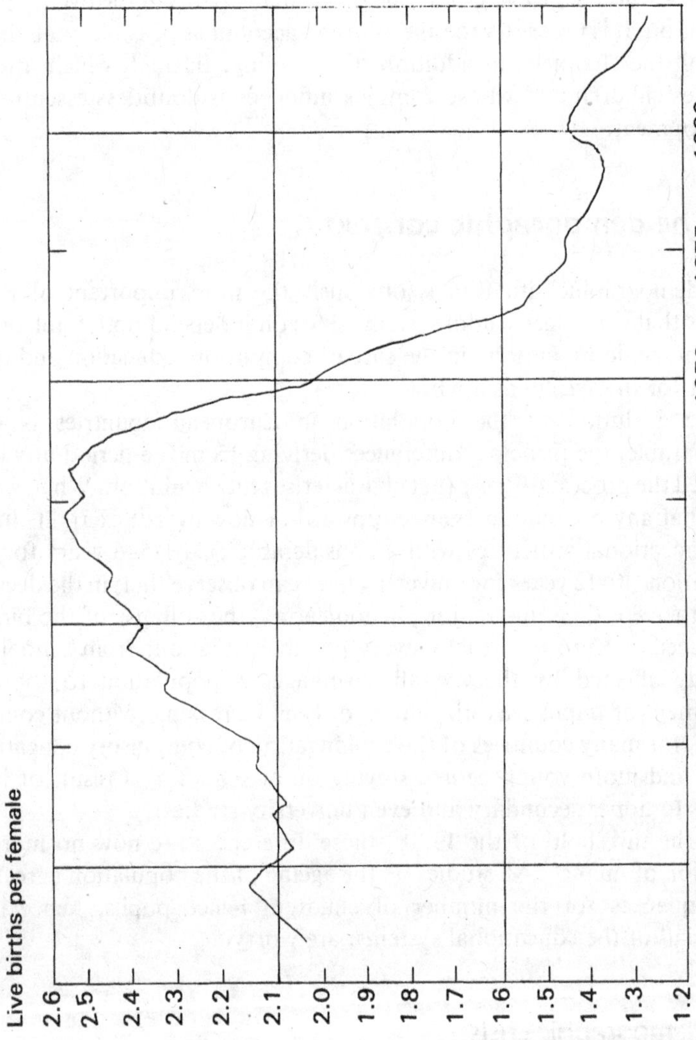

Figure 1.2.1a Evolution of the reproduction rate in the Federal Republic of Germany

Figure 1.2.1b Evolution of the population balance in the Federal Republic of Germany

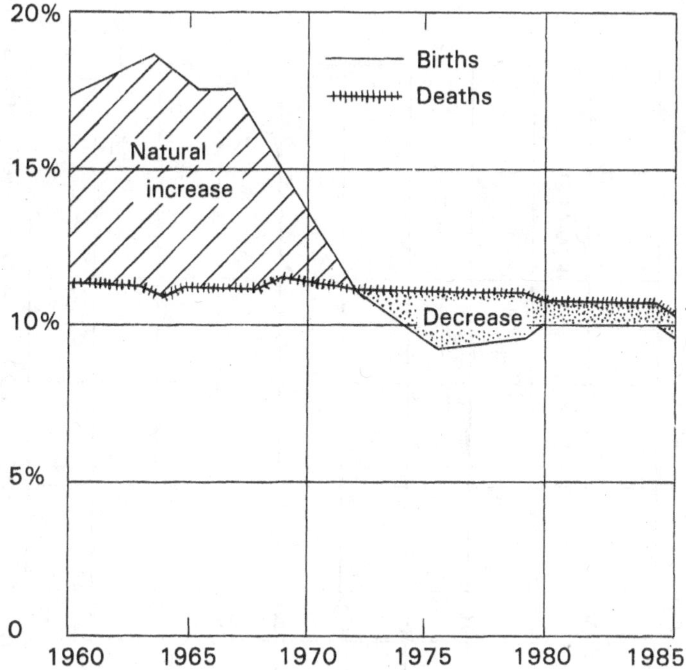

Kingdom. It should be recalled that the population renewal rate is 2.1 children per female. In many countries of our old Europe, this rate is now far from being achieved (in 1985, 1.8 children per female in France, 1.78 in the United Kingdom, 1.7 in Spain, Finland, Norway and Sweden, 1.6 in Portugal, 1.5 in Belgium, Austria, Switzerland, the Netherlands and Luxembourg, 1.4 in Italy and Denmark, 1.27 in the Federal Republic of Germany). It is already easy to discern the reduction in the number of young people and at present there is no sign of a reversal of the downward trend with a significant and lasting rise in birth rates.

The social consequences are incalculable and go far beyond the school itself. Whether dealing with questions related to a general ageing of the population, with the concern to maintain or renew the active population, or with the increase in social benefits (see section 2 below), all the analyses are in agreement: the 'sensitive' age-group, the subject of study and concern by both academic researchers and the public authorities, is changing before our eyes from those under 20 to those over 65 years old. The age pyramid of a country like France, where this population trend came relatively late (Figure 1.2.2), or the foreseeable evolution in Europe of the over-65-year-old age-group during

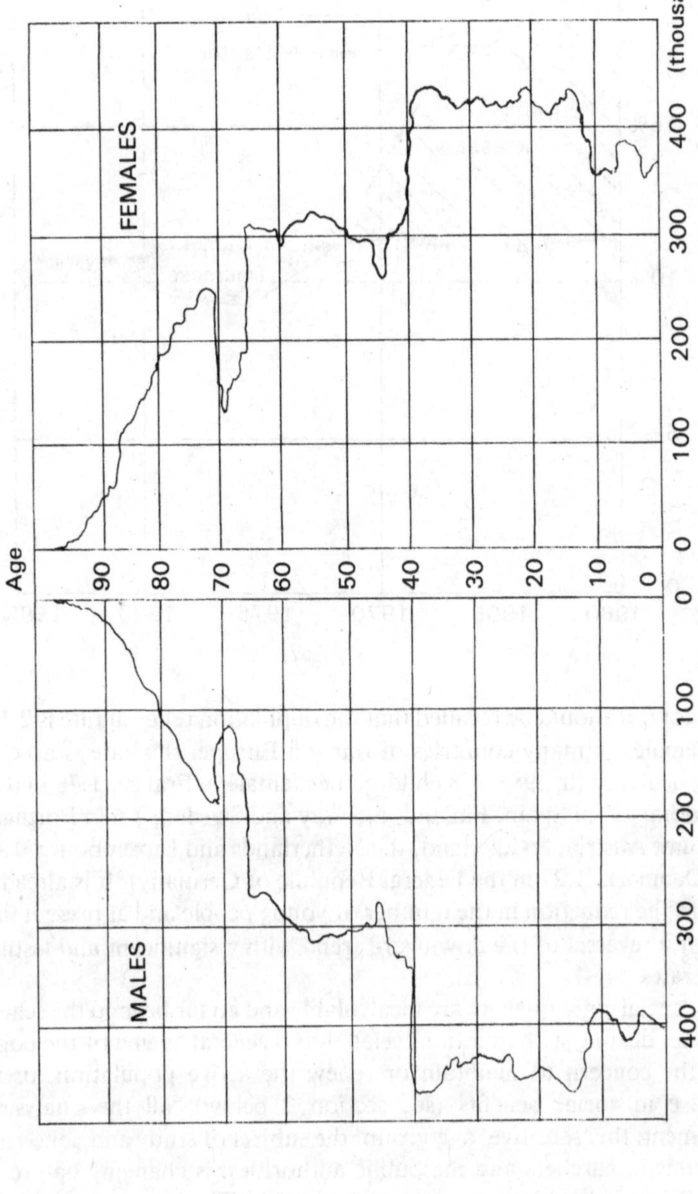

Figure 1.2.2 Age pyramid of France as at 1 January 1987

Table 1.2.1 Population aged 65 years and over (1980–2020) as a percentage of total population

	1980	*2000*	*2010*	*2020*
Austria	15.5	14.9	17.5	19.4
Belgium	14.4	14.7	15.9	17.7
Denmark	14.4	14.9	16.7	20.1
Finland	12.1	14.4	16.8	21.7
France	14.1	15.3	16.3	19.5
Germany (West)	15.5	17.1	20.4	21.7
Greece	13.1	15.1	16.8	17.8
Iceland	9.9	10.8	11.1	14.3
Ireland	10.7	11.1	11.1	12.6
Italy	13.5	15.3	17.3	19.4
Luxembourg	13.5	16.7	18.1	20.2
Netherlands	11.5	13.5	15.1	18.9
Norway	14.8	15.2	15.1	18.2
Portugal	10.2	13.5	14.1	15.6
Spain	10.9	14.4	15.5	17.1
Sweden	16.3	16.6	17.5	20.8
Switzerland	13.8	16.7	20.5	24.4
United Kingdom	14.9	14.5	14.6	16.3

Source: OECD

the next 20 years (Table 1.2.1) are highly significant. In this general context, it should be noted that the Republic of Ireland has long been, and continues to be, an exception. Thanks to the highest reproduction rate in Europe (over 2.5 children per female), the birth rate in that country is continuing at a very high level (19 per 1,000 in 1985) and the natural surplus remains large, with the result that the age-groups in school form a relatively large proportion since one-third of the population is under 15 years old. However, in Ireland as in the other European states, the number of pupils in primary education is beginning to drop after peaking in 1986 (see Ireland's national report in Chapter 2.2).

Owing to the delayed action referred to above, together with the already mentioned fact that everywhere in Europe the 1970s were characterised by the attempt to democratise education, the postponing of the age of entry into vocational training and a general lengthening of school careers, the two decades from 1960 to 1980 were still decades of quantitative expansion, in which pupil enrolments continued to rise, in some cases more or less smoothly but often with impressive jolts that caused a lot of worry for the authorities in charge of organisation and management. The outward signs and the effects are well known; two of them in particular cut across frontiers: the widespread increase in public expenditure devoted to education (and of the proportion of public expenditure in total expenditure on education), and the development of economic theories that raise education to the rank of a factor accounting for growth (Lesourne 1987).

The 1980s have been years of demographic recession; they have also been years of questioning about quality. In ten years, from 1977 to 1987, the total number of pupils fell by 5 per cent in Europe. Taken country by country, the change is even more remarkable: 12 per cent fewer pupils in the United Kingdom, 12 per cent fewer in the Federal Republic of Germany, only 1 per cent fewer in France; but if we consider the numbers in primary education alone (cf delayed action effect analysed above), the figures become vertiginous: during those same ten years, 37 per cent fewer in the Federal Republic of Germany, 24 per cent fewer in the United Kingdom, 8 per cent fewer in France. And the figures for Denmark, Italy, Norway, the Netherlands and Sweden, to mention only those countries, are comparable.

Later on we shall examine the consequences of such a situation for the educational systems, particularly in regard to the number of pupils per class and the recruitment of teachers. But it is important to realise here and now the seriousness of the problem thus confronting the systems and the general climate of concern prompted by the existence of this problem.

Population movements

Population movements provide the indispensable correctives to the above description of 'natural' trends (difference between birth rate and death rate).

Internal migration

The distribution of the population inherited from the nineteenth and the first half of the twentieth centuries brings out stronger contrasts in all areas, with economically active and highly populated zones coexisting alongside human deserts. Despite recent efforts at a deliberate and concerted planning of the economically less developed regions, nowhere do we observe a significant reversal of the trend; at best, the exodus of the population from rural and disadvantaged areas towards the industrialised cities has slowed down, but it has seldom stopped.

The interior of the United Kingdom (the mountainous areas of Wales, the Pennines, the Southern Uplands and the North of Scotland) accounts for 40 per cent of the territory but only 10 per cent of the population. The mountainous districts of east Portugal (Tras os Montes, Alentejo) have population densities 20 times lower than the coastal areas of Estremadura or the Algarve. In eastern and southern France, wide overpopulated valleys and coastal plains lie shoulder to shoulder with virtually empty regions. The examples could be multiplied at will, always with the same result: generally speaking, everywhere in Europe, the mountainous regions, the traditional suppliers of manpower for the low-lying and coastal areas, are continuing to lose their populations. Even if the Italian Mezzogiorno is now tending to halt this haemorrhage of able-bodied men and women towards the north of the country and abroad, the legacy is such a burden that it would be impossible to wipe out its effects quickly.

Everywhere this sharp inequality in the distribution of the population poses particular problems, such that we cannot measure the problems of a school in a rural or mountainous area by the same yardstick as those of an urban school (staffing ratio, size of classes, travel of the pupils, facilities, equipment, etc). For the highly centralised systems, which are based, even more explicitly than other systems, on geographical equality in the 'supply of education', this provides a major challenge and is still very much a problem.

International migration

The first point to note – which justifies our placing it after internal migration – is that international migration seems fated to reinforce the impact of internal migration. It helps to widen the gap between highly populated areas and areas losing their population: in the traditional countries of emigration it is above all the inhabitants of the less active areas (rural regions, mountainous areas, the highlands, etc.) who leave; for a long time this step was taken after an initial stay for a relatively short period in the towns and more developed areas of the country itself; increasingly often they now leave directly. In the host countries it is necessarily the active regions, those offering job opportunities and already the most highly populated and manpower-hungry, that attract the immigrants, first the worker and then his family. This concentration of migrants in very particular geographical areas (a phenomenon, let it be said, common to all migratory movements throughout the world in all periods of history) obviously has direct repercussions on the school and on the composition of the school population (Bastide 1982).

Beyond the general problems encountered by foreign children in the host countries, problems that we shall discuss later (the break, wound even, caused by the migration itself, contact with other cultures and civilisations, etc.), this origin of the migrants often poses real problems for the schools in which their children are placed, problems very familiar to primary teachers: these children, coming from little developed regions with usually inadequate school facilities, find in the school as institution, in its rules, its manner of operation and its particular 'culture', an additional difficulty that is sometimes impossible to overcome.

There are three qualifications that need to be made to this general presentation. Not all recent and on-going migratory movements in Europe are exclusively 'for work'; far from it. From the end of the 1950s the various upheavals, some of them dramatic, produced by the splitting up of the empires and decolonisation brought into the European mother countries (the Netherlands, the United Kingdom, France and, a little later, Portugal) a wave of populations from their former colonies. It is interesting to remark that, although the geographical origin remains the same, the composition of this flow of immigrants changes with time; from the return home of nationals frightened by the newly acquired independence of the territory in question (a movement often rather like political asylum) to the establishment of traditional migrations in search of work, only one factor remains common to all: the special links between the former metropolis and the former colony. Striking examples from among many others are the flows from Jamaica or India to the United Kingdom, from Algeria to France or from Surinam to the Netherlands.

The second qualification concerns political refugees. The geographical origin of such refugees is highly diverse (their common trait being flight from authoritarian regimes of which, alas, there has been no shortage in the last 30 years) but such refugees represent a mass movement only in the case of departures prompted by situations of post-colonial war: Southeast Asia, black Africa (in particular East Africa), Bangladesh, etc., whence the migrant flows faithfully reflect, at least initially, the former colonial link (France for refugees from Laos or Vietnam, the United Kingdom for those from Uganda or Pakistan, etc.).

Political refugees are to be distinguished from the mass of work-seeking migrants by at least two points, extremely perceptible at school:

- the departure affects all professional and social categories of the population (indeed, the first to leave are often the most wealthy categories);
- the mythical idea of the 'return' is much less strong and sometimes even absent.

This makes it easy to understand why the school does not treat them in the same way or reserve for them the same destiny as in the case of 'ordinary' migrants. On the other hand, political refugees, when seeking work in the host country, augment the geographical concentration of immigrants mentioned above.

The last remark has to do with the traditional distinction between country of origin and host country, which we know, just as traditionally, over-simplifies situations that are in fact diverse. This statement can easily be illustrated by means of two examples:

- First example: Portugal is both a country of departure (towards Latin America for a long time, then towards France and the Federal Republic of Germany) and a host country (Cape Verde Islanders, Angolans, etc.); Italy, for a long time a supplier of manpower for the mines and industries of Northern Europe is in the same situation, and its economy employs more than 500,000 workers from North Africa.
- Second example: a number of workers – and sometimes their families – migrate from one host country to another depending on job opportunities, the legislation on foreigners and the possibilities of reuniting the family. A large proportion of the Turkish community in France thus comes from . . . the Republic of Germany.

'One of the dominant themes in the history of mankind is migration. The large-scale European migrations in the post-war period can thus be considered a fresh manifestation of a phenomenon as old as mankind' (Lithman 1985).

There can be no question of dealing here with all the questions that this influx of migrants has posed and continues to pose to the societies of Western Europe. When we take the point of view of the school, which is our argument, two of these questions stand out with special acuteness: one concerns the straightforward demographic situation (number of migrants, place of settlement, number of children per family), and the other, an infinitely more complex and sensitive issue, concerns the meeting (or better, all the subtleties of the meeting) of different cultures.

From the demographic point of view, foreign children constitute a significant proportion of enrolments in primary education, often close to 8–10 per cent, but exceptionally 30 per cent and over (Luxembourg). As we have seen, this figure conceals profound regional disparities and, within a region, a municipality or even a local district, no less profound local disparities. In Europe, against a background of demographic recession where nationals are concerned, it is generally speaking no exaggeration to say that foreign children and children of foreign origin have in many cases made it possible to maintain, and sometimes to open, classes or even schools (and hence posts for primary teachers, headmasters, etc.). This point, not always properly stressed in national or international reports, has in contrast great importance for local authorities and the primary teachers themselves.

It is obvious that with enrolments in hundreds of thousands (in each country) or in millions (at the European level), the term 'foreign pupils' covers an extremely wide range of situations related of course to the type of migration (see above) but also to the nationality of origin and to how long ago the migration took place. Many of the most long-established migrant groups present an age pyramid (school population) that is inverted – relatively narrow at the base and gradually widening towards the top (a pyramid similar, or identical, to that of the nationals). In contrast, the most recent immigrants have a pyramid that is wide or very wide at the base, narrowing rapidly towards the top.

The fact is that the more or less positive attitude to reproduction of the immigrant populations changes in the host country, occasionally with spectacular speed. Though here again qualifications are needed owing to the great diversity of the populations concerned and their cultural practices, the overall picture for Europe is fairly concordant. After a few years, the immigrant populations adopt, as far as the number of children per female (or pre-school for infants at a nursery school or kindergarten) is concerned, patterns of behaviour similar to those of the native populations. Indeed, although the reproduction rate of immigrant women remains higher than that of native women, at least for the 'first generation', the trend towards assimilation of the host country's demographic behaviour is very rapid.

At the cultural level, the challenge is obviously quite different. Here we are faced with a real social problem which goes far beyond the primary school framework. It should be noted, however, that this problem is not new and that, with the Italian, Spanish or Polish waves of immigration at the beginning of the century, Europe experienced cultural conflicts that, in the expression of xenophobia and racism, more than matched the present-day outbreaks.

If the demands made upon the primary school through the presence of foreign children are felt to be – as, objectively speaking, they are – so severe, this is because the success of those children at school, inferior to that of national children, serves as a cruel indicator (the 'magnifying-glass effect' dear to the sociologists of education) of a number of dysfunctions.

First of all the non-success of migrant children echoes, for the school, the non-success of disadvantaged socio-professional categories. Whatever the system, the school norm remains primarily that of the liberal professions, middle-level and senior executives, and . . . teachers. Beyond the cultural conflicts (integration/assimilation, teaching of the host/native language, more open curricula, etc.), the fact that numerous foreigners come from civilisations different from that of Europe (Islam, India, Far East, Africa, etc.) exposes the school's difficulty in resolving the great dilemma of education for all/education for each individual, or how to reconcile the unity and universality of the education offered with the legitimacy of the recognised right to be different. Whether considered at the level of the class, of the school or of the systems as a whole, they are problems that continue to be highlighted whenever the subject of immigrant children is raised: the children's problems in adjusting to the system and not the system's problems in adjusting to the children. A very interesting, and significant, reversal of the argument.

Is this due to the efforts of international organisations (the concept of 'intercultural', which has proved to be so rich, originated in the work of the Council of Europe, and the Commission of the European Communities, like OECD or UNESCO, have carried out numerous substantive studies and pilot projects on the school success of migrants), to national efforts or to individual efforts? Or is it due to a sort of weariness and to the fact that the school systems have other challenges to face? The great interest in migrants during the 1970s and early 1980s seems to have gone rather out of fashion without any confidence that all the problems have been solved. And yet the policy of 'educational priority areas' in the United Kingdom, France or the Netherlands has made it clear that this struggle for the school success of foreign children (and of national populations from the same socio-professional categories) involved a constant renewal of efforts to match the rapid renewal of the populations in the areas considered.

In sum, the demographic context at the end of the 1980s is one of crisis and recession. It should be noted that this drop in the number of school-age children is not necessarily in itself a negative factor; yet it cannot be denied that it is often perceived as such by people involved in or attentive to education systems. One of the reasons for this stems from the limitations placed on the recruitment of teachers accompanying the drop in enrolments, limitations that result in an ageing of the profession, corresponding fears over the capacity for adaptation and innovation of the systems as a whole (at a time when the shock of the new technologies brings fresh worries), and the possible undermining of job security. Like any crisis situation, it raises questions as to what should be kept and what should be abolished – basic questions that are accompanied by a no less basic questioning concerning the criteria of decision.

2. The social and family context

Since 1973 the demographic crisis has been supplemented by a difficult economic context in which, from one oil crisis, monetary crisis and social conflict to the next, the western economies are searching for a firm and lasting stability and further growth. The direct and indirect impact on the school is considerable, both in terms of the expectations of parents and in terms of the public and private financing of expenditure on education.

Work and the employment of young people

Unemployment, the growth or persistence of which at very high rates (8–12 per cent of the active population in most European countries, 15 per cent in Italy and around 20 per cent in Ireland and Spain, but less than 2 per cent in Sweden, Switzerland, Iceland and Luxembourg) are perceived as one of the most serious consequences of the crisis, is not without repercussions on the school. It is even one of the issues that brings out most clearly the complex and subtle interactions between any large-scale social phenomenon and the world of education.

The concern over employment has been aggravated by the fact that the unemployment of young people is much higher than that of adults, and it is not very easy to see how this situation can be changed, as one of the characteristics of times of crisis is the attempt to safeguard and hold on to the advantages inherited from times of prosperity. Although all the countries possess young graduates having difficulty in finding a job, it is the large body of those leaving the school systems without qualifications that suffers the most from the difficulties in obtaining their first job; thus, for the 15/16–24 age-group the unemployment rates reach 7 per cent in Sweden, 21 per cent in the United Kingdom, 26 per cent in France, 37 per cent in Italy and 42 per cent in Spain (but only 7 per cent in the Federal Republic of Germany owing to its 'dual' system of vocational training).

The first direct consequence for the school is that, since young people are having such difficulty in finding work on leaving school, the trend is to continue their education, in more or less disguised forms of vocational training modules when it is not bluntly a matter of re-enrolling young people who have already left the system in an attempt to give them in a few months the basics of a general and vocational training that the school had, over a number of years, failed to provide them with. And it is no real paradox that this often meets with success owing to a context and motivation for learners and teachers quite different from the traditional school setting.

However, it is important to note - second consequence - that this prolongation of schooling or re-enrolment is costly, particularly in countries in which recurrent training is not very well organised. The cost of these various measures to promote the social and vocational integration of young people forms part of the redistribution of social expenditure accompanying the economic crisis (see below).

The third consequence is of another kind, but the pressure it exerts on the school is no less great, and is perhaps a vital factor. The anxiety caused by adult and youth unemployment is leading many parents to wonder whether the school really pays dividends in terms of access to the labour market for their children. Their expectations and demands *vis-à-vis* school systems are being modified as a result, more stress being laid on the acquisition of immediately operational tools rather than on personality training through a broadly based liberal education <DECS/EGT [87] 23>. I shall return later to this point, which is at the heart of the school/society relationship.

The fourth and last consequence is more indirect: the means used to combat unemployment form part of a general redistribution of the amount of available work, a redistribution that is expressed in particular in an increase in part-time work (especially for women). The impacts on family life will be examined later; it can be observed, however, that this new organisation of time (work time and leisure time) sometimes enables certain parents to have 'more time' to devote to the studies of their children and relations with the school.

The welfare state and priorities in social expenditure

The two aspects are connected: one of the most powerful manifestations of the welfare state is indeed the organisation of vast transfers of wealth, in some cases to provide for the development of some sector deemed of priority status and sometimes to ensure the subsistence of disadvantaged or needy social categories. Through the amount of funds which a state, increasingly powerful and regulating economic and social life to an increasing extent, sets aside for a given sector of public life, we glimpse the real priorities of a given moment, especially when the concept of the welfare state is accompanied by an approach to social problems that puts more emphasis on management than on politics (Keyes 1981).

The demographic problems confronting Europe and the serious social problems arising from the economic crisis have led many states to get down to rethinking their system of social, and hence budgetary, priorities and values. The educational sector, in the broad sense, has thus found itself increasingly in competition with other sectors considered, in these difficult times, of even higher priority (hence that odd but common expression 'the priority of priorities'). Unemployment, the employment of young people, social protection and the revival of economic activity have become, one after the other, of higher priority than education.

Here the ageing population (see above) is of particular significance. A recent forecast by the OECD shows that the total cost of social expenditure is expected to increase by one-third, in real terms, over the next 50 years on the assumption that the volume and scale of benefits remain unchanged and that expenditures will rise and fall in proportion to the number of beneficiaries. This overall rise of one-third conceals very sharp inequalities between sectors: a drop of 20 per cent in expenditure on education, of 15 per cent in family allowances, a rise of 40 per cent in expenditure on health and of 100 per cent in the cost of retirement programmes (Maguire 1987)!

Faced with such a situation, very strongly sensed by the rank and file of the education systems, it is very difficult to persuade people that today education still constitutes the 'priority of priorities'; this redeployment of budgetary resources formerly spent on education towards other sectors indisputably serves as a brake on the functioning and dynamism of the education systems.

The new organisation of the family

The family is at the core of two different triptychs whose poles are in one case the family, the school and the work of one or both parents, and in the other, the family, the school and the children and adolescents themselves. In these two triptychs, any change made to one of the poles rebounds on the whole; this has been the case, for example, with the observed changes in the social 'status' of the wife or of the young person, but also with the way in which family ties are slackening or with the rising number of single-parent families.

> Three major trends appear to be shared by all western countries. Individualism is progressing and reinforcing a demand for personal expression and self-realisation, for self-fulfilment, which goes naturally hand in hand with a greater tolerance towards other people and a more evident interest in social relations, friendship and good neighbourliness. In every country the family is being transformed in the same way, though to a varying extent, but this does not prevent it from being still as highly if not more highly regarded by its members. Authority is losing its intrinsic value, its legitimacy. Social divisions are becoming more numerous, engendering a greater variety of groups, which are no longer organised like a pyramid. (Mendras 1987)

The rise in the activity rate of women is one of the most visible indicators of this change in the organisation of the family. More and more women are taking jobs outside the home, with the sometimes spectacular growth in female employment accounted for in particular by a clear preference for the tertiary (service) sectors, in which employment has continued to expand. Quite obviously this entails a number of changes in the family's daily routine, first and foremost the straining of relationships between husband and wife and between parents and children. Here it should be noted, however, that part-time work might provide an answer to the difficulty of reconciling the mother's job with the maintaining of ties with her children: in France in 1986, it accounted for 25 per cent of active women (and less than 4 per cent of men).

The slackening of intra-family ties has many consequences that are too obvious to relate. One of them, however, deserves to be mentioned because it is usually insufficiently stressed: 'the time spent by children and adults speaking with one another is liable to decrease because of the reduced availability of parents who both work; when we say "speaking", we are thinking in wider terms of the interaction and intercommunication within the family, whatever the form (channel) taken by this communication' <DECS/EGT [87] 23>. Realising the importance of all these forms of family communication for the development and personal equilibrium of the child, we have to admit that there lies a real problem, primarily affective but also to a large extent social.

The number of children per family is dropping (see above), with the result that families are becoming more demanding for each of their children; at the same time we find a loss of stability and a weakening of the 'conventional' (nuclear) family cell inherited from the middle-class social model of the mid-nineteenth century (Shorter 1975): parents married, children born in wedlock.

The rising number of divorces is another highly visible indicator of changes in the family. In Sweden, for example, it would appear that half the marriages contracted today will break down, probably ending in divorce, and that perhaps half the children born of marriages entered into this year will see their parents divorced before they are 18 years old (Lithman 1985)! And Sweden's divorce rate per 100 marriages is far from exceptional in Europe.

Although less visible than divorce or co-habitation (and procreation) without marriage, an important change is affecting the function of the family. One of the characteristics of the family unit is that it was for a long time, and perhaps primarily, an economic production unit (in agriculture, craftwork, business, etc.). This absolutely essential function has, before our eyes, if not disappeared altogether at least been reduced to a marginal status; and it is more and more exclusively ties of an affective and sentimental nature that unite the members of a family, in many cases completely replacing the economic ties but without, perhaps, the same strength.

In any case, one thing is certain: the consequence of this change in the production function of the family is that each of its members is less economically dependent on the unit as a whole and on each of the other members. This brings us back to the growing individualism referred to above.

Here again a qualification is needed. Even as young people are becoming more and more economically independent of their family, they are tending to live longer and longer with their parents; this fact, observed in many European countries, is of course related to the economic crisis and the difficulty of finding a first job. It none the less reveals the danger of over-simplifying a social change as sensitive as that affecting the family.

In short, are we moving towards a 'break-up' of the family framework or simply towards new definitions of intra-family relations? It has at all events turned out that the family, as a mode of social existence and as a point of reference in the midst of emotional uncertainties, continues as this century draws to a close to be a 'haven of security', even though it has also turned out that it is less and less often the sole arena in which individual success stories are constructed.

3. The cultural context

It is probably the cultural context that confronts the school with basic questions, questions of ethics and policy and not of management.

> It is almost as scandalous to write about the relations of the school with culture and ethics as it is to say nothing.
>
> To take the first path is to run the risk of deciding arbitrarily the content of the future culture, forgetting that any culture is a living creation and that, in any society, there are always several cultures existing side by side; one is also exposed to the danger of an *a priori* definition of the school's moral outlook because one disregards the permanent need to question the goals that are agitating the foundations of our society.
>
> And yet to choose the path of silence would be even worse, for where, if not in culture, can the knowledge, skills and behaviour patterns be rooted and on what can the meaning of the goals be based if not on the preoccupations of ethics? (Lesourne 1987)

I have already noted the complexity and ambiguity of a society's relationship to its school. On such a sensitive issue as the transmission of 'values', this relationship is blurred and sometimes conflict ridden.

The school, a focal point of culture?

Here we need to be reminded briefly of a few important points concerning the respective roles of the family and school in the absorption of the cultural heritage. Many of those who have studied this subject agree with the tradition of giving the school a special role as the main route from family life to employment, i.e. as a bridge between two milieux with a strong socialising influence. From this point of view the school is an institutional channel and not a focal point of culture, and its primary contribution to the socialisation of children is to open up and broaden, through general, even universal, knowledge, any excessive narrowness of those two milieux, one coming before and the other after. Indeed, the school as an institution has everywhere laid great emphasis on the freedom this implies for the training of individuals.

> Upstream from the school is the private world of the family, which plays the main role in education. Downstream is a series of social and professional milieux which are known to have their rules, norms and systems of approbation but from which the school is determined to remain free. Between them lies the school itself, which should be the world of knowledge, instruction and reason. The job of the school is therefore situated between two root systems and, for that very reason, the school has to run the risk of damaging those roots since its chief function is to open up knowledge and possibilities for the children. This clearly makes it a social and not a cultural model. (Touraine 1986)

This model possesses such strength only because the school is the sole social arena through which an entire age-group passes (and stays for longer and longer).

Both the upheavals in the family and the new facts of the labour market are introducing radical changes into this pattern and, almost in spite of itself, the school is finding itself entrusted with educational responsibilities that the family assumes to a decreasing extent (see above, the section on intra-family relations) and that the world of work assumes imperfectly and at a later and later stage. Here we have a reversal unwanted by the school, and not necessarily welcome to teachers, who are often very attached to its traditional role; it is a situation that the school as institution has a duty to assume even though it is not always technically equipped to do so and that, rather paradoxically, ends up by considerably increasing the sometimes insistent demands made upon the school and its teachers at a time when the latter, instead of desiring these new responsibilities, regard themselves on the contrary as victims. It is hardly surprising that relations between parents and teachers are not straightforward.

It is interesting to perceive that the school is no more a true focal point of culture in this new situation than it was in the previous model. It is only slightly affected by (with, it is true, notable differences from one country to another and even from one school to another) the major mass media of today (television, radio, hi-fi, etc.), which have, on the other hand, invaded family life and play a primary role in the dissemination of culture: the fact is that the piecemeal nature of the information conveyed by these media is in opposition to the whole tradition of learning at school (see section 4 below).

The cultural attitudes of young people

The school is no longer the place where the forms of 'youth culture' are expressed and it is even easy to defend the argument that it was against the school as institution that this youth culture came into being. Much has been written, often in violent terms, on this culture of young people, either to refute it or to defend it. It should be set in the context of the present-day explosion of cultural forms, each with its own language and insignia and brought into being either through a break with the past in the traditional cultural fields of literature, music and the plastic arts or by the creation of new cultural fields (film-making, radio, television, narrative, cartoons, fashion, publicity, etc.).

A few features common to the cultural attitudes of young people, which are displayed chiefly from adolescence onwards and remain characteristic of the age-group until the age of 24–25 years (but which, through family osmosis and the desire to imitate older children, also have a big influence on the under-10s) are as follows:

- Young people are consumers with their own not negligible resources (pocket money, birthday money, odd jobs) and are often a specific target for mass consumption products such as clothes, bodily hygiene and beauty products, gadgets, personal stereos, hi-fi equipment, etc.).
- This group is highly sociable, whether it is a matter of relations with their 'mates', of going to cafes or of involvement in local associations. Their external appearance, or 'look', is very important to them and results in an over-consumption of clothes, in quantity but also in quality (especially by young males), jewellery, toileteries and perfumes.
- Young people 'get about' a lot: for example, a lot more young people than adults spend their holidays or leisure time visiting a foreign country, usually camping.
- Lastly, young people are characterised by their high expenditure on leisure and culture: cassette recorders, hi-fi equipment, musical instruments (guitars, keyboard instruments, etc.), much more frequent visits to the cinema and concerts (not only rock concerts) than adults, and a slightly greater interest in the theatre, spectator sports, etc.

Mention should also be made of what knits the group together, the forms of expression it chooses in order to stand out. Here an essential role is played by language, music and the powerful and widespread sense of solidarity between young people.

Clearly, none of this has much to do with school, and if one can even speak of an opposition it is because, in contrast with these cultural forms, which value creativity, difference, change and the output of technology (with perhaps much that is superficial and excessive), the school appears as the custodian of traditional values and rules, lagging so much behind the times that it even seems insipid and antiquated. For an ever-increasing number of young people the 'utilitarian' function of school takes pride of place: they expect it to guide them towards a job and for that they are often much more willing to accept its rules than their elders of one or two decades ago. Being at school is already work; going to lessons is a preparation for going to a job. Life and culture are elsewhere.

What is expected of the school?

The very ambiguity of these expectations expresses clearly the social and cultural disarray of our age. In the first place, as many surveys have shown, young people expect school to equip them for professional life and job-hunting. This directly utilitarian vision, which is completely understandable in view of the omnipresent image of youth unemployment in many countries, leads them on the whole to do their best in their 'profession of pupil'. And their parents? What are their expectations?

Before trying to answer this question we must briefly return to the fact that the problematical or unproblematical perception of the school and its results (and therefore of the expectations expressed about the school) naturally depends to a large extent on the social and cultural context, but it also depends on the overall context of expansion or recession. Mention has already been made of the expansion of the school systems in the 1960s and 1970s; the effort needed to win the battle of numbers has, except in the case of a few specialists, blinded people to educational failures, especially in view of the possibilities of varied employment for young people even without qualifications.

In the present phase of recession, such failures become unbearable. And here again it is no minor paradox that the school finds itself being reproached so severely for abandoning as failures (or causing the failure of) 10–20 per cent of an age-group (depending on the system and country), at a time when there is a willingness to maintain that it has everywhere considerably improved its performance over the last 20 years and that 20 years ago such failures would have appeared almost normal, or at least would not have caused such disquiet on the part of the public authorities and such anger on the part of parents.

The questioning takes two forms. Outside the education system (i.e. among parents and public opinion in general), the trend is towards nostalgia and 'iron rations', in other words the OECD's 'back to basics'. Let the school do its best to carry out its function of instruction, help all pupils to master the basic languages (correctly written mother tongue and arithmetic) and transmit the major historical and moral values and it will have fulfilled its contract. It is against this backcloth that we see the development of the struggle against 'school failure' but also, as in France between 1984 and 1986, the emotive recollection of the end of the nineteenth century and the beginnings of compulsory education for all. Few are those who lay stress on the development of the individual and on the adaptability that will later become necessary for the future adult in his professional and personal life.

Within the systems, the positions taken are more varied, often going as far as verbal attack and occasionally anathema. Nostalgia for the traditional approach has just as many fervent supporters as an open-minded education centred on the individual needs of the learner-pupil. Agreement is difficult to reach between the practitioners of teaching and the false quarrel that artificially opposes formal knowledge to skill and moral qualities is visibly gathering momentum. A geography of the pedagogical approaches taken by the school in Europe to achieve its objectives has never been attempted; it is, however, permissible to advance the hypothesis that, within the shared overall concern to give everyone the maximum chance of success, a meticulous examination of pedagogical policies would show that the dividing line closely reflects the consideration accorded politically to the individual; and here the age-old split between Latin countries and Germanic countries is still to some extent relevant.

At all events, the school is today a major cultural and social challenge everywhere (even when, as we have seen, it is no longer the top financial priority). And the picture is further confused by questions about the coming society of technicians and the impact of the new information technologies.

4. The transformations in technology

In the eyes of future historians the years between 1960 and 2000 will doubtless be the ones in which the information society took hold, in which the symbol replaced matter and energy as the salient image of a period. We are clearly dealing with an all-important change, which is fundamentally transforming, before our very eyes, the whole system of relations between the social, economic and technical dimensions of society.

It is a phenomenon on a planetary scale that goes well beyond the question of teaching methods or the use of new information technologies in education, though it naturally embraces both of them.

So much has been written on this information society that I will be forgiven for concentrating here on only the few characteristics most relevant to my argument.

This information society is rooted in the emergence of a vaster system in which sciences and production techniques (or goods and services) are more and more closely related and even affect each other directly. In this system, innovation is no longer so much a question of constructing new machines but one of mastering a greater (and increasing) quantity of information: in the classical example of the computer and the logician, for example, the innovation is now centred much more on the software than on the hardware.

It is also quite remarkable how technical innovations make their way into numerous sectors of activity (one has only to think of the vast range of uses, at work and at home, for electronic chips) and interact with each other to engender fresh innovations.

It goes without saying that, however difficult it is to see ahead in this field, these transformations will have repercussions on tomorrow's professional skills and hence on the importance of an initial training that facilitates adaptation (again and again) to scientific and technological changes. The first requirement, which no one disputes, is to raise the level of skill of the active population, both adults and young people. But two points must be kept in mind:

- There are at present big differences between the states of Europe, clearly revealed by an indicator (with its strengths and weaknesses) such as the percentage of an age-group that completes its upper secondary studies with the necessary qualifications to be admitted to university: less than 30 per cent in Austria and Portugal, about 30 per cent in the Federal Republic of Germany, the United Kingdom, France and Denmark, nearly 50 per cent in the Netherlands and more than 80 per cent in Sweden and Norway. In other words, the reality underlying a massive increase in the level of skill is not the same in each of these countries.
- For a young person there is a kind of contradiction between the desire for specialised vocational training, which is effective in the short term but fragile, and a solid general training which develops the aptitudes for independence and adaptation necessary for a successful career but is less and less helpful for finding a first job (see above, the section on the expectations of young people).

The questions posed to education systems by a general rise and change in vocational qualifications and skills are obviously of major importance. Yet they are not the only ones raised for education systems by the advent of an information society. Against the backcloth of this radical change, the school, which is itself essentially an information system, is directly challenged. It is in fact a double challenge: how should the school handle the new information technologies as a subject to be taught (in particular, should it treat them as separate 'disciplines' and teach them as such, or should it design a sort of 'trans-disciplinary' course for them?), and what upheavals are the new information technologies likely to provoke in teaching methods?

Though the first question may concern only present or future 'specialists', the second obviously affects all teachers and, through the equipment to be purchased and the training courses to be provided, all education systems.

At a time when attention is centred, particularly in primary schools, on the computer and its possible uses, it is interesting to consider what 30 years of stormy relations between the school and the audio-visual media have taught us about this clash between 'school' and 'parallel school' and its consequences.

More than films and photographs, it is television that is the focus of the hostility of a high proportion of teachers to the 'culture of the image' (with of course, I repeat, big differences of emphasis from one school to another, one country to another, even one primary teacher to another), and the simplistic opposition between the 'Gutenberg galaxy' and the 'MacLuhan galaxy' is highly revealing of relationships that are felt in terms of competition rather than complementarity.

Without going into too much detail, since much has been said and written on the subject, we can note a few points that underpin the general relationship between the school and the world of the media.

- All the media, in particular radio and television (chiefly television), offer pupils (but also people in general and hence teachers in particular) information and knowledge, entertainment and subjects to think about. All this reaches the person addressed outside school and in forms (those of mass communication) very different from the ones that shape and are developed by the teaching relationship to be found in schools.
- Although the school is not a focal point of culture, it has a strong sense of its role in the transmission of culture. Objectively it is entrusted with the function of introducing and transmitting cultural values and, subjectively, it feels this function to be its true mission. It goes without saying that the emergence of other cultural circuits represents a risk that it would be dispossessed of its role, a risk that it interprets moreover as a danger for the nation. Faced with the media culture, this 'third culture' (in the sense of Third Estate) of Edgard Morin or 'sub-culture' according to numerous primary teachers, the initial quasi-visceral reaction of the education systems is one of hostility, admonition and exclusion. This feeling is strengthened when the modes of cultural diffusion are considered, in particular the role played by the 'opinion-makers' or 'cultural mediators' in a two-step flow of communication such as Katz highlighted over 30 years ago.

  It is clear that the teacher represents the cultural mediator par excellence in the diffusion of an erudite culture. On the other hand, the media foster the emergence of a new type of cultural mediator based on the characteristics of mass culture. These guides cannot be teachers inasmuch as teachers consider the media as 'different', non-erudite, a 'sub-culture'. Naturally, the dangers of conflict, and hence of mutual exclusion, are aggravated.
- We must now face up to the differences in educational reasoning (or simply in reasoning) that characterise respectively the message of the school and the message of the media, particularly television. Even if MacLuhan's distinction between 'cold' media and 'hot' media is as debatable as it is renowned, it has the immense merit of focusing attention on the role of the addressee in the reception and comprehension of the message. It is a dual contrast involving both the form and the organisation of messages.
- The child's 'activity' at school is often compared with his/her 'passivity' in front of the television set. This is of course true but nevertheless requires considerable qualification. Generally speaking, the information dispensed by the school is very carefully prepared and elaborated beforehand, predigested so to speak, and thus ready for reception and assimilation by the pupil–recipient; this indisputably gives the recipient many reasons to remain passive, even if we consider his or her passivity unintended by the teacher and an unwanted side-effect of the teaching relationship.

  The visual and televisual message is quite different. It requires great activity in the eye (and therefore brain) of the recipient so that it can be decoded and interpreted. This is technically true for the television image owing to its 'resolution' into a number of points which make the viewer construct the image s/he sees by making use of only a proportion of those points; it also applies to any image, a coded and ambiguous language that pupils master less effectively than speech. All these are forms of activity behind the bodily passivity often engendered by television.

- Closely interwoven with this difference in the nature of the messages appears a no less fundamental contrast in organisation. The school organises its work in terms of structure, courses, reasoning, and respect for the pace and progressive processes of learning. The media, and once again television in particular, are characterised by chance, freedom, instantaneous and direct reactions but also by a disordered and even fragmentary approach. They use a completely different logic in the organisation of messages, well illustrated by the distinction, totally pertinent in its simplicity, that Moles made 20 years ago between 'network culture' (that of the school) and 'mosaic culture' (that of the media) (Moles 1968).
- Lastly, the inevitable question: is the influence of the media the same for all children–recipients? In particular, what is the impact of the family and cultural surroundings? The few reliable scraps of knowledge we have on the subject do indeed tend to show that, like the school (but without necessarily following in detail the same sharp divisions), the media exert a highly differential influence, with the socio-professional and socio-cultural category of the parents playing a major role.

Computers provoke few modifications to this general picture, except in one major respect: a computer requires extreme logic in reasoning and programming since no error is forgiven; for some people this means the impoverishment of thought, especially creative thought, while for others it assists the structuring of thought and fosters an awareness of the need for exactness. The quarrel shows no signs of abating.

On the whole, though sometimes with reluctance, the world of education has nevertheless opened up to the new information technologies and there is no evidence that it will not continue slowly but surely in that direction. For that purpose, a few points must be made perfectly clear:

- Like books, the new information technologies (including to a great extent computer science) are aids for the teacher whose work they can facilitate or refresh, but they cannot in any circumstances replace him or her.
- The new information technologies, particularly computer science, are already capable of giving the individual, both learner and teacher, more independence, more opportunities for innovation (see above) and possibly more creativity. For the teacher at all events they considerably extend the range of available teaching aids and tools.
- Lastly, the development of the new information technologies calls for considerable investment, in equipment of course, but also and above all in brains, for the design, preparation and making of films, broadcasts, television programmes, educational software, data banks, etc. before the actual teaching itself takes place.

5. Conclusion

A changing educational landscape of contrasts? The Europe of 1990 offers an educational panorama whose diversity continues of course to be a source of enrichment, but the similarity of the relationships between the major social, cultural and economic factors and the school is more striking. As the twentieth century draws to a close, the problem facing the education systems in Europe is not the problem of numbers; that battle has been won on all fronts. The problem at the heart of the question being raised today, the problem of quality, is just as difficult to resolve since the context is not really helpful: budget priorities slipping towards other sectors, anxiety of those involved in the system, the school's role as sole cultural mediator called into question, and, at the same time, the pressures exerted by young people, their parents, the state and the whole society to obtain greater success for everybody. The questioning of the school as an institution and of its objectives is a recent development that is often unwelcome within the education systems, but whose full-blooded power is helping Europe to limp along in step in the search for solutions.

SECTION 2

ORGANISATION, POLICY AND PRACTICE OF PRIMARY EDUCATION IN EUROPE

Introduction

Alan Blyth

Section 2, the longest in the book, embodies the 22 national reports submitted on behalf of each country by the relevant national authorities. Chapter 2.1 introduces the reports, indicating something of how they came to be written and analysing some aspects of the material that they present; Chapter 2.2 comprises the reports themselves.

In essence, this Section portrays primary education in Europe from the standpoint of those responsible for organising, financing and maintaining it. In other parts of the book, independent material and opinions are presented from the vantage-point of expert knowledge and experience, but in this Section the reports, and the editorial comment on them, are confined to the issues on which, largely as an outcome of the Vaduz Conference held in 1982 <DECS/EGT [83] 64>, the member states were invited to concentrate. This, then, is the authentic voice of governments and administrations, with an editorial gloss.

CHAPTER 2.1

The National Reports: Analysis and Comment

Alan Blyth

1. The submission of the reports

In 1982, the Council's 21 member states, joined for this purpose by Finland, were each invited by Project No. 8 to submit an account of primary education in their own country, under three main headings: Basic Information; Problems and Trends; and Recent Important Studies of Primary Education.

In the light of the Vaduz Conference <DECS/EGT [83] 64>, it was suggested that the first section on 'Basic information' might include data such as:

- The aims of primary education.
- The responsibility for the organisation of primary education at national, regional, local and school level.
- The links between pre-school and primary education, and between primary and lower secondary education.
- The number of primary school pupils and teachers. The arrangements for grouping pupils, and the official class sizes.
- The length of primary schooling and of the school day, the school week and the school year.
- The major branches of the primary school curriculum.
- The main methods of pupil assessment.
- Arrangements for the basic and further training of primary school teachers.
- The support services available to primary schools, e.g. doctors, psychologists, social workers and advisers.
- The institutional links between the primary school, parents, and the community.

However, it was left to each state to implement this brief in the way that its authorities considered most appropriate and, as will be evident from Chapter 2.2, they exercised considerable discretion when deciding the format in which their submission should be made to the CDCC. Some adhered quite closely to the actual headings suggested, while others made use of existing documents, or improvised more freely on the themes suggested. A few may have taken it for granted that the most characteristic features of their national systems were too familiar to require re-stating. Some kinds of statistical information were almost universally furnished, but it must be emphasised that, owing to the method used for data collection, this is one of the instances in which it is necessary to exercise the caution referred to in the Introduction, before attempting any quantitative comparisons between states. Fortunately, there exists in many cases other material with which the reports can be supplemented. Elsewhere in the reports, the style becomes rather more discursive, ranging from the citation of legal provisions to individual and corporate opinions about the effectiveness of current procedures.

There is comparable diversity in the material provided under the heading 'Problems and trends'. In some cases this information is closely woven into the discussion of basic information, while elsewhere it is presented as a series of issues and sub-issues that have clearly been engaging the attention of the national authorities concerned. In once instance, that of Switzerland, a vigorous action-research programme had given rise to a set of theses or hypotheses intended for further investigation.

The third part of the original set of suggestions, the one asking for information about recent important published studies, was rather patchily answered. Some countries appeared excessively modest in their claims, for nothing of importance was reported. Others listed mainly, or even exclusively, government publications. Only in one or two instances can the coverage of published material be regarded as comprehensive. Therefore no systematic

Table 2.1.1 Dates of submission of national reports

Member state	*Date of original submission*	*Date of revised submission*
Austria	1984	1988
Belgium	1984	1988
Cyprus	1984	1988
Denmark	1984	—
Finland	1984	1988
France	1984	—
Germany (West)	1984	—
Greece	1985	—
Iceland	1984	1988
Ireland	1984	1988
Italy	1987	—
Liechtenstein	1984	—
Luxembourg	1987	—
Malta	1986	—
Netherlands	1986	—
Norway	1986	1988
Portugal	1984	1987
Spain	1984	—
Sweden	1984	1988
Switzerland	1984	1988
Turkey	1986	—
United Kingdom	1987	1988

analysis of this third category of response is practicable, but all the material supplied under this heading has been listed in Appendix 1. The present chapter will therefore concentrate on the replies to the first two sections of the enquiry.

The answers to this enquiry were originally sought in 1981–2, and submitted to the CDCC in 1984. However, when this Handbook was being planned, member states were invited to send, if they so wished, amendments to their original submissions, or even entirely revised statements. Table 2.1.1 indicates the dates of the original and amended submissions. Comparison of the original with the revised data reveals some interesting trends, even over a short period of time, particularly in the case of member states that had undergone substantial political change during those years. In each case, the report reproduced in Chapter 2.2 is the latest version, but, in the following analysis, differences from the earlier versions have been borne in mind.

2. Plan of analysis

The analysis presented in this chapter follows much the same pattern as the headings previously listed. The greater part of it is concerned with the 'basic considerations' mentioned in that list, and thus includes some issues, notably in relation to the primary curriculum, that do not figure among the topics singled out for specific attention elsewhere in the Handbook. Problems and trends are considered subsequently, with particular reference to those issues that appear to concern a number of countries. Finally, some observations are added about other issues which, though not prominently represented in the national reports, do nevertheless appear relevant to the public provision of primary education in Europe today and tomorrow.

Since all of these issues are important, there is a considerable body of relevant literature that could be cited in respect of any one of them. A major analysis and interpretation of the reports would be a most worthwhile task, but one that would require time and effort and publication space on the scale of Dottrens' and Schultze's earlier studies (Dottrens 1962; Schultze 1968). The present analysis is necessarily more modest in scope and intention. Some reference is made to particularly relevant studies carried out by or for the CDCC. Project No. 8's Final Report <DECS/EGT [87] 23: henceforth referred to without further citation as 'the Final Report' > has been borne in mind during its compilation, but is not fully quoted because many of its themes, some of them the subject of further studies under the project, are developed in later chapters in the Handbook.

3. Frameworks, aims and objectives

The contributing states considered that any proclamation of aims should be prefaced by a statement about the legal framework within which primary education is conducted. In some instances the legal structure is fully spelled out; in others it is more impressionistically presented.

Every state has a public system of primary education, though there are varying degrees of private provision outside the public system. Such provision is of two kinds. The first is a fee-paying sector, catering for small minorities of pupils. Of the countries that give such details, Italy and Greece state that between 5 and 10 per cent of primary-age children are educated in schools outside the public system, while in Ireland the percentage is below 2 per cent and in Sweden below 1 per cent. Other countries indicate that they have private schools of this kind, but do not state the percentage of pupils for whom they cater. However, in political units such as Belgium, the Netherlands and Spain, and with analogies elsewhere, there is a large sector of privately run denominational schools, in which costs are substantially borne by governments; private schools in this sense may cater for between 30 and 60 per cent of the total child population of primary-school age. Project No. 8 included among its activities a Netherlands case study in the co-ordination between the public and private sectors in such circumstances <DECS/EGT [87] 18>.

Turning now to what is in most countries the much larger and more significant system of public primary schools, the relevant statistics for most countries, derived from the most recent versions of the reports, are shown in Table 2.1.2.

These figures serve as a reminder of the very big differences in size between the member states. Allowing for the discrepancies in age-levels between one country and another, it is still noteworthy that three countries (France, Spain and Turkey) each claim more than 5 million primary pupils, while Cyprus (the Greek sector) and Iceland each have only about *one-hundredth* of that number; the three countries that did not provide figures (Liechtenstein, Luxembourg and Malta) are clearly in the lower rather than the higher child-population band. As for the ratio between numbers of schools and numbers of pupils, this clearly reflects the geographical pattern in some countries where, as they indicate elsewhere in their reports, there are many small rural schools in remote areas. However, this ratio may also reflect levels of resourcing, and deliberate policies about school size, which cannot be deduced from these figures alone.

Aims, as expressed in the reports, are fully considered in Chapter 1.1 and in consequence only a few observations will be made here.

The actual formulation of aims by different member states is itself significant. For some countries, the right to primary education and even to particular aspects of primary education is actually enshrined in their written constitutions. In others, there is a Basic Law or its equivalent that figures as a sort of educational constitution and includes, perhaps as a preamble, a statement of educational aims. In the remainder, aims are stated with an assumption of national consensus but without legal or administrative referents.

It is noteworthy that in almost every instance there is some statement to the effect that the formation of citizens is an explicit aim. This is usually coupled

Table 2.1.2 Numbers of primary schools, pupils and teachers in member states (as far as supplied)

Member state	*Number of primary schools*	*Number of primary pupils*	*Number of primary teachers*
Austria	3,395***	342,378	28,454
Belgium**	4,618	801,771	45,590
Cyprus	361	52,066	2,236
Denmark*		709,623	59,939
Finland*	3,863	378,000( )	
France	60,000( )	6,037,000( )	180,000( )
Germany (West)		3,100,000( )	124,000( )
Greece	9,000( )	800,000( )	32,000( )
Iceland*	217	44,000( )	3,000( )
Ireland		567,272	21,205
Italy	25,928	3,607,628	280,716
Liechtenstein			
Luxembourg			
Malta			
Netherlands**	8,400( )	1,500,000( )	69,000( )
Norway	3,500( )†	530,000( )	
Portugal (1984)		1,084,055	56,933
Spain**	20,198	5,500,000( )	189,985
Sweden*	4,700( )	914,000	92,000( )
Switzerland		373,245	23,890
Turkey	50,000( )	6,500,000( )	211,797
United Kingdom		4,500,000( )	205,800

* Figures apply to comprehensive schools with age-ranges extending beyond the primary level
** Figures include publicly funded private schools
*** Total includes private schools
† Total includes some comprehensive schools extending beyond the primary level
( ) Approximate figures

NOTES Age-levels vary from one country to another, and figures are the most recent supplied but not all apply to the same year.
Some countries other than those marked with ** include in their totals schools not wholly provided from public funds.

with the maintenance of national identity and cohesion, but raises problems both for countries with a federal structure and for those that, though unitary in governmental structure, manifest divisions in language or culture, sometimes compounded by the presence of considerable numbers of temporary migrant workers or of more permanent immigrants, some of them not only from outside the country but from outside Europe. In some cases this civic aim is coupled with the maintenance of a religious orientation, which is complicated by the same set of considerations.

Many countries reflect, in some measure, the Final Report's emphasis on the importance of some degree of differentiation and individuation of programmes to meet the needs of particular children and groups. However, no country declines to state any aims or objectives at all for its primary education.

This may seem almost self-evident, but it stands in contrast to some avowed expressions of educational purposes in contemporary society, according to which any precise pre-specification of aims and objectives runs contrary to what should be the essence of progressive primary education. Maybe it would be difficult for any government to subscribe to such a philosophy. In fact, no government did.

4. Patterns of organisation

Perhaps because they are easy to objectify, national patterns of organisation are systematically expounded in the reports. The principal data on this topic are summarised in Table 2.1.3.

From Table 2.1.3, despite the lack of uniformity of presentation, certain variations between member states are immediately apparent. The first of these is the age-span of primary education itself. The range 6–12, preceded by a linked pre-school programme, is the most usual. It is followed by those countries, notably in Scandinavia, whose entry age is 7, but which have comprehensive schools covering most or all of compulsory education. Entry ages below 6 are mostly confined to Ireland and to the United Kingdom where, as in Switzerland and West Germany, there are local variations in entry and transfer ages.

The movement of children through the national systems also shows some variation. In some, 'promotion' is by age alone; in others, some measure of successful performance is also required, though there is a trend against this practice, especially in those countries that have a non-selective system of secondary education. There is thus quite a contrast here between European practice and normal procedures in, for example, North America. However, almost all member states report a considerable proportion of schools, especially in rural areas, that have so few pupils that they are bound to stay in one class for at least two years and sometimes more.

Another important variation is to be found between centralised unitary systems: those that allow a considerable measure of local or regional autonomy; and those that are avowedly federal in character or even, as in the United Kingdom, comprise more than one national system. In some cases, such as Denmark and the Netherlands, a strictly centralised framework is combined with a high degree of local autonomy under which the implementation of policy has to be delicately negotiated with parents and others. Indeed there is a general tendency to emphasise differences between centre and periphery (McLean 1988), so much so that the Final Report warns against too marked a polarisation of this kind which might overlook the roles of intermediate participants. In the Netherlands again, as in Belgium, the very substantial participation of religious denominations in non-fee-paying primary school provision introduces another tier of negotiation, which has partial counterparts elsewhere; one instance mentioned is that of Northern Ireland.

Table 2.1.3 Organisation of primary education in member states

Member state	*Basis**	*Central administration*	*Local administration*	*Nature of pre-school education*	*Grouping** in primary schools*	*Age-range 1950s‡*	*Age-range 1980s*	*Class size (average)*	*School patterns Year*	*School patterns Week*	*School patterns Day°*	*Other features*
Austria	L	Federal Ministry of Education, Arts and Sports	District and provincial boards	Deferred entry	Age-graded where possible	6–14	6–10	20	Sept–June	5 or 6 days	Varies – 6 hours max	Preparation for selective secondary education
Belgium	C/L	Ministry of Education	Provinces and municipalities; Churches	Optional (90%) kindergarten	3 levels 6–8–10–12	6–14	6–12	20	Sept–June	4½ days	6 hours	Preparation for leaving examination
Cyprus	L	Ministry of Education	(parents' groups)	Optional kindergarten	Age-graded where possible	(not supplied)	6–12	34 max	Sept–June	6 mornings	4½ hours per day	
Denmark	L	Ministry of Education	Municipalities; negotiations with parents	Provision 0–6	Age-graded	7–14	7–15†	19	(40 weeks)	5 days	5–6 hours	Continuity into secondary phase
Finland	L	Ministry (and National Board) of Education: Council of State	Municipalities (local discretion)	Social emphasis	Age-graded where possible	7–16	7–13†	20	Aug–May	5 days	5-6 hours	Continuity into secondary phase
France	L/A	Ministry of Education	*Départements*; municipalities; parents on school boards	*Ecoles maternelles*	3 levels 6–7–9–11	6–14	6–11	23	Sept–June	4½days	6 hours	Growing power of school boards
Germany (West)	L/A	Federal Ministry of Education; also Ministry in each *Land*	Communities	Private kindergarten	2 levels 6–8–10	6–14 or 6–15	6–10‡	(varies)	(40 weeks)	5–6 half-days	4 hrs per ½ day	Allocation to selective secondary education
Greece	C/L	Ministry of Education	(some local autonomy)	Optional 3½–5½	Age-graded	6–12	5½–11½	30	—	5 days	c.5 hours	Recent political change

Iceland	L	Ministry of Education and Culture	Regions; districts; boards	Social emphasis	Age-graded	7–15	6–16†	30	Sept–May	5 half-days	4 hrs per $\frac{1}{2}$ day	Continuity into secondary phase
Ireland	C/L	Department of Education	Individual boards	4–6 for most	Age-graded	6–14	6–12	30	—	5 days	5 hours	Lack of intermediate level of administrati-on
Italy	L/A	Ministry of Education (and National Education Council)	Regions; provinces; localities	3–6 (some)	Age-graded	6–14	6–11	—	—	30 hours	—	Recent and current reform
Liechtenstein	(L)	Central Board of Education	(some local powers)	5–7 (some)	Age-graded	(not supplied)	7–12	—	—	—	—	
Luxembourg	L	Ministry of National Education	Municipalities	4–6 (some)	Age-graded	6–14	6–12	c.20	Sept–July	6 mornings, 3 afternoons	$3\frac{3}{4}$ hours $2\frac{1}{4}$ hours	Preparation for selective secondary education
Malta	L	Education Department	(some local initiative)	3–5 (some)	2 levels 5–8–11	(not supplied)	5–11	30	—	—	—	Preparation for selective secondary education
Netherlands	C/L	Ministry of Education and Science	Provinces; municipalities; religious bodies	(now basis school from 4)	Age-graded	7–13	4–12	—	—	—	—	Integration of pre-school
Norway	L	Ministry of Church and Education	Regions; municipalities	Substantial pre-7	2 levels 7–9/10–12	7–14	7–12	28 max	(37 weeks)	5 days	3–6 hours	Emphasis on school class as a social unit
Portugal	L/A	Ministry of Education	Districts; municipalities	Some pre-6	2 levels 6–8–10	7–13	6–10	25 max	Sept–June	5 days	$4\frac{3}{4}$ hours	Local control of 1st stage

Table 2.1.3 Continued

Member state	Basis*	Central administration	Local administration	Nature of pre-school education	Grouping** in primary schools	Age-range		Class size (average)	School patterns			Other features
						1950s‡	1980s		Year	Week	Day ø	
Spain	C/L	Ministry of Education and Science	Autonomous regions; provinces; religious bodies	Some pre-6	3 levels 6–8–10–13	6–12	6–13	32	Sept–June	5 days	5 hours	Basic general education runs from 6 to 13
Sweden	L	National Board of Education	County boards; local boards	Some 0–6	2 levels 7–10–13	7–14	7–16†	21	Aug–June	5 days	4–5 hours	Continuity into secondary phase
Switzerland	L	Cantonal directorates with federal oversight	Communes	Some pre-6/7	(varies by canton)	6–7 to 15–16	6–7 to c.12§	19	34½ to 40½ weeks	10 half-days	3¾–5¼ hours	Sharp cantonal variations
Turkey	C/L	Ministry of National Education, Youth and Sports	Provinces; districts; villages	1.5% 4–6	Age-graded	7–12	6–11§	40 max	Sept–June	—	—	Concern about length and effectiveness of school attendance
United Kingdom	L	Separate Departments for the component nations	Different local administrations in each component nation	Extensive 3–5	Age-graded	5–15	5–11 or 5–12§	25	Sept–July	5 days	3–4 hours minimum	Introduction of national curriculum

* C = Constitutional L = Legislative A = Administrative
** In small schools, age-grading is often restricted
‡ Dottrens (1962) (figures apply to whole age-range of compulsory education)
† Comprehensive (primary and lower secondary) school
§ with some exceptions
ø Where two figures are given, the lower applies to the younger children
— data not supplied in national reports

There are notable differences between countries in the way in which the school year is arranged. The most usual pattern is for a start to be made in September and for the year to run until the following June, with two or more short breaks at times considered appropriate. Latitude exercises an influence here, for the northernmost countries allow a rather longer summer break while the hours of darkness are fewer. In the United Kingdom and in Luxembourg, the summer break is shorter than elsewhere. However, the request for information on this point was framed in such a way that some countries notified the total number of weeks' schooling required in the year, without indicating how those weeks are distributed, and in those instances it is necessary to supplement the information given in the reports from other sources.

Time-patterns within schools show differences of another kind. In Iceland, and rather similarly in Austria and West Germany, it is the current practice, for various reasons, for some or all primary-age children to attend school for half-days only. Elsewhere, the school day occupies the morning and at least a part of the afternoon, five days per week, with a shorter working week for the youngest children. In a few instances, Saturday mornings are included in the programme without increasing the total number of hours' attendance. In some states - France, Belgium, West Germany, Malta, Norway, the Iberian countries, Sweden and the United Kingdom - the primary phase as a whole is subdivided at one or more age-levels.

All of these variations reflect geographical, historical and cultural differences between the member states. What appears normal within countries sometimes seems strange to onlookers from outside. A synoptic view of practice in Europe as a whole may serve to challenge each national unit to think again about the reasons for its own procedures and to decide afresh how justifiable they are, in the light of different practices elsewhere. This, of course, is one pragmatic reason for any form of comparative study.

5. Continuity and transfer

One related topic on which information was specifically sought is the set of procedures used by each country to facilitate transfer from pre-school to primary school, and from primary to secondary school. This issue was considered particularly important in view of the increasing emphasis on developmental considerations that characterised Project No. 8, an emphasis epitomised by a research workshop held in Madrid in 1985 <DES/Rech [85] 61> (see also Chapter 4.3 below).

The first of these transfers, from pre-compulsory to compulsory education, is of interest in the context of Project No. 8, because of the CDCC's earlier concern for the pre-school phase (Woodhead 1979, 1981; Van der Eyken 1982). If a common theme can be traced from these earlier statements through the national reports, it is that 'harmonisation' between the organisation and ethos of pre-school provision and primary education has been a major feature of policy, involving as it does the bringing together of what have hitherto been, in many cases, quite different professional traditions. In the Low Countries, indeed, this process of harmonisation has been taken a stage further, through the introduction of the idea of the *basis-school* within which the pre-school age-range would be comprised. In Belgium, this has been considered in two projects, one in the Flemish-speaking region (VLO Project) and one in the French-speaking area (Cycle 5–8 Project). The Netherlands has already gone farther and has actually integrated the 4 year olds within the complete 4–12 primary school. At the same time, countries with a normal entry age of 7 present a different style of harmonisation; in Sweden, for example, where the welfare of under-7s has hitherto been the responsibility of authorities other than those concerned with school education, and also in Norway, a lowering of the entry age to 6 is being considered. Meanwhile in Ireland and in the United Kingdom, an entry age of 4 to primary education itself is not unusual.

There is encouraging evidence that the impact of transfer on individuals and groups is being given attention. So, even if there is no universal evidence of long-term cognitive gains from an expansion of pre-school provision (Van der Eyken 1982, ch. 4), there is considerable confidence that the social advantages of expanding pre-school provision are substantial.

The other transition, from primary to secondary education within the compulsory age-range, raises quite different issues. Significantly, in connection with Project No. 8, the CDCC commissioned a report by Jean Petite on *Expectations at secondary level and trends in primary education in Europe* <DECS/EGT [85] 64>, which drew upon opinions of a wide range of secondary school teachers expressed through their international organisation FIPESO. The report indicates that, in the past, the views of secondary teachers have been largely those of teachers in academic schools (grammar schools, *lycées*, *Gymnasien*, etc.) and that this has resulted in a gulf between their outlook and that of primary teachers. However, a recent FIPESO survey in seven CDCC countries (France, West Germany, United Kingdom, Norway, Denmark, the Netherlands and Portugal) had shown a considerable change towards a joint developmental view of the educational process and towards a recognition of the significance of such an approach in different aspects of curriculum – a reversal of the trend towards separate perceptions about which the Final Report expressed concern. However, Petite's survey had also indicated the danger that this alignment of view between primary and secondary teachers could result in a joint displacement of responsibility for children's lack of progress from the school on to the social environment. It had also, incidentally, thrown light on the problems encountered by member states in the actual implementation of reforms.

The national reports themselves show that the administrative aspects of transition do vary between selective and non-selective systems. In both, the maintenance and effective transmission of school records is important, but in selective systems these records, sometimes supplemented by formal testing, are used as a means of routing pupils into different schools or tracks, as for example in Austria, some *Länder* in West Germany, Luxembourg, Malta and Portugal. Where, as in Scandinavia, there are comprehensive schools spanning most or all of the compulsory age-range, there is no parallel transition between phases. Most member states indicate the procedures employed to ensure effective administrative transition; some have devoted considerable attention to the experience of children moving from one stage to another, with the attendant shift in styles of pedagogy and teacher–pupil relations; few have actually stressed the positive consequences, for children, of feeling that they are moving into a new stage on the road to maturity.

6. Curriculum

There is no doubt about the central importance attached by all member states to the question of curriculum, which is the one aspect of primary education to be made the subject of a previous world-wide survey (Dottrens 1962). Table 2.1.4 has been constructed in such a way as to indicate which, among the most usually stipulated curricular areas, are represented in the various national reports. A further column has been added for more general comments, but a three-dimensional diagram, and more consistent data from the reports themselves, would be required in order to show with any adequacy how curricular patterns within states change as children grow older.

There is considerable consistency in the pattern of primary curriculum found among member states. This no doubt reflects a curricular history that all European countries hold in common, though it is interesting to see that Austria, at least, actually claims to have modified its approach to curriculum along lines suggested during the currency of Project No. 8.

Not surprisingly, mother-tongue teaching occupies pride of place in this analysis of curriculum, though in some countries the definition of the mother tongue itself gives rise to problems of one sort or another; Belgium, Ireland, Luxembourg and Switzerland all encounter difficulties well known to those who are familiar with the political and cultural situations in those lands. Minority languages make demands of their own, whether on account of long-standing indigenous speech communities such as the Welsh or Gaelic speakers in the United Kingdom, the Sami/Saami in northern Scandinavia, the Frisians in the Netherlands or the Catalan-/or Basque-speakers in Spain, or because of migrant populations bringing Turkish or Slav speech to Germany or Bengali or Urdu to the United Kingdom. In every case there is concern for the preservation of minority languages, coupled with a recognition of the functional importance of the country's major language or languages, and some indication that there is flexibility of approach both to the teaching of language and to the place of literatures within the primary curriculum. One of the research workshops conducted, at Tilburg, under the auspices of Project No. 8 <DECS/Rech [86] 80; DECS/EGT [87] Misc 19> was in the field of mother-tongue teaching; it was concerned with reading and writing skills.

Table 2.1.4 Basic components of the primary curriculum in member states

Member state	*Mother tongue and related skills*	*Other languages*	*Maths*	*Science*	*Geography*	*History*	*Art*	*Music*	*Crafts*	*Physical education*	*Religious education*	*Moral education*	*General comments*
Austria	✓	From age 8	✓	*Sachunterricht*			✓	✓	✓	✓ (option after 8)	(not explicitly)		Flexibility. Drama option after 8. Traffic education compulsory
Belgium	✓ according to region	✓	✓	—	✓ (national)	✓	✓	—	✓	—	—	(alternatives)	Some optional subjects too
Cyprus	✓ (Greek)	English	✓	✓	Social studies		✓	✓	Home economics	✓	(not explicitly)		
Denmark	(no specific stipulation: democratic interpretation of national guidelines)												
Finland	Finnish, Swedish, Saami	From age 9	✓	Environmental studies' biology and geography			✓	✓	✓	✓	Religion, ethics, life skills, civics		Much emphasis on basic subjects; flexibility in the arts
France	✓	—	✓	Introduction to natural and social sciences			Artistic activities		✓	✓	Ethics, civics, sensitivity training		3 main categories: French & maths; PE; all others
Germany (West)	✓	(✓)	✓	*Sachunterricht* including traffic and sex education			Artwork		✓	✓	✓	✓	Emphasis on *Sachunterricht* as basis for disciplines
Greece	✓	—	✓	Environmental study			Aesthetic education		✓	✓	Social and political education		
Iceland	✓	Danish/ English	✓	✓	Social studies		✓	✓	✓	✓	✓		Wide conception of social studies

Ireland	Irish and English		✓	Social and environmental studies			✓	✓	✓	✓	✓		
Italy	✓	✓	✓	✓	✓ and social studies	✓	✓	✓	✓	✓	optional		
Liechtenstein				(no specific data, but emphasis on centrality of values)									
Luxembourg	German, French and Luxembourgeois		✓	(limited study from age 8)			✓	✓	✓	✓	✓		Free expression specified for ages 6–8
Malta	Maltese and English		✓	✓	✓ also social and envir. studies	✓	✓	✓	✓	✓	✓		Recent revision of curriculum
Netherlands	✓	English (and Frisian)	✓	✓	✓	✓	Expressive activities			✓ and health ed.	Social relations and religious movements		Also social skills
Norway	✓ (inc. Sami)	English after 10	✓		civics		✓	✓	✓	✓	✓		Home economics after 10
Portugal	✓	From age 10	✓	✓ and technology	Social studies (hist. after 10)		Creative studies			✓	Catholic religion and optional ethics		
Spain	✓	(Regional languages)	✓	✓	Social sciences		Art education			✓	Religious or ethical instruction		Progressive differentiation with increasing age
Sweden	✓	English	✓	Natural and social orientation subjects				✓	✓	✓	(✓)		Some domestic science from age 10
Switzerland	✓ (per canton)	Other Swiss	✓	✓ Knowledge of the environment			Creative and musical ed.		✓	✓	✓		
Turkey	✓		✓	✓	(Practical life studies till 10) ✓	✓	✓	✓		✓			
United Kingdom	✓	(some Welsh or Gaelic)	✓	Ideas involved in topic work			✓	✓	✓	✓	✓	Personal/ social	Recent introduction of new national curricula

Note Proportions of time allocated to subject areas in some countries are shown in the reports as shown in Chapter 2.2.

Second-language teaching also figures substantially in the primary curriculum in a number of countries. In countries with two, three or even four languages in substantial current use, either by different populations or, as in Luxembourg, sometimes for different purposes by the same population, the choice of second languages for school purposes is largely predetermined, but in several others there is a firm policy of second-language teaching, partly in response to increases in international travel as the Final Report emphasises. For such purposes time may have to be subtracted from what is available for other meritorious purposes. English is always the most likely claimant for inclusion as a second language; the compliment is not repaid by the United Kingdom.

Next to language, predictably, mathematics occupies the most prominent position, though with little indication of how it is approached – surprisingly so in view of the controversies that have raged about the teaching of mathematics and the widespread, if rather exaggerated, worries expressed about competence in basic numeracy. There is also little indication that mathematics is linked with computer education, though in the responses to the enquiry about problems and trends, reported under (10) below, several states indicated that this was becoming a preoccupation. This theme was also pursued at a research workshop at Edinburgh in 1984 <DECS/Rech [84] 58> and a conference at Lyngby in 1986 <DECS/EGT [87] 48>. Two of the project's case studies, in Leeds <DECS/EGT [85] 24> and at Bar-le-Duc <DECS/EGT [85] 44>, were concerned with the introduction of microcomputers into primary schools. schools.

The 'New Basics', discussed below in Section 3 of the Handbook because they had been designated by the CDCC for particular consideration, comprise not only language and mathematics, with computer education, but also science and technology. A perusal of Table 2.1.4 indicates that this 'basic' has not hitherto been given the same central importance as language and mathematics. Although some countries have treated primary science as a distinct curricular element, it has more usually been combined with the humanities in some composite area of study entitled, according to national tradition, 'social studies', 'environmental studies', '*Sachunterricht*' or 'topic work'. This does not imply that the scientific component within such studies has been overlooked; rather, that the unified primary curriculum, the legacy of Pestalozzi, Froebel and Dewey, is particularly upheld where social and environmental studies are concerned. However, the introduction of 'New Basics' thinking may result in some reconsideration of this legacy. One of the symposia held in Cambridge under the auspices of Project No. 8 <DECS/EGT [86] 59> was concerned with these issues in relation to primary science and technology.

The remainder of the primary curriculum also shows a considerable measure of similarity from country to country. Other aspects of the field of social/environmental studies feature to some extent in all the national programmes, sometimes with separate study of history and geography added to, or substituted for, an inclusive programme. Occasionally, as in Norway, a component of civics is specified, though elsewhere civics is sometimes linked with moral education. In nearly all cases, and explicitly in West Germany, it is assumed that, where there is a composite programme of social or environmental studies, this will lead into more systematic studies (often of history and geography and science separately) in the upper primary school or at any rate in the secondary school. Although the whole of the social/environmental studies area was not specifically designated for attention in Project No. 8, it has continued to figure prominently in the Final Report and in other activities of CDCC, notably through its programme of teachers' seminars held annually at Donaueschingen. In these seminars, attention was paid to modern trends in primary history, in 1983 <DECS/EGT [84] 1>, and to primary geography as a resource for international understanding, in 1985 <DECS/EGT [85] 47-E>, while other similar seminars have been concerned with related issues in primary schools, such as development education and education about the urban environment <DECS/EGT [84] 40-E; DECS/EGT [84] 42-E>, indicating how history and geography, among other subjects, can figure in an approach to wider social issues.

The arts receive systematic treatment in all the countries concerned, though the actual approaches vary, with the emphasis sometimes on creativity and sometimes apparently on performance or on appreciation. In some cases, for example in the Netherlands, the various arts are jointly considered; elsewhere the emphasis is on the individual arts. Where this separate emphasis is laid, the subjects offered are usually visual art, music and crafts: drama and movement are rarely specified. Project No. 8 paid particular attention to the arts, in relation to environmental education, in one of its innovatory case studies, in Athens <DECS/EGT [85] 56>.

Physical education, linked sometimes with sport and health education, figures almost universally, though it is not an area singled out for particular attention in Project No. 8.

The same is true, in general terms, of moral education and religious education, whose varying treatment inevitably reflects the cultural histories of the member states but also confirms the continuing vitality of Europe's Christian traditions in many countries. In several instances it is evident that recent changes, especially in countries facing new multicultural and multi-faith developments, have led to a more tolerant, though no less serious, attention to the basic issues involved.

There are indeed explicit references to the importance of cross-curricular issues such as multicultural education and the education of children with special needs, as well as to the education of the children of migrants and travellers, which was extensively treated in Project No. 7. These issues are further examined in Section 4. Others mentioned in the Final Report, such as informatics and media studies and general environmental issues, receive more scattered reference. But in this chapter, attention is focused on what administrations are saying about their own systems. It is evident that, already, official thinking about the primary curriculum is developing on similar lines among almost all the member states. As they face the realities of individual differences and cultural pluralism, all countries have to resolve the basic dilemma of any curriculum noted in the Final Report, namely that of reconciling the needs of a society with the legitimate concerns of all of its citizens.

7. Assessment

Almost every national report indicates some specific policy for assessing progress among primary pupils, and in the very few exceptions where no details are given (France, Greece, Luxembourg), the context makes it clear that a similar situation exists.

Within this general policy of positive assessment, there is however a wide variation in approach, ranging from informal appraisal and observation to formal summative testing. Generally, the amount of actual testing is small, and decreasing. The most usual pattern of assessment consists of continuous observation of individual children, against a firm background of a clearly defined national curriculum. This observation is usually formalised, perhaps twice a year, in records of grades communicated to parents. Where there are selective systems of secondary education, or where differentiation occurs within all-age comprehensive schools as in the Nordic countries, there are actual examinations at particular age-levels, though these are frequently referred to almost apologetically by the national authorities concerned. In a few instances, including those of Cyprus, the Netherlands and Switzerland, mention is made of the importance of children's self-assessment as a significant part of the process. In most countries, assessment if confined to attainment, but in the report from Finland there is explicit reference also to 'behaviour and diligence', and there are many indications, for example from the Netherlands, that these matters are not neglected elsewhere. There are also some statements of policy, for example from Portugal, to the effect that the efficiency of teachers is also liable to assessment.

8. Teachers

The importance of teachers to the success of primary education is axiomatic; and this is generally recognised, whether or not it is subjected to official assessment. Tables 2.1.2 and 2.1.3 above include incomplete data about numbers of teachers and average class sizes and these are reproduced, as far as possible, in Table 2.1.5, with an added column giving approximate teacher–pupil ratios where these can be derived.

These data are not only inadequate, in the sense that the information

Table 2.1.5 Primary teacher statistics in member states (as far as supplied)

Member state	*Number of primary teachers*	*Average class size*	*Pupil–teacher ratio (approx.)*
Austria	28,454	20	12
Belgium**	45,590	20	16
Cyprus	2,236	34 (max.)	23
Denmark*	59,939	19	12
Finland*	—	20	—
France	180,000( )	23	21
Germany (West)	124,000( )	***	12
Greece	32,000( )	30	26
Iceland*	3,000( )	30	15
Ireland	21,205	30	26
Italy	280,716	—	13
Liechtenstein	—	—	—
Luxembourg	—	c.20	—
Malta	—	30	—
Netherlands**	69,000( )	—	21
Norway	—	28 (max.)	—
Portugal (1984)	56,933	25 (max.)	19
Spain**	189,985	32	28
Sweden*	92,000( )	21	10
Switzerland	23,890	19	15
Turkey	211,797	40 (max.)	30
United Kingdom	205,800	25	21

* Figures apply to comprehensive schools with age-ranges extending beyond the primary level

** Figures include publicly funded private schools

*** Each *Land* determines its own

( ) Approximate figures

NOTES Age-levels referred to vary from one country to another, and figures are the most recent supplied but do not all apply to the same year.

Some countries other than those marked with ** include in their totals schools not wholly provided from public funds.

supplied is not uniform. They are also incomplete, because no questions were asked about the proportions of women to men, or of older to younger teachers, or of senior to junior posts (though Switzerland did provide such information), or of differences in qualifications where these are to be found, or of levels of remuneration in real terms. Such matters are clearly important when estimating the well-being of primary education in individual countries. Official statistics often yield information on some at least of these variables; these issues are discussed in general in Section 5 of this Handbook.

Another question not covered fully in the national reports is that of qualitative differences between countries in the basic and post-experience education of primary teachers, which is also considered in Section 5. However, the procedures devised for these purposes by individual countries are stated, though with some omissions, in Table 2.1.6.

Table 2.1.6 Patterns of primary teacher education in member states

	Basic (initial) provision			*In-service (post-experience) provision*		
Member state	*Location*	*Duration*	*Nature*	*Location*	*Duration*	*Other details*
Austria	Teacher-training academies	3 years	General	Provincial institutes		
Belgium	Municipal, state or private colleges	2 years	General	State or private inspectorate	Short, and some long' courses	Emphasis laid on updating
Cyprus	Pedagogical Academy	3 years	General	School, local area, or Pedagogical Institute	Short, and long' courses	Updating; scholarships for higher degrees abroad
Denmark	(actual detail not provided in report)			Royal Danish College of Pedagogical Studies	Short and long courses and higher degrees	Staff concerned with initial training must qualify here
Finland	University	5 years	Up to Master's degree level	(no further information given)		
France	Teacher-training colleges	3 years	DEUG and primary teachers' diploma		Equivalent of one-year's entitlement during career	
Germany (West)	University or college, then school attachment	$2\frac{1}{2}$ years in all	6 months' degree work; 2 years in school	In-service centres		
Greece	University (formerly colleges)	4 years	General	Pedagogic Institute		
Iceland	Teachers' Training College	3 years	General	Teachers' Training College of Iceland	Short and longer courses	Courses are arranged by College, ministry or region
Ireland	University–validated colleges	B.Ed. 3 years	General	Ministry; colleges; university; teachers' unions	Summer courses	
Italy	*Istituti magistrali* and universities	3 years	General			Organised by central administration

Liechtenstein	(no specific information given)					
Luxembourg	University or Higher Institute of Education and Educational Research	3 years	General	University or Higher Institute		
Malta	University of Malta	B.Ed. (Honours) 5 years as worker–student	General	Department of Education	Short and longer courses	Scholarships and bursaries for study abroad
Netherlands		(no specific information given)				Some higher qualifications recognised
Norway	(no specific information given)					
Portugal	Colleges of education or universities		General	Organised, as entitlement, through colleges and univs.	(May include sabbatical years)	Emphasis laid on updating
Spain	University teacher–training colleges	3 years	1st year general; thereafter more specialised	University institutes of educational science	Short courses	Inspectoral guidance
Sweden		(no specific information)		University	Short and longer courses	Participants mostly chosen by local admin.
Switzerland	Mostly teacher–training colleges	4–5 years	Academic, pedagogical and practical studies	Cantons and teachers' groups	Compulsory and optional courses	Optional courses are in teachers' own time
Turkey	Institutes of education linked with universities	2 years	General	Ministry		Emphasis laid on updating
United Kingdom	Universities, polytechnics, colleges of education	Degree + 1 year, or 4-year B.Ed.	General	Inspectors, Advisers, higher education	Short and longer courses and higher degrees	Emphasis on current policy needs

Only relatively few, cautious, conclusions may legitimately be drawn from Table 2.1.6, though these can be underpinned more confidently when supplemented by journals such as the *European Journal of Teacher Education* for 1982, *Western European Education* (vol. 19, issue 2, 1987), and other articles such as Broadfoot *et al.*'s (1987) comparing certain French and British teachers. What does appear evident from even a cursory examination of Table 2.1.6 is that there is considerable variation in the length and nature of basic training, and that, in spite of frequently reiterated claims about the importance of professional updating, in some countries it is difficult for more than a few teachers to be sure of any form of post-experience education. This not only limits the horizons of individual teachers and renders them less capable of innovation (the central theme of Project No. 8) or of the role-changes identified as important in the Final Report, but it also minimises possibilities of exchanges of facilities between member states, a matter that could become more important in Europe as a whole and especially, for the EEC countries, after 1992.

9. Institutional links

The last of the basic questions in the original list referred to the relationships of primary education with other official support services, and also with parents and with community organisations. Here, a distinctly encouraging picture emerges, though there are differences in detail between countries. Most depict harmonious and mutually helpful relationships with medical, dental, paramedical, psychological, social and legal services, which are seen working together for the benefit both of children and of their families. There is considerable variation of provision for children with special needs, the topic of Chapter 4.4. Here, a major issue is the extent to which these children are catered for in mainstream schools as urged in the Final Report or, as in the Netherlands, in a substantial variety of special schools, which nevertheless aim to return them to mainstream schools whenever possible. Occasionally, as in Spain, regret is expressed that such relationships had not been developed earlier.

Community participation in primary schools is mentioned by several countries, notably Portugal. Some initiatives in the field of community relations are particularly interesting, especially where parental participation and the extent of parental control is concerned, a matter that is further considered in Chapter 4.1. Official encouragement is widely given to parent–teacher co-operation, though this takes different forms in different countries and may, as Beattie indicates in his studies of the United Kingdom, France, West Germany and Italy, become a focus for quite acute political controversy (Beattie 1985).

Other forms of community link are more spasmodically, but just as interestingly, discussed. Communities themselves have different kinds of significance in different countries. Contrasts appear especially between predominantly rural and predominantly industrial areas, but also according to particularising geographical circumstances such as Scandinavian fjords, Alpine valleys and Mediterranean bays. Historical, economic and cultural circumstances too have impelled a distinction between Catholic and Protestant in West Germany, the Netherlands, Switzerland and Northern Ireland, between politically contrasted locations in, for example, France and Italy, and between language communities in countries such as Belgium, Luxembourg and again Switzerland. So links between primary schools and communities can be a delicate matter, and it is encouraging to see how far they have, nevertheless, developed. The self-sufficient isolation of the primary school is becoming a thing of the past, with clear implications for changes in the teacher's role; yet it seems that this evolution is being achieved without the opposite danger that schools might become mere replicas of the parochial visions of a thousand separate subcultures.

10. Problems and trends

The questionnaires yielded a picture of present and future problems and trends seen as important by the relevant authorities in the 22 countries. Their perceptions of what is important may not entirely coincide with those that other bodies, such as parents or teachers, might have offered, but these are particularly significant, since these are the ones on which legislative and administrative action is being, or is likely to be, brought to bear.

The original intentions of the CDCC would have been more directly fulfilled if the 'problems' and 'trends' had been separately considered. But, in practice, the distinction between these two categories was not consistently maintained, and it has proved more feasible, for purposes of this analysis, to combine them.

To some extent, each country's problems and trends are peculiar to itself. For example, Austria's concern with the modernisation of Germanic script, and Iceland's misgivings about the dual use of school premises, do not find ready counterparts elsewhere. Six of the member states - Belgium, Denmark, Greece, the Netherlands, Spain and Switzerland - replied to this part of the enquiry mainly in terms of the major political and administrative changes that they were planning or had actually introduced. However, a number of themes recurred from country to country, and these are embodied in Table 2.1.7. Of course, this table is little more than a checklist of trends and problems, and makes no attempt to quantify their scale or intensity or to indicate how those problems and trends are perceived in the various countries concerned: the detail required for this purpose is to be found in the individual reports in Chapter 2.2.

Table 2.1.7 Some problems and trends in European primary education regarded as important by national authorities in the member states

Member state	*Organisation*										*Curriculum*										*Other*						
	Demographic change	Rural problems	Migration to cities	Relations with local authorities	Length of primary schooling	Length of school day	Pre-school provision	Selection	Grading and transfer	Teacher availability	Motivation; truancy	Developmental emphasis	Balance and quality	Curriculum reform	Central planning	Particular areas	Language	Computer education	Multicultural education	Gender issues	Special needs: mainstreaming	Assessment	Teacher education	Migrants	Minorities	Deprivation	Links with society
Austria						✓			✓												✓	✓		✓			
Belgium																						(VLO and Cycle 5–8 Projects)					
Cyprus		✓			✓																		✓				
Denmark											(not specified)																
Finland				✓								✓															
France																✓					✓			✓		✓	✓
Germany (West)	✓ (falling)												✓	✓										✓			✓
Greece											(implementation of school reform)																
Iceland		✓				✓				✓				✓									✓				
Ireland	✓ (rising)		✓																		✓						
Italy						✓				✓						✓						✓					
Liechtenstein					✓	✓		✓													✓						
Luxembourg																✓	✓				✓		✓				
Malta							✓		✓			✓				✓						✓	✓				
Netherlands				✓														✓	✓	✓			✓				
Norway	✓ (falling)			✓			✓						✓		✓			✓		✓					✓		
Portugal		✓									✓																
Spain				✓	✓								(implementation)			✓							✓				
Sweden											✓	✓											✓	✓			
Switzerland														✓		(SIPRI Project)						✓	✓				
Turkey		✓		✓	✓						✓												✓				
United Kingdom	✓ (falling)				✓					✓						✓											

From this table it is apparent that a relatively small number of themes stand out as being of widespread concern, for the present and the future. Among organisational issues, the most prominent are the relations between central, regional and local authorities in the implementation of policy, and modifications in the span of primary education and in the length of the school day. Rural schools, and especially small schools with their specific difficulties, including the consequences of internal migration of population noted in Chapter 1.2, give rise to considerable concern. Falling total population, also analysed in Chapter 1.2, is seen as presenting both difficulties and opportunities. The opposite case of Ireland's rising population, noted as an exception in Chapter 1.2, emerges here also and gives rise to problems of its own: a sharp contrast to the days a century ago when Ireland was characterised by massive overseas emigration.

The second group of problems and trends is concerned with curriculum. Here, there is quite substantial emphasis in some of the national reports on liberalisation and on movement towards a more balanced programme based substantially on children's development. Linked with this there is some concern about levels of motivation and truancy, and the tenor of the reports as a whole indicates that this concern may be more widespread than Table 2.1.7 shows. This is, of course, an issue that gives rise to controversy about how far answers to such problems can be sought in curriculum, and how far they are dependent on developments in society as a whole. It is noteworthy that Project No. 8 explored the specific question of underprivileged families in relation to motivation in primary school work <DECS/EGT [85] 21>. Meanwhile, some countries have paid close attention to specific areas of curriculum: France lists six of these (reading, music, arts, history, civics and ethics). Cross-curricular issues too, such as multicultural education, are taken seriously, once again more so than the entries in Table 2.1.7 alone might suggest.

A set of miscellaneous issues is also embodied in Table 2.1.7. Of these, three (assessment; special needs and mainstreaming; and one that emerges with uncomfortable prominence, namely teacher education) have been discussed earlier in this chapter, while the two latter figure also in Chapter 4.4 and in Section 5. It is encouraging to see the importance of these issues so substantially recognised, but it is also sobering to realise how far governments and administrations regard them as problems whose solution is totally dependent on considerable commitment and effort, notably from teachers and teacher-educators, who are widely expected to perform social miracles without the aid of an Aladdin's lamp of genius or a cornucopia of resources.

It may be this official confidence in teachers' superhuman powers that accounts for the absence from Table 2.1.7 of one particular issue, that of lack of resources; only Turkey actually specifies this as a problem! But, to be just, throughout the reports there are plenty of indications that it is a widespread concern. In recent years there has been something of a world-wide retreat from the extension of public expenditure on education, and in such circumstances there could be a danger that the primary sector might be liable to the most severe cutbacks. Yet in practice it is encouraging to observe that most member states, having firmly embedded primary education in their national structures, appear determined to preserve its slice of the national cake, even when the cake itself is less lavishly baked.

11. Regional patterns?

In view of the historical, geographical and social differentiation of Europe outside the socialist bloc, the possibility suggests itself that regional patterns might be detected among the national reports.

In general, this appears not to be the case. The nearest approach to such a pattern appears among the five historically linked Nordic countries, with their later ages of entry (hitherto) to compulsory schooling, their comprehensive schools spanning the years from 7 to 16 (with possible extension envisaged), their long summer intervals and dark winter days, their generally progressive approach to curriculum, and the occasional social strains that they encounter in pioneering innovation. The two Iberian states have in common their relatively recent emergence from the relics of Fascism, so that they are characterised by a consciously reformist policy, though Portugal does not share Spain's problem of regional languages and cultures. The other southern countries differ too sharply from one another, both politically and culturally, to permit the designation of a common Mediterranean approach. Fortunately, the lag in literacy levels in southern Europe when compared with the northern lands, pointed out by Dottrens in 1962, is no longer noteworthy. A thread of similarity does run through the three smaller Alpine countries (Austria, Switzerland and Liechtenstein), with their interesting interplay between innovation and tradition. Meanwhile Belgium and that seat of innovation, the Netherlands, also present some common features, especially their initiative in bringing some of the pre-school age-band within primary schools and, differently, in their approach to the question of religious diversity. Luxembourg does not follow its neighbours closely in these policies. Of the remaining outer countries, Ireland has an image of its own, though conscious of a former semi-colonial status reflected in its educational history, as is the case also with two other outer islands, Cyprus and Malta; this has left a rather different legacy from the situation in other countries in which nations or groups have been affected through political control by others. British legal and administrative influence has affected, in some ways, developments in all three of those countries, though the Atlantic island has little else in common with those in the Mediterranean. The remaining, larger, countries all epitomise important elements in the European educational tradition, but stand out as self-sufficient units or federations rather than manifesting any collective qualities beyond those shared with the rest of the Council's members.

So there is relatively little support for the notion of regional differences within the CDCC's area. Almost as much variety could in fact be found between regions in a politically more homogeneous unit such as the USA, or even within some of the plural CDCC states themselves. It is, incidentally, interesting to note that no discernible lines of division in primary education can be drawn between those countries that have adhered to the European Economic Community, or to NATO, and those, mostly among the smaller members, that have not. This relative absence of sharp territorial differentiation bodes well both for the continuing effectiveness of European co-operation in primary education, and for the development of mutual understanding.

12. Some additional considerations

The national reports were intended to reflect the concerns expressed by the CDCC and the Vaduz Conference. They cover a wide and comprehensive range of topics. Yet when these are set against the whole canvas of concerns raised nowadays by practitioners and students of primary education, there are a few rather scattered gaps where the canvas shows through.

In view of the centrality of the encounter between children and the curriculum, more attention might well have been paid to how children learn. Experiment and research have been focused on this issue since the days of Pestalozzi, yet in a number of these reports the learning process is rather taken for granted, and figures only fleetingly among the problems listed. In particular, the question of biorhythms in relation to learning, a matter that gave rise to considerable discussion at Vaduz <DECS/EGT [83] 64, pp. 9–11 > has been almost overlooked, and little attention is paid to the metacognitive elements in learning, and in the disposition to learn, which figured substantially in the Final Report and in Project No. 8's research programme (see Chapter 6.1).

In similar vein, it is implied that the official curriculum is all that needs to be stated. Nowadays, it is commonplace that the whole range of considerations collectively known as the 'hidden curriculum' must also be taken into account (Blyth 1984, ch. 7). There are hints, themselves sometimes rather hidden, that governments are aware of this, particularly where an atmosphere is to be created for the pursuit of moral, civic or religious education. However, there is little overt recognition that the organisation and conduct of schools may themselves convey lasting messages to the children who attend them, particularly where those messages epitomise what a school really thinks of them and of other people.

One particular message of this kind that has attracted much attention in recent years is what it means to be a boy and a man, and what it means to be a girl and a woman, and how far girls should be treated differently (and often made to feel less important and less ambitious). These gender issues are by definition universal and therefore of at least as great importance as that of multicultural education but, in spite of the few noteworthy mentions in Table 2.1.7 and the airing of relevant considerations at the seminar on *Equal opportunities for girls: the role of the primary school,* held at Donaueschingen in 1987 <DECS/EGT [87] 37–E>, neither the reports, nor indeed the Handbook as a whole, pay these matters the attention that they deserve.

As was pointed out under (9), the question of links with communities could also have been more thoroughly explored. The Final Report lays great stress on this issue. On the one hand, the mobilisation of the human and material resources of communities in support of primary schools could be given more official encouragement. On the other hand, curricular links with local communities, long established through, for example, the tradition of *Heimatkunde* in German-speaking lands (stripped of the perversion that it underwent in Nazi times) and of environmental studies in the United Kingdom, could be extended to include progressive understanding of life in the community itself. Indeed, these two aspects could be brought together, as is done in a number of countries including Denmark, by bringing primary education within a comprehensive process of community education and development in which children, adolescents and adults all take part.

Europe, and the rest of the world, are moving into a 'post-progressive' age in primary education, one that is less readily self-confident, and one in which a more cautious and pragmatic approach is required than in the heyday of psychological and sociological positivism. As the century draws to its close, there is an awareness that the continent has been twice devastated since 1900 and has narrowly escaped destruction more than once in times of technical peace, together with a consciousness of political, technological and ecological trends that still threaten the vulnerable fabric of *fin de siècle* society. At the same time, primary education, sometimes seen in the past as one of the most menial or social activities, and at other times greeted almost reverentially as the harbinger of Utopia, is coming to be perceived as the unpretentious, yet indispensable, base on which any society must rest its plans and its hopes. The national reports, whatever their diversities may be, have in common a recognition of this fundamental significance of primary education now and for the future. They show, too, a determination to turn away from any kind of parochial complacency, and a growing recognition that primary education should be conceived in, and should present, a world perspective, within which the spiritual and material heritage of Europe can interact constructively with current political, social and technological changes in the shaping of the future of mankind. Moreover, through its response to the spirit of innovation promoted by Project No. 8, primary education itself demonstrates just the combination of realism with optimism and of experience with flexibility that it aims to promote in society as a whole, as the new millennium approaches.

CHAPTER 2.2

Texts of the National Reports on Primary Education in the Member States

Edited by Alan Blyth

These reports are presented in alphabetical order, in their most recent versions, and with their wording scarcely altered. However, as indicated in Chapter 2.1, lists of publications on primary education submitted by some national authorities in response to the original CDCC invitation are not included in the versions reproduced in the present chapter; they are grouped together in Appendix 1. In the material that follows, covering the sections of the original enquiry concerned with 'Basic information' and with 'Problems and trends', statistical tables have been retained, except where very considerable detail was included in the report as submitted. In some cases, where it appears to be of considerable general interest, there is quite extensive reference to recent research as well as to policy initiatives.

A word is required about the arrangement of notes in this chapter. Where they occur in tables of data, the related references have been retained immediately adjacent to the tables. However, where they figure as comments on the text of a report, they are collated not at the end of the report concerned but, as is the practice throughout the Handbook, at the end of the chapter. The number of such references is small.

1. AUSTRIA
<DECS/EGT [84] 104 rev>

1. Basic information

1.1 The school system in Austria

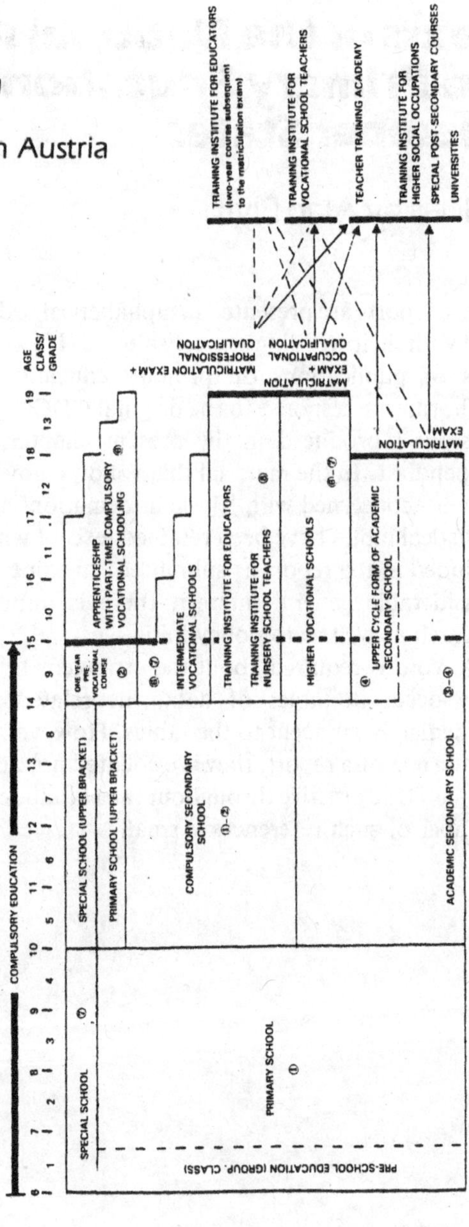

1.2 School organisation

In the School Periods Act it is stipulated that all children having their permanent residence in Austria are liable for compulsory schooling. It starts with the September 1st following upon the date when the child has completed his or her 6th year of age, and lasts nine school years.

Basic schooling comprises, in addition to the pre-school stage (pre-school group, pre-school class), the first four grades of primary school. In addition there are special schools for mentally or physically handicapped children which specifically take account of the various handicaps of children.

1.2.1 Admission to primary school at the beginning of compulsory school attendance

The admission to primary school of children compelled to attend school (i.e. those children who have completed their 6th year of life by August 31st of the following school year) is effected upon registration of the pupil. The deadlines for such registration shall be fixed by the responsible provincial schools boards on the basis of local requirements; however, the period allowed for such registration shall end, at the latest, one month before the beginning of the principal holidays. Parents or guardians have the duty of registering in due time their children compelled to attend school; if possible, they have to present them personally.

1.2.2 Early admission to primary school

Children ready for school and born between September 1st and December 31st of the current calendar year may be admitted to primary school early, in so far as parents submit a written application to this effect to the head of the primary school concerned within the period allowed for registration. A child will be considered ready for school if it may be justifiably assumed that the child will be able to follow instruction in the 1st grade without being subjected to undue physical or mental stress. Such early admission of children who are not yet of compulsory school age may be cancelled until the end of the current calendar year, if, after the admission of the child to the 1st grade, it becomes apparent that he or she is not ready for school after all. These children may afterwards be registered by their parents for attendance at a pre-school educational institution.

1.2.3 Deferral from school attendance of children of compulsory school age

Attendance in the 1st grade of primary school for children of compulsory school age is to be deferred if they do not show the necessary maturity for school. Such deferral may be pronounced *ex officio* or upon application of the children's parents. Children thus deferred from school attendance must or may (depending on how far away they live from the nearest pre-school institution) fulfil their first year of compulsory schooling in the pre-school stage (pre-school group or pre-school class.) In the case of children liable for compulsory schooling but not yet ready for school, both the time in which the child attended the pre-school stage and the time in which the child was deferred from school attendance will be included in the length of compulsory school attendance. In the case of children admitted early whose admission is cancelled later on, this time is not included in the length of compulsory school attendance.

1.3 The official aims of primary education

The official aims of Austrian schools are stipulated in the School Organisation Act of 1962.

According to the School Organisation Act of 25 July 1962,

> it shall be the task of the Austrian school to foster the development of the talents and potential abilities of young persons in accordance with ethical, religious and social values and the appreciation of that which is true, good, and beautiful, by giving them an education corresponding to their respective stages of development and to their respective courses of study. It shall give young people the knowledge and skills required for their future lives and occupations and train them to acquire knowledge on their own initiative.
>
> Young people shall be trained to become healthy, capable, conscientious and responsible members of society and citizens of the democratic and federal Republic of Austria. They shall be encouraged to develop an independent judgement and social understanding, to be open-minded to the philosophy and political thinking of others, they shall be enabled to participate in the economic and cultural life of Austria, of Europe and of the world and to make their contribution, in love of freedom and peace, to the common tasks of mankind. (Section 2)

Beyond this, the aim of the elementary school with its four grades is to give all pupils a basic general education (see section 1.9 below). Within the lower secondary cycle, the upper elementary school aims to build on the common elementary education for all pupils offered by the elementary school and to give pupils an extended education, possibly also a complementary education. Thus pupils are to be prepared for practical life as well as for continuing their educational careers.

1.4 The responsibility for the organisation of primary education

Legal authorities for school inspection are in most cases the district school boards, the provincial school boards, and – as the supreme authority – the Federal Ministry of Education, Arts and Sports.

Compulsory general schools are supervised by the district school boards, which are under the authority of the provincial boards. These are responsible to the Federal Ministry of Education, Arts and Sports.

The compulsory general schools are maintained by the communities, which means that the communities have to pay for the school buildings and their maintenance. The teachers' salaries, however, are paid by the state.

1.5 The links between pre-school and primary education and between primary and lower secondary education

Pre-school classes serve to promote the attainment of school maturity by children who, though liable to attend school on the basis of their age, are deferred from school attendance for one year.

Pre-school classes were pilot projects, but with the 7th Amendment of the School Organisation Act they became compulsory in 1983.

After the 4th grade of elementary school pupils have to go either to the compulsory secondary general school or the academic secondary general school.

1.5.1 Transfer to schools leading to higher forms of education

In the course of the 4th grade, either towards the end of the first semester or at the beginning of the second semester of the instruction year, parents or guardians are informed about the further educational career recommended for each individual child on the basis of his or her interests and past achievements.

The prerequisite for admission to *Hauptschule* (compulsory secondary school) is the successful completion of grade 4 of primary school. There are no further admission requirements, since allocation to achievement groups is effected in *Hauptschule* itself after an observation period of 8–12 weeks.

The prerequisite for admission to *allgemeinbildende höhere Schule* (academic secondary school) is the successful completion of grade 4 of primary school, an additional condition being that the child must have received the grade of 'very good' (1) or 'good' (2) in the subjects German, reading and mathematics. However, this is not necessary if the school conference states that, in spite of a grade of 'satisfactory' (3) in these compulsory subjects, the child will be able, judging from his other achievements, to meet the requirements of the *allgemeinbildende höhere Schule* (AHS). Children failing to meet these requirements may be registered by their parents or guardian within a period of two weeks with the school head of an *allgemeinbildende höhere*

Schule for an admission test. The aptitude requirements will be waived if the admission test is successfully completed.

1.5.1.1 Admission test

This admission test covers the subject matter discussed in the 4th grade of primary school at a slightly more difficult level. It comprises both a written and an oral test. This admission test may not be repeated.

1.6 The number of schools, pupils and teachers

Primary schools[1] in 1986/7

	Schools	*Classes*	*Pupils*		*Teachers*	
Burgenland	211	735	M	6,292	M	349
			F	6,104	F	756
			Tot.	12,396	Tot.	1,105
Carinthia	339	1,429	M	14,258	M	525
			F	13,429	F	1,709
			Tot.	27,687	Tot.	2,234
Lower Austria	653	3,237	M	31,995	M	1,030
			F	30,198	F	3,981
			Tot.	62,193	Tot.	5,011
Upper Austria	597	3,226	M	33,299	M	1,106
			F	31,300	F	4,522
			Tot.	64,599	Tot.	5,628
Salzburg	184	1,124	M	12,056	M	327
			F	11,016	F	1,440
			Tot.	23,072	Tot.	1,767
Styria	590	3,055	M	28,840	M	808
			F	27,306	F	3,856
			Tot.	56,146	Tot.	4,664
Tyrol	407	1,633	M	15,739	M	814
			F	14,802	F	1,567
			Tot.	30,541	Tot.	2,381
Vorarlberg	167	893	M	8,833	M	441
			F	8,521	F	992
			Tot.	17,354	Tot.	1,433
Vienna	247	2,196	M	24,961	M	345
			F	23,429	F	3,886
			Tot.	48,390	Tot.	4,231
Austria	3,395[2]	17,528	M	176,273	M	5,745
			F	166,105	F	22,709
			Tot.	342,378[3]	Tot.	28,454

1. Private schools (about 2.3%) are included.
2. Includes 34 schools with an upper bracket of primary school included.
3. Includes 9,307 pupils attending pre-schools, of which 3,810 with renounced early admission.

There are 3,395 primary schools with 28,454 teachers. In about 27 per cent of these schools two or more forms are taught by one teacher only.

1.7 The arrangements for grouping pupils and official class sizes

Usually pupils are grouped by age, but in some federal provinces with sparsely populated areas there exist also classes in which there are pupils of different age. One teacher teaches all subjects to his/her class except religious instruction and handicraft. The official class sizes are between 10 and 30 pupils, the average being 20; in optional activities like music (choral and instrumental music) and physical education there are from 12 to 15 pupils in one group.

1.8 The length of the school day, the school week and the school year

As a rule, instruction must not start before 8 o'clock and it may last maximally six periods in the morning, if the afternoon is off. The total number of periods per week has to be distributed by the school head as evenly as possible over the individual days of the week.

Schools operate from Monday to Friday or from Monday to Saturday. This has to be decided by the teachers and parents. There are different models for decision-making in the federal provinces, but as a rule one can say that if more than 20 per cent want to change from a five-day week to a six-day week (or the other way round) there has to be another vote.

The number of periods during a week varies between 20 and 26; there is one additional hour of remedial instruction for pupils who have learning problems. A period lasts 50 minutes; between the individual periods a sufficient number of breaks lasting between 5 and 20 minutes have to be scheduled.

In the federal provinces of Burgenland, Lower Austria and Vienna, the school year starts on the first Monday, in the other federal provinces on the second Monday in September and lasts till the beginning of the following school year, the summer vacations (July and August) included. So the school year has about 40 weeks.

1.9 The major areas of the primary school curriculum[1]

The syllabus of the primary school only constitutes a frame to be filled in by the teachers' pedagogical work, rather than containing a codification of educational subject matter and content in a fixed amount and precisely defined sequence. While this permits the application of a nationwide syllabus even for primary schools, limited shifts of subject matter, collections of locally relevant subject matter and additional content resulting from local conditions are also possible. Thus the numbers of weekly periods assigned to individual compulsory subjects may be determined, within the limits given in the distribution of class periods, by the provincial school board depending on local conditions. Moreover, there is the possibility of offering optional subjects and optional exercises, which are intended to cater to individual talents and preferences, as well as to remedial instruction.

In the syllabus of the primary school, the grades are combined into two 'cycles' covering grades 1 and 2, and grades 3 and 4, respectively. This subdivision is based on the recognition of the different developmental characteristics of the age-brackets and on a desire for a cautious modification of the system of single-year classes.

Primary schools provide the following compulsory subjects: German, reading, writing, factual instruction German, reading (3rd and 4th grades), mathematics, music education, arts education (1st and 2nd grades), arts education, writing (3rd and 4th grades), handicraft and physical education. Starting with the 3rd grade, a foreign language (English or French) is offered as a compulsory subject (without achievement grading). In the 1st and 3rd grades traffic education is also a compulsory subject; in addition to this, optional subjects such as choral music, instrumental music and physical training are offered in all four grades, and drama in the 3rd and 4th grades.

1.10 The main methods of pupil assessment

The basis of assessment in primary education is the permanent observation of pupils; oral examinations do not exist at the elementary level. But there are six written tests in the mother tongue and in mathematics in the 4th grade. Besides, dictations are possible in the mother tongue and standardised tests are available, although small in number.

1.11 Arrangements for the initial and in-service training of primary school teachers

The teacher-training academies train teachers for the primary school and for all other types of compulsory general schools (six semesters). For further training of teachers, authority mainly rests with the teacher-training institutes in the federal provinces.

1.12 Support services that are available to primary schools

The support services that are available to primary schools are psychologists and a free school medical service.

The psychologists have to assist the teachers in the field of testing children to ascertain whether they are able to attend primary school or should be sent to special schools.

The school medical service is free and a school physician visits each school periodically for medical checks and vaccinations. In the field of pilot projects there exist other support systems for teachers, e.g. '*Psychagogen*' and 'advisory teachers'. These are psychologically trained teachers who support the class teachers in cases of deviant behaviour of children; advisory teachers also advise the parents.

In classes with a high rate of migrant children there is an additional teacher ('accompanying teacher') for some periods a week to work with foreign children to handle their difficulties in learning German. Also in classes covering more than one grade the class teacher is accompanied by another teacher for about half of the periods a week to teach all the children of the same grade.

1.13 Institutional links between the primary school, parents and the community

In many primary schools there exist parents' associations which have legal standing. In theory their function is mainly advisory in certain educational matters (e.g. in the choice of textbooks); in practice they also have a social function. Their fundamental aim is to support co-operation between parents and school.

In the 4th Amendment (1986) to the School Instruction Act, institutionalised school community was extended in compulsory general schooling in addition to already existing parents' associations.

So one can distinguish between:

- already existing parents' associations.
- talks between the class teacher and parents about educational questions, about assessment, about the further educational career and health education (*Schulgesundheitspflege*). The number of these meetings is not limited. They should take place as often as necessary.
- the class forum, which is formed by the parents and the class teachers. On the one hand, this body has to decide upon certain matters, for example school skiing courses and school country weeks, house rules, and discussions on health education. On the other hand, it has to give advice on essential questions of teaching and education, in planning school activities and the dates of consulting hours for parents and for teaching materials.
- the school forum has to discuss all questions concerning more than one single class.

2. Problems and trends in primary education

2.1 School entrance phase (1st–2nd grade)

Entry into primary school raises a number of questions. About 13 per cent of the children have to be deferred for one year, more than 1 per cent of pupils voluntarily repeat the 1st grade, although every pupil is allowed to enter the 2nd grade regardless of his or her achievement. And at the end of the 2nd grade more than 2 per cent are unable to pass on to the 3rd grade and have to repeat a year. Therefore you can say that our school entrance phase is highly selective.

Now, in the field of pilot projects, models are implemented that give pupils two or three years to complete the first cycle. That means that class grouping on the basis of the pupils' age will not be the chief criterion any more, but flexible pupil-grouping arrangements.

2.2 Pilot projects to change pupils' assessment

At present, 1st grade pupils get a mark for all subjects (excluding religious instruction) at the end of the first semester (very good, good, satisfactory, sufficient, insufficient). At the end of the 1st grade, marks from 1 to 5 are awarded in each subject, although each pupil is allowed to go on to the 2nd grade even if some learning processes are not finished before the end of cycle 1, e.g. the ability to read fluently is one of the goals that should be reached at the end of the 2nd grade. As this is a very unsatisfactory situation, school experiments tend towards pupil assessment in the reports at the end of semesters and school years. In many projects all over Austria the marks 1–5 are replaced by a verbal evaluation or both forms are combined. Most pilot projects concern cycle 1. In the federal provinces Vorarlberg and Vienna they also include cycle 2.

2.3 Children with special needs

In several federal provinces, projects are undertaken to integrate handicapped children into normal classes. In these cases, the class teacher and a teacher of a special school plan together the instruction (team teaching) and in some periods they work with the whole class and others only with groups. At present these projects are merely at their beginning and we have only limited experience in this field. But this is a branch of pilot projects which is strongly demanded by parents. As Austria has a long tradition of special schooling, e.g. the blind and the deaf, and a very differentiated school system, these projects cause a lot of problems. One has to consider whether schooling in normal classes is the best way of helping pupils with special needs or not. To some extent it is a question of supplying specially trained teachers and special teaching materials, but it is also a financial question. Beyond this, the question of what integration really means is under discussion.

Though it is not possible to give a definition, one can say that pupils of both groups should be able to work together for a longer phase of the lessons, to fulfil more or less the same tasks, to solve the same problems, to do the same work, and so on. Just sitting together in the same classroom is not really integration. Nor is it integration if the handicapped child only serves as a means for learning processes of the other pupils.

2.4 Successful teaching as intended by the new primary curriculum

After a period of broad democratic involvement of about 1,000 teachers all over Austria in developing a new curriculum (1983–6) now a phase of thorough in-service training for primary teachers has begun to implement the main ideas of this new curriculum in daily school life and to change teaching methods. Especially, pupil-oriented methods should be put into practice, learning by playing and by doing, differentiation, learning as discovering, and individual learning in free choice periods, and so on. Austria thus wants to change teaching at the primary level and to create a humane school, better suited to the needs of the pupils.

2.5 Morning school versus day school

The regular Austrian elementary school (up to 26 periods a week; see p.89) is a morning school. So in 1974 pilot projects were started in which the daily attendance was extended to 8 hours. This type of school[2] provides integration of prep lessons and recreational periods within the school day. It offers the possibility for parents to drop their children off at school as early as 7.15 a.m. and to collect them as late as 5.30 p.m., because before and after school there are special courses supervised by teachers. In this school the so-called 'parallel teaching system' has been developed, the aims of which are to distribute all classwork, recreational courses, prep lessons, lunch hour supervision, etc. between two teachers as evenly as possible. It aims at ensuring complete equivalence of both teachers in the pupils' eyes, thus eliminating the danger of regarding form masters more highly than teachers of recreational classes. Furthermore it is intended to open new and more effective ways of classwork through complete co-operation and partnership of two teaching-partners. Opportunity is given to the children to relate to two equal but different teaching-partners, similar to the situation in a family.

Though these pilot projects have been successful, Austria is trying to find other models that are not too expensive and would make it possible to involve more than 5 per cent of the schools as now, because there is a great need for whole-day schools.

2.6 Pilot project on handwriting

The alphabet of handwriting which has been used up till now dates from 1924. While many European countries have changed their handwriting to a simpler form, Austria has changed only some letters. Now Austria is undertaking a broad pilot project in about 220 classes with about 5,000 pupils all over Austria to change the form of handwriting (see Appendix 1, Boyer 1986, p. 15). In this project, universities as well as teacher-training institutes are involved.

2.7 Migrant workers

In some classes in urban areas more than 50 per cent of the pupils are children of migrant workers. This causes a lot of social friction, not so much among the pupils as among the parents. Many Austrian parents feel that the quality of instruction in such classes suffers because too much attention is paid to these children's learning difficulties, which are mainly caused by the language barrier. There are different models to improve this situation: additional instruction in German to help them to tackle the language problem, e.g. German as a foreign language, or to have a second teacher in these classes to support the class teacher. For about five periods a week the so-called 'accompanying teacher' works with those migrant children who cannot speak German at all.

2. BELGIUM
<DECS/EGT [84] 88 rev>

Part 1

1. Official objectives

The Act of 29 June 1983 extended the compulsory education period to the age of 18. So primary schooling, which used to be self-contained and was the only education received by the majority of pupils, has started to focus on preparing pupils for secondary education.

Primary education aims at the harmonious development of all pupils and is preceded in 90 per cent of cases by optional kindergarten attendance. Various types of support exist to ensure that children from different walks of life have equal chances and a social life suited to each age. In addition to the most functional teaching possible in basic techniques, primary schools provide manual and aesthetic education.

2. Primary school organisation

Since Article 17 of the Belgian Constitution stipulates that 'education shall be free', primary schools are organised by various authorities: the state, the provinces, the municipalities, and private institutions. Among the latter, Catholic schools are by far the most important. The state takes full financial responsibility for its own schools, whereas the other organising authorities, official or private, may be subsidised in conditions laid down by the law.

Parents are free to choose whatever school they wish, whether it be a state or a subsidised private school. The composition of these systems varies according to the language area.

1. *French- and German-speaking sector*:

Official education	– state	20.03%	
	– provincial	4.94%	57.04%
	– municipal	32.07%	
Private education			42.96%
TOTAL			100.00%

2. *Flemish-speaking sector*:

Official education	-	state	17.82%	32.50%
	-	provincial	1.53%	
	-	municipal	13.15%	
Private education				67.50%
TOTAL				100.00%

Schooling is free in all primary schools and teachers' salaries are paid by the state, while the organising authorities receive an annual working grant of some 6,750 BF per pupil. Schools attached to the various organising authorities have virtually the same curriculum in the compulsory subjects, for which no minimum timetable is laid down.

Each organising authority enjoys freedom in its programming and methods. The state issues a curriculum for its schools, as do the large cities and the Catholic Education Federation. State inspectors visit the subsidised schools, as a guarantee of the standard of teaching and source of advice to teachers and school authorities.

3. Liaison between primary school and infant school

Children of 2½–6 are admitted to the kindergartens attached to primary schools, which are under the authority of the Ministry of Education. In the last few years efforts have been made to improve the integration of these two levels: play methods have been extended to primary education, teachers take part in the process and there is a greater wealth of teaching material. The 'Project VLO' (VLO – reformed primary education) in Flanders and the 'Cycle 5–8' in Wallonia are experiments in bringing the two levels of basic education closer together.

When a primary school is attached to a public or private secondary school, the transition to secondary education is easy. Moreover, as the choice has been delayed by the introduction of the first two observation classes, adjustment is facilitated.

Children who have failed to obtain a primary school certificate are admitted at the age of 12 to class B, known as the 'reception class'.

4. Number of pupils and teachers

Year	*No. of pupils*	*No. of schools*	*No. of classes*	*No. of teachers*
1. *In the Flemish-speaking region*:				
1977–8	499,345	2,575	22,858	27,349
1981–2	443,386	2,323	21,569	26,744
1986–7	429,822	2,470	—	25,839

2. *French- and German-speaking region*:

1977–8	379,169	2,553	17,419	19,135
1981–2	358,385	2,295	17,219	18,846

In Flanders the average number of pupils per teacher fell from 18.25 per cent in 1977–8 to 16.57 per cent in 1981–2, and in Wallonia from 19.81 per cent to 19.01 per cent. Remedial teachers and principals relieved of class responsibilities are not included in these ratios.

5. The grouping of pupils

Over the six years of primary schooling, the course is divided as follows:

- level 1, two years, for 6–8 year olds;
- level 2, two years, for 8–10 year olds;
- level 3, two years, for 10–12 year olds.

Three-quarters of the children attend schools with more than three qualified teachers. They are divided into age-groups and most classes cover only one year of schooling. However, mixed age-groups do exist for pedagogical reasons, and are even formed at times for certain school activities in the basic subjects.

6. School timetable

Primary education involves a minimum of 28 hours of lessons per week. The school year comprises 182 school days, each week consisting of nine half-days. It begins on 1 September and ends on 30 June.

7. Subjects taught

The compulsory subjects are laid down in Section 50 of the relevant Act. They are: reading in the language of the region, writing, simple arithmetic, the legal units of measurement, elementary French, Dutch or German according to local needs, the geography and history of Belgium. Only in schools in the Brussels conurbation and a few schools along the language frontier is a second language a compulsory subject (3 hours per week in the third and fourth primary years and 5 hours per week in the fifth and sixth primary years). Subsidised organising authorities may add subjects to the curriculum or appoint special teachers at their own expense (e.g. for music, drawing or handwork).

Public schools must also offer a free choice between a course of secular moral education and one of four courses of religious education (Catholic,

Protestant, Jewish and Islamic), each involving two or three hours of tuition per week.

8. Pupil assessment methods

The directives and advice issued show that assessment is designed to promote the continuous progress of each child. In the 'VLO' schools and the 'Cycles 5–8', the accent is on pupil observation and individual records are recommended. However, oral and written tests and examinations are a feature of the majority of schools. The totting up of marks is not recommended, but this practice is still frequent in school reports, which have not been standardised.

In pursuance of the royal decree of 15 June 1984, schools award a primary education certificate to pupils who have successfully completed their primary schooling by passing their sixth-year examination, which is the same for all schools in most towns.

In pursuance of the royal decree of 15 June 1984, the same certificate may be obtained by pupils who pass the cantonal examination. Catholic schools hold a similar test in each language area.

9. Initial and in-service teacher training courses

Two-year courses for holders of the upper secondary education certificate are provided in the official (municipal or state) primary teacher–training colleges or equivalent subsidised private institutions. These courses cover thoroughly the branches of primary education, as well as child psychology, educational method and the history of education.

They include some 16 weeks of practical training in primary school classes.

For in-service staff two days of training per annum, known as pedagogical lecture days, are organised by the ministry's inspectorate or by pedagogical advisers appointed by the subsidised private education authorities. Since 1978–9 Flemish teachers may take half a day off per fortnight for retraining without any cancellation of lessons for their pupils. Higher schools of education organise two- and three-year courses which are attended by some 10 per cent of teachers. The same applies to the seminar held by the ministry in the Easter holidays under the name of 'pedagogical week'.

10. School support services

Every school must be attached to a school medical inspection centre and may also be attached to a psycho-medico-social centre of CPMS (350 throughout the country), while the state schools combine both services.

At the mental health and rehabilitation centres depending on the Ministry of Public Health or the Ministry of Social Affairs school children in psycho-social care are treated, partly during school hours, by speech therapists, kinesitherapists and social welfare workers.

11. Institutional links between school, family and community

The two parents' associations (for public and private schools) are represented on the two reform commissions set up by the ministers. Parents are free to form their own groups and, at any rate in state schools, to take part in school management. Some schools associate parents closely with educational support activities such as remedial courses, group work, workshops, handwork, class excursions, etc. In the early primary school classes, a third of the schools organise open days. Before a school can try out a pedagogical experiment such as the 'Cycle 5–8' or the 'VLO', the consent of both parents and teachers is required.

Part II: Problems and trends

Reform movements

In Wallonia since 1971 and in Flanders since 1973, the three school systems have launched a concerted series of experiments for the reform of basic schooling, including:

1. The 'VLO' scheme, which this year covers 274 Flemish schools, and whose four features are:

- concern for the continuity of schooling for the 3–6 year olds and 6–12 year olds, in order to achieve a consistent education for all;
- differentiation measures at the two levels of schooling, tutoring and remedial teaching in cases of difficulty;
- family–school co-operation;
- activities to promote creative expression and harmonious development.

2. A pedagogical scheme known as the 'Cycle 5–8' combines in a large group the third-year kindergarten children (5 year olds) with the children in the first two primary classes (6–8 year olds), under a team of three teachers (one kindergarten and two primary school teachers), who are responsible for the continuous progress of 45 to 59 children over a period of three years.

This experiment, now operative in 67 French-speaking schools, is based on the following principles:

- offering the best chances of development to a maximum number of children;
- preventing too many cases of repeated years;

- smoothing the transition from kindergarten to primary school;
- responding to the child's interests by helping him to understand his natural, social and technical environment;
- abolishing premature cognitive learning in the third year of kindergarten and avoiding excessive intellectual emphasis at the first level of primary education.

3. CYPRUS <DECS/EGT [84] 95>

1. Aims, content and organisation

1.1 Official aims

The general aim of education in Cyprus is the development of free and democratic citizens with a fully developed personality, mentally and morally refined, healthy, active and creative, who will contribute with their work and their conscientious activity in general to the social, scientific, economic and cultural progress of our country and to the promotion of the co-operation, mutual understanding and love among men and peoples for the prevalence of freedom, justice and peace.

Education in Cyprus helps the new generation:

(a) to assimilate the spiritual and other achievements as well as the fruitful elements of the past,
(b) to capitalise on all the possibilities of the present, and
(c) to proceed to new achievements, in all sectors of social activity, drawing lessons from the past.

More specifically the basic objectives of primary education are:

- The full mental, physical and emotional development of pupils, through the acquisition of knowledge, skills and attitudes necessary for contemporary life.
- The proper understanding of the world, through systematic observation and study of the surrounding natural and social phenomena.
- The knowledge of history, particularly national, and the achievements of civilisation.
- The training of pupils for the right use of the language and the development of their ability to express themselves clearly and with precision.
- The development by pupils of:
  - love for their country, humanitarian ideals and democratic attitudes;
  - respect for work, social conscience and responsibility;
  - conscious discipline and ability to safeguard and exercise their rights;
  - understanding, respect for other people's ideas, initiative, co-operation and friendship;
  - interests, talents and inclinations.
- The preservation and development of pupils' health and the necessary skills and attitudes.

- The aesthetic education and systematic acquaintance of pupils with the works of art of the national and international civilisation.

1.2 Responsibility for the organisation of primary education at national, regional, local and school level

The Cyprus educational system in general is centralised. The Ministry of Education (Department of Primary Education) is responsible for the formulation of educational policy in all areas (administration, curricula, books, etc.) and through its inspectors evaluation and supervision are exercised. The system, however, gives opportunities to interested parties (teachers' and parents' associations) to participate in the process of policy formulation.

1.3 Links between pre-primary and primary education and between primary and lower secondary education

Pre-primary education is the responsibility of the Department of Primary Education; thus an easy transition of children from the kindergarten to the primary school is maintained. Some kindergartens are in the same buildings as the primary schools, so close contacts exist among children and teachers of the two levels.

Lower secondary grades belong to the Secondary Education Department and so, apart from some efforts at co-ordination of curricula at the central administration level, very few official opportunities exist for contacts and ties between primary school and lower secondary education. In fact, some gaps are sometimes observed, mainly in the methodology approaches, because of the lack of prescribed procedures for co-operation. Recently, compulsory education has been extended up to the 15th year of age (six years primary and three years secondary), and serious efforts are in progress for the preparation of a unified curriculum for the nine years of compulsory education.

1.4 Numbers of primary school pupils and teachers

During the school year 1986–7, the number of primary schools in Cyprus was 361 with a total pupil population of 52,066. The number of teachers during the same year was 2,236.

1.5 Arrangements for grouping pupils and official class sizes

Pupils are grouped for instruction according to age (grade level), regardless of ability. Only pupils with severe retardation attend special schools. Special needs of certain pupils are met in their regular classroom through individualisation of instruction by the teacher. Very rarely some pupils leave their regular class-group for a short time each day to have individual help from a special teacher.

This is the rule in schools where there are enough pupils of the same class to form a group. In the rural schools, however, where the number of pupils is very small, multi-age grouping is employed. In such schools, groups are formed by 1st and 2nd graders, 3rd and 4th, and 5th and 6th. In smaller schools we find groups of 1st, 2nd and 3rd graders and of 4th, 5th and 6th graders, while in even smaller schools the whole elementary school, all six grades, forms one group with one teacher.

The official class size is 34 pupils maximum. For the single-teacher school the maximum number of pupils is 25 and for the two-teacher school, 50.

1.6 Length of the school day, the school week and the school year

Lessons in the primary schools start on 15th September each year and finish on 28th June. There are two weeks of vacation for Christmas and another two for Easter. The number of working days is approximately 210. The working day lasts from 8.00 a.m. to 12.30, every day, for six days a week.

1.7 Major areas of the primary school curriculum

The major areas of the primary school curriculum are: language (Greek), mathematics, science, social studies, art, music, physical education, home economics and English.

1.8 Main methods of pupil assessment

The assessment and evaluation of pupils' performance is achieved mainly by the following methods:

- continuous observation and record keeping by the teacher;
- testing (formative and summative evaluation);
- self-assessment on the part of the pupil.

Emphasis is given to self-evaluation by the pupils and to the progress that each individual makes, in relation to his/her previous standards.

1.9 Arrangements for the initial and in-service training of teachers

1.9.1 Initial training

All primary school teachers are graduates of the Pedagogical Academy (teachers' training college) of Cyprus, an institution of tertiary education with a three-year programme of studies.

1.9.2 In-service training

It takes many forms, such as the following:

(a) *Meetings of teaching staff*: They are called by the headmaster once a week for the discussion of subjects arising from school work.
(b) *Seminars held in small areas*: These are organised by the inspectors regularly throughout the year. Some of these seminars deal with subjects concerning school administration and are attended only by headmasters. The majority of seminars, however, deal with topics which interest all teachers such as: classroom atmosphere, the teaching of various subjects, pupil evaluation, grouping of pupils, etc.
(c) *Courses organised by the Pedagogical Institute*: Many short courses are organised every year by the Pedagogical Institute on a variety of subjects, and are attended by teachers on a voluntary basis. Sometimes experts from abroad conduct these courses, within the framework of educational exchanges with other countries and UNESCO programmes.
(d) *Scholarships*: A small number of teachers each year have the opportunity for further training abroad, through scholarships.
(e) *Radio and television broadcasts*: Both radio and television broadcasts are used for in-service training of teachers.
(f) *Independent study*: Teachers are encouraged to keep abreast of new developments through independent study. To facilitate such study the Ministry of Education keeps an education library. Also an *Education Bulletin* is published regularly every two months, and is distributed free to all teachers.

1.10 Support services

(a) A school medical service operates more or less adequately in the towns, where doctors and school nurses visit schools and examine children. The schools in the rural areas, however, are less often served by such units.
(b) There are seven psychologists in the 'Counselling and Guidance Service' of the Ministry of Education, who examine cases of primary school children with mental or general behaviour problems, and advise headmasters and teachers accordingly.
(c) Advisers (for each subject) visit schools regularly and work with the teachers, helping them with demonstration lessons, teaching methods and materials.

1.11 Institutional links between the primary school, parents and the community

The basic links between the primary schools and the community and parents are the 'school committees' and the 'parents' and teachers' associations'. The school committees' role is mainly concentrated on school buildings, furniture, equipment and their maintenance, whereas PTAs cater for the welfare of the pupils, and in general they demonstrate a keen interest in the whole school programme. The 'school for parents' is another institution which plays an important role in the education of parents on matters relevant to their children's school life and their general development.

2. Problems, trends and intended changes or reforms

(a) The main problems in primary education are:

- the many small rural schools and the opposition presented by parents to the efforts by the ministry to consolidate them;
- the in-service training of teachers;
- the provision of special education to persons who need it, and who are scattered in small rural communities.
- the short duration of the children's attendance at school;
- teachers' evaluation.

(b) A major trend is the more active participation of both children and parents in all aspects of school life. This is encouraged by the system because it is believed that through this participation responsibility is developed and the democratisation principle is adequately served.

A second trend is the 'mainstreaming' idea. Children, regardless of ability, are grouped together, when they are of the same age. Only in cases of severe retardation do children attend special schools.

(c) The expansion of the duration of the school day, in combination with the abolition of Saturday work, is a change which currently is under serious consideration.

4. DENMARK <DECS/EGT [84] 94>

The Folkeskole in Denmark

The aim of the *Folkeskole* is – in co-operation with parents – to give pupils the possibility of acquiring knowledge, skills, working methods and ways of expressing themselves which will contribute to the all-round development of the individual pupil.

In all of its work, the *Folkeskole* must try to give possibilities to pupils to gain in experience and in self-expression, to allow them to increase their desire to learn, expand their imagination, and develop their ability to make independent assessments, evaluations, and form personal opinions.

The *Folkeskole* shall prepare pupils to take an active interest in their environment, to participate in decision-making in a democratic society, and share responsibility for the solution of common problems. Thus, teaching and the entire daily life in school must be based on intellectual freedom and democracy.

The Danish *Folkeskole* – the primary and lower secondary school – is a comprehensive school in which pupils are in principle kept together in the original classes throughout the entire period of compulsory education. However, it is possible for pupils in top forms to choose between a number of options.

The Danish *Folkeskole* is characterised by being decentralised to a considerable extent. Such decentralisation implies that the content of teaching is not decided upon at the central level. Thus, the subject matter taught may vary from one municipality to another, as well as from school to school.

The content of teaching is based on the locally adopted curricula for the different subjects. However, these local curricula are generally drawn up on the basis of guidelines issued from central quarters, and in many instances the central and local curricula are the same.

A curriculum in the Danish *Folkeskole* lays down the framework for the content of teaching. This framework may be an indication of activities to be pursued in the subject, and examples may also be given. A list of such examples is in most cases open-ended, thus offering an opportunity for adding more examples.

A curriculum may be more or less specific. Thus, it may comprise areas that *must* be taught as well as some that *may* be taught. However, generally speaking, some kind of framework exists which the teacher must respect. On the other hand, the teacher can be sure of being given sufficient freedom of action within this framework, in that such freedom *must* be provided in pursuance of Section 16 (4) of the Primary and Lower Secondary School Act: 'The more detailed planning and organisation of the educational activities, including the decision on teaching forms, methods and material, shall to the widest possible extent take place in co-operation between the teachers and the pupils.' It should be noted that the wording is 'to the widest possible extent' and not 'as far as is possible', i.e. there is a possibility that must be utilised.

Two conditions in the *Folkeskole* must thus be met for a subject area to become a reality in teaching practice. First, the locally adopted curricula must offer the possibility - i.e. the subject matter must be within the framework - and secondly the possibility must be exploited by a decision taken in the classroom itself.

Only in rare cases will the framework be an obstacle. This also means that the introduction of a subject area is actually a very complicated democratic process in the Danish *Folkeskole*. It is a process that has a formal basis, but no formal rules as to the procedure governing it.

Is it not dangerous to let such matters be decided upon in such an informal, democratic process? Well, the *Folkeskole* is at any rate not afraid of doing so.

What we have tried to explain applies in principle to much of the subjects taught, i.e. all the topics in the curriculum that do not bear the tag *shall*.

In this way the subject matter does not easily become something traditionally included in the lessons, with the ensuing risk of becoming tedious and of seeming irrelevant. It will be included in the curriculum as a result of a collective decision-making process ensuring commitment to the subject. Thus the school will become a mirror image of life outside the school gate, and that is just the point!

But how can examinations be worked out at the central level when the content of teaching is decided upon at the local level through locally adopted curricula?

The task of the ministry was to fill in the framework for the examination system laid down by the Primary and Lower Secondary School Act. This could be done by issuing further regulations, and this is where the examination standards come into the picture. Such standards are based on the teaching, as it is taken for granted that it is the teaching that will decide how the examinations are to be, and not the other way round. While drawing up a list of examination standards, we have had to recognise that it is not possible to draw up examination standards that are as specific as is desirable, and we have also had to recognise that it is no easy matter to distinguish between examination *requirements* and examination *forms* in all fields. However, we should like to say, as a general rule, that the examination requirements must be constant, one of the reasons being that it is essential for the teacher's planning of his instruction, while it is desirable that the examination forms be developed to such an extent that they become as expedient as possible.

As we mentioned earlier, continuing development is a characteristic feature of the Danish *Folkeskole* and much development takes place at the local level – in the individual municipalities. We cannot frame the development behind closed doors in the Ministry of Education; it is our task to update the system, listen to grass roots opinion, find the schools where the system works well and try to make the others follow suit.

Figure 1 Educational provision in Denmark

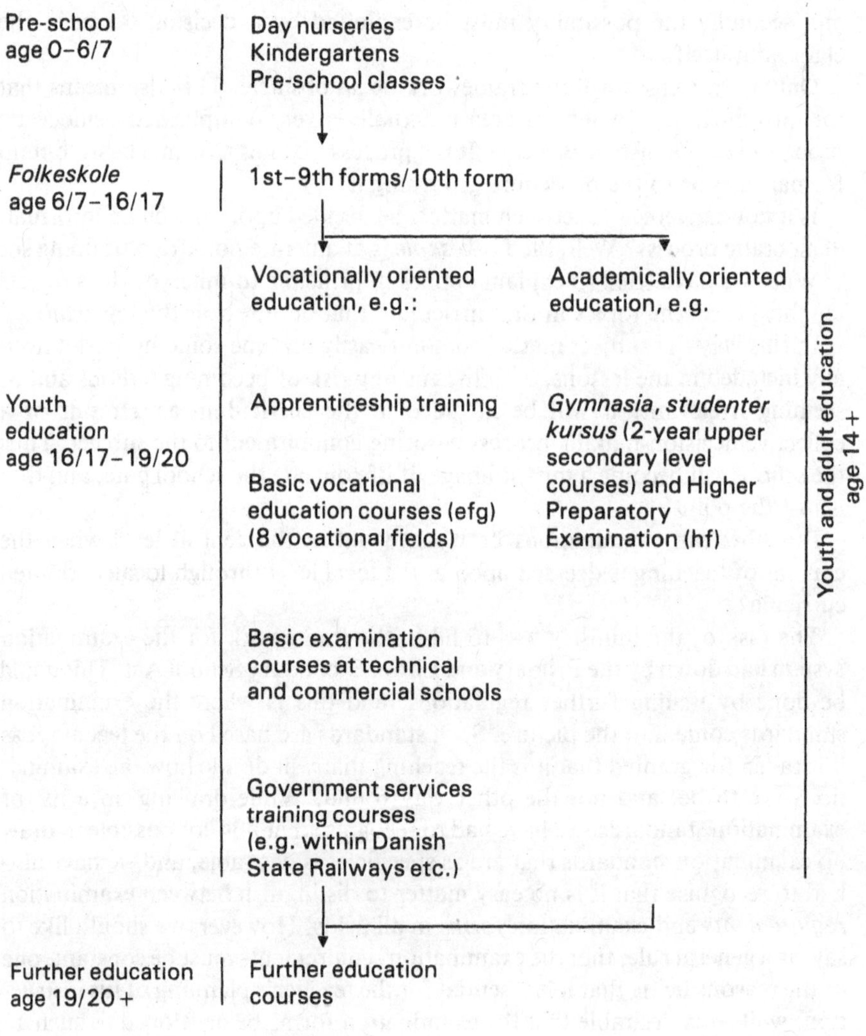

Appendix

I The number of primary and lower secondary school pupils and teachers

School year 1981/2: 709,623 pupils
59,939 teachers

II The arrangement for grouping pupils and official class sizes:

School year 1981/2: 3,868 classes
class size 19.1

III The length of the school day, the school week and the school year:

Form	*Maximum number of hours*
1	4
2–3	5
4–5	6
6–10	7

Form	*1*	*2*	*3*	*4*	*5*	*6*	*7*	*8*	*9*	*10*
Minimum number of lessons according to the Act	15	15	18	20	23	24	24	24	24	24
Maximum number of lessons according to the Act	20	20	23	25	29	30	30	30	30	30

The school year lasts 40 weeks of 5 days each, i.e. 200 school days in all. Some days can be used for school camps, field trips, practical trainee work or similar activities:

Form	*Maximum number of days*
1–7	10
8	20
9–10	30

IV The major areas of the primary and lower secondary school curriculum

(Details not supplied)

V The main methods of pupil assessment

Parents are naturally interested in knowing what their children are learning, which is why they must be informed of their child's progress, as the school sees it. This is to be done regularly, and not less than twice a year.

The manner in which it is done - orally or in writing - is determined locally. However, any pupil leaving school after the 7th form is given a Leaving Certificate containing his or her marks in certain subjects.

In the 8th–10th forms, performance marks, and marks for the year's work, are given in the same subjects in which they can take leaving examinations. Pupils may present themselves for examination in one or more subjects and be given marks in these. No particular mark is required for passing.

VI Arrangements for the initial and in-service training of primary and lower secondary school teachers

The DLH (Royal Danish College of Pedagogical Studies)

The DLH is a unique institution of its kind. Its beginnings date back more than a century. It employs a considerable staff (150 full-time teachers and 800 part-time). On average, it accepts (both at its headquarters and in its eight branches) 35–40 per cent of the 45,000 teachers practising in the sector for which it is responsible. A state institution, responsible to the Ministry of Education, it has the status of an establishment of higher education entitled to award qualifications up to doctorates in the educational sciences.

Its principal task is the advanced training of teachers of all disciplines in the compulsory schooling sector (including the arts and dress design, but not physical education and woodwork, for which there are special institutions) and also that of their trainers in the training colleges and of the teachers in the demonstration schools.

The DLH also provides training for teachers in the special education given to children in serious difficulties, school librarians, career advisers and school psychologists: these represent forms of training slightly different from in-service training, since the courses are compulsory for eligibility for the functions concerned.

It also organises special courses for headmasters.

VII The support services which are available to primary schools, e.g. doctors, psychologists, social workers, advisers

Special aid offered by the school - psychological counselling

Today all municipalities have either established their own school psychological centres or have established counselling offered by school psychologists in co-operation with other municipalities, and in some cases in co-operation with the county.

Psychologists and consultants for remedial education are attached to the school psychological centres.

This psychological counselling is attached to the school system as a whole and is advisory to the school as well as to the parents and to the authorities.

The school psychological centres co-operate with the social services.

Referral to school psychological examination is in most cases made at the request of the class teacher following discussion with the pupil and the parents, but the parents may also take the initiative, as may the pupil. At many schools the school psychologist has fixed office hours.

The school psychologists are not a decision-making body, but are only an advisory service.

Health in schools

The health service provided by the school comprises the school doctor, the school nurse and the school dentist.

The school medical services are not responsible to the *Folkeskole*. The school doctor, the school nurse and the school dentist are administratively placed under the social service administration of the municipality.

The *school medical officer* does not give treatment; his work is based on direct contact and consists in referring to the appropriate specialists, in co-operation with the school - including the pupil himself - and with the home.

Many schools employ *school nurses* who assist the school doctor in his work and give the children routine medical examinations, give first-aid in the case of accidents, and treat small injuries which may occur while the children are at school; the nurse also goes to the home if she feels the need to discuss the health of a pupil with his or her parents.

Most municipalities have established *school dental clinics* for the pupils' annual examination. In municipalities where there are no school dental clinics, co-operation has been established with local dentists. The school dentists examine and treat the children's teeth and straighten teeth. Many school dentists also participate in preventive work by giving lectures to the children and their parents on the care of teeth and on the importance of food for dental health. The school dentist also arranges periodic fluoride rinsing for the children.

VIII The institutional links between the primary school, parents and the community

The municipal council has the final decision concerning how the educational plan at your child's school is to be formed. As a parent, you have a special opportunity to exert your influence in educational matters in your municipality. You are one of those who decides who is to represent the parents on the school board which supervises your child's school. From among its members, the school board elects representatives to the educational committee which supervises the municipality's entire school system. In other words, you have indirect influence on who is to represent the parents on the educational committee.

Figure 2

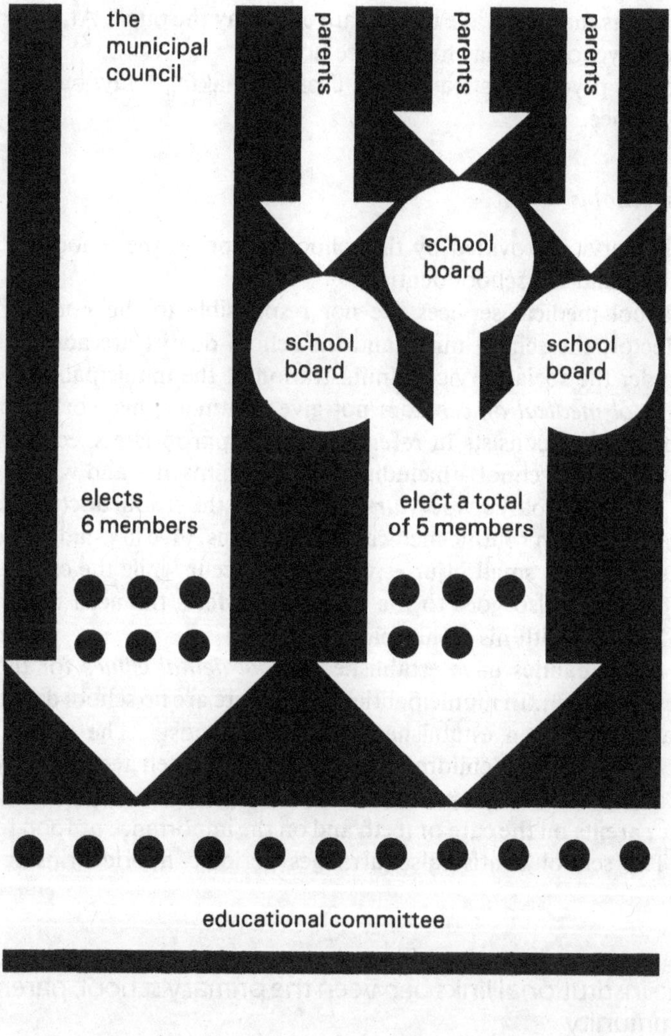

Figure 2 illustrates the system in a somewhat simplified manner. The educational committee drafts educational plans. The school board must comment on such a draft before it is discussed by the municipal council.

Through the school board, you have influence on a number of questions, e.g. the distribution of subjects among the school's teachers; the distribution of lessons throughout the week.

As a parent you are free to decide on the following matters:

- whether or not your child will attend the *Folkeskole* at all, or be taught in some other way;
- whether or not your child should repeat a form, if this is suggested by the school;
- whether or not your child is to be exempted from Christian studies. If your child is 15 years old or more, he or she must agree with your decision.
- what educational materials are to be used;
- the school rules;
- how large the school's budget should be;
- how the money should be used.

On the following questions, a decision cannot be reached until they have been discussed by the parents, the pupils and the school together:

- what subjects your child should choose;
- what courses your child should choose;
- whether or not your child should continue school after the period of compulsory education is at an end (i.e. after nine years of instruction).

5. FINLAND
<DECS/EGT [84] 89 rev>

Introduction

1. In Finland compulsory schooling begins at age 7 and lasts ten years, unless the student has completed the comprehensive school before that.

2. In Finland compulsory schooling consists of a nine-year comprehensive school course, which is divided into a six-year lower stage and a three-year upper stage.

3. The current comprehensive school legislation dates from 1983.

Tasks and objectives of the comprehensive school

4. The tasks and objectives of the comprehensive school are laid down in legislation, which stipulates:

(a) *The tasks*
- The comprehensive school is nationally unified and provides citizens with a basic education.

(b) *The objectives*
- The comprehensive school aims at educating its pupils into balanced, fit, responsible, independent, creative, co-operative and peace-loving human beings and citizens.
- It should also teach its pupils to be decent and well-mannered and otherwise prepare them for life.

(c) *The instruction*
- The instruction and education given by the comprehensive school should provide students with the knowledge and skills they need in order to be able to develop personally, to function in social and working life, to make career choices and pursue further studies, to protect the living environment and nature, and to promote national culture and values as well as international co-operation and peace. This education should also promote equality between the sexes.
- The instruction must be in keeping with the students' age and abilities.
- The comprehensive school must strive to support the family in the rearing of the children.

5. These statutory aims are specified in more concrete terms in the

comprehensive school curriculum and in the various subject syllabuses. The objectives laid down in the relevant legislation apply to the comprehensive school as a whole and are not defined separately for the lower and upper stages.

6. The comprehensive schools are maintained by municipalities, which also draw up local curricula. The National Board of General Education, which is directly subordinate to the Ministry of Education, issues directives concerning the curricula and confirms the subject syllabuses. These documents leave the municipalities scope for decision on the organisation and content of teaching.

7. As already mentioned, compulsory schooling begins when a child turns 7. Before that, education is generally arranged by the social authorities. Comprehensive schools may, however, be authorised by the Ministry of Education to arrange pre-school education. This form covers a relatively small number of 6-year-old children at present. In most cases such education is arranged in connection with the two first classes of comprehensive schools situated in sparsely populated rural areas, where the social authorities would have problems with practical implementation of pre-school instruction. The general principle adopted in Finland is that pre-school education provided by the school authorities complements in sparsely populated areas the pre-school activities organised by the social authorities.

8. Co-operation between the day-care system (including the pre-school classes) and the comprehensive school takes the form of school visits arranged in the spring for 6–7-year-old children who will begin school in the autumn. Instructions concerning curriculum have been issued for both forms of pre-school education. These instructions underline the importance of developing general skills the children need in school.

9. During the school year 1987/8 there were a total of 378,000 children in the lower stage of the comprehensive school.

10. In the school year 1987/8 there were a total of 3,863 lower-stage schools in Finland. The majority of them were small school units with combined classes. Some 68 per cent of the schools had one to three teachers, but, owing to the small size of the classes, the pupils in these schools represent less than 20 per cent of the total number of lower-stage pupils in Finland. It is a good indication of the tendency to support small schools that the minimum number of students needed to keep a one-teacher school is six.

11. The formation of teaching groups is governed by a lesson hour quota system defined in the Comprehensive School Act. Each lower-stage school has a certain number (quota) of lesson hours per teacher post, part of which must be used for remedial teaching. In addition to this, each municipality has a certain computational quota that can be divided between schools in the area. In the school year 1987/8 the average quota was 29.7 lesson hours per class

teacher post. Each school decides on the size of its teaching groups within the framework of its lesson hour quota. When the whole class is taught by its class teacher alone it uses up one lesson hour; if the class is divided into two groups taught by different teachers it uses up two lesson hours, etc. The average size of a lower-stage teaching group (class) was 20 pupils in 1987/8.

12. The pupils' school day may not exceed 5 hours in grades 1–2 and 6 hours in grades 3–6. A teaching hour is 60 minutes, but only 45 minutes of it are used for actual teaching. The minimum lunch break is 30 minutes.

The pupils go to school five days a week, from Monday to Friday. In grades 1–2, the weekly number of study hours is 19–21, in grades 3–4, 23–25 hours and in grades 5–6, 24–26 hours.

The school year is 190 school days, beginning in August (usually mid-August) and ending on 6th June at the latest.

13. The subjects to be taught in the lower stage of the comprehensive school are defined in legislation. The Council of State decides on the distribution of lesson hours between the subjects. Within this framework each municipality makes its own work schedules. A great number of municipalities have left it to the schools to decide on their own schedules in the scope defined by the Council of State. This means that different schools in one municipality, or even different classes in the same school, may have different distributions of lesson hours. The different emphasis placed on subjects reflects the pupils' interests and their parents' views.

14. The subjects and the weekly lesson hours are shown in Table 1, which is based on a decision taken by the Council of State in 1985.

Table 1

Subjects	*Grades* 1	2	3	4	5	6
Mother tongue	7	7	5–6	5–6	4–6	4–6
Foreign language or second national language	—	—	2	2	2	2
Environmental studies, biology and geography	2	2	2–3	2–3	3–4	3–4
Civics and citizenship	—	—	0–1	0–1	0–1	0–1
Religion or ethics and life skills	2	2	2	2	1	1
History	—	—	—	—	1–3	1–3
Mathematics	3	3	4	4	4	3
Music	1–2	1–2	1–4	1–4	1–4	1–4
Art	1–2	1–2	1–4	1–4	1–4	1–4
Handicraft	1–2	1–2	2–4	2–4	2–4	2–4
Physical education	1–2	1–2	2–3	2–3	2–3	2–3
Maximum number of hours per pupil	19–21	19–21	23–25	23–25	24–26	24–26

The mother tongue is either Finnish or Swedish. The foreign language is English, German, French or Russian. Religion is usually either Evangelical-Lutheran or Orthodox, or possibly some other religion; pupils who have no religion are taught ethics. Civics and citizenship include student guidance. In the area where the Saami population lives, the mother tongue may be Saami or Finnish, and instruction may be given in Saami in other subjects as well.

15. The pupil's behaviour and diligence, as well as his/her skills in each subject are assessed at the end of the autumn and spring terms on a scale 4–10. The attainment of pupils in grades 1–3 may be assessed in a descriptive written report. The emphasis is on a continued formative assessment of the pupil's progress.

16. At the lower stage pupils are generally taught by a class teacher in all subjects. Only foreign languages are usually taught by subject teachers. Class teachers have a Master's degree in education (a five-year university training). According to an agreement reached in teachers' collective bargaining, teachers have three days of in-service training each year.

17. In Finland school psychologist services are not statutory, but schools in larger towns and cities provide these services. Finland has a network of educational counselling maintained by the municipalities, which also comprises a psychologist's and social worker's services. These services are intended for pre-school children, too.

In co-operation with health care stations, the local school authorities arrange medical and dental services. Each school district has a school nurse. In sparsely populated areas, medical services are arranged with the help of mobile clinics.

School meals are provided by the municipalities.

18. Each school is governed by a seven-member board of directors appointed by the municipal council. At least three of the members are pupils' parents, one represents the school's teachers and one the rest of the staff. Two or more schools may also have a joint board of directors. The board of directors has a considerable influence on school work, since it takes decisions on the work plan (which includes the use of the lesson hour quota and, in some cases, the distribution of lessons), on textbooks, on school rules, etc. Apart from various administrative tasks, the board of directors has a duty to further the education given by the school by developing co-operation between the school and home.

The responsibility for local school administration belongs to the municipal school board.

The situation in school development and future prospects

19. The present school legislation, which was passed in 1983, has introduced a considerable increase in the scope the municipality and the school have for

deciding educational content and teaching arrangements. The municipalities adopted new curricula in 1986 and 1987. One of the central goals of the legislation is to support the municipalities in continuous development of curricula. The municipalities are encouraged to include more material on local culture, industry and economy, and nature and to keep the curricula up to date. As regards work in each school, the goal is to encourage a distinctive approach and an innovative methodology. It is considered important for the municipalities and schools to carry out continuous development and not be content with mere administrative changes required by the new legislation. The National Board of General Education has launched projects intended to support further curricular development.

20. One particular development object at the lower stage is integration of subjects. In this, the aim is to make use of pupils' activity in the learning process and to give a comprehensive picture of different phenomena to pupils. Although the existing regulations and statutes give a relatively large scope for such integration, some experiments have been launched to explore the need and possibilities for developing legislation in this respect.

6. FRANCE
<DECS/EGT [84] 20>

Aims

According to Section 3 of the Education Act of 11 July 1975, 'the function of primary education is to teach the basic skills: speaking, writing, reading and arithmetic; to foster the development of intelligence, artistic feeling and manual, physical and sporting abilities; to provide an introduction to the plastic arts and music; and to teach ethics and civics in conjunction with the family'.

The decree of 26 December 1976 adds that 'the specific features of the local or regional environment may be taken into account in primary education'.

Schools and classes

Primary education is *compulsory* for children between the ages of 6 and 11 years. It is provided in primary schools built and run by local authorities. The state takes care of the actual education, i.e. decides its content and trains and pays the teaching staff. Schools vary considerably in size: 12,500 schools still have only one class, about 28,000 have two, three or four and 20,000 have five or more.

'Educational mapping' – i.e. the opening and closure of classes and other organisational measures affecting schools – is done annually by the educational authority inspectorate of each *département*, after consultation with the joint councils representing staff and administration. The inspector is also in charge of school teachers and heads of schools throughout the *département*. The Ministry of Education controls the inspectors responsible for supervising and counselling primary school teachers in each *département* as well as the teaching staff and heads of teacher-training colleges, which provide the greater part of the primary school teachers' initial and further training.

In 1981–2 state primary education accounted for 3,850,000 pupils at elementary level and 122,000 in special education, which, added to the 2,065,000 pupils at pre-elementary level, amounted to a total of 6,037,000 pupils.

Estimates for 1982–3 indicate a slight drop in numbers at elementary level: 3,723,000 pupils.

At elementary level the average number of pupils per class is now 23.5.

Tuition

Primary education comprises five consecutive levels divided into three courses:

- preparatory course: 6–7 years
- elementary course: 1st year: 7–8 years
  2nd year: 8–9 years
- intermediate course: 1st year: 9–10 years
  2nd year: 10–11 years

At each level the curriculum provides for 27 hours of classes a week.

Educational continuity between the various levels is essential. Links between classes must be flexible to enable pupils to progress continuously without significant breaks and without repeating more years than strictly necessary.

Likewise, the earlier transition from nursery school to primary school and the subsequent transition from primary to secondary school must be effected smoothly:

- at one end, frequent contact between nursery school and primary school teachers facilitates follow-up;
- at the other, continuity between primary and secondary school is assisted by introducing the beginnings of a multiple-teacher system and by accustoming intermediate-level pupils to a more individual, independent style of work both in class and outside school hours.

Primary school activities are divided into three main educational areas:

- 1st area: French: 9 hours
  maths: 6 hours
- 2nd area: sensitivity training (7 hours) – ethics and civics, manual work, artistic activities, introduction to natural and social sciences (history, geography).
- 3rd area: physical education and sports: 5 hours.

The 27 weekly hours of activities are spread over nine half-days. The school year lasts 35 or 36 weeks.

The curriculum content of the various primary school courses was recently revised to reflect the conclusions drawn on the basis of policy discussion and methodological experimentation:

- in 1977 for the preparatory course
- in 1978 for the elementary course
- in 1980 for the intermediate course.

The learning aims defined for each course and each sphere of activity (French, maths, sensitivity training, PES), together with detailed teaching instructions, replace the former syllabuses.

School life

In each primary school the parents' elected representatives form the parents' committee, which, together with the teachers' committee, forms the *school board* under the chairmanship of the head. The local authority representative and the primary education inspector for the *département* are also members of the board.

The board is expressly consulted on school regulations, arrangements for remedial work to help pupils with difficulties, arrangements for a two-way flow of information between families and teaching staff, school transport, child-minding outside school hours, canteens, out-of-school and after-school activities and health care.

The responsibilities of school boards are currently being extended beyond the problems of school life to cover a school's educational work as a whole.

Teaching staff

Tuition is provided by primary school teachers, who currently number just over 180,000 at elementary level (i.e. excluding nursery school and infant classes).

Teachers are trained at teacher-training colleges. They are normally recruited by means of a competition open to those who have passed the *baccalauréat*; however, as a temporary measure arising from the large number of posts to be filled (particularly those created since 1981), a special competition is held in some *départements* for persons possessing a DEUG (diploma awarded at the end of a two-year university course), who will be able to start work sooner.

Major changes in the vocational training of primary school teachers have been made since 1979.

Training now lasts three years and comprises a year's basic training, at the end of which trainee teachers undertake to serve the state, and 2 years' advanced training linked to higher education and leading to the DEUG – a university diploma – and the primary school teacher's diploma. It includes numerous practical activities and opportunities for teaching practice.

In addition, advanced training courses have been provided for primary school teachers since 1972; each teacher is entitled to the equivalent of a year's training spread over his or her entire career.

Problems and plans

Action to reduce inequalities and failure at school may be regarded as the focal point of the various measures envisaged to improve the functioning of primary schools. Discussion currently centres on children in the learning process at school, the problems they encounter and the resources provided by the educational system to help them overcome their difficulties.

Main target areas at school

Following action on PES, specific campaigns have been launched to boost activities whose importance has hitherto been underestimated or to remedy methodological deficiencies:

- the *reading* problem remains the chief concern and a wide range of measures to improve training, awareness and classroom activities in this area continue to be applied;
- sustained efforts to promote *musical* and *artistic* education are still under way;
- new steps are to be taken on *history*, civics and ethics, which are a basic element of primary education.

Priority zones

These have been set up to make selective inroads on educational failure among children in difficult situations of one kind or another. As the difficulties they encounter are never purely educational, it is planned to adopt an overall approach to the various problems (improvement of living conditions and community, sports and cultural facilities, increase in aid to families), as well as relying on the work of the actual educational teams.

Action to help migrant children

The number of migrant children in primary schools has increased considerably. Some of the children, who do not speak French on starting school, need special teaching for a limited period to bring them up the minimum threshold level in French before starting to attend normal classes. In addition, as it is considered essential for foreign children to retain links with their languages and cultures of origin, they receive tuition in their own languages either outside school hours or as part of sensitivity training.

Integration

A major effort has been undertaken to promote the integration of handicapped children, or children with serious difficulties, into the educational system. The idea is to increase school capacity by improving teachers' skills and using a variety of methodological approaches, and to educate handicapped children in conditions as near normal as possible. A prerequisite of success is naturally to pursue the psycho-educational work done so far, for instance by increasing the number of psycho-educational aid groups (GAPP).

More effective integration of school into society

If these measures are to succeed, each school must of course develop its capacity for educational initiative and accordingly enlist the help of the various partners in education, who will be required to share joint management of the school on the basis of increased decentralisation: parents, local authorities, out-of-school educational groups, leading figures in the economic, social and cultural spheres, etc.

Hence the need for in-depth policy discussion, with the participation of all those concerned, to enable schools to adapt to their environment and present conditions.

7. GERMANY (WEST) <DECS/EGT [84] 93>

Section I

At the age of 6 children enter the age-group in which school attendance is compulsory and are enrolled in primary school. All children attend primary school together. As a rule primary school comprises grades 1–4 (grades 1–6 in Berlin).

1. The objectives of primary education are determined by the needs of the children of this age-group, by personal, individual and social requirements, and by the insights of educational research. Primary education attempts to provide basic cultural skills and all-round development for all children. It tries to improve equality of educational opportunity, particularly by placing strong emphasis on helping those children who show poor scholastic achievement. It imparts basic skills and abilities, in particular the 'three Rs', i.e. reading, writing and arithmetic, and serves the purpose of preparing the student in a non-specialised phase of education for the specialised teaching awaiting him in secondary education. The intention is to enable primary school students to experience and to structure the world around them in a manner befitting their age-group and to promote the development of their psycho-motor capacities, their interest in learning, their creativity and their social behaviour patterns.

2. The entire school system is under government supervision. Legislative and administrative responsibility for education, and thus for primary schools as well, lies almost entirely in the hands of the individual *Länder* as provided for in the Constitution. As such, teachers are civil servants in the employ of the various state administrations. The schools themselves are primarily institutions financed by the local communities. The supervision of primary schools is generally decentrally organised in the different *Länder* and takes place at the lower administrative level.

3. All of the *Länder* have provided special educational measures to facilitate the transition from the pre-school sphere to primary school. Initial teaching in primary education is designed to effect a gradual transition from learning by playing to learning in a typical classroom situation. Co-operation is sought between pre-school and primary school teachers, and co-ordination of methods and content in both areas is considered necessary. In terms of the way they are organised pre-school education (mainly kindergarten, privately financed, optional attendance) and primary education are quite different.

Apart from the situation in Berlin, grades 5 and 6 are part of lower secondary education. They are an orientation phase. Building on the basic education begun in the primary sector, these two years are designed to keep the decision on the student's further school career open until the end of grade 6, in order to have a more reliable basis for making such a decision.

The orientation phase can be organised independently of school types or can be school-type-dependent, relating to the *Hauptschule*, *Realschule* or *Gymnasium*, as the case may be.

4. In 1979 the number of students enrolled in primary schools was 3.1 million, the number of full-time teachers 124,000 and the ratio of students to teachers 25 to 2.

5. Primary school education is divided into four grades, of which grades 1 and 2 (initial education) and grades 3 and 4 (continuation of non-specialised education) are grouped together. Despite the fact that separation is potentially possible, the four grades are divided up into fixed classes. The individual *Länder* have laid down maximum limits for class sizes. Lessons involving more than one grade or class at the same time are rare except in the case of physical education and religion.

6. The vast majority of general education schools in the Federal Republic of Germany are half-day schools. The school day for primary school students consists of up to six lessons of 45 minutes each. The number of lessons per week ranges between 16 and 28, depending on the grade involved. There is school at least five days a week and in many cases still six. The school year consists of 40 teaching weeks and is divided up into two halves.

7. In addition to imparting the basic cultural skills of reading, writing and arithmetic, teaching in primary education is dedicated mainly to religion, German, *Sachunterricht*, mathematics, artwork, sports, crafts and textile work. In *Sachunterricht* an introduction is given to the fundamental concepts of what will later be the subjects of geography, history, physics, chemistry, biology and social science, providing variable focuses. Traffic safety training and sex education represent special aspects of this teaching. A foreign language may also be taught in primary school.

8. All primary school students receive reports at the end of the school year. Beginning with grade 3, all primary school students are given reports at the end of each half of the school year. The certificate handed out at the end of the school year contains a remark indicating whether or not the student has passed. Assessment of scholastic achievement is based on the observations of the teachers in question and their appraisal of the students' oral and written work during the school year.

9. The qualification of primary school teachers is generally based on a six-month degree course at universities (teacher-training colleges) and two years of practical teachers' training. State examinations must be taken both at the end

of university studies and after completing the period of practical training. In-service education courses are offered for teachers at the individual schools or school systems or in supraregional in-service education centres. Enrolment in courses of this kind is voluntary.

10. As far as this is necessary in each individual case (e.g. in determining whether or not a child is ready for schooling), the school doctor, the school psychology service and the educational advisory staff of the institution in question work together. They are generally responsible for all school types and levels and not just for primary schools.

In all of the *Länder* there are special regulations to secure the co-operation of parents and schools.

Section II

The development of primary schools has been determined by various factors over the past few years.

The decrease in the number of children in the population has done more than just bring relief to the primary schools. In the case of many such schools, especially in rural areas, this fact has endangered their future existence. All of the *Länder* have taken measures to avoid the closing of schools if at all possible and to safeguard the local availability of good primary education.

Special attention is being given to the rising number of foreign children in primary schools. Foreign children with the necessary knowledge of German are always placed in classes and school types corresponding to their ages and achievement levels. The majority of children who were born in the Federal Republic of Germany and have attended a kindergarten can be enrolled in the first year of school together with German children. However, they still require special assistance. This includes remedial measures to improve their knowledge of German. On their certificates these children receive a description of their German language skills instead of a grade. In teaching, account is taken of their cultural and linguistic backgrounds.

Criticism of the primary school reform introduced at the beginning of the 1970s was triggered mainly by the curriculum reform. The demands made by the various sides are aimed at reducing the amount of material taught and reversing a trend towards an inappropriate academic approach in the various subjects, particularly mathematics and *Sachunterricht*. The questions of weaknesses in reading, spelling and writing present a special problem area. In general, what is involved is the creation of a teaching style that is more strongly oriented towards the child, in which instruction and behavioural training are carried out at the same time. For this it is necessary:

- to achieve a balanced relationship between cognitive, emotional, creative and social learning;

- to avoid any overload of learning material;
- to put a stronger emphasis on artistic education and forms of education that promote creativity.

Corresponding measures have already been introduced in part.

Important for the further improvement of work in primary schools are:

- co-operation between parents and schools;
- special attention for students who manifest learning difficulties or weaknesses in the form of supplementary or remedial classes or differentiated teaching;
- co-ordination of the educational and behavioural training concepts in the pre-school and primary school sectors;
- co-operation with specialist personnel in both areas.

GREECE
<DECS/EGT [85] 63>

Background

1. *Development and characteristics of the educational system*

The creation of an independent Greek nation state in 1830 led the country to turn both to her own history and to western sources for a guide in the development of education theory and practice.

Two major influences have dominated the development of the educational system since the country attained its independence.

First should be noted the role of the Greek Orthodox Church, as it is the only one which introduced the concept that the Greek Orthodox faith was allied with the creation and growth of the state. The second major influence was the adoption, in 1834, of the Bavarian plan for a centrally dominated education system. Even today the system is centralised, to a great degree resulting in curriculum and teaching style conformity. Nevertheless, it always allows room for a reasonable diversity regarding teaching, teaching methods and school management.

In the 1950s and 1960s a change took place aiming at an expanded, rationally designed, efficient and modern education system that could play an important role in the efforts for economic prosperity and the creation of a better life.

The first five-year plan of 1960–4 considered the development of human capital and technical education basic desiderata in order to accelerate the transformation of the structure of the Greek economy from agricultural to industrial and raise living standards ‘to the level of highly industrialised European countries’.

A new draft law, already submitted to parliament, aims at upgrading nursery, primary and secondary education on two dimensions, vertical and horizontal. As regards the first, the aim is to facilitate the transition from one stage to the next through proper curriculum and teaching methods. As regards the second, its aims are to integrate the school with community life through a network of two-way relations.

2. Population structure

The historical evolution of the Greek state and the continuous addition of new population have created the preconditions for the over-expansion of the capital city at the expense of the other regions. Migration abroad and a strong urbanisation movement, mainly towards the Athens region, have greatly influenced the distribution and structure of the population. This shift of the population distribution from rural to urban areas was accompanied (a) by a shift in the distribution of the economically active population to the major sectors of the economy, (b) by an increase in the participation of women in the labour force, and (c) by a decrease in the proportion of the economically active population in the urban, semi-urban and rural areas.

Out of the approximately 10 million total population of Greece, the urban population is about 6 million, the semi-urban 1 million, and the rural population about 3 million people.

3. Education as a social function

Article 16 of the Greek Constitution contains the following provisions:

a. Art and science, research and teaching shall be free of impediment and it shall be incumbent on the state to develop and advance them. Academic freedom and freedom in teaching shall be subject to the provisions of the constitution.
b. Education shall be a fundamental concern of the state. Its purpose shall be to develop national awareness and to provide for the moral, intellectual, physical and vocational education of the Greeks, and to engender their upbringing as free and responsible citizens.
c. Compulsory education shall last for not less than nine years.
d. All Greeks shall be entitled to free education in the state institutions, at all levels. The state shall support distinguished students and those in need of assistance or special care according to their abilities.

The educational policy of the Greek government rests on the basic assumption that

> education is a social good and something to which every citizen has a right. The state has an obligation to ensure this provision for every young person as an urgent priority, in every corner of our land, with the same level and quality of preparation, the same upright, transparent and objective procedures, the same reliable and complete provision of information about opportunities and conditions of study at all levels, about the specific needs of the economy, and about the employment situation.
>
> One of the basic objectives of our educational policy is to seek out and develop the creative abilities and talents of our young people, to give these people a systematic preparation for shouldering the difficult task of regene-

rating our country and ensuring its progress, in a responsible way, with critical understanding and, above all, to educate socially conscious workers and citizens equipped with adequate scientific and technical expertise.

The structure and operation of the educational system

Education is divided into three levels: primary education, secondary education and tertiary education, which encompasses studies at university-level institutions (AEI) and at other higher technical and vocational institutions below university level. Compulsory education lasts for nine years (six years at a primary school and three years at a *gymnasium*).

Nursery school

Infants entitled to attend are $3\frac{1}{2}$–$5\frac{1}{2}$ years of age. Attendance is optional.

Primary school

Primary school attendance is compulsory and lasts for six years ($5\frac{1}{2}$–$11\frac{1}{2}$).

Pupils are grouped according to age only. No grouping according to ability or other criterion takes place. The school is comprehensive throughout the grades in the whole country. Pupils are graded (assessed) according to the following designations: very good (A), good (B), average or below (C).

It is normal for children to progress upwards through the grades (classes) without being kept back for a year. The primary schools vary from being single-teacher schools to establishments with up to 15 teachers, based on an average of 30 pupils per teacher. The schools operate a five-day week. Grades 1 and 2 receive 23 hours of instruction and the other grades 25 hours weekly.

For grades 1 and 2 the subjects taught are: study of the environment, modern Greek, mathematics, physical education and aesthetic education. For the remaining grades the curriculum includes: Greek language, history, religious education, physics, geography, mathematics, social and political education, aesthetic education and physical education.

In 1983 the total number of primary school pupils attending state schools was nearly 800,000. The same year the total number of state school units was approximately 9,000. The total number of state school teachers was 32,000, and the pupil–teacher ratio 26.

The private sector of schools caters for about 5 per cent of the pupils.

The 1982 innovation in primary school

(a) Definition of aim

The aim of primary and secondary education is to contribute towards a multi-faceted, harmonious and balanced development of the intellectual and psycho-physical abilities of pupils, so that, independently of sex and social origin, they have the possibility to develop into an integrated personality and live creatively.

In particular, primary schools enable pupils:

- to broaden and rearrange their creative relationships with objects, situations and phenomena they study;
- to build up the mechanisms helping assimilation of knowledge, to develop physically, to improve their physical and psychic health, and to cultivate their kinetic abilities;
- to comprehend basic concepts and gradually to acquire the ability to move from perception to abstract thinking;
- to acquire the ability to use oral and written language correctly;
- to gradually adopt moral, religious, national, humanistic and other values, and organise them into a system.

(b) Curriculum and methodology innovations

These innovations refer to the subjects: language, study of the environment, mathematics, and social and political education.

Language

This subject is for the first time treated as an area of learning in itself and not as a means of teaching history, religion and traditional values. Grammar is no longer taught as a separate subject, with its own textbook, but in relation to text. Thus the principle of functionality is emphasised. Specially prepared text-books for pupils and guidance books for teachers have been published.

Composition writing aims at encouraging pupils to express their own ideas in a spontaneous and creative way. In the pre-innovation period the emphasis was put on syntaxis and the structure of writing. The subject covers all grades.

Study of the environment

It is taught in grades 1, 2, 3 (and 4 next year). It is a skilful integration of subject areas from the physical and social environment in their internal inter-relations. Learning is obtained through discovery and active participation of pupils. The process rather than the product is emphasised. Pupils do not memorise any concrete details, but they arrive, by themselves, at cognitive schemes, being able to assimilate knowledge within a large area relating to each scheme. Textbooks for pupils and guidance books for teachers have been prepared.

Mathematics

In the pre-innovation period, traditional mathematics gave emphasis to routine calculations, rather than to understanding structure. The innovation aims at a proper balance between the comprehension of concepts and structure and competence in mechanical calculations. The mathematical concepts of set, classification, seriation, correspondence, inclusion, conservation, are taught for the first time in Greek primary schools. Textbooks for pupils, as well as guidance books for the teacher, have been prepared.

The whole innovation plan was carried out by a team of experts at the KEME, a centre for education studies and research.

(c) Teacher training

Up to now, primary school teachers have been trained at a college of education for two years. From now on these teachers (as well as nursery teachers) will receive their initial training in a university department for four years.

Up to now, primary school teachers could receive, if they wanted to, in-service training: (a) at the Maraslion *Didaskalion* for two years, after successfully passing an entrance examination, or (b) at SELDE for one year, after drawing lots for entrance. In future, in-service training of teachers (primary and secondary), as well as research responsibilities, will be taken over by a new institute, the Pedagogic Institute.

(d) The school adviser institution

Up until the 1982 administration, scientific guidance and pedagogic supervision of primary schools were the responsibilities of the well-known school inspector. With the 1304/1982 law the institution of the inspector was abolished. The administration of schools is now the responsibility of the *proistamenos* of the schools of one area, while the school adviser has undertaken the duty of giving advice to teachers in different educational matters regarding curriculum, teaching methods, pedagogy, etc.

Secondary education

Secondary education is divided into two cycles: *gymnasium* (three years) and *lykeion* (three years).

Attendance at the *gymnasium* is compulsory. Pupils who have completed the six-year primary school are automatically promoted (without examinations) to the *gymnasium*. Pupils throughout the country follow a common course of instruction. Textbooks are provided free. Assessment is based on oral examination and written work on the day's lesson.

Holders of the *gymnasium* leaving certificate have the automatic right of admission to a *lykeion*. It may be a general *lykeion* or a technical and vocational one. At an experimental stage there exists a new type of *lykeion*, a comprehensive one (*polykladiko*).

Special education in Greece

Until a few years ago special education was provided for only a few children, mainly as students of residential homes run by various charitable foundations. In recent years, however, with the creation of the necessary legislative infrastructure (laws in 1981 and 1982) the provision of – in general terms – properly trained staff and the founding of a number of special schools covering the whole country, this sector has been given systematic attention.

Present and immediate future trends in primary education

Since 1981, when our Socialist government came to power, many drastic and far-reaching innovations have been put into practice. Efforts are being made towards the effective implementation of these innovations.

9. ICELAND <DECS/EGT [84] 91 rev>

I. Aims, organisation and content

1. Compulsory education in Iceland is stipulated by an Act of Parliament no. 63/1974. All children have to attend school from the autumn of the year in which they reach the age of 7. The same act stipulates the following about pre-schools:

> Local councils may permit comprehensive schools to establish classes for 6 year old children, and 5–6 year old children, if the Ministry approves their plans, accommodation and equipment. Pre-schools are budgeted in the same way as comprehensive schools.
>
> Comprehensive schools are permitted to allocate part of their premises to organise pre-school classes. Private pre-schools are not permitted without the consent of the district school supervisor concerned.

This Act of Parliament defines the aims of schooling in this way:

> In co-operation with the home, the school must prepare the children for life in a modern democratic society. The schools should therefore be guided in their work by tolerance, Christian values and democratic co-operation. The school should endeavour to widen the children's horizon and develop their understanding of their environment, social conditions, the characteristics and history of Icelandic society and the obligations of the individual to society.
>
> The school must endeavour in its work to meet the demands and needs of the child and give each individual an opportunity to develop intellectually and physically.
>
> The school must enable the children to gain knowledge and develop their skills and methods of work, in a constant effort to gain mental and physical maturity. The school must therefore foster independent thought and co-operative attitudes.

In accordance with the objectives of the comprehensive school, work in all grades is to be closely related to the world outside the school walls through observation and activities.

The Ministry of Education issues a general curriculum in which there is a more detailed exposition of the educational objectives of the school and the organisation of its work. It is stated that special care should be taken to give all children equal opportunities as far as this is possible, while trying to meet and accept their differences in personality, maturity, ability and interest.

2. Most of the Icelandic primary schools are state schools and under the authority of the Ministry of Education. The country is divided into eight school regions. Each region is controlled by a board of education and the regional educational office, supervised by the director of education. The board of education and the regional educational office are responsible to the district authorities and the Ministry of Education.

The regions are divided into districts. The number of schools within each district varies considerably. Individual schools are controlled by a school board. The headmaster/mistress in co-operation with the teachers' council, appointed by the teachers, is responsible for the internal running of the school.

3. Children below the age of 6 have a choice of day-care institutions or play-schools; these are found mainly in urban areas; both whole-day and half-day care are offered. These play-schools are run by the local authorities but receive some state support. Until recently there have hardly been any links between play-school and primary education, mainly because they are separate institutions and the educational qualifications for the staff are different. But there is now increasing interest in co-operation between these institutions.

However, there are considerable links between primary education and lower secondary as most pupils in Iceland continue at the same school. There is no break between primary and secondary education.

4. There are 217 comprehensive schools in the country with pupils from 6 to 16. The average number of pupils in each school is about 190. Of the 217 schools there are 70 with more than the average number of pupils, the biggest enrolling 1,280. This shows that there are a great number of small schools in the country districts. There are about 4,200 pupils in each year-group and there are about 3,000 teachers working in the comprehensive schools.

5. According to the law the maximum number of pupils in a class is 30. In Reykjavik, the most populous district, there are about 24 children on average in each class of 7–12-year-old children, 18 in each class of 6 year olds, whereas in rural districts there are often only a few children in each grade, so vertical classes are common. In most urban areas pupils are divided into groups according to age; however there are some exceptions. One of these is an open plan school for the primary stage. Some comprehensive schools are carrying out experiments in vertical teaching for the first three or four grades (6–9 year olds).

6. The school year is 8–9 months depending on whether the school is in an urban or rural area, within the period from 1 September till the end of May. The school week is five days covering:

880 minutes in grade 1
960 minutes in grade 2
1,080 minutes in grade 3
1,280 minutes in grade 4
1,360 minutes in grade 5
1,400 minutes in grade 6

In most of the schools, two classes use the same classroom, one in the morning, the other in the afternoon. 97 per cent of all 6-year-old children attend primary school, but the length of their school day/week/year varies from a minimum of 16 lessons a year to a maximum of 840 lessons (1 lesson = 40 mins), the average being 396 lessons.

7. There is a legal obligation on the Ministry of Education and Culture to expand the provisions of the Law and General Curriculum and also to decide what study material is to be selected for the schools, its arrangement for the grades and the number of class hours for each subject. The study material and its arrangement for the grades appears in the curricula, but the number of class hours for each subject is decided by regulations, which the schools may however vary if circumstances make it necessary. Generally speaking, schools have considerable opportunity to organise their own timetable and to alter the weight of individual subjects in the first grades.

Icelandic, mathematics, social studies and arts and handicraft have been given the greatest weight as far as number of class hours is concerned. These subjects are taught throughout this school level. In grades 1–6 these subjects are on the average allotted about 60 per cent of the available time, the division being as follows:

Icelandic	25%
Mathematics	13%
Arts and crafts	12%
Social studies	10%
Other subjects	40%

The primary school curriculum includes Icelandic, mathematics, social studies (i.e. a combination of environmental studies, Icelandic history, world history, geography and sociology), biology, physics, religious instruction, Danish, English, domestic science, art and craft, music and physical education.

In Iceland individual schools usually do not formulate their own policy or write their own curricula. Even those few schools that are markedly different from the rest owing to special methods or organisation, e.g. open or half-open schools and experimental schools, have not issued a special, formal curriculum. Their policy, however, appears in their work, organisation and methods, but the contents do not markedly deviate from the core curricula.

8. The regulation on evaluation no. 65/1985 states as its purpose:

(a) to supply pupils with information on their progress,
(b) to encourage pupils,
(c) to provide teachers and pupils with feedback on various aspects of their work which could lead to improvement,
(d) to inform teachers, parents/guardians about the progress of the children.

In the primary schools the children are usually given marks in a separate report book twice during the school year. The report states how successful the child has been in reaching set objectives, and often a report is given on the child's progress, attendance, etc. The children show this report to their parents or guardians and the report may be discussed at interviews between parents and teachers.

9. The initial training for primary school teachers is three years at the Teachers' Training College. During these three years the students have 12 weeks of practical training in primary schools.

In-service training is mainly carried out during the summer. The Teachers' Training College of Iceland is responsible for the summer courses. There are also several in-service courses or short workshops during the school year. The Teachers' College and the Department of Educational Development of the Ministry of Education and the regional educational offices arrange these courses.

10. Children entering primary school have a medical inspection by a school doctor or nurse, and they are examined once a year after that. All children in comprehensive schools get free dental care from the first school year.

To meet the requirements of a regulation concerning consultancy and psychiatric services in comprehensive schools dating from 8 January 1980, a separate department is to be established at each district educational authority entitled 'Psychology Service for Schools'.

Preventive work is emphasised and coherent service for children and their families.

The situation as far as remedial teaching is concerned varies a great deal according to educational districts. The most populous district of Reykjavik gives special assistance to about 20 per cent of children; in the lowest grades this especially applies to reading and mathematics. This assistance amounts to about 14 per cent of the total teaching in Reykjavik. In the country as a whole the percentage amounts to 4–7 per cent.

11. If the headmaster, the teachers' association or the parents wish to establish a parents' association in order to support work at the school and strengthen the links between school and home then the head is obliged to call a meeting.

A representative from the parents' association has the right to attend staff meetings with freedom to speak and make proposals. In Iceland there are now parents' or parent–teacher associations at 115 primary schools.

II. Changes

There have been considerable changes in Icelandic schools the last 10 to 15 years. In 1966, the Department of Educational Research at the Ministry of Education was established and its main task was the revision of materials and teaching of individual subjects in primary and lower secondary schools.

New legislation for Icelandic comprehensive education was enacted in 1974 and in 1976 the ministry issued a general curriculum. It included pedagogical policies, i.e. the role of the school, teaching methods and evaluation. The new curricula and the new teaching materials call upon different and varied teaching methods and activities in a lively and stimulating learning environment.

During the last few years, changes have been most obvious in the first grades (6–9 year olds), whereas the upper primary classes (10–12 year olds) have been more conservative.

There are, though, some trends now towards more open education with emphasis on the child's individual development and that every child should receive tasks suitable for his/her ability. But there are many problems to deal with, both financial and professional, such as:

- lack of educated teachers, mainly in the rural areas;
- frequent changes of teachers, again in the rural areas;
- lack of sufficient in-service training;
- the short school day for the first grades, which results in a lack of creative work at this level;
- lack of sufficient teaching materials, including equipment, books, libraries, aids, etc.;
- the school buildings in many areas are not suitable for the kind of education we would like for children today, there are not sufficient classrooms or they are often too small, there is a lack of special rooms for arts and crafts, music, physics, etc.;
- most classrooms have to be used by two classes on a shift basis.

In November 1979 the Ministry of Education appointed a commission to investigate the problems facing pre-schools.[3] The commission was to make policy proposals and recommend what steps should be taken in the near future. The commission found that they were unable to separate the pre-schools completely from the first grades of the comprehensive schools and in their work they looked upon the pre-school as 'school commencement' or part of the continuous education of 6–8-year-old children. Consideration was given to the position of the youngest school children particularly because of the ever-increasing rate at which *both* parents go out to work.

The commission delivered a report in December 1981 (*Skýrsla Forskólanefndar, menntamálaráðuneytið, desember 1981*). The report contains the following:

I. *The development of pre-schools in Iceland*
Origin–preparation–motivation. A survey of the pre-schools 1970–80.

II. *The pre-schools today*
A diagnosis of the present status of the pre-school; its external and internal organisation, methods, content, co-operation with parents and others, etc. Particular emphasis is laid upon the problems facing the pre-schools today with regard to educational and social considerations.

III. *Policy premises*
- social
- attitude to knowledge and education
- equal opportunities (urban–rural)
- psychological premises
  (a) intellectual development of 5–8-year-old children
  (b) children with special needs
- the status of the pre-school and its ties with the comprehensive school.

IV. *Ways and means*
1. Objectives (6–8 year olds).
2. Organisation; e.g. the link between pre-schools and comprehensive schools.
   - hours per day, size of classes
   - environment
   - methods and scope of study.

   The main emphasis is on organising the school in such a way that each individual benefits from his work there, that the children are active and find enjoyment in their activities, that the environment is stimulating, and that the children's education is continuous and directed at the intellectual and physical level of each child.
3. Co-operation of the pre-school with various parties such as:
   - parents, nurseries
   - psychology service, medi-care and other institutions
   - special emphasis is placed upon co-operation with parents/guardians.

V. *A plan of action for the next few years*
The proposals include e.g.:
- comprehensive approach to infant education
- increased number of lessons for the 6 year old to approximate those given to 7–8-year-old children
- to strengthen the link between nurseries and schools.

Teaching qualifications were also dealt with. Proposals were made for continued work, concerning both the teachers' education and the curriculum and teaching materials for the first three years (6–8).

III. Trends/developments

The development of education in Iceland during the last 10–15 years has been a period of almost unprecedented growth. The organisation of the primary school and the content of education have been radically changed in a relatively short time. There are more doubts about teaching methods, and there are various instances where original expectations concerning changes in school organisation following new teaching materials have not been realised as quickly and definitely as hoped by many in the beginning.

In this connection it should be remembered that this involves the basic education of a whole nation which has been radically changed in about a single decade. Although there is much left to be done, most of the main changes have come through. The main lines laid down in the late 1960s and early 1970s have become clear. Of course, problems of secondary importance and unforeseen difficulties are constantly becoming apparent.

The General Curriculum is now under revision. The main emphasis is on clearly stated aims and objectives which include directives on content. The methods and organisation of school work are in the hands of headmasters and teachers. The draft of the General Curriculum is now being examined by an editorial board appointed by the Minister of Education (March 1988).

The new proposals for core curricula on the other hand not just open up possibilities for individual schools to form their own policy and plans, but in fact demand it within a given framework. The reason for this change in policy is based on the belief that the centralisation of the education system should be loosened up to a point and also the belief that more freedom and responsibility of the school is likely to bring about positive reforms in school work.

Formally it is the concern of the ministry to supervise schools and ensure that they perform their task according to law and regulations. There is actually very little supervision of the inner workings of the schools. The regional educational directors and the directors of studies in the Ministry of Education are those mainly concerned with professional and methodological supervision; up to the present they have, however, regarded themselves more as guides, assistants and co-operators with the teachers rather than as supervisors or judges.

Formal supervision appears in the form of the results in centralised examinations and exploratory survey tests. Centralised examinations are, however, held in only four subjects by the end of the primary comprehensive school, while exploratory survey tests are few and without general organisation.

The Teachers' Union has recently issued an Educational Policy. Clauses concerning school work do not in any major matters conflict with the official policy of the ministry. Emphasis is on school-based innovations.

A proposal for new laws for teacher education is now being considered by the government. The proposal includes changes in the structure and organisation of teacher training, four years of training instead of three, and more emphasis on in-service training and further education opportunities for teachers and heads.

At the invitation of Icelandic authorities, a group of experts from OECD visited Iceland in 1986. The Examiners' report on education policy in Iceland was discussed at the 36th meeting of OECD's Education Committee in June 1986. The report has been published in Icelandic and distributed to all schools.

Series of conferences based on this report are being planned. As far as compulsory education is concerned, questions were raised about facilities, content and teaching, which are now being discussed in a search for improvements.

10 IRELAND <DECS/EGT [84] 18 rev>

Preamble

The Irish Constitution recognises the right of parents to provide for the education of their children 'in their homes or in private schools or in schools recognised or established by the State'. While parents may not be compelled in violation of their conscience to send their children to any particular type of school, the state, as guardian of the common good, must see that children receive a certain minimum education. To this end, the Department of Education provides for education free of charge. In fact, at primary level, the great majority of children receive their education in state-supported schools which operate within a system established in 1831 and are termed national schools.

Attendance at school is compulsory for children between the ages of 6 and 15 years and optional for those over 4 years. In general, children transfer to second-level education at the age of 12 years. While the great majority of primary schools are denominational in character and denominationally controlled at local management level, no child may be refused enrolment on the grounds of religion in any school in which there is accommodation available.

All schools, irrespective of the religious denomination of the management, receive equal treatment and equal support from the state, which contributes the major proportion of the cost of primary education and at the same time exercises a large measure of control over its operation. The cost of building, equipping, renovating and maintaining primary schools is met by state grants, amounting to about 85 per cent overall, which are supplemented by local contributions. The state pays teachers' salaries in full and the operating costs of the schools in large part. State aid, however, is conditional upon the school being operated in accordance with Rules for National Schools under the Department of Education which give the Minister for Education certain powers, among them the power to prescribe the curriculum, the qualifications of teachers, the teacher–pupil ratio, the length of the school day and year, teachers' salaries, etc. and which provide inspection by the Department of Education. The functions of the inspectorate include monitoring teachers' work and reporting to the minister on the operation of the system. The government of the school is the responsibility of the local board of management, which appoints teachers on individual contracts subject to approval by the Department of Education. Teachers take their professional courses in colleges of education, which are recognised colleges of universities. Standards of entry to these colleges are set by the Department of Education.

Section I: Basic information on the aims, content and organisation of primary education in Ireland.

1. The official aims of primary education

As indicated above, the vast majority of primary schools have a religious denominational ethos and, as might be expected, religious instruction in both the doctrinal and the moral behavioural sense is a fundamental part of the school course.

Elsewhere, the Primary School Curriculum (1971) expresses the view that 'the aims of primary education may briefly be stated as follows:

(a) To enable the child to live a full life as a child;
(b) To equip him to avail himself of further education so that he may go on to live a full and useful life as an adult in society.'

2. The responsibility for the organisation of primary education at national, regional, local and school level

The primary education system in Ireland, being centralised, has two levels only, the central authority and the individual school. Ireland's written constitution acknowledges the family as the primary and natural educator of the child and obliges the state to provide for free primary education. The Department of Education (headed by the Minister for Education) is the state agency charged with such provision. It deals directly with each individual school and there are no intermediate structures.

Subject to the budgetary and political control of Parliament it provides the vast bulk of school funds, makes and enforces the rules under which schools operate, prescribes and revises the curriculum, inspects schools, etc. Many interested bodies such as churches, teachers' organisations and school management representatives, although they have no statutory right to influence policy making, are nevertheless consulted on the operation of the system.

Each school is managed by its board of management, which consists of parent representatives, teacher representative(s) and nominees of the patron. In most cases the patron represents a particular religious denomination. In recent years however, some schools of an interdenominational character have been recognised. The board of management is charged with the maintenance of the school and its equipment, the provision of further equipment, the appointment of teachers and, generally, with ensuring that the school is run in accordance with rules for national schools. In practice the day-to-day running of the school is very often left in the hands of the principal teacher.

3. The links (a) between pre-school and primary education and (b) between primary and lower secondary education

(a) In Ireland, the majority of children attend primary school from the age of 4+ years. During their first two years in school they are enrolled in grades referred to as junior infants and senior infants. These grades are an integral part of the primary school. Scarcely any educational provision has been made from public funds for children before they enrol in primary school. In recent years, however, the state has made some educational provision for children under 4 years in a small number of exceptional situations and mostly on an experimental basis.

(b) Although the Department of Education has much the same relationship with post-primary education as it has with primary education, particularly in the areas of finance, curriculum and inspection, no close link exists between the two levels of education and pupils experience an abrupt change on transfer from the child-centred primary school to the subject-centred and examination-oriented post-primary school. Some progress was made towards aligning the two systems when, following upon the publication of the Report of the Pupil Transfer Committee in 1983, it was decided that pupils might transfer from primary to post-primary school only on completion of the primary school course up to and including 6th standard or its equivalent and that normally they would be 12 years old by the 1st September of the year of entry to post-primary school. The formation (1987) of the National Council for Curriculum and Assessment, under whose auspices revision of both primary and post-primary curricula is taking place, may be expected to result in the further alignment of the systems.

4. The number of primary school pupils and teachers

	1983–4	*1985–6*	*1986–7*
Teachers in national schools:	20,732	21,144	21,205
Pupils in national schools:	567,495	567,064	567,272
Teachers in non-aided (private) primary schools:	Information not available		
Pupils in non-aided (private) primary schools:	11,969	9,512	8,734

5. The arrangements for grouping pupils and official class sizes

The number of teachers employed in a school depends on the number of pupils enrolled and is in accordance with a schedule issued by the Department of Education. The grouping of pupils and the deployment of staff are the responsibility of the principal teacher. The Department of Education does not specify class sizes, which average about 30 and range from about 15 to 44. Usually pupils are grouped by age and the one teacher teaches all subjects to his/her class. Streaming by ability is discouraged but within his/her class each teacher is expected to practise some individual and/or group teaching to provide for the different needs of a mixed-ability group. As a rule such individual and/or group teaching is used for English reading and for mathematics.

In some newer schools, some of the accommodation has been designed for co-operative teaching and this has had effects on the grouping of pupils.

6. The length of the school day, the school week and the school year

One of the major constraints on the system of primary education in Ireland is the length of the school day. Rule 56 of the Rules for National Schools provides for a minimum of 4 hours and 10 minutes for secular activities each day. A further period for religious instruction is compulsory, but its length is not specified by the Department of Education: in practice it amounts to 30 minutes. Schools operate a five-day week, Monday to Friday, with a minimum school year of 184 days.

7. The major areas of the primary school curriculum

During the eight years of primary schooling, the pupil is exposed to an integrated, child-centred curriculum involving the following areas of activity:

Religious instruction
Irish
English
Mathematics
Social and environmental studies
Art and craft activities
Music
Physical education

It must be emphasised that the Irish primary school is bound by regulation to teach two languages, i.e. Irish and English.

8. The main methods of pupil assessment

There has been no state examination for primary school pupils since 1967. Pupil assessment since then has been school-based and has usually been carried out by the class teacher. Some standardised tests are available, particularly for Irish reading, English reading and mathematics, and are used regularly in some schools. Teachers in all schools supplement subjective assessments based on day-to-day performance by the pupil with assessment tests that they themselves devise. Pupils are also assessed in the course of national surveys and school inspection, but assessing the individual pupil is not the purpose of these exercises.

The recently established Review Body on the Primary Curriculum (1987) has the question of assessment included in its terms of reference.

9. The arrangements for (a) the initial and (b) the in-service training of primary school teachers

(a) The basic qualification for primary teachers is the Bachelor of Education Degree awarded either by the University of Dublin or by the National University of Ireland. Candidates for the B.Ed. degree pursue a three-year full-time course at one of the colleges of education.

(b) While some in-service courses are conducted during the school year, most such courses are made available during the school summer holidays by such bodies as the Department of Education, teachers' unions, teachers' centres, colleges of education and the universities. Teachers attend on a voluntary basis. For teachers who qualified prior to 1976, a two-year in-service degree course has been available since 1985.

10. The support services which are available to primary schools

(a) A comprehensive and free school medical and dental service is provided by the regional health boards, through regular school visits by medical personnel and through the community health centres. Pupils who suffer from various types of learning, physical and emotional handicap may be referred to appropriate clinics for assessment. Remediation is provided in remedial and special classes in ordinary schools, by peripatetic teachers, in special schools, through attendance at extra-school centres and clinics for specialised attention and by means of home tuition programmes. These services are free.

(b) About 20 teacher centres established throughout the country provide advisory and material support for teachers.

(c) Finally, support and advice to teachers in the classroom is a major element in the work of the Inspectorate.

11. The institutional links between the primary school, parents and the community

The board of management of each school includes two elected parents, and many schools have parent–teacher associations, arrange parent meetings and communicate with the home in a variety of ways. Usually, parents are made to feel welcome and indeed are encouraged to visit the school and meet the principal and class teacher. Most schools include a policy in respect of parents as an element in the school plan and most adopt a positive attitude towards enlisting the help and the goodwill of parents in the interests of the child and of the school. While school/community links are informal, they are nevertheless effective and fruitful as a rule.

Since its establishment in 1985, the National Parents' Council has given parents nationally a strong, independent voice in the education of their children.

Section II: Problems and trends in primary education

The Irish primary education system has laboured under financial constraints since its foundation. As recently as 1961 the overall teacher–pupil ratio was 1:36.1, as much as 25 per cent of school stock was classified as obsolete and facilities in the remainder were often basic. Since then, the financial strain resulting from the effort to remedy the situation has been aggravated by a significant expansion in pupil numbers, while at the same time a population movement from countryside to town and from inner city to newly built suburbs has emptied schools in some areas and made necessary the building of completely new schools in others, thus duplicating expensive stock.

The more important problems and trends in the Irish primary education system in recent years include:

A. Structure

1. Increases in the number of pupils enrolled:
   1969: 489,559
   1981: 551,319
   1984: 567,495
   1986: 567,064

A decline in enrolment is now beginning to manifest itself.

2. Increases in the number of teachers:
   1969: 15,318
   1981: 19,465
   1984: 20,732
   1986: 21,144

50 per cent of teachers are under 35 years and 25 per cent of teachers are male.

3. Improvements in the teacher–pupil ratio:
   1969: 1:32.0
   1981: 1:28.0
   1984: 1:27.3
   1986: 1:26.8
4. Substantial investment in school buildings and changes in school design.
5. Increases in the provision of ancillary school services.
6. The elimination of corporal punishment in 1984 and the publication of the Report of the Committee on Discipline in Schools in 1987.
7. The introduction on an institutional basis of parental involvement in the management of schools.
8. A switch from separate schooling for boys and girls to co-education.
9. The establishment in 1985 of the National Parents' Council.
10. The establishment in 1987 of the Primary Education Review Body, reporting to the goverment.
11. A declining enrolment presenting both challenge and opportunity.
12. A scheme of career-breaks for teachers introduced in 1985.
13. The establishement of multi-denominational schools independent of church management in response to parental demand.

B. Curriculum

1. Greater provision for the intellectually, physically or socially disadvantaged, including an extension of the service available to children with severe and profound mental handicap.
2. Curricular changes, taking account of universal participation in post-primary education and a more child-centred approach in the primary curriculum itself, leading to the creation of a more pleasant atmosphere in schools.
3. A move towards the removal of sex bias from school textbooks and a requirement that both sexes be represented on interview boards involved in the appointment of teachers.
4. The establishment in 1987 of the National Council for Curriculum and Assessment whose brief covers both primary and post-primary education.
5. The establishment in 1987 of the Review Body on the Primary Curriculum under the auspices of the National Council for Curriculum and Assessment.
6. The creation, in response to parental demand, of a significant number of *Scoileanna Lán Ghaeilge*, schools situated outside the *Gaeltacht* or Irish-speaking areas yet teaching the entire curriculum wholly through the medium of Irish.
7. The obligation to teach two languages in the course of an exceptionally short school day: a particularly noteworthy feature.
8. The *Report of the Working Party on the 'Primary School Curriculum and the Disadvantaged Child'*, issued to all schools in 1985.
9. A pilot project on the role and function of computers in primary schools (1984–6) resulting in the provision of increased in-service education in this area.
10. A pilot project on the teaching of basic science in primary schools (1984–6) resulting in the preparation of a report for the Department of Education.
11. A greater awareness of the need for educational research and a greater willingness to support it, culminating, with the setting up of the National Council for Curriculum and Assessment, in a move towards the rationalisation of the work of the various educational research agencies.

11. ITALY
<DECS/EGT [87] 15>

Figure 1 Structure of the education system in Italy

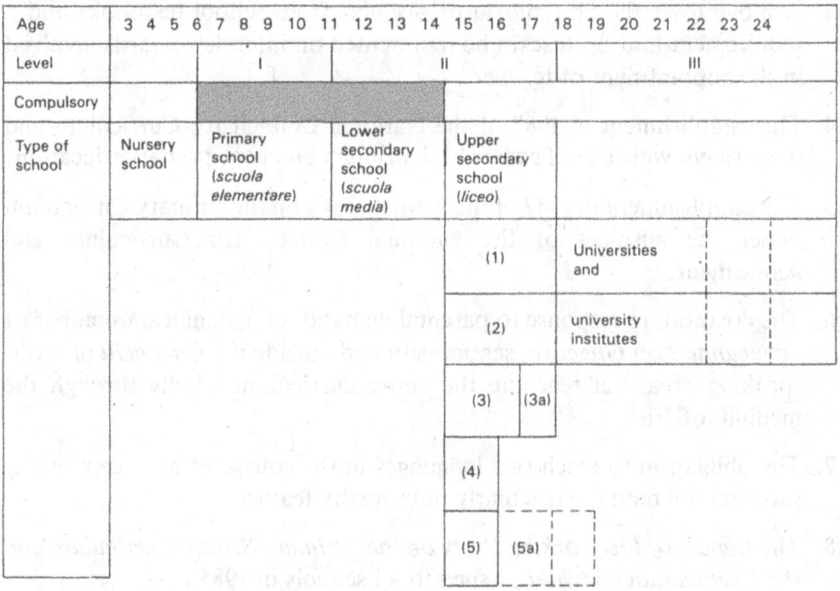

(1) (a) Classical
    (b) Scientific
    (c) Technical
    (d) Linguistic
(2) Technical schools.
(3) Art schools and primary teachers' training colleges (*instituto magistrale*).
(3a) University integration year.
(4) Training colleges for nursery school teachers (*scuola magistrale*).
(5) Vocational training schools.
(5a) Two- or three-year 'integration' courses leading to the secondary school-leaving certificate (*maturità*).

Powers and administration

In Italy, all official primary, secondary and higher education is centrally administered by the Ministry of Education.

This does not mean that teaching in Italy is totally under state control; in addition to the network of state schools, there is a large network of state schools not under state control (run, for example, by local authorities) as well as private schools. During the 1984–5 school year, the percentages of pupils attending private schools were as follows: 7.7 per cent in primary schools, 4.6 per cent in lower secondary and 10.5 per cent in upper secondary.

All schools, state-controlled or otherwise, public or private, must comply with national legislation as well as with Ministry of Education decrees and regulations.

Schools not under state control as well as private schools that follow the state's curricula and provide teaching of adequate quality may be approved by the state, with all this implies as regards the legal status of pupils, the recognition of curricula, etc.

The Minister of Education is assisted by under-secretaries, who do not have any powers of their own, as their responsibilities are delegated by the minister; they act on the minister's behalf whenever he is absent or otherwise engaged.

Pending the planned reform of the public administration, the principal units responsible for organisation are the nine general directorates, whose responsibilities cover: primary education; secondary education (grade I); training of teachers for classical, scientific and primary education; technical education; vocational education; university education; cultural exchanges; personnel and administration; buildings and equipment.

Specific sectors, such as sport and physical education, arts teaching and pensions, are under the control of three inspectorates.

Another important unit at ministerial level is the Studies and Planning Department (*Ufficio Studi e Programmazione*). This is the national unit for coordinating research, teachers' in-service training and experimentation. Pre-primary education comes under a special department, the Pre-primary Schools Service.

The Minister of Education is not only the head of the central administration of education; he is also chairman of the National Education Council, which is the supreme advisory body for all questions concerning education below the higher level.[4] The council consists of 71 members elected for five years. Three-quarters of the members are teachers, elected at national level by school principals, teachers, non-teaching staff and education administrators.

The council's task is to assess school activities and facilities and draw up curricula. The Minister of Education has to consult the council on all proposed legislative and administrative measures of any importance.

In practical terms, central power in the Ministry of Education is exercised by ministerial delegations and branches at regional and provincial level. For each of the 20 Italian regions, there is a regional superintendent appointed by the minister. The superintendent's powers are as follows:

- organisation and administration of competitive examinations for teaching posts in secondary education;
- co-ordination between the central administration and regional and local policies.

On the whole, it can be said that the influence of the central administration on regional authorities remains very strong. However, the influence of the regional authorities is tending to increase, particularly as regards the determination of regional priorities in education.

At provincial level, the minister is represented by provincial directors of education, who are, as it were, the local branches of the central administration.

The importance of the provincial directors of education and their departments is considerable. Their main task is to ensure the implementation of statutes and regulations relating to primary and secondary schools, both private and public. The principals and teachers of primary and secondary schools are directly answerable to the provincial directors of education, who are also responsible for supervising adult education.

Provincial directors of education are required to seek – though not follow – the advice of provincial school councils (made up of representatives of teachers, parents and provincial and local authorities) on teaching problems in the province in question.

In 1974, a new Act required regional governments to make provision for educational districts enjoying administrative autonomy and able to raise funds for that purpose. The districts must consist of rural and urban regions with common social and economic characteristics.

Compulsory education

In Italy, compulsory education currently starts at the age of 6 and continues until the age of 14, consisting of five years of primary school and three years of lower secondary education. The government has proposed that the duration of compulsory education be increased from eight to ten years, i.e. to the age of 16.

Compulsory education is governed by national acts and regulations applicable throughout the country, i.e. to both public and private establishments. In the public education sector, compulsory school is free of charge.

Primary education

Introduction

The following account, which summarises the system of primary schools in Italy, is necessarily sketchy and provisional owing to the measures recently introduced or being promulgated in 1986–7. Approval of the new primary school curricula by the competent minister (Presidential Decree of 12.2.1985, No. 104), has resulted in:

1. a radical change in the subjects taught and in the content of teaching;
2. the need to modify the structure of the school system.

As regards point 1 above, it should be added that the entry into force of the new curricula has been scheduled for 1 September 1987 (i.e. the beginning of the 1987–8 school year). As regards point 2, it should be pointed out that the reform of the primary school system will be introduced first on an experimental basis and not uniformly throughout the country. Consequently, the details given below should be regarded as provisional, since it is impossible to describe a structure that will not be complete until the statutory stages have been gone through and the new Act becomes applicable throughout Italy (1989–90 school year).

Structure of primary education

The new curricula recently approved will enter into force in the 1987–8 school year. They are compulsory for all public or private schools in the country. The aims and objectives of primary education are determined at national level.

The new curricula are the result partly of various partial reforms over the past 15 years and partly of innovations suggested by progress in the theory of education.

Indeed, the first reform was carried out as early as 1971 by Act No. 320, which introduced new subjects into primary school curricula (complementary activities and special courses) and authorised the adoption of more flexible timetabling (from 24 hours a week to a maximum of 48 hours a week in the case of full-time attendance). Subsequently, in 1974, the parent–teacher boards were introduced as part of a reform of the criteria governing the programming of teachers' activities and, in the area of participation, the assumption of direct responsibilities by pupils' parents.

Lastly, Act No. 517 of 1977 introduced a number of other major innovations, viz: the admission of disabled children to ordinary classes; new principles for pupil assessment together with the abolition of marks and the adoption of a 'personal record' for each pupil; and new teaching methods (open classrooms) aimed at various forms of collaboration between teachers and pupils in different classes.

All the foregoing has been permanently and systematically incorporated in the texts of the new curricula. The latter confirm the division into cycles (the first cycle consisting of the first and second classes of the five primary school classes; the second one consisting of the remaining classes). The original system of organisation, with one teacher responsible for each class (a fixed group of pupils), has been perpetuated for the first cycle; the principle of 'plurality of teachers', those without tenure being collectively responsible for the organisation of teaching (grouping of pupils, differentiation of methods, diversification of activities), is to be introduced into the second cycle.

Under the new curricula, the following subjects are compulsory: Italian, a foreign language, mathematics, science, history, geography, social studies, art, music and physical education.

Religion will be an optional subject in future: it will be taught only to pupils requesting it at the rate of 2 hours a week. Pupils who do not wish to study religion will be offered other subjects.

The weekly number of hours' teaching, which is currently 24, will almost certainly rise to 27 with the introduction of the new curricula. In two years, it is due to increase again (perhaps to 30 with the start of a foreign language). For moving up the next class, pupils are no longer assessed according to their marks. Their capacities and abilities are evaluated on the basis of observation by the teacher during the school year and are entered on a personal record designed to provide a detailed picture of the pupil's personality.

The present assessment form has come in for some justified criticism after 10 years in use, and a review of assessment principles and methods is now planned, in line with the spirit and aims of the new curricula.

During the 1984–5 school year, 3,607,628 pupils were enrolled in the 25,928 Italian state primary schools, i.e. 92.3 per cent of those required to attend such schools. In the same year, pupils enrolled in private schools numbered 301,737. The reduction in the number of primary school pupils (owing to the well-known decline in the birthrate) was 12.1 per cent over the last five years.

During the 1984–5 school year, 280,716 teachers with tenure and others without tenure were working in state primary schools. The national ratio of pupils to teaching posts was 12.9.

12. LIECHTENSTEIN <DECS/EGT [84] 92>

A. Main ideas

I. Aims

Education, the formulation of a personality, maturity, development in a general sense, are lifelong processes and cannot be restricted to the time of school attendance. The main responsibility for the formation of the developing personality is borne by the family and by the individual child. Schools are able to assist, to continue or to correct what is fundamentally created in the family sphere. The bounds of their possibilities of influence vary greatly and depend a great deal on the individual pupil, but also on the family, on the teacher and on the environment as a whole.

The main task of the school is to assist the pupil in his all-round development as a human being, helping him to develop harmoniously his physical, mental and intellectual skills and abilities. Naturally such targets are not undisputed. The question arises, for example, whether a highly industrialised mini-state can afford high-brow expressions such as 'all round development as a human being'. Some say a mini-state has to place top priority on high-quality work because of its almost entire dependence on export.

Liechtenstein is considered to be a Catholic homeland. The influence of the Church has now strongly diminished, after being extremely important – especially in the field of education – until the 1960s. Since then it has become difficult to define the concept of human being in a society which is getting more and more pluralistic. No educators, however, can do without such definition.

If you are concerned about education as well as about the imparting of knowledge, you will soon realise how difficult it is to formulate, in a pluralistic society, aims of education that are accepted by the majority. Therefore it is not by chance that religious instruction is in a serious crisis in our country. Certain fundamental values are laid down in the constitution of every country. Can these be reflected somehow in our schools, in their everyday life?

II. Means

1. School system

(a) The present school system is to be further developed emphasising the following aspects:

- more security for the pupils (improvement of the system of class teachers, better pupil guidance and care);
- greater consideration for particular circumstances;
- fewer organisational rules and restrictions.

As a matter of principle, small unities easy to survey will have to be aimed at.

(b) With regard to the planning and the organisation of the schools great emphasis will have to be placed on the right of co-determination of parents and teachers. However, the right of co-determination with respect to the co-operation of the parents will have to be clearly defined. In respect of the syllabus and the teaching aids, mainly the teachers and the school authorities are duly qualified.

(c) If a pupil has to change schools (maybe he has to be transferred to a special school), the right of co-determination of the parents shall be assured.

(d) In our primary schools we do not appoint subject teachers. However, an interchange of subjects among the primary teachers, on a voluntary and sensible basis, should not be excluded.

2. Syllabus, teaching aids, teaching methods

(a) The main aim of primary school is not the imparting of knowledge but the education of the pupil. In the subject matters chosen, those values (aims of education) shall be stressed with which the pupil can identify himself.

(b) The flood of teaching aids, hardly manageable any longer, will be brought under control. If pupils of the first or second form of the primary school are carrying huge files filled with worksheets, then too much of a good thing is being done, as they also have textbooks for the different subjects. One is almost inclined to exclaim: 'Back to the textbooks!' One further example: at the GCE exams one occasionally gets the impression that the texts put before the pupil for appreciation or translation and so on become increasingly difficult every year. Formerly the examining teacher had to copy these texts on his typewriter and could only duplicate them afterwards. While copying he occasionally hesitated. He had to reflect on whether certain terms were not too difficult. Nowadays there are photostatic machines in all schools. One could say, with some sarcasm perhaps, that reflection has become superfluous as photocopying is all the teacher has to do.

3. *Organisation of learning*

(a) The burdening of the pupil through lessons and homework has to be kept within limits so as to give him enough time for the regular pursuit of his personal interests. A critical perusal of the syllabuses and the timetables is urgent.

(b) The present-day widespread aversion to learning, is it also due to our common timetables involving, at times, a change of topic every 45 minutes?

4. *Appraisal of pupils, performance, selection*

There is no need here to enter into further details about the pros and cons of the marking system. But the question arises whether one could not do without any marks, at least at the first level of the primary school.

As to the selection for particular educational branches and special schools, there is a statement below.

5. *Teachers and teachers' training*

(a) The learning process at school is to a great extent dependent on the personality of the teacher. The latter should view himself as a human being called upon to work at his personal development.

(b) To a much greater extent than hitherto teachers should strive for didactic and pedagogic co-operation in the same school building and among colleagues. Many teachers isolate themselves and retire to their classrooms.

(a) Co-operation between the school and the parents is of paramount importance. The teachers have to be prepared, more efficiently still, to establish contact with the parents.

(b) Lately one gets the impression on several occasions that the schools have to take responsibility for many things. Undesirable developments conditioned by society are being blamed one-sidedly on the schools. For example, people admit only reluctantly that unfavourable family backgrounds become painfully apparent at school too.

B. Specific problems in the principality of Liechtenstein – a few examples taken from the current debates

1. The procedure of selection

Pupils changing from primary to secondary school are subjected to the so-called 'procedure of admission' consisting of three parts:

- Performance tests
  These examinations in the native tongue and in arithmetic give information about the actual level of the child's performance.
- School aptitude test
  In contrast to the performance tests the school aptitude test gives information not about the level of the pupil's knowledge but about the actual efficiency of a pupil.
- School marks, teacher's judgement.

In order to be able to be able to take into consideration performances over some length of time, the school marks of the whole 5th form are taken into account. In the so-called 'teacher's judgement', personal traits of the pupil are shown relevant to his successful passing to a secondary school. For the assessment of the total result the several parts of the examination are attributed different weights:

- performance tests 30%
- school aptitude test 15%
- school marks, teacher's judgement 55%

I must admit that even this combined and scientifically well-founded procedure of admission to other schools has come to show some disadvantages which are strongly emphasised in the current debates. Let me briefly deal with these in the following:

(a) Subject stress

Critics of the above-mentioned procedure of admission point out that, because of its subject stress, subjects connected with fine arts and science get the worst of the deal at the intermediate level of the primary school, especially in the 5th form (i.e. the year of transfer).

(b) Mutual competition amongst the teachers

Primary teachers are anxious to send a maximum number of pupils to the grammar school or to the middle school (*Realschule*), which means to the more demanding secondary schools. That is to some extent understandable, as the teachers are, in many cases, judged by the parents according to the number of pupils they can get into the grammar school, for example.

(c) Avoidance of the 'lower' type of school

When the transfer of pupils to the different types of schools occurs, parents would like to avoid, as far as possible, the *Oberschule* (being to some extent an advanced level of the primary school). It is not taken into consideration that the *Oberschule* might be the appropriate type of school for some pupils because handicrafts and practical life experience play an essential part in it. The *Oberschule* is considered to be merely a last resort.

(d) Pressure from the parents

Occasionally great pressure is brought to bear on teachers by the parents. Thus a 3rd form teacher was menaced by parents who told him that they would contact the school authority if he did not succeed in transferring their child to the grammar school after the 5th form. As a consequence of such an attitude on the part of the parents, fewer and fewer primary teachers will want to be in charge of a 5th form.

(e) System of recommendation

A commission appointed by the government is actually dealing with the question whether we should not introduce a 'pure' system of recommendation. This would mean that the assignment of the pupils to the different types of secondary school would be solely delegated to the primary teacher (without performance tests). We would be interested to know which European countries are acquainted with this system, and what sort of experiences they have had with it.

2. Questions of structure

(a) *Prolongation of the primary school by one year*

The question whether the primary school should be extended by one form is being discussed rather vehemently in Liechtenstein. It would then again comprise six forms as it did before 1972. It is maintained that the shortening of the primary school by one form has transformed it into a 'rump' school. It is held furthermore that the centralisation of the secondary schools has had an unfavourable influence on the structure of the villages. Hence the slogan resounds again: 'Home to the villages!' Just think of it! That happens in a small country where the largest central school accommodates only about 650 pupils. The numbers of pupils at the remaining central schools range between 200 and 300.

There are a lot of debates about the disadvantages and drawbacks of school centres in this country. A conclusive assessment is not possible yet because this innovation was only introduced nine years ago. On making preparations for the new school structure (dating from 1973), the following *advantages* of school centres were envisaged:

- increased possibilities of differentiation in teaching;
- introduction of the system of optional and alternative subjects;
- better equipment with specialised classrooms (including sports facilities and teaching aids);
- school attendance at the same site for pupils belonging to different types of schools, e.g. for pupils of the *Realschule* and the *Oberschule* (no change of premises in case of a transfer to a 'lower' type of school);
- better utilisation of classrooms in a school centre.

On the other hand, the disadvantages were not withheld either:

- rather high expenditures for the school bus service;
- supervision of pupils in school centres more difficult;
- disadvantages concerning the organisation of family life (the pupils are only at home for lunch for a short time or not at all);
- rather large numbers of pupils and, hence, monitoring difficulties (the teacher no longer knows every single pupil);
- difficulties arising from the co-existence of two school types;
- one-sided emphasis on performance and neglect of the educative aspect at school centres.

At the beginning of the 1970s, faith in progress and science was still strong. The necessity for starting rather early with the system of subject teachers was accordingly urged by many. Nowadays certain counter-currents are to be felt to the effect that e.g. pupils of the 6th year are said to be better looked after at the primary school in the village community.

(b) *Abolition of the grammar school catering for the whole age-range of secondary education and installation of a lower level of the grammar school at the Realschule.*

With some justification, people reason occasionally that selection for the grammar school at the age of 12 years is too early. All prospective pupils of the grammar school should have to go through a stage of orientation, as it were, within the *Realschule*.

(c) *The Liechtenstein school law dating from 1972 has a few centralising trends.*

Thus, for example, the communities are given far fewer powers than in Switzerland. In many concerns a homogeneous solution, wherever realisable, was envisaged. As a consequence, a great many decisions, also of a pedagogic nature, were left to the central school authority or the central school board of the country. At the moment it is being envisaged that some decisions could be delegated back to the localities. The headmasters too should once more be given more decision power.

(d) *Integration or segregation of pupils attending special schools.*
Pupils who are not able to follow normal instruction are admitted to the school for children with learning difficulties. It was already in the mid-1970s that the segregation of these pupils from the others was queried. This trend towards integration has not only intensified up to the present day but has also seized the domain of the school for handicapped children.

3. Homework – the pros and cons

The question of homework, for example, shows clearly how strongly the opinions of parents may differ. It is an astonishing fact, however, that teachers who do not give any homework or rather rarely are not popular. Parents fear, as you must know, that in such conditions their children will not be able to adopt the right working attitude.

Appendix

Figure 1 The school system in the principality of Liechtenstein

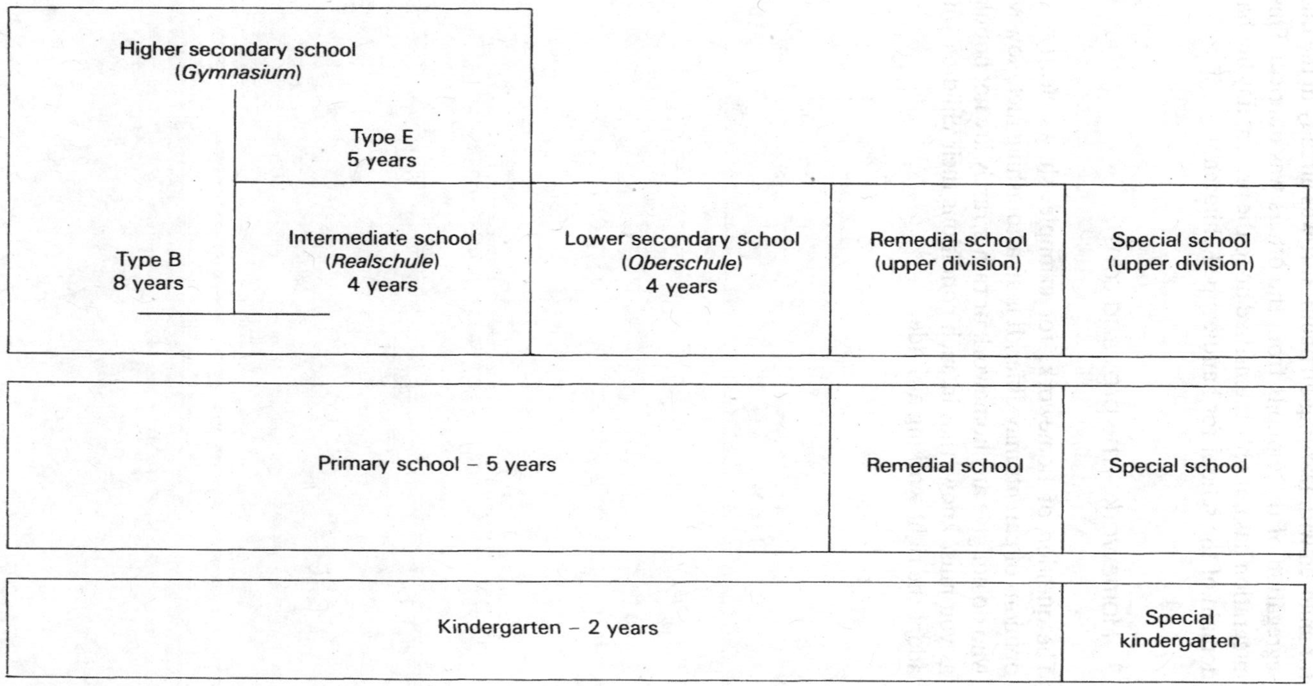

13. LUXEMBOURG <DECS/EGT [86] 86>

Primary education in the Grand Duchy of Luxembourg is governed by the Act of 10 August 1912 on the organisation of primary education, amended by the Acts of 1958 and 1963 and, more recently, 6 September 1983.

Pre-school education covers two years, the second of which is compulsory.

Compulsory education covers nine years, six years of primary education followed by either three years of complementary education or by study at secondary or technical secondary schools.

Outline of education in Luxembourg

Age range (at the beginning of the school year)

Pre-school	*Primary*	*Complementary*
4 5	6 7 8 9 10 11	12 13 14
		Secondary
		12 13 14 15 16 17 18
		Secondary technical
		12 13 14 15 16 17 18

In primary education, most classes form a single unit; occasionally, for reasons of distance between home and school or numbers, the first year is combined with the second, the third with the fourth or the eighth with the ninth, etc. In larger municipalities, schools serve particular districts, while in rural regions the transport of pupils is organised for one or more municipalities.

In primary and complementary education the number of pupils in classes may vary between 10 and 25. Most classes have fewer than 20; there are few with more than 25.

Introductory classes are temporarily attended by foreign children who have difficulty in adapting to Luxembourg schools.

There are special classes for maladjusted children of school age who, though capable of receiving education, are permanently or temporarily unable to pursue ordinary education successfully.

More seriously handicapped children are educated in special institutions.

Children who at the end of the sixth year wish to continue education in a general or technical secondary school have to take one of the two admission examinations. These written examinations consist of a mathematics paper, two German and two French papers. More than four-fifths of pupils in this age group take one or other of the examinations. Pupils who, after the sixth year, do not continue their education in a secondary school, whether technical or otherwise, attend complementary classes. It is possible to move to a secondary or more likely technical secondary school during or after the three years of complementary education.

After the examination that completes general or technical secondary education after seven years of study, pupils may begin higher or university education.

University courses in Luxembourg enable students to complete an initial university year in law and economic sciences, arts and human sciences or natural sciences. This first year of study is recognised by foreign universities. It is compulsory for future teachers.

Beyond that first year, university studies in all disciplines are pursued in a foreign university of the student's choice. Diplomas obtained in universities are confirmed and registered in Luxembourg.

The Higher Institute of Technology provides a three-year course of study for technical engineers in mechanical engineering, electro-technology, civil engineering and applied data processing.

The Institute of Education used to train pre-school and primary school teachers in two years. Since 1983 the course has been extended to cover three years, at the Higher Institute of Education and Educational Research which has replaced the Institute of Education. The new institute selects students on the basis of results obtained in the school leaving examination.

Public education in Luxembourg is free.

Teaching branches in primary education

	1st	*2nd*	*3rd*	*4th*	*5th*	*6th*
Religious instruction	3	3	3	3	3	3
Luxembourg language	–	–	½	½	½	½
Free expression	3	3	–	–	–	–
French language	–	3*	7	7½	7½	7
German language	9	7½	4½	4½	4½	4
Mathematics	7	5½	5½	5	5	5
History	–	–	–	–	–	1
Local environment	–	–	1	–	–	–
Geography	–	–	–	1	1	1
Painting and drawing	1	1	1	1	1	1
Handwork	1½	1½	1½	1½	1½	1½
Music	½	½	1	1	1	1
Sport	2	2	2	2	2	2
Recreation	2¾	2¾	2¾	2¾	2¾	2¾

* from 1 March

The weekly timetable comprises 27 hours of education, 24 of which are non-religious (three lessons are set aside for religious and moral education). Lessons in non-religious moral education are provided in some municipalities. Almost half of these 24 lessons are taken up with language study.

Recreation takes up a further 2.45 hours per week, giving a total of 29.45 hours.

Pupils may be exempted from religious and moral education lessons provided they have an appropriate written statement from the person legally responsible for their education.

Typical timetable

Slight variations are accepted to fit in with school transport.

	Morning	*Afternoon*
Monday	8–11.45	14–16.30
Tuesday	8–11.45	free
Wednesday	8–11.45	14–16.30
Thursday	8–11.45	free
Friday	8–11.45	14–16.30
Saturday	8–11.45	free

Holidays

The school year begins on 15 September in all schools and ends on 15 July. At All Saints there is one week's holiday; at Christmas two weeks; in Lent one week; at Easter two weeks; and at Whitsun one week. There are three other holidays: 1 May, Ascension and the National Holiday.

Supervision of primary education

As far as the state is concerned, supervision is carried out by the government and, on its instructions, the Board of Education, the Inspector General and primary education inspectors; as far as local authorities are concerned, supervision is carried out by the municipal administrative authority and the schools board. Parents are represented on the Board of Education and the municipal schools boards.

Supervision of religious education is the responsibility of the head of the church concerned.

Supervisory bodies and bodies providing consultation and information services

- the Board of Education of the Grand Duchy;
- municipal schools boards;
- the schools inspectorate: an inspector general and, at present, 14 regional inspectors;
- the National Schools Medical Board and its regional and local boards;
- the Higher Institute of Education and Educational Research with its various departments – initial and in-service training, documentation, psychology and research, remedial education;
- the Higher Council of National Education;
- Schools Guidance Service and Social Services.

There are two teachers' trade unions:

- the National Union of Teachers (Syndicat National des Enseignants, SNE), previously the Amalgamated Association of School Teachers (Association des Instituteurs Réunis, AIR);
- the Education and Science Union (Syndicat Education et Sciences, SES) previously the General Federation of Luxembourg Schoolteachers (Fédération Général des Instituteurs Luxembourgeois, FGIL).

Both unions publish regular bulletins and prepare textbooks and teaching material.

Private education

There are very few private schools at primary level in Luxembourg. At all events government authorisation is required to set up a private school for children of compulsory schooling age. Private primary schools are subject to inspection by the authorities responsible for the supervision of public education.

Problems

1. the linguistic situation,
2. the high percentage of foreign children.

The linguistic situation of Luxembourg raises complex problems particularly at school. Luxembourg is in effect a trilingual country:

- In the Grand Duchy the language spoken by all levels of the population on all occasions, even in the Chamber of Deputies, is the Luxembourg language, which is a Franco-Moselle dialect. This is the native national language of the Luxembourg people and is an expression of their identity and a symbol of their will to remain independent. But it is a language of limited usage; it is not much written or taught and is not very suitable for abstract expression. Spelling was loose for a long time and was officially laid down only in 1976.

- German is the language used for written communication – the newspapers of the country appear mainly in German, particularly where articles and items are intended for all readers. Despite the fact that Luxembourg and German are very close to one another, German is looked upon as a foreign language. Since the end of the Second World War German has been gradually replaced in church by Luxembourg.
- French is the official language of government, law, courts and international affairs in the Grand Duchy. It is the language used by the intellectual groups in written communication. Lastly it is the language used on ceremonial occasions and for public notices.

The three languages are thus used concurrently and in the same way from family to family and from region to region, while each is required to fulfil different functions.

Luxembourg is the language used in the two years of pre-school education, except in cases where there is a large number of foreign children in the class and it may be necessary to use French or even Portuguese.

In primary school, reading and writing are taught in German, which becomes the teaching language for the other branches of education, except French. Owing to the use of Luxembourg in families and in the Luxembourg environment, the study of German causes serious difficulties to Luxembourg children and even more so to foreign children, the majority of whom come from Latin countries. Oral French begins in the second half of the second year and in the third year the regular study of French occupies an important place in the timetable in Luxembourg schools.

The Luxembourg language is used in various school activities until children are able to use German. In practice it remains the language used for artistic and recreational subjects.

Integration or assimilation of large numbers of foreign children is a major problem in Luxembourg schools. Of a total population of about 367,000, about 96,000 are foreigners, i.e. 26 per cent. About 39 per cent of children receiving pre-school education and 35 per cent of children attending primary school are foreigners. In the city of Luxembourg almost 55 per cent of school children are foreigners; in the city of Esch over 50 per cent. It should be added that a certain number of these children were born in Luxembourg and that many children are partly integrated, but it is still true to say that the school has a responsibility to see that these foreign children progress educationally and socially, at the same time as it has to cope with the problems of trilingualism. For most foreign children the first language learned is French, as the vast majority (85 per cent) come from Romance language countries (Portugal, Italy, France, Belgium and Spain).

Every kind of experiment has been conducted to find out the best form of schooling for foreign children; new experiments are to be conducted. The problem is especially serious as a large proportion of these children are from disadvantaged socio-cultural environments.

Trends

As schools are bilingual with a large number of lessons devoted to language study, the timetable is subject to imbalance – there is necessarily less time given to the preparatory teaching of history, geography and the sciences and to self-expression than in countries where schools are unilingual. Attempts are being made to modify the timetable and bring curricula 'up to date' so as to give more time to science, history, self-expression and current affairs and as far as possible include the language and culture of foreign children.

In this way a new set of timetables are under study which should make it possible to reallocate the time allowed for school subjects. Redistribution of this kind will necessarily entail revision and adaptation of curricula and text-books.

Since September 1986 an amended timetable has been tried out in several schools; this comprises 30 lessons of 50–55 minutes each (instead of the current timetable of 27 lessons described above). Under the new timetable three lessons a week are reserved for physical education, there is an introduction of science and science lessons proper, in the fifth year an extra lesson is reserved for history, and over the whole six years one optional lesson is written into the week to allow for discussion of current affairs or an introduction to technology. Moreover, two lessons a week of intercultural education are planned, devoted primarily to the language and culture of foreign children in places where there is a need for this.

In December 1985 the Ministry of National Education and Youth set up a commission to revise the curriculum. The commission is split into working parties, each chaired by an inspector.

The link between pre-school and primary education is being examined anew, especially since the second year of 'kindergarten' has become compulsory and pre-school teachers receive the same basic training as primary school teachers.

The new book for teaching the alphabet takes full account of the basic linguistic situation, the presence of a great many foreign children and preliminary learning done in pre-school classes, where more suitable teaching material has now been introduced.

Early teaching and systematic study of French have been revised and re-evaluated following a review of the objectives of French teaching at the various levels of primary and post-primary education.

Continuous efforts are made to improve the preparation for working life of pupils who do not go to secondary or technical secondary school or who are not successful in those schools.

Everyone responsible for education gives full attention to the problem of the transition of children from primary school to the various post-primary educational facilities.

As far as handicapped children are concerned, experiments are being carried out to integrate or reintegrate them into normal classes as far as possible.

An Act which came into force in 1983 governs the initial and in-service training of pre-school and primary school teachers. It provides for:

(a) reform of primary school teacher training,
(b) foundation of a Higher Institute of Education and Educational Research,
(c) modification of pre-school and primary education.

The main aims of this Act are to extend primary school teacher training so that it covers three years, to improve the quality of primary school teacher-training studies, to institutionalise in-service training and to create a Higher Institute of Education and Educational Research.

Since this Act became law, pre-school and primary school teachers have been trained at Luxembourg's University Centre and at the Higher Institute of Education and Educational Research.

It must be said in conclusion that the Education Act referred to above is to be revised and adapted to the present situation in schools, the family and society. Many people have been consulted and preliminary work is under way.

14. MALTA
<DECS/EGT [86] 30>

A. Innovation in primary education

1. Recent developments

Although many changes have taken place over the past years at all levels of education in Malta, I shall limit myself to defining recent areas of innovation introduced in primary school.

1.1. With the implementation of the 1974 Education Act, education became compulsory for all Maltese children between the ages of 6 and 16.

Article 9 of the same Education Act ensured that education provided in government schools is free by law. Besides free tuition at all levels of kindergarten, primary, secondary and trade schools, technical institutes, new lyceums and the university, this Act ensured that henceforth all students would have:

(a) *free loan of textbooks*: at kindergarten, primary, secondary and trade school levels;
(b) *free writing materials* – at kindergarten and primary levels;
(c) *free transport* – for all students up to compulsory school age;
(d) *free midday-break supervision* for all full-time students below university level;
(e) *free milk* for all students;
(f) *free school medical service*, which is composed of school medical officers and school nurses. This service, which is run for the Education Department by the Medical and Health Department, keeps a constant check on the health of all children in kindergartens and primary schools by means of regular visits. Students in secondary and trade schools benefit from this service as and when the need arises or when referred by the head of school.

1.2. *Special education in primary schools*
The 1974 Education Act (art. 17) also specifies where a child, for whom education is compulsory, should, owing to some mental, emotional or physical handicap, receive education in a special school. The parent is to register the child who shall have to attend the special school best suited for him.

The Education Department runs a number of special schools and services for handicapped children. These include:

- special schools, or units, for handicapped children – the educationally subnormal, the maladjusted, the impaired of hearing, the visually impaired and the physically handicapped;
- hospital classes;
- integrated classes for the educationally subnormal;
- a peripatetic service for home-bound children.

It is the policy of the Education Department to open integrated 'opportunity' classes for handicapped children in primary schools where this education is to the greatest benefit of the child.

Thus, full attention is also being given to the needs and to the instruction of physically and mentally handicapped children. Home teaching to below-school-age handicapped children and advice to their parents have also recently been expanded. Children who have to stay away from school for long periods because of sickness receive regular lessons at home or in hospital.

In line with modern educational developments in this field, educationally subnormal children are, as far as possible, being given special treatment in normal schools so as to give them the opportunity to integrate with other children. Such schools have been equipped with the necessary facilities to cater for these children.

B. The education system in Malta

Kindergarten and primary education

1.1. The expansion of the educational system in Malta during the 1970s included the introduction of kindergarten facilities for children aged 4 years in a number of towns and villages. (This service has since been made available to children all over the island.) Thus all children, including those from culturally deprived sections of the community, were enabled to receive early formative preparation for their school years. This service also made it possible for working mothers to continue in productive employment.

It is intended to further expand kindergarten centres, particularly in new residential areas and large districts where the number of children of kindergarten age has risen considerably. It is also expected that, in the early stages of the plan, kindergartens will be able to take 3 year olds as well.

Kindergarten centres are, in most cases, attached to existing primary schools, but are administratively run by an education officer in charge of kindergarten and infant education. Classes, or kindergarten groups, are looked after by kindergarten assistants and the maximum number in these groups does not exceed 25 children on the enrolment register. Attendance at such classes is voluntary.

Kindergarten classes run on a whole-day basis and follow the normal primary schools' opening and closing times. The aim of kindergarten education is to socialise the child and to provide opportunities for guided intellectual, emotional and physical development. Play and activity methods are promoted. There exists no formal curriculum, but due attention is given at the proper time to preparing children for primary education.

1.2. The organisational structure of the existing school network at the primary level has also been updated to take due account of the significant increase in the number of children of primary school age. At the same time, due action has been taken to improve and modernise both the content and teaching methods of primary education in line with international trends. Among other innovations, greater emphasis is being placed on group work to stimulate collective activity while preserving the child's autonomy and sense of responsibility.

A programme to modernise equipment and facilities in primary schools has also been launched while locally-produced teaching materials, aids and textbooks are being used to the fullest extent possible.

Primary education begins at age 5 and lasts for six years, that is, Year 1 up to Year 6. Primary schools generally cater for the population of a particular self-contained community or parish. In the smaller concentrations, one school caters for all grades - Year 1 to 6, including kindergartens. In the bigger centres, schools are generally divided into 'A' schools, which cater for kindergartens and Years 1–3, and 'B' schools, which cater for Years 4–6. This division also reflects the emphasis in the curriculum and the general approach to teaching.

C. Areas of innovation in primary schools

With a view to making the educational system more dynamic and effective, several educational innovations have recently been introduced. Areas of innovation include curriculum development, structure of classes, integration of subjects, individualisation of instruction, pupil assessment, teacher training and school-home communication.

1.1 The school curriculum

A major innovation in primary education has been the development of a suitable curriculum that constitutes a broad guide for the teacher over the scholastic year. The primary school curriculum consists of the following subjects: Maltese, English, mathematics, physical education, religion, social studies, history, geography, environmental studies, nature study and elements of science, art and craft, music and singing.

In the first three years the emphasis is on reading, writing, numeracy and English. More formal studies (to include history, geography and elements of science) are introduced in the third and fourth years. Activity and creativity methods, together with extra curricular activities, are promoted.

The new curriculum underlines the idea that there is no fixed or stable curriculum for every school. Teachers are encouraged to modify and adjust it according to their environment and the needs of their particular class. Teachers are also reminded that the curriculum should be under continuous development.

1.2 Structure of classes

The construction of spacious new school premises during recent years has made it possible for classes not to exceed 30 pupils each, and in rural schools the teacher/pupil ratio is even lower. The primary school teacher teaches all subjects of the curriculum and is in charge of his class for the whole time. There are, however, peripatetic services to help teachers in physical education, art and music. Remedial education on a withdrawal system is available in some schools, while in others integrated classes of educationally subnormal children (strictly speaking belonging to the special education sector of the Education Department) are functioning.

1.3 Pupil assessment and promotion policy

Classes are generally streamed by ability depending on the size of the school. Half-yearly and annual examinations are used to assess pupils' achievements. From Year 3 upwards, annual examinations are run on a national basis (the same paper on the subject is set for all children in the same grade).

Notwithstanding the above, a general promotion policy has been established since we strongly believe in the 'individualisation of instruction' policy and the many shortcomings of 'retention' or 'class repetition' practice. Children are made to repeat only in exceptional circumstances and after serious consultation among teachers, parents and the education officer in charge of special education. Pupils who perform at a very low level are further 'screened' and placed in special classes with a curriculum more suited to their abilities.

With the implementation of the Education Act, secondary education was made available to *all* children who complete the six-year primary school course. Education at this level is available in two types, namely:

(a) the recently introduced selective secondary education in Junior Lyceums for the brighter and more promising students (admission to such schools is through a competitive examination), and
(b) non-selective, general, comprehensive secondary education based on area schools.

In the two types of school, the course is of five years' duration and leads, in the case of the Junior Lyceums and more motivated students in other secondary schools, to the General Certificate of Education and the Malta Matriculation examinations at 'Ordinary Level'.

1.4 Teacher training

With the introduction of the worker–student system, the course of studies leading to the degree of Bachelor of Education (Honours) of the Faculty of Education of the University of Malta was extended over five years. The system alternates 5½ months of study and 5½ months of work. The work phase is carried out in the Education Departments, during which students gain first-hand experience in actual classroom situations.

The course is organised on the unit credit system and comprises five major subjects or areas, namely:

(i) educational theory and pedagogy (educational psychology, socio-cultural aspects of education, pedagogy)
(ii) main subject specialisation (content, pedagogy)
(iii) subsidiary subject
(iv) teaching practice
(v) dissertation.

The general principle underlying teacher training is that the primary school teacher is a generalist who teaches all subjects of the curriculum. However, all teachers do not receive identical training. They are given the opportunity to make certain choices which give them different competences. They also specialise in particular subjects or areas of study.

1.5 Continuing education of teachers

The Education Department and the Faculty of Education also run a number of in-service courses for teachers independently of or in collaboration with each other. These courses are mainly of an *ad hoc* nature and are held according to needs. These include:

(a) Evening diploma courses for teachers, which are of two years' duration. They are generally intended to update/retrain teachers.
(b) Day-release in-service courses for teachers intended to update teachers in the subjects that they teach.
(c) Seminars and lectures organised by the Education Department and given by visiting foreign lecturers.
(d) Courses for the initial and recurring in-service training of kindergarten assistants.

Besides the above courses, great use is also made of scholarships and bursaries abroad, often provided by foreign governments and institutions through bilateral agreements for the further training and updating of Education Department personnel in the principles and methods concerning educational developments and curriculum subjects.

1.6 School inspectors

The education officers (former inspectors of schools), whose main role was the inspection and evaluation of teachers, have now assumed the role of advisers and animators. The emphasis is given to guidance and staff development through individual advice, organisation of in-service courses and the preparation of textbooks suited for local needs. They also monitor school progress and plan curricula and syllabuses. They work in close collaboration with the Ministry of Education.

1.7 School–home communication

Close communication has of recent years been established between schools and homes by the setting up of parent–teacher associations in schools. It is believed that strong links between these two components will make children and parents see school as an important part of their life, as something for which they should feel responsible and which they will want to improve.

Since the life of children is mainly divided between two environments, that is, the home and the school, it is in these two places that children pass the greater part of their time. Consequently, the home and the school are the most important elements that could have the greatest effect on the moulding of the character and personality of children.

When encouraging the setting up of parent–teacher associations in schools, the Education Department had this main objective in mind, that is, 'that parents and the teachers of their children associate together and get to know one another better to ensure the best academic education and proper upbringing of children'. Parents are kept informed about school decisions and activities through school bulletins or specially convened meetings at which the education and upbringing of children are discussed according to their diverse duties. The PTA, as a body united in a common ideal, strives to find ways and means to be of moral and material help to the school.

The main aims and objectives of innovation in primary education

It is a fact that innovation in primary education in Malta was prompted by radical changes in contemporary society and the challenge children have to cope with owing to new discoveries in science and technology. Children's greater exposure to the mass media, their vulnerability in the face of changing patterns of family life and their earlier maturation, all call for the urgent need of innovation with a view to adapting teaching to the new demands thus ensuring the necessary pedagogical and teaching continuity.

The main aims of innovation are to:

- ensure, apart from the acquisition of fundamental skills, the awakening and development of all skills, attitudes and knowledge necessary for the development of the child's capabilities and for his well-balanced life in society;
- lay the foundations and knowledge of skills in order to ensure the success of future studies;
- develop individual autonomy, a commitment to democratic values and a sense of social responsibility;
- help the child acquire an active attitude towards problems and help him adapt to new situations;
- develop the child's eagerness to learn, his reflective ability, curiosity, self-reliance, creativity and sense of responsibility.

The process of implementing educational innovations is a slow and laborious one which presents many difficulties. A certain amount of resistance is also put up by those teachers who have to adopt new methods and approaches to their teaching techniques. However, through persuasion, goodwill and personal involvement of all those concerned, I am confident that such innovations will eventually produce the desired results.

15. NETHERLANDS <DECS/EGT [86] 67>

1. General principles of the Dutch education system

In the Netherlands, education has been governed by law for more than a century. Developments in the educational system have resulted in new legislation.

Until the nineteenth century educational matters were regulated only at the local level. At the beginning of the nineteenth century the first national legislation governing education was passed.

1.1 Constitution

Two issues dominate the political discussions about education:

- freedom of education or the freedom to found a school on the basis of one's own principles, and
- equal state support for public as well as for private schools.

In 1848 the political opponents agreed upon the freedom of education. The Constitution of 1848 declared that education was free. So the permission of the government was no longer required for founding a school.

In 1917 a new article for the Constitution was drafted and accepted which called for placing publicly run and privately run schools on an equal financial footing.

Other important principles, inserted in the Constitution, are:

- Education shall be the constant concern of the government. This provision dates from 1815 and indicates that the social function of education is deemed to be of such vital importance to the community that it is the duty of the government to uphold it.
- All persons shall be free to provide education, without prejudice to a few restrictions that may be placed upon it. This provision dates from 1848 and embodies the constitutional right of everyone to provide education.

  Interference by the authorities is prohibited under the Constitution except with regard to supervision and to requirements concerning the moral integrity and competence of teachers. The legislator (and only the legislator) decides that such restrictions are desirable.

- Publicly run schools must be regulated in such a way that they pay due respect to everyone's religion or belief.
- The standards required of publicly run schools and privately run schools financed from public funds must be so regulated that in both the standards are fully guaranteed.
- The standards required of privately run schools must give due regard to the freedom to provide education according to their religious or other principles (case law in the Netherlands regards private education as education based on one of the religious or other principles to be found in Dutch society). The Constitution explicitly mentions two areas in which this freedom is to be respected: in the choice of teaching aids and in the appointment of teachers. These matters are therefore the sole concern of the competent authority of the educational institution in question.

1.2 Education acts

The present educational system for children aged 4–12, which came into force on 1 August 1985, is based on two laws: (a) the Primary Education Act, which has replaced the earlier Primary Education Act of 1920 and the Nursery Education Act of 1955; (b) the Interim Act for Special Education and Secondary Special Education, which replaced the Special Education Decree of 1967.

According to the law, the former nursery schools (age 4–6) and ordinary primary schools (age 6–12) are now integrated in new primary schools (age 4–12).

Special schools are schools for children with physical, sensory or mental handicaps (which prevent them attending ordinary primary schools) who require a predominantly orthopedagogic and orthodidactic programme.

Rights and duties of teachers are laid down in special decrees. Beyond that there are numerous decrees and 'general administrative measures' which regulate the practical implementation of the various laws.

1.3 Compulsory education

In the Netherlands, school attendance is compulsory for all children aged 5–15. So they have to attend a primary school or a special school, without having to pay for it.

1.4 Participation

In addition, there is an Act that guarantees parents and teachers having influence in educational matters and in running the school.

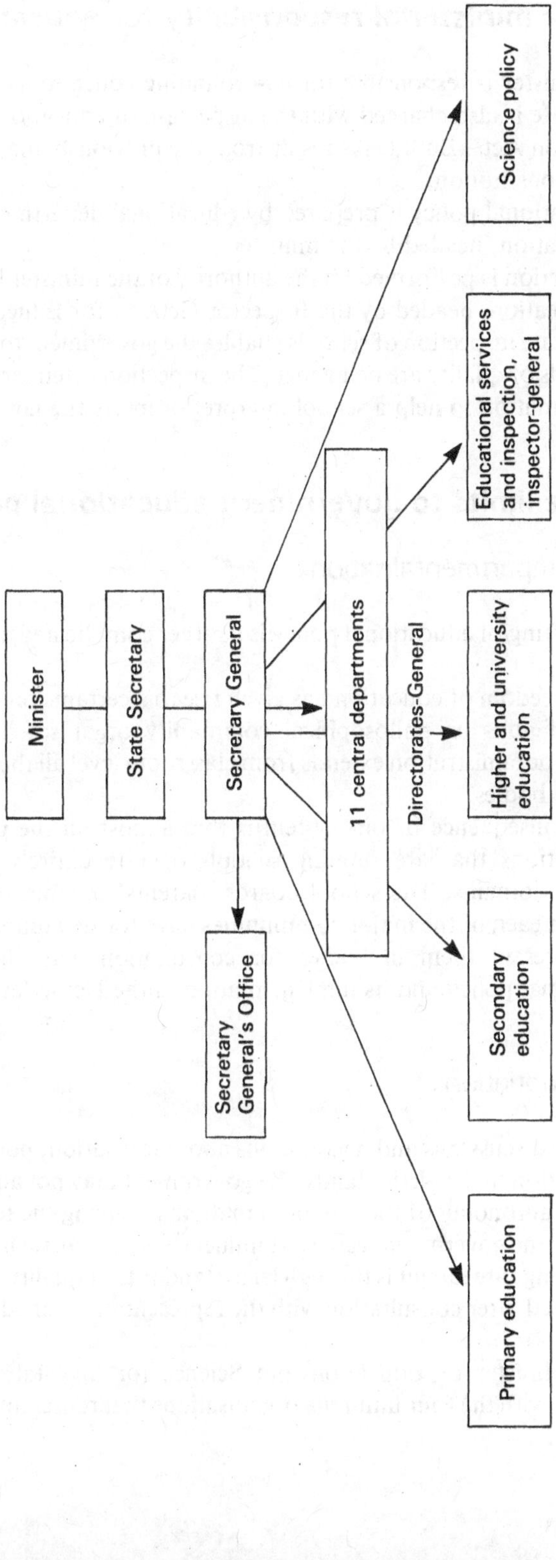

Figure 1 Administrative structure of public education in the Netherlands

2. The ministerial responsibility for education

The minister is responsible for co-ordinating educational policy and science policy. He is also charged with the inspection of education under the various Education Acts. Both tasks result from the previously mentioned regulations in the Constitution.

Educational policy is prepared by educational departments in the Ministry of Education, headed by the minister.

Inspection is performed on the authority of the minister by the Inspectorate for Education, headed by the Inspector General for Education.

The state inspection of schools enables the government to see whether or not standards of quality are being met. The inspection often serves also as a source of information to help a school interpret properly the laws and regulations.

3. The limits to government educational policy

3.1 Compartmentalisation

The drafting of educational policy is a rather complicated affair in the Netherlands.

The freedom of education has given rise to a certain compartmentalisation. Each religious or philosophical community organises its own education; separate administration extends from classroom level all the way to the highest advisory bodies.

The consequence of our system is that almost all the parents' or church organisations that are running schools operate entirely within their own separate domains. The school boards, parents' organisations and teachers' unions in each of the major communities have formed umbrella organisations that represent them in bodies for consultation with the government on educational policy and its implementation in the Netherlands.

3.2 Negotiations

In all the discussions and negotiations about legislation, policy and regulation of education in the Netherlands, the government may not and cannot interfere with the autonomy of the school in matters involving the teaching itself. The only way the government can exert influence on the curriculum and the way in which things are taught is through legal standards of quality. But even these are formulated after consultation with the representatives of educational organisations.

The Minister of Education and Science (or his State Secretary) meets regularly with the four umbrella organisations that represent public education, general private education, Roman Catholic education and Protestant education. All governmental proposals concerning education are examined most critically, especially by the organisations of the privately run schools, particularly when either the subject matter or the methods of teaching are involved. Governmental proposals that call for major changes in laws or regulations regarding education are always viewed as sensitive issues. This perhaps explains why the state government in the past has always been very conservative when it comes to proposals for educational reform.

3.3 Educational reforms

Every Minister of Education and Science knows that attempts to reform education in the Netherlands will succeed only through close, regular consultation with the educational establishment. Each organisation in which the school boards, parents' associations and teachers' unions are represented has its own political affiliation. The larger political parties represented on municipal councils, provincial councils and in parliament in fact share a common political history with the major educational communities.

4. Primary schools

4.1 Statistics

There are:

- 8,400 primary schools, of which approximately 35 per cent are public-authority schools run by the municipal authorities, 30 per cent are Protestant, another 30 per cent are Catholic and 5 per cent are private non-denominational schools,
- approximately 1½ million primary school children aged 4–12, and
- some 69,000 teachers.

4.2 The impact of the Primary Education Act 1985

Despite the previously mentioned limits to government policy, the government succeeded in getting the new Act accepted in parliament.

Primary education is regulated by the Primary Education Act, a framework act incorporating:

- general guidelines on teaching arrangements;
- great stress on the individual responsibility of those involved;
- detailed regulations for a highly standardised system of financing;
- a certain degree of decentralisation in the implementation of the Act, with specific reference to school accommodation.

The government's main objective is to establish primary education facilities that allow children to undergo an uninterrupted process of development from the age of 4 to about 12.

As mentioned before, the role of government in steering processes of development and change is limited. The Primary Education Act provides only a framework. The schools themselves decide on the day-to-day activities with which they will achieve the objectives and the principles outlined in the law.

A central feature of primary education is the school work plan, which has to be drawn up by the staff and approved by the competent authority every two years. Within the framework of the objectives formulated in the Act, schools describe what will be taught in their particular school, the methods to be used and the means of assessing whether the desired results have been achieved.

Emphasis in government policy on creating favourable conditions, stimulating developments and initiating activities to encourage schools to achieve the objectives inserted in the new Act.

Recently the government announced its intention of determining national standards regarding school curricula. These standards will spell out the subject matter and pupil achievement (skills, knowledge, behaviour) at which school curricula have to aim.

The government also started a debate about school self-appraisal. Probably proper instruments for schools will soon be developed.

4.3 Objectives

The crucial parts of the Primary Education Act are to be found in sections 8–11, which describe the content of the new-style primary education.

Section 8

Primary education must ensure that pupils can follow an uninterupted process of education and development and that this is attuned to the development of the individual pupil (i.e. independent of other pupils' progress). In all instances the teaching will aim to promote the development of the emotions, the intellect and creativity and the acquisition of essential knowledge and social, cultural and physical skills. The underlying assumption must be that children are growing up in a multicultural society.

Section 9

The following subjects must always appear on the syllabus in the new-style primary schools, preferably related to one another: sensory and physical exercise; Dutch; arithmetic and mathematics; English; expressive activities; development of skills necessary for daily contact with others, such as road safety; the promotion of healthy living; and a number of specific subject areas. These subject areas will always include geography, history, science (including biology), social relations (including civics) and religious movements.

Section 9 goes on to define what is meant by expressive activities: the use of language, drawing, music, handicrafts, play and movement. This section also specifies that the Frisian language is a compulsory subject in the province of Friesland (unless special exemption is granted) and that lessons may be given in Frisian, other living local dialects or, in the case of children with a non-Dutch cultural background, their own native language.

Finally, section 9 allows schools to obtain exemption from teaching certain subjects, for example in order to carry out specific innovatory projects.

Section 10

Section 10 lays down additional provisions for pupils with a different language or cultural background. The school work plan can, if necessary, allow room for classes in a different language or culture, which may also be attended by pupils from the other schools.

Section 11

Section 11 deals with the content of the school work plan. The school work plan provides an annual review of the organisation and content of teaching. It is based on the assumption that in principle children can proceed through the school in eight consecutive years.

The school work plan should also state what links the school has with other institutions, such as school counselling services or welfare organisations. The school work plan will be developed within an annual programme of activities, which will specify what is to be done in a particular period, when the school holidays and days off are to be and the length of the school day or week.

4.4 Policy themes

The following are the main themes of policy:

- The further development of the school work plan is encouraged by designing programmes for the adoption of tried and tested means for achieving specific goals of the Primary Education Act. Schools receive facilities to take part in these programmes. Broadening the schools' scope for meeting pupils' needs is an important aspect of every programme.
- Broadening schools' scope for meeting pupils' needs is also improved by supplementary teacher training. As reading problems are the major reason for pupils having to leave regular schools and enrol in special schools, one of the first training programmes is a reading programme. By this programme

teachers learn to diagnose reading problems quickly and accurately and then to remedy or even prevent them.

- Further development of the school organisation and school management. A very important aspect of management is the role of the head teacher in carrying out the reforms and in achieving the objectives specified in the Primary Education Act.

  The task of the head teacher is even more complicated because the school work plan should be a team document, the result of a bottom-up decision-making process.
- The promotion of intercultural education. Insight into other cultural backgrounds must form the basis for mutual respect and equality, which eventually lead to social integration.
- Educational priority policy involves extra measures for schools in neighbourhoods with pupils who have the most serious educational disadvantages.
- Reducing the traditional sex-role patterns, to make sure that girls take more advantage of education. This is very important to give them better qualifications and consequently better chances in the labour market.
- Explore the possibilities for using computers in primary education (computer-supported education and computer-managed instruction).
- Regional primary education councils are initiated as discussion forums for matters of primary education that transcend individual schools, like the programming of supplementary courses for teachers and support activities, matters involving co-operation between schools, etc.

4.5 The educational support system

The educational support structure consists of general and specific support institutes.

General institutes are the local or regional guidance centres, the teacher-training centres and the national pedagogical centres. Their work encompasses guidance and development activities, evaluation and providing advice and information to schools. Local and regional centres provide direct support for schools. National centres mainly provide support for the local and regional centres. The teacher-training centres provide for supplementary teacher-training programmes in needs of schools.

Specific educational support institutes are: the National Institute of Educational Research (SVO); the National Institute of Curriculum Development (SLO); and the National Institute for the Development of Tests (CITO). The SLO develops curriculum models and school work plan models.

5. Special schools

5.1 Statistics

There are:

- 1,000 schools for children who require a predominantly orthopedagogic and orthodidactic approach – about 25 per cent are public schools, 20 per cent are Protestant, 35 per cent are Catholic, and 16 per cent are private non-denominational schools;
- some 102,000 pupils;
- about 16,000 teachers and specially skilled staff.

5.2 The relationship between ordinary education and special education

Some children are unable to function optimally at ordinary school. This may be because of a physical handicap, a mental handicap, a serious learning and/or behavioural difficulty or a combination of factors.

There are 15 different types of special primary school and special secondary school. Each of these specialises in accommodating and teaching a particular category of handicapped children. Teachers have usually had additional training, while the size of classes and the buildings have been adapted to the specific requirements of each target group.

5.3 Referral and admission to special schools

Children can be referred to special schools in two ways:

- parents register a child with a special school because he has a serious physical or mental handicap which makes attendance at an ordinary school out of the question;
- a child has attended an ordinary school for some time (either primary or secondary school) and has been referred by that school to a special school.

The Referral Boards attached to schools draw up reports on whether a child is eligible for admission to a certain type of special school. The competent authority of the school concerned decides on admission or rejection of pupils. Pupils attending special school are retested every two years.

5.4 Types of special school

There are schools for children with sensory handicaps, physical handicaps and mental handicaps, with learning difficulties and behavioural difficulties, and with other handicaps.

5.5 Special primary education and special secondary education

Special primary education is designed for pupils up to the age of 12–13. The curriculum runs parallel to that at ordinary primary school as far as possible so that children can be readily transferred back to ordinary primary schools or can proceed to ordinary secondary schools. Special secondary education is designed for pupils aged 12–20.

5.6 Training prospects of pupils at special primary and secondary schools

Many special secondary schools provide courses comparable to those in ordinary secondary schools so that children can sit regular examinations. More and more special secondary schools are co-operating with ordinary junior vocational secondary schools (lbo) with the aim of providing vocationally oriented programmes in technical and theoretical subjects, taught by lbo teachers, for those special school pupils who are eligible to take lbo courses.

5.7 Re-referral

Government policy aims at having as many special school pupils as possible return to ordinary schools to promote integration and improve their chances. A prerequisite for achieving this end is that ordinary schools must be prepared to and capable of offering an adjusted approach to children who require it. This policy is referred to as a policy of 'widening the area of concern'.

Special schools are sometimes awarded additional facilities to enable staff to provide former pupils with guidance in ordinary schools.

6. Conditions of employment of staff

6.1 Appointments

Municipalities are responsible for appointments in publicly run schools. School boards are responsible for appointments in privately run schools.

Teachers are not civil servants as they are in Germany or France for example.

Requirements for appointment are that candidates should possess:

- a certificate of proficiency;
- a certificate of adequate pedagogic and didactic preparation;
- a certificate of good behaviour;
- a medical certificate to the effect that they are free of disease or disability.

6.2 General conditions of employment

Numerous conditions have been adopted from those applying to civil servants:

- pension scheme
- early retirement scheme: 61 years
- sickness benefit
- redundancy pay
- holidays (for non-teaching staff)
- holiday allowances.

6.3 Conditions of employment specific to teachers

- school holidays (about 60 days)
- dismissal as a result of falling rolls or closure of schools.

6.4 Salary system

The salary of teachers (i.e. salary scales and the amount of salaries) depends on the following criteria:

- type of school
- level of qualification
- age
- post (teacher, assistant head, head)
- number of hours for which appointed.

Each type of school at the moment has separate salary scales.

Nursery, primary and special school teachers are placed, according to the level of their qualifications, on one of the scales appropriate to the type of school in which they are to work. Their salary is fixed at the step on the scale appropriate to their age. Salary does not depend on experience, years of service or other criteria such as good or poor performance in school. The top of the scale (the maximum salary) is usually reached at the age of 47. It is not possible to progress to a higher salary scale on the basis of age or years of service, though it can be done by obtaining a similar or higher qualification.

Separate salary scales apply to school heads.

Assistant school heads are salaried in accordance with teacher scales plus an allowance. Formally there are no other posts.

Teachers whose appointment is not full time are salaried accordingly.

The same salary scales apply throughout the country – there are no regional salary weightings. No distinction is made between salaries in publicly run and privately run schools.

Salaries are adjusted each year in accordance with the index for civil servants. Salary reviews, however, may be arranged by the Minister of Education after consulting staff organisations. An attempt has been made to simplify the salary system because of the numerous problems in fixing the right salaries (for one thing because of the diversity in qualifications) and because of the numerous different scales and cutbacks in salaries.

On 1 January 1985 a revised system was introduced. Some features of the new system are:

- salaries will be paid according to post and no longer according to level of qualification;
- salaries will be paid according to years of service and no longer according to age;
- primary education will be subdivided into a few salary levels;
- the number of salary scales will be restricted and brought into line with the civil service system.

6.5 The nature and extent of teaching duties

It has already been pointed out that formally there are three posts, those of teacher, deputy head and head. These posts involve activities that are not teaching in the strict sense and that are not remunerated separately, but for which 'time units' are usually awarded to a school. Time units release teachers from some of their teaching duties to allow them to perform other activities for which they have been given responsibility.

In special education it is not uncommon for specialist help to be appointed, e.g. remedial teachers and speech therapists. They are not regarded as teachers and they are salaried and financed in a different way.

16. NORWAY <DECS/EGT [86] 84 rev>

Basic school education

Provisions relating to compulsory basic education have existed in Norway since the first part of the eighteenth century (1739). Compulsory schooling of nine years' duration was established by law in 1969.

According to the Basic School Act of 13 June 1969 and the supplementary Act of 13 June 1975, the purpose of the basic school is:

> . . . in understanding of and collaboration with the home, to help give the pupils a Christian and moral upbringing, to develop their mental and physical abilities, and to give them a good general knowledge, so that they can become useful and self-reliant human beings both in their homes and in the community. The school shall further freedom and tolerance for the creation of productive forms of co-operation between teachers and pupils and between school and home.

Through a revision of the Basic School Act in 1975, handicapped children have also been entitled to teaching provided in the regular basic schools. The fundamental principle of this revision was to integrate as far as possible all handicapped children into the ordinary nine-year comprehensive basic school. For certain groups of severely handicapped pupils, specialised institutions will necessarily be maintained in the future also. Special schools for different groups are mainly run by the state.

It is worth mentioning that the nine-year basic school is completely comprehensive with very little organised differentiation in practice outside the classroom. The aim of the basic school is to offer all children an education that is adapted to the individual's ability and that is within the individual's capabilities. This principle applies equally to the education of children with learning difficulties and handicaps and to children with particular learning abilities, be they theoretical, practical, physical or aesthetic. Everything that takes place in the school must take this principle into consideration, and the school must see to it that the principle of suitability of the education offered to every pupil is upheld and integrated into the day-to-day life of the school.

Each class is kept together as a unit at least from the 1st to the 6th grade, and in many cases even to the 9th grade.

In Norway, there are three levels of public administration: the national level, the regional level and the local level.

Local authorities

Norway has 454 municipalities, or local government units, which are responsible for ensuring that all children receive education and that compulsory schooling is carried out in accordance with the general directions drawn up by the Education Act and regulations drawn up by the Ministry of Church and Education. The municipalities are responsible for building and organising and maintaining primary and lower secondary schools.

The supreme authority in local administration is the local council, a body elected by popular ballot for a four-year period. The council appoints a school board to deal with educational matters. The board may have between 7 and 35 members, depending on the size of the area in question, and the political parties are represented in the same proportion as on the directly elected council. Its tasks include, for example, the appointment of teachers, decisions about priorities in financial budgeting, curriculum and teaching. The board also appoints a School Superintendent for the municipality. His or her office serves as the secretariat for the school board. The composition of the school board reflects the relative strength of the local political parties.

Regional level

In order to ensure that the development of compulsory schools is properly coordinated, a Director of Schools is appointed in each county. The director is appointed by the Crown and represents the government.

One of the duties of the School Director is to ensure that laws and regulations applying to the basic school are observed by local authorities. As more authority has increasingly been transferred to the local school boards, the school directors have been given more pedagogical functions. Such functions include assistance to local school authorities in matters concerning innovation in schools and in-service training of teachers.

Another important task is to supervise the equality of education provided throughout the country.

National level

The National Assembly has the supreme political power in the country. As far as education is concerned, this involves legislative and budgetary authority at all levels of the system. Through legislation, the National Assembly determines the basic pattern of education by laying down the aims, structure and contents of education to be provided.

The Ministry of Church and Education is the supreme administrative authority for compulsory education. An advisory body, the Basic School Council, assists the ministry in developing education within the compulsory schools.

Organisation of schools

Compulsory education in Norway is organised and run by public authorities, with very few exceptions. With the passing of the 1969 Education Act, compulsory education was extended from seven to nine years. According to this Act, the compulsory school is divided into a primary stage comprising grades 1–6 and a lower secondary stage comprising grades 7–9.

Classes 1–6: primary (age 7–12)
Classes 7–9: lower secondary (age 13–15).

The links between primary education (stages 1–6) and lower secondary education (stages 7–9) are good. More than 1,000 of 3,500 schools combine primary and lower secondary stages in the same school building.

Figure 1 The administration of the basic school

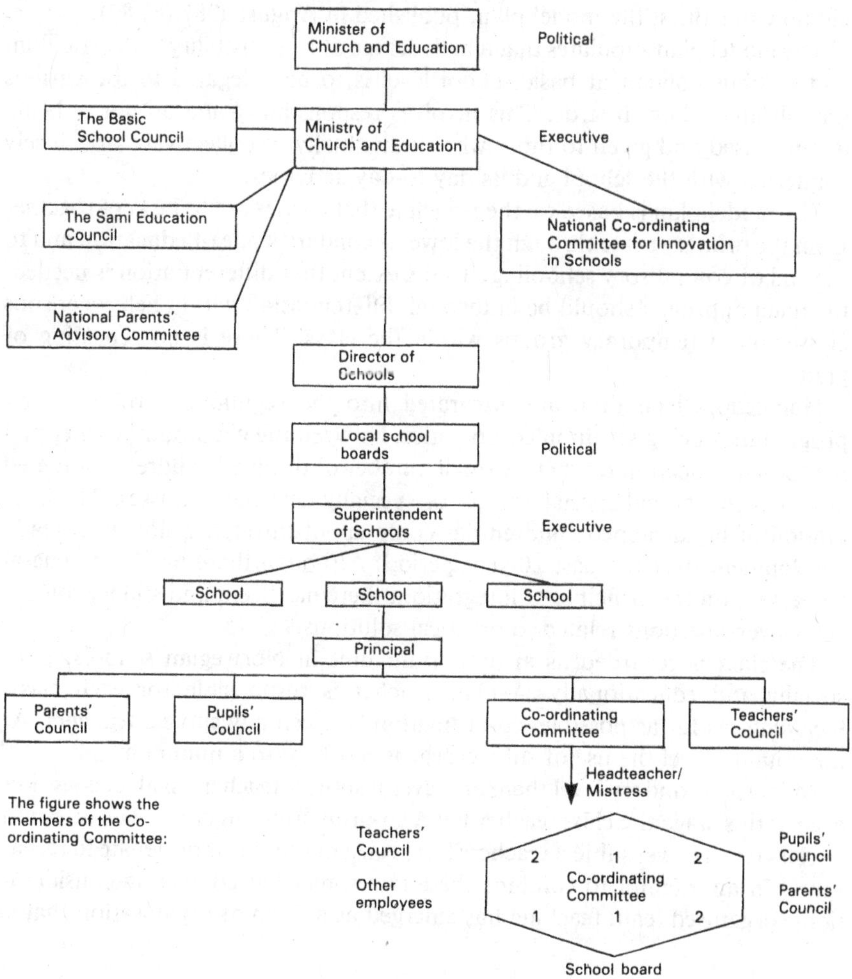

Curriculum Guidelines (The model plan, M 87)

The Basic School Act authorises the Ministry of Church and Education to draw up a model plan for teaching in the basic school. In 1984, the Ministry of Church and Education decided that the then current Curriculum Guidelines from 1974 should be revised. The task of revision was given to the Basic School Council. A draft document was developed and distributed to all schools and educational bodies in Norway, the resulting comments and reactions worked into the Guidelines and the final version delivered to the Ministry of Church and Education in 1985, as a recommendation from the Council.

The National Assembly wanted to discuss the Guidelines before they were published. In response to this request, a preliminary edition of the Guidelines was published early in 1986, parallel with the preparation of a White Paper to be submitted to the *Storting*. The debate held in the *Storting* early in 1987 formed the basis for the wording of the ultimate revised edition of the Curriculum Guidelines, the model plan, published in August 1987 (M 87).

The model plan stipulates that a high degree of responsibility for curriculum and syllabus content at basic school level is to be delegated to the various schools and school boards. This involves responsibility and authority being decentralised and given to those who, individually or collectively, are closely connected with the school and its day-to-day activities.

The model plan is based on the principle that classes are to be kept together from the primary stage through the lower secondary stage of education and to the end of compulsory schooling. To the extent that differentiation is needed, the main approach should be individual differentiation within heterogeneous classes or in temporary groups within the class. There is no repeating of grades.

Handicapped children are integrated into the regular classrooms, their programmes being set up in co-operation between the classroom teacher and the special education teacher. A small number of disabled children, estimated at 1 per cent, attend special schools or specially designated classes. The integration of handicapped children has come about through a slow but steady development over the past 20-year period. Although there has been general agreement on the principle of integration, there has been, and still is, controversy over questions related to practical solutions.

The class is regarded as an important unit in Norwegian schools, both socially and educationally. A class teacher is responsible for each class, including, as far as possible, co-ordination between any subject teachers. At the primary level the use of subject teachers is kept to a minimum.

At lower secondary level there are several subject teachers in all classes, but even at this stage the class teacher has a co-ordinating function. The question of class teachers vs. subject teachers has been a matter of some debate in recent years. In an attempt to combine these two somewhat conflicting considerations, organised team teaching has emerged as a form of organisation that is now recommended. Team teaching may be organised in various practical ways, but quite frequently we find a form of organisation where three teachers share the responsibility for teaching and co-ordinating the work of two classes.

One of the underlying principles of the Curriculum Guidelines is the necessity to take care of the basic human needs of the pupils. Pupils must feel that they belong, and that they have a part to play in the whole - a part that includes taking responsibility for and having a say in what happens in the school. Therefore, the principle of pupil participation is given increased importance in relation to the 1974 Guidelines, and is to be found integrated throughout the whole of the Curriculum Guidelines.

Co-operation between school and home

Related to this principle is the emphasis on the interactive relationship between home, school and the local community, all of which have a responsibility as regards the environment in which young people grow up. There is genuine concern that parents should have a real influence on what happens in the school, and that the school should respect and take into account the differing values that children meet at home, be they religious, political or cultural. Co-operation between home, school and the local community is regarded as necessary if pupils are to see school as meaningful and related to their past and present experience outside the physical surroundings of the school building.

Sami education

The Curriculum Guidelines include a special section on Sami education, with the teaching hours and the subjects being distributed in a way that takes account of the right of the Sami people to an education that is non-discriminatory seen in relation to the rest of Norwegian society. In addition, Sami history and culture are included in the Guidelines as topics that all Norwegian pupils should be familiar with.

Minority groups

Other language minorities have also been taken into account. These include small groups who have lived in Norway for a long time as well as the more recent immigrant minority groups. Emphasis is put on the necessity to provide teaching in both the child's mother tongue and the Norwegian language. Children of minority groups must be given the same opportunities as Norwegian pupils, and the school has a central role to play in fostering understanding, acceptance and respect for those with different backgrounds.

Assessment and evaluation

The model plan lays down the main guidelines for evaluating basic school pupils, while detailed regulations for parent–teacher contact, reports and marks are to be found in the instructions for the basic school.

In relation to previous curricula, the present Curriculum Guidelines propose broader and more varied forms of assessment at all levels. Emphasis is put on forms of assessment that are suitable for providing guidance to pupils and stimulating and supporting the learning process.

It is stressed in the instructions that the school must maintain good contact with parents and guardians. At least twice a year parents and guardians must be informed of their child's progress at school, either through personal meetings or by means of written reports.

At the junior stage (i.e. for the first six school years) no marks are given. At the lower secondary stage (years 7 to 9) pupils are given marks for compulsory subjects twice a year.

Formal assessment at the lower secondary level used to be related to group norms. Presently, we are in the process of shifting the emphasis from norm-related assessment to assessment related directly to the educational objectives of the Curriculum Guidelines. The challenge is now to develop practical assessment material and tools which can encompass the whole range of aims and objectives presented in the Guidelines.

Distribution of subjects and periods – allocation of teaching periods

In the basic school the school year consists of 37 weeks for pupils and 38 for teachers. This means that teachers are to spend one week – i.e. 40 hours – in the course of the year in in-service training or on organised planning.

The school week is five days, and the time pupils spend at school per week varies from age-group to age-group, ranging from 15 to 18 lessons per week in the first year to 30 lessons per week in the final year. The weekly minimum of lessons for all years at the primary level (grades 1–6) taken together is 138; for the three years of lower secondary school the minimum is 90 weekly lessons.

The allocation of time to the various subjects is given in the Curriculum Guidelines in terms of weekly lessons per subject for each of the three year-blocks of compulsory education, presented in Table 1.

Problems and trends in primary education

During the last few years a trend towards greater decentralisation of educational authority from the ministry to regional/local education authorities has been further implemented. This is now being applied even to the financial sec-

Table 1

Subject	*Primary stage*			*Lower secondary stage*
	Years 1–3	*Years 4–6*	*Total years 1–6*	*Years 7–9*
Religious instruction	6	6	12	6
Norwegian	17	16	33	14
Mathematics	11	11	22	11
English		7	7	9
Civics	6	15	21	
Social studies				9
Natural science				8
Music	3	6	9	3
Arts and crafts	4	12	16	5
Physical education	4	6	10	8
Home economics		3	3	4
Optional subjects				11
Pupil and class council	30*	60*	90*	2
Practical, social and cultural work	50*	75*	125*	150*
Total	51	82	133	90
At local disposal			5	
Total			138	90

* Total number of lessons in the three-year period.
The activities are integrated into all subjects.

tor, allowing the municipalities to have a greater influence on how sums of money allocated to them are to be spent.

Previously the government covered its part of the expenditure for the operation and construction of basic schools through a highly differentiated system of 'ear-marked' subsidies. As from 1 January 1986, most of these subsidies have been abandoned and replaced by a sector grant system. This means that the central education authorities no longer have the same financial means of controlling educational expenditure at the local and regional levels.

At the same time, it is essential to balance the policy objective towards greater local autonomy with the need of ensuring equal standards throughout the country. The latter objective will now have to be catered for mainly through legal provisions, and a number of amendments of the school Acts have thus been adopted.

Experiments will be launched with a view to getting a more gentle transition from pre-school to primary education. The government considers that all children from the age of 6 should gradually be enabled to receive pedagogical training according to their maturity. One of the options may be to lower the school starting age from 7 to 6, and thus in the long term possibly to extend the duration of compulsory education from nine to ten years.

According to the Curriculum Guidelines, both local education authorities and individual schools have more freedom to develop their own local curricula, or more precisely to adapt the national Curriculum Guidelines according to local needs and conditions. The policy of decentralisation is also pursued in the field of research and development work. This implies greater freedom for individual schools to initiate innovative programmes.

After a period characterised by major structural reforms, attention is now being paid to the content and quality of educational provisions, and more emphasis is being laid on the school's responsibility for transmitting skills and knowledge required in all ways of life.

Due to a marked reduction in the birth rate in recent years, the annual national intake in Norwegian basic schools is rapidly decreasing, a trend that will continue in the years to come. As for the school year 1985–6, the annual intake was about 530,000 as compared to 590,000 in 1980–1. The annual intake makes it possible to raise educational standards in certain priority areas.

The allocation per pupil has at the same time increased. For the school year 1985–6, the number of pupils decreased by 15,000 (2.8 per cent), whereas allocations decreased by only 0.7 per cent. There has also been a general improvement of standards in the sense that the maximum number of pupils per class has been reduced from 30 to 28, first in the lower grades. Similarly, the teaching duty of the teachers at the primary level has been reduced from 29 to 27 lessons. Resulting from this reform, 1,400 new teaching posts had to be established from the 1984–5 school year.

A programme of action for equal status between the sexes was concluded in 1985. However, resources have been allocated in the budgets with a view to ensuring a continued effort towards equality of opportunity in education. This applies especially to measures aiming at motivating girls to choose untraditional patterns of training.

A four-year programme for the introduction of computer technology in schools was launched in 1984. The implementation of this programme is a top-priority area. Data equipment is now being purchased for a number of experimental schools, teachers are undergoing an extensive programme of in-service courses and software is being developed, taking into account national values and traditions.

An important amendment of the Basic School Act applies to the education of Sami pupils – pupils belonging to an ethnic minority group mostly to be found in the northern regions of the country. As from 1 August 1985, all pupils with a Sami background who live in the central Sami districts are entitled to be educated in their mother tongue in all subjects.

It is worth mentioning that the teachers' organisations have expressed dissatisfaction with their working conditions and levels of salary. A certain drift of qualified teachers from the school to the private sector has been observed. Some school boards, especially in remote and sparsely populated areas, have experienced difficulties in attracting a sufficient number of qualified teachers. In order to stimulate teachers to seek employment in these areas, the Ministry of Education has adopted a series of measures (additional salary, paid leave of absence, etc.).

Private schools

The Norwegian educational system is predominantly a public one. There are however a limited number of private schools at various levels, which operate with the help of state grants, pursuant to law. A new Act on state grants to private schools has been put into force from 1 January 1985. When proposing this Act the government made it clear that private schools have a right to exist side by side with public schools, i.e. state, county and local authority schools. However, according to the government's view, private schools shall primarily be considered as supplementary and are not supposed to compete with the public school system. One of the implications of the new Act is that schools based on an alternative pedagogy, such as the Steiner schools, are now entitled to government grants.

17. PORTUGAL <DECS/EGT [87] 12>

I

1. Basic education in Portugal consists of nine years of schooling in three stages, the first lasting four years, the second two years and the third three years.

Basic education is compulsory for all (i.e. for all children between the ages of 6 and 15) and free of charge (in state schools, in private and co-operative schools under contract, and in centres receiving TV education broadcasts for stage 2).

2. *Objectives of basic education*

- to provide a common general education for all Portuguese children, designed to ensure that they discover and develop their interests, aptitudes, reasoning ability, memory, critical faculty, creativity, moral sense and aesthetic awareness and to further individual self-fulfilment in harmony with community values;
- to establish a balanced relationship between knowledge and skills, theory and practice, and school culture and everyday culture;
- to stimulate physical and motor development, to cultivate interest in manual skills and to emphasise artistic education aimed at making pupils receptive to the varied forms of aesthetic expression and at detecting and stimulating their aptitude in this domain;
- to teach one foreign language and to provide an introduction to another;
- to ensure that pupils acquire the basic knowledge they will need in order to continue their studies or to enter vocational training; to help them to acquire and develop the methods and equipment used in individual and team work, with emphasis on the human aspects of work;
- to bring about a national awareness of the world situation, from a standpoint based on universalist humanism, solidarity and international understanding;
- to cultivate knowledge of and respect for the characteristic values of Portuguese identity, language, history and culture;
- to expose pupils to experience designed to further their civic, social and emotional maturity by fostering positive attitudes and habits of communication and co-operation, conducive both to good family relationships and to a thoughtful, responsible involvement with their environment;

- to cultivate independent thinking with the aim of creating a citizenry capable of participating in the life of the community in a spirit of civic responsibility and democratic involvement;
- to establish suitable conditions for the development and self-fulfilment of children with special educational needs, due in particular to physical and mental handicaps;
- to encourage pupils to take satisfaction in keeping abreast of new knowledge;
- to participate with the pupil's family in providing educational information and guidance;
- to allow basic civic and moral education to be acquired with complete freedom of conscience;
- to establish the conditions that are necessary for pupils to succeed in their schooling and education.

II

1. Basic education is organised by the central departments of the Ministry of Education, which include:

- the General Directorate of Basic and Secondary Education, responsible for deciding pedagogical policy for these levels;
- the General Directorate of Administration and Personnel, responsible for all matters pertaining to teaching, administrative and auxiliary staff;
- the Institute for Socio-Economic Support, responsible for welfare assistance;
- the General Directorate for Educational Facilities, responsible for buildings and equipment.

2. In the case of stage 1, the administrative decisions of these departments are put into effect through the agency of the district and municipal bodies.

Where stages 2 and 3 are concerned, regional structures providing the whole range of Ministry of Education services are in the process of being set up.

The organisation of stage 1 education in the school itself is the responsibility of school councils (the entire teaching staff of one or more schools).

The task of organising stage 2 and stage 3 education falls to the governing boards and pedagogical councils.

III

1. Co-ordination between pre-school and basic education is mainly effected through joint activities designed to alleviate the difficulties involved in transferring from one educational level to another.

2. The following differences exist between the stages within basic education:

- Stage 1 education is of a general nature; classes have a single teacher, although others may be called in for specialist subjects.

- Stage 2 education is broken up into interdisciplinary fields within the basic syllabus; classes generally have a different teacher for each field.
- Stage 3 education consists of a standard curriculum, which includes a variety of vocational fields; classes have one teacher for each subject or group of subjects.

3. The co-ordination between stages is based on a steady progression, in which each stage is designed to complete the previous stage in depth and in breadth, so that there is an overall unity in basic education.

4. The specific objectives for each stage are related to the general objectives for basic education stated above, to the age-groups concerned and to the principles below.

(a) The stage 1 curriculum is designed to develop oral self-expression and to provide an introduction to and steady progress in reading, writing, basic arithmetic, the physical and social environment and self-expression through the plastic arts, drama, music and movement.
(b) Stage 2 includes the arts subjects and creative arts, physical education, sports, science and technology; it is designed to give pupils skills of assimilation, interpretation, criticism and creativity so that they master the methods and equipment for working and gaining knowledge that they need in order to continue their education; emphasis is placed on developing their involvement in and awareness of the community and the main problems facing it.
(c) The objective for stage 3 is a systematic and discriminating approach to the acquisition of present-day culture through the arts subjects, literature, creative art, physical education, sports, science and technology, which are essential requirements whether a pupil is to seek employment or to continue his studies; this stage also includes the requisite educational and vocational guidance so that the decision to start work or to stay at school can be taken without curtailing the individual's scope for self-determination.

5. In specialist basic education schools, some components of the creative arts syllabus, or of physical education and sports, may be given special emphasis without any weakening in the basic curriculum.

6. A certificate of basic education is delivered upon successful completion of compulsory schooling. Successful completion of a given school year or stage of schooling will be certified upon request.

IV

1. Stage 1 education is divided into two two-year phases. Classes consist, on average, of not more than 25 pupils. The pupil–teacher ratio may vary in some cases, for example in open plan schools, in schools applying experimental teaching methods or in schools where certain classes comprise handicapped pupils.

2. In stage 2 and stage 3 education, the number of pupils per class ranges from 26 to 34 in classrooms measuring 40 m^2 and from 15 to 20 in those smaller than 35 m^2.

Classes have a certain age-spread but divergences are not great. They are fairly heterogeneous, that is to say, pupils are not grouped according to criteria such as school performance or adjustment difficulties.

V

In stage 1 education, the school day lasts 4 hours 45 minutes, making a weekly total of 23 hours 45 minutes.

The school year normally begins on 21 September and ends between 10 and 30 June, with breaks for the Christmas holidays (two weeks), Carnival time (five days) and the Easter holidays (two weeks).

In stage 2 and stage 3 education, classes last 50 or 110 minutes and are separated by 10-minute intervals. They are so organised that there are never more than five consecutive classes.

VI

Curricula

1. *Stage 1 education*

- Interest-arousing activities designed to:
- facilitate the child's adjustment to the school;
- constitute a general introduction to future studies;
- permit general observation of each child in order to detect possible handicaps and forestall any future maladjustment.

Portuguese language
Mathematics
Physical and social environment
Plastic self-expression
Self-expression through movement, music, self-expression through drama (1st phase) and musical education (2nd phase)
Physical education
Catholic religion and ethics (optional)

2. *Stage 2 education*

Portuguese
Social studies/history
Foreign language (choice between French, English and German)
Mathematics
Natural science
Visual education

Handicrafts
Musical education
Physical education
Religion and ethics (optional)

VII

1. Progress in stage 1 education is measured by a system of continuous assessment, the final overall assessment being entered in the pupil's school record at the end of the first and second phases (i.e. of the 2nd and 4th years of schooling). Passage from the 1st to the 2nd year and from the 3rd to the 4th year is automatic.

Assessment is selective at the end of each phase.

It is not only the pupils who are assessed, but all those involved in the teaching/learning process. The following are also forms of assessment:

- verification that the work schedules drawn up by the teacher with the help of the class have been completed;
- daily and/or weekly inspection of the work performed by the class;
- daily and/or weekly inspection by the teacher of each pupil's personal work;
- 'classroom discussion' of work done by a pupil or group of pupils (exhibitions, albums, talks, reading of texts, essays, etc);
- direct observation of pupils.

2. The system of continuous pupil assessment is also employed in stages 2 and 3. It presupposes that education is a process of change and its purpose is to ascertain the degree of success achieved. Each assessment thus represents a stage in the teaching/learning process, of which it forms an integral part.

Assessment is based on:

- direct observation;
- partial examinations (work cards, tests, short exercises, etc.);
- final performance tests (longer exercises, full-scale final examinations, etc);
- individual pupils' records, in which each is given a mark according to criteria specific to the various disciplines.

Pupils in stages 2 and 3 are given a mark on a discontinuous scale ranging from 1 to 5 (3 = satisfactory). A pupil will be promoted to the next class provided he does not have a mark under 3 in more than two subjects.

VIII

1. Initial teacher training

1.1 Teachers for basic education obtain their professional qualifications by taking courses designed specifically for their type of training, matching the syllabuses for the corresponding levels of education, or by attending university departments of education.

The following principles apply:

(a) Teachers for basic education stages 1 and 2 are trained at the college of education;
(b) The teachers referred to in (a) may be trained at universities delivering the same diplomas of education as the colleges of education;
(c) Basic education stage 3 teachers and secondary school teachers are trained at university.

1.2 Teachers of professional, vocational and artistic subjects within basic education receive their training by taking the appropriate vocational courses in education, where they are also given method training.

1.3 Degree-holders (*licenciados*) with the scientific qualifications required for in-service teacher training may also qualify as teachers for basic education stage 3 by attending a suitable in-service course.

1.4 The teacher-training courses for basic education stages 2 and 3 are '*licenciatura*' degree courses.

2. Continued training

2.1 All teachers and other education professions are entitled to take continued training courses.

2.2 The continued training must be sufficiently diversified to deepen, broaden, and bring up to date the trainee's previous knowledge and teaching proficiency, and to provide him with career mobility and advancement.

2.3 Continued training is provided chiefly by the same institutions as initial training, and in close co-operation with the establishments in which the trainees are employed.

2.4 Teachers are allowed special periods for continued training; these may take the form of sabbatical years.

IX

There are no regular support services in stage 1 schools, apart from the school health services and medico-pedagogical services.

Schools teaching stages 2 and 3 receive medical assistance from the medico-pedagogical centres, and some schools have the services of a doctor and welfare assistants for a few hours a week.

Educational psychology assistance is provided by the educational guidance services of the General Directorate of Basic and Secondary Education, through the agency of their own staff or in collaboration with psychologists.

Mention should also be made of:

1. the socio-economic support services, which seek to create equal educational opportunities for all pupils, whatever their socio-economic situation or place of residence,
2. the services providing assistance to handicapped pupils attending ordinary schools:

- the 'special education teams' composed of specialist teachers, therapists and other technicians. Their work is performed either in the field or in special halls or centres. Their aim is the handicapped child's integration in the family, school and society;
- centres producing equipment;
- technical support services (deafness branch).

X

The schools conduct and stimulate certain activities in the context of school-family-community relations, for example:

- parents' meetings – to discuss educational problems, guidelines for class work, curricula and other questions necessitating the opinions and collaboration of parents, guardians or other persons *in loco parentis*;
- general meetings – to familiarise parents with school life. Such meetings are also convened whenever particular problems so warrant;
- interviews with individual parents, in order to keep them informed of their children's progress or problems;
- exhibitions of work and school celebrations;
- information visits to bring pupils into touch with their immediate physical and social environment, and school outings to give them insight into physical or social realities further afield;
- participation of members of the public in school work, for example, in environmental studies, sports or scientific and artistic activities.

By way of integrating schools in their environment and supporting the community in which they are located, the General Directorate of Basic and Secondary Education is taking steps to alert teaching staff and parents to certain problems, advising them, *inter alia*, on:

- how to deal with drug-dependence and other similar problems in schools;
- food education;
- how to combat smoking and alcohol consumption;
- nature conservation, etc.

XI

The Ministry of Education has the following services at its disposal for ensuring that all children fulfil their obligation to attend school and really have an equal chance to enjoy the universal right to education:

- a socio-economic support service, which provides welfare assistance to all pupils in state or officially sponsored education; this assistance may take the form of direct grants, subsidised meals, school transport networks, lodging facilities, etc.;
- indirect stage 2 education programmes broadcast by television for the benefit of areas that have no stage 2 schools, owing to their isolation, their small school population or lack of appropriate premises.

There have nevertheless been difficulties in implementing this policy, e.g.:

- as regards means of access:
  - the possible absence of motorable roads or the shortage of available vehicles;
  - the distance to be covered and the long waits for a bus – which inevitably affect pupils' academic performance;
  - the shortage of accommodation facilities at the state's disposal or the precariousness of possible alternative solutions;
- as regards motivation, the difficulties lie in the resistance of some families to compulsory schooling – particularly after the first four years – which may be ascribed in particular to the following factors:
  - recourse to child labour for agricultural or domestic work;
  - opposition to removing children from their home, especially when it means lodging them in another locality;
  - financial difficulties and the fear that schooling will be too costly;
  - ignorance of the importance for their children's future of obtaining a school leaving certificate.

In order to overcome these difficulties, the Ministry of Education has taken steps to inform the public about the welfare assistance provided to pupils.

18. SPAIN <DECS/EGT [84] 48>

I The educational system

1. Structure

1.1 There are four main levels in the Spanish educational system: pre-school (age 2–5); basic general education (age 6–13); higher level (age 14–16) and university education (preceded by a university guidance course at age 17), plus vocational training which is divided into three grades (first-, second- and third-grade vocational training).

1.2 Basic general education (BGE) embodies what used to be primary education and the equivalent of the first part of secondary education.

BGE is compulsory and free. It is divided into three courses: an initial course covering the first two years of compulsory schooling (age 6–7), which is closely related to pre-school education; a middle course (age 8–10); and a higher course (age 11–13).

1.3 At the end of BGE pupils are awarded either a diploma entitling them to continue their studies at the upper level or a certificate of education if they have not completed their eight years of schooling satisfactorily. In the latter case they must continue their studies in a first-grade vocational training course.

2. Objectives

2.1 The profound political and social transformation occurring within our country over the last few years has naturally had repercussions on the educational system and its objectives. The main lines of the regulations governing education are laid down in Article 27 of the Constitution, as follows:

> 1. Everyone is entitled to education. Freedom of instruction is recognised.
> 2. Education shall have as its objective the full development of the human personality compatible with respect for the democratic principles of coexistence and for fundamental rights and liberties.
> 3. The public authorities guarantee the right of parents to ensure that their children receive religious and moral instruction compatible with their own convictions.

4. Basic education is compulsory and free.
5. The public authorities guarantee the right of everyone to education, through general planning of education, with the effective participation of all parties concerned and the setting up of teaching establishments.
6. The right of individuals and legal entities to set up teaching establishments is recognised, provided they are compatible with respect for constitutional principles.
7. Teachers, parents and, when appropriate, pupils, shall participate in the control and management of all the centres maintained by the administration with public funds, under the terms to be laid down by the law.
8. The public authorities shall inspect and standardise the educational system in order to guarantee compliance with the law.
9. The public authorities shall help teaching establishments which meet the requirements to be laid down by the law.
10. The autonomy of the universities is recognised, under the terms to be laid down by the law.

2.2 The general objective of BGE is to provide full education which is essentially identical for all, adapted as far as possible to each pupil's aptitudes and abilities.

This full training is designed to cover: the acquisition, development and functional use of habits and instrumental techniques of learning; the exercise of imagination, observation and reflection; the acquisition of religious or moral concepts and habits; developing the ability to coexist and reinforcing the feeling of belonging to the local, national and international communities; an introduction to aesthetic and artistic appreciation and expression; the development of civic and social responsibility; the development of physical abilities and abilities for sport.

These general objectives are reflected in fields of educational activity that are all-embracing during the first two courses (age 6–7 and 8–10) and moderately diversified in the third course (age 11–13). These fields are: language, mathematics and natural sciences, social sciences, art education, religious or ethical instruction and physical education.

2.3 Following the introduction of revised syllabuses from the educational year 1981 onwards, the different contents were rearranged into a number of 'subject blocks', subdivided into 'work topics' that can be tackled independently, thanks to their specific nature. In turn, each work topic is subdivided into several 'basic reference levels' (BRL), which serve as landmarks enabling the teacher to diagnose his pupils' situation in relation to the basic content of the different subjects.

3. Organisation

3.1 Public and private establishments coexist within the Spanish education system, private schools being wholly or partially subsidised by the state.

During the educational year 1981–2 the total number of establishments was 20,198, able to accommodate 6.5 million pupils; in fact there were 5.5 million pupils and 189,985 teachers. About 65 per cent of this total came under the public system, with private establishments accounting for the remaining 35 per cent.

3.2 Until very recently the Spanish educational system was highly centralised and it remains so in the regions that have not yet been granted full autonomy. The Ministry of Education and Science is the state organ responsible for drawing up guidelines on educational policy, managing budgets, creating and closing down educational establishments, managing and inspecting all educational institutions coming under its aegis, etc. In each province there are a provincial directorate of the Ministry of Education and Science and an inspectorate, which are responsible for managing, co-ordinating, programming, implementing and inspecting the ministry's powers in the province.

However, in the case of regions and nationalities that have already been granted their autonomy, all powers relating to education have been placed in the hands of the regional government, although the state reserves the sole right:

(a) to lay down general regulations governing the educational system;
(b) to devise minimum curricula and to determine the conditions for the award, issue and recognition of academic and vocational diplomas which are valid throughout the country;
(c) to operate the higher inspectorate and any other functions designed to guarantee that the authorities are fulfilling their obligations.

3.3 As has already been said, BGE is compulsory and free. It comprises eight years' schooling. In order to be admitted, pupils must have their sixth birthday during the calendar year in which the school year begins. The year generally begins in mid-September and finishes at the end of June or in the first fortnight of July (depending on the province); there are two holiday periods of some 15 days at Christmas and 10 days at Easter. In law the educational year comprises 220 days' teaching but in practice this number is reduced. Children attend school for 5 hours a day, usually from 9 to 12 a.m. and from 3 to 5 p.m., five days a week.

At the same time as the syllabuses were reformed in 1981, BGE was reorganised into three courses, which are adapted to the child's stages of development and which allow greater flexibility as regards the organisation of the establishments and the progress of pupils.

The initial course (age 6–7) is very closely related to the pre-school period and is designed to replace it when pupils have been unable to attend nursery school.

In the initial and middle (age 8–10) courses each group of pupils has a single teacher. In the last course (age 11–13) there are three teachers for languages, mathematics/natural sciences and social sciences respectively, each acting as a tutor for one group of pupils.

3.4 The average number of pupils per class is 31.7. However the national average does not mean much since there are many substantial variations: some classes have fewer than 10 pupils and some have 40 or more (especially in big cities or in expanding suburbs). However, it can be said that all children now attend school in fairly satisfactory conditions.

To a great extent the course has replaced the educational year as a pedagogical unit. Organisation, programming and assessment are based on each course and are carried out by the teaching team assigned to the course.

Flexible regrouping, tailoring education to individual needs, team work by teachers and continual assessment and progress of pupils are ever-present principles in the spirit of the reform that has been undertaken, although there is still a long way to go.

Pupils are assessed by the teachers of their establishment, who rely on the fairly detailed standards and guidelines issued by the ministry and on supportive instruments in order to complete this task. Pupils are assessed at three stages: initially when admitted to the school, continually throughout the educational process, and finally at the end of each course and the end of BGE.

3.5 Relations between schools and the community or between schools and parents have been extremely limited so far. The administration has attempted to extend and encourage such participation. At best, participation used to be limited to supporting what the school was doing without any scope for intervening in its organisation and running, even indirectly. The governors of each establishment, recently made subject to the Statute on Educational Establishments, now include four representatives of the parents' association, which gives such associations a say in programming teaching activities, supervising the running of the school and administering its budget.

Relations with local authorities are not very extensive, as the process of decentralisation has not yet reached the municipalities, but such participation should increase markedly in the near future.

4. Teachers

BGE teachers are trained at university teacher-training colleges, to which they gain admittance after obtaining the higher-level diploma and following a university guidance course.

The course lasts three years: the first year is devoted to common studies, and in the second and third years the student specialises in philology, sciences, humanities, pre-school or special education. The subjects common to all these specialities comprise: teaching technique, psycho-sociology, Spanish, mathematics, artistic expression, music, physical education and teaching practice.

The BGE teaching diploma entitles its holders to teach in public or private establishments at this level, but they must take a competitive entry examination in order to teach in the former.

Currently there are an excessive number of BGE teachers and it is proving extremely difficult to find jobs for them.

Practising teachers are guided in their work by basic education inspectors (who number 616 for the whole of Spain) and they have the opportunity of taking further training and refresher courses organised by the institutes of educational science which are found in all universities. Over 150,000 teachers have attended such courses in the past 10 years.

II Problems and trends

The two main questions affecting BGE at present are, first, the revision and improvement of educational standards and, secondly, the completion of the decentralisation process and the transfer of educational responsibilities to the different regions and nationalities.

5. Educational standards

Now that the serious problems of infrastructure that had to be faced in the last few years have been settled, or are on the point of being settled, increasing attention is being paid to problems concerning teaching standards.

5.1 The 1981 reform must be seen in this light. This involved organising BGE into courses and gradually introducing revised syllabuses designed to adapt compulsory schooling to the demands of a new, democratic, pluralist society, to cope with a high educational failure rate and to modernise the whole system by effectively incorporating principles such as team work, flexible regrouping, continual assessment and progress, personalised teaching, etc., emphasis being laid on instrumental subjects.

5.2 In order to support and assist teachers in introducing this reform, the ministry is organising further training courses, short-term projects in establishments and technical meetings with inspectors, and is also preparing and distributing:

- *supportive documents*, such as the pre-school teacher's handbook and guides for teachers of languages, social sciences, mathematics, natural sciences, etc.;
- *instruments of assessment* for the initial, middle and higher courses, enabling teachers to ascertain how far objectives have been reached;
- *multi-media programmes*, new teaching materials in prototype form designed to help teachers introduce new techniques and to facilitate independent work by pupils.

The ministry is also:

- modernising establishments' teaching equipment;
- encouraging teachers to participate in implementing innovatory projects (programme for the testing and distribution of new educational techniques, 'EDINTE programme');
- making the best use of provincial educational and vocational guidance services, etc.

5.3 The reform aims to make free pre-school education universally available, not just for social reasons but because of the growing awareness among families and society in general of the decisive importance of education in the first years of life.

5.4 The reform also aims to raise the school-leaving age to 16, even though a large proportion of pupils who do not undertake secondary studies already attend school up until this age, either at first-grade vocational training colleges or in BGE establishments. A project is already under way here.

5.5 Lastly there is a very advanced project concerning a possible reform of the curriculum for initial teacher training, a change in the ground covered by the competitive entry examination that must be taken in order to become a state-registered BGE teacher, and bringing the retirement age for teachers down from 70 to 65 years.

6. Regional autonomy

The decentralisation process, at the end of which the country will comprise 17 autonomous regions or nationalities, is having repercussions on education and will continue to do so in the future. The governments of Catalonia, the Basque country and Galicia already have full powers in educational matters, with the exception of the powers reserved for the state indicated above. This is expected to be the situation shortly in all the other regions, marking the end of a long process of major importance in the political, social, cultural and educational life of the country.

19. SWEDEN
<DECS/EGT [84] 105 rev>

Primary education in Sweden is a part of the compulsory comprehensive nine-year school system which was established in 1962. The municipalities are mandated to offer pre-school facilities to all children at the age of 6 but pre-school attendance is voluntary. Compulsory schooling starts at the age of 7.

The comprehensive school has two three-year levels of primary education – the junior level (grades 1–3) and the middle level (grades 4–6) – and a lower secondary level – the senior level (grades 7–9). The first two levels have a system of class teachers who teach almost all subjects. At the senior level, teachers specialising in generally two or three subjects each are used. Subjects such as music, arts, physical education, etc. at the senior level and often at the middle level are taught by teachers specialising in only one of the subjects each.

Figure 1 School structure in Sweden

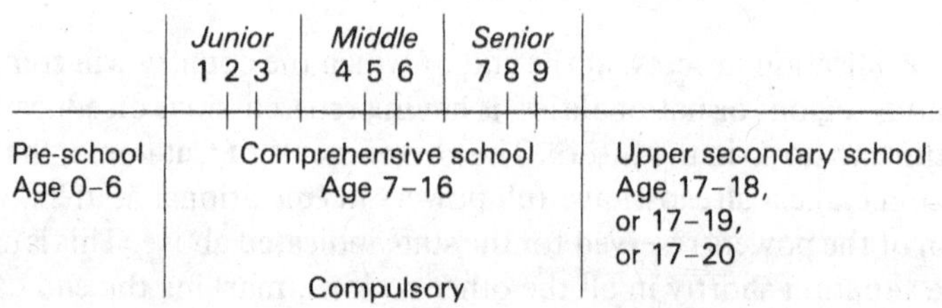

Almost all children in Sweden attend the public comprehensive school. Private schools are very rare in Sweden though the Education Act is liberal towards private persons or groups wanting to establish private schools. Less than 1 per cent of children attend private schools.

Teacher training in Sweden will be reformed from the academic year 1988/9. Teachers for the comprehensive school will then be trained for teaching either in grades 1–7 or in grades 4–9 (overlapping each other in four grades). The first category will teach almost all subjects in grades 1–3 but then concentrate on fewer subjects. The second category will teach more subjects than the senior level teachers of today do.

The school year starts at the end of August and ends in mid-June. It comprises 40 weeks (Monday–Friday) and is divided into two terms, called the autumn term (20 August – 20 December) and the spring term (10 January – 10 June). The exact dates vary from one school year to the next and are not the same in all school districts.

The time-schedule gives the total sum of periods per week (one period = 40 minutes) for the level as a whole. Each school has to decide its own distribution of periods over the three grades of each level. The local school board has the right to adjust the time-schedule within the limits of the levels. That right is used almost only to postpone the start of learning English from grade 3 to grade 4. In grade 1 there are 20 periods per week (ppw), in grade 2, 24 ppw and in grade 3, 30 ppw. In the rest of the grades there are 33–34 ppw. (See Table 1.)

Table 1 Time-schedule of the comprehensive school

Subject	*Junior*	*Middle*	*Senior*
English	2	10	9[2]
Physical education	6	9	9
Mathematics	13	15	12[2]
Music	4	5	2
Orientational subjects[1]	18	21	32
Social orientation subjects	—	(15)	(17)
Nature orientation subjects	—	(6)	(15)
Handicrafts	2	9	5
Swedish	29	26	12
Drawing		6	5
Domestic science		1	4
Child care			1
Options			11[3]
Total	74	102	102

1. Orientational subjects at the middle and senior levels are divided into two groups, social orientation subjects (geography, history, knowledge of religion and social sciences) and nature orientation subjects (biology, physics, chemistry and technology).
2. Pupils have a choice between a common or a special course in English and mathematics at the senior level.
3. Either a three-year course in French or German or locally decided courses – at least one term long. Immigrant children can also choose their mother tongue as an option.

In the comprehensive school there are no examinations. Regardless of options a complete nine-year school course qualifies pupils for studies in the upper-secondary school in any of the subjects. Marks are given in grade 8 and grade 9 at the end of each term in all subjects, with 5 as the highest and 1 as the lowest mark. The main reason for the marks is that they form the basis for admission to upper secondary education when there are more students wanting to follow a given specialisation than there are places for.

In 1980 the *Riksdag* (parliament) passed a government bill on a new curriculum for the nine-year comprehensive school. That curriculum has been in force since the school year 1982/3.

The meaning of the word 'curriculum' differs from one country to another. In Sweden the 'formal' curriculum consists of three parts:

- goals and guidelines;
- syllabuses for subjects or groups of subjects;
- time-schedule.

The general goal for the comprehensive school is set out in the first paragraph of the Education Act:

> The purpose of the education which society provides for children and young persons is to impart knowledge to the pupils and to develop their skills and, in co-operation with their homes, to promote their development into harmonious individuals and into competent and responsible members of society.

The opening sentences of the goal chapter in the curriculum say:

> Compulsory school is a part of society. The curriculum reflects the view of the democracy on society and man, the implication being that human beings are active and creative and that they both can and must assume responsibility and seek knowledge in order to co-operate with others in understanding and improving their own living conditions and those of other people. The content and the working methods must be designed in such a way that they promote this attitude towards people and society. It is the duty of schools to give their pupils increased responsibility and powers of co-determination as they grow older and become increasingly mature.

The goals and the guidelines are formulated in general terms. They are thus not measurable, and express rather a direction for the work of schools than what schools shall attain.

In the syllabuses for subjects or groups of subjects, goals for the work in these subjects or areas are also expressed. They have to be read in parallel with the general goals and guidelines. The goals of the subjects are also formulated in rather general terms. The syllabuses also contain the main items of the subjects for each of the three levels of the comprehensive school – also fairly generally expressed.

The curriculum also includes extensive commentaries to support local development work. These commentaries are going to be published, revised and updated on a continuous basis. They do not include any regulations as such. Instead they are intended to describe current problems and difficulties as experienced by people working in schools, and on this basis to discuss alternative methods of tackling these problems and difficulties and working in the direction indicated by the goals laid down for schools. Experience and research findings will successively be fed back into revised versions of the commentaries, and various goal conflicts will be elucidated.

According to the curriculum, each school[5] has to make a plan for its work. This local plan should reflect the aims and the ambitions of the school. It can be seen as a development programme and a form of local curricular work. A catalogue of problems should be the basis for the plan. There is naturally no standardised structure for the local plans, and the experiences of the first year show great differences between those local plans.

Initially current problems in the Swedish comprehensive school are mainly seen at the senior level, but there are of course problems in primary education too. In Sweden as in many other western industrialised countries, there are problems with truancy, drop-outs, vandalism, etc. A report claiming that 8 per cent of pupils do not complete their compulsory schooling has caused a discussion on whether the figure is too high or not; nevertheless, there are pupils who leave school without having reached a level of knowledge and skills that they need, in spite of the fact that substantial efforts with compensatory teaching are made. Experience shows that increasing the responsibility and influence of pupils in school has some effect in trying to solve these problems.

For a few years now, Swedish school authorities have paid extra attention to the situation relating to children's school start. A number of schools have had the opportunity of receiving an extra state grant for local development work at junior level. This drive has mainly been concentrated on co-operation between pre-schools and comprehensive schools, on higher quality in teaching basic skills, and on co-operation between the school and parents. As from the present year (1987–8), the extra state grant is aimed at the middle level and especially at teaching in Swedish and in mathematics.

The policy of migrant education has the objective that migrant children will develop a bilingual competence, mastering both their mother tongue and Swedish. The majority of immigrant children are individually integrated in ordinary Swedish classes, but when there are many migrant children of the same origin in a school at the junior and the middle level they often form bilingual classes called home-language classes, or classes with one-half Swedish-speaking children and one-half speaking another language. In those classes, the home language is the predominant language of instruction in the lower grade, but gradually Swedish takes over as the language of instruction.

Democratisation, increased effectiveness in studies, a deeper responsibility towards pupils with difficulties and handicaps and decentralisation are the main trends in the reformation of the comprehensive school. Both the new curriculum and other rules are expressions of those aims. In addition, basic skills are more stressed in the current curriculum than in the former.

In order to support the implementation of the new curriculum there has been in-service training for headmasters and deputy headmasters for many years. Another support was a special state grant for a period of four years to all schools – the two years before what was then the new curriculum and the first two years when it was in force. That has enabled groups of teachers to undertake preparatory work in their schools.

The reform of comprehensive schooling was paralleled by a reform of the state school administration from the fiscal year 1982/3. The division of roles can be described as follows:

- The central political level (the government and parliament) lays down the goals and guidelines, indicates frameworks in which these goals are to be realised and decides on financial resources.
- The central administrative level (the National Board of Education) has overall responsibility for advice and control of the realisation of the goals and provides a basis for change in these goals and strategies.
- The regional administrative level (the County Board of Education) is responsible for development, co-ordination and planning in the county and has regional responsibility for advice and control of the realisation of the goals and guidelines.

In the municipalities, the local education boards are responsible for the day-to-day administration of the activities of schools and for the development of education activities, having regard to plans and development aid from the state authorities.

The number of comprehensive schools in Sweden is comparatively high but many of the schools in sparsely populated areas are small. In the 284 municipalities there are approximately 1,400 school districts (administered by one headmaster each) with approximately 4,700 schools.

The number of pupils in comprehensive schools diminished from 1,037,799 in 1979/80 to 914,200 in 1985/6, but as from 1986 the birth rate has been increasing.

Table 2 Number of pupils in comprehensive schools

1980/1	*1981/2*	*1982/3*	*1983/4*	*1984/5*	*1987/8*
1,026,100	1,012,700	996,200	975,100	958,000	914,000

The number of teachers in the comprehensive schools is approximately 92,000 (1987/8).

Since the school year 1978/9 there are no regulations on class sizes, but approximately 75 per cent of the state grants are distributed on the basis of 25 pupils per class at the junior level and 30 pupils at the middle and senior levels. The mean class sizes in 1983/4 were 20.5 at the junior level, 23.2 at the middle level, and 26.6 at the senior level.

A substantial part of the teaching takes place in smaller groups thanks to the fact that approximately 25 per cent of the state grants are distributed per capita and can be used for mainly two purposes: extra support to pupils with difficulties, and teaching in smaller groups to facilitate individualisation. The pupil–teacher ratio in the comprehensive schools is approximately 10.

A new system has been in force since the fiscal year 1982/3 for the in-service training of teachers. The municipalities get state grants for local development work; 60–80 per cent of that state grant is to be used for in-service training.

The training is arranged mainly as university courses. The local boards of education decide who can participate. 20–40 per cent can be used for different kinds of development work in accordance to local needs. In-service training can also be a part of that development work.

School welfare activities take place at two levels, work being done in the course of everyday life of school and carried out by specialists.

At the first level, every teacher has responsibility. The work is mainly of a preventive nature, but it also includes extra attention for pupils with difficulties of different kinds. In units of generally two or three classes the planning of school welfare activities is integrated in the planning of the rest of the daily work.

At the second level, the headmaster, the school nurse, the school doctor, the school psychologist and the school social worker form a team (the pupils' welfare team) within which planning is done for the cases that cannot be handled at the first level.

The establishment of day homes, nursery schools, kindergartens and corresponding pre-school care institutions has predominantly been seen as a social welfare enterprise. Centrally, and usually also locally, pre-school institutions are managed by the boards of health and social welfare and not by the boards of education.

Compulsory school does not start until the age of 7. An earlier start has long been discussed. In 1973, parliament decided to retain 7 as the starting age, but also that pre-school should be available for all children of 6 ('common pre-school year'). The issue of earlier school start was investigated by a government committee some years ago, but no change has yet been proposed by the government.

The treatment of pre-school care and education as primarily a social question has given Swedish pre-school institutions some specific features: they are run mainly by municipal authorities; they have a low child–adult ratio (seldom more than six or seven); they also have a special responsibility for children with difficulties and special needs (for instance, migrant children).

The responsibility of the local municipalities for pre-school care and education was not laid down by law until 1967. The establishment of pre-school institutions had come late and is so far incomplete. The following statistics are from 1979:

Children in full-time day homes,	0–4 years	71,000
	5 years	25,000
	6 years	25,000
Children in nursery schools,	0–4 years	2,500
(some part time)	5 years	18,000
	6 years	88,000

These figures should be seen in relation to the birth rate in Sweden, which in recent years has been about 100,000 per year.

Co-operation between pre-schools and primary education is expanding. Experiments have been made with a total integration of children from the age of 6 to the age of 9. The experiences are positive. The problems are caused mainly by the fact that pre-schools and comprehensive schools belong to different administrative systems. How co-operation could be promoted is also a matter for the governmental committee mentioned above.

Co-operation between home and school can be illuminated by quoting the curriculum:

> The primary and principal responsibility for a pupil's care and upbringing rests with the home. School activities must support the home in its provision of an upbringing shaped according to the fundamental democratic values of our society. It can be very important for differences regarding norms and opinions on various questions to be discussed between schools and parents, so as to resolve any clashes that may occur.
>
> Experience has shown that it is difficult to establish contact with all parents. In this case, schools themselves must take active measures to get in touch with the parents concerned and to establish the necessary co-operation.
>
> Parental contacts with a school should not be confined to a couple of occasions per year. Schools are also duty-bound throughout pupils' school career to keep their parents informed of matters concerning the organisation of compulsory schooling, the curriculum and working methods, and the further education opportunities or career opportunities which are available.

20. SWITZERLAND <DECS/EGT [84] 21 rev>

Part I

1. Official objectives of primary education

The objectives of primary education in the 26 cantons of Switzerland are set out in each canton's Education Act, often in a brief paragraph, where they are generally formulated in a fairly abstract way. However, they are formulated in a more explicit manner in many curricula – either by way of an introduction or as guiding principles.

The objectives and curricula of primary education can be summarised as follows:

- During the 1st school year pupils must progress from play to a set activity and submit to a certain discipline. This first year is designed to develop oral expression and vocabulary, as well as provide an initiation in reading and mathematics.
- During the 2nd and 3rd years the mother tongue has pride of place (in German-speaking Switzerland the aim is to progress from the spoken dialect to the written language), alongside mathematics, knowledge of the environment, creative activities, writing, music and physical education.
- The intermediate level (4th, 4th–5th, or 4th–6th school years, depending on the canton) plays a special role for the purposes of pupil selection for secondary cycle I of compulsory schooling: history and geography are added to the subjects taught hitherto.
- The 7th, 8th and 9th classes of primary schools (upper primary level, terminal classes, practical sections of orientation cycles) are designed to supplement knowledge of those pupils who will not be continuing their schooling and to prepare them for practical life. The following subjects are therefore added: civics and general education, book-keeping, etc.

2. Bodies responsible for primary education at national, regional, local and school level

The federal government's powers are very limited in the field of primary education. They are designed solely to ensure the implementation of Article 27 of the Federal Constitution, which requires the cantons to provide primary education of adequate standard under the exclusive control of the civil authorities. Such education is compulsory and free of charge in publicly owned schools.

The authorities really in charge of public education are the cantons, which are responsible for finance, organisation, management and supervision. They delegate some of their duties to the municipalities ('*communes*').

Each canton has its own Education Act, defining the various powers as well as the school system as a whole at all levels. Most cantons have an education directorate (with variable powers), usually headed by the Director of Public Education.

At municipal level, schools are often run by school authorities elected by the people.

3. The transition from the pre-school period to primary education and from primary to lower secondary education

The transition from the pre-school period to primary education takes place at the age of 6 or 7. There are considerable differences between the aims and functions of preparatory schools and those of nursery schools and between German-speaking Switzerland on the one hand and French- and Italian-speaking Switzerland on the other. In German-speaking Switzerland the two institutions are quite separate and each one's teachers undergo very different training. In French-speaking Switzerland there is closer liaison between pre-school education and the initial classes of primary schools. In the canton of Geneva, for example, the first and second classes of infant schools and the first and second levels of primary schools form part of the same cycle and are jointly administered.

In addition to the upper cycle, which is divided into sections, most cantons have an undivided upper primary cycle which takes children up to the end of their compulsory schooling. The transition from primary school to secondary level I takes place after the 6th year of primary school (in 18 cantons), after the 5th year (in 4 cantons) or after the 4th year (in 4 other cantons). In most cantons, entering secondary level I means moving from a homogeneous class with a single teacher to a structure divided into several sections with varying requirements. Although, in some cantons, secondary level I is fairly selective and allows only limited freedom of movement, either vertical or horizontal, other cantons have an orientation cycle of a more open kind.

4. Statistics on pupils and teachers

The number of pupils for the 1986/7 school year is shown in Table 1.

Table 1

		Total	Girls
1P	All cantons	69,916	34,574
2P	All cantons	70,332	34,381
3P	All cantons	69,971	34,215
4P	All cantons	70,043	34,654
5P	(Excepting the cantons of Berne, Basle-Urban, Vaud and Jura)	52,286	25,550
6P	(Excepting the cantons of Berne, Basle-Urban, Vaud, Jura, Aargau, Basle-Rural, Neuchâtel and Ticino)	40,697	20,004
	Total	373,245	183,378

Table 2
(a) Breakdown of primary school teaching staff into age-groups

Age-group	Number (school year 1986/7)	%
20–29 years	7,430	31.1
30–39 years	8,616	36.1
40–49 years	4,710	19.7
50–59 years	2,589	10.8
60 years and over	545	2.3
Total	23,890	100.0

(b) Breakdown of primary school teachers by age and sex

Age-group	Male teachers	%	Female teachers	%
20–29 years	2,445	32.9	4,985	67.1
30–39 years	4,001	46.4	4,615	53.6
40–49 years	2,215	47.0	2,495	53.0
50–59 years	1,312	50.7	1,277	49.3
60 years and over	339	62.2	206	37.8
Total and average %	10,312	43.2	13.578	56.8

Average number of pupils per class (1986/7): 18.8 (the cantonal averages range between 15.7 and 21.0 pupils per class).

Number of classes during the 1986/7 school year: 21,144, of which:

- 16,366 single-level and
- 4,778 multiple-level classes.

Statistics on teachers employed in compulsory schooling were published in 1987 and are summarised in Table 2. Although the average proportion of women for Switzerland as a whole is 56.8 per cent, the figure varies considerably from one age-group to another; it also differs widely from one canton to another – from 34 per cent (Grisons) to 92.6 per cent (Vaud).

5. Sections, divisions and composition of classes

Normally children of the same age are grouped together in single-level classes. Multiple-level classes, i.e. classes grouping together pupils belonging to two, three, four or more levels, are chiefly found in sparsely populated regions, where there are a very small number of pupils in each class.

6. Length of the school day, week and year in primary education

On the basis of the average annual number of hours during the first year of primary school (i.e. 750), the daily total is $3\frac{3}{4}$ hours. This number increases steadily, reaching about $5\frac{1}{4}$ hours in the 6th year of primary school.

Schools operate in both the morning and the afternoon. Depending on the canton, pupils are free either all day on Saturdays or on Saturday afternoons plus another half-day or on Saturday afternoons plus another whole day.

The school year comprises $34\frac{1}{2}$–$40\frac{1}{2}$ weeks. Long holidays (5–9 weeks) are granted in summer in all cantons.

7. Main branches in the primary school curriculum

The mother tongue and mathematics are the main subjects in the primary school curriculum. Then come the following branches: creative and musical education, natural sciences and knowledge of the environment. Lastly come religious education, physical education, handicraft and domestic science.

8. Pupil assessment

In most cantons pupils are still assessed by means of marks. Two or three times a year they are given a report showing their results in the various subjects. The average marks obtained at the end of the school year – either in all subjects or in some major ones – constitute the criterion for promotion, either permanent or temporary, from one school level to another. Experiments in teaching without marks in the early years of primary education are under way in several cantons.

9. Basic and further training of primary school teachers

In roughly half the cantons, future primary school teachers are trained at teacher-training colleges after completing their secondary education.

In a few cantons (Geneva, Basle-Urban, Zurich, Neuchâtel, Vaud, Aargau), pedagogical and didactic training is available after the award of the secondary school-leaving certificate ('*maturité*'); the same arrangement is planned in Ticino and Valais. Other cantons offer both possibilities of training.

Courses at teacher-training colleges last five years (four in some cantons), beginning upon the completion of compulsory schooling (from age 15/16 to age 19/21).

In addition to an examination in specific subjects, candidates must demonstrate their moral, intellectual and physical aptitudes and their abilities in singing, music, art and gymnastics.

In teacher-training colleges providing a single four-year cycle of studies, general knowledge and specific vocational knowledge are taught in parallel. Those whose courses last five years usually comprise two cycles: a lower cycle covering general knowledge and an upper cycle providing more specifically pedagogical, psychological and didactic training.

Courses include practical work and teaching practice.

The cantons regularly organise compulsory or optional further training courses in close co-operation with teachers themselves. Compulsory courses take place partly during teaching hours and partly on days off; optional courses take place almost exclusively in teachers' free time.

10. Para-educational services

The following services are provided in primary schools: regular medical examinations of pupils and teachers; dental care; tests of academic maturity; early detection of academic problems, assessment of and support for children at risk whose behaviour or development show anomalies; educational counselling (a psycho-pedagogical team); transport of pupils; special tuition for migrants' children in the language of the host country as well as in the language and culture of origin.

11. Institutionalised contacts between primary schools, families and municipalities

Co-operation between teachers, schools and families depends to a great extent on the teacher's own initiative (meetings with parents, visiting days or open days, individual interviews with parents). There are few parents' associations. However, parents have an opportunity of influencing the running of school affairs thanks to the democratic voting process (election of teachers and school authorities, participation during the construction of school buildings, etc.).

Part II – Trends and reforms

Reforms in specific subjects

- Teaching of the second national language at an early age: lengthy trials have been conducted in the teaching of French in the 4th or 5th year of primary schools in German-speaking Switzerland; in French-speaking Switzerland, German is taught to a limited extent even in the 3rd year.

  In 1975, in the light of the reports of a committee of experts as well as the results of a broad consultation, the Swiss Conference of Cantonal Directors of Public Education (CDIP) recommended that the cantons 'introduce, renew and co-ordinate the teaching of the second language for all pupils undergoing compulsory education' and make provision for the necessary back-up.
- Introduction of new mathematics, either experimentally or permanently, and provision of appropriate training for primary school teachers: in September 1973, after lengthy experimentation, new mathematics was introduced in French-speaking Switzerland in all 1st year classes. There is now a full syllabus covering the first six years.

  In the CDIP, a 'mathematical forum' has been set up for the purpose of organising a continuous exchange of information.

  This year, after consulting all interested bodies, the CDIP recommended that cantons align their new programmes on a series of 'points of convergence' and 'guidelines' as regards the teaching of mathematics during compulsory schooling.
- The mother tongue has also been the subject of reforms in several German-speaking cantons as well as in French-speaking Switzerland, where 'renovated teaching in French' has been introduced. This new way of teaching the mother tongue is aimed at developing ability to communicate and encouraging personal discovery of the language.

Reforms of assessment and transition arrangements

Many experiments in teaching without marks are being carried out in the early years of primary education; as a result, new tools of assessment are being devised. By means of transitional classes (where one year's teaching is spread over two years) or the provision of educational support (the 'fluidity' experiment in Geneva), attempts are being made to ensure a smooth transition from the pre-school period to lower primary school.

Moreover, wide-ranging experiments are under way with a view to replacing the traditional entrance examination at secondary level I by different transitional arrangements.

Curriculum reforms

It is envisaged prefacing the new or renovated curricula with some *idées-force* with the aim of laying down guiding principles for the structure and development of schools.

Similarly, attempts are being made to adapt curricula in order to guarantee equality of opportunity to girls and boys in respect of training (following an amendment to the Federal Constitution).

The SIPRI project

When the Swiss Conference of Cantonal Directors of Public Education (CDIP) recommended in 1975 that cantons introduce teaching of the second national language earlier, in primary schools, the Conference of Swiss Associations of Teachers (CASE/KOSLO) asked for an overall review to be made of the Situation in Primary schools (= SIPRI). In 1978, the Plenary Assembly of the CDIP agreed to go ahead with the SIPRI project, appointed two directors and a chairman to supervise it and endorsed a rough draft breaking the project down into four study themes:

- objectives of primary education: aims and realities;
- functions and forms of assessment;
- transition from the pre-primary period to primary school;
- contacts and co-operation between schools and families.

The purpose of the SIPRI project was to identify the main aspects of the present situation in primary schools in Switzerland and to propose and test practical improvements to the system, in close liaison with school staff and educational researchers and authorities. This would require an in-depth debate at the inter-cantonal level on the problems of primary schools.

Selected 'contact schools' were used for observation and experimentation in conditions approaching real life in schools. Four working groups made up of researchers, representatives of school authorities, teachers' associations, parents and teachers in the contact schools carried out the research work, calling upon scientific experts when necessary.

The results obtained were made public as the work progressed and widely disseminated in the educational environment during special study meetings, seminars or intensive courses. The publications issued to date seem to indicate that SIPRI has largely achieved its prime objective of describing the situation in schools in the four selected areas. Furthermore, the numerous working documents and the research survey reports contain many concrete proposals for improving primary schools.

The final report[6] summarises the results obtained. All the arguments it puts forward are based on the various SIPRI publications. The aim of the report is not to provide an exhaustive description of primary schooling or to list major current development trends, but to deal exclusively with the features covered by the SIPRI project.

We have deliberately avoided describing the current situation of primary schools in Switzerland in this final report because the situation varies considerably from one canton to another and from one region to another.[7] We decided to present the results of our research and deliberations in the form of *theses*, fully aware that some of them have been achieved long since or are nearing completion in several cantons, while in others they are still at the project stage. Some cantons will therefore be reassured by our findings or our recommendations with regard to the innovations they have carried out in their schools, others will be all the more motivated to pursue their efforts in the chosen direction, while others will find ideas in the report which may prove useful to them in the future.

The report comprises *six chapters*, each with an introduction. The main core of each chapter is made up of a statement of the thesis, by way of a title, followed by an explanatory text. Each thesis is accompanied by corollaries for the attention of specific groups or institutions, such as teachers, headmasters, local authorities, etc.; they propose a range of measures for putting the school objectives set out in the theses into action. At the end of each chapter there is a bibliography referring the reader to more detailed documentation on the content of each thesis and the reasoning behind it.

The *22 theses* developed in the six chapters of the report are as follows:

1. Schools on the move

1.1 Schools and life
The role of schools is to help all children develop the aptitudes, attitudes and knowledge they need in order to understand the world they live in, and solve the problems they come across autonomously. Schools and teaching must therefore forge a dynamic link between the pupil's current environment and the world he/she will eventually live in.

1.2 Education and values
Schools teach the basic rules of conduct for compliance with the fundamental values and standards of society. These values and standards affect what is taught and how it is taught, as well as relations between the people concerned by the educational process.

1.3 Schools – places for development and continuous education
Schools are constantly undergoing changes at the communal, cantonal and inter-cantonal levels. A single teacher cannot cope alone with all this change, so it is up to the local school community to deal with it. The teaching staff of a school is the educational unit which implements projects on continuity and development in schools.

1.4 Schools and flexible policies in the cantons
The extent and efficiency of innovation in the cantonal school system depends on the extent and efficiency of innovation in the different local school communities, which each have their own specific requirements. The canton provides the basic legal framework, leaving enough leeway so that the different communes and schools are able to develop in their own way.

2. *Schools and parents*

2.1 Contact with the family: collaboration and duties
Contact with the parents of pupils is one of the obligations of every teacher: the ethics of his profession makes it a permanent duty. It is left to the appreciation of the teacher primarily, and also of the school community (and of the parents) to decide how this contact should be approached.

2.2 Discussing teaching objectives and pupil guidance
Dialogue has to take place between those most directly involved in educating children if they are to agree on basic matters of educational concern such as the essential aims of education, or how children develop and progress throughout their schooling.

2.3 Collaboration project involving teachers, parents and school authorities
The collaboration takes place at each level within the school community (class, school, commune, district) and materialises through teachers, parents and school authorities at the communal, cantonal and inter-cantonal levels. School authorities at every level support the collaboration projects and create suitable conditions for their implementation.

3. *Universal nature of the educational process*

3.1 Co-operation within the school
Teachers view their pedagogic role with regard to their pupils as an integral part of the children's schooling and of the educational effects of school in general. In each school community, teachers at various levels work in close collaboration to guarantee the continuity of the educational process and a pedagogic climate based on common standards and values.

3.2 Reducing hierarchical differences between schools
Every stage in the teaching and training of growing young people is equally important. The general educational role of schools requires this principle of equality to apply also to the initial and further training of teachers, to their collaboration at the communal or cantonal level and to conditions in which they work.

3.3 Infant school[8] attendance: two years
The infant school is a stepping stone from early childhood, during which the

family educates the child, to the primary school. It generally prepares children for their compulsory schooling, including children with various learning problems and handicaps. It is important that every child should be able to attend an infant school free of charge for two years.

3.4 Smooth transition between infant school and primary school
Close collaboration between infant school mistresses and primary school teachers makes for better understanding and mutual adaptation and eases the transition of pupils from one level to the other. If teaching in both infant and primary schools is personalised, based on active global methods which provide for the child's welfare, the child will get a feeling of continuity between the two levels: this will help him/her adapt to the new content of teaching in the primary school.

4. *Educational content*

4.1 Correcting unintentional hierarchies in teaching content and objectives
It is part of the role of schools to distinguish between the contents objectives of their teaching in terms of importance. The criteria that determine their scales of importance are based on the need to develop the knowledge and behaviour of the pupil and on their fundamental educational objectives. They must not be based unthinkingly on tradition, on how easy it is to test pupils in a subject or on the demands of post-primary school structures.

4.2 Functional integration of knowledge
Teaching and school syllabuses continue to be organised into separate subjects. It is important at the primary school level, however, to make frequent use of methods spanning several subjects at once. This teaches the pupils a broader approach to things, facilitating the integration of knowledge.

4.3 Basic education
From the variety of paths open to it, the primary school chooses those elements that are necessary and vital to basic education and lead to:

- development of the aptitudes and attitudes defined in school legislation;
- the learning of basic knowledge;
- the ability to transfer knowledge to new situations;
- a broadening of basic cultural references;
- consideration of the major needs and interests of the pupil.

5. *Assessing pupils' work*

5.1 Distinguishing between different kinds of assessment
Assessing the work of pupils is useful when methods and functions are clearly defined. It is particularly important to distinguish informative assessment from other kinds such as summative assessment.

5.2 Assessment as an aid to learning
The ideal conditions for learning exist when the pupil is fully aware of the objectives pursued and is regularly informed of the progress he/she has made. From this point of view informative assessment is the most satisfactory kind of assessment.

5.3 Assessment as an aid to planning
Assessment enables teachers to pinpoint their pupils' particular learning difficulties and to adjust their methods to the potential of their pupils.

5.4 Self-assessment by the pupil
A pupil's efficiency and sense of fulfilment and responsibility at school depend upon him/her having a realistic idea of his/her own possibilities. One way of achieving this is to make the pupil responsible for his/her own learning process through a self-assessment scheme geared to his/her development.

5.5 Assessment and parent information
Teaching is a task shared by schools and families. Frequent information on the progress and difficulties a pupil is experiencing enable the parents to help the child with his/her studies and to make more informed career choices.

6. Quality of teaching/workload

6.1 Organisation of teaching, a driving force
Teaching must be organised in such a way as to avoid any hindrance to learning, either from stress and overloading or because the pupil is not given enough to do and lacks stimulation. Building up a climate propitious to learning requires:

- unconditional respect and support from the pupil;
- creating a space in which individual interests and working habits can be developed;
- active learning methods;
- informative assessment methods which encourage learning and include self-assessment schemes.

6.2 Differential teaching
Differential and personalised teaching methods often require the teacher to deviate from traditional methods involving group teaching and group progress. Differential teaching means adjusting the content, objectives, methods and pace of lessons to suit the needs of each pupil or group of pupils. The responsibility for planning, managing and supervising their work is then shared by the pupils.

6.3 Teacher capacity and workload
It is becoming increasingly important for the number of teachers, their working capacity and their enthusiasm for the job to be kept at a high level. The level can be sustained and developed through high-level training and

education of teachers, by constantly bolstering their self-confidence, by giving them a certain amount of freedom to make their own decisions, by pedagogic efforts based on objectives and values (guidelines) and by the social support they receive from colleagues and school authorities. Furthermore, teachers must be in a position to take a constant look at their teaching activities and their workload, which means being able to take an occasional break from their daily routine (sabbatical year, training courses and so on).

The SIPRI project covered primary schools. The results of this extensive report, however, are equally applicable to other levels of education. Schools should be interested, for example, by our conclusions regarding transition from infant school to primary school, and also by our comments regarding collaboration between school and family for the assessment of pupils' work. We sincerely hope that the SIPRI report will be appreciated and will give rise to pedagogic debate far beyond the primary school.

The considerable means invested in the SIPRI project by the CDIP (Swiss Conference of Cantonal Directors of Public Education) and the Swiss cantons will only have served a useful purpose if school authorities in the cantons and regions, and particularly teacher-training and further training institutions and teachers' organisations adopt and follow up the ideas and proposals put forward by SIPRI so that they outlive the end of the project, for the SIPRI project proper has now come to an end. Its true impact will be measured in terms of the number of suggestions that are actually put into practice in schools by those in a position to do so.

The BICHMO project

In 1987 the pedagogic commission of the CDIP was commissioned to carry out a project entitled BICHMO (Bildung in der Schweiz von Morgen, or education in Switzerland tomorrow). This study is (1988) currently in its initial phase and should lead to a number of recommendations and guidelines on educational policy for the attention of the CDIP, cantons and training institutions. It should give a clear picture of future development prospects in compulsory schooling, the various types of post-compulsory schooling, adult education and their role within the educational system as a whole. There would seem to be little future in the educational field for studies concentrating on one type of organisation, like schools, for example; on the one hand, schools are only one part of the education system and, on the other hand, insufficient attention is given to relations with society at large. That is why the BICHMO project not only looks at schools but also intends to adopt a much broader approach, open to the outside world, with the help of experts from every field.

The LEFO project

The LEFO project (short for Lehrerfortbildung, or further training for teachers), which has just got under way in 1988 in Switzerland, should come up with some fresh ideas for improving and revising further training courses for teachers on the basis of an inventory drawn up by cantons, regions and teachers' associations. Further training for teachers has been on the increase in all cantons over the last 20 years and the CDIP has contributed greatly to defining the pedagogical justification and orientation of this further training. It would seem that increasing demands on teachers and the importance of further training in keeping abreast of new teaching methods will continue to be the driving force behind further training. The problem today is to improve the quality and the range of services, by exchanging information, systematically following up the more promising developments and clarifying fundamental questions, to help cantons and teachers' associations to adjust further training courses for teachers to suit changing demands.

21. TURKEY <DECS/EGT [86] 87>

I. Basic information on the Turkish educational system

General characteristics of the system

Education in Turkey is operated and financed largely by the state. The Constitution of the Turkish Republic defines the role and responsibilities of the state in education. A specific article lays down the principle of compulsory primary (elementary) education for boys and girls free of charge in public schools.

The legislative power is vested in the parliament (the Grand National Assembly) and this power cannot be delegated to any other authority. All legal actions taken by the parliament are executed by the central government. The Ministry of National Education, Youth and Sports, on behalf of the state, is the main organ with powers and authority to guide, control and supervise the educational system in the country. The Basic Law of National Education dated 1973 enumerates the tasks and responsibilities of the Ministry of National Education, Youth and Sports. These include permission for the establishment of any school as well as preparation or approval of the curricula of all schools including private institutions of learning.

Central and provincial organisations were reorganised according to the present conditions and needs and this reorganisation was finalised with Decree No. 179, which came into force on 14 December 1983, and with Decree No. 208, which amended some articles of the previous decree. As can be understood from the title of the decree, the Ministry of Youth and Sports, which had been a separate ministry until then, was joined to the Ministry of National Education.

The present educational system in Turkey includes both formal and non-formal education. Essentially, formal education comprises basic/elementary school and junior high school/secondary and higher education.

Non-formal education covers all learning activities organised within and outside formal education institutions. It caters for those who passed through the formal education system without acquiring reading and writing skills, in addition to those wishing to improve their general education or to undertake vocational training.

The Ministry of National Education, Youth and Sports is headed by a

Table 1 Statistics of pre-school education in Turkey

	Pre-school class			*Kindergarten*			*Nursery*		
School year	*Class*	*Teacher*	*Pupils*	*School*	*Teacher*	*Pupils*	*Class*	*Teacher*	*Pupils*
1973–4	245	336	6,093	8	43	912	186	—	3,284
1974–5	394	374	8,185	8	42	912	202	425	4,293
1975–6	—	—	—	—	—	—	251	—	4,479
1976–7	—	—	—	9	44	842	255	—	4,817
1977–8	984	1,087	17,986	11	57	988	262	—	4,882
1978–9	1,372	1,572	26,559	12	63	1,000	271	550	6,051
1979–80	1,519	1,833	29,098	12	52	811	275	618	6,368
1980–1	1,606	2,024	32,779	12	59	1,128	280	634	6,601
1981–2	2,118	2,634	44,819	14	77	1,525	283	643	6,617
1982–3	2,294	2,724	46,793	17	87	1,609	292	669	7,227
1985–6	3,071	4,545	85,153	16	138	1,720	276	834	7,499

minister, who is a member of the Cabinet. An under-secretary assists the minister in his executive functions. There are a number of departments (general directorates) in the ministry, established mainly to implement policies and programmes.

Structure of the formal education system

The essence of the formal education system in Turkey has for a long time been a five-year primary school at the first level, followed by a two-cycle secondary education, each cycle lasting three years, completed by universities, academies and specialised schools of higher learning. After reorganisation efforts, which took place between 1973 and 1977, reforms and new approaches in the structure of the educational system are now under way.

One of the important consequences of this reform was the integration of the primary school and middle school under the name of 'basic education'. Basic education consists of two cycles: a lower cycle of compulsory primary school for five years and an upper cycle of optional middle school for three years. Primary school covers the education of children between 6 and 14 years of age. The Basic Law of National Education allows primary schools and middle schools to operate separately or to be unified under the same administration. It is expected that the new system will result in better articulation of primary and middle school programmes under basic education.

Pre-school education continues to be an optional part of formal education. Pre-school institutions, which serve 4–5-year-old children, consist of preparatory classes, kindergartens and nurseries. Preparatory classes are located in the primary schools and prepare children for elementary education. (See Table 1.)

II. The aims, organisation and content of primary education

Primary education has been a target of development both in quantity and in quality since the declaration of the Turkish Republic in 1923. The primary education reform has been considered as a continuous matter by governments, educators and laymen. The rate of schooling has risen from 25 per cent in 1923 to 98 per cent in 1986. However, need for progress in quantity as well as in quality is still recognised.

Official aims of primary education

The aims and tasks of primary education may be defined thus:

1. to enable every Turkish child to acquire all the necessary basic knowledge,

skills and habits required for effective citizenship and to raise him in a manner commensurate with national ethical concepts;
2. to train every Turkish child in a manner commensurate with his interests, abilities and aptitudes and prepare him for further education.

The organisation of primary education

It is the duty of the Ministry of National Education, Youth and Sports to organise primary education all over the country. One of the major departments in the ministry is the Directorate General of Primary Education. This department is charged with responsibility for administering the primary schools, middle schools, basic education schools and pre-school education under its competence.

Turkey is divided into 67 provinces. In these provinces, local organisation of education is headed by the superintendent (Director of National Education, Youth and Sports) who is responsible directly to the Governor. The superintendent has a professional administrative staff and a body of supervisors (inspectors) for the institutions of primary education. In addition, elementary education councils established in the villages, sub-districts and provinces deal with the problems of primary schools.

Links between various stages of education

The traditional middle school is considered to be part of basic education in the new system. Therefore, the articulation between primary and middle school programmes is expected to improve in the coming years. At present, a primary school diploma leads to automatic admission to middle schools.

The number of primary school pupils and teachers

There were about 50,000 primary schools and over 6.5 million pupils in these schools in the 1985–6 school year. In the same school year, the total number of primary school teachers amounted to 211,797 (122,387 were male and 89,410 were female).

Grouping procedures

According to the Law of Elementary Education dated 1961, the maximum number of pupils in a classroom in the primary schools is 40. Children are grouped on the basis of age. All pupils are enrolled in the 1st grade and then every year they are promoted to the next grade. Special classes are also arranged for children with learning difficulties.

The length of the school year

The length of the school year is 160 working days in villages and 180 working days in towns and cities approximately. Primary schools are generally opened in mid-September and closed at the end of the first week of June in urban areas. Village schools are closed 3–4 weeks earlier. There is a two-week vacation in the middle of the school year (1–15 February). Opening and closing times are defined according to a schedule prepared by the Directorate General of Primary Education and approved by the Board of Education every year.

The primary school curriculum

The subjects in the primary school curriculum include Turkish, life studies, social studies, science, mathematics, religion and ethics, drawing, music and physical education. (See Table 2.)

Table 2 Weekly distribution of primary school lessons

	Weekly programme by class				
Subject	*I*	*II*	*III*	*IV*	*V*
Turkish	10	10	10	6	6
Mathematics	5	5	5	4	4
Science	—	—	—	4	4
Social studies	—	—	—	3	3
Practical life studies	5	5	5	—	—
Religious instruction and ethics	—	—	—	2	2
Art	1	1	1	2	2
Music	1	1	1	1	1
Physical education	3	3	3	3	3
TOTAL	25	25	25	25	25

The primary school curriculum aims at behavioural change in accordance with the objectives of national education. Children in the first cycle of the school, which covers grades 1–3, gain knowledge and skills in reading, writing, arithmetic, life studies, basic sciences, taught together with arts, music and physical education. The content gets comparatively specialised in the last two years.

The psychological structure of the content is emphasised in the primary curriculum, that is, knowledge and skills are selected and organised according to the developmental tasks and needs of children of 6–14 years old. The general approach is to establish natural links around life problems rather than to teach individual subjects separately. Extra-class activities in primary schools are also organised around actual life situations and carried out in and out of the school building.

Projects and problem-solving as well as group techniques are used largely in primary schools. Provision of technical and didactic aids is the state's responsibility. However, in many places local and parental support is obtained.

Methods of pupil assessment

Children in primary schools are evaluated continuously, with great emphasis on the total development and success of the pupil. There is no graduation examination as such at the end of fifth year; the child completing the five-year schooling with satisfactory marks in each grade receives a diploma.

The scale of marks in the primary school is a numerical five-point scale with values from 1 to 5. Five is the highest mark. In the middle school a ten-point scale is used. Marks are awarded at the end of each term. The marks awarded at the end of spring term are the final judgements on achievements during the whole school year. Special measures are taken or techniques are used for slow learners and retarded children.

Training of teachers

Primary school teachers previously received training in normal schools with a duration of four years' education based on the middle school. When the Basic Law of National Education introduced the principle of higher education for all teachers, two-year institutes of education were established in 1973 to train primary school teachers. Thus, a higher-quality training for teachers has been legally determined. Since then, all primary school teachers are trained in these institutes, which have been recently attached to universities. In addition, the ministry introduced training on the job for primary school teachers who graduated from teacher high school in co-operation with the Open University in the school year 1985–6.

The support services

The Law of Elementary Education requires every province to have health supervisors, school and regional doctors. In addition to this, in many provinces there are centres of guidance and research. These centres provide primary schools with medical and social services through doctors, psychologists, social workers and educational advisers. All pupils are examined once or twice a year by school or regional doctors.

School and community relations

At present, there are two types of institutions to establish and to improve relationships between schools, parents and communities. One of these is the School–Family (Parent–Teacher) Association, the other is the Association of School Protection.

The basic aim of the School–Family Association is to strengthen relations between school and parents and to ensure a better educational environment for children. Each primary school in Turkey has a School–Family Association. All teachers and parents are *ex officio* members of this association.

The Associations of School Protection, on the other hand, are organised by local people who are interested in the physical development and financial problems of the school which serves their community. The director of the school, and teachers, may be active members of this organisation.

III. Problems and trends in primary education

Problems

Although the schooling rate at the primary level is over 98 per cent, still great numbers of children are not enrolled in any school because of lack of facilities in some places.

Transition of pupils from primary schools to middle schools remains to be improved. Only 54 per cent of the graduating students from primary schools move on to the middle schools.

Recent studies relating to enrolment and graduation at various educational levels indicate that some regions maintain an advantage while others lag behind.

Especially in rural areas school absenteeism is a problem caused by socio-economic factors and lack of transportation facilities.

Lack of proper educational aids and equipment and inadequate school buildings and facilities are also major handicaps in providing effective elementary education in some areas.

Turkey has the shortest duration of primary education amongst the European countries. It is felt that schools at this level have to be extended in the immediate future.

Trends

The above-mentioned problems and increasing social pressure required improvements and innovations to be made relating to the organisation, content and methods of elementary education.

A continuing trend is to integrate primary schools with the middle school and extend elementary education to eight years. Parallel to this reorganisation, the upper division of eight-year school will offer some practical courses. A pilot project called 'Life-oriented basic education project' is under way, covering more than 600 schools in 1986.

Another trend is to increase the number of regional boarding schools of eight-year duration as a measure to meet the needs of several surrounding communities in rural areas. Thus, a better-equipped school environment is created in these boarding schools. The boarding schools place particular emphasis on vocational skills demanded in the localities.

An important goal is to realise universal education at the elementary school level. New school buildings are established each year by the state and by the contributions of voluntary organisations as well as by donations from individuals. It is estimated that the goal of universal education at the primary school level will be achieved before 1990.

Raising the quality of teacher education is another trend which has been discussed thoroughly in the recent meeting of the National Education Council, the highest consultative body of the Ministry of National Education, Youth and Sports. Concrete action in this direction is raising the duration of pre-service training for elementary school teachers.

22. UNITED KINGDOM <DECS/EGT [87] 4 rev>

Section I: Basic information

1. The aims of primary education

The fundamental aim that primary schools should meet the educational needs of every pupil is embodied in the 1944 Education Act's reference to the duty to secure education suited to each pupil's age, ability and aptitude. It is widely accepted that primary education should be concerned with the following broad educational aims:

- to help pupils to develop lively enquiring minds, the ability to question and argue rationally and to apply themselves to tasks and physical skills;
- to help pupils to acquire understanding, knowledge and skills relevant to a fast-changing world;
- to help pupils to use language and number effectively;
- to help pupils to develop personal moral values, respect for religious values, and tolerance of other races, religions, and ways of life;
- to help pupils to understand the world in which they live, and the interdependence of individuals, groups and nations;
- to help pupils to appreciate human achievements and aspirations.

2. The responsibility for the organisation of primary education

The following paragraphs show some of the variations in the education system in the United Kingdom.

England and Wales

The education service is distinctive in its distribution of responsibility between central government, local government and the teaching profession. The instrument of central government is the Department of Education and Science, at the head of which is the Secretary of State for Education and Science. He or she is a member of the government of the day and has overall responsibility for education in England and for universities throughout England, Wales and Scotland. The Secretary of State is usually assisted by several ministers.

Responsibility for schools and non-university education in Wales rests with the Secretary of State for Wales who is a member of the United Kingdom Cabinet and it is exercised through the Welsh Office.

The Department and the Welsh Office are concerned almost entirely with the formation of national policies for education. They are responsible for controlling educational buildings and the supply, training and pensions of teachers, but they do not lay down schools' detailed schemes of work nor do they run the schools and colleges.

Local government administers education through the local education authorities, of which there are 105 in England and Wales. These are responsible for over 89 per cent of national spending on education. Some 46 per cent of their education expenditure they receive directly from central government, but the remainder they raise from the rates (local taxes). The local education authorities administer the routine working of the education service, it being their duty to provide and run the schools and colleges in their areas and to employ teaching and ancillary staff. A chief education officer is in charge of each local education authority's administration and he or she is assisted by professional and administrative staff.

The 1988 Education Reform Bill[9] proposes that there will be a national curriculum in contrast with the present situation whereby the control of the secular curriculum rests with the local authority, or in the case of voluntary and independent schools with the school governors or providing body, but the detail of the work, the choice of textbooks and the planning of the timetable are usually left to the head of the school, with the methods of day-to-day teaching being decided by the individual teacher. In effect, at present, what is taught within schools depends on the partnership of the local authorities, the head and the teachers, and the governing body.

The Education Reform Bill specifies certain common curriculum elements to be offered to pupils of compulsory school age by maintained schools. These elements are: the core subjects of mathematics, English and science; the other foundation subjects of history, geography, technology, music, art, physical education and (for secondary pupils) a modern foreign language and in Wales, Welsh, which will be a core subject in Welsh-speaking schools and a foundation subject in the other schools. The Bill will have other far-reaching effects; for example, each local education authority will be required to submit to the Secretary of State a scheme for allocating their aggregated schools' expenditure between all the schools they maintain. The schemes must include details of the authority's arrangements for delegating to governing bodies of all secondary schools and primary schools with more than 200 pupils responsibility for managing their school's budget. The governing bodies of schools with delegated budgets will be responsible for deciding, within the total resources available to them, how many teachers and non-teaching members of staff the school will have. Governing bodies will have greatly increased powers in respect of appointing and dismissing staff. It is also proposed that, following a ballot of parents, the governing bodies of large schools may apply for grant-maintained status and, to that extent, break away from the local education authority. By these and other measures within the Bill, the government intends to increase parental involvement in the schools and, through competition, introduce a new dynamic into the schools system.

The structure of the education system in Wales is identical with that in England. The existence of the Welsh language however, spoken by about one-fifth of the total population and by about one-seventh of pupils in primary schools, means that Welsh is used as the sole or main medium of instruction in 355 primary schools, partly as a medium in a further 242 schools, and as a second language in a further 779 schools.

Scotland

Public sector education in Scotland is a partnership between 12 regional and islands councils and central government. The Secretary of State for Scotland is a member of the Cabinet and is responsible to Parliament for central government policy on a wide range of issues, including the overall supervision and development of the education service through the Scottish Education Department.

The elected regional and islands councils have a statutory duty to ensure that there is an adequate and efficient provision of schools and further education in their areas, and for this purpose are known as education authorities. They are responsible for the construction of buildings, the employment of teachers and other staff, and the provision of equipment and materials. Their responsibility for the curriculum taught in schools is normally delegated to individual head teachers; guidance is however issued from time to time by the Secretary of State on the advice of Her Majesty's Inspectors of Schools and the Consultative Committee on the Curriculum (CCC).

Northern Ireland

Northern Ireland has a four-tier arrangement of educational administration. The tiers are: the schools with their boards of governors and principals, responsible for the day-to-day operations; the five education and library boards funded by the Department and responsible for the administration of the service in their respective geographical areas; the Council for Catholic Maintained Schools, which has responsibility for all maintained schools under Roman Catholic management; and the Department of Education, accountable to the Secretary of State for Northern Ireland who is a member of the United Kingdom Cabinet and is responsible to Parliament.

3. The links between pre-school and primary education and between primary and lower secondary education

In the United Kingdom, compulsory schooling begins at 5 years of age. Before this there is a variety of pre-school provision, and an increasing number of children receive nursery education either in a nursery school or in a nursery class in a primary school. The links between pre-school and the primary stage vary from school to school. Frequently the nursery teachers and the primary teachers meet to discuss curricular objectives and continuity between the two stages; the needs of individual children are discussed, and assessment and record cards are sent on to the primary school. At the time of transfer, parents of nursery children are encouraged to visit the primary school, the head talks to them about the work of the school and they usually have an opportunity to talk to the head individually. There is other pre-school provision which is voluntary but this does not have the close links outlined above. It is often the case that a large number of primary schools 'feed' one secondary school. The majority of local authorities require the primary school to pass on a record card for each pupil. Apart from this, the links established vary considerably from one group of schools to another. Most schools organise a range of contacts in the summer term. Heads of primary schools and heads of first year in secondary school meet and discuss pupils' abilities and prospects. Parents visit the secondary schools and pupils visit their new school - usually for half a day.

4. The number of primary school pupils and teachers

In the school year 1985–6 there were about 4.5 million pupils of compulsory school age in maintained primary schools in the United Kingdom. In 1985–86 there were approximately 205,800 teachers involved with this phase of education.

5. The arrangements for grouping pupils and the official class sizes

In most cases primary school classes have a wide ability range and the learning takes place in these mixed-ability groups, though in England frequently there is a regrouping by ability for the 10 and 11 year olds for the teaching of mathematics.

Information on the distribution of primary pupils by size of class is not readily available for the United Kingdom as a whole. Table 1 below shows the percentages of primary school pupils in five categories of class size in England, Scotland and in Northern Ireland.

Table 1

	Class size					
	10 or under %	*11–20* %	*21–30* %	*31–40* %	*41 or over* %	*Total* %
England (1985–6 data)	0.9	9.2	65.1	24.6	0.2	100
Scotland (1984–5 data)	0.4	10.1	71.4	17.9	0.2	100
Northern Ireland (1986–7)	15.8		62.0	22.0	0.2	100

6. The length of the primary phase, the school day, the school week and the school year

Most children in England and Wales spend between six and seven years in the primary phase of education. Variations occur because children are first admitted to school at different times in the academic year according to their birthday. At present about half of all the first entrants are less than 4 years 9 months and many are just 4 years old. The primary phase is often subdivided: first an infant department/school followed by a four-year junior department/school with transfer when the children are 11. However, a minority of education authorities follow a slightly different pattern of 'first' schools for the age group 5–8 or 5–9, followed by four-year 'middle' schools for the 8–12 or 9–13 year age-group.

In Scotland, education authorities are free to adopt more than one intake of children per school year. However, the practice has been to arrange for a single intake of children between the ages of 4½ and 5½ years. Transfer to secondary education takes place between the ages of 11½ and 12½ after a seven-year primary course.

Because of the high degree of independence given to local authorities for the administration of schools, there are very few common rules for the organisation of the school day and week or for the quantity of teaching to be given. For children under 8 years of age, 3 hours of instruction per day are prescribed. Pupils of 8 years and over are offered at least 4 hours. This teaching has to be divided into morning and afternoon sessions unless exceptional circumstances make this undesirable.

Most of the United Kingdom schools teach five days per week in morning and afternoon sessions. If a school meets on six days in the week, as is the case for many independent and boarding schools, one day may consist of one session only.

There are only a very limited number of administrative regulations for the organisation of the school year. The regulations simply state that maintained schools must meet for no less than 400 sessions per year from which may be deducted no more than 20 sessions for closures during the educational year. Since one session in the United Kingdom educational system corresponds roughly to a half-day, the minimum number of teaching days per year is about 190. In practice, many schools still follow the 'term' system, allowing two weeks holiday at the end of the first term (Christmas), between two and three weeks at the end of the second term (usually around Easter) and some six weeks at the end of the school year, which normally closes in the second half of July.

In Scotland, education authorities are required to arrange that the schools under their management be open for a minimum of 190 days (excluding Saturdays and Sundays) in each school year. Individual authorities can make application to the Secretary of State for Scotland for his consent to a reduction in the number of openings.

7. The major areas of the primary school curriculum

Primary schools give high priority to English and mathematics. In Wales many schools give high priority to Welsh and in Scotland provision is made for the teaching of Gaelic in some areas of the country. Beyond this, the curriculum encourages children to develop an understanding of the world, of their place in it and of how people live and work. This involves an introduction to some of the many ideas derived from historical, geographical, health-related, scientific and technological issues. Time is given to aesthetic and practical subjects such as art and craft, physical education and both instrumental and vocal music, and to religious education. In most schools children are introduced to using a computer.

Finally, schools are concerned with the personal and social development of their pupils in the widest sense of the children's awareness of themselves as individuals and the way they relate to others in the context of the culturally and racially diverse society of Britain today and of the European Communities.

8. The main methods of pupil assessment

In most classes, teachers keep records of their pupils' attainment in numeracy and literacy. Many education authorities now test all children in these two major aspects of the curriculum and in verbal and non-verbal reasoning, in some cases twice or three times during the primary phase. Most schools are required to complete a record card for each pupil showing the results of such tests, relevant facts to do with the health of the child and broad comment about attainment, interests and general attitudes to work. These records are passed on from school to school; in some cases they are supplemented by samples of the pupils' written and graphic work.

In 1974 an Assessment of Performance Unit (England and Wales) was set up within the part of the Department of Education and Science concerned with curriculum and examinations to promote the development of assessing and monitoring the achievement of children in schools and to seek to identify the incidence of under-achievement. It has published reports on pupils' performance in English and mathematics at 11 and 15 and in science at 11, 13 and 15. In these subjects the Assessment of Performance Unit reports are helping to build up a national picture of achieved educational standards and are providing valuable information on curriculum and assessment which can be used on a variety of in-service courses for teachers.

In Scotland, the Assessment of Achievement Programme was started in 1982 to assess pupils' performance in selected areas of the curriculum. Mathematics was tested in 1983 at P4 and P7 as was English in 1984, and science at these stages in 1987. The results from the testing of mathematics have been circulated to all schools in Scotland in the forms of folders containing sets of cards. Booklets for teachers giving the findings from the English project are in preparation. It is planned to retest in each of the main subject areas after five years in order to provide an up-to-date picture of what Scottish pupils know and can do.

The Education Reform Bill (1988) specifies common curriculum elements (see the references under the heading 'the responsibility for the organisation of primary education') and proposes to establish attainment targets and programmes of study. It is also proposed that arrangements shall be made for assessment, to be specified as appropriate, at four key ages – 7, 11, 14, 16.

9. Arrangements for the initial and in-service training of primary school teachers

There are two main forms of initial training for teachers in primary schools in England and Wales. Those who hold a degree, following a three-year course in a university or institution of higher education, can take a one-year Post-Graduate Certificate of Education (PGCE) in an approved institution, normally a university, college of higher education or polytechnic. The main route into primary teaching is a four-year course leading to the degree of Bachelor of Education. Most Bachelor of Education (B.Ed) degrees combine one or more academic subjects with professional and educational studies in a concurrent programme, and courses must meet the criteria set down by the Secretary of State. In total, primary training provided about 13,750 primary teachers in the year 1986–7, a minority by the PGCE route and the majority by the B.Ed. route. There is mounting pressure to extend the length of the PGCE course.

In Scotland, there are two forms of initial training for teachers in the primary sector. Those who hold a degree of a UK university (including the

Open University) or of the Council for National Academic Awards or a qualification of equivalent standard can take a one-year postgraduate course in a college of education. Alternatively students may take a four-year course in a college of education leading to the Bachelor of Education degree, which replaced the three-year college of education course leading to a diploma in primary education.

Opportunities for in-service training for primary teachers vary widely in nature and content. In the past four years the government has provided educational support grants for developments in inner urban areas and in rural areas and to encourage higher standards of achievement in mathematics and science. Most local education authorities offer a programme of short courses through their own advisory services. These range from courses for newly trained teachers to advanced training for experienced teachers and heads. Universities, colleges and polytechnics offer courses leading to the award of certificates, diplomas and masters' degrees covering a wide range of subjects and aspects of education. Teachers' centres, subject associations and other agencies provide further opportunities for professional development through courses, conferences and workshops. In England and Wales, the government departments, through Her Majesty's Inspectorate, offer a substantial programme of national short courses covering a wide range of subjects each year. In Scotland, courses are offered principally by colleges of education.

10. The support services which are available to primary schools, e.g. doctors, psychologists, social workers, advisers

The 1981 Education Act set a new pattern for educational provision in respect of children with special educational needs. The particular requirements of individual children are assessed, and as far as possible appropriate provision is made within normal school so that these children are taught with their peer group. Legislation calls for the school's close co-operation with the parents of those children whose educational needs require special help. Schools generally maintain good links with the health services and the school nurse provides a valuable link with the doctor who may visit once or many times a year according to need. Relationships between doctor and school are generally good. Doctors discuss individual children with the head and relevant information is transmitted to the class teacher.

Approximately 1,300 psychologists are employed by local education authorities and are available to the schools, and in Scotland there are a further 180. Their duties vary widely but in many cases include the assessment of individual pupils, working with teachers in devising learning programmes, participating in in-service training for teachers and providing guidance and support to children and their parents.

Local education authorities appoint their own officers to ensure that the duty of securing attendance at school is carried out and that children should be able to benefit from such education. The welfare element has long been recognised and these officers are designated education welfare officers, school attendance officers or even, but less commonly, education social workers. Many of these officers are fully qualified social workers. Education welfare officers function in the following principal areas: ensuring school attendance, the provision of free meals, school uniform and clothing in cases of need, provision of maintenance grants where appropriate, non-accidental injury to children of school age, the welfare and transport arrangements for handicapped pupils and the employment of children. In carrying out these functions, education welfare officers and heads co-operate with social workers employed by the social services department of the authority and, in some cases, by other agencies.

Each local authority employs educational advisers who inform the Chief Education Officer or Director of Education about resources and the work of the schools. Most advisory services include primary school specialists but the pastoral work of visiting the primary schools is usually shared with subject specialists. The advisers are key figures, as they influence and lead the in-service training programme for the teachers, they supervise the work of newly qualified teachers, and draw together groups of more experienced teachers and heads to discuss educational methods and curriculum development. In some cases they are involved in appointing teachers, advising on equipment and teaching materials and writing reports on individual schools.

Northern Ireland has a small number of primary advisers in the education and library boards. These advisers undertake support work in primary schools but have no responsibility for monitoring of standards. The Inspectorate of the Department of Education is involved in both support and monitoring of all primary schools.

11. The institutional links between the primary school, parents and the community

The Education Act (1986) increased the influence of parents in the running of their children's schools. In the governing bodies of primary schools there are now an equal number of parents and local authority governors and provision is made for representatives from the local business community. All parents receive an annual report from the governing body and have the chance to discuss this at an annual meeting. Many primary schools have parents' associations or parent–teacher associations. Recent research on the important effect parental support may have on pupil performance in, for example, reading skills has further encouraged primary schools to involve parents in the work of the school and there have been many projects to take pupils out into the local community, and to bring members of the local community into schools.

In Scotland the nearest equivalent to governing bodies are the school councils, provided for in terms of the Local Government (Scotland) Act 1973. Membership of the school councils is at the discretion of the education authorities, subject to due representation of parents of the pupils attending the school(s) served by the council, at least one person interested in the promotion of religious education and, by nomination or appointment, at least one teacher or member of other educational staff. The functions of the school councils are also to a great extent determined by the authorities. The legislation directs the authorities to appoint school councils to discharge, subject to any directions given by them, such functions of management and supervision of educational establishments or groups of educational establishments as the authority shall determine.

In March 1988 proposals were laid before Parliament in the form of the School Boards (Scotland) Bill, which will have the effect, now that this Bill has become law, of establishing school boards for each primary and secondary school administered by local education authorities in Scotland. When these boards are established, they will replace school councils. The boards will comprise elected parents, elected teachers and co-opted members of the local community, with a majority of parents. Head teachers will not be board members but will advise and liaise with the board. The proposals will give boards basic functions and powers, including the right to approve expenditure on books and materials, rights to information from their local education authorities and involvement in senior appointments to the school. Boards will be able to take on additional delegated functions as they develop. Boards will not have the power to control the curriculum or to dismiss staff. It is intended that boards should be operational from the beginning of the 1989/90 school year, i.e. from August 1989.

Section II: Some problems and trends

Although there has been an 'up-turn' in primary pupils' numbers since 1985, a number of matters that give cause for concern arise directly from the interplay of the fall in number of pupils in the years before 1985 and the effects of economic constraint, factors that directly influence the total number of teachers and the supply of equipment and materials. Where schools become smaller, this may lead to an increase in the number of mixed-age classes. The Inspectorate's national survey of primary schools in England indicated that children in mixed-ability classes of 25, or more, did less well in tests of reading and mathematics, and work in other subjects was less well suited to their abilities. A fall in the number of teachers in a school can create difficulty in providing expertise to cover all parts of the curriculum.

In recent years the fall in the overall numbers of teachers brought with it the problems of redeployment, one of which is that a redeployed teacher may not be able to offer the subject strengths required by the school. However, there is evidence that many local education authorities are now giving more attention to the management of aspects of the education service such as policies relating to the curriculum and staffing, the role and function of the local advisers and the matching of teachers' in-service training to the identified needs of the service, the schools and individual teachers. In some cases this is facilitated by centrally provided resources being targeted on specific developments.

These changes, together with the findings of recent surveys and studies, have led towards greater awareness of the need for each school to have a staff of teachers who can offer different curricular strengths and expertise. An associated trend is the increasing attention given to issues of management and leadership and to coherent planning of the curriculum.

In English and mathematics, recent major studies have added weight to the evidence that children learn language and mathematical skills most effectively when they recognise the application of these skills to everyday life. There is evidence of renewed interest in the teaching of science and environmental studies in primary schools and the beginning of a sharper awareness that some art and craft work for primary children might be of a simple technological kind aimed at designing and making things that work.

In recent years, an increasing number of 4-year-old children, some of them only just 4, have been admitted into school and so there is a need to provide appropriately for these young children in terms of resources, teaching approaches and the curriculum offered. In some cases, the needs of 4 year olds have received insufficient attention and this has been so particularly where they are in classes together with children of statutory school age.

NOTES

1. This curriculum was changed in 1986 and the contents were developed along the lines of Project No. 8.
2. One of these schools was involved in the Contact School Plan.
3. Pre-school means *6 year olds* in this report.
4. For higher education in Italy, there is a separate university council, whose composition and activities are identical.
5. School is here seen as the administrative unit – one or more schools administered by one headmaster.
6. *ECOLE PRIMAIRE SUISSE – Une école pour apprendre. 22 thèses pour le développement de l'école primaire – PROJET SIPRI*, comp. Jean-Pierre Salamin (Berne: CDIP, 1986).
7. The best example of this is the different procedures for passing from primary school to the first year in secondary school.
8. 'Infant school' here refers to pre school.
9. The Bill's proposals are now substantially embodied in the Education Reform Act, 1988.

SECTION 3

THE NEW BASICS IN PRIMARY EDUCATION IN EUROPE

Introduction

Maurice Galton

In this Section we review some of the recent developments that have taken place within recent years in member states of the Council of Europe. Increasingly in member states, the idea of basic primary education has been extended to incorporate the use of computers into mathematics education and to stress the need for all children in this age-range to have first-hand experience of science and technology.

In the first chapter, Roger Hartley considers recent developments in the use of computer packages, including problem-solving approaches based upon the programming language LOGO. He points to the difficulties of classroom organisation when computers still constitute a very limited resource in most primary schools, and goes on to raise serious questions about teaching methods and assessment procedures. In most European countries, efforts are being made to steer the content of primary mathematics courses away from straightforward computational activities towards the use of these procedures in practical 'real life' situations. The difficulties facing teachers in making this transition are not often realised by those responsible for policy making. Problem-solving classrooms present much greater challenges to teachers in terms of their management and control techniques and Hartley is right to emphasise the need for well-resourced innovation strategies.

Chapter 3.2 discusses the move in all European countries to increase the proportion of time devoted to science in the primary curriculum. Joss Elstgeest demonstrates how these trends have developed out of the secondary school curriculum reform movement of the 1960s and the growing appreciation that this style of teaching and learning needs to begin before children move on to secondary education. Elstgeest also stresses the lack of appreciation by many policy makers of the radical change in teaching methods that a process approach to primary science demands of schools. He strongly criticises the current tendency for national authorities to emphasise the minimum standard that pupils must attain, arguing that this will deter teachers from encouraging children to extend their understanding to the full limits of their capacity.

In the final chapter of this Section Mogens Jansen traces the influence of developmental psychology on controversy about how to teach reading effectively. He notes the division between Scandinavia and other countries and makes the interesting point that the stages of the developmental model chosen often correspond closely to the stages at which children transfer from the pre-primary to the primary and from the primary to the secondary school in different countries. He draws attention to the fact that, although the different countries start reading at different ages, the research evidence suggests that there is little difference in performance by the age of 11 or 12. Indeed, he argues that children who start later are generally reading more often than those who start at an earlier age.

Overall, although each of the chapters concentrates in detail on recent developments within only a few countries within the Council of Europe, a clear understanding emerges from the discussions that all countries have more in common with each other than the different systems of education that they operate would suggest.

CHAPTER 3.1

Numeracy and Computer Education

Roger Hartley

In recent years, developments in computer technology and the widespread demand for its applications in society have brought hardware and software costs within the budgets of primary schools, and have forced a serious consideration of the educational potential of microcomputers. However the situation is complex. Currently, some experience has been gained in using computers for interactive learning, but should such applications support conventional curricula, or should they become more strongly innovative? One development is that of computer education, but is this to be conceived as a separate study, or interpreted as information technology and introduced through a variety of curriculum domains? And there are other considerations. Using computers for information handling can influence assessment and record keeping; connecting computers through local area and wide area networks allows schools and education offices to communicate through electronic mail and file transfer systems. How should these facilities be best exploited? There are various ways users can interact with computer systems, eg. through joysticks, concept keyboards, touch screens, and mouse-controlled screen pointers, as well as the keyboard. What are the benefits of these direct manipulation interfaces, particularly for children with special needs? At the same time, it should be noted that home/school links can emphasise the poorer access to computers that is found in less prosperous areas, and the general male dominance in computing (which gives a particular challenge to the introduction of computers in primary schools) can also cause significant problems.

Thus, the scale and potential of computer applications in primary education require careful planning (and resourcing) of equipment provision, of curriculum developments, and of training (both initial and in-service), and these decisions must be informed by classroom-based research with effective dissemination. In short, any review and discussion of mathematics and computer education in the primary school should make reference to these larger issues.

1. Technological change and primary education

There are several reasons why computer technology is requiring a reappraisal of the aims of primary education, and this realisation, perceived across Europe, has led to a series of commissioned studies and symposia (e.g. Jensen 1986; Council of Europe Memorandum 1987). A first consideration is the changes that the new technologies are causing in society and the place of work. Although these might appear to be well removed from young children, 'primary education is the foundation of their learning, and this foundation must equip them to develop in an ever-changing society'. Important applications include information handling seen in wordprocessing systems, in graphical packages for the design office, in records maintained through databases, in spreadsheets and modelling systems for helping decision making, and in expert systems for working out the consequences of complex rule-sets. A second aspect is the computer control of machinery in the factory and for devices in the home. Another is communication that embraces not only electronic text-based mail systems, but fax facilities and the transmission of pictures via satellites. Finally, and not to everyone's liking, is the entertainment industry with its computer-based games, designed for immediate visual impact and giving the user direct manipulation through devices such as joysticks and pointers.

These aspects, of information processing, control systems, communication and interaction, are general themes that technology will bring to the curriculum, and that will impinge directly on computer education and mathematics (with its special relationship to computing). All delegates at the Council of Europe Symposium accepted that this awareness of technological innovation must be a significant educational objective, though how it should be worked out in the curriculum and in teaching methods is a matter of debate.

What makes the computer of particular interest to education is that it can itself serve as a teaching/learning instrument. The same packages that are used in the workplace can become devices for instruction; for example, the database software that stores school records can be used for projects in subject areas such as biology, mathematics or the social sciences. As well as storing information about the domain (e.g. socio-historic data on local towns and industry), school children can seek out and collect their own data, learning not only about social studies or elementary statistics but how to arrange and organise information so that types of enquiries can be answered and relationships observed in a large data-set.

Similarly, spreadsheets and modelling packages can be used in simple ways by primary school children in projects set up by the teacher and the class to suit their particular interests and needs. Spreadsheets provide an interconnected sequence of calculations (for example, linking length, breadth and height dimensions to the volumes of regular solids). Changing values shows the effects on other related variables, and with modern spreadsheets the effects can be displayed graphically.

Computers are programmed with languages (e.g. Basic) and these can be employed (usually by the experienced programmer or commercial developer) to build simulation exercises for investigation-type projects. There are also specially designed languages like LOGO, used as a learning laboratory with young children to develop their problem-solving skills (Papert 1980).

Calculators and elementary statistics packages, as well as wordprocessing systems, are service tools for the classroom; author languages can be used to develop adaptive drills and practice exercises, in addition to test–teach and assessment materials, and adventure game packages to stimulate both imaginative and logical thinking. In short, the computer, an instrument of technological change in society, can assume a wide range of educational roles. But to focus and develop this potential, the aims of primary schooling have to be re-examined in relation to these roles within the curriculum. The connecting links are the classroom intervention and organisational strategies that are employed by teachers.

In discussing objectives, the Lyngby Symposium (which also included delegates from Switzerland and Scandinavia) was well aware of the influence of information technology and the demands of society, but considered also the psycho-emotional development of the child within the learning process (Jensen 1986). It noted the needs for continuity between the stages of education, and for differing teaching/learning approaches to suit the individuality of the child. These policies need a curriculum that can foster the acquisition of skills in selecting and organising information, and in applying and using knowledge through problem solving, reasoning, investigation and planning. A further aspect concerned attitudes, particularly those directed towards an awareness of the learning process itself. Hence, learning tasks that foster skills should also stimulate the development of values and interests, encourage co-operative working so that children explain their ideas, interchange and test opinion, and thus acquire motivation and confidence in their learning.

These objectives, as might be expected from a thematic symposium, were set at a general level and covered knowledge skills, values and interests which can be interpreted within a wide range of curriculum disciplines, each providing its own working contexts. Indeed the publication *Will mathematics count*? (Ball *et al.* 1987) notes similar aims of flexible problem-solving skills, co-operative working, communication of concepts, and enjoying and valuing the learning process. It also provides the opinion that 'styles of teaching which involve microcomputers can aid greatly the acquisition of these important high level skills, which are exactly those which will be required in the future by our industries and by our citizens'.

The European Symposium also considered that mathematics should 'be an experience providing the pupil with a means of seeing, discussing and representing real-life situations in mathematical terms, and thus, of being able to resolve problems and gradually to acquire self-confidence' (Council of Europe Memorandum 1987). In computer education/information technology, the aims again emphasised a range of skills 'for the collection of data, formulation of problems and ideas . . . making active use of technological means to achieve these goals' (ibid.). More controversially, the symposium suggested that it will be necessary to consider the influence of formal programming languages on the development of children's natural language, though hastened to point out that there is much more interest in teaching the social aspects of technology, and in using technology to support the curriculum rather than in teaching about hardware or programming languages.

Having agreement on general aims does not imply a similar consensus on the teaching/learning methods by which those objectives might be achieved. At the European Symposium, some educators maintained that the computer could have a detrimental effect on pupil–teacher interactions, aware perhaps of those applications using self-sufficient practice packages or tutoring programs, or learning environments such as LOGO, where the role of the teacher is less dominant and harder to define. Larsen (see Jensen 1986) emphasised that the need was 'not for a more sophisticated technology, but a more sophisticated way of using existing technology'. It was recognised that these innovative techniques needed more examination and action-based research, for they might not easily co-exist with conventional or established methods and hence might not always be welcomed by teachers.

This point, underlining the gap between promise and practice, is discussed by Jackson *et al.* (1988). Although conclusions are drawn from questionnaire data collected from a particular region of the UK, the observations seem likely to apply to wider experience in Europe. In Jackson's 1984 survey, even though a National Microelectronics Education Programme (MEP) had been initiated in 1980, only 15 per cent of primary schools had been using microcomputers for more than a year, and 24 per cent either had not yet obtained a microcomputer or had not started using it. By 1986 the percentage of primary schools having experience with microcomputers had risen to 90 per cent, but the majority (55 per cent) had still only one machine. This lack of resources was a main reason given in the questionnaires to explain the pattern of use in schools.

The main aim of teachers working with microcomputers in the classroom was to develop 'computer awareness', and this was followed by the 'reinforcement of school work'. Developing logical thought, and extending school work came next, with problem solving being given a lower level of support. Only approximately 20 per cent of teachers gave 'teaching computer skills' as an objective. However, those teachers who had been on training courses, or who were more experienced in using microcomputers, gave significantly more support to extending cognitive skills of reasoning and problem solving.

Most of the software applications in the primary school curriculum tended to be associated with mathematics (though the language/literary domain was increasing rapidly). Drill and practice packages were used by more than two-thirds of teachers, followed by problem-solving materials (56 per cent),

LOGO/Turtle graphics (34 per cent), with data-handling and wordprocessing systems being used by approximately one-fifth of the primary teachers. Again, trained and/or experienced teachers were more likely to use LOGO, problem-solving materials and the data-handling packages. Those teachers were also more likely to report an increase in children's motivation, a finding that was not apparent with the drill and practice software. Further, this more open-ended and child-directed software could sustain co-operative learning in groups (particularly with the older children), and promote social skills of turn-taking in argument, and shared responsibility for decision making.

These data, showing some of the aims and practices of teachers when computers are brought into the classroom, contrast with the aspirations of educators noted in the European symposia. Practice programs supporting current school work play down the innovative roles of the computer but underline day-to-day concerns with curriculum and performance standards. An interesting feature, though, is the change brought about by training and/or experience with computer-assisted methods. Presumably, increasing confidence in using problem-solving materials, LOGO and database software (which require the teacher to simulate, monitor and devise suitable intervention strategies with the children) allows a greater emphasis on cognitive skills and co-operative learning methods. The data show there was an extension of current school activities, with the learning attracting and sustaining a greater motivation from pupils.

2. Computer education

The objective labelled 'computer awareness' was most prominent in the questionnaire, with over 80 per cent of primary school teachers giving this a prime place in their selections. But the term is somewhat vague, and the interpretations teachers had in mind, or how these intentions were given a practical form, are not recorded. The European symposia considered that technology or computer awareness should be introduced *across* the curriculum; computer-based learning and problem-solving materials, and/or database software, would be useful in this regard but, presumably, the main aim would be to use these programs to support curriculum understanding. Even if skills of enquiry or information handling are introduced, the intention would be to promote cognitive development rather than changing focus and pointing out the data-processing and control features of the computer. In short, much more consideration should be given to what is involved in computer education for primary school children, and how this can be achieved in a direct way 'across the curriculum'. Indeed, few experiments have sought even to establish the perceptions of children when they are working or programming the microcomputer.

A preliminary study, supported by the Council of Europe, was undertaken in France (Dieschbourg 1985). It concerned intermediate pupils at primary schools and the teaching followed two main approaches. The first concentrated on computer awareness, with pupils using software packages in projects relating to real-life themes. One of these was 'computers and money' and teachers collaborated with a local bank whose staff arranged visits so that the children could follow the progress of (fictitious) cheques through various accounts. Other preparation included an outline of the history of money, and follow-up activities had the children identify the information exchange between branch and central bank and note how this information was coded and controlled. Simulation exercises on the microcomputer took place periodically. A second example developed the theme of 'data-processing in business'. The actual context was house-building materials, and the teaching followed a similar approach with simulation activities involving the production of invoices and till receipts.

The second technique of introducing computers again concentrated on data-processing, but was computer oriented and focused on the flow of information and its control in time and space through the different hardware/software components. Visual aids were used and children were taught the rudiments of a programming language (BASIC), which they used to solve simple numerical problems. The computer was seen as a machine to carry out commands (referencing variables/data) put together in a program (i.e. a controlled set of instructions) stored in the computer memory.

These approaches were informally but independently evaluated. Clearly, reliable conclusions cannot be drawn from one small study, though a noteworthy feature of the first applications projects was the co-operation between teachers, lecturers and the bank/business firms. Further, the rich nature of the themes allowed the teaching of mathematics, language and the humanities in ways that were authentic, motivating and innovative. Group working on the tasks also seemed to benefit the children's 'socialisation and communication'.

The programming project was ambitious and led to several difficulties. The most important was limited access to equipment, and one computer lesson each week was a minimum for achieving some progress. Less than this and pupils had problems even in using the keyboard to copy programs; for them the course was of little benefit. These difficulties, and the need to manage a whole class of working groups, led teachers into adapting a directed approach. The project also underlined the need for preparatory training courses for teachers as well as pupils.

One of the most important developments, which can span objectives of developing computer awareness as well as promoting cognitive skills of problem solving, is the programming language LOGO. The approach has been well advocated by Papert (1980) and need be no more than briefly outlined here, particularly as its use in France and the UK (as well as America) has led to a variety of supporting texts and discussion papers on its classroom use (e.g. Balacheff 1987).

LOGO provides users with commands which in Turtle graphics, for example, move a floor robot-turtle or drive a cursor on the display screen. In direct command mode, children can translate their own body actions in pacing out or drawing a shape into a sequence of forward <amount> turn <amount> instructions for LOGO. These instructions are directly executed as they are typed, providing immediate feedback with opportunity for correction. However, the instruction sets can be stored as a program in a form that invites experiment, and leads to computational notions of variable, procedure/subprocedure, repetition and recursion (Hoyles and Noss 1987; Sutherland 1987). For example, what if the command amounts were altered, patterns of instructions repeated, sequences of commands stored as program-procedures and then used within larger programs? Thus, LOGO allows children's knowledge to be organised from their experience in procedural forms (Lewis 1988). Problems are solved by analysing them into smaller units (e.g. geometric patterns into their constitutent parts) and refining and improving the solutions. The learning approach is one of experiment, with the direct action-effects and feedback of LOGO maintaining progress and motivation. The point here, though, is that LOGO uses computational ideas; it is a programming language and seems a more appropriate vehicle for introducing computer education into the primary school than is BASIC (see, for example, O'Shea and Self 1983). Since LOGO can drive robots, notions of control can be clearly demonstrated, and LOGO environments are now readily available in Turtle graphics, arithmetic, word/sentence manipulation, and music. However, such work depends critically on pupils having ready access to microcomputers and the software. It also requires training for teachers so that they become familiar enough with the language and its approach to exploit its potential creativity. Perhaps these requirements (and the limited facilities in number/word LOGO, which restrict its curriculum overlap) explain why in many European countries LOGO is not used adequately or extensively.

In summary, the notions of computer education and its placing in the primary school curriculum remain to be worked out. The consensus view of developing information processing with themes across the curriculum seems worthwhile, though current packages (e.g. databases, spreadsheets) will need modification if they are to serve primary school children adequately. At present, LOGO seems the best way of making stronger links to the operational characteristics of computing systems. However, if these innovations are to be successful, it is clear that much greater access to microcomputers is needed, and that there are considerable implications for the in-service and initial training of teachers.

3. Numeracy

Although educational practices and curricula on mathematics are not static and can adjust to changing requirements in today's technological and multicultural society, there has been increasing concern across Europe that these adjustments are not sufficiently responsive. Indeed, almost all European countries have invited commissions or projects to review the functions, curricula and resourcing of mathematics teaching, and several conferences and publications have commented on these developments (e.g. Blanc 1984; Plomp *et al.* 1987; van der Klauw 1987; Verhagen 1987; Department of Education and Science 1988a, Appendix 4).

One common concern, perhaps felt more strongly in the UK, is that standards of mathematical performance and skills are not improving and in some respects may be in decline. Evidence for this has referenced data from the Assessment of Performance Unit (APU) survey in the UK and international studies, which tend to show Japanese school children performing more strongly than pupils in Europe and USA. Calculators and computers can easily carry out routine arithmetical work, and some educators consider this could lead to a further erosion of skills rather than to a strengthening of performance. On the other hand, calculators/computers can bring school children closer to the principles of mathematics. Hence, the place of these technological aids in the primary classroom has been the subject of special discussion (Blanc 1984; Jensen 1984).

Proposed changes in the curriculum see mathematics retaining a pre-eminent position with its contributions across school subjects being underlined (Beeler 1984). Mathematics is a means of representing, organising and manipulating information and data; with the curriculum approach becoming more thematic, the mathematics of school can extend its range and application to the world outside. But such applications, set in these contexts, require general skills of seeing relationships, reasoning and problem solving. The particular power of mathematics is shown in the way it can process information (through its concepts and rules) in a variety of descriptive and symbolic forms. Thus, the communication or mapping of contexts and ideas into mathematical language, and vice versa, becomes another important objective.

These changing emphases, which reflect in part current perceptions of the nature of mathematics, can remain in tension. The European seminars reflect this, together with the view that all the educational components of objectives, curricula, technological innovations, teaching methods, assessment, teacher training, dissemination and teacher support are interlinked and are engaged in the mechanisms of change: hence the need for co-ordinating national or regional plans. However, viewpoints and intentions have to be given a practical form in the classroom, and many of the participants at the seminars came from training and administrative institutions. Arguments are often based on 'indirect experience' rather than collected data, and the need for action-based research and classroom demonstrator projects to guide developments was noted, though in general terms. A further theme, singled out for special attention, was the changing functions of assessment and evaluation, and difficulties in implementing such schemes (Cardinet 1984; Jacquet 1980).

The curriculum is more than a structured sequence of topics directed towards educational objectives; it includes tasks and materials to enable learning interactions and teaching strategies to initiate and control them. England and Wales have opted for national curricula to be established, and in mathematics topics are set in domains (number, algebra, measures, shape and space, and data-handling) and levels which are to guide the development of performance. Levels 1–3 are arranged for pupils aged 5 to 7 years, and levels 2–6 span the remaining years (7 to 11) of primary education. Programmes of study are constructed (covering conceptual and procedural knowledge, and problem-solving applications) so that various attainment targets can be reached by different categories and abilities of pupils. The curriculum employs both short and extended tasks using concepts and their properties that make up the knowledge domains (i.e. number, patterns, quantities, shapes and data). The emphasis is focused on skills so that 'all pupils should, at their own level, be able to use mathematical language, recognize patterns, make generalizations, model situations, make conjectures, attempt proofs and perceive their relevance, criticize arguments, formulate, tackle and solve problems and acquire the ability to recognize a mathematical concept in a given situation' (DES 1988a, p. 72).

The Report of the Council of Europe (Blanc 1984), after discussing national reports from Belgium, Denmark, Finland, France, Germany, Greece, Italy, the Netherlands, Switzerland and the United Kingdom, had proposed similar views and sought to move mathematics 'from an emphasis on structural, content oriented aspects to those more directly related to the natural (activity) sphere of the child'. Within this schema, national reports emphasised their own particular concerns, often influenced by the degree of centralisation in their educational systems. These varied from France with a high degree of curriculum control, through countries such as Belgium where administrators of grant-aided schools can adapt the state syllabus under ministerial approval, to Switzerland and Germany where control is placed regionally.

The Belgian authorities have developed a system similar to that of England and Wales (Habran 1984). However, new syllabuses for primary mathematics, introduced by 1983, were reinterpreted by the public and private organising authorities on the grounds (shown by a survey) that teachers considered the curriculum 'overloaded and overambitious'. The result was that non-traditional topics tended to be neglected. To control this diversity in content and methods, particularly between primary and secondary education, a list of minimum skills to be acquired in the primary phase was prepared. These covered numbers and numerical operations, quantities, geometry, problems, sets and relations. However, 75 per cent of samples of teachers drawn from those instructing sixth (i.e. last) year primary and first year secondary agreed on the competence of their pupils on only 23 per cent of the basic skills. In short, the criterion of competence 'appears to mean very different things' to these groups of teachers. On the other hand, 75 per cent of teachers at both levels agreed on 75 per cent of the skills as necessary requirements for their pupils. Following these data, the Ministry of Education has prepared a basic syllabus of skill objectives 'which must be regarded as a course of learning': the England/Wales scheme, which has performance levels charting a development through primary and secondary education, with assessments reporting on these levels, is thus in agreement with conclusions from the Belgium experience. In Germany, where the curricula of the independent regions are different, the Conference of Ministers of Education is also trying to bring about greater co-ordination and harmony (Lauter 1984) by emphasising teaching methods that develop mathematical skills.

The move towards unification of objectives and skill-based curricula in mathematics has required greater attention to teaching/learning methods. Italy, following its partitioned curriculum of arithmetic, geometry and measurement, logic, statistics and data-processing, has provided teachers with very full method guidelines. France, since 1977, has prepared new curricula for each of its five years of primary mathematics, set out in terms of objectives and accompanied by 'very full notes for teachers suggesting one or more means of achieving each objective' (Blanc 1984). Other countries have made methodology and the renewal of teaching materials their main priority. For example, East Switzerland, rather than altering curriculum topics, 'conserved the spirit of the traditional syllabus' (i.e. arithmetic, relations and functions, equations, geometry, problem solving, statistics and probability, mathematical language and representation) but reviewed and updated teaching/learning methods, reinforced by the introduction of newly prepared textbooks (Kriszten 1984). Greeçe has followed a similar approach.

However, commissioning new textbooks and the production of learning materials can be both expensive and unduly prescriptive. Most European countries have preferred teachers/authors to use established publishers and local authorities or schools to develop their own schemes within the curriculum. This is difficult without adequate time release and training for teachers, particularly when higher-level skills (such as the learning of generalisations, and problem-solving applications) and the introduction of new technologies are involved. The Swiss materials have attempted to deal with the former in an adaptive manner, through graded and interlinked exercises and problems that can be partitioned into stages and steps. Weaker pupils can thus be given more help in a controlled manner or only attempt one module of the exercise. In generalisation and problem-solving exercises (e.g. dealing with number patterns) methods of algorithm building or flow-charting are used as a technique for representing and refining procedures. Thus, explaining the result when 519 (say) is used in sequence to write 519519, and this number is then divided by 13, then 11, then 7, or (a harder task) when 565656 is divided by 37, then 91, then 3, requires pupils to see that successive divisions can be replaced by a single step and that, in the first example, multiplying 519 by 1001 gives 519519.

Such techniques and materials/textbooks are useful, particularly with numerical, data-processing and procedural types of tasks. However, it is harder to be prescriptive when there is a strong tendency towards pragmatism, for example in mathematics problem-solving applications that encourage the use of local contexts, or when computer software is being introduced into the curriculum. In this circumstance (with the exception of drill and practice programs), preparation and follow-up, intervention and discussion by the teacher, encourage the active engagement of pupils in more open-ended tasks, and this makes the direction of learning less predictable. The teaching control, while operating under a curriculum scheme, is more directly driven by the pupils' own working and knowledge base.

This tension, between covering a common curriculum stream and developing instruction from pupils' work patterns, is made more obvious with computer-aided learning which is able to change the sequence as well as the emphasis of learning. For example, as Ball *et al.* (1987) point out, computer graphics packages allow pupils to start by examining graphs of (linear) functions before considering equations. Computer-assisted methods can also introduce new topics or allow them to have greater prominence; for example, simple iterative numerical techniques, statistics and probability, logic, number (pattern) theory, and mathematical modelling. Further, it can change the learning emphasis through calculating packages (say) and provide a greater range of representational techniques, e.g. Turtle graphics with its procedural descriptions of geometry and where the notion of variable can be an interesting preparation for the algebraic concept (Sutherland 1987). Mathematical links to other subjects can also be made more rewarding through the use of databases and spreadsheets (Beeler 1984). However, the potential for computer-based methods to be an innovative influence arguing for a more adaptive curriculum structure (and the difficulties in developing this potential) are not yet adequately recognised. Current schemes only lightly reference these techniques and, when they do, it is in general, stereotypical ways. Scandinavia has recognised this situation (Gjone 1984) and useful comments are provided by Fyfe (1984) and by Ball *et al.* (1987).

Number and number patterns

Number (from counting, assigning values, learning operations and rules to manipulate them, and searching for patterns and generalisations as a preparation for algebra) occupies a notable place in the primary school curriculum, and arithmetical performance is readily quoted as an indicator of 'standards'. Computer-based practice packages are available and survey data show they are one of the most popular types of program currently in use. On the other hand, although they can deal with the learning of relevant number facts, indicating errors and providing right answers are not likely to be effective with children who have misconceptions, e.g. with place value. Such remedial teaching can, and should, be handled by the teacher, but the diagnostic capabilities of programs that use pre-stored examples are limited and not able to alert the teacher in an informed way. Recognising that a response is wrong falls far short of recognising the mal-rule or misconception that caused the error. It is these limitations of pre-stored programs, which seem to insist on practice rather than understanding, that are causing some disquiet. Work coming from artificial intelligence is relevant here. The program BUGGY-DEBUGGY (Brown and Burton 1978; Friend and Burton 1980; Burton 1982) is able to diagnose arithmetic subtraction errors in the form of mal-rules, i.e. misunderstandings represented as when <these number conditions hold> then this <operation> is applied. These diagnoses can be checked by the program generating related test questions. Hence the mal-rules are more general but summary hypotheses of how the errors arise. Indeed the BUGGY program evolved from experimental studies (the best account is given by van Lehn 1982) which caused Brown and van Lehn (1980) to propose a Repair Theory of Error. In brief, they argue that when pupils meet an impasse, a 'patching' process (from operational rules that appear plausible and are correct in other circumstances) takes place that allows them to proceed. For example, when faced with subtracting a larger digit (n_1) from a smaller (n_2) a pupil might assume that $n_1 - n_2 = n_2 - n_1$. The program can produce these mal-rule patches by altering correct procedural rules; BUGGY-DEBUGGY has also been used in initial teacher training to sharpen discrimination of error. The main point is that having such interpreted information about a learner allows the teacher to give particular tuition to eradicate the misconceptions.

There are some fears that calculators/computers will lessen the need for practice in numerical operations, which may lead to a greater dependence on such aids and result in a poor knowledge and understanding of those number functions that are performed by calculators. This need not be the case; indeed, computers can assist agility and accuracy in arithmetical skills, principally through the use of number games, which can be presented in an attractive format. For example, the program WEST has participants move down numbered tracks in a type of snakes-and-ladders. The computer provides three single-digit numbers randomly, which the pupil can arrange in any arithmetic expression (using operators and parentheses) which, when evaluated, determines the number of forward steps. Sometimes it pays to arrange the move (if possible) to arrive at a marked location which gives a forward short cut, or arrive at the same point as an opponent, who is then penalised by a backward move. Thus, as well as composing moves that are arithmetically accurate, there are strategically good and less good moves (which the computer can recall and then provide comment in a review panel). Pupils can play each other individually or in pairs, or play against the computer program, which can be pre-set at two levels of competence. This program, from the same stable as BUGGY-DEBUGGY, is highly motivating and engages pupils in discussion both on strategy and on the typing and evaluation of arithmetical expressions. Also, tutorial sequences concentrate on types of errors made by pupils. The program has been well reviewed in the classroom (Sanger 1988).

Of course, similar types of number games have been designed for conventional use, and some in the Netherlands follow the 'Wiskobas' technique of teaching/learning. These use more extensive problem settings, broken down into stages with flowcharting and algorithms providing a framework for trial and amendment and for generalisation (Goffree 1984). The computer, though, helps the presentation of such games and, through its evaluation of responses and feedback, aids learning in a more direct fashion. As a final comment, using the computer/calculator as a tool brings more realistic examples within the experience of the class, but also requires arithmetic flexibility (and understanding of operators) from pupils in order to estimate and check that computer values are reasonable and the command sequences valid. In this respect, and used in conjunction with number games, the computer/calculator is likely to improve numeracy.

Conceptual understanding

The development of conceptual understanding (e.g. of operators and place value) at the primary level usually involves direct manipulation with apparatus. Interfaces to arithmetic computer programs, through typing at the keyboard, make learning less direct but the *concept keyboard* can give some improvement. In effect, this allows the teacher to fit an overlay to a flat keyboard connected to a microcomputer and divide it into response 'areas'. Thus, the overlay may have teacher-drawn diagrams of various groupings of objects in the areas, for example; the pupil can choose and press these in response to other material and questions presented on the display screen. Such devices can be particularly useful for programs with younger children or those with special needs who find it difficult to manipulate the conventional keyboard. However, there is still a physical separation between the concept keyboard and the display screen.

Modern interfaces can be controlled through mouse-drive cursors that manipulate windows, icons and menus (e.g. in the AppleMacintosh), and these facilities move closer to the idea of using direct manipulation in learning. The aim is to present *on* the screen a simpler visual 'world' that the pupil can directly manipulate (and thus explore) using the mouse and display icons that have been programmed into this 'world interface'. The technique has been used to create interactive animated simulations in science, and also for supporting a range of skills and concepts in primary arithmetic (Hennessy *et al.* 1988; O'Shea *et al.* 1988). The latter application takes the form of an adventure game (called 'Shopping on Mars') where pupils, playing individually or in pairs, and against each other or against the program, face particular 'danger' situations, which have to be solved by selecting and purchasing appropriate equipment to overcome the difficulty. Generated displays show the available goods in the shops, a purse with the (remaining) money, and a calculator is also pictured (and available to use) with a scratchpad to help learners keep track of their working and to make amendments. The presentation is vivid and animated, and all moves and working are controlled through the mouse-pointer. The program has some adaptive help/tutorial features, but the main point is that all interactions directly manipulate visual representations (e.g. the money of different denominations), thus relating the pupils' mental operations more closely to experience. (The authors maintain that preliminary evaluation data confirm these benefits.)

Problem solving

Problem solving and investigatory modes of learning place control with pupils for the direction of activity and the organisation of knowledge. Experienced problem solvers are able to recognise significant features in the problem description and use them as the basis for developing their solutions, whereas novices tend to apply remembered algorithms suggested by the problem goal. On occasions, therefore, it is advantageous to have pupils discuss or investigate a problem context through open-ended exercises before setting more specific problems that use (parts of) this knowledge (Kulkarni and Simon 1988; Sweller 1988). However, it is difficult for teachers managing a class to follow these schemes and give guidance, as their time has to be distributed amongst pupils whilst their interventions have to be prompt and well judged. The computer can help by providing learning environments useful for open-ended problem solving, but that allow pupils to represent their knowledge in structured forms: this leads to further experiment and amendment. LOGO is one of the best examples. Pupils can write their procedures when investigating open problems concerned with shapes or number patterns (say), and then use them as components when forming program-solutions to more specific problems – perhaps concerned with symmetry.

This way of learning by constructing organised knowledge structures, sometimes known as microworlds (Lewis 1988), has been investigated (see, for example, Balacheff 1987); and Hoyles (1986) and Hoyles and Noss (1987) have proposed interpretive models that employ skills of using, discriminating, generalising and synthesising. More generally, Robert (1984) has provided a useful comment on the considerable French experience in using LOGO.

To what extent pupils should be taught 'mathematical programming' is an open question. The advantages are that algorithms and computational ideas can be used in problem solving; for example, with older children a simple FOR-NEXT can be a useful approach for finding the root of an equation, and numerical methods, which have general applications and may well become more imporant in the curriculum, are easily represented by a programming language. Also, programmable calculators which use a version of BASIC are now cheap (less than £70) and have small screens which can show graphs of functions for example. On the other hand, BASIC has disadvantages for educational use, particularly in the primary school, and the arithmetic/ numeric facilities of LOGO are also inadequate.

As European seminars have noted (Adams 1984), there is a need for research that disciplines anecdotal evidence by relating principles of mathematics learning to the design of software systems and to effective strategies for their use in the classroom.

Assessment

The changes in mathematics curricula are also shifting attention to teaching/learning methods and to techniques of assessment. However, there are considerable difficulties in deciding the exact purposes of evaluation, the data needed in its support, and the generality of conclusions that can be reached. (Cardinet, 1984, has provided a useful comment on these issues when summarising the evaluation of mathematics teaching in French-speaking Switzerland.) Performance data are produced by pupils but, even if the objectives and test items are closely specified, the results reflect not only on children's abilities and work habits but on teaching methods, time distribution and the curriculum that has been followed. Given more practice with better diagnostics and supporting teaching materials, performances would clearly improve, and this relativism is recognised especially with problem-solving assessments. The domains in which problem-solving skills can be exercised are numerous and have to be sampled, but the quality of a pupil's solutions can vary considerably depending on the particular contexts in which the items are placed.

Schemes of national or regional assessment have tried several methods of educational/curriculum control, and have employed various statistical techniques, including Rasch scaling and multi-levelled models deriving from generalisability theory (see, for example, the APU Technical Reports of the National Monitoring of Mathematics and Science Performance Surveys available from the Department of Education and Science, London). However, our main concern is with classroom practice and, as Cardinet points out, teachers in the classroom are continually making assessments with various degrees of formality. Indeed, it is these diagnoses and impressions that guide the approach and pace of teaching and the types of supporting materials that are used. In short, the assessment exercise becomes one of *formative evaluation* under feedback control. The data from the class (including interview and judgemental assessments of communication skills and attitudes, perhaps) allow the teacher to adjust and develop, while the results of an individual pupil – showing what was correct and what was in error – allow that pupil, too, to correct and re-plan. Cardinet notes that difficulties arise when purposes change from formative evaluation to strict assessment, i.e. when one pupil has to be compared and graded in relation to another.

4. Mechanisms of change

Reformulating the curriculum nationally or regionally requires considerable resources and support, especially when innovative technologies and teaching methods are involved. Even when agreement on principles has been reached, longer-term mechanisms of change have to be worked out, including provision of equipment and curriculum materials, teacher-training schemes and methods of dissemination. In Europe, two sorts of models have been used for innovation. The first, shown in the national schemes of the United Kingdom (except Scotland) and France, have made arrangements with industry for placing microcomputers in each school. Schools have equal opportunities to participate and by 1985 in France over 10,000 primary schools were included in the scheme; each had small 'home computers' on a local network linking between six and ten of them to a professional type of microcomputer. Typically, a network centre serves three or four primary schools and, under local authority control, they are made available to the general public outside school hours. In the UK, British microcomputers were used, and 14 regions were set up under the national Microelectronics Educational Programme (MEP), which operated from 1980 to 1985. (Originally focused on secondary education, primary and special needs were incorporated into the programme at a slightly later date.) Each of the regions had co-ordinators for the main activities of computer-based learning, control technology, computer studies, information systems and primary education. These activities were co-ordinated through a National Panel. The main objective was the introduction of computers into schools and this work embraced teacher training, provision of curriculum materials and software, and dissemination. France took similar aims, but placed more emphasis on opening up the information technology centres to the general public.

In teacher training a cascade model was followed. Regions selected teachers who received special courses, and whose functions were to act as trainers for other teachers through courses and through day-to-day working contacts in schools. The difficulties were those of scale. Resources of money and manpower were not enough to meet the demand, particularly in training teachers to use software packages such as databases, spreadsheets and LOGO, and to exploit them in the classroom. Further, those teachers who were to act as catalysts with their own and nearby schools could not gain enough time from their conventional teaching. The plans in France were to train teachers, including those in higher education, during an intensive 50-hour course in such a way 'that the normal routine of the school is not interrupted'. It was estimated that by 1986 'nearly a quarter of all teachers at schools and universities had received an introduction to computing and the practical use of hardware and programs' (Plomp *et al.* 1987).

Developing computer-based materials for the primary curriculum presents several difficulties. Teachers must be involved but require time away from the classroom, and (usually) technical support for program design and coding. Even then, software needs evaluation trials, and arrangements have to be made for its publication (with copyright) and its continuing maintenance. The process can be complex and expensive, and is unlikely to be economically self-sustaining. These problems were not overcome satisfactorily by MEP, although the primary domain had some success and a national curriculum group was established in mathematics. Dissemination of materials and information about programs is still not satisfactory. In the UK most local authorities have teacher centres where software can be examined; some maintain databases of published materials and collect opinion on the suitability of programs in the classroom. However, licensing arrangements between publishers and local authorities are still the exception rather than the rule and, although communication networks are becoming available within individual authorities and nationwide, the cost/benefits ratio is judged too high. Hence the take-up and utilisation, though growing, are still relatively low.

France has taken a more organised and directed approach. Curriculum/programming teams have been formed in liaison with distributors, and education authorities commission projects (avoiding duplication) that make their materials available to the public sector. A National Courseware Library is maintained, providing on-line access to a database. Schools are offered a points chequebook, which can be used for buying any program in the national catalogue. This points system 'enables the Ministry of Education to make a bulk purchase of programs at a very advantageous price and re-sell them on a preferential basis without being obliged to state the real cost' (Plomp *et al.* 1987).

In contrast to the UK and France, most European countries have adopted a more cautious model of innovation. They have targeted resources into chosen pilot projects, and developed those that are successful into larger-scale demonstrators whose methods and materials can then be disseminated more widely. This approach is more restrictive but directs its efforts at those institutions and teachers who are prepared to make a commitment to the work. Although progress quickly outdates any survey of achievements, a useful European synopsis up to 1986 is given by Plomp *et al.* (1987, pp. 103–56).

The Netherlands is concentrating on initial and in-service training, with three teachers from each school engaged in projects that are funded until 1989. Developments at the primary level focus on methods of using learning environments (LOGO) and software tools (e.g. wordprocessing). LOGO-like systems have also featured in the primary school projects of Italy,

Luxembourg, Spain and Portugal. In general, primary education attracts less interest and funding in the national schemes, and research and educational institutes play a larger part in directing the work (e.g. the MINERVA Project involving 40 primary schools in Portugal, with five centres managing the work; and the five-year ATENEA initiative in Spain, with 100 primary schools being co-ordinated from a national centre set up at the City University Madrid). Germany, with its devolved regional control, is encouraging information technology across the primary curriculum, with software houses, publishers and teachers' groups producing materials following recommended design standards. Denmark has the difficulty that the school market is not big enough to attract publishers into software development; also most teachers have not enough technical experience to easily ensure that their materials are up to publishers' standards. Therefore, the projects have given more attention to the use and development of open software, such as simulation packages, databases and educational programming languages.

In summary, curriculum developments in mathematics are following broadly similar themes throughout Europe, though their emphases and methods are different depending on national administrative structures and perceived needs. The role of the computer and its innovatory influence within primary mathematics, and across the curriculum, is only in its formative stages. Many useful ideas are available, but they need working out in an organised and examined fashion. The initial prerequisites must include adequate access to computers/software and, above all, systematic programmes of in-service and initial teacher training.

Acknowledgements

The author acknowledges helpful discussions with Malcolm Byard during the preparation of this chapter.

CHAPTER 3.2

Science and Technology

Joss Elstgeest

1. Children *must* do science

Children are born into a material world. They belong to it, and they depend on it for their livelihood. It is in their nature to try and find a footing in this world. They orient themselves by attempting to make sense of it all and by figuring out how things fit together. Dominating features and recurring events become 'landmarks' to aid this orientation, so that the children can accommodate themselves among their varied fellow creatures, living as well as non-living, and come to terms with the powers and forces that control them. Like every human being they look for relationships, connections, explanations, re-assurance and familiarity. This universal human trend may be the basis of their endless curiosity, but it is, after all, a matter of survival. And children do survive, partly because they grow up in the protecting company of caring adults, and partly because of their attempts to master their world by understanding.

A combination of these external influences and the urge to conquer from within, through a stimulating education, will certainly advance a child's chances not only of survival, but also of controlling, with insight and wisdom, their own interaction with the surrounding world. Part of this good education consists of fertile teaching that brings out the best in each child – independent thinking and self-reliance through the confident use of one's own intellectual faculties and resources.

Although these paragraphs summarise the goal of all good education, they have a particular bearing on the rationale for science education in school, because this is directly concerned with the workings of living and non-living nature. We shall endeavour to describe how good science teaching to young children is a form of education that enables them to bring order into the multitude of impressions that assail them in their daily existence. Science education should start early and introduce children to an orderly process of learning from and about the world in which they are growing up.

'The world in which they grow up' must be on the scale of the children's perception: its boundaries are confined to the familiar environment in which the children play, skip and run around, in which they hide and seek, in which they are given food, and which they share with family, school and friends. Whatever lies beyond these bounds is of no interest to the child until it comes into their view on account of their expanding horizons, or when it is consciously perceived after being brought deliberately into their world by parents, by teachers, by books, or by other media. 'Learning about' implies forming and retaining concepts and ideas that are then used to build up knowledge and understanding by linking these into appropriate relationships with each other and with already existing ideas. 'Learning from' indicates that this knowledge comes about through direct interaction with the reality of things, through encounter and 'dialogue' which is the suitable application of scientific process skills.

According to David Hawkins (1965), we can distinguish three active elements in education which ought to be in constant interaction with each other in a triangular fashion:

1. There is the child who, full of wonder and query, interacts with the things s/he encounters and is confronted with and that are sometimes identified with 'subject matter'. At the same time this child also interacts with the teacher who subtly intervenes whenever there is a need to do so.
2. There is the teacher, also with an ever-inquiring mind, who approaches the object under study (subject matter) with the confidence, not of omniscience, but of knowing one's way about. Thus the good teacher is able to guide children on their path to knowledge by asking the right question at the right time, by indicating relationships that the children, if left to themselves, might well overlook.
3. There is the 'subject matter', which in science is always a distinct component of the child's physical world. It may fascinate the child by its own intrinsic challenge, or the teacher will manage to introduce it as a matter of immediate and real interest.

This tripartite interaction is the essence of teaching. Letting children mess about for ever may lead to a very enjoyable interaction between children and learning matter; the matter of learning, however, is likely to remain questionable. A well-timed intervention by the teacher not only sanctions a certain amount of 'messing about' as a means of getting to know new and unfamiliar materials, but also raises the spontaneous exploration to purposeful investigation (Hawkins 1974).

The teacher, on the other hand, who leaves out the lively encounter with the reality of things, and looks upon such activity as a burden, may lecture pupils with wise words till he is hoarse in the throat and red in the face, but this one-way interaction with children may well become for them a boring experience, and leave their learning equally incomplete.

It is a proper balance between the children, the things of science, the acquainting interaction, the concept-forming 'dialogue' and the timely intervention by the teacher which creates the admirable atmosphere within the classroom that results in learning in the children's minds so that teaching and learning go naturally together.

2. Watching some classes of children

I attended a lesson on 'changes and the agents that cause them' in a top class of a primary school. Questions such as why sugar dissolved in water and why old milk turned sour, had been raised, and at a certain point the groups of children were given the famous ball and ring apparatus with which William Jacob Gravesande nonplussed his audience many years before. The class was to perform 'the experiment on thermal expansion'. The teacher lit the burners on the tables, and in each group one child was to hold the ball over the burner after having ascertained that the ball slipped through the ring, held by another child. The rest of the group looked on. When the teacher considered the balls to be heated sufficiently, the children were told to put the balls through the rings once more. They stuck of course, as they should, and the teacher asked the children. 'What have you observed?' And the children dutifully answered: 'We see that the ball has expanded, sir.' 'Good,' responded the master, 'repeat your experiment.'

There was little to repeat: the balls had not yet cooled enough to fall through the rings and, anyway, to what purposes should they 'repeat the experiment'? There was no problem left: the balls did what they were supposed to do. There were no lingering doubts in the minds of the children which could have been resolved by repeating the experiment. In fact there was nothing left to experiment about! So, the teacher told them to cool their balls in water and slip them through the rings once more, but even that was no real experiment.

No child had seen the ball expanding. What they had seen, but did not say, was that the ball would not pass through the ring. Confronting the children with a phenomenon like a ball behaving oddly after being heated is a perfect way of starting a scientific discussion:

- What exactly did you do with the ball?
- What did you do with the ring?
- How long must the ball be heated before it gets stuck?
- What happens if you heat the ball and the ring?
- What do you think has happened to the ball after heating?
- How could you get it to pass through the ring again?
- Would an unheated ball pass through a ring that has been very much cooled in the freezer?
- Would you be able to measure the ball before and after heating, other than by means of the ring (. . . which is a gauge, after all)?

Questions like these not only start a discussion, but also stimulate further action: more refined and purposeful interaction with the ball and the ring and the heat. That is what is meant by the 'teacher's interaction with the things at hand and with the children', complementing the interaction between children and things, and thus closing the triangular relationship.

The same teacher had also set up a distilling apparatus for this lesson. It was an impressive-looking vessel, of copper, and because it would take quite some time before anything happened the teacher had previously lit the heat source, and then ignored what was happening for the time being. Just about the time that the children were engaged with their ball and ring activity, the 'thing' began hissing, and the teacher had to pay attention to the process of distillation. This demonstration was to show the double change, water into steam, and steam reverting to water once more. Alas, although the copper thing looked impressive the children could see neither the water nor steam. The only thing visible was a slow lazy drop of water forming at the tip of the spout, and leisurely dripping into a tiny beaker. Although this 'experiment' was intended to crown the lesson, it passed the children by because they were busy slipping balls through rings. There was no reaction from the children, for a slowly dripping spout in front of the classroom draws very little attention. Neither did the teacher interact with children. Although he showed a lively interaction with the still, and attempted to explain to the class the unseen mysteries of the still's heated innards, the children were more impressed by the things they could handle. In this lesson the balance between the teacher, pupils and the materials was upset, which was a pity, for the teacher had obviously prepared this lesson well and deserved better results.

In another class, the children had been working with solutions and during the lesson I attended they were introduced to the idea of saturation. The children were given sufficient equipment to work with, and they worked in six groups. The aim of the lesson was stated as 'Accuracy and reliability in experimenting', indicating that the exercise of a scientific process skill was to lead to some insight into the saturation of a solution. The problem, as it was presented to the children, was written like this: 'Saturation. How many spoonfuls of salt dissolve in a glass of water?'

There was, of course, no way of finding an answer than by the children doing an experiment. Without any encouragement the children raised the problem that not all 'glassfuls' of water contained the same amount. They began a discussion about how to make sure that everybody would use the same amount of salt in the same amount of water. They agreed to use one measure of water and to pour that into each glass. Next they agreed that a 'spoonful' should be a level spoonful of salt.

Next the teacher asked: 'What do you expect if we all carefully stick to these rules? Would each group get the same result?' 'Naturally!' the class exclaimed, and the children set about measuring the water and adding level spoonfuls of salt until no more salt would dissolve. After a while the results were recorded on the blackboard. They were, to say the least, a little surprising.

Group 1: 4 spoonfuls
Group 2: 10 spoonfuls

Group 3: 6 spoonfuls
Group 4: 8 spoonfuls
Group 5: 9 spoonfuls
Group 6: 7 spoonfuls.

These results were not all the same, and the children were disappointed. They had all done the same thing, used the same measurements, and yet got vastly differing answers. 'Did you do the same thing and did you use the same measures?' asked the teacher, 'Let us discuss this'. Another lively discussion followed. It appeared that group 1 had used a bigger spoon than the others. Group 3 had much finer salt than all the rest (they had brought salt from home to school with them). Group 2 had counted the spoonful of salt that brought the solution to its saturation point, which the others had discounted. And, finally, group 5 had stirred the water with same spoon with which they added salt. It had made their salt moist and sticky so that, on levelling it, they pushed more salt off their spoon than they should.

Now there was a good reason for repeating the experiment. The discussion at the beginning of the lesson had taken into account the more obvious variables; the less obvious ones came to light during the activity. There is no better way of learning to appreciate variables (or to recognise them in the first place) than by experiencing their effects. I liked this lesson very much, because the triple interaction was in steady balance. The unreliable results of the interaction between the children and the solutions were turned into a powerful lesson by the teacher who was interacting with both – the children and the unsatisfactory situation.

The lessons that I have just described do not just show the relationship of the tripartite interaction of the child's world and the teacher. They occurred in an ordinary school, on an ordinary day, and were not specially set up for my benefit. They were part of an existing curriculum, performed by a regular teacher, and they had nothing to do with any particular development project. Therefore these lessons may also be regarded as illustrations of the ways 'new trends in primary science' can gain a foothold within the existing school tradition, with varying measures of success.

More and more teachers, provided they are given the necessary encouragement, are moving away from purely factual instruction and dry rote learning towards a greater involvement of the children in a 'do-it-yourself' approach to science. These trends are also penetrating the consciousness of people to whom teachers are held accountable – the parents of the children, the school/inspectors, and even the policy-making authorities. National politicians wielding educational batons tend to totter along the line between 'back to basics' and 'basics first', for in educational politics sense and nonsense are not always identical. This political dimension accounts for the significant differences between the way science is taught in various countries. At primary level, the development of science education is more quickly achieved in the 'creative' minds of educational progressives than in the reality of the primary classroom, where busy teachers have to accomplish this work while coping with many other varied demands.

3. New trends in primary school science

The 'new trends in primary school science education' are, however, no longer all that new. These trends were set during the early 1960s when, almost simultaneously in several countries, well-funded new science programmes appeared on the educational scene, causing significant perturbations to ripple around the world. Some people now suggest that this was a reaction in the West to some technological *tour de force* perpetrated by the other side of the cold war front, but that would be too simple an explanation for the sudden spate of research and development programmes in science education at secondary level and, a little later, also at primary level.

These whispering tongues, though, had a point, even if we reject the idea that the source of this development was called 'Sputnik'. The Second World War caused a gigantic leap in technological progress, unleashing unknown and unfamiliar forces and power. As a result, the demand for technical and scientific personnel with high qualifications became very great. The educational system could not keep pace with the technological and scientific strides made by post-war industry. Yet the application for peaceful uses of the many new inventions, and the investigation of possibilities, needed prompt attention.

It was also felt in many countries that the high levels of specialisation isolated scientists from the community. There developed a lack of understanding, or too much misunderstanding among the populace of what science and technology was about. This created a widening communication gap between the scientists and the majority of non-scientists among their fellow citizens. This in itself could threaten scientific progress, as most of the political decision and policy makers were and still are non-scientists. However, apart from these considerations, scientists, because they are human, share the common urge to talk about what occupies their mind, what keeps them busy and justifies their existence. Lack of sensible dialogue threatened to curb this urge to communicate, and a new educational aim was therefore formulated for all who attended school: the goal of scientific literacy.

Scientific literacy is broader than scientific understanding. Nobody can hope to know all that human scientific endeavour has revealed and continues to unveil day after day. Nobody can hope to find out by themselves even a tiny fraction of the vast complexities that make up our universe. Personal experience will never be sufficient to learn what everyone needs to know in order to maintain themselves in our diversified technological society. We need the results of the scientific work done by others.

Providing children with a structure of abstract generalisations, to be learned by rote and unrelated to the children's experience (as older textbooks tended to encourage), was seen as vain and useless. Children should, it was argued, be given many broadly selected concrete experiences to provide a basis for (later) generalisation and understanding. Nevertheless, these scientific 'basics' would be insufficient, too, if they were not fitted within a context of a growing conceptual framework. Basic and diversified experience, together with the subsequent formation or adjustment of concepts, build upon this conceptual framework. Future experiences could then be accommodated within this scheme, as could other ideas encountered through written or spoken communication.

Scientific literacy, therefore, is knowing how to find one's way around the world of scientific discovery and technological achievement. An individual does not have to master the details, but needs to follow and appreciate the bold lines of the process of inquiry as well as of the outcomes of the scientific toils of others (Karplus 1964). In other words, scientific literacy enables people (and children in increasing measure) to benefit from scientific literature, texts and books because they have learned, and are learning better, to interpret what they read in the context of a broad conceptual framework built up out of their experiences and enlightened by good teaching.

The 'enlightenment by good teaching' is, of course, what the programmes of innovative science teaching were concerned with in their various approaches. This takes us back to the tripartite interaction between the child and their world (experience) and the teacher who selects or pinpoints and provides guidance on the subject matter, interacting with it and the children. The good teacher encourages or initiates purposes, relationships, explaining connections, clarifying problems and indicating ways towards solutions. In doing so the teacher will also refer to others who have grappled with similar problems and who have communicated their way of finding an answer.

This reference to others, however, need not apply solely to textbooks and scientific monographs written by established scientists. Literacy is not exclusively passive. A literate person knows how to communicate with others in discussion as well as in reporting. When children report and discuss their experiences, experiments and findings, however simple they are, by word of mouth and demonstration as well as in writing and display, then they practise literacy. This communicative aspect of scientific literacy deserves, therefore, a high priority in science lessons.

There was during the late 1960s a certain amount of dissatisfaction with the state of affairs in schools – the textbooks used, the equipment available and the didactic approach to science in pre-university teaching. This led originally to an overhaul of secondary school curricula where strong emphasis was placed on greater student involvement in the laboratory in genuine scientific activity. In many ways, however, this was reduced to the scientific process of collecting and preserving information knowledge. Series of selected, well spun out, carefully graded, but genuinely scientific laboratory exercises, observations and experiments, requiring a high degree of accuracy, alternated with the introduction of sound texts and theory around broad concepts of science in a particular discipline. This was characteristic of the pioneering secondary school curricula in the United States as well as in the United Kingdom.

It was, however, correctly argued that children coming up to secondary schools were not starting with a blank educational sheet, and that it would make sense to begin an innovative programme of science education in the primary schools. Thus the quest for a suitable primary science curriculum was started. The 'practical involvement' of children in the processes of science had already become the guiding principle of innovative science education at secondary level and it was taken also as the basis for primary science. Prevailing theories on how children learn and develop intellectually had a strong influence on the shape of the various new didactic approaches. It is difficult to establish who took the lead in primary science innovation, as chronology is not necessarily the best measure of influence. By the time the general public became aware of what was happening, a number of projects or programmes were operating simultaneously, each having considerable influence on each other.

It is beyond the scope of this chapter to enumerate and comment upon the many serious attempts at primary science curriculum development since the 1960s. A few of the most influential programmes should be mentioned as they are now regarded as trendsetters. Famous names, like Gagne, Bruner and Piaget, were associated with these pioneering programmes, not just to lend them prestige but to help place them within recognisable theoretical perspectives.

Gagne's theories, for example, shaped the programme sponsored by the American Association for the Advancement of Science, which was known as 'Science – A Process Approach'. This emphasised introducing children to the processes of science as a way of arriving at the facts of science.

The Science Curriculum Improvement Study of the University of California, Berkeley, was based upon Bruner's (1966) hypothesis 'that any subject can be taught effectively in some intellectually honest form to any child at any stage of development'. The material coupled active involvement with things to be handled with broad scientific concepts or generalisations, thereby placing a child's scientific experiences into a unifying intellectual perspective or broad conceptual framework.

The Elementary Science Study (ESS) of the Education Development Center, Newton, Massachusetts, approached the world of direct experience of children in a very open-ended way. Selecting 'tempting' topics of science and presenting them in the form of attractive little packages, called 'units', it left the options for further elaboration open to the awakened interest of the children together with their teacher. Jean Piaget may be considered the theoretical 'godfather' of ESS's way of working, which also served as a model for another large-scale project: the African Primary Science Program. An approach similar to the Elementary Science Study was meanwhile being developed in Great Britain as Nuffield Junior Science. It too had a direct influence on the form and the philosophy of the African Primary Science Program (Richmond 1971).

These trendsetters have, to some extent, shaped people's thinking about primary science throughout the world. As an illustration of how fundamentally different the science activities and their effects upon children can be in a science lesson within this newer tradition, as compared to the situation that preceded it, I will relate the following story. It is a small episode from the African Primary Science Program, far removed, perhaps, from the European landscape, but all the more revealing for its delightful simplicity of a child interacting with a plain, common little creature.

It happened in the fifth class of the primary school of Kirakala, a small settlement in the neighbourhood of Morogoro, in Tanzania. The children were studying antlions. Antlions are very common in tropical lands. They are the larvae of a fascinating flying insect that you hardly ever see, for it is nocturnal. The larvae, however, live all round in loose sand or soil, in which they make conical pits of a few centimeters in diameter. Unaware ants often stumble over the edge and slither down to the bottom when they lose their foothold on the dry slope. At the bottom of the pit the antlion larva awaits them, pierces them with fearsome pincers, sucks them empty and discards the useless shells over the edge so as not to clutter up its trap and home. To children these larvae, which do not look like worms but like proper wingless insects, are completely harmless. Because they are hardy, sturdy, clean and safe, they can easily be handled by children, and so they form a perfect object for direct observation of their behaviour, and for careful experimentation.

A little boy in the class had kept an antlion in a tin, and had looked after it well, giving it a generous daily ration of fresh ants. One morning during their lesson the children started to shake out their antlions in order to continue their explorations and investigations, and so did the boy. Out of his tin, however, there rolled a sandy little ball, but no larva. However carefully he searched his tin, there was no antlion there. The boy was rather upset and called his teacher. She had never seen anything like it before, and she had no idea what the sandy ball was, or where it came from. The teacher and her children guessed that it was an egg sack, and the little boy and his mates decided to leave it alone and see what would happen. But this did not solve the mystery of the missing antlion!

After a day or two the boy could not stand it any longer, he had to check one way or another. Perhaps he suspected that the answer might be found within the egg sack, so he carefully opened his sandy ball, which appeared to have an inner lining of white silk. To his delight, and that of the whole class, there were no eggs inside it, but in the silken shroud lay his vanished antlion. But it had changed. It looked strange, longer, thinner, and had little stubs on its back that looked like folded-up wings. It wiggled its tail end. The little boy put it gently back into the tin with sand, but kept it lightly covered so it could not escape once more.

Now the whole class was off on a new line of research. They started feeding their antlions more than before and, sure enough, soon there were more balls all over the place. Within a short time, starting with the first one of the little boy, adult antlions emerged from what now were revealed to be pupae. The adult creature had an elongated abdomen and transparent, gauzy wings, and flew with a silent fluttering flight, to the delight and wonder of the children as well as of their teacher.

The mystery of a creation, a metamorphosis, a coming into being, unfolded itself here in front of the children in a natural, unsophisticated manner. They did not fathom the mystery, but they were confronted with the reality of it, and it fascinated them immensely. They were very deeply and very personally involved in the event. Granted, there was an element of luck, of chance, but there was also the regularity of a pattern of development: larvae do turn into adults. The reaction of the teacher – 'perhaps it is an egg sack. Keep it, and watch what happens' – had been a blessing, for now the discovery, the revelation, belonged to the children. Teaching and learning melted together here. Who would prefer the older style of teaching requiring pupils to remember an encyclopaedic smattering of words like thorax, abdomen, antennae and appendages from books that took up all the space on our desks, in contrast to the exciting study of real living things?

4. Primary science in Europe

Within the Council of Europe, ministries, institutes, departments and schools of education have all engaged in adopting, adapting or developing teaching materials and curricula for primary science education based upon these ideas. From the easternmost fringe of Europe in Cyprus to the extreme western shores of the United Kingdom and Ireland, teachers are being made fully aware of the need for good and sound child-worthy science education. Everywhere there is greater appreciation of the innovative nature of these new active child-centred approaches. Thankfully no attempt has been made to assemble a universal curriculum, but there is much dynamism, much exchange of ideas and experiences and useful lessons have been learned as the results of evaluation research in different countries become more available.

The vagueness of the early formulations of goals and aims such as 'to imbue the child with a spirit of enquiry' or 'to educate the children towards a greater self-reliance in thinking and problem solving' has narrowed to clearer and more manageable objectives. A good example of a well-considered scheme is to be found in the United Kingdom project 'Science 5/13', which had an accompanying booklet entitled *With objectives in mind* (Ennever and Harlen 1972). The particular merit of this project is that it developed teaching and learning materials with children in schools around these stated objectives. Not only were the general objectives of process-based science education carefully formulated but immediate objectives for every detailed activity were also clearly stated. Because the objectives were identified with the involvement of the children, their value could be assessed immediately. This evaluation being part of the project could then lead to improvement and refinement in the formulation of these objectives. The result is a vast array of broad and specific objectives, well ordered and logically arranged for quick and easy reference at the end of each teaching unit. 'Science 5/13' emphasises children's practical work, and its objectives are expressed in terms of skills and attitudes, as well as of ideas (cognitive achievement), in line with stages of intellectual development emerging from the theories of Jean Piaget (Schools Council 1975). The directness of the objectives gives teachers a means of clarifying what they wish to achieve.

At a later date, and of different heredity, are the efforts undertaken in the Netherlands to reform science education in the primary schools. The Dutch Institute for Curriculum Development (SLO 1988) has produced a well thought out scheme of work which, supported by theoretical reasoning and justifications, has been presented to schools under the title of 'Science education in broad outline'. It is the result of an extensive development project in which children and schools from all corners of the country have taken part. The broad outlines safeguard the creativity and initiative of the teacher, who can build up his or her own programme and plan of work. Children are expected to work mostly with real materials and things, and desired skills and attitudes are included in well-stated objectives. Teachers also get the support of a thrice yearly publication full of tips, suggestions, ideas, background articles, reports of class activities and an exchange of correspondence.

On similar lines, but with more direct links to international pioneering programmes like the Elementary Science Study and the African Primary Science Program, teaching and learning materials have been produced by the Regional Pedagogic Centre, Zeeland. These are based on the strategy of 'ask it of the things themselves'. Through operational questions and open-ended suggestions, these source materials offer ways and means of using living and non-living things as real sources of information, for children and teachers alike, thereby requiring both to exercise scientific process skills (Elstgeest 1987).

Over these and similar programmes hangs a 'sword of Damocles' in the form of imposed national minimum requirements produced in the guise of final goals. This threatens to minimise effort, and therefore the effective execution of new primary science programmes. Some schools, as a result, will aim to maximise results in terms of these national goals. However, 'with objectives in mind' is something quite different from 'working towards minimum standards of attainment'. Children have a right to be given the chance of making the most of their opportunities, but with minimum requirements schools may play safe and concentrate on getting as many pupils as possible through the targets rather than encouraging some to undertake work that is in excess of the national standard.

UNESCO, with its powerful influence all over the world, has monitored attempts in many countries to innovate or improve science curricula during the last 20 years. A wealth of information has been collected and made available by international publications such as the 'New Trends Series'. *New Trends in Integrated Science Education*, published in five volumes over the period 1971–8, gives a broad account of all the tests that have been developed, thought about and implemented in primary education throughout many countries. A less descriptive but more practical and explanatory volume entitled *New Trends in Primary School Science Education* was published in 1983 and included several European initiatives in the accounts of innovation.

The Council of Europe, through Project No. 8, has also produced some important ideas concerning the teaching of science and technology at primary level. Although Project No. 8 was much wider in scope and intention, science education was given significant attention <DECS/EGT [87] 23>. The Council established the need for good and sound primary science education. Documents on related activities of the Council bear witness to this awareness. Two important papers that particularly emphasise the need for sound science education are represented in the conclusions of two research workshops, one held in Edinburgh (Scotland) in 1984 <DECS/Rech [84] 58> and another held in Madrid in 1985 <DECS/Rech [85] 61>.

In the context of Project No. 8, a symposium on Science and Technology in the Primary School was held at Cambridge in the United Kingdom during August 1986. The document to emerge from this meeting with the same title as the symposium outlines the background to and the content of the United Kingdom government's policies for science and technology education for the age-group 5–16 in England and Wales. A brief quotation from this report not only characterises the British policy on primary science and technology but also illustrates the implementation of the main trends described in this chapter.

> The policy statement [from the symposium] stressed that science should be part of the education of all pupils of compulsory school age and that, therefore, all children should be properly introduced to it in the primary school. Learning to think scientifically was a crucially important aspect of this introduction. To do this, children needed to be given opportunities to:
>
> - make observations;
> - select observations relevant to their investigations for further study;
> - seek and identify patterns and relate these to patterns perceived earlier;
> - suggest and evaluate explanations of the patterns;
> - design and carry out experiments;
> - communicate and interpret written and other material;
> - handle equipment safely and effectively;
> - use their knowledge in conducting the investigations;
> - bring their knowledge to bear in attempting to solve technological problems. <DECS/EGT [86] 59>

The report further outlines the main conceptual areas of primary science together with some criteria for selecting content.

The general ideas on science education emanating from these specific activities related to Project No. 8 have been summarised by Gerard van den Hoven and Dook Kopmels in an appendix to the Final Report of Project No. 8.

> Science is concerned particularly with increasing children's understanding of the natural world but also of the world as modified by human beings. At the primary stage it seeks to develop skills and competencies associated with science as a process of inquiry....
>
> Links between science and technology are particularly close at the primary school stage, where scientific knowledge and understanding can be harnessed along with other human and material resources to solve realistic practical problems... (van der Hoven and Kopmels 1987)

Discussion at the Cambridge Symposium, as in other gatherings of a similar nature, tended to produce a large measure of agreement concerning the principles of science teaching, while emphasising the difficulties and obstacles of putting these principles into practice. These difficulties are around the observed lack of, and subsequent need for, proper (primary science) teacher training. This problem, of course, is not a new one. The International Council of Scientific Unions through its Committee for the Teaching of Science has also expressed serious concern on this issue. The Sub-Committee for Elementary Science has begun to aim its recent activities towards those responsible for teacher training in order to reach as wide a field of influence as possible among those responsible for providing the training for a new generation of primary science teachers.

Although all European countries have included science and technology education in their curricula, there still remain differences in emphasis. Science and technology topics are often 'hidden' in the more general curriculum, of which the state syllabuses of *Sachunterricht* in various states of the German Federal Republic are a good example (Mayer 1985). Other governments, like the British and the Dutch mentioned earlier, make explicit provision for science and technology in their curricula and confirm it by a definite policy of promotion and support.

Cyprus offers another example of such practice (UNESCO 1988a). A specific basic objective of primary education with respect to science is expressed as follows: 'The proper understanding of the world, through the systematic observation and study of the surrounding natural and social phenomena.' A set of textbooks, developed by the Pedagogical Institute of Cyprus and issued by the Ministry of Education, gives teachers guidance and ideas. Although the texts can be followed strictly, they leave enough scope for alternative topics and/or additional activity. It is stated (in Greek) at the beginning of these books that teachers should regard the processes of science as the most important aspect of primary science education, and that the literal content of the textbooks matters less. The children should reach the content through the process. Learning content by rote is a mistake and not good science education. If the teacher is not able to get through all the content in the textbook, no harm is done as long as the children have *done* science and have undergone the process. A dedicated staff of tutors at the Pedagogical Institute run a regular schedule of seminars for teachers throughout the year in various places throughout the country. These courses are meant to help teachers develop a programme of active science, on an agreed basis of both content and pedagogic approach: a process approach.

5. Some characteristics of the innovative science curriculum

What, then, are the characteristics of the innovative primary science curricula that are finding their way into European schools?

In the first place, children are confronted, more consciously and more consistently, with the physical reality of living and non-living things, with forces that affect them or with events or phenomena that directly involve them. These statements of abstraction must be translated into the reality of a child's hand and eye which can cope with an earthworm, a magnet or a spoonful of salt – things and events occurring in the child's immediate environment. This confrontation is in the nature of a carefully devised 'encounter' where the thing itself can freely interact with the child. Everything, from the fly buzzing up the window-pane to the cloud passing overhead, emits its own challenging message: 'Come and get to know me.' Questions, the ground on which curiosity feeds, emerge from the interaction between the real thing and the child. Whatever catches the attention or interest of a child provokes some question: 'What is it?' 'What can it do?' 'What does it feel like?' 'What can I do with it?' (Elstgeest 1985).

The reaction to this stimulus is more than just curiosity: active exploration is the normal reaction. Exploration is a 'getting to know you' activity aiming at a more than superficial acquaintance. Exploration is still open-ended, which means that it keeps detailed options open. When children explore something, they want to know 'everything' about it; they just start finding out about it and see how far they get. Often they do end up with some information, but also with a number of questions. When such a question or problem becomes acute, when some unknown detail becomes important, then the exploration may turn into an investigation. That is the point where it can become science. That is the point where science education brings order and discipline into the learning process. That is, therefore, the point where the child learns to exploit scientific process skills so as to approach the problem (the problematic subject) in a scientific way – orderly and systematically.

Children are placed in a problem situation. Instead of being given a solution, they are shown a direction, a way along which they can find the solution, or at least part of it. Where appropriate, helpful information or instruction is provided, or the problem may be related to earlier experiences. The children are thus given the keys with which to discover their world.

The learning activity, the children's science, occurs between the question and its answer: between the problem posed and its solution found. As soon as the answer is obtained or a problem solved, the quest has come to its end and the learning activity stops. In all probability a new question will arise from it, which will call for renewed action and fresh learning, and so the scientific process continues.

It is clear that the emphasis is laid very strongly on the learning and practice of scientific process skills, but we should always remember that learning skills cannot be practised in a vacuum, without learning something, without making knowledge. That 'something' sits at the point where learning and knowing reach out and touch. That 'something' is that with which the child is actively and skilfully occupied, which he is manipulating, with which he has entered into a dialogue, an interaction. That something is nothing less than the flower in his hand, the antlion in his tin, the magnet in his fingers, the storm wind round the building, the willow behind the school, the fish in the pond, the spider in its web, the batteries in the circuit, or the spoonfuls of salt in the glassfuls of water. That 'something' is always close at hand, and very concrete. Children practise their skills on something touchable, visible, feelable, physical; not on our abstractions, like 'nature' or 'magnetism' or 'flora'. They work on things that they can handle. On these they sharpen their intellectual tools during science activities, for they are real and measurable.

What, then, are these process skills?

An essential process skill in science is the skill of raising questions. This sounds superfluous, for where there is no question there is no quest to find out and know. However, having questions is no skill. Formulating them the right way is a skill, for a well-posed question is or indicates the first step toward its answer. A good, scientific, operational question not only invites activity, it also points at what activity will be most appropriate (Elstgeest 1985).

A 'What?' question leads people to observe. Observation is a basic process skill, for it penetrates all scientific activity. By it we consciously absorb information, in direct interaction with the things around, through the senses of sight, smell, sound, touch and taste. Where the questions ask for quality and comparison, the observer zooms in to similarities and differences. Where questions relate to quantities and magnitudes of space and time, the observational skills refine themselves into the skills of measuring, calculating and computing, which in turn call for the skills of manipulating instruments, materials and equipment effectively.

The accumulation of factual information obtained by observational skills often leads to questions that ask for clarification or explanation or insight in specific relationships, like cause and effect. 'How?' and 'Why?' questions are of this nature, and a direct answer is seldom available. Further gathering of information through observation must be selective and carefully organised. The selection will be made on the basis of a hypothesis. Hypothesising is a very special skill in the continuity of the scientific process. It can be circumscribed as 'attempting to explain', which is suggesting reasons for certain events on the basis of previous experiences or on well-founded notions or ideas. A hypothesis is a conditional statement that makes sense, but that also asks for verification. A wild guess, sometimes masquerading as a hypothesis, would end by itself, being unverifiable.

Whereas a straightforward 'What happens if . . . ?' question calls for simple and direct experimentation (Do what comes after 'if'), the hypothesis requires the exercise of yet other skills, namely those of devising and planning experimentation, and carrying out experiments. This, in turn, may evoke the creative skills of designing necessary equipment or setting up experimental situations.

Past experiences, particularly those crystallised in recorded outcomes of investigations, may often be bundled into generalisations, relationships and patterns, making inference beyond actual experience possible. Past experience and conceived patterns reinforce the (time-saving) skill of predicting what the outcome of certain actions, or the concurrence of certain circumstances, will be (Harlen 1985; UNESCO 1988b).

Finally, to give permanence to one's own learning, and to support that of others, the skill of communicating clearly and effectively must have a high priority in science education. Communication, of course, has two faces: the ability to present information so that others understand it, and the ability to understand the information conveyed by others (scientific literacy). The form of communication is manifold: using concise but lucid and unambiguous language; using and interpreting graphs, diagrams, maps, cross-sections and other graphic representations. In the totality of children's education, though, to which science makes such a valuable contribution, the communication goes as far as expressing oneself through the multidimensional means of descriptive prose, of poetry and of pictorial art.

The conciseness of the above description of scientific process skills makes it all look rather abstract. It seems like a tall order for primary children to achieve. However, the art of teaching is characterised by the ability to translate our adult abstractions into concrete activities for children. We do not usually 'observe' with children; but we look and turn over and squeeze and rub. When children match their heartbeat against the time it takes for a candle to extinguish under an inverted jar, they measure time. We seldom 'hypothesise' with children; they 'suppose if'. Anybody who has seen children working with concentration, their brows furrowed, and heard their heated arguing around the evidence they claim to have uncovered, will agree that the best of their science consists of progressing from the question to its answer, and practising any appropriate skill in between. From practising they become skilful; but the teacher must make them practise.

Process-based science education obviously requires skilful teachers who have themselves been exposed to process-based learning. The experience of learning from sources other than a teacher or a book, the analysis of one's own work and progress through process-based learning, the realisation of having genuinely grasped some content by practising scientific skills, may provide teachers with enough confidence to carry over their learning through scientific processes to their teaching of children. This has implications for teacher training (UNESCO 1985).

6. Technology in the primary school

Lastly I would like to add some notes on 'technology' in the primary school. Science and technology tend to be mentioned in one breath, particularly there where 'something useful' is given priority in curriculum making. 'Technology' is, of course, a somewhat heavy proposition for young children, but 'something useful' is not. A main distinction between science and technology is that science is concerned with understanding things, while technology is related to making effective use of things (Harlen and Tanuputra 1985). Solving problems in science hopefully leads to (better) understanding, while solving problems in technology hopefully leads to meeting some (immediate) need. Children can use a thermometer (technology) long before they understand that it works through thermal expansion (science). Children can weigh and measure with balances (technology) before they make a problem of how the balance works (science). Yet, having worked out 'the rule of the balance' (science), may well enable children to make more accurate use of it (technology) so that they can tackle new scientific problems. The little boy I saw sitting under his desk and using two mirrors in order to keep an eye on his teacher's movements had in fact solved a technological problem by 'inventing' the rudiments of the periscope. His classmate, who wanted to know if sunlight reflected from a mirror through a magnifying glass would heat a piece of paper sufficiently for it to catch fire, tackled a scientific problem, although its technology might be put to later use.

Even though there is a clear distinction of purpose between science and technology, even in primary classes, both are learned through activity, through working with materials, and by the exercise of appropriate skills. Besides, science and technology interact towards mutual improvement. If they do not fit within the same breath, they certainly do fit within the same curriculum, where a balance between the need to understand and the need to do 'something useful' is kept on the lines of the children's interests and the legitimate desires of the community of which the children are a part.

Problem-posing science education and problem-solving learning go together and benefit the creative person in each child. The interplay between the urge to understand and the wish to do something with it feeds this creativity. It is the privilege of the primary school teacher to coax children along the lower reaches of their ascent to wisdom. The teaching of science at the primary school means educating children through the processes of science, and that requires great personal effort, dedication, application and devotion throughout. It is a demanding profession, and teachers deserve all the support that can be given them – a sound teacher education, the opportunity to organise active science classes, sufficient equipment, appropriate materials, and above all: confidence.

CHAPTER 3.3

Literacy

Mogens Jansen

In this chapter importance is attached to viewing literacy in primary education against a background of literacy in society. Moreover, an attempt is made to view the teaching of reading within primary education in the light of the previous experiences of the child and in connection with their subsequent education.

1. When the world was simple and primary education was clear

Two or three generations ago, it was possible to describe quite precisely when it was that children first encountered 'literacy'. Surveys investigating the start of formal schooling contained brief notes describing the child's first six months of education. A reasonable account of the children's initiation into reading was available. Within this framework the roots of literacy were described in such a way that most children in most European countries were included in the survey.

During this same period, however, a society based largely on agriculture and trade was gradually replaced by one based upon industry. This industrial society gradually became dominated by automation, so that what we now call the 'service society' has become typical in most European countries. This service society has given rise to what we might term the 'know-how' society, which is information dominated. Thus the appropriateness of describing the roots of literacy by means of formal surveys analysing the beginnings of formal schooling is now somewhat questionable. The information society is so dominated by literacy that the child's initial meeting with reading now takes place long before the start of formal education.

As early as 1900, it was recognised that 'in studying foreign systems of education we should not forget that the things outside the schools matter even more than the things inside the schools and govern and interpret the things inside'. One practical value of the serious study of foreign systems of education is that it can result in our being better able to study and understand our own. In his scholarly descriptions of education in Denmark, France, Great Britain, the United States of America, the Soviet Union and India, King (1979) substantiates the strength of this approach and supports the analysis that follows.

2. The beginnings of literacy

In her description of *Young fluent readers*, Clark (1976) documented in detail the importance of children's domestic conditions in the development of reading ability. In doing so Clark presented an account of the general information already possessed by teachers experienced in the reception class of the elementary school. The environment of the very young child is of great importance for emergent literacy and thus for primary education in general. The work of Marie Clay (1976), based on familiarity with linguistic and general development of New Zealand and American children, also points in this direction. Clark's (1976) studies were followed up by Danish researchers and exhibited a similar pattern of results.

This body of research, however, has been interpreted differently by theorists and by practitioners. Some have claimed that the results support teaching children to read at the earliest stage possible. In contrast, others have emphasised the importance of the general development of children, arguing that their maturing linguistic development should be well established before a formal reading programme is started.

The first group is often referred to as being 'head start oriented', and it is true that a great deal of research that has been carried out in the United States has been on these lines. However, other countries have adopted similar strategies. The Soviet Union lowered the school age by one year in 1986. The French kindergarten is also very school oriented in comparison with Scandinavian practice. French schools have a common team of teachers for the 3–10-year-old range and a formal curriculum.

Typical examples of the second approach can also be found in the United States, as well as in Scandinavian countries where the tradition of play is maintained as far as possible up to the age of 6. However, there is not necessarily a complete contrast between the view that the prerequisites of literacy are formed very early in the young child on the one hand and the view that a formal education in reading should await the appropriate linguistic and cognitive development of the child on the other.

As far as the majority of the pupils are concerned, the formal learning of reading rests on a systematic reading education based on a reasonably well-developed spoken language, on a conceptual apparatus that is sufficiently broad, according to the age, and gradually on a certain familiarity with written language. The stage of examining the written language – writing words and letters, etc. – is reached by individual children at very different age-levels.

Figure 3.3.1

Children reach a stage when they want to know 'what it says' in the text. A connection with the spoken language is experienced, and differences between spoken and written language can be taught.

The roots of literacy are developed from the day when the child becomes fascinated by the total experience of an adult making the child comfortable, while holding pieces of white paper with black print or colour print, and speaking soft and friendly words. The child may be 13 days or 13 weeks old when this happens for the first time. The familiarity with literacy increases as the child crawls around among model cars, picture books and dolls, experiencing something about the different characteristics of these toys. Some of them move and make noises, some of them are meant to be cuddled, and some are commented on and referred to by adults. This phase in the growing-up of the child and in the development of literacy cannot be ignored. Figure 3.3.1 illustrates not only this phase, but also reading development during the first 10–11 years.

3. How does literacy begin in the information society?

The earlier traditional and often heated discussion in Scandinavian countries concerning the question of whether children ought to have learned their letters before starting school, or whether they should wait until encountering a teacher who was knowledgeable about the best way to teach reading, has now subsided and in some places disappeared altogether. Such discussions have become unimportant because in the present information society the world of the child has undergone rapid change. Naturally the essence of the first steps in learning to read still requires that the child must learn to read letters, words and sentences. However, it is also important for the teacher to ensure when the child is learning letters and single words that these are spontaneously connected with concepts with which the child is already reasonably familiar.

Another reason why the intensity of the debate about when to start reading has declined is the general acknowledgement of the very considerable individual differences of children when they begin school. At the same time it is also generally recognised that when children learn to read they learn more than simply letters and words.

Today most children in Europe grow up with the knowledge of letters and words. They may 'wallow in writing' but still they do not necessarily learn to read. This situation is even worse among the Third World countries where texts are available but there are no teaching materials. Neither do such conditions motivate people to learn to read. To wish to read and write, an individual must learn to connect writing with experience and information as well as with knowledge and instructions. It is necessary to learn that writing gives a more elastic meaning to well-known things and that in other cases it defines more clearly something with which the individual thought they were familiar. In fact, the use of writing in society has become so broad and varied that there is a gap of more than four or five generations in the range of written materials that are available today. For past generations the familiar letters and syllables were taken from the Ten Commandments and the Lord's Prayer, while for the current generation the omnipresent texts of today's advertising boards, TV, newspapers and popular magazines continually influence their lives.

To summarise, the child must learn to enter into co-operation with the written language to understand both form and content and gradually come to terms with writing that is unfamiliar. The reason for this is that it is a well-known paradox that when children begin learning to read, they are not able to read anything which they do not know beforehand and thus do not know what it says in the text. On the other hand, the more well-structured the concepts that the child encounters in the writing and the better the child's knowledge of and familiarity with the spoken language, the better the child is able to acquire knowledge and experience through the written language.

The educational movement that is occasionally referred to as 'governess education' had a prominent European representative in Ragnhild Söderbergh (1977, 1979, 1982, 1986). Söderbergh and other linguistic-oriented researchers have called attention to the desirability and the many possibilities of an early formal reading education. They argue that linguistically well-equipped pupils have always existed and always will exist. The governess tradition is not new and it also builds on other things. Its starting point is to actively 'push' the child into reading using the greatest possible kindness while taking into account all possible knowledge of the individual. As a method it can be very effective, but it presupposes that in the typical school surroundings such instruction is feasible. In practice, such optimal learning conditions are probably rarer than both the researchers and educationalists who support this strategy would like them to be. The main issue is not, therefore, whether reading education takes place in early childhood but whether this education is formal or informal. Furthermore, there are essential questions of what the subject matter of this education should be and when children should first be taught formally by professional teachers.

The answers to such questions as not only 'how' but also 'when' should be considered in the light of the different systems of schooling that exist in different European countries. Some educational systems start formal education rather late. Schooling begins at the age of 6–7 years and the teaching of reading at the age of 7–8 years. Yet these schools 'deliver' 10–11-year-old pupils whose reading standard is not inferior to that of pupils from other education systems starting at the age of 4 or 5. What is even more remarkable is that, in general, the pupils who were late starters subsequently read considerably more than other pupils who began reading earlier. It is difficult, therefore, to give unambiguous answers to the two questions of 'how' and 'when' because the response of the child appears to be dependent on the context in which schooling takes place and its effects on the emotions and the self-image of the child when confronted by the initial difficulty of learning to read. Thus the matter is highly complex and the expectations of the participants must also be allowed for. For these reasons it is difficult to make any firm predictions about the best age at which to begin to learn to read formally.

4. Reading seen in a developmental perspective

From many points of view developmental theories have aided both researchers and teachers in primary education on matters of reading. A useful and interesting starting point is the language experience approach (LEA) developed by Ulrika Leimar and others as a special Swedish-Norwegian approach. From their perspective, conversation, reading aloud and written expression are regarded as 'extroverted' activities. Indeed, almost any form of reading is regarded as an external phenomenon, including starting to read. Using this approach, children learn to read because they know the meaning of the words and are able to read the text in front of them. In this way the concepts of the words they need do not exceed their expressive capability.

Concurrently with this 'reading method' other researchers argue that knowledge and routines must be built up so that reading becomes an internalised function. The educational conflict between these two approaches is a clash not only between different teaching methods but often between different teaching personalities and educational traditions. It is no coincidence that the language experience tradition argues strongly for children's activity, with the use of workshops based upon experience, while the second approach desires primarily to convey experience and knowledge. The first approach is built up strongly around the teacher and the class in a social situation, while the latter method attaches importance to making the child meet the written language and acquire knowledge and experience independently of others as soon as possible. It is also of interest that the language experience approach is strongly based on the American and British 'do-it-yourself' tradition of primary education, while the second method follows the Northern European, particularly the Danish, tradition of placing books for independent reading very centrally in the reading area of the school or the classroom. In practice it is difficult, probably impossible, to maintain a clear distinction between these two approaches to the teaching of reading.

5. The psychology of development relevant to reading

When the reading development of the individual is considered in relation to the ideas of child development held by a number of researchers, the influence of certain psychologists such as Piaget, Vygotsky and Bruner can be clearly seen.

By way of example we can consider Piaget's view that the intellectual development of children takes place in certain stages – the sensorimotor stage, the pre-operational stage and the concrete operational stage. Reading researchers have shown interest in the phase development approach to reading (Chall 1983b, Jansen 1959, Jansen *et al.* 1978, Sundblad *et al.* 1981, Lundberg *et al.* 1988 and Dalby *et al.* 1989 all consider this issue). It is hardly a coincidence that in Europe these views are strongly represented by researchers from the north, as it corresponds closely to the northern tradition outlined earlier. However, researchers other than developmental psychologists have also argued in favour of this approach (Frith 1979; Chapman 1987), as have a great many experienced teachers who have in their work followed the same pupils over a number of years. It is characteristic of this approach that:

- all agree on the need to work with development on different levels,
- all accept the idea of plateaus and all accept there is a rhythm in reading development.

It is also characteristic of this approach that the domestic educational system of the researcher's country is reflected in the developmental stages they propose. The more divided the years of early childhood schooling, the greater the predicted number of stages in reading development. For example, Lundberg's scheme of structuralisation, which draws inspiration from many sources, still corresponds closely to the main structure of the Swedish educational system (the *Fork Scholar*, *Lagstadie*, *Mellanstadie* and *Hogstadie*), while the even more minute gradings of Sundblad and Allard correspond closely to the grades within Swedish schools. Chall's groupings correspond closely with the structure of American schools, and the tradition of testing from one grade to the next appears to have a massive influence on the proposed structure. Chapman's varied divisions, with clear specification of transition stages, are not untypical of the structure of many British school systems. The work of the Danish researchers is generally based on a four-stage division covering the period from early childhood to adulthood and quite closely relates to the educational system. It includes an early childhood stage, prior to compulsory education, and subsequently (like Lundberg, Sunblad and Allard) follows the pattern of the Danish comprehensive school through the early years of youth up to the adult stage. Figure 3.3.2 illustrates this structure as described by Jansen (1988).

It is a common feature, therefore, of any strongly divided educational system that there is a constant need to categorise pupils when moving from one educational stage to the next. Transition procedures are therefore established in order to enable pupils to adapt to the new stage with minimum disruption. Sometimes entrance examinations or failing procedures are introduced into the transfer process. In the Danish educational system there is a long and continuous period of schooling involving the same teachers and without any kind of entrance examination or leaving procedure from the age of 6 to about 16.

Figure 3.3.2

Reading development: ▸	Symbol reader	A Word guessing reader 1st–2nd (3rd) grade	B 'Transition reader' (2nd)–3rd–(4th) grade	C Content reader c.4th grade and up

Examination procedures do not therefore exert any appreciable influence and a fundamentally different developmental process operates. In the Danish system, however, a phenomenon discovered in the 1960s and known as the 'Matthew effect' has been observed (Stanovich 1986, 1988). The 'Matthew effect' reflects a trend whereby the standard of the better pupils improves and the numbers of such pupils increase, while at the same time the numbers of weaker pupils also increase. The trend is illustrated in Figure 3.3.3.

Obviously primary schools would wish to take credit for the fact that the good readers increase in number and that it is not only the very best pupils who improve. At the same time, therefore, it is difficult not to place the responsibility with the primary school for the fact that the number of poor readers also increases throughout the years in primary school. It must be accepted that the 'information society' also exerts an increasingly important influence upon reading performance, not least during the years prior to the beginning of formal education. In cross-national discussions between reading researchers the growth of the 'know-how' society is usually cited as a possible general accelerator behind this 'Matthew effect'. There is every possibility that the number of conceptually and linguistically strong individuals will increase in a society that largely depends upon reading for knowledge.

If this reasoning is sound, then the issues raised by these trends ought to be the subject of serious discussion leading to action, especially in very early childhood and in primary education. Danish studies show, for example (Jansen *et al.* 1987), that the serious damage resulting from the division into two groups of successful and unsuccessful readers seems to be established by the age of 5. At the same time it appears that these differences become fixed by the age of 10 or 11 years. It is difficult to ignore the fact that, as society changes, the 'Matthew effect' seems to increase and to give cause for either satisfaction or worry depending on the particular group of children under investigation.

Chall argues that the transition from primary education to the secondary stage appears to mark the point where most literacy campaigns become ineffective (Chall 1983a). At this transition far too many pupils have not yet reached the stage of functional readers. This is true of primary education in most European societies. It is also true of primary education in developing countries with literacy programmes aimed at adults. From a reading developmental point of view, it is always the transition year where the greatest number

Figure 3.3.3

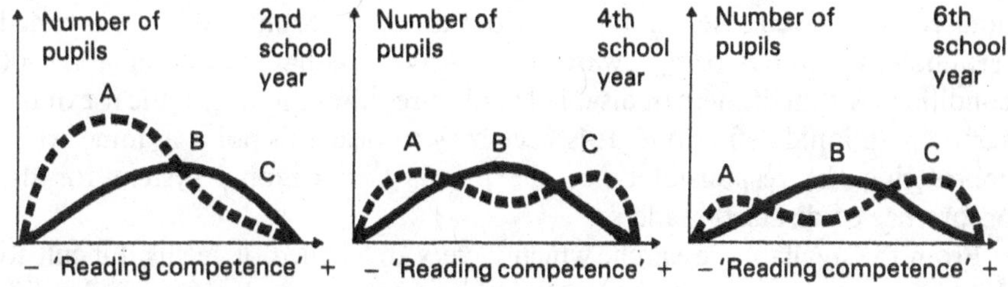

Roughly outlined, the development of reading abilities among Danish children looks like this in grades 2, 4 and 6 – earlier and now.

(1) generally, they read *later* (not 'better' – not 'worse');
(2) they all read *more* (cannot be seen here);
(3) there are *far more* better readers.
(4) there are also some who read *too badly* (are 'reading handicapped').

of difficulties are encountered, irrespective of the age of transfer. The number of highly qualified readers of late youth and adult age seems to be connected with the attitude towards reading established in very early childhood prior to the first attempts to teach reading.

It is not difficult to conclude that, apart from linguistic competence and similar factors, attitudes, motivation and related concepts, although very difficult to test, seem to be important in determining whether groups of pupils will read a lot or very little. At the moment there seems to be too little relevant reading matter of suitable degrees of difficulty for weak readers that might aid their motivation.

6. The disabled reader: a many-sided problem

The pupils on the left side of the distribution shown in Figure 3.3.3 are all disabled readers. A few of them can be diagnosed as alexic. Some of them will probably be characterised as dyslexic, others as reading retarded and some as weak readers. They are all functional illiterates. The terminology used in connection with disabled readers causes problems, especially in comparative research studies on reading. Even in a dictionary of reading produced for an international audience, such as that by Harris and Hodges (1981), the definitions are limited and relate only to the English language. It is true that the book contains an appendix attempting to collate the more general reading definitions in English, French, Spanish, German, Danish and Swedish. The attempt has not been successful. By way of example, the word 'dyslexia' is paralleled with *dyslexie* (French), *dislexia* (Spanish), *Legastheni* (German), *dysleksi*, *ordblindhed* (Danish), and *dalig lasning* (Swedish), respectively. While these translations are not totally incorrect, they are not always used unambiguously. Even research reports from the same country often use varied terminology without being aware of it. Any cross-national comparison of conditions within the field of disabled readers requires the systematic use of the same operational definitions. It is necessary to bear this point in mind when considering the responsibility of the primary educational system for the occurrence of disabled readers.

From the available research, which is very diversified, it seems difficult to deny the occurrence of *dyslexia* when this is defined as decoding difficulties caused by insufficient phonetic development. Hereditary factors play a part in the occurrence of dyslexia, the ratio between boys and girls being often reported as 1:4. In Scandinavia it would be difficult to identify dyslexic pupils before about the age of 8, when their difficulties become obvious on entry to school. Many of these pupils will have learned compensating techniques when discovering earlier that they were not able to read like other children. In countries where formal education is started sooner it may be possible to make a diagnosis at an earlier age.

Pupils who are retarded in their reading have decoding difficulties on all linguistic levels. Irrespective of their country of origin, such pupils are usually referred to as pupils with severe reading difficulties. Hereditary factors are not usually thought to be the main cause of these problems. When this handicap is related to age it is a characteristic of essentially later linguistic development compared to the remainder of the peer group. In Denmark, the diagnosis of a reading retarded pupil is not usually made until after at least two years of formal education.

The reading difficulties of such pupils often seem explainable on a semantic basis. It is rarely a matter of inheritance and it is usually difficult to achieve a precise diagnosis until after a number of years in formal education. All reading disabled pupils will, in most cases, be in mainstream primary education, with the result that their handicaps often cause still more serious problems concerning both reading and behaviour. As other activities are incorporated into the routines of the curriculum, disabled readers generally experience greater stress. Even a subject such as mathematics involves reading examples and is therefore stressful at every level. Manual subjects like woodwork and creative art cause fewer problems depending on the extent to which written instructions are provided. In many countries there are also problems during leisure-time activity which is available in addition to the formal education provided within the system.

There is little doubt that it would be desirable if an early and clear diagnosis could be made for these various forms of reading handicap. However, in this connection diagnosis should be seen more as a hypothesis that provides the opportunity for special education. This special education then helps to determine whether the hypothesis was reasonable. Furthermore, it should not be forgotten that it is the children's current development and not their potential that is being assessed. The risk of an erroneous diagnosis has prevented most teachers and school psychologists from attempting diagnosis at an early stage of primary education, even though there has been no lack of suggestions of methods for carrying out such testing. Vellutino (1987) restricts diagnosis to one area, dyslexia, where, in fact, diagnosis is often superfluous.

Generally, there is no doubt that an information-oriented society based upon reading could well give these problems more attention. For example, in Denmark the National Association for Severely Disabled Readers provides a small yellow card on which is written 'I am word-blind'. This description is used widely in Denmark to designate the most severely disabled readers. The intention is that disabled readers should show the card when they have to fill out papers at public offices such as the post office. Other public services have also written to their employees to the effect that the card should be taken seriously.

7. Awareness of written language

In recent years there have been many references to awareness, with different meanings attached to the concept. It seems difficult to deny that phonological awareness is one of the prerequisites of reading competence. Lundberg, Frost and Petersen (1988) argue that this is especially true of the earliest stages of learning to read. Some researchers who have focused on general linguistic relationships tend to speak more about general linguistic awareness (Downing 1973) and many concentrate their attention on cognitive factors. Similarly, graphic artists and others working with visual aspects of reading (Christiansen *et al.* 1987) speak about visual awareness. Basing their conclusions on experience rather than research they argue that visual factors are essential in learning to read. It appears that pupils who lack visual awareness are not necessarily the same as those with difficulties in relation to linguistic or specific phonological factors.

In the classroom, the teacher has little choice but to use the broadest possible strategy in providing linguistic training and organising the teaching so that a variety of methods is on offer and the majority of pupils are presented with sentences, words and letters that they gradually assimilate and thus learn to read. It goes without saying that when a pupil with specific learning problems is involved then the methods and materials must be evaluated in quite a different way taking into account the specific needs of these pupils as a result of the diagnosis of their difficulty. In order to prevent pupils with various forms of linguistic awareness problem becoming functional illiterates it is important that they are not subjected to the kind of teaching that has the consequences shown in Figure 3.3.4. This gives rise to a vicious circle whereby the reading

Figure 3.3.4

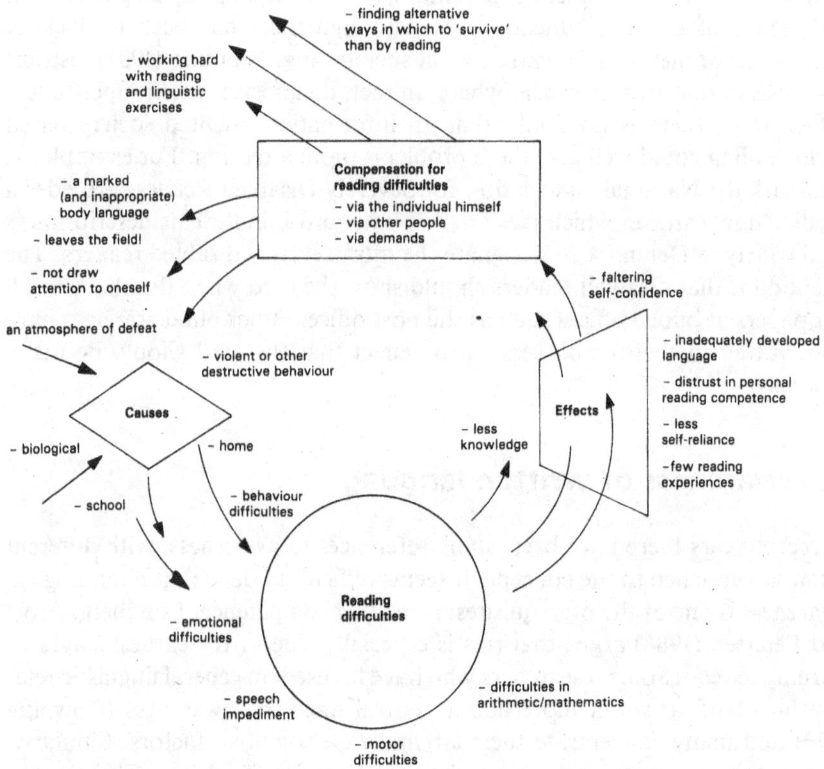

difficulties produce faltering self-confidence, which forces the child to find other ways to survive without reading. The resulting frustration can then develop into violent or destructive behaviour causing emotional difficulties that then act as a barrier inhibiting the effectiveness of any diagnostic reading programme.

Danish, Swedish and Austrian studies repeatedly emphasise that it is important for pupils to read as much as possible as soon as there is a basis that makes possible the teaching of independent reading. In Denmark, at present, this process usually does not take place until relatively late, generally not until a child is 8 or 9 years old. However, the availability of easy independent reading matter from well-stocked libraries situated at the school and near the home no doubt facilitates the pupils' progress in reading. It is particularly important that the teacher should not accept the claim of a pupil that they are uninterested in reading. If this lack of motivation in poor readers is not overcome there is a considerable risk that they will eventually become functional illiterates.

8. The school as an educational laboratory

In primary education of the future, teachers will need to become involved in educational research, the aim of which is literacy development. Such research does not involve classical laboratory experiments and it would be unthinkable and unethical to disadvantage some pupils by placing them in the placebo control group. Fortunately, however, it is possible to simulate a kind of laboratory experiment by looking at different traditions in a number of countries with similar environmental and social backgrounds. If these variables are similar then the educational practices of the different countries concerned can be compared. One obvious example of this procedure concerns the Scandinavian countries. In what follows, the briefest description of the instructional practices in each country is provided, together with the other ways in which reading development, although not presented directly through teaching materials, is made available.

Teaching methods in reading

The same terms, for example 'phonetic method', have different meanings in the different languages and sometimes even within the same language (Heiberg and Crogh 1983). Any comparison of the extent to which a phonetic method is used as against the 'look and say' method is only meaningful, therefore, if the teaching methods represented by these terms are defined extremely precisely and preferably illustrated by means of examples. Even then the reader in a particular country will interpret such accounts more or less using their own definition of reading methods. At one level it is possible to distinguish between phonetic and 'look and say' methods if the terms are defined operationally as follows:

- One method (phonetic) mainly attaches importance to learning sounds and builds upon the introduction of sounds and letters.
- The other method (look and say) mainly presents single words or brief sentences supported by pictures and frequent repetition of the words.

It is, however, one thing to describe the approach of the teacher, but this may be quite different from the experience of the pupil who is being taught to read. This pupil experience may also be very different from the previous experience of pupils when confronted by reading material prior to formal schooling (Jansen 1968).

A further issue to consider is that behind all teaching approaches is a basic educational ideology, which is firmly anchored in a conscious or unconscious view of the nature of man. As Figure 3.3.5 indicates, unlike a machine, which can be programmed to reproduce certain educational routines, individual teachers will always, to some extent, vary a particular teaching method according to their particular educational ideology. Further, this ideological standpoint will be influenced by the teacher's knowledge of linguistic psychology, child development and other aspects of psychology and sociology. In the classroom, however, what we observe when pupils are learning to read is a process of interaction between the children and the adults. It is the outcome of these interactions (which are described by what the pupils are actually observed doing) that, in practice, defines the method by which the children learn to read.

Given these reservations, it is possible to describe the range of different teaching methods used during the first years of formal reading education. Previously it was generally argued that in any given language the smaller the gap between the sound and the letter the more satisfactory it was to use a phonetic method initially. Some researchers also argued that this approach led to relatively fewer reading problems at later stages of schooling. Among the Scandinavian countries the use of the phonetic method would be most appropriate in Finland where the correspondence between the letter and the sound was estimated to be in a ratio of 1:1. Moving from Sweden to Iceland, Norway and Denmark this ratio worsens until in the Danish language, as for English, it is impossible to infer sounds from letters to any extent.

By this analysis it could be expected that fewer reading difficulties would occur in the early years of Finnish education than in Danish. In the 1950s it was claimed that there were almost no reading problems in Finnish-speaking schools in Finland compared to those Finnish schools where Swedish was spoken. However, as better methods of diagnosis became available and as the size of classes became smaller, teachers were able to devote more time to individual children and became better acquainted with their problems. Differences between Finland and Denmark are now far less drastic than they were a generation ago.

For a very long time in Sweden the phonetic method was generally used for beginning reading instruction. In Denmark the method remained dominant primarily in certain parts of the country where the German influence was strong. This was because the southern part of Jutland was adjacent to the German empire from 1864 until 1920 and up to the period between the two world wars it was still possible to trace the German influence, which was sustained by tradition and by the approach adopted in the teacher training colleges. Phonetically oriented texts, which for the most part were also moralising in tone, were often translations or adaptations from German originals. These texts did not disappear completely until the beginning of the 1960s. After 1945, however, theories about the desirability of working with a

Figure 3.3.5

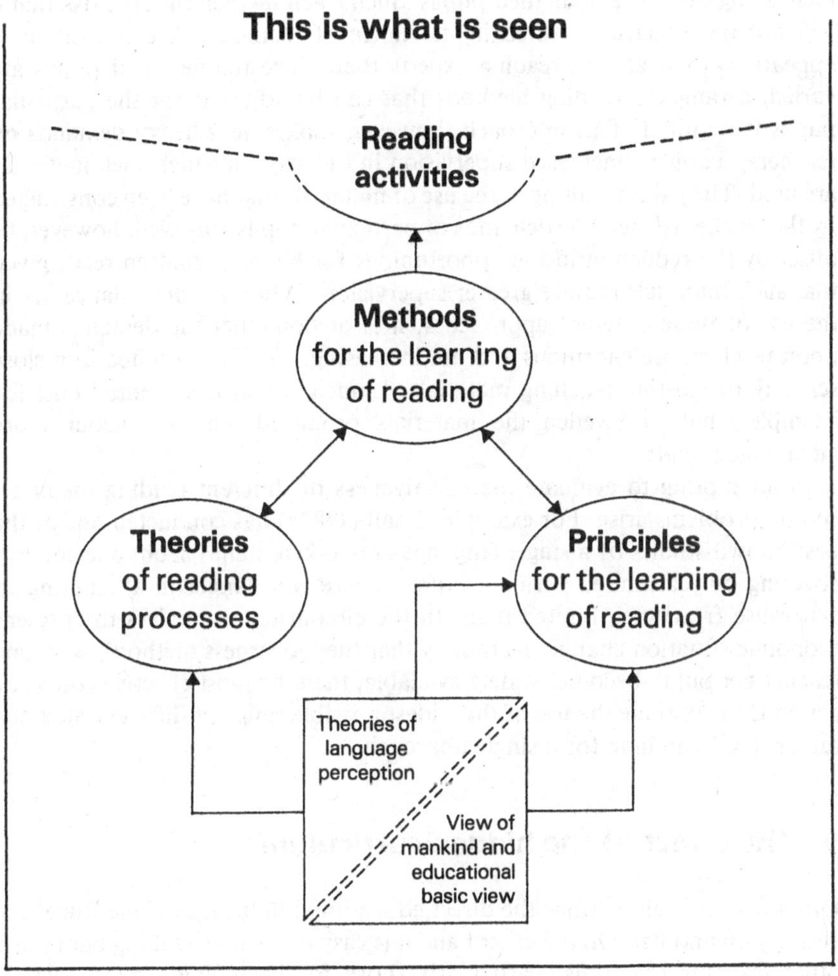

'non-incidental' (i.e. accounted vocabulary) began to permeate most parts of Northern Europe. This influence from the United States and the very strong influence of the English-speaking world in the aftermath of the Second World War stimulated the growth in the 'look and say' method, most particularly in Denmark but also in Sweden and the other Scandinavian countries.

As the style of teaching has shifted towards an activity, topic-centred approach and more of the materials used are produced by teachers, in co-operation with parents and pupils, it becomes more important that the teachers understand the methodology behind particular approaches to reading. Most European countries can testify to the principle that, without the active engagement of pupils with the reading materials, little learning will take place. Without sound knowledge of linguistics the teacher is not capable of identifying the needs of all their pupils. Such teaching then runs the risk that it will not be sufficiently varied in its choice of methods. A consensus now appears to exist among reading experts that, since the needs of pupils are varied, a range of reading methods that can be adjusted for the particular pupils is required. This approach, however, makes very heavy demands on teachers, requiring increased supervision in the ways in which such materials are used. The gains resulting in the use of materials that have been constructed by the teacher to meet the demands of particular pupils may well, however, be offset by the reduction in the opportunities for hearing children read, given that such materials require greater supervision. Wherever the balance lies in the use of these different approaches, it is obvious that the demands made upon teachers are enormous and are increasing. This has resulted in a close scrutiny of existing teaching materials. Lindell (1982) has pointed out, for example, that in Sweden the materials produced tend to favour more advantaged readers.

In attempting to evaluate the effectiveness of different reading methods, certain problems arise. For example, Chall (1983a) has conducted one of the best-known studies of a single language area taken mainly from one country covering only a limited period of time. There is a danger in attempting to generalise from such limited data. In the circumstances, unless the present economic situation changes so rapidly that the 'governess method', with one teacher per pupil, becomes widely available, then the most effective course of action is to continue the use of the widest possible range of different methods rather than searching for a single approach.

9. The effect of the hidden curriculum

Often it is difficult to trace the direct educational influence of one European country on another. On the other hand it is easy to see how reading books and other teaching materials, particularly those for beginning readers, clearly reflect the nature of the society in which they were produced and in which they are used. There are, for example, the rather garish examples of primary texts produced in Nazi Germany. Swedish primers reflect the world of royalistic Swedish society around the First World War, while in British texts there is much relating to the glory and decline of the Empire. Textbooks, in other words, rarely reflect the period when a new era is being established. The books tell of yesterday rather than of today. Such influences also increase towards the top end of the school.

This theme is discussed by Herbert Kingston, the Swedish historian. Kingston argues that, although from our school days we remember history books with three or four names on the title page, a study of these texts shows that the contents of the books can change appreciably from edition to edition. He describes the result of his study of these books as 'bizarre' and notes cases where a change of regime in a country has necessitated a quick revision. For example, he describes a number of Austrian and French textbooks where the recommended form of government (monarchy, democracy, dictatorship) changes from edition to edition without any substantial alteration to the names on the title page.

In Scandinavian countries there have, for many years, been both official and unofficial endeavours to remove nationalistic illustrations, terms and attitudes from textbooks. Originally this concentrated on history books but later was extended to geography texts and then to other subjects. In the aftermath of the Second World War there have been increased efforts by all Western European countries to adopt similar practices.

One way of demonstrating dramatically the national influence on the content of books is to represent the dimensions of each individual country in proportion to the number of pages devoted to each country. When this was done for Danish supplementary primary readers in 1970 (in Denmark the first seven grades), then Denmark was equivalent to the United States and Africa combined. Similar patterns emerged for other countries such as Sweden, Germany and France. From their reading of textbooks, for example, French children might easily gain the view that the map of the world was dominated by France and the then existing French colonies.

Such features of the content of reading texts constitute a hidden agenda that extends beyond issues such as the place of one's country within the remainder of Europe and the world. An increasing number of studies show that texts have built-in biases with respect to gender roles. Even granted that there is now a greater awareness of such matters, reform of textbooks seems to take place very slowly. Other descriptions giving rise to religious, geographical and historical bias also require attention. A detailed study of Danish textbooks (Jansen 1969) concluded that minority groups were presented very infrequently in reading books and that reference to minorities such as the handicapped were almost non-existent. In America, however, the demand for full representation of minority groups according to different sex, colour of skin and age has formally changed the hidden agenda of American readers. At the same time, the large publishing houses agreed informally to prohibit the use of picture stereotyping wherby Southern European-looking North Americans always appeared in the villain's role while Northern European persons usually represented heroes. As a result, life has no doubt become more difficult for illustrators and artists, but whether attitudes have changed as a result of this co-operation on the part of publishers still remains to be seen. The content of the reader is determined by the hidden agenda of the particular society and this factor is particularly influential in books for the primary phase, where the literary contribution is traditionally the weakest part.

10. Mother tongue and other languages

As a result of the migration of groups within Europe, attention has increasingly been focused on the needs of ethnic minorities who settle in other countries. In Sweden, for example, more attention is paid to Turks than to Finnish immigrants living in Sweden who are also attempting to maintain their own language and culture. The curriculum is presented in the official language but the domestic language of many pupils is very different. This phenomenon is not new, but in the last decade many countries where previously such 'foreigners' were almost unknown are now having to face the problems of assimilating ethnic minorities. For hundreds of years, large German-speaking groups have lived in Romania, Hungary and the Ukraine. For many hundreds of years the frontiers between the northern parts of Sweden, Norway and Finland have been inhabited by the Saami who represent a constantly moving element in northern Scandinavia. However, in previous centuries it was never the main objective for a society that everyone should learn to read. Many immigrants of today appear to take a similar attitude.

Among such groups there are likely to be variations of dialect. During their first few years of primary education these children will therefore need to learn to listen to, speak, read, write and understand a language that they may not even be familiar with in any great detail. A clear example of these 'mother tongue' problems can be seen at the frontier between Germany and Denmark. In this area German is the domestic language but the people also learn Danish. Parents wish their children to qualify in both German and Danish and this is made possible within the framework of the educational system where children attend Danish schools. In some cases the situation is more complicated because, although German is the official language, the school is Danish and the language spoken in the home may be either a local dialect or another separate language such as Frisian. Although exceptional, such cases are not altogether rare. Making the transition from mother tongue to a foreign language is not simply a question of learning skills but also involves strong emotions.

Contexts also affect the way in which a language is used. This can be illustrated by reference to the use of Danish in the 1950s. At that time, Danish was the language of the working class in large parts of Schleswig, an area just south of the German–Danish frontier, which meant that speaking the language was not considered very prestigious. In the same decade, however, Danish was the language of the local upper class and of the administration in Greenland. Thus the same language, admittedly with different social influences, functioned very differently in two different places, while in Denmark itself it functioned in yet another way. There are other examples involving the German and Danish languages where differential effects exist as a result of local linguistic conditions. While in both countries attempts are made to secure equality between the different languages, the national and cultural differences still complicate attempts to teach these languages in the primary school. In fact these national and cultural conflicts exert a much greater influence in the debate concerning the way to teach language than do the methodological issues discussed earlier.

11. Mother tongue and formal teaching of foreign languages

Despite the difficulties discussed in the previous section, it is clear that in the foreseeable future literacy competence will include the ability to use at least one other language besides the mother tongue. In the past the need to speak several languages was confined to countries whose language is not used widely. Now, however, it is also becoming more important for the populations in the larger countries such as Germany, France and the English-speaking community.

Mastering a second language is of great value because it provides conceptual variation and a more flexible handling of the world and its ideas. Mastering a second language can be a difficult task and the methodology used in teaching must take into account the age of the pupils. For example, a didactic approach to foreign language would be unacceptable within the tradition of primary schooling that is now established in most countries.

Countries also differ in the importance that they attach to the national language. In France, for example, there is a ministry that attends to the status of the national language, while in Denmark the teaching of Danish has received less attention in proportion to the time given to the acquisition of the languages of neighbouring countries. However, the French model is now becoming more popular among politicians and educators in Denmark, who now want more attention paid to the national language. Nevertheless, much damage has been done, particularly for those citizens who have passed through school in the last twenty years when the authorities reduced the teaching of Danish in schools by as much as 45 per cent.

These variations point once again to the fact that the debate about foreign language teaching, in relation to the mother tongue, brings with it emotional overtones that exert a considerable influence on policy in different countries. Nevertheless, the trend is now for more people to become competent in a foreign language on a functional level. This inevitably leads to the question of how soon the teaching of foreign languages should begin. Here opinions differ, but the general conclusion is that the more time spent on teaching a foreign language the better the results. Even more important, where the ability to speak, read and write in the mother tongue is well established, less time needs to be spent on the foreign language in order to achieve competence. If, therefore, there are sufficient resources, then it is best for foreign language teaching to begin at the earliest opportunity. If, on the other hand, resources are limited, then competence in the mother tongue should be the first priority.

When proficiency in the mother tongue is roughly equivalent to the teaching level in the foreign language, then progress for all but the linguistically able is likely to be slow. While it is easy to find cases, mainly drawn from examples of the expert linguists' own children, of the existence of language mechanisms in early childhood that allow a foreign language to be learned at the same time as the mother tongue by means of simulation and play, it is extremely difficult to generalise about this for the majority of pupils. While a programme of foreign language teaching in the use of grammar in the written language and the development of a wide vocabulary should only be introduced after primary education has been completed, there is no reason why a programme of activities based upon conversation, audio tapes, TV and visits to foreign language speaking areas should not be introduced much earlier.

In summary, therefore, the appropriate policy of foreign language teaching depends primarily on the resources available and the need to avoid damaging the acquisition of the mother tongue language with linguistically weaker pupils. A generation ago it was possible to assess the benefits of introducing foreign language teaching, but now, as foreign language teaching has become more varied and as English becomes well used in many other countries, particularly in Scandinavia, then previous research results will need to be re-evaluated and new studies begun. At the present time, however, it is difficult to argue in favour of an early start to foreign language teaching unless it can be sustained by considerable funds, can be delivered by highly competent teachers and receives strong support on the part of the pupils and their parents.

12. Reading and the new technology

Throughout the entire history of teaching reading the introduction of new materials has always resulted in increased expectations and thence an increase in literacy. Developments in technology therefore are having an influence on reading and on the teaching of reading.

The early stone carvings were comparatively few and were of little practical use. This situation changed with the invention of Roman letters and the use of parchment to transmit instructions around the Empire. The invention of print further improved communication. Martin Luther's 'theses' when posted on the door of the chapel in Wittenberg were, as tradition demanded, written in Latin. They were, however, subsequently printed in German and their message spread like wildfire, thus gaining a larger public than any earlier criticism of the papacy. The use of computers for wordprocessing is a further technical development in the refinement of materials and techniques that have sustained literacy for over 7,000 years. Many other factors have, however, remained unchanged over this period; for example, the use of the alphabet to convey the written word. Nevertheless, technological developments over the last decade have resulted in many changes and further advances may be expected in the next few years.

Despite improved technology, children will still need to grow up in literate societies. Although, for example, it will be possible to transcribe speech directly into print, reading will still need to take place. Children will still have to learn linguistic, audio and visual skills in order to cope with written language and they will still need to develop cognitively in order to understand the content of what they read. Thus children will still need to receive a formal education in school, although during this process they will need to become familiar with a range of techniques that at present are not yet invented. None of this will alter the fact that all children will still have to learn to read.

13. The meaning of illiteracy in Europe of the future

In 1985, it was estimated tht 890 million adults were illiterate, more than a quarter of the total adult world population. These figures should be set against the fact that more than 100 million children between the ages of 6 and 11 did not go to school at all. On this world-wide scale the illiteracy problems in European countries can be thought of as minor ones. If groups of immigrants, the handicapped and the very young age-group are left out of the count, then in most countries the figures for illiterates are negligible. However, while in general terms such minorities can be ignored, this position is unacceptable from the point of view of human rights. Moreover, the issue now is not only that the entire population, above a certain age, should be able to read but that each person should be able to read well enough to function in a society in which reading is now an essential part of everyday life.

Standards that were acceptable in the earlier agricultural and industrialised societies are no longer sufficient in a modern 'information' society. It is now necessary for a person to be able to read and to understand. A minimum requirement is therefore that reading should be of use. Hence the need to introduce the idea of functional literacy, which can be defined in several ways. Gray (1956) argued that a person is 'functionally literate when he has acquired the knowledge and skills in reading and writing which enable him to engage effectively in all those activities in which literacy is normally assumed in his culture or group'. In the following year, however, a UNESCO (1957) report stated that 'literacy is a characteristic acquired by individuals in varying degrees from slightly above none to an indeterminate upper level. Some individuals are more literate or less literate than others but it is really not possible to speak of literate and illiterate persons as two distinct categories'. More recently, Levine (1982) has written that 'it appears that a functional competence in literacy has been defined so that it is merely sufficient to bring its possessor within the reach of bureaucratic modes of communication and authority', while in the United Nations it has been argued that by 1990 the functionally illiterate will usually be able to read but at a level that is inadequate to find a job in a modern society or to participate effectively in increasingly complex societies.

The problem, then, is becoming serious because the demands of society are increasing. Unless a relative growth in reading competence is achieved, these increasing demands will mean a relative reduction in reading competence. Consequently more people will in practice become functional illiterates. In most countries this creates a problem and what happens during primary education is important because it is at this stage that attitudes to reading are shaped. With this in mind, one of UNESCO's aims, which is to do away with illiteracy by the turn of the millennium, has important consequences for primary education in Europe.

There is another reason why Europe should take up the issue of functional illiteracy. In the near future many of these countries will have to accept a large number of immigrants because in the course of the next decade there will be a decline in the population group in active employment. While it is true that at present there is temporary and perhaps continuous unemployment for large numbers of citizens, the decline in the proportion of the indigenous working population will eventually create the necessity for high levels of immigration if senior citizens are to retain their pensions and to live out their lives with dignity. This fact places a huge responsibility upon primary education because it is here that immigrant children, many with a language and a culture unlike the European, will need to be taught to read. These children arrive in schools under considerable risk of being impoverished both linguistically and culturally. The potential of such children is in sharp contrast to those who have the ability to learn two languages and therefore enjoy a rich conceptual world. In the future, the foreign language problems of children of first-generation immigrants may be more serious. Many people are beginning to express concern about these 'second-generation' problems of children with a weak mother tongue and conceptually weak linguistic skills.

Those who regard illiteracy as a socio-cultural phenomenon are probably right when they argue that any 'intervention' will need to take into account the cultural context in which this illiteracy is present. It will not suffice simply to teach these new Europeans to read. They will also need to learn how to use this reading. Ideally the same wide selection of texts ought to be made available as are offered to 'mother tongue' children. However, it is easier to argue for this objective than to achieve it, since not everybody looks at illiteracy in this way. There are those who argue that illiteracy could be eliminated if politicians would agree to do so, while others seem to see the phenomenon as a medical problem, arguing that 'the germs of illiteracy must be wiped out'. From a cultural analysis perspective, however, eliminating illiteracy hardly appears to be as simple as these solutions would suggest.

14. Primary education and the future of reading

Many people, researchers, teachers, journalists and politicians look at the future from two different points of view which are not easily compatible.

Alexis Carrel (1936) warned against the negative consequences of technology and science in modern society. He pointed out that intelligence was becoming dull and character weak. The intellectual elite was not growing in a way that could match the new way of life. 'Nobody has ever asked themselves how to stand the enormous increase of speed in the rhythm of life which is due to the faster means of transportation, the telegraph, the telephone, modern methods of trade, machines, writing and calculating and other people doing all the domestic work of previous days.'

Other people, however, look at the future with the optimism of Jules Verne. During the decades in which a new technology is introduced into the world of reading there are obvious parallels to the fifteenth century. Gutenberg was one of the key people in creating a reading technological turning point that proved to be of great significance for many hundreds of years thereafter, helping also the Catholic Church to achieve spiritual control of the souls of the European people. No doubt, at the time discussions took place in the proper circles as to where the mass production of bibles might lead to. Some people saw the monopoly of the interpretation of the Bible and therefore the control of both souls and literature to be endangered. The consequences of the new technology were unpredictable both to Gutenberg and to the clergy. Printing, as such, was neither bad nor good. It could be used and it could be, and was, abused.

The new technique of printing created limited possibilities of learning for a relatively few people. Only in the last few generations have large numbers in the populations of most European countries been able to read usefully. However, history is now about to repeat itself as we encounter a new technological breakthrough which is having a decisive influence on all our lives. In some countries, television is constantly gaining ground at the expense of reading while in other countries such as Sweden there is still some resistance to this trend (Jönsson 1985; Sonesson 1987). In Denmark, indeed, books have still been gaining ground throughout the years of televison; today the children of Denmark read more than they did a generation ago. The issue of library books is very stable, although tastes change and more textbooks are being borrowed. Schools therefore have a unique opportunity of making each new generation of children, including those from homes where very limited reading takes place, become accustomed to regular reading on a routine basis.

During the last few years, data have been obtained from a number of places in Denmark to the effect that the 'Matthew effect' is not part of nature. The creation of a stable domestic environment together with a well-organised education programme carried out by well-trained teachers seems to be producing readers who continue to develop from the very first beginnings. With such contributing factors as the availability to very young children of books through the public library system, it would appear that the vicious circle of illiteracy can be broken to some degree.

The leisure-time reading of children is, in countries such as Denmark and Austria, far more extensive than the reading done for homework and other reading set by the school. This again can no doubt be attributed to the well-developed school library system and the growth in the number of children's books available in homes. In Denmark and other Scandinavian countries, the systematic use of subtitles on all foreign language television programmes is another contributing factor.

In countries such as the United Kingdom and Denmark, competent spelling is a sign of a sound education, since in both languages it is difficult to spell correctly. In other countries, flawless pronunciation and the use of correct grammar in written language (with the proper placing of accents) is characteristic of a literary elite. In the Scandinavian countries reading has avoided becoming an elitist activity; it is something that everybody must learn to do because everybody needs to use it. It is to be hoped that, for as far as can be seen, this will continue to be the case in the future.

SECTION 4

THE ADAPTATION OF EUROPEAN PRIMARY EDUCATION TO SOCIETY

Introduction

Roger Merry

Section 4 moves away from an examination of curricular issues themselves towards a consideration of some of the external factors that are having major effects on the primary education systems of Europe.

For various reasons, increasing co-operation between home and school has come to be seen as important and desirable, and parental participation is the subject of the first chapter in this Section. Chapter 4.2 turns from the family to a wider social issue that has also been increasingly recognised, to the extent that it should be regarded as part of the actual curriculum – multicultural education and the way it has evolved within the differing traditions of Europe. The next chapter looks at the importance of continuity for children just coming into primary schools and for those about to leave, considering links between the home and the school at one 'end' and links between primary and secondary schools at the other. The final chapter in this Section turns to another area that has been increasingly emphasised over the last few years – the education of children with special educational needs, and the role of 'ordinary' primary schools in meeting such needs.

Clearly, the ways in which any educational system adapts to meet change depend to a great extent on the sorts of factors discussed in the first two Sections – on objectives and philosophy, on demographic trends and social, cultural and technological developments, and on different organisational policies. In spite of the obvious differences between countries, these four chapters indicate some of the common themes that do emerge when one considers how the various primary educational systems are adapting to meet the changing demands of European society.

CHAPTER 4.1

Home–School Relations and Parental Participation

K. Schleicher

1. Introduction

At the primary school level the value of close co-operation between home and school is regarded as indisputable today. Although the nature of the relationship varies across nations, subcultures, socio-economic strata, communities and schools, there has been an overall trend in all European countries since the 1970s to pay more attention to home education and matching home and school education. And this seems to be an irreversible trend, resulting from research insight into the sweeping influence of the home as socialising agent, an overall rise in educational standards of the population and a political re-evaluation of the family.

In the nineteenth century, schools were expected to educate the younger generation beyond parental competences, while parents were responsible for sending their children to school and for their moral upbringing. Generally little interest in home contacts existed with the exception of some educational reformers. In addition, some twentieth-century ideologies and theories favoured state education in order to limit home influence on the children – either to overcome the family as a 'social relic' (as with Soviet socialism in 1918, 1920, 1928) or to reduce 'social stratification' (as with the early Swedish or compensatory education policy) (Liegle 1970). However, not only reform pedagogy in the 1920s pointed to the need to inter-relate children's home, school and environmental experiences. The Soviet Union also reversed its family policy in the face of growing child neglect and juvenile crime in the 1940s and has favoured home–school links since the Second World War. Finally, compensatory education quickly learned in the mid-1960s that co-operation with the home was the most promising way to cope with the socialisation and education of disadvantaged children.

So, although co-operation between home and school had occasionally been favoured in earlier centuries, particularly in periods of social change, there had never been such a unanimous trends towards parental involvement in different countries as over the last two decades. This trend was due to the coincidence of four overlapping factors: first, social unrest linked with demands for 'participatory democracy'; secondly, as a result of widespread secondary education many parents had equivalent academic backgrounds to teachers; thirdly, research results pointed to great family influences on the learning process; and fourthly, a certain disappointment with educational planning was linked with a demand for a more situation-specific teaching method or with accountability. Often all the aspects were inter-related.

On the whole, European countries paid more attention to home education. They developed new organisational frameworks for co-operation and they explored means to cope with the specific social, educational and attitudinal obstacles to co-operation. With regard to educational aspects co-operation has been stressed since the late 1960s:

- to optimise children's education by reducing competitive and conflicting educational goals,
- to make teaching more effective and counteract the schools' retreat from pastoral duties,
- to bring remote subjects more in touch with the child's life experiences,
- to interconnect the school with other socialising settings in society in order to overcome its alienation,
- to stimulate parent education through participatory learning,
- to take changes in the family and school structure into consideration, and
- to facilitate educational reform and/or further democratic involvement.

Through co-operation, educationalists tried to inter-relate the different functions and obligations of home and school, i.e. to amalgamate the educational professionalism, subject competence and educational equality on the part of the schools with home responsibility for the individual child and his or her closer relationships with the neighbourhood.

Depending on different demands and tasks, the forms of co-operation differ considerably. Often they tend to be confirmatory (e.g. supporting school aims), to a certain extent they are compensatory (to make up deficits on both sides), but generally they have to be complementary (e.g. with regard to the overall education process). Such co-operation is all the more important the younger the children are, the more children are challenged by transition from home to school and from one educational level to another, and the stronger educational conflicts are in periods of educational reform or social change.

What is expected from co-operation, how it is organised, its acceptance by home and school and its aims, all depend quite strongly on the different traditions and objectives of co-operation in various countries, on the social context, the legal framework, ideological focuses and the situational demands. Formal discussions about pseudo-participation, partial participation and full participation are often too narrowly oriented towards competition between the participating groups or to administrative and legal aspects of co-operation. Instead the child's well-being and development should really be the central point of departure for choosing between different ways of non-formal and formal co-operation (Paulig 1983).

However, adequate ways and means of co-operation have not yet been fully explored. Instead, most strategies are still to some extent deficient. Sometimes co-operation is too school oriented and learning dominated – respectively too little concerned with a psychologically healthy education or with the matching of educational, cultural, social and ethnic differences between home and school. Sometimes parental participation still leads to too many unnecessary conflicts amongst the participants, or too great cleavages exist between public expectations of and logistic support for co-operation. Thus considerable conceptual and structural improvements are needed: to overcome resistance on the part of the schools (e.g. in view of extra work or inadequate training), to cope with the lack of parental engagement (e.g. because of little self-confidence or interest), and to avoid unnecessary conflicts between home and school (e.g. because of insufficient administrative support or inadequate planning).

It should be considered right from the beginning which old problems and new challenges have really to be met, in order to set the stage for further discussions. On the one hand, research and educational policy have not really come to terms with the following problems:

- To what extent do value and behaviour patterns, which children learn from home, school and environment (including the media), influence one another, and how could – and should – they complement each other?
- How to achieve a community- and child-oriented co-operation, if schools as well as teachers have fewer links with the community, and if curricula are geared towards national policies or demands for 'equal opportunities'?
- Can home–school relations be made an integrative part of subject and didactic studies, if teachers and their trainers discuss co-operation only in a few specialised courses?

On the other hand, new challenges have to be met, for example, in view of the falling birth rate or increasing co-operation in pre-schools (Woodhead 1979; Fowler 1983).

- Since in some countries parents have the right to choose among different schools, shall parents increasingly decide which schools remain open in view of falling rolls?
- What will be the consequences for co-operation if ageing school staff get out of touch with parents who are almost a generation younger, and who might even have been their pupils?
- Can primary schools ignore the fact that many parents have experienced co-operation at the pre-school level? How can they harmonise these parents' experiences and expectations with their own concepts and strategies?

Generally, future developments in home–school links depend on the extent to which these problems and challenges can be dealt with. However, one should not ignore the fact that the fundamental relationship between the socialising role of the family and that of the school is determined not so much by parents and teachers on pedagogical grounds as by political decisions.

2. Historical and social context

Although there have been great changes towards closer co-operation since the late 1960s, there are no exciting new departures except in specific areas (e.g. with regard to reading and involvement of minorities). In order to realise the scope of present-day co-operation with all its similarities and divergences, the developments have to be viewed against the historical background, against public attitudes towards the family, and with regard to different ideological contexts.

Tradition of home–school relations

Demand for better co-operation has quite a long history, though it has never been a continuous trend, and was closely tied to periods of social change (Dolch 1928; Schleicher 1972). Comenius attempted as early as the seventeenth century and Pestalozzi in the eighteenth, to reduce the fencing off of the school from family life, and Süvern tried to put Condorcet's plea for greater parental participation into practice when the Prussian school system was reformed after the French Revolution. The intention then was to give every father and citizen a share in supervising the school and to secure equal rights for home and school in education. Furthermore, after the mid-nineteenth century, Grundtvig's concept of parent participation in 'free schools' was legally accepted in Denmark, and after the turn of the century educational reformers like Dewey and Petersen clearly realised that parental participation was indispensable for a pedagogical renewal of primary schools in terms of a child-centred education.

Then, the destruction of the Second World War made parental support and co-operation a *sine qua non* for a quick reconstruction of schools in accordance with democratic principles – and to a certain extent with children's needs. However, as soon as the educational systems were re-established, as a welfare state mentality spread and as socialisation research pointed to the home influence on social stratification, the co-operation waned considerably under the impact of educational planning and curriculum developments. The pendulum however did swing back in favour of parental participation after the mid-1960s, when social unrest spread and citizens' participation in decision making on the factory floor emerged, when political discussions on participatory democracy spread to the education system, and when new insight into early childhood and compensatory education stressed the need for parental involvement. It is open to debate to what extent co-operation started to suffer again in the 1980s under the impact of the freeze and the increased competition for good examination results to safeguard employment. Generally, today's parents want more contact with schools, teachers' attitudes are more favourable than in the past, and administrators as well as politicians are at least more aware of the demand for co-operation.

On the whole, the demand for co-operation has been discussed throughout history from three different points of view:

- On the one hand, there were arguments in favour of parental rights. In all EEC countries parents are legally responsible for the upbringing and well-being of their children. In addition, most countries allow parents to choose private schooling, and some countries even do not insist on compulsory school attendance but only demand adequate education. Debates about parental rights mainly emerge as soon as school policy touches too strongly on questions of religious faith, philosophy of life or on ideological matters. That such debates are still current is manifest in French demonstrations in favour of the '*école libre*' in 1984, which proved to be a major factor in the change of government.
- On the other hand, active parental co-operation was demanded during periods of democratic reform and social change in order to encourage participatory democracy at grassroots level if the institutional structures and/or state requirements no longer met the interests of larger social groups. The claim for participatory democracy was quite in vogue in the late 1960s, although sometimes it served less the children or parents than the legitimisation of political goals and educational planning (Zubke 1980, Boppel and Kollenberg 1981).
- Thirdly, parental involvement was quite strongly promoted whenever traditional school subjects and teaching methods did not really meet children's needs and educational requirements. The demand to make schools more pedagogical and more open institutions through parent participation found resonance with 'progressive education'. It to some extent merged with a trend towards clientele 'accountability' and the de-schooling movement in the late 1960s. Among the expected benefits were improved attitudes towards school, improved learning achievements and improved homework. In some countries, this view was taken to support educational reform, for example by giving parents more influence (as in Denmark) in choosing schools outside the local school district or deciding on combinations of certain optional (or advanced) courses. (Ministry of Education, Denmark 1979).

Generally speaking, the history of parental involvement shows that the demand for parental co-operation has been closely associated with periods of social change and inter-related with political, social and educational dimensions. Thus it is insufficient to discuss home–school relations only in practical terms, i.e. with regard to crisis contacts, group relations or legal provisions.

However, there are differences between the intentions behind home–school links (e.g. in terms of education and democratisation), which legal provisions are made (e.g. in terms of parental involvement in decision making), and what organisational structures are chosen (e.g. informal or formal). It all depends on the socio-political system in a given country, on the ideological (*weltan-*

schauliche) context of the co-operating groups, on the educational concept of a school and on the changing attitudes towards the family.

Changing expectations towards the family

Children's lifestyles, learning attitudes, social behaviour and norms are strongly influenced by the family and its changing structure – this is the unanimous view in research. The conclusions drawn from the findings, however, differ considerably according to different times and philosophies of life.

But before summarising some time-specific interpretations and perspectives of the family and its socialisation and considering their repercussions on the family's role in home–school relations, some changes in the family structure have to be taken into account (Van de Kaa 1976; Le Bras 1979).

Since the Second World War the long-term trend from extended to nuclear families, with fewer children and more affective relations, has accelerated. In addition, economic changes and reduced working hours encouraged the development of the weekend family and social and normative changes led to a higher status for the wife and children. This could suggest both that parents have more time for and interest in their children, and that they are ready for extended co-operation with the school – as some literature seems to confirm.

Simultaneously, however, rates of divorce and remarriage increased considerably (in Britain about 1 in every 3.5 children might be caught up in parental divorce before leaving school). More mothers with young children joined the workforce, and parental partnership often became at least as important as relations with children. With regard to home–school relations this suggests that fewer children means less experience with child development and the school, and that single-parent families often have difficulties in co-operating with the school. Generally, behavioural disturbances in children are strongly associated with family discord and disorder (see Boocock 1975; Ashford 1987).

Thus the prerequisites for home–school co-operation – i.e. the possibilities, need and willingness on the part of the family – are rather complex and difficult to handle by legislative and administrative means.

But co-operation between home and school is at least as much influenced by public attitudes towards the family as by the changing family structure. Public expectations towards the family changed with social developments. Immediately after the war there was a strong trend to reverse the downgrading of the family by the totalitarian regimes. On the one hand, its function was revalued in the context of the 'Human Rights Declaration', and on the other the family was urgently needed, since the educational system had to be re-established and the home had to act as a substitute for a missing or still insufficient welfare system. But the more the social structure and welfare state developed in the

1950s, the more the family's private function was stressed. Gradually, however, criticism of the family grew in the early 1960s because of its social isolation, because the deprivation cycle was related to its socialisation, and because it was regarded as an obstacle to educational planning. The situation changed again in the 1970s when open curricular and ecological approaches in education came to the forefront, and when scepticism about social engineering increased. Since the mid-1970s many countries have come to regard the family and its educational function as extremely important for personal and social development - partly encouraged by financial constraints in the welfare state and the demand to remove young mothers from the labour market (Hobbs *et al.* 1984).

During the same period, the educational role of the school changed almost inversely to the revaluation of the family. After the Second World War the school was expected, first to foster children according to their ability (in the 1950s), then to guarantee equality of opportunity (in the 1960s), and finally to help children in dealing with out-of-school challenges - e.g. in terms of preparing them for leisure activities or for family life.

Today most countries support the family - including some 'preparation for family life' - as a profitable investment. In our highly specialised, impersonal and efficiency-geared society, with poorly integrated welfare agencies, the family - in spite of its deficiencies - more than any other social group facilitates personal and group identity and a certain balance between personal needs and satisfactions. It continuously leads to day-to-day problem solving in real-life situations, and it transmits extra-functional competences. Therefore the Conference of European Ministers for Family Affairs, for example, stressed its educational role 'in preventing socialization deficits and other serious troubles in the adults of the future' (Schleicher 1982).

Generally, western societies expect families to lay the groundwork for later education, to give love and security to the child, to develop mutual attitudes of fairness, helpfulness and responsibility, and to offer a certain model for co-operative partnership. There is less reflection about the extent to which families are up to these expectations. It must also be recognised that the realisation of these expectations differs in a multicultural society and that society to some extent contradicts these expectations, since it itself is dominated by principles of competition, by hierarchical structures and by group egoism. Thus conflicts arise in home-school relations, when schools expect altruistic attitudes from parents (to care for all children and not only their own) while school and society are organised on competitive terms.

All in all, since the family is highly valued today, co-operation between home and school is not only favoured (with quite distinctive tasks) but also regarded as indispensable to compensate for shortcomings on both sides, to protect the child from competitive and conflicting educational goals, to counterbalance unfavourable social conditions, and to make education more effective.

Ideological aims and impact

Ideological positions influence the debate about parental participation quite strongly. The aims and practice of co-operation differ not only according to socio-political systems but also with regard to political points of view in all pluralistic societies.

In more socialistic states - and particularly in those with a one-party system (as the USSR or German Democratic Republic) - co-operation is considered and organised as support for schools, but it must also submit to the educational aims of the state - if not to its ideological policy. To a certain extent the school even exerts a controlling influence on parents - e.g. in the case of their educational shortcomings. In the GDR, for example, parents have no influence on the school and its organisation at all, although parent representatives are 'elected' and although the constitution gives parents the right and duty to educate their children (Art. 37, 40, 44). According to the ideology, parent representatives only have the task of explaining and enforcing decisions of the Communist Party conventions in order to guarantee the development of a socialist society (Mitter 1972; Busch 1972).

In contrast, more pluralistic democracies - and particularly decentralised and community-oriented democracies (e.g. the Netherlands or USA) - acknowledge parents' rights in education and to a certain extent approve participatory models of co-operation. Sometimes parents even attain a joint right (*Mitentscheidungsrecht*) to decide on school matters (e.g. in Denmark or the Federal Republic of Germany) or to influence curriculum decisions (as in some parts of Norway or Denmark). In the FRG, for example, family and school have competitive fundamental rights in education (cf. Art. 6, 7), and, in the regional state of Hessen, parents even have the constitutional right to take part in educational policy decisions at the school and regional level (Seipp and Haugg 1954; Taylor 1958).

Apart from these almost contradictory conditions in Eastern and Western Europe for parental participation, considerable political and ideological differences also exist amongst pluralistic societies themselves and also within most countries. Great differences exist between countries like France and the Netherlands, for example, because of their different school, social and political history.

In France, the central education bureaucracy controls almost all curricular and financial matters, the achievement-oriented teaching profession allows little parental intervention, and primary school parents have hardly any influence on the *conseil d'école*, which is chaired by the head teacher. So, despite the 1968 troubles, the 1975–8 reforms and the 1981 socialist impact, the situation has changed little. At best, national parent organisations (with few grassroots links) serve as consulted pressure groups, and local school councils - or subordinate class councils - are primarily concerned with peripheral areas of school life (i.e. extra-curricular activities and school transport) (Beattie 1985).

In almost complete contrast is the situation in the Netherlands with their locally organised and socially well-integrated school. The country's liberal tradition and religious stratification mean that parents have a large say in choosing and influencing the school. Since the 1920 primary school law, public and private schools are equally state financed and parents have the right to set up their own school if certain requirements are met. The consequence has been that about two-thirds of parents choose private institutions. Public schools (which are supported by local communities) and private schools (mainly church-related) have to set up parent committees at the school and community level (oudersraad 1964/medezeggenschapsraad 1983), which have to be consulted with regard to employment of the principal, school finance and change of curriculum. However, home-school relations are not only legally established, but well practised – for example, parents are welcomed to demonstration lessons (e.g. MacBeth 1984; Rupp 1972).

Beyond the national differences, co-operation varies in all pluralistic societies according to group-specific and ideological positions. The extension of 'participation' beyond the shopfloor level for example became a political slogan during the political turmoil in the late 1960s, to increase the responsiveness of social institutions, to legitimise educational policy and educational associations, and to further the interest and responsibility of citizens. In this context, trade unions and parent associations mainly pleaded for the idea of expanding 'representative democracy', while more radical democrats and educational reformers argued in favour of a 'participatory democracy' (of the directly affected groups) at grassroots level.

On the whole the following trends can be observed in western pluralistic societies over the last two decades. Generally speaking:

- liberal democratic groups were more likely to admit wider parent participation in decision-making;
- conservative groups have been quite careful to restrict professionals' expertise and schools' authority, because they feared lower teaching standards and group conflicts;
- socialist-oriented groups either tended to limit parents' influence in order to secure equality of opportunity and uniformity of the school system, or they stressed parental co-operation in order to reform or revolutionise the education system.

Obviously, home-school relations are linked to ideological perceptions and political systems. Thus, they generally change according to historical circumstances and reflect social and educational demands. Therefore there is no simple and straightforward answer as far as the aims, organisational structures or practice of co-operation are concerned.

3. Need for co-operation today

In spite of all national and ideological differences, the educational role of the family has been re-evaluated, co-operation has been supported by research and the framework for collaboration has been extended over the last 20 years.

Educational functions of home and school

Generally, expectations of family socialisation and education increased when the social and educational systems were in trouble (in the late 1940s and 1970s), while scepticism rose in periods when the welfare and educational systems expanded and the possibilities of formal education were overestimated (as in the 1960s).

Today some consensus exists with regard to the impact and importance of the home in educational matters. It is clearly recognised that the family - quite often a one-parent or one-child family - is more vulnerable and less able to bear stress than in the past. On the other hand, it is acknowledged that a child (till age 16) spends most of his/her time in the sphere of the home environment (compared to 14 per cent of his time at school), and that familial socialisation has a greater impact on children's attitudes, extra-functional capacities, learning readiness and even on subject competences than the school. And this home influence is particularly strong at the primary school age, when practical application of what is 'learned' is easiest and most meaningful in the child's everyday life experience (see Douglas 1969; Peaker 1971; Kifer 1975).

Therefore the declaration of the Council of Europe conference - amended and adopted by the Committee of Ministers in 1981 - reads: 'All services with a contribution to make to the development of young children - especially health, education and social services - should work with, and through the family to provide continuity of experience for the child' (Van der Eyken 1982).

The educational role of the home is regarded as complementary to that of the school, because both fields of education are separate with little joint planning, and because schools alone cannot safeguard equal educational opportunity. Moreover, the child's declining learning motivation after the first years of schooling - the time of increasing school stress - has to be compensated for. The public are also less and less ready to accept professional expertise and bureaucratic decisions as the exclusive authority in education.

So, if the time-specific evaluations of the role of the school and home are related, it is easy to understand why co-operation concepts changed considerably during the last few decades. In the 1960s - when school education was highly respected and the family little appreciated - co-operation often meant nothing more than parental support for school learning. In the 1970s - when home and school were both regarded as insufficient institutions for education - co-operation was envisaged as inter-relating their capacities and balancing their shortcomings. Today the overall opinion – with regard to primary education – seems to be that close co-operation is necessary because the complex school system with its differentiated subject areas tends to deviate from the children's experience and their environmental context. On the other hand, small or emotionally strained families often need supplementary guidance and their children need opportunities to mix with peers. It is largely accepted that:

- children need more help than ever to integrate school and out-of-school experiences;
- the strain on children increases notably if they are faced with conflicting education styles, value judgements or life patterns;
- their education depends at least as much on the development of extra-functional capacities (e.g. the abilities to communicate with their environment or to cope with the media) as on school knowledge;
- teachers as well as schools will be more effective if they encourage parental involvement in school life and learning.

A holistic, well-integrated and life-relevant education can only result from better home-school and neighbourhood relations. Therefore the Council of Europe recommended that 'Parents should participate in the implementation of all measures which have a bearing on conditions of work and conditions of life in school. They ought to be represented at all levels, local, regional and national and in all branches of teaching and, in a wider sense, of education.' And this view after all is in line with research results (see Maddaford 1972).

Research demanding closer co-operation

A rapidly growing literature on home–school relations has appeared in the last decade. Although research is still much more concerned with learning in the school than in the home or from the environment, nevertheless growing attention is paid to non-formal and informal education, to the learning climate and environment, and to the consequences of matching or mis-matching educational inputs. Therefore the need for home–school co-operation is no longer simply deduced – either from socialisation and developmental theories or from learning and participation theories, which often concentrated on home inadequacies (and their demographic implications), parent education or political aspects of participation (Halsey *et al.* 1967; Birch and Gussow 1970).

As long as research was primarily concerned with problems of home deficits and partial home effects on school learning, it tended to subordinate family involvement to school aims or it favoured co-operation in order to intervene in family education. Since the mid-1970s, however, research increasingly related psychological and sociological aspects of learning with institutional and environmental conditions for learning. It asked *why* socio-economic status, cultural differences and parent education influence learning so strongly, or *how* conflicting aspirations, attitudes and experiences of home and school can be avoided. Consequently more complementary forms of home–school collaboration were developed.

Several studies have identified parental involvement as a key factor in effective schooling and some studies even proved that teaching and curricula had weaker correlations with children's school achievements and learning process than the home did. The home situation, for example, explains a larger part of the variance in the mathematical, linguistic or political knowledge of children at age 10–11 than do school conditions or even teacher competence. In addition, 'the most obvious indication of a school's attitude to academic work is provided by its use of homework' (Kifer 1975). And the home influence on school achievement not only correlates higher with the psychological support in the home than with the socio-economic status of the family, but it is also strongly related to the extent of parental co-operation with the school. Finally, it has been argued that 'educational success under the comprehensive system depends on the support the child receives from home . . . the home thus takes on a central and not merely a peripheral role' (Plowden Report 1967; Fehrmann *et al.* 1987; Lynch and Pinlott 1976).

Although the overall effect of the home is beyond question, some particular research results did not pass unchallenged. The critics rightly stress, for example, that schools also have an impact on children's demands on the home, e.g. on the educational orientation of the parents and parental attitudes towards school and co-operation (Postlethwaite 1974; Marjoribanks 1980; Douglas *et al.* 1968). To what extent parents are at least indirectly influenced by the school is evident from studies showing that parents largely defend – notwithstanding their age and the date when their children left school – the educational opinions prevailing at the time when their children went to school.

Moreover, the literature – which deals explicitly with the co-operation problem – demonstrates that intensive parent participation reduces discipline problems in schools and strongly correlates with good grades. In addition, continuous co-operation seems to be a prerequisite for attitudinal changes of children and for successful work with disadvantaged children. Finally, reviews of intervention programmes and attitudinal mismatch of parents and teachers show that discontinuous and controversial interactions with the child are restricting the development not only of minority children but of all children (Gordon 1970; Schleicher 1975; Hansen 1986; Henderson 1981).

On the whole it is evident from research that parental involvement is indispensable for children's educational progress and does not really interfere with the teacher's autonomy as long as the co-operation is reasonably well planned and organised as a continuous process. A shortcoming in research still is that it offers too few integrated practical suggestions for how parents' competences can be made useful for co-operation. Moreover, many well-established forms of co-operation with parents of handicapped children have not yet been adapted to the context of primary school.

Structural framework for co-operation

Generally, all EEC countries have some similar legal arrangements, giving parents the overall obligation for their children's upbringing, setting up schools for instruction of the children, and arranging some consultation and co-operation between home and school. In the early 1970s several countries (e.g. Denmark, France, Germany, Italy and Norway) responded to the new educational and social demands with extended legal arrangements for parental participation particularly at the class and school level (Suessmuth, 1973).

At the school level the participation must distinguish between personal relations (concerned with the individual child) and group contacts (more concerned with administrative affairs).

Most extensive are the contacts at the personal level, which may be fairly informal or institutionalised. According to a European survey, principals in several EEC countries stated that parents contact the school about twice a year by phone and 2.5 times by meeting the teacher. Moreover, parents' visits to classes in session, if the teacher is consulted beforehand, seem to be possible in about 60 per cent of European schools (with a range from 88 per cent of German schools to 36 per cent of the French), while unexpected class visits are mentioned for an overall 35 per cent of schools (ranging from 52 per cent in Ireland to 4 per cent in Germany). Furthermore, about 50 per cent of parents are said to have access to the school records of their children in Belgium, Germany, Italy and the Netherlands. Beyond such statements on home–school contacts, parents are legally entitled to personal contact in some countries. In Denmark for example, they can expect regular information on their child's progress and they may participate in selecting optional courses for their children, while French parents have to be consulted at the end of the *cycle d'observation* and *cycle d'orientation* with regard to the child's further schooling (with a right to appeal against the school's final decision) (MacBeth 1984).

At the level of institutionalised group contacts principals assume – according to the EEC survey – that about 50 per cent of the schools generally send information to the parents prior to the first day of schooling (in Germany and the Netherlands more than 75 per cent, in France about 16 per cent); that about one-third of EEC schools contact parents prior to sensitive teaching periods (e.g. sex education), and that schools arrange about two class meetings per year. In some countries (e.g. Germany and Italy) such meetings are obligatory.

How parents are involved in class or school councils becomes clear from Table 4.1.1 (which does not cover optional arrangements as e.g. in Belgium) (MacBeth 1984). The effectiveness of parent participation at class or school level varies according to the national situations – for example, how strongly and formally parents are represented, whether their participation is restricted to consultation or includes some decision-taking power, and what problems

Table 4.1.1 Statutory regulations for parent–school co-operation

		Class level	*School level*	*District group of schools*	*Region/province or federal state*	*Region/province or National*
Denmark		G	A ---	A		
France:	public primary schools		A			
	Catholic schools	(S)	A			
Germany:	Hamburg	A ---	A ---	A ---	A ---	
	N-R. Westphalia		A ---		A ---	A (Parents' organisation)
	Baden-Württemberg	A ---	A ---	A ---	A ---	
Italy		A/G ---	A ---	A ---	A	
Luxembourg:	primary schools			A ---		A
Netherlands:	public schools		A			A
	private schools		A ---		G ---	G
Ireland:	primary schools		A			
Britain:	England & Wales		G	S		
	Scotland			G		

A = always, G = generally, S = sometimes, () local differences, --- = formal/technical relations are put on the agenda (e.g. extra-curricular activities, school rules, or even the employment of teachers and principals). At least parent participation in school councils helps to clarify school policy, and to increase parents' awareness of teaching aims and of themselves as educators.

Last but not least parents are organised at the national level in many countries. Although the situation of the parents' associations might be complicated if several associations compete with one another, or if they have party inclinations or church affiliations, they nevertheless constitute a complex information network, they enrich and diversify the professionals' point of view, and they may be consulted as a pressure group (Beattie 1985).

On the whole, parental co-operation at the personal, class and school as well as at the national level has increased parents' interest in, and concern about, school education. The contacts have helped to make schools more socially integrated and neighbourhood related, and they have furthered a matching of home and school education.

4. National differences

Great divergence exists in the conceptualisation and organisation of home–school links in different countries. Some national priorities and fields of action will be indicated in order to avoid stereotyping European developments on the basis of one country's experience. How the differences follow from educational traditions and socio-political preconceptions will be evident from summaries of Finnish and Norwegian as well as English and Swiss developments. These countries have been chosen because education policy in Scandinavia has traditionally been more centralised than in the two oldest European democracies, England and Switzerland.

Co-operation in more centralised education systems

Great steps towards closer co-operation have taken place in all the Scandinavian countries over the last decade. These changes are probably most far-reaching in Denmark, although the ongoing process of change is more evident from developments in Finland and Norway.

Finland

In Finland, a strong demand for closer home–school and neighbourhood links results today from the great mobility over the last decades (which uprooted many families), from rapid urbanisation (which led to depersonalised living conditions), and from a centralised education policy (which favoured large school systems and homogeneous curricula that left little room for parental participation). These demands came to the attention of policy makers in the mid-1970s, who then initiated some basic research, which proved quite influential in reshaping the policy on home–school relations.

Several surveys analysed parents' and teachers' expectations of attitudes towards, and experiences with home–school co-operation. The results, which pointed to the need for more horizontal continuity in the children's education, indicated several things (Korpinen *et al.* 1980). First of all: home–school contacts are most frequent among educated parents, they are more frequent in the 1st than the 3rd grade, and they happen least when a child is doing well. Moreover, Finnish schools tend to arrange at least one parent meeting per year at the school level, 70 per cent of the teachers set up parents' evenings and 27 per cent offer 'open days'. But 'parent committees' at the class level are quite rare (3 per cent). Finally, about 10 per cent of teachers think that teacher training gave them sufficient skills for co-operation, and at least 2–4 per cent of teachers have received *compensation* for the time they spend on co-operation.

As far as the functions of co-operation are concerned, parents and teachers rate them rather differently. While teachers favour 'personal discussions' with parents, because they make mutual understanding with the pupils easier, parents are more ready for co-operation when the children are not doing well or are transferred to another level of schooling. Interestingly enough, parents from cities regard co-operation more often as insufficient, although city schools offer more formal contacts than do rural schools. Essential obstacles to co-operation seem to be too big classes and schools from the teachers' point of view and too rigid school structures from the parents' point of view. Both sides complain about the 'subject teacher system' and the 'lack of experience or inability of teachers' to co-operate with parents.

Nevertheless, parents and teachers are increasingly willing to co-operate if schools encourage and support their efforts. Almost 50 per cent of parents welcome personal contacts with the form teacher at least once or twice a year, and many experienced teachers state that 'personal discussions' with parents generally have quite a positive influence on co-operation with the home. This readiness to co-operate is largely due to increasing problems in education. But it also reflects the European disillusionment with educational planning and the Finnish change in educational policy (Pekkala and Koivumäki 1982; Kananoja 1984).

Since the mid-1970s, educational authorities have been increasingly concerned with home–school contacts. The National Board of Education launched a 'verbal reporting system' on children's learning success (with a feedback slip for parents to answer), which obviously increased discussions between home and school. Furthermore a booklet on home–school co-operation was sent to schools in 1979 to explain the aims of co-operation and give practical advice for setting up parent–teacher conferences. In 1981 a ministerial subcommittee recommended that *teachers should be paid* one period per week for home–school co-operation and that special attention should be given to co-operation 'in the skill and arts subjects'. Finally, the new 1984 School Law stressed that the comprehensive school (in order to fulfil its task) 'has to try to achieve a close mutual understanding and collaboration with the home by supporting the home in its educational task' (Korpinen and Lang 1979; Koivumäki *et al.* 1980).

Norway

In Norway, educational policy has been increasingly concerned with home–school relations since the end of the 1960s. Until then the organisation of the educational system had been quite centralised and allowed only limited scope for parental involvement. The 1969 Basic School Act however stated right from the beginning that the school should educate 'in understanding of and collaboration with the home' so that children 'become useful and self-reliant human beings both in their homes and in the community' (Norwegian Ministry of Church and Education 1975). Correspondingly, the establishment of parent councils was required at each school in 1969. Since the mid-1970s, 'a number of responsibilities previously in the hands of the Ministry of Education have . . . been delegated to regional and local education authorities' to give greater decision-making authority to school boards and to strengthen the links between home, school and the local environment. This intention was surely easier to put in operation in Norway than in many other European countries since almost 30 per cent of the population live in rural areas and since schools are relatively small (the maximum number should not exceed 450 pupils) (Norwegian Ministry of Church and Education 1982; Ingeborgrued 1984).

However, to speed up home–school communications the Ministry of Education initiated some pilot projects in 1982 to sway traditional reservations amongst parents and to compensate for the shortcomings of teacher training with regard to co-operation. In the southern project, three advisers (one parent and two pedagogical consultants) offered guidance to parents and schools on how to co-operate in mutual respect of each other's competence (parents are regarded as 'experts' too), how to build on existing forms of co-operation (in terms of children's, parents', teachers' and neighbourhood needs), and how to help co-ordinate life and school 'learning' through complementary action (Council for Cultural Co-operation 1983). This approach had quite an impact regionally because of its group dynamic concept, which helped teachers as well as parents to start from their own life situations and to experience co-operation problems beyond the arrangement of formal parents' evenings. As a result of the initiative some schools immediately developed some home-visiting schemes, with parents participating in language and mathematics lessons during the 1st grade. A follow-up 'competence scheme' involved parents either in more practical subject areas (e.g. craftsmen in the crafts area) or as information sources (e.g. elderly people in on local history lessons). On the whole the initiatives helped to enrich the teaching, to make learning more relevant to the children, and to integrate school and community affairs (Sannes 1984).

At the national level, the new activities led to some important results – for example, a campaign against 'mobbing' (demanding mutual support from home and school, see page 341), and an international training camp for parent representatives, school administrators and teachers. This proved that a group dynamic approach can be very useful because participants not only discuss methods for home-school contacts but also practise them simultaneously.

Generally, the need for cross-generational and cross-educational co-operation is strongly felt in Norway because the number of children and families with special needs is increasing. (In some areas of Oslo, almost 50 per cent of first-graders are children of non-European migrant families.) Moreover, 'a lot of children and young people do not have adequate relations with adults and thus fail to receive valuable guidance and insight' (Ingeborgrued 1984).

Obviously, in the more centralised countries of Norway and Finland the governments took the initiative to increase parent involvement. The Finnish government primarily aimed at better co-operation to improve learning standards and to decrease the schools' alienation without giving parents any decision-making power in school affairs. The Norwegian authorities, however, were inclined to entrust more responsibilities for school management to the local level – rather than to parents – because it was recognised that the children's in- and out-of-school activities should be more inter-related.

Co-operation in more decentralised education systems

Contrasting the above developments with home-school relations in countries with long traditions of grassroots democracy gives some insight into the extent that political structures are important for parent involvement.

England

In England parents have the 'right' to provide suitable education (even in terms of private tutoring), so that school attendance is not compulsory in the formal sense. Thus one might well assume that parental participation in schools affairs was well established throughout the country – and this even more so because English primary schools are strongly child oriented and because British research has emphasised quite conclusively that good home-school relations are indispensable for healthy and successful development in the emotional, social and cognitive domain (Schleicher 1972; Sharrock 1970; Tizard *et al.* 1981; Warnock 1978).

However, home-school relations were not well established in the past, and progress has been relatively slow compared to many other countries. Low parent participation was complained about in the mid-1960s (e.g. Plowden Report), a spreading of contacts was demanded at the turn of the 1970s (e.g. Department of Education and Science 1962), and a greater proportion of parents on schools' governing boards was recommended in the late 1970s (Taylor Report). Obviously change was slow because of the traditional fixation on personal forms of co-operation (98 per cent of primary schools offered open days for parents but a comparatively small percentage had parent teacher associations) (Taylor Report 1977; Bassey 1978). Home–school relations became an important issue because the awareness had spread:

- that young children, particularly from priority areas, needed a better matching and complementing of home and school education, and
- that as the consensus on educational policy and confidence in professional authorities diminished, new forms of legitimation and consensus were needed.

So – backed up by spreading literature on home–school relations – new channels had to be developed for communicating parents' concerns. On the one hand many primary schools increased their contacts with parents, while on the other hand voluntary organisations tried to vitalise parent involvement in school affairs (e.g. the Advisory Centre for Education, the Confederation for the Advancement of State Education, or the Home School Council). Finally the government took some action.

These manifold activities led to important changes. While in the early 1970s only 17 per cent of primary schools had PTAs (Plowden Report), such associations could be found in 35 per cent of schools in the late 1970s. According to a primary school survey meanwhile, 34 per cent of schools invite parents to workshop meetings to discuss their children's progress, 43 per cent offer opportunities to see their children at classes in session, and more than a third involve parents with special knowledge to give talks. In addition, another study stated that now 95 per cent of teachers arrange parents' evenings and open days, 92 per cent invite new parents before their children start school and 50 per cent send written reports to parents (Cyster *et al.* 1979; Department of Education and Science 1978b; Wolfendale 1983).

However, co-operation still concentrates on the personal level, the extent of co-operation is at the schools' discretion, and the contacts are strongest with middle-class parents. In the face of these developments, changes in educational policy became overdue. After the Taylor Committee (1977) suggested a format for the composition of governing bodies (which should include parents as well as older pupils), the 1980 Education Act required that all schools have parents' and teachers' elected representatives on the governing body. But, while the Education Act hesitated to touch on the overriding power of the local education authorities (Department of Education and Science 1982; Liell and Saunders 1986), the 1984 Green Paper finally proposed 'policies for raising standards in schools by enabling parents to improve the work of the school', i.e. by giving them 'the right to form the majority of the governing body' and by establishing some 'lay oversight and control' of schools. Important sections of the government's Green Paper read:

- 'The governing body should be able to determine, in consultation with the headteacher, the main policies and lines of the development of the school', although 'the professional responsibilities of the headteacher and the staff . . . should be respected.'
- In curriculum matters the 'governing body would have the duty to determine the statement of the school's . . . aims and objectives' while the head teacher would be responsible for organising the syllabuses and the local education authority had to implement the regional curricular policy.
- Moreover, the governing body should have 'a powerful and effective influence . . . at every stage of the selection process' if a new head teacher or new teachers had to be engaged (e.g. by participating in 'interviewing and recommending an applicant to the LEA for appointment').
- And finally, if laymen are to be involved in such important and complex responsibilities, then the 'governor cannot be expected to discharge them effectively without some training', which the LEAs should provide (Department of Education and Science 1984).

The impact of these proposals should not be exaggerated, though they met with considerable criticism. For experience shows that parents themselves welcome professional competence in the governing bodies, that the board clerks tend to be staff members of the LEAs, that parent nominees generally serve not more than two years compared to four years for the LEAs' representatives, and that increasing centralisation in education is complemented by only some local diversification (Kogan 1985).

On the whole the English developments show that a well-established political democracy and decentralised education system do not necessarily lead to participatory democracy at the school level, and that strong research pleas for parental involvement may have limited effect on their own.

Switzerland

Another well-known example of a decentralised, participatory democracy is Switzerland. Here again there has been little interest in home–school links, although school affairs largely are a concern of the cantons and local communities. Partly this may be a consequence of the feeling that all citizens are represented at grassroots level, i.e. at the local level. However, since school districts have become larger (about 50 per cent of the population live in urban communities today) and since educational bureaucracy has increased (as in other countries), the traditional structures hardly meet today's educational needs and parental interests (Vogel 1980). Thus the demand for better home–school links grew in the face of the new structures – accelerated by social changes (with increasing divorce rates, working women and guest workers), influenced by international research on socialisation processes, and responding to experiences of parent self-help groups in early childhood education.

A 1979 analysis of parent initiatives and participation in the French- and German-speaking areas of Switzerland shows that local parent groups or parent organisations – which seldom existed before the mid-1970s – quickly spread around urban areas. These local parent groups regard themselves and their inter-group contacts as indispensable because in most cantons parents have no legal right to participate in school matters and because no more than 10–15 per cent of parents are members of political parties. Thus almost 90 per cent have hardly any opportunity to be elected as members of the school administration. In addition, parents obviously get little information about school affairs from administrators and teachers, and most home–school contacts are limited to the personal level. The parent groups were not started to interfere with teachers' and bureaucracies' functions; rather they concerned themselves with parent information, guidance and contacts with schools and local bureaucracy. Until now however, the groups have by no means been powerful organisations for the following reasons:

> At elections for local administration candidates are generally presented by political parties, so that parent groups almost never succeed in nominating a candidate of their own. Moreover they rarely get regular invitations to meetings of the local school administration, and even their limited proposals (regarding homework, holidays or the establishment of parent councils at the class level) are seldom successful. (Schweizerische Studiengruppe 1980)

Certainly, home–school links do not entirely depend on institutionalised contacts; teachers' attitudes towards parent involvement are just as important. But surveys on teacher training for primary schools and in-service training show consistently that

- regional school laws almost never require training institutions to prepare for co-operation with parents;
- the training staff have little practical experience in home–school co-operation itself;
- and neither special training nor in-service courses on home–school relations are open to teachers, parents and administrators simultaneously. (Schweizerische Studiengruppe 1982)

Nevertheless it is widely accepted by the training institutions that preparation for co-operation should be an important aspect of the teachers' professionalism and that most student teachers apparently appreciate such a training. So the preceding findings – discussed in four regional hearings in 1982 (including representatives from teacher training institutions and from school administration) – led to the following recommendations:

- joint courses on home–school relations should be offered to parents, teachers and administrators (although teachers had a strong need to start discussions by themselves);

- preparation for co-operation appears to be easier and more relevant in in-service rather than at the initial training level;
- some guidance institutions should be set up, which could give advice to schools, parents and administrators on practical problems; and
- revisions of school laws with regard to home–school relations were regarded as desirable. (SIPRI 1983)

Finally, the Swiss Study Group for Co-operation between Parents, Teachers and School Administrators presented a proposal for future action. Although the Swiss constitution and law emphasise the importance of 'educating the individual' (in terms of *Erziehung*), most curricula specify only teaching and learning goals. Thus parents - who are in charge of an overall education and upbringing - should demand a more integrated education, which takes their functions and opinions into account. Furthermore, parents as well as teachers should be represented at the school and administrative levels (local, cantonal and national). First signs of some forward-looking developments are: in 1979 the canton Basel-Land revised its school law, making parents' evenings compulsory and including parent representatives on advisory school councils. Moreover, new parent organisations (e.g. Schweiz. Vereinigung der Elternorganisationen since 1977; Schweiz. Studiengruppe Zusammenarbeit Eltern–Lehrer–Schulbehörden since 1978) became active in advising local parent groups, in offering parent education, or in co-ordinating parent and teacher groups at regional levels.

These developments illustrate the fact that parental involvement in school affairs is not yet well established beyond the level of individual contacts, because in the past the principle of democratic representation stood in the way of parental participation.

The experiences of the four countries can be summarised. On the one hand, there exists an overall trend towards closer home–school relations, particularly at the class and school level. But often parental participation is still limited to consultation and to participation in extra-curricular activities. On the other hand, it is evident that the aims and means of co-operation differ considerably according to national traditions and concerns, and that more decentralised countries are latecomers in organising formal parental participation while more centralised countries might find it difficult to allow too much local divergence. Against these national backgrounds the next section contrasts some immanent concepts and consequences of different co-operation strategies.

5. Concepts and strategies

The emphasis in home–school relations has changed from individual- and crisis-oriented to more process- and collective-oriented forms of co-operation over the last few decades. Accordingly laws were passed in many European countries stating that parents should be represented on school boards if not on regional or national councils (e.g. in Denmark, Norway, the Netherlands, Federal Republic of Germany, France and Italy) (Suessmuth 1973; Commission of the European Communities 1983). But to what extent legal and formal frameworks come to exist depends as much on the underlying or immanent concepts for co-operation. Two pairs of underlying patterns (or hidden curricula) will be exemplified – first 'learning vs socialisation concepts', then 'school- vs home-oriented concepts'.

Learning- vs socialisation-oriented concepts

The differences between the two concepts can be illustrated by overall trends in the United States of America and the Federal Republic of Germany. (The USA is included here because its 'learning-oriented concept' influenced not only European research for a while but also many co-operation projects.) Although the overall aims for co-operation are stated as being rather similar in the USA and FRG, they are quite different in practice. Common to both the countries are the aims: co-operation shall make education a joint process, shall strengthen local self-regulation, shall support school learning, and shall help parents to cope with educational reforms. The implementation, however, differs according to the social needs and the way schools see themselves in both nations. For example, it makes a great difference:

- whether co-operation is intended to increase the child's learning or to safeguard an integrative socialisation, and
- whether parents are treated as schools' clients (in a systems theory approach) or as semi-professionals (in a communications theory approach).

In the United States the dominant approach is a learning-oriented concept of co-operation. Reasons are easy to find. Until the 1950s schools had to cope with a considerable percentage of semi-literate parents and were committed to the 'melting pot ideology'. Then compensatory theories and rather closed curricula came to the forefront, and today society as well as schools demand a better preparation for job competition and/or 'excellence' (Schleicher 1972; Sexton 1961). This learning-oriented concept dominates despite the fact that locally elected school boards generally decide on school regulations, subjects and education taxes. (Several 'local' boards are no longer local in the original sense but serve large urban areas.)

This concept certainly does not prevent 93 per cent of superintendents and school board presidents from regarding teachers' working with parents as part of their job. 90 per cent of teachers regard strong home–school links as desirable, and 80 per cent of parents would welcome monthly parents' evenings (to discuss their children's progress) (National Education Association 1981). Nevertheless, parental influence on schools is extremely indirect at best, since parents have few collective rights of participation, because a wide discrepancy exists between the reported willingness to co-operate and the limited opportunities available for participation. The great majority of parents have no say in curriculum planning (except parents of handicapped and minority children) and teachers seldom explain their teaching concepts to parents (even when the teachers are interested in parent co-operation). So, whenever parents are really involved beyond school displays, etc., then it is as direct teaching supports (Gallup 1980; Davies 1987; Epstein 1987; Burns 1982).

What schools really expect from parents becomes perfectly clear from a survey analysing what 3,500 primary school teachers and 600 principals expect from co-operation. They identified areas in which parents could and should support their children (see Table 4.1.2; Epstein and Becker 1982). These data are in line with developments in Idaho and West Virginia, where over 60,000 certificates were given out to primary school parents who read with their children at least 15 minutes per day, five days a week for 9 weeks.

The overall impression (supported by literature on home contracts and reading programmes) is that supervision of learning activities at home is regarded as the most effective form of parent co-operation. In comparison, PTA councils and classroom volunteers are considered of minor importance, since few parents - and not the most needy - participate. Thus, the immanent attitude towards parent involvement in the US can be summarised as follows: in spite of the US tradition of participatory democracy and community-aligned schools, parents are largely looked upon as a worthwhile source of instructional activities.

In comparison, the Federal Republic of Germany is socially far more integrated, less dominated by competitiveness and educationally at least as much geared to extra-functional competences (*Bildung*) as to specific skills. Furthermore, parents not only have individual right of access to the school (according to the constitution), but they also have a collective right to participate at the level of the class, the school, and - for most - at the regional (*Länder*) level (the *Länder* have legal authority in educational affairs). Parental

Table 4.1.2 Active use of selected techniques of parent involvement

Techniques	*Principals who encourage (%)*	*Teachers who use actively (%)*
Read aloud or listen to reading	76	66
Informal games at home	45	21
Contract with parents on student projects	33	25
Loan books to parents	31	41
Teach parents techniques for tutoring and evaluation	24	21
Parent contracts to reward or punish behaviour	12	13
Parent-led discussions of TV shows	12	2

participation rights are most far-reaching in the *Land* Hessen where parents even have to agree to the introduction of new curricula and examinations before they become obligatory. But as important as this framework for co-operation is the change of emphasis in home–school relations. The main emphasis has changed over the last 15 years from legal and institutional aspects towards endeavours for a better balance of home and school socialisation (Roebbelen 1966).

This matching of socialisation processes is regarded as being of the utmost importance for the child's development and for greater dynamism in the educational system. Therefore the *Länder* more or less demanded that teachers should give reasons for their teaching content and methods, and should allow more parental suggestions on school affairs (e.g. Baden–Württemberg). Further demands were that:

- parents should have opportunities to sit in on classes (e.g. Saarland);
- parents and teachers should consult each other with regard to homework, learning assessment and educational planning (e.g. North-Rhine Westphalia); and
- discussions should be encouraged between inspectors, headmasters, teachers and parents (e.g. Hamburg). (Grabbe 1983)

Such developments at least increased interest in and readiness for parental involvement. According to two studies,

- parents generally feel 'well-informed' or 'informed to some extent' about their children's school success (77 per cent + 21 per cent),
- they are 'well' or 'somewhat' acquainted with the schools' arrangements for supporting children's special needs (35 per cent + 36 per cent), and
- they feel informed about the new didactics (e.g. in mathematics 22 per cent and languages 33 per cent).

In primary schools, about 77 per cent of parents participate regularly in parent meetings, while another 20 per cent do so from time to time. Co-operation on a mutual basis appears to be the easier since parents do not give high priority to the school's teaching of the three Rs (35 per cent) but expect as much education for independence (35 per cent). Simultaneously parents do not regard themselves as teacher substitutes, even if they are involved as teacher aides, as in the area of Hamburg, so that about 75 per cent of teachers welcome their support and advice (Boppel and Kollenberg 1981; see also Günther and Heitmeyer 1981).

To what extent teachers are satisfied with the form of legalised parent participation is illustrated by an empirical study comparing teachers' perceptions of parent involvement in Germany with that of teachers in Ireland, where schools are more learning oriented. The study summarises from its data: 'despite the rights of German parents to engage in activities such as observing lessons and making suggestions about lesson plans – rights which many Irish teachers would be unprepared to countenance – the attitudes of German teachers with respect to parents are much more favourable than those of the Irish' (Pritchard 1981).

Obviously, the school in Germany is no longer perceived as an inaccessible sovereign institution. Teachers are increasingly aware of parents' concerns and influence on socialisation, and parents are as much interested in school didactics and teachers' problems as in an overall education. So it is not too difficult for both groups to agree on *reciprocal support* (e.g. with regard to environmental, health or media education), and, in view of a better integration of outsiders amongst children, parents or teachers, to avert bureaucratic intrusions on education. One may wonder whether some relapses into old habits may follow under the influence of the freeze and increasing unemployment.

The comparison elucidates that co-operation is strongly influenced by 'hidden' concepts and needs a broader perspective than school success if the child's home, school and environmental socialisation are to be smoothly amalgamated.

School- vs home-related areas of co-operation

In order to avoid a narrow focus on special elements of co-operation which limit the participants to special roles, some school- and home-related areas will now be contrasted.

Co-operation in school-related areas is generally based on the view that poorly educated parents cannot help themselves and that teachers alone cannot deal with the diverse learning problems. Therefore schools should give practical suggestions to parents on:

- how to support their children's school learning (e.g. by daily reviews of homework), and
- how to strengthen or train certain abilities (parents even may get 'home learning recipes' or computerised instructions). (Moles 1982; Shuck *et al.* 1983)

The overall aims of such strategies are to make parents aware of their children's learning difficulties, to train them in school supportive functions and to increase certain skills of the children (e.g. in reading and calculation).

At the primary school level various countries have organised home activities to support the schools' aims and learning success, particularly with regard to reading (e.g. the Parent Plus Program in Chicago, the home-enrichment program at the Hebrew University or the Lothian Educational Home-Visiting Scheme in Scotland). Such schemes spread after similar programmes for disadvantaged children confirmed improvements in their abilities.

In England, reading activities are a central emphasis in co-operation. For example, about 44 local education authorities reported some informal reading co-operation with parents at the primary school level (i.e. preparing material for home reading), with some schools following more formal programmes. In one local education authority no less than 27 schools make reading suggestions and exchange reading cards about what children actually have read. Some consequences of these activities seem to be:

- that parents understand school activities much better,
- that they share more knowledge of their children with the teaching staff, and
- that the attainments of their pupils improve. (Jowett and Baginsky 1988; Tite 1987)

Some scepticism however was raised by the Scottish home-visiting scheme. After self-critical observations it was mentioned that perhaps parents are forced 'to feel that they should adopt a more directive "teaching" stance', and 'mothering skills' which appear to be important 'may be further de-valued and undermined', so that society in the long run may 'be the loser if it [the child] is deprived of a wide variety of human concerns and abilities . . . ' (Raven 1980). Such scepticism helps to bring one-sided forms of parental involvement back into equilibrium.

If co-operation goes beyond skill training, then home-related areas of co-operation must be included, because children have as much to cope with with out-of-school as with in-school affairs, and parents need as much support for their education as teachers do. Such home-oriented co-operation is urgently needed in spite of the common reluctance to encourage public interference in private affairs (which is fundamental to western democracies). How it is possible will be exemplified with regard to media education and in stemming bullying.

As far as media education is concerned, home and school functions overlap a great deal. Generally children have a wide range of media at their disposal in the home (television, cassettes or video-games), even before they start school. Therefore the teacher is on the defensive as far as the children's socialisation through the media is concerned. Nevertheless, parents expect him/her to make important contributions to the children's media education. According to research, a co-operative education is particularly important at the primary school level, because:

- children already tend to be fairly independent media-users at puberty,
- teachers are generally poorly acquainted with the children's media habits and can do little more than teach 'about' the media, and
- parents are not only faced with the children's media use and with the imitations of their own media consumption but they may also be acquainted with the problems of media education. (Havlicek and Steinmann 1980; Hill 1983; Feilitzen 1975).

Thus, children as well as parents and teachers need more than isolated initiatives and more than traditional forms of home–school relations to cope with the media's challenge. An effective media education – which tries to arrive at an age-related media usage – requires child-oriented collaboration, with mutual information and agreement about his/her media consumption, or with reciprocal support for home and school strategies. For a teacher the consequences may be that s/he includes more competent parents in developing the syllabus, that parents and teachers arrange for joint in-service training sessions, or that they offer agreed alternative life experiences to the children.

As important for really reciprocal co-operation are the problems of bullying or mobbing, which generally happen outside the school. Although harassment or mobbing are not new phenomena, they seem to spread with violence in society and the media. In Norway, for example, long-term and systematic use of mental or physical violence amongst pupils is reported for 5 per cent of children aged 7–16 and in the area of the Inner London Education Authority about 20 per cent of children (aged 10–11) seem to be affected. In spite of these alarming figures, school authorities tend to be reluctant to admit problems for their school or area, teachers seem to do little to combat it (because rewards or punishments are not readily available), and parents either lack knowledge about it (particularly if their children are bullies) or they feel unable to handle it (particularly if their children are victims).

In order to counteract these problems the Norwegian authorities, for example, started a national campaign to increase public awareness and demanding its support. However, the situation of 10–11 year olds even worsened thereafter. Thus it became clear that crisis-management demands closer co-operation between homes and schools, and that parents have to be accepted as equal partners. On the whole, parent involvement seems to be most cost-effective (Council for Cultural Co-operation 1988).

In retrospect, it becomes evident from the comparison of some underlying concepts of co-operation that parental involvement should not be directed one-dimensionally to learning and school affairs but is as important with regard both to home-related areas and to a better match of socialisation.

6. Different role expectations

While the stage for co-operation is set by formal structures and hidden concepts, its realisation depends quite strongly on the attitudes of the participants, i.e. what headmasters, teachers and parents respectively actually expect from co-operation, and which functions are assigned to parents.

Role-specific views on co-operation

Expectations and attitudes towards co-operation first of all depend on the educational priorities of the participating groups and how they value their educational function in comparison to that of their concurrent educators.

As far as educational goals are concerned, an earlier English study (Schools Council 1968) shows that parents are particularly interested in their children's school success (e.g. in terms of grades) and so-called life-relevant aspects of education (e.g. sex education). In contrast, headmasters are more concerned with personal development and an overall education (in terms of character development and getting on with others), while teachers take a stance between the groups (although closer to the headmasters' point of view). Moreover, the participants have different views on their respective functions in the educational process, as another English study confirms (Davies and Davies 1985). Parents, for example, regard social education as their particular domain but cognitive training and an encompassing moral education as the school's function. Teachers, however, do not regard moral education as one of their major responsibilities but feel obliged to further social skills. These findings illustrate how different role perceptions of the co-operating groups are, although the evaluation is by no means representative of all European countries. (In fact, even in England parents' views differ according to their children's age and their own cultural background; see Davies and Davies 1985).

Although different attitudes towards co-operation are quite normal – because parents, teachers and principals have different functions and competences – they nevertheless have important repercussions on co-operation.

On the one hand, headmasters organise and represent the schools within more or less hierarchical school systems so that they are to some extent in a leadership position as far as home–school relations are concerned. Even if they delegate some of their authority to advisory bodies, they hardly feel ready to relinquish their own responsibility for the school. And by tradition headmasters tend to live with a self-image that makes them reluctant to encourage lay involvement in school management.

On the other hand, teachers see themselves as professionals who have to respect curricular and teaching standards, and who have to impart important elements of their subjects to the children. From their point of view, parents appear as educational laymen who have to provide a good upbringing and should control homework but not interfere in teaching. Generally their perception of parental functions changed little until school criticism and discipline problems increased greatly, and until the socialisation theory pointed to the enormous influence of the home on school success.

Finally, parents tend to look at school more with personal concerns than collective ambitions, and they often do not understand the importance of their support for school teaching and an overall education. It is therefore easy for them to feel inferior to the school's expertise – particularly if they live close to impressions of their own school days. Even after public concern for parental involvement increased greatly in the 1970s, for the most part parents still react to school initiatives or leave their 'right to say' to the well-educated and highly motivated parents and to parent representatives.

Table 4.1.3 Views on school councils' functions

	In matters of school discipline:		*In curricular matters:*		*In appointment of teaching staff:*
	Favour some advice or deciding	Favour some decision making	Favour some involvement in subjects to be taught	Favour some involvement in the methods of teaching	
Head teachers	59%	13%	32%	23%	32%
Teachers	66%	18%	36%	22%	27%
Parents	86%	29%	80%	68%	47%

The group-specific attitudes towards school education and co-operation are reflected in a Scottish study, which analysed their different perceptions of the tasks of school councils. In Scotland, school councils have been mandatory since 1973. The majority of them are responsible for a secondary school and its primary feeder schools. Such council meetings are – according to the analysis – primarily concerned with general home–school issues (30 per cent) and non-curricular school issues such as discipline (25 per cent), while problems of staff appointment (5 per cent) or curricular matters (1 per cent) are seldom made an issue. The group-specific expectations of the councils' functions are reflected in Table 4.1.3 (MacBeth *et al.* 1980). Despite the great differences, all participants unanimously appreciated the councils' activities, wherever schools had difficulties in handling educational problems. On the whole, the data provide some evidence that institutionalised co-operation strongly depends on attitudes of the participants.

So, what could or should be done to make co-operation at the school and class level easier and more effective? Perhaps Northern Ireland has developed a forward-looking strategy, supplementing the school councils by the appointment of 'home–school links teachers' (now more than 100 for primary schools) who help to organise parent–teacher and inter-staff contacts, and try to involve parents who normally do not participate (Department of Education for Northern Ireland 1976).

On the whole, however, some attitudinal changes are needed on the part of all participating groups. Headmasters' roles, for example, need to be redefined according to the degree of parent co-operation intended (e.g. whether parents should advise, participate or decide in school affairs). In addition, teachers need more training and in-service training to further co-operation in home- and school-related areas and this on a more mutual basis. (In particular, they need to be less concerned about parents' interference since the great majority of parents do not really intend to subject teachers to parents' demands.) Finally, parents have to develop a more self-reliant 'co-operative attitude'. This could be facilitated through an enlarged sharing of responsibility from the class to the school level, from joint efforts in media education and more involvement in curricular matters (Sass and Holzmueller 1977).

It can be summarised that home–school contacts cannot really be established by legal regulations alone. Besides, attitudinal changes by the participating groups are as important for establishing mutual trust, interactive communication and efficient school councils.

Functions assigned to parents

In all pluralistic societies, three different though overlapping functions are assigned to parental participation.

First, parental involvement is regarded as participation of citizens. The importance of such civilian participation increases the less the social welfare state and the education systems are able to respond to individual needs or those of certain minority groups. In order to counterbalance this overall trend towards alienation, at least some participatory democracy is worth striving for. This is because parents have a greater competence to share educational responsibility with schools than any other group of clients has with regard to its social institution.

This type of co-operation is regarded as an opportunity to increase parents' educational and political competence through 'participatory learning', to make school structures more democratic, and to improve the neighbourhood relations of schools or to develop them into community centres. The idea of citizen participation in areas of particular concern is the basis of collective parent involvement (e.g. for their representation on school or administrative councils). However, a mandate for parental involvement is a necessary but not a sufficient condition for positive home–school relations.

How the participatory concept may be put into operation is evident from English pre-school developments and from Dutch as well as Danish parent participation in school education. In England, the pre-school playgroups (strongly supported by Lady Plowden as a useful alternative to nursery schools) were organised by parent self-help groups according to public minimum requirements and with a training possibility for the parents in charge. With regard to primary schools, Dutch parent groups have the right to establish publicly financed 'special schools' (which care for about two-thirds of primary school children), while Danish parents have some participatory rights with regard to curriculum decisions and on the distribution of subject hours (Plowden 1973; Van Ham 1983; Centraal Bureau voor het Katholiek Onderwijs 1982). Small steps towards parental co-operation as a citizens' right have been made in most countries.

A quite different role for parents exists if their participation is regarded as a support system for school teaching. In particular, compensatory education and educational planning in the late 1960s encouraged this kind of parent participation. Here the schools are seen as agents for social change which should influence or even educate parents, so that parents are to some extent pressed into a consumer role according to the schools' learning goals and teaching programmes. Since the mid-1980s this form of parental involvement has been growing again, because schools have increasing difficulties in meeting several obligations under the present economic constraints (in England, for example, with regard to school meals, materials and uniforms), and because parents are increasingly anxious to support school achievements in the light of youth unemployment or qualification requirements.

The consequences for the primary school situation are that the educative function of the home is somewhat subordinated to formal learning functions, either in terms of the schools' demand for parental control of homework or home application of some didactic games and support techniques (e.g. for reading).

A third type of co-operation can be distinguished, which may be called child centred or socialisation oriented. Here the environmental, developmental and personal dispositions of the children are put to the forefront, rather than specific learning goals or aspects of parental representation. This format not only demands a more open and flexible approach to synchronising school- and home-related areas of co-operation, but it also demands long-term concern by parents beyond crisis management. Such child-centred co-operation is of particular importance when children start school, if they are handicapped or belong to minority groups. The importance of the approach increases the stronger the influence of concomitant educators such as the media, the greater the psychological lability of the children, and the weaker the educative function of the school.

This third approach, which is continuously stressed and sometimes indirectly practised, is extremely difficult to carry out beyond the personal contact level. Since no universal prescriptions can be given, some practical experiences of the city of Hamburg are summarised. In Hamburg, parents have been involved for more than 15 years as teacher aides throughout all subject areas in more than 170 primary schools (sometimes on a rota basis) (Bürgerschaft der Freien und Hansestadt Hamburg 1982). Partly parents give technical assistance (e.g. with swimming), partly they present their own experience to the class (e.g. if leisure-time matters or environmental problems are discussed), and partly they tutor small groups or individual children (never their own) during lessons, because they otherwise would not get sufficient attention from the teacher. On the other hand, parents counsel themselves with regard to minor family and educational problems. Although parents from all social strata co-operate, it has not been researched to what extent the approach favours children from different social strata and leads to attitudinal changes in home education.

The child-centred approach stems from the view that schools need a better understanding of the children's overall life experience and the school's effect on the home, and that parents need personal experience of the school's teaching and learning situations and a better estimation of their own child's development in relation to his/her peer group. The view also proposes that children need a better integration of different socialisation procedures and communicaton styles, more personal attention than the teacher can provide and more opportunities to learn participatory attitudes from the co-operation amongst adults.

At first the approach met with considerable scepticism, particularly on the part of teachers (because of additional work and conflicts) and above all on the part of trade unions (because of the involvement of 'uncertified lay teachers'). Since then, however, the co-operation strategy has become widely accepted, because of its careful planning, its step-by-step introduction, and its open-minded feedback. Generally it improved the school climate, allowed more individualised instruction, furthered the personal stability of the children, and made teachers more aware of how worthwhile home and neighbourhood experiences are for the children's learning (Freie und Hansestadt, Hamburg 1981).

On the whole, it is important that the different role expectations and the different types of parent assignments are fully considered by all participating groups, because otherwise many unnecessary conflicts follow.

7. Practical experiences

Although there are some well-established areas of co-operation (for example, when a child starts school) and although other areas at least find great approval (for example, that minority children need mutual support), many schools still leave parental involvement to chance and many teachers are afraid of conflicts (for example, that parents might trespass on their territory). The following examples therefore illustrate why co-operation is not at all unreasonable, the extent to which it supports the teachers' work, and how it could generate fewer conflicts than expected.

Establishing contacts in the first grade

The first period of schooling usually implies a lot of expectations and frustrations for children, parents and teachers. Children tend to react to the new challenge with a significant increase in curiosity, interest and anxiety; mothers either come up with high demands on their children's learning after a half-day's routine work in an empty nest or they feel stressed in the face of unclear school demands at the end of a long working day; and teachers generally become uneasy in situations with large groups of unknown children (not so in England because of individualised school entry), and they may retreat to class teaching from the front (Grothloh-Amberg 1971).

Getting off to such a bad start can be avoided through early and child-centred co-operation. The goals of such early contacts are:

- to inter-relate the children's prior experiences with the schools' goals,
- to give teachers an early chance to be acquainted with the children's motivational, social, and cultural background, and
- to help parents to cope with their changing family situation and to understand the present-day school's didactics. (Gordon 1970)

There are many examples of how co-operation could be initiated in kindergarten or at least before school begins. They show that mutual co-operation is facilitated if teachers are provided with short biographies of the children before school starts (as in Gloucestershire) or if early contacts are established in kindergarten or the home environment (as is usual in the Rudolf

Steiner schools). And parents could be set at ease if they meet with the children's future teacher before school starts (as often happens in Denmark), if they can exchange ideas with the then 1st grade parents to see how other parents have settled (as some projects in North-Rhine Westphalia do), or if they are informally drawn into class activities on a rotation basis soon after the beginning of school (as in many of Hamburg's primary schools; see page 346).

However, co-operation should not be limited to individual contacts and parents' evenings. Rather, it should be established as a continuous process of mutual orientation, guidance and support. This may come about by co-ordinating out-of-school activities, via common seminars for kindergarten nurses, parents and teachers, or by joint activities to help children and families in need. All these and similar activities are particularly important in the first period of schooling because the early forms of co-operation determine to a certain extent whether sub-groupings of parents and/or children from different social, ethnic or educational backgrounds can be avoided, whether the children can assimilate and integrate the different learning experiences in home and school, and whether a mutual co-operation style with the teacher and amongst parents will be developed for the future (e.g. Raven 1980).

In any case parents and teachers should be aware of why and how they need each other. For example, 1st graders tend to substitute parents' authority for that of the teacher but the children's school enthusiasm and learning interest rapidly decline in the 2nd grade, so that good contacts can help both sides at different times considerably.

Despite the many encouraging examples of close home–school contacts in the first period of schooling, there is little continuity in the following grades and a co-operation problem generally arises with the child's transition to secondary education. On the whole, schools and society are still too little concerned with horizontal discontinuity – i.e. between home and school – compared to vertical discontinuity – i.e. with transitions from one educational level to the next (Arbeitsgruppe Elternarbeit 1981; Borgmeier *et al.* 1980).

Integrating minority families

As important as an early start in co-operation is the attention paid to minority parents since they are burdened with additional difficulties. On the one hand, their children tend to be isolated in school (if they are not trapped by competing educational styles), and on the other hand parents do not easily fit into the usual home–school relations (so that they often withdraw immediately). Thirdly, schools expect the children to have learning handicaps and to increase teaching difficulties (which shows that schools do not sufficiently adapt themselves to the needs of children).

Given these difficulties it cannot come as a surprise that many early intervention programmes failed because they started from the children's difficulties at school and demanded home support – for example, with regard to enforcing language and skill training. The problem of cultural differences (e.g. in terms of learning interest and value orientation) was hardly taken into consideration. Gradually these failures led to a more complex understanding that minority parents often understand neither school expectations nor their children's difficulties at school, that primary school teachers are too seldom bilingual and acquainted with the problems of multicultural education, and finally that children often cannot communicate their particular needs. Beyond this, some uneasiness might exist amongst majority parents if they fear that teachers will diverge from normal school procedures and achievement standards (e.g. Birkelbach 1982; Flesza 1982).

The sooner other co-operation projects took cultural differences into consideration, the more they involved parents in a considerable share in arranging school activities and curricular matters, and regarded co-operation as a chance to tap home and school resources for the child's development. These approaches appeared to be more efficient, since the extended contacts allowed more in-group safety for all children and supported minority children and their parents in understanding learning strategies and handicaps. In addition, if minority parents felt accepted as partners they were more willing to draw on the teacher's and other parents' experience (Compagnoni 1982; Olmos 1983; Cetinsoy 1983; Huart 1982). Finally, the approach made it easier for teachers to cope with the children's and families' attitudes and to establish an accepting class climate ready for a multicultural give and take.

Even these strategies did not completely fulfil expectations, because minority parents tend to be more easily satisfied with the schools' arrangements and teaching programmes than majority parents even though the latter participated to a greater extent. According to a US case study, about 85 per cent of minority parents felt welcome to observe classroom teaching but not more than 43 per cent did in fact participate; and although 60 per cent of minority parents knew that their children's records were available for review, not more than 18 per cent actually examined them (Lynch and Stein 1987).

In the face of such experiences, the scope of co-operation was sometimes extended to home-related areas in order:

- to increase the minorities' motivation in participation,
- to acquaint teachers and majority parents with the culture and concerns of the minorities (e.g. to what extent Turkish fathers and boys accept female teachers), and
- to develop a co-operative out-of-school climate that allowed – if not appreciated – cultural differences.

With regard to such broader concepts of co-operation much can be learned from co-operation strategies used with handicapped children. Those concepts often begin developing communication channels for trusting relations or involve parent-to-parent services or home-visiting schemes (the latter are reported for one in five English primary schools) and recognise the powerful influence of parents on school learning. In the long run, these strategies are obviously quite effective, so that American legislation strongly demands that parents of handicapped children have the right to participate in the assessment and programme planning process for their children (see Public Law 94–142 and the Education for All Handicapped Children Act of 1975) (e.g. Hannon and Jackson 1987; Buchan *et al.* 1988; Hornby *et al.* 1987). Perhaps the advantages should not be limited to handicapped children and all parents should be accepted as real partners of the professionals.

In general, extended co-operation (supported by parent advisory schemes or parent teachers, etc.) is all the more needed, the greater the shortage of multilingual teachers, and the more the social fabric in Europe changes in the near future. The question arises as to why extended co-operation should not be advantageous for all children. Extended co-operation certainly helps to reduce the often existing mis-match in education between home and school and to limit or avoid much unnecessary conflict.

Accepting and avoiding conflict

Co-operation can only be successful if conflicts are neither overestimated nor underestimated and if their social, institutional and personal causes are distinguished. Generally, schools and homes should be more aware that new endeavours to intensify home–school links tend to imply new conflicts. Such conflicts may result from social problems, inadequate frameworks, initial contact difficulties and false expectations or participants' personal shortcomings. Although some conflicts tend to be insoluble (e.g. if they result from the repercussions of competing social or political structures), nevertheless many of the other conflicts can be reduced, if they are due to the school's framework, to role perceptions or to limited experience with group dynamics. Insight into the reasons for the conflicts is a prerequisite for improvements in co-operation.

Some conflicts tend to be insoluble if contradictions between social and educational demands have repercussions on home–school relations, as the following example illustrates. On the one hand, our competitive social and economic structure strongly rewards qualifications so that parents are compelled to concentrate on their children's school marks and success. On the other hand, schools expect parents not to be too occupied with grades but to strive for an overall education of their children (Huelshoff *et al.* 1979). So certain conflicts in home–school relations are almost inevitable and they increase proportionally with the influence of examination results on life chances, particularly in times of youth unemployment. However, if such socially inbuilt conflicts are clearly recognised, it becomes much easier for parents and teachers to avoid misplaced blame.

In addition, conflicts may arise if co-operation does not limit itself to parental support for school learning, but also deals with the children's general development and overall questions of pedagogy and educational policy. Such conflicts obviously have to be accepted since they are nothing but a reflection of our pluralistic society where educational aims are no longer uncontroversial. Another set of conflicts must follow from the differing educational roles, functions and priorities amongst parents and teachers, because parents have to undertake the overall and personal education of their child in the face of subject specialisation in the schools. On the other hand, schools have to respect the aims of educational policy and have to pay attention to curricula and to organise learning in a class situation.

Such existing conflicts are too often suppressed instead of being accepted because teachers and schools traditionally have little experience of coping with them. Such conflicts, however, exist in all pluralistic societies (much more often in other spheres of life than in schools). They cannot be solved by formal administrative measures and their suppression only leads to distrust and hinders real co-operative compromises.

In any case, the most widespread and common conflicts are so-called soluble conflicts, which could be either smoothed over or avoided. They tend to result from misjudgements of the different educational functions, from insufficient planning of co-operation and from inadequate behavioural patterns. Probably, home and school links are most severely hindered by the fact that the participating groups rely too much on fixed roles. Schools tend to function too much according to institutional structures, set curricula and self-images. Teachers often have too little training for co-operation and they are generally not really familiar with adult pedagogy. Sometimes they even refrain from co-operation because their weekly teaching load does not include time for parent contacts (as in Finland) or because they still live with a tradition that blamed parents for their children's difficulties. Finally, parents often focus quite narrowly on momentary or personal problems and their attitudes towards teachers may even be impeded by their own school experiences some 20 years previously. Generally, parents are a somewhat unstable factor for an institutional partnership (Davies 1987). Nevertheless, according to many experiments much unnecessary anxiety, distrust and conflict can be reduced or avoided:

- if co-operation is started in the spirit of 'confidence-establishing measures' (e.g. by furthering group problem-solving abilities, including the skill of seeing ourselves as others see us),
- if contacts are furthered amongst parents (perhaps mediated by liaison teachers) and co-operation includes home-related areas as well as school-related areas,
- if parent volunteering in the classroom is something normal (so that parents are acquainted with the teacher's work and his/her enormous difficulties), and

- if teacher training pays more attention to home–school co-operation (so that teachers know how to consider the cultural, social or intellectual gaps between home and school).

All in all, conflicts can be reduced to a large extent by making parents and teachers more familiar with positive examples of co-operation, by depersonalising and defusing the socially inbuilt conflict potential, by opening up more areas of practical interaction, and by some joint in-service training.

On the whole, co-operation between home and school has greatly improved since the 1970s. Mutual collaboration has become well established in some areas (e.g. in the 1st grade) and considerable efforts have been made in others (e.g. with regard to minority families). Nevertheless, there still exists too much stereotyping amongst the participating groups and undue anxiety with regard to conflicts.

8. Summary

Although mutual co-operation had been favoured by educational reformers in earlier centuries and repeatedly been in vogue in periods of social change, there had never been such a unanimous swing towards parental involvement as in the 1970s. This trend was due to four almost overlapping factors: first, social unrest linked with demands for more 'participatory democracy'; secondly, better educated parents; thirdly, research pointing to the great home influence on children's socialisation and learning progress; and fourthly, increasing disappointment with educational planning and the impersonality and specialisation of schools.

Today the main objectives of home–school co-operation are: to promote the child's social well-being and learning development by a better fit of both educational spheres; to stimulate the educational and social competency of parents through pedagogical information and participatory learning; and to reduce the schools' social isolation and counteract the remoteness of school subjects, bringing them more in touch with the child's experience.

How co-operation is organised depends on national traditions, social demands and ideological positions. Since the late 1960s, however, most European countries have required some parental involvement at the class and/or school level. Parent representation at regional or national levels is less common and seldom demanded. Particular differences exist among countries with regard to the function of parental involvement and representation – whether they should be informed, consulted or participate in decision making.

Beyond the formal framework, the scope, concept and direction of co-operation strongly depend, first, on 'immanent concepts', which favour co-operation sometimes with regard to school achievement and sometimes with regard to a better-balanced socialisation. Secondly, co-operation depends on role-specific expectations, attitudes and competences, which finally decide how principals, teachers and parents co-operate. Thirdly, it depends on public attitudes towards the family and its educational function.

Conclusions with regard to more effective and less conflicting co-operation should be:

- A *legal framework* is needed everywhere, to guarantee parental information on their own children (including some access to school records) and to facilitate or clarify the function of parent participation at different administrative levels.
- *Financial support* would greatly improve co-operation, if it allowed teachers some time off for intensified contacts, and/or made home-visiting schemes or liaison teachers possible (first of all in view of minority parents' needs).
- *In-service training* should pay more attention to home–school relations (including adult pedagogy and conflict solving) and should offer some joint sessions for parent representatives, staff and administrators.
- *Schools' manpower* should be better exploited with regard to co-operation in making more use of parents and teachers with special experiences (e.g. with home-related aspects of co-operation) or by establishing parent-to-parent services.
- Finally *research* should be encouraged, to compare the consequences of different co-operation strategies in terms of their long-term repercussions on child development, on parents' and teachers' attitudes and on the learning climate.

CHAPTER 4.2

Multicultural Education within European Traditions

Marcel Leurin

1. A backward glance

> Education should help young people to acquire a better knowledge of the world and its inhabitants and form attitudes which develop in them a spirit of appreciation and mutual respect for other cultures, races and lifestyles. Education should throw light on the relationship between the environment and lifestyles and standards of living. While presenting objectively the differences which exist in particular in political, economic and social systems, it should stress the common values, aspirations and needs in the lives and consciences of different peoples. Education should show that progress in human knowledge has been achieved by contributions from various peoples in the world, and that every national culture has been and continues to be enriched by contributions from other cultures.

The International Conference on Public Education held in Geneva in 1968 unanimously adopted this recommendation.

Directive 77/486/EEC (25 July 1977) on the education of the children of migrant workers does not confine itself to issuing moral exhortations; it imposes an obligation on member states of the European Community to take a series of three measures for the benefit of such children:

- help with initial reception so as to enable them to obtain benefit from attending schools in the country where they are resident;
- organising, in association with their countries of origin, courses in language and culture which will enable them to preserve their identity and make their return possible;
- special training for teachers who are to receive such children in their classes.

In Dublin in May 1983 the Standing Conference of Ministers of Education – we now go beyond the frontiers of the European Community into the 21 member states of the Council of Europe – unanimously adopted a resolution recommending an 'education with an intercultural dimension'. That type of education is recommended for children of migrant workers and also for all other pupils.

In Strasbourg on 25 September 1984, the Committee of Ministers of the Council of Europe adopted (with the exception of the United Kingdom delegate who did not oppose the recommendation but reserved the right of her government to comply with it or not) Recommendation No. R (84) 18 on 'the training of teachers in education for intercultural understanding, notably in a context of migration'. That means, in the context of the Council of Europe, that all teachers should be trained for intercultural education, even though more attention may be given to regions with a migrant population.

2. The intercultural approach

The Geneva recommendation and the EEC directive use no specific terminology when describing the objectives. The Dublin resolution and Recommendation R (84) 18 explicitly refer to intercultural education.

Moreover, sociologists, politicians of all tendencies, educational theorists and teachers employ, either indiscriminately or with different meanings, various terms with the same root 'cultural' but with different prefixes: 'multi', 'pluri', 'inter', 'trans'.

This confusion is particularly regrettable as well as inexplicable since from the end of the 1970s highly qualified experts of the Council of Europe have expended much effort to reach a unanimous and precise definition of those terms in order to remove any ambiguity in the semantic field and in the methodologies to be introduced in the various sectors of social life where the matters addressed under these various labels are considered.

Multicultural is used to describe the situation of societies, groups or social entities in which many sub-groups or individuals belonging to different cultures live together, whatever lifestyle they have adopted – they may have chosen to be integrated into the society of the majority or to live in self-sufficiency with no connection with members of this society. Example: London has a multicultural society.

Pluricultural is almost a synonym; it is used in the same circumstances to indicate that a particular situation exists. But instead of stressing the existence of a large number of cultures in contact, attention is simply drawn to their plurality. Example: in a school the entertainments committee is pluricultural.

Intercultural is not limited to describing a particular situation. This term provides a precise definition for:

- a procedure, an approach, a dynamic process of a social nature (in politics, teaching, education, . . .) to which the partners are positively committed – groups or individuals belonging to different cultural communities – and aware of their interdependence. Example: in this school education is intercultural;

- the thinking, philosophy, policy, etc. behind the adoption of such an approach. Example: intercultural philosophy has resulted in the school committee drafting new curricula;
- the option itself. Example: the intercultural option has increased collaboration between teachers of different ethnic origins.

Transcultural is hardly used at all in the Council of Europe. This term, like the one above, designates a movement. But whereas 'intercultural' implies exchange, relationship, reciprocity, or mutual recognition, 'transcultural' indicates a unilateral movement, the passage from one cultural situation to another. Example: a minority community abandoning its traditional dress and conforming to the local customs is a transcultural phenomenon.

With these definitions available, it becomes clear that, of the four documents mentioned earlier, Directive 77/486/EEC is not based on intercultural concerns: its unilateral aim is to 'do something for the benefit of the children of migrant workers' (e.g. schooling, preserving their identity, possible re-integration) without any regard for the cultural enrichment that the presence of their communities might contribute to the native population.

3. Relevance of the intercultural approach

Before adopting such an approach, even if recommended by the eminent international authorities, we should be sure that intercultural education has sociological relevance – is it appropriate to the social conditions we are familiar with in our countries? We should also be sure that it has economic relevance – in the light of current developments is this teaching approach realistic or does it appear idealistic? It must have ecological relevance – does it meet the requirements of man's relationship with the environment in which he lives? And finally it needs ethical relevance – are we likely to approve of the values which this type of teaching helps to inculcate?

Sociological relevance

Most European countries introduced measures during the 1970s in order to reduce or stop immigration. But the ease with which more and more people can travel has made the effectiveness of such measures purely relative. As a result, the proportion of foreigners in classes and in schools, particularly in large densely populated city areas, is often very high.

But it is not only migrants who bring about the cultural heterogeneity of our societies. Inequalities in economic levels give rise to subcultures that develop distinctive features based on common characteristics, and it is only right that the school should take these into account because it is concerned to raise every child, for his/her own benefit and that of society as a whole, to the highest level of his/her intellectual abilities.

Finally, the way states have developed and the connections they have come to build up have resulted in fairly large ethnic minorities finding themselves in an enclosed situation in many societies. Recent conflicts in East European countries, in southern Africa, in the Far East and in the United States are proof, if such is required, that those phenomena are not to be found exclusively in Western European countries.

There is no space here to deal at length with the problem of demographic inequalities in the various communities making up our societies. I shall therefore simply point out that it helps to increase the relevance of what we are discussing.

In societies containing such unequal elements it is in everyone's interest and essential for social harmony to develop mutual understanding between their constituent communities. The intercultural approach helps to make this possible.

Economic relevance

For a long time the school was regarded everywhere as simply a dispenser of knowledge, at first only to those whose membership of certain social classes bestowed on them privilege, and later on to everyone, but only by a process of cultural adjustment on the part of the newcomers who had no other choice but to adapt themselves to the system and the content of the education provided. Unskilled employment was so plentiful that the economic structure enabled those who were unsuitable to be absorbed. Their failure was simply noted and attributed to their lack of intelligence or to laziness.

The increasing use of more and more high technology requires a significant raising of the level of training of the workforce as a whole. In addition, economists have been astonished at the poor return on the substantial sums invested in the 'educational machine'. Thus, the requirement for qualified manpower and the need to reduce the cost of education concur in seeking to raise the school success rate – in other words in seeking the success of children hitherto resigned to failure, including the children of ethnic or cultural minorities and the children of immigrant workers.

The development of this approach is to a large extent dependent on intercultural teaching.

Ecological relevance

The information we receive daily through the media demonstrates that the health and survival of people in a particular country or region depend frequently on events occurring thousands of miles away.

The extraction, production and marketing of raw materials can no longer be left to simple market laws, or controlled by the use of armed force. For example, a nuclear reactor in a power station got out of control and caught fire in Chernobyl and contaminated clouds throughout the entire world make fruit and vegetables inedible. And if freon continues to be used as a propellant gas in aerosols, the destruction of the ozone layer in the atmosphere will result in an increase in skin cancer throughout the world.

People must come to understand one another beyond frontiers and cease to fear each other. That will be achieved by better mutual understanding, which the intercultural approach encourages.

Ethical relevance

The children of immigrants and of ethnic or cultural minorities are frequently assimilated to the educationally disadvantaged of the indigenous population for whom special arrangements are made to keep them afloat. This is because the institution is generally focused not on the learners but on the standardised results - knowledge and competence - that they are required to achieve in a certain time.

When the teaching process recognises the basic aptitudes and needs - linguistic, psychological, social - of the learners it discovers that it has to take account of specificities disregarded up to that point. And over and above the study of the pupils' culture it becomes involved in analysing the culture it conveys through its language, its curricula, its books, its ways of doing things . . . .

The discovery of their own ethnocentricity leads anybody interested in humanity to compare cultures in contact and to discover that what appear to be cultural hierarchies are without any rational foundation, and are simply the outcome of relationships based on economic strength resulting in the culture of those who perform manual tasks being regarded pejoratively and the culture of those who have power being grossly overvalued.

Thus intercultural teaching, by providing everyone with the opportunity of comparing their culture in a practical way with that of others, also has ethical relevance.

4. Intercultural education

But what is this intercultural approach, which I have said is highly recommended and of great relevance in many ways?

A little history

What does the school generally do with its minorities, of whatever kind? In its desire to achieve the - mythical! - homogeneity of classes, it counts on the acculturation of all those who are in its care, whatever the official statements may say about objectives: independence, responsibility, social sense, curiosity, experimental attitude, etc. Moreover, teaching is organised in terms of curricula and timetables, almost exclusively on the basis of cognitive norms. And what is done about the pupils who lag behind? Attempts are made to bring them up to standard by means of remedial teaching. If the therapy fails the willingness to bring them up to standard ceases and they are transferred to a special teaching class which will do what it can for them.

In schools and countries where the most concern has been shown about adapting to an influx of foreign children, measures have been introduced that have always followed the same lines.

From the outset, the absence of knowledge of the teacher language has always been regarded as the sole obstacle to the assimilation of the children of immigrants. Was there no better solution, in order to enable them to benefit fully from compulsory schooling, than to put them together temporarily in initiation or adaptation classes and give them intensive language courses?

At first, those courses were mounted with staff in the school who were unqualified for this kind of work. It quickly became clear that the methodology used to teach the mother tongue was not appropriate for these pupils. The next step was to employ audio-visual methods for learning a foreign language . . . only to find that they were too far removed, because of their cultural content, from the daily life of the pupils concerned.

The next step was that teams of the most lively and most willing teachers prepared audio-visual material based on situations actually experienced by the pupils, in the hope that effort could be saved by using the material again with other pupils. They soon discovered that the hope was ill-founded, that the cultural nearness of the content was not enough to make the message effective, and that the way to make the effort worthwhile was to base the material on the pupils' experiences.

And that is in fact how intercultural teaching began. It means that, in a multicultural environment, pupil-centred teaching is bound to result in taking account of widely differing individual needs and interests and comparing them.

The other approaches described above are characterised by their standardising and unilateral nature: new arrivals have to be changed in order to make them conform to the accepted standards of the national school system – which amounts to assimilation.

Principles

While dominant groups are naturally inclined to absorb any foreign bodies, the intercultural approach condemns any policy designed to assimilate migrants and cultural minorities by the country in which they live. This is based on the principle that the migrant phenomenon brings into contact individuals and groups none of whom is *a priori* superior to another, and none of whom represents *a priori* a danger to another.

Interculturalism is not therefore a matter exclusively concerned with migrants; intercultural teaching is relevant to all children, and not only those belonging to an ethnic or cultural minority. Society has to make what amounts to a difficult choice, in the context of a world that, if it is to survive, must opt for interdependence instead of retreating into a defensive posture.

Inevitably, activities arising from an option covering such an area frequently encounter obstacles erected by special interests, and are confronted with many difficulties. But the essence of the intercultural approach is that none of the problems it gives rise to is capable of a unilateral solution.

Is the intercultural approach culturally neutral?

Clearly, the objectives of school education are laid down by the general policy of governments which in turn depend on the values underlying what people believe and how they live out their daily lives.

Edward T. Hall has made a very successful study of this phenomenon and has described it in a number of significant works. The following comments are based on one of them (Hall 1976).

Some peoples have a poor cultural context while others have a rich one. In the case of the first (generally speaking, in the western countries) a high value is placed on independence and individual responsibility; in the second, behaviour is linked to each situation and takes place within a strict and unchanging context (a chain of actions where one action leads to the next), with society exerting continuous control.

It follows that interculturalism, based on the perception and mutual acceptance of cultures in contact, is closer to the way of life and customs of societies with a poor cultural context than to that of societies with a rich cultural context. Consequently, the distance to be travelled to adopt the intercultural approach is immensely shorter and easier for Europeans of the west – and in particular for those living in towns – than for migrants and members of ethnic minorities.

That does not remove in any way the need to adopt this approach; the cultural enrichment of all, the improvement of mutual acceptance, and the raising of the rate of success at school are dependent on it. But teachers must appreciate that the effort required by some pupils is enormous and that they must endeavour, by increasing contacts with families, to bridge as far as possible the gap separating the principles governing school activities and the concepts prevailing in the family unit.

Cross-breeding?

It is not unusual for politicians or teachers to jibe at adopting the intercultural approach; they are attached to their own culture and are afraid they might have to give up some of its features and adopt the cultural characteristics of other communities.

Their fears are groundless and stem from a misunderstanding of the problem. The following good definition will be found in the *Little anthropological and sociological glossary of immigration* by Antonio Perotti, Director of the Centre for Information and Research on International Migration in Paris (cited by Baio 1985).

> Intercultural society: A political project which, arising from the cultural pluralism already present in a society - a pluralism limited to the juxtaposition of cultures and resulting solely in the enhancement of the status of cultures based on ethno-groups - tries to develop a new cultural synthesis. In contra-distinction to syncretic fusion or a 'melting pot' which leads to a fusion (confusion) of various cultural models with the loss of their own identity, and in opposition to the cosmopolitanism transmitted by the international market in cultural goods, the project for a new cultural synthesis means that original models generated by the cultures in contact — without however being restricted to any one culture - would be grafted on to the basic national culture, thereby strengthening and renewing it.

In this intercultural approach nobody is subjected to the slightest pressure, no one has to abandon their identity or the values they hold dear. But everyone, whatever their origin and cultural characteristics, sees themselves 'perceived' as a person marked by the imaginary and the symbolic which have made that person what they are. It is not possible to develop in a balanced way and to become harmoniously integrated into the society in which you live if your very existence is negated (Baio 1985).

But although no one is compelled to give up any part of their culture, there is no doubt that lifestyles, habits, even beliefs, by close contact in a context of mutual understanding, influence one another, modify one another, and contribute in so doing to the formation of that cultural synthesis described by Antonio Perotti.

Facets of intercultural education

Intercultural education clearly cannot be taught. It is not a new course taking its place alongside existing courses. Teachers at any level who are simply content with dispensing knowledge could never have access to it because the intercultural approach would in that case be emptied of its very substance.

Attempts by some schools to introduce original aspects of minority cultures in their curricula are not sufficient to establish intercultural education even though the process may be suitably initiated in this way. This thematic facet of the intercultural approach is nevertheless the best and almost the only means of introducing the subject where culturally homogeneous classes or schools are concerned. But that type of situation is and will be increasingly exceptional. It is appropriate to recall that one of the advantages of the intercultural approach is that it produces a situation in which pupils, teachers and parents can stand back and look at any sort of knowledge or belief, can compare their knowledge, and can question certainties of all kinds that continue to pit people against each other. Even in a homogeneous environment it is possible for any teacher fascinated by the human scene to evoke many points of view and show pupils and parents by means of this plurality of views that Manichaean attitudes can never be justified.

If intercultural education is to develop, communication between communities should be instituted inside and outside the classroom, and relate not only to children and adolescents but to all teachers and to all parents.

The use of the communication aspect can only happen in so far as school activities allow it. Schools must open their doors to the study of situations drawn from real life. Study of this kind, in addition to bringing about a functional approach to the subjects in the school curricula, leads to a comparison of the cultures in contact. The term is used here with its everyday meaning, which is sometimes disregarded by the thematic approach when all it offers pupils are thoughts about the prestigious, and the most unchanging, aspects of culture.

We now come to the third facet of the intercultural approach, the methodological facet. The children of migrant workers and of ethnic minorities frequently come from working-class backgrounds where learning is not surrounded with a prestigious halo and where things are only really interesting when they possess immediate usefulness.

By sinking its roots into the daily lives of the children the school gains in two ways: it forestalls lack of interest in study, a frequent source of premature detachment by the pupil, and it enables comparisons to be made of representative contributions from the many cultures existing side by side within the host society and creating what are more and more often called migrant cultures.

Awareness by the school of its pupils' cultures, when it happens in a multicultural environment – simply using 'the school open to life' teaching approach of the Decroly, Freinet and others like Paolo Freire – will inevitably develop into intercultural teaching.

Practical illustrations

While the intercultural approach is essential in all school subjects, some are particularly suitable for it: history, literature, music, geography . . . .

The most frequently used situations in nursery and primary schools are based on what some people disdainfully call 'food or folklore teaching': festivals or various national 'weeks' are organised in order to promote national or regional foods, songs, dances, ways of dressing, etc. Introducing specific folklore characters from one or another community can go even further (e.g. the Turkish puppets Karagoz and Haçivat who appeal to adults just as much as to their children).

History is taught so as to show how highly relative are the value judgements expressed by one side or the other: the Crusades, the Arabs in Spain, the Yom Kippur War, the Intifada, the 1914–18 and 1940–45 wars . . . .Other aspects of this subject have been illuminated by analogies discovered in events occurring a long way apart in space and time (for example, the foundation and development of Brussels, with shipping on the Senne, and of Fez, with camel transport in caravans, show unsuspected and remarkable parallels).

Classes are involved in special occasions of importance to the families of pupils belonging to various communities - Haïd el Kebir, Ramadan, Lent, marriages, births . . .

When starting to compare various types of living accommodation, a comparison can be made between the living conditions and the family in the Maghreb countries and in countries of Western Europe.

Many examples of this interchange within the school can be given to illustrate the relevance of this approach. Questions raised on one side or another can lead to dossiers being assembled, or audio-visual aids being prepared. These can be circulated and enrich the knowledge and general culture of all concerned, comparing lifestyles, stimulating the discovery and acceptance of otherness.

Intercultural workshops, sponsored by the free university of Brussels, have been successfully organised in three nursery schools.

Films (fictional or documentaries) in the original language with sub-titles are shown in some secondary schools on one day a week during the mid-day break. They can stimulate interesting comparisons with certain countries' distinctive ways of life.

The theatre is one of the most fruitful sectors for this purpose both in the primary and in the secondary school. Thinking up a play, writing it, designing the scenery, organising the lighting and wiring for sound, then producing and performing it, provide opportunities for involving a number of school subjects while highlighting the cultural specificities of each community.

There are many cases where activities organised as part of an intercultural approach go beyond the strictly teaching sphere. The school then becomes open to the outside world and is brought into contact with the social aspect of intercultural studies. Many examples of this exist and have been the subject of case studies published by the Council of Europe. Three of them are briefly described below.

The Frais-Vallon (Marseille, France) Project

Taking the view from the outset that situations arising to a large extent from socio-economic deficiencies cannot be rectified exclusively by teaching, this project is focused on collaboration between the school and the neighbourhood. The strategy is based on the establishment of networks of activity centred on the school and involving families, communities, public institutions and associations. The activity fits in with the public authorities' plans to bring about a social revival of the neighbourhood by refurbishing its buildings and establishing a facility for continuous education.

Sponsored by the CEFISEM (Centre of research, training and information for the teaching of children of migrants) and with the collaboration of the centre's staff, people active in schools, political representatives and social workers have come together to work out how to utilise a whole range of resources and locate the most suitable sectors in which to deploy them: public libraries with activity organisers, sports clubs, day nurseries, various types of workshop, literacy classes, etc.

All the staff of the nursery and primary schools (60 people) were trained in the use of intercultural teaching methods by means of combined theoretical and practical training courses. Cultural excursions and festivals helped to bring people of different communities together. Moreover, people are seen to have fewer fears and prejudices. The vandalism that was rampant in the neighbourhood is diminishing considerably, and school results are improving.

The Zürich (Switzerland) Project

Here again the school is at the centre of the project, a project that has grown out of the need to cope with a large number of school failures and with the channelling of a large number of children of Italian origin into low-level streams.

The first stage consisted of showing, with the help of a psychologist of Italian origin using non-verbal or Italian language tests, that these pupils had a normal intelligence. This demonstration was brought about by the persistence of the parents' associations.

Once that operation was concluded, the next step was to bring Italian culture to the school. This was achieved by the joint efforts of the education authorities of the canton and of the very numerous associations of Italian immigrants in this region.

Two intercultural methodological techniques used in this project are noteworthy for the tremendous impact they had on the whole of the school's activities:

- the production of a trilingual journal (in German, Italian and French) containing articles for outside readers prepared by the pupils together with information relating to the various communities in the city;

- interviews conducted by the pupils with craftsmen and elderly members of their families; comparisons drawn from statements and documents obtained.

Coventry (United Kingdom) Project

The schools in the centre of the city have 50–80 per cent immigrant children, most of whom come from Ireland, India, Pakistan or the West Indies.

The project is targeted on both children and adults and is designed to bring about a considerable increase in intercommunity contacts. It is based on centres with well-defined objectives, as follows:

- a teacher training centre: in-service training of teachers (primary and secondary);
- a support service for minority groups: English language classes taught by peripatetic teachers;
- five community education centres whose aim is to encourage co-operation between the school and parents, especially mothers;
- two first-level community schools: out-of-school activities, leisure pursuits, continuing education for adults;
- five second-level community schools, open from 9.00 a.m. to 10.30 p.m. and offering many kinds of activities for all ages;
- in-house English language courses for business firms;
- home-taught courses.

Courses in the 'language of origin' are organised as part of the schools' activities and taught by teachers from the immigrant population paid by the public authorities. There are joint training courses for teaching staff to prepare appropriate methodologies, design curricula and devise teaching materials.

It must be clear from the above list that the training of teachers - of all teachers - for intercultural education is one of the major problems to be tackled in this approach. And it is not a simple problem to solve.

But important issues are at stake. The first is if we want to be consistent about building a citizens' Europe in the next few years that transcends economic considerations, however significant they may be. The second goes even beyond the frontiers of Europe and the wider nationalism that is sometimes to be discerned, if we wish to see all mankind, without distinction of any sort, treated fairly.

For useful information on the characteristics and requirements of this type of training, see Council of Europe publications (Rey 1986; Council for Cultural Co-operation 1983 <DECS/EGT [83] 62>; Symposium on *The intercultural training of teachers* <DECS/EGT [82] 61>).

The role of teachers of language and culture

Many emigrant countries organise courses in the language and culture of origin for their nationals, often in collaboration with the host countries. In the case of member states of the European Economic Community, Directive 77/486/EEC stipulates that such courses shall be organised (see section 1, above). In some cases (including the Netherlands, the Scandinavian countries and 6 of the 11 *Länder* of the German Federal Republic), the immigration countries organise such courses for the children of immigrants so that they will not be cut off from their roots. Minority ethnic groups sometimes make such arrangements themselves for the children of their community.

Whoever is the promoter, the organisation of courses in the 'languages and cultures of origin' is not necessarily a step in the right direction. When such courses are 'deferred' (French term), 'parallel' (Belgian term) or 'out-of-school' (EEC term), they become a burden for the pupils, possibly hampering their normal school progress and even their development.

It is not enough for a course to be inserted in the normal timetable of a class to become thereby an integrated course. When a teacher comes to a class to take away his young compatriots to another place to teach them his language and culture while the other pupils continue with their normal activities, the language and culture courses do not form an integral part of the whole, but are simply inserted instead of other activities. And in such cases it cannot, *a fortiori*, be described as intercultural education.

It is therefore better to abandon the term 'integrated courses' and substitute the expression 'inserted courses' when it is simply a matter of inserting them in the timetable.

We have therefore, by increasing degree of collaboration:

- *out-of-school courses*: outside the normal timetable for the pupils as a whole (whether or not the courses take place on school premises);
- *inserted courses*: appearing in the normal class timetable but simply inserted alongside other activities;
- *integrated courses*: appearing in the normal class timetable and forming an integral part of all activities.

Article 3 of the EEC Directive talks about promoting the teaching of the mother tongue. Mother tongue is easily said. In many migrant families the spoken language differs appreciably from the official language of the country of origin; can this official language be termed the mother tongue of the children of these families? And what is the mother tongue of young Turkish children born in Belgium, who, when playing with each other in the street, talk not Turkish, but French; and this even if their parents continue to speak Turkish at home?

The same article also speaks about promoting the culture of countries of origin. How far is it justified to speak of THE culture of a country? What is common about the culture of a Galician peasant, an Andalusian shopkeeper, a Madrid civil servant and a Basque fisherman; and what can the Spanish teacher of language and culture display in attempting to give an artificial unity abroad to what is locally so diversified? Moreover, it is incorrect to speak about 'culture of the country of origin' when referring to children born abroad.

The school system in various countries, by the choice of curricular methods and structures, eliminates the culture of groups that are economically, socially or numerically dominated; there is no other solution for the members of these groups but to be assimilated by the dominant population or to be rejected through failure at school. This highlights the fact that the intercultural approach is not only essential between migrants and indigenous populations. It is also vital that intercultural teaching between countries and within countries must be based on people as they are and not on the fictions they are supposed to conform to (learner-centred teaching).

Are language and culture courses designed exclusively or primarily to strengthen pupils' links with their countries of origin, or those of their parents, compatible with the intercultural approach?

Replying to such a question requires careful thought. It depends first of all on the relevance of such an objective. It is devoid of any intrinsic value and only deserves to be considered as a means of building a balanced personality, rooted in a stable environment that is full of meaning and serves as a symbolic anchorage. It depends, too, on the age of the child on arrival in the host country. The piece of earth in which children put down their roots is the neighbourhood of a town or a village much more than a country. Exposing children to the culture of the country of origin of their parents may be as far removed from their emotional needs as assimilating them to the standard culture of the host school. In short, what is required is to direct activity in this field towards the pupils' needs so as to fill any gaps that may occur and forestall the risk of cultural anomie.

Is it not the case that the nationalist objectives pursued by certain countries of origin are totally incompatible with the intercultural approach and are therefore to be totally condemned? The countries of origin and the host countries must negotiate the measures to be taken for the education of children of migrant workers. Are the real interests of these children properly taken into account in such negotiations?

It is likely that, without stating it in so many words, the authorities of the host countries hope that foreigners in general and their children in particular will merge nicely into the indigenous population. It is likely that, without giving it any more publicity, the authorities of the countries of origin hope that their nationals will maintain strong links with their homeland and nurture a strong desire to go back there. The economic advantages of such links are obvious. It is likely that this double and contradictory intention underpins the bilateral negotiations undertaken by the countries' respective diplomats.

Where in such encounters are the real interests of the pupils to be found and how can the teachers of language and culture take account of them? Those interests may be summarised by stating that all teachers must work together to give a coherent character to what they are doing and enable each child to develop a balanced personality. The main indicator of their success should be the pupils' achievements in the local school system.

Where the school has authentic intercultural teaching, the teachers of minority languages and cultures can play an extremely important role, in so far as their courses are properly integrated into the activities as a whole. That implies co-operation with the teaching team and is only conceivable when they have perfect command of the teaching language. Their contribution in such cases is beneficial in several ways:

- By being a member of the team they enhance the value of their culture in the eyes of the indigenous teachers, pupils and parents, and for the members of their community, usually regarded pejoratively because of the socio-economic status of most of its members.
- By the resources they supply (information, materials, etc.) they help with compiling dossiers and preparing intercultural activities.
- By being present and intervening in cases of conflict they improve relationships in the institution and so reduce tensions and vandalism.
- By acting as intermediaries between the school and families, they help the parents of minority groups to understand the working of the institution and diminish their fear of it; and they draw them into taking a greater part in the educational process of their children.
- By the combination of all these activities they help to increase the motivation for study of the children of their community, with invariably pleasing consequences in their school results. They assist those children and society as a whole, which will benefit both from their better vocational qualifications and from their better integration.

5. Conclusion

Every day we discover a little more that the survival of our world is bound up with the interdependence of those living in it. But every day too those who live in it are engaged in a ferocious competition which makes this interdependence more and more uncertain. By helping to lower the frontiers of all kinds – regional, national, language, ethnic, social, religious, philosophical, etc. – which separate people, intercultural education helps them to know one another and themselves better, makes their society more congenial and opens the doors to the 'anthropo-ethic' (Morin 1981).

Everyone who takes some responsibility or plays some role, however modest it may seem, in this immense movement of educational reform will be justifiably proud of having been part of such an undertaking.

CHAPTER 4.3

Continuity: A Necessity in Education

Monica Gather Thurler

Throughout Europe and the rest of the world, children in industrialised countries are faced with a very strange reality: never has the adult world known so much about children, never has there been so much literature and so many training and refresher courses on offer to 'professionalise' teachers, or indeed to form 'good' parents; never has such a variety of teaching materials, games and TV programmes been available; and never has there been such a wide range of school and out-of-school activities. And yet, never has there been such a feeling of duress, as witness the lower and lower age at which children start attending nursery schools (private, on a co-operative basis or official) to become 'socialised' and acquire pre-learning skills; or the spread of pre-school education, compulsory between the ages of 4 and 5, to prepare children for primary school. There is the further constraint of fixed timetables, fragmented school days, the necessity of adapting to the very varied demands of the new teacher and new classmates at the beginning of each school year, and the abrupt changeovers between school and family life, out-of-school activities and family weekend breaks. Lastly, many children are extremely apprehensive about the selection procedure at the end of primary education for the purpose of channelling them into the appropriate secondary stream and are distracted from their school work.

Some of these problems are undeniably caused by unrealistic and inappropriate attitudes, or expectations, on the part of parents, or else by the child's failure to adjust to the school's demands, but both researchers and actual teachers are looking hard and critically at the school itself.

Obviously, the problem is complex, and there is no simple solution: it embraces all the historical, political and social dimensions of the school. For instance, schools have great difficulty in assimilating new theories on the child's chronobiological development. According to specialists (Montagner 1983), the organisation of the school year (long summer holidays, holidays in October, the school year beginning in autumn, and the weekly timetable) fails to cater for the child's natural rhythm. It still reflects the needs of the late nineteenth-century agrarian society, which first and foremost employed children on a multitude of agricultural tasks (especially in summer), releasing them for schooling almost as an afterthought.

Furthermore, over the years schools have taken society as a model for their internal structures and hierarchies, which often push into the background the school's main aim of educating and instructing the children in its charge, fostering their specific abilities and fulfilling their individual needs, with a view to their optimum development.

This state of affairs may be explained in a variety of ways. Depending on the geographical, social and economic context, the various educational sections - pre-elementary, elementary and secondary - and the subjects themselves, develop independently of each other. In most cases this divergent development is reinforced by the sectoral organisation of school administration. Lastly, the parents' widely varying social and cultural interests help to maintain the hierarchical organisation of the different grades.

It may seem inevitable that the school should adopt the established sections into which learning is divided up and that each country or region should do so in a way that is partly arbitrary. Any anthropological or psycho-pedagogical investigation would find exactly the same. However, it has not yet been understood why the school adopts one mode of apportionment rather than another, why it changes over to another mode, or why in one particular case it splits up the sections and consequently the teachers and children, while keeping them together in another particular case, and vice versa.

Let us not forget here that the teachers themselves occasionally tend to forget their educational task in order to defend professional interests: prejudice, pettiness and jealousy among teachers from different educational sections or even levels hamper mutual understanding and disrupt communication and co-operation. This situation is aggravated by the particular institutional and political conditions applied to different categories of teachers. Differences in training, contracts of employment and salary conditions obscure the real basic equivalence of the act of teaching, irrespective of the school section or level in which it is carried out.

The children, for their part, have no hierarchical organisation in their lives and have no inkling of the school's formalised structure. Children's lives cannot be split up into life as a child and life as a pupil, into infant and junior school level, or into summer and winter life. They have a global, continuous perception of existence, but their development is a process that is neither continuous nor homogeneous. Not every aspect of their latent personality develops in exactly the same way. Although progress is its salient characteristic, children's development also has periods of stagnation or indeed regression. *Discontinuity in development may give rise to problems in the learning process, especially in the absence of a differentiated, individualised teaching method*. Discontinuity in educational and teaching assistance is bound to intensify learning difficulties, so that it is necessary to seek continuity in a child's education.

Again, each changeover into a new world brings with it the pleasure of new expectations but also an element of insecurity and anxiety; each transition also sets off a process of adjustment which may take a long time. The same is true of starting school and changing classes, levels or sections. Some children are very quick to overcome the problems of adjustment, while others take longer to regain their self-confidence, establish good relations with the new person of reference, decipher his/her reasoning, anticipate his/her expectations and be able to perform the requisite tasks.

Consequently, continuity in the primary school should be reflected in structures (both ordinary and special teaching), content, co-operation among the teachers involved, and lastly between school and outside or family life.

I shall therefore be looking in more detail into these fields in which more continuity in children's education might be sought, and attempting to illustrate my recommendations by presenting experiments that have been or are being conducted in the various member states of the Council of Europe. Since the purpose of this chapter is not to offer the reader a comparative study of the various existing systems (for such a study see Chapters 1.1 and 1.2), I thought it preferable to examine 'symptomatic' or original experiments aimed at putting the various exigencies of continuity into practice and demonstrating the difficulties involved in such undertakings.

I shall begin with the two 'key areas' in primary school: first, the transition from pre-elementary to elementary education, and secondly the transition to secondary education. In most countries these sections are kept very much apart. Although there are isolated experiments in unification (I shall mention some of these), it will be interesting to see the extent to which transition can be facilitated in cases where such changes are clearly going to be difficult or are at present impossible at the structural level.

I shall then consider the problem of continuity in primary education itself: the changeover from one class to another, from one level to another, and from one subject to another, continuity perceived as a problem of learning integration, and continuity as between ordinary and specialised teaching; and, in the third section, continuity between primary school and the outside world. I feel that this is the area where the greatest endeavours must and can be made.

1. Continuity between the main sections in education: pre-elementary, elementary and secondary education

The problems caused by transition differ according to the structure in question, and most of the solutions being developed are bound to remain local. However, a certain number of intermediate 'strategies' exist which might be developed with the adoption of more fundamental approaches, and this is the main type with which I shall be dealing.

Harmonious transition between pre-elementary and primary education

Many children have real difficulties when they move from pre-elementary to primary school, the reason being that there is frequently a rupture between the two levels. And yet pre-elementary and elementary education share many major objectives, particularly such general aims as concentration, behavioural strategies and social skills. They also share a large number of problems, such as motor instability, restlessness, aggressiveness, rivalry, etc. Consideration should therefore be given to the case for joint, continuous choices in connection with the methodological and educational approach.

What principally distinguishes primary from pre-primary education is that elementary education in most European countries tends to follow a set curriculum and have mandatory learning objectives. Since all primary school children need to attain specific educational objectives, they can easily become overworked. There is a risk of the more play-oriented learning contents and forms, where the aim is not only knowledge and skills but also the beginnings of independence and co-operation, for example, being pushed into the background.

Here, pre-elementary teaching methodology can come up with a variety of approaches for encouraging independent work at primary school as well, such as the principle of motivating children to develop their skills in the light of their own level, to co-operate, and to complete the work they have begun (preparing them for a primary school approach based on active individualisation). There is also the desire to give the widest possible scope for creative expression, flexible organisation of activities, less tension thanks to games, use of equipment familiar to the child and well-rooted in his family experience, etc.

Consequently, the continuity principle implies continuing to use and further develop in primary school everything learned at the pre-elementary stage, and tackling anything new only gradually and gently.

If links between pre-elementary and elementary education are to be improved, the same institutional framework is needed for both educational levels, which is not yet the case in all Western European countries.

The model of single education: the 'basis-school' in the Netherlands

In 1985 in the Netherlands, a system of unified schools, known as 'basis-schools', was set up to cater for children from 4 to 12 years of age. Integration of the two types of education, until then separate, is to be effected at the level of schools. The government has instituted a number of measures, spread over several years, to provide back-up for the process of implementing the new basic type of teaching, whose main objectives are the following:

- an uninterrupted development process centred on each pupil's individual development;

- phasing out the traditional system of classes determined by chronological age, automatically ending the system of repeating a year;
- more intensive supervision for children with learning difficulties;
- extending the range of educational and training opportunities.

The specialists (AVT 1988) commissioned by the Netherlands authorities to report on the progress of the operation, have highlighted the difficulties attached to implementing legislation, one of whose ambitious aims is the educational integration of nursery and primary school. They particularly point out that:

- teachers are too unprepared for applying differentiation, individualisation and the techniques of examination result analysis to be able to translate the aims of the legislation into concrete terms;
- progress towards differentiation and individualisation, and the actual implementation of continuous programmes, is long and arduous;
- although there are good methods of applying differentiation and individualisation in teaching, many teachers continue to teach along traditional lines, being unable to discard a mentality that 'still too often operates in terms of either pre-primary or primary teaching'.

It would appear that there has not been much progress in the educational integration of pre-primary and primary school since 1985. It has not yet been implemented in 35 per cent of schools, and at the same time it is uncertain whether the 65 per cent of schools that have adopted it are really putting it into practice, since the split between nursery school and primary school apparently continues in the Netherlands basis-schools.

The Geneva solution (Switzerland): 'Fluidity'

The Geneva reform assigns the nursery school a new ambitious role as a compensatory instrument designed to neutralise handicaps, in the quest for greater equality of educational opportunity.

This new dimension, together with the determination to make the first school years into a harmonious whole where *each child can* integrate easily, *prepare for, start out on and proceed with learning without a break, without having to change their attitude and with the same resources*, is the basis of the 'fluidity' approach, which was tried out between 1974 and 1977 and is in current use in all Geneva schools (Feyler and Hutin 1981). The approach, which involves adapting structures, curricula and educational attitudes as a whole to the child's character and living conditions, moves away from the traditional notion of 'one school for all' towards the more recent idea of a diversified school able to adapt to each pupil's particular potential and needs. It has therefore to develop between two clearly opposed poles, that of biological and cultural inequalities among children and that of the equality of their basic education.

In keeping with this spirit, the pre-elementary section has been extended to the second year of primary school to form one continuous educational process – with the title '*Division élémentaire*' (elementary section) – embracing the four stages of basic learning.

	Elementary section			*Middle section*
1 PE	2PE	1P	2P	3P to 6P
Emphasis on: socialisation	pre-learning	learning	learning consolidation and continuation	

This new structure, based on adequate training for teaching staff, makes it possible to envisage most children moving up from one grade to the next without the risk of having to repeat a year and with maximum equality of opportunity for succeeding.

Nevertheless (as is also the case with the Netherlands model), introducing a system allowing children to move up automatically until the second year of primary school can only be considered in close conjunction with the establishment of foundations for properly understood remedial education based on differentiated educational activities tailored to the specific expectations of individual pupils, both the achievers and the under-achievers. The basic elements in the procedure – which follow from each other – are the following:

- teaching based on differentiation,
- evaluation to be formative,
- global educational back-up.

Difficulties have emerged in accurate evaluation of the experiment because the people involved – teachers and inspectors – vary widely in character, both in their personal conception of the school's role and aims, and in their approach to the problems of this first phase of school education. I shall do no more here than list the difficulties that have impeded realisation of the objectives:

- drawing distinctions between differentiated methods of teaching and those based on active individualisation;
- understanding that developing a differentiated type of education – as to when learning should start and what educational procedures, activities and resources should be used – is not incompatible with preserving identical joint objectives, e.g. children being able to read by the end of the second primary year;

- not only acknowledging differences but agreeing actually to take them into account;
- promoting and maintaining good relations between the regular class teacher and the ancillary teacher; such relations should be seen as the basis for the continuation and reinforcement of the educational process in class and for joint work on the part of both teachers to promote each child's development.

Nevertheless, before some countries or regions could achieve structural integration like that currently being realised in schools in the Netherlands and Geneva, they would still have to overcome a number of structural and organisational difficulties. The main difficulty, however, lies in the area of teacher training: teachers have scant knowledge of the major educational trends and the various directions in which teaching and learning methods are moving. Most of them seem to have acquired one single teaching method and only a few are able to take the 'pupil learning' dimension into account in their practice, closely geared to teaching.

This is probably the main reason why many countries (e.g. the Federal Republic of Germany, Austria and German-speaking Switzerland) are today still attempting to solve the problem of the transition from pre-primary to primary teaching by means of special classes (known as integration classes, small classes, etc.). I do not have enough room here to elaborate on curricula and methods in these special classes; nevertheless, they pose a number of important questions:

Does a pupil learn only with the teacher?

It should be noted that I am in no way questioning the usefulness of such classes, whose smallness above all promotes a special teacher–pupil relationship. What I do refute is the underlying educational ideology which posits that children can learn only with the teacher. If we really take seriously the idea that children learn a lot from one another and would learn even more in given educational and methodological contexts, we can hardly remain attached to the principle of grouping together in one class a large number of children with problems of a 'psycho-affective immaturity' or 'language disorder' nature. This, in my view fundamental, consideration is compounded by two further questions:

How are problems of diagnosis to be resolved?

The transition from pre-primary to primary school is a very important event in a child's life. All parties concerned have high hopes when this new chapter of life opens. Any measure or element making entry conditions more difficult, such as psychological tests, etc., and any change to a general entry procedure, trigger major defensive reactions. Some parents simply reject tests, while others question the measures proposed and interminable pleadings and discussions demand much time and energy. Selection machinery invariably prompts argument about the methods used, especially where such sensitive events as entry to primary school are involved. Relations among parents, nursery school teachers and education authorities deteriorate, making the start of school life even more difficult for the child.

What is the best way of dealing with the stringencies of selection?

Special classes inevitably involve a number of regulations. Who is to decide which child must attend a special class? What are the criteria for this decision? Do parents have a right of decision? Who is to decide, if a ruling is challenged?

We have absolutely no means of forecasting a child's future development, whether they will do well or badly at school; nor are we ever likely to have, given the wide range of inter- and intra-individual differences. Selection criteria are vague, difficult to determine and usually elastic – hence the danger of special classes being 'filled' with children presenting a wide range of problems for the sake of ensuring that such classes are continued in years when the numbers drop.

These few considerations show the full value of the above-mentioned experiments in the Netherlands and Geneva, despite the difficulties of implementation.

Harmonious transition between elementary and secondary education

Here we find problems of similar complexity to those described in connection with the changeover from nursery to elementary education, and also the need for educational rather than political and administrative solutions in the transition period (or rather the lack of transition period) from primary to secondary education, which brings with it difficulties that are almost insuperable for some children. While it is essential that primary education should take into account the demands of the child's subsequent education, a number of changes are still required in the first few years of secondary education if the two types of education are to be successfully bridged.

Many children are apparently disturbed by contradictions between the two educational approaches when they move from primary to secondary school. Primary school is usually characterised by its child-centred approach (which tends to be more so as time passes), its classroom-centred school life (where children stay in the same, often highly personalised room), with one teacher per class. Secondary education is characterised first by its subject-centred approach, with more than one teacher, and the often standardised (and impersonal) use of different premises.

There is something artificial in this gulf between the two systems, as in others: the supposed gulf between content and method, between types of knowledge, know-how and life skills, between general and specific objectives, and between the establishment of independence and socialisation. Continuity does not mean uniformity, and the different aims assigned to primary and secondary education can very well be adapted to differing approaches, provided they are complementary. What should be avoided is an abrupt break anywhere in the chain of school life, which inevitably unsettles certain children.

This is why some countries are aiming at continuity in children's education from the age of 3 to 16, by means of a genuine basic school covering pre-primary education and the whole compulsory school period. For example, we should remember that, in the 1960s, the United Kingdom and Sweden were among the first European countries to introduce major reforms in the lower secondary school section. From being selective (grammar and secondary modern schools) almost all British state schools are now comprehensive, i.e. they take in all the pupils from one catchment area under the same roof instead of splitting them up into different schools according to their academic standard (Harland and Lawton 1988). Similarly, the Swedish school system was reorganised with the aim of setting up a comprehensive form of education with two objectives in mind: equality of opportunity, and educating the citizens of a modern pluralistic and democratic society (Lundgren 1988). Research began showing as long ago as the 1970s that the reforms were not producing the expected level of equality. First, social stratification has proved to be a much more persistently decisive factor than had been thought. Secondly, teachers tended to perpetuate earlier learning and teaching patterns pertaining to an 'aristocratic and selective' type of education, instead of adopting new patterns better suited to the requirements of a heterogeneous population.

A number of countries are currently seeking solutions to such problems through experiments based on a more educational and less 'egalitarian' rationale. The experimental school in Bielefeld, Federal Republic of Germany, provides an example of a global approach to the problem. The children remain together throughout the entire period of compulsory schooling. The common core principle is adhered to as far as possible, the inevitable teaching problems being solved by intensive individualisation of teaching. The school has also made use of the following structural and methodological resources: longer periods are spent at each educational level (which means more time for achieving the set aims); different contents are linked on the basis of areas of experience (i.e. subjects are grouped according to transdisciplinary themes cutting across all subjects); daily, weekly and yearly teaching is judiciously organised so as to alternate between a variety of learning forms – discovery, project and mastery learning; there is also a complex system of optional subjects to complement the basic compulsory teaching for all pupils. This structure provides considerable scope for internal differentiation.

Other countries, however, have opted for keeping differentiated tracks, particularly for 11 or 12 year olds. We should note that this approach, which aims at solving the problem of heterogeneity, results none the less in very heterogeneous tracks through which the principle of the same progress rate is imposed on all pupils.

However, I shall leave the matter at that, since it is more vulnerable to social, economic and political fluctuations than to educational considerations and proposals. I might simply state that 'single' structures covering the whole compulsory schooling period are very unlikely to become the norm in the near future. What will probably happen is that lower secondary school sections will be kept separate, although they will share the primary school's educational concerns more than in the past (e.g. internal differentiation, catering for individual needs, etc.). I might quote a few of the very many experiments that are being or have already been carried out in this field: the *Scuola Media Unica* in Italy and Italian-speaking Switzerland, the AVO (abteilungsübergreifende Versuche an der Oberstufe) model in the canton of Zürich (Switzerland) (Oertel *et al.* 1986). These experiments all share a concern to make transition more harmonious, either by abolishing all forms of selection after primary school (all children indiscriminately moving up into a single comprehensive structure as in Italy and Italian-speaking Switzerland), or by replacing the examination at the end of primary school by a negotiated decision between the primary and secondary school teachers and the parents. The children are channelled into one of the streams of the secondary school section, so that the course chosen is not final but can be changed according to individual needs following consultation with all parties concerned (the method advocated by AVO).

In the light of the above, then, I shall attempt to pinpoint the means whereby it is possible to guarantee continuity in the transition from primary to secondary education. In practical terms, the continuity principle means that:

- teachers from the various school sections should engage in dialogue and co-operation, especially before and after the transition period;
- education should be organised in as global and transdisciplinary a manner as possible, with considerable room for social interaction;
- teaching should draw on the pupils' real-life experience and use practical activities to enable them to grasp abstract concepts;
- teaching should be largely individualised, with working periods to be used at will by the pupil for activities chosen and planned with the teacher;
- part of the teaching should be devoted to activities promoting a corporate class spirit;
- the learning approach should emphasise individual, autonomous activities;
- evaluation should mainly be formative and individualised, and based on observation of the learning processes.

All attempts to achieve greater continuity throughout the compulsory schooling period should provide a better response to pupils' expectations when they enter each new section and avoid disappointing them in their desire for new learning experience.

2. Continuity within primary teaching

It might seem surprising that I have decided to devote a special section to this subject. Surely primary education constitutes a self-sufficient whole, which might have all sorts of problems, but certainly none to do with continuity? And yet such problems do emerge in primary schools. The often rigid pupil grouping systems do not necessarily correspond (and are often an obstacle) to the pupils' individual rates of development and assimilation; the same applies to the excessive fragmentation of education across the various subjects. Again, there is currently much critical debate about internal selection as it is actually practised by means of a whole parallel set-up, which comes into operation when there are too many inter-individual differences for the teacher to cope alone. It is nevertheless interesting to note that primary education is tending to cast doubt on a number of principles belonging to the revered legacy of the 1960s.

Graded course structuring

In primary education, as in most secondary school tracks, pupils must follow a course whose structure comprises successive grades, each covering a one-year curriculum designed to prepare pupils for moving up to the following grade. Only in the nineteenth century did such an organisation seem obvious and natural. Originally, several grades co-existed (and still co-exist in small schools in peripheral regions) in the same class group. With urban expansion, the tendency arose to lump pupils of the same grade together in one class group. And now pupils in most European countries, particularly in urban areas, are presented with the curriculum for one single grade, which they are supposed to assimilate at the same rate as their classmates. At the end of the year, they either move up one class or must repeat the year. Some school systems 'remix' the new classes in order to prevent social phenomena such as in-groups, the halo-effect of the 'poor class', etc.

Whatever the considerations - disciplinary or merely administrative - accounting for or even justifying such discontinuity, the fact remains that the children affected by such measures must spend a great deal of time and energy trying to adjust to their new teacher's methods, understand his/her expectations and decipher the operation of the class dynamics. Nor should we forget the energy expended by children in rural regions in travelling to the often remote 'school centres'.

There is the further point that contact between the various grades often becomes difficult because of teachers' lack of experience and ignorance of their colleagues' problems. Initial and further teacher training courses often have different contents. Teachers may have personal contact only with colleagues teaching the same educational grades, and problems affecting other grades interest them only when pupils are moving up from one grade to the next. Yet the primary school's educational mission demands the very opposite, i.e. that the educational contribution of all its various agents should aim to safeguard the continuity of the child's education in terms of teaching standards, methods, objectives and content.

It would appear that such objectives cannot be achieved without a radical re-organisation of the actual education system. If continuity in educational responsibility for the child became the rule, a type of organisation would be required that, although less simple and therefore more difficult to design and manage than the current type, would make 'customised teaching' a distinct possibility.

One of the most interesting aspects of such reorganisation is the formation of 'mixed age-groups' taking in children with two- or three-year age differences. Unlike 'traditional' multi-level classes, which teachers divide into 'sub-classes' based on the annual curriculum for each grade, children in mixed age-groups share a wide range of activities, split up into smaller groups, or else work on their own, depending on the activity proposed and individual levels of development. The children remain in one group for more than one year (often two or three years) and may change groups several times during the year. These groupings have the following advantages:

- They provide more opportunities for development at the *social and affective* level. The children acquire experience by changing social positions within the group and regularly moving from one group to another. They therefore find themselves several times in the position of the 'newcomer' requiring help in becoming familiar with a new situation, or of the 'veteran' able to provide help having been through the whole system. The children generally remain with the same teacher for about two years.
- Mixed age-groups provide children with better education for contact with others because the very great differences in development among the children make the individual learning process more important than the class average, which pupils too often tend to use as a yardstick in conventional systems.
- Work in mixed age-groups makes for greater development continuity. The sense of success or failure at the end of the year is removed because instead of moving up from one class to the next every year pupils can transfer two or three times each school year.
- In mixed age-groups there are no links between the yearly objectives and the 'school year' and consequently fewer of the difficulties encountered by many children in the conventional system.

Several European countries (United Kingdom, Norway, Sweden, Netherlands, Denmark) have introduced or are introducing, or indeed extending, this new method of grouping pupils. Obviously, such a measure is unthinkable without considerable resources for the retraining and in-service training of teachers, most of whom are ill-prepared for managing such groups with these new aims in mind and are in danger of reverting to the old practice of varying the treatment of subject matter according to the 'sub-classes' represented.

Continuity in the functional integration of knowledge

Despite being occasionally challenged, encyclopaedic knowledge maintains its pride of place in study programmes, teaching resources and schemes of work, thus preventing schools from pursuing other learning objectives (both new and old). More emphasis is put on verifiable, mechanical knowledge than on thought, imagination and problem solving. Feelings, helpfulness, honesty, credibility, dedication and endurance have little to do with academic success. Artistic and craft activities, knowledge of the environment and physical activities are regarded as secondary or even recreational sectors in any discussion of school timetables. They are always placed below 'serious' sectors such as mathematics and the mother tongue.

The almost canonical definition of the aims and content of primary education (and, of course, *a fortiori* of secondary education) has its origin in classical studies (Latin and Greek). The broad lines of this definition today are still a reflection of the university's scientific disciplines, and it is by pure historical chance that some subjects have entered the state school timetable.

There are intermediate solutions to the dilemma of the inflexibility and narrowness of current subject-based teaching and the almost intractable complexity of wider, overall approaches to education. In compulsory education it is possible, and wherever there are more than six teaching domains perfectly safe, to attenuate the discontinuity and dissipation of subjects.

Theme-centred teaching should periodically be organised on outline activities or centres of interest calculated to keep pupils busy over a certain period. If more emphasis were put on transdisciplinary concepts in study programmes and teaching resources, teachers would be able to grasp the relations between the different subjects. In fact, it would be a great service to education if teachers were able to welcome all the questions that come into pupils' heads: such questions always reflect a global perception of a phenomenon, problem or experience, demanding a global reply, interpretation or further analysis. Among the many experiments that are being or have been conducted throughout Europe in the field of continuity in the knowledge integration process, I might mention two national projects at opposite ends of Europe: Iceland and Greece.

The Icelandic Social Science Curriculum Project is a response to the school authorities' wish gradually to change study programmes based on taxonomic objectives (Bloom), which were felt to be too fragmented, into curricula more geared towards interactive learning, using a constructivist, psycho-social approach to the child's cognitive development based on the theories of Dewey and Piaget. Launched in 1974, this project covers subjects such as Icelandic and world history, geography and civics, and has the following aims:

- to prepare pupils for active participation in democratic society; to prepare pupils for the problems of life, and enable them to make decisions either on their own or with others;
- to acquaint pupils with the world around them, its history, its various social realities, and the basic principles of human relations;
- to enable pupils – either on their own or jointly – to obtain the necessary information on the socio-cultural context, assess it and make a number of deductions and inferences. (Jónsdóttir 1988)

A project launched in 1983 by the Greek Ministry of Education and jointly executed by five primary schools (including a special school for handicapped children) and one of the country's colleges of education attempted to combine the teaching of art with knowledge of the environment (Eriksson 1985). The aim was to improve communication, socialisation and inter-pupil relations through a climate of tolerance and mutual understanding; another objective was to improve co-operation among the school teachers, teachers in the educational district and the education authority, and promote the teaching of art and knowledge of the environment.

What these two experiments have in common is obviously an attempt to establish transdisciplinary teaching, with objectives based less on content than on the development of a number of practical and life skills in the various parties involved – primarily the pupils, but also teachers, training and administrative staff. Analysis of the evaluation of the various participants indicates another joint feature: the teachers find it hard to make proper use of the educational material and methods corresponding to the underlying principles (active discovery education in Iceland, and development of spontaneity, improvisation and creativity in Greece).

It is obviously no simple matter to persuade teachers to give up their compartmentalised thinking habits, which, it must be admitted, often help us to comprehend the phenomena of this world. However, they limit our perception and ability to resolve complex problems and often prevent us from making full use of our instincts, intuition and spontaneity.

It must nevertheless be noted that, despite its obvious disadvantages, the subject-based education system also has advantages that a completely open system might very well bring into question. Here I might usefully comment on the 'objectives-based educational approach'. This often severely criticised area of research has frequently been linked to the learning theories inspired by the behaviourist school, which are not really compatible with the methods of European psychologists such as Piaget, and more recently Perret-Clermont (1979), Cardinet (1986) etc., who emphasise activity, awareness, the building up of knowledge and representation of reality.

I might counter these stereotypes by pointing out that defining a teaching objective in no way entails teaching by objectives, at least not in the sense of each objective requiring separate, compartmentalised school work. Objectives may be used for guiding evaluation and in so doing help to pilot more individualised educational action, without thereby fragmenting school work. Defining teaching objectives does not as such compel the choice of any particular learning theory; in particular, it remains perfectly compatible with an interactionist, constructivist approach.

Excessive fragmentation has nevertheless shown that it is better to stick to *general objectives* such as reading, writing, arithmetic, reasoning, time planning, command of the body, command of a foreign language (see Kopmels 1987), etc. Each of these can obviously be broken down into more specialised skill areas for analysis; but in the end all that matters is that they should be complementary and functionally integrated.

Knowledge should also be multi-purpose: the only valid objective is a type of basic learning providing a command of general areas of proficiency. We should also counter the school's natural tendency to devote a lot of energy to mastering very specific routines and skills that are difficult to transpose into other contexts.

It is impossible to propose a satisfactory conception of teaching objectives in a few lines, let alone define their content. However, enough has been done to enable us to continue resolutely in this direction (see Huberman 1988).

Continuity between ordinary and special education

Inequality of educational opportunity is a reality: social background, sex and various other factors have a decisive effect on a child's chances of doing well at school, from the first year at school up to the most advanced stages of degree courses. In any event, in a society with differing living conditions and lifestyles, it can never be pure chance that one child succeeds while another underachieves; it invariably depends on the resources, ambitions and support resulting from background, family and personal history.

It is today generally agreed that each child has a specific learning capacity regardless of content, generally referred to as a 'learning aptitude or style', which can also be described as a particular way of operating and using learning strategies. The reference here is to general skills, such as the use of anticipatory and planning machinery, capacity for self-assessment and utilisation of information and feedback from the environment.

This ability to adapt and learn is to a large extent transmitted ('cultural transmission') by such mediators as parents, primary school teachers and school friends. Depending on the cultural features and modes transmitted, however, some children do not possess the decoding instruments required in order to understand the rules of the game in school society, to advance by means of a system of self-correction and consequently to adapt their behaviour to the new context and data. They neither know nor understand what is expected of them; for example, they cannot see any point in learning to read. Schools cannot entirely level such inequalities for the simple reason that they have little influence on pupils' or their families' approach to school.

One of the main challenges in education is to combat under-achievement and this has prompted numerous European countries, over a period of many years, to give extensive help to children suffering from various physical, mental or social and cultural handicaps, who had long been thought incapable of attending ordinary schools. The general trend has been to set up a special educational network for them with curricula that allow for their difficulties.

However, such special schools have always had their opponents, and over recent years the idea that this type of education should be confined to severely disabled children has been gaining ground. Several European countries have thrown their full weight behind this option and, taking the differentiated education concept to its logical conclusion, consider that the place of such children is primarily in the company of school children of their own age.

I must emphasise that the process must be gradual, with close co-operation between ordinary and specialised education, before the final step of integration is taken. *Combating educational failure and marginalisation means pursuing neither a meaningless equality of opportunity nor an illusory equality of education.* It simply means giving the pupil a command of a minimum amount of basic knowledge and skill, with optimum development of his/her aptitudes, personality and social integration; in fact it means practising active individualisation. Although this practice is widespread in special education, the opposite is true in ordinary education.

It is interesting to note in this connection that the latest efforts at integration have been aimed at involving special education more. In Switzerland (Zürich), the education authorities are currently assessing two models (Hildbrand 1987):

- *Model A*: complete integration of a predetermined number of pupils with learning problems into a 'normal' class with a maximum number of 20 pupils. The class teacher and a special teacher work in close co-operation and alternate their teaching on an individual and collective basis, depending on the required degree of individualisation.
- *Model B*: keeping special classes for children with severe learning handicaps. With a view to promoting their social integration and instruction in specific domains, such children attend ordinary classes for certain subjects. Conversely, the special class takes a limited number of pupils from ordinary classes with learning problems necessitating special attention.

We should note that these are only two among many conceivable variants. What is important is that they should be adjusted in such a way as to cater for local conditions that are outside the scope of overall solutions (teaching opportunities and abilities of staff, availability of classrooms, existing therapy provision, co-operation among neighbouring municipalities, special attention for the individual pupil, etc.). Once acknowledged and put into practice, *the*

diversity of the educational contributions would thus become an asset rather than a process stigmatising pupils as outcasts. In a structure that seeks to make the most of such contributions by stressing continuity instead of discontinuity, that has clear objectives and encourages individual progress towards these objectives, the important thing is what the individual knows, not how, where or when they acquired the knowledge.

3. Continuity between primary school and the outside world

Schools do not have a monopoly on the transmission of knowledge. Children learn in their families, from their neighbours, on the streets, from their friends, from the radio, by reading or from the television or computer screens. Although not all they learn in these ways appears in the school curriculum, there would be even greater discontinuity if we deliberately excluded from the curriculum everything that interests young people outside school.

Towards extending the educational environment

Even, and especially, when outside sources overlap with the curriculum, schools tend to play down lessons thus learnt that are beyond their control; for example, they are often contemptuous of electronic gadgets and television. And, when they do adopt radio and television or computers, they generally only do so in order to subordinate them to the contents and established forms of school work.

These trends are difficult to reverse, but reversed they must be. Although the lessons that children and teenagers learn outside school are extremely varied, accentuating their inequalities *vis-à-vis* the school, this presents a problem only for non-differentiated types of education. In the present school system, children who already know what they are supposed to be learning can be a problem: they often get bored, interrupt, fidget and, finally, lose all interest. In a system with differentiation as a rule, everything learnt in the family and generally outside school would be acknowledged as experience gained, enabling the most advanced to progress faster and aim at new types of learning, and providing other pupils with more resources and time.

Towards improving continuity between school and the family

For some 20 years now, relations between the school and the family have been the subject of much discussion. Some circles (Perrenoud and Montandon 1987) have proclaimed that dialogue between the two is impossible. For 10, 15 and sometimes 20 years, depending on the child's career, families are brought face to face with the school, its demands, judgements, the emotions and constraints it creates every day, and its examinations, fraught with consequences for the future.

Academic success has become a major issue for most parents, who expect the school to discipline their children without bullying them and educate them without depriving them of their childhood. The school is under close scrutiny by parents from all backgrounds who are increasingly demanding an individual or collective say in the way the school treats their children.

Schools react in a variety of ways to the emergence of parents as active, organised and sometimes almost militant negotiating partners: at times they anticipate the expectations of the most demanding parents by opening up the school, in tandem with other innovations such as curriculum reform or the quest for more active educational approaches. Efforts are made to improve direct relations between parents and teachers, and relations between the family and the school are debated in public. There is perhaps a danger in so doing of forgetting that the pupil, the go-between or messenger to and from his two main environments, daily weaves a fabric of indirect relations between school and family. This backdrop of daily communication and interdependence as mediated by the pupil is the hidden part of the iceberg, the background for encounters between parents and teachers and discussion of the real issues in talks, meetings, breakdown of relations and other forms of direct contact.

Let us not forget that school is in very many ways part of the family: it determines how the family spends its time; it requires effort and expenditure; it provides a basis for the educational action and control exercised by parents over their children. School radically transforms children, at the risk of dispossessing their parents, and at the same time exerts continuous influence on the climate of family life, etc. (Perrenoud and Montandon 1987). Yet families do not remain passive in the face of such influences. Every family has its own specific conception of school and education, its own way of dealing with events, setting dialogue, devising strategies for coping in the light of which, or because of which, the child's role as 'mediator' will change. S/he will act sometimes as a lightning conductor and sometimes as an amplifier by developing strategies for protection or even dramatisation.

To stress that the child plays an active role in mediating the influences exerted by school on the family is to reiterate that the commonly adopted divisions are analytical and do not take sufficient account of mutual influences, interactions and interdependence. Any attempt to institute or improve educational continuity between the school and family consequently stands to gain from taking account of these various parameters, standing back to examine the daily interplay among them, and subsequently introducing effective co-operation strategies.

It has emerged that difficulties encountered in experiments in improving relations between school and family, such as the Norwegian national project launched in 1983 (Kratochwil 1985) or the Swiss SIPRI IV project (1970–86; SIPRI IV 1986), have mainly been connected with changing pre-conceptions about parents' and teachers' roles. The project leaders' theory that implementation of new forms of co-operation between school and family would really help children's cognitive, social and affective learning processes, and influence their mental representations of school work, still requires verification.

One thing is certain: if the school were less defensive and formalistic in its relations with parents, if parents felt more at ease in approaching the school (see Kopmels 1987), and if teachers felt sure enough of their competence to stop talking down to parents and accept a dialogue, then family and school could join educational forces instead of cancelling them out.

CHAPTER 4.4

Special Needs Education

Roger Merry

1. Introduction

The education of children with special needs is currently receiving considerable attention throughout most of the countries of Europe. Even a cursory examination will show that in some cases quite radical steps have been taken to change educational provision, and some common themes can be traced which suggest the beginnings of a widespread change in our attitudes towards those with special educational needs. Such developments, however, need to be seen in two contexts. First, they need to be seen against the background of underlying demographic trends and social, cultural and technological changes such as those discussed in Chapter 1.2. Second, changes in special needs education need to be seen in the context of educational systems as a whole.

This chapter, therefore, begins by looking briefly at three examples of wider social changes in Europe and how they might affect the education of children with special needs. It then goes on to consider how special needs education fits into the context of the different educational systems of Europe. Finally, it focuses on three particularly important issues – the integration of children with special needs into ordinary schools, young children with special needs, and working with parents and with other professionals.

2. Special needs education in the wider social context

As examples of the wider social context and its possible effects on the education of children with special needs, three factors have been chosen that are having important repercussions throughout Europe. There is clearly considerable overlap, and the relationships between the three are complex, but they are presented separately for reasons of clarity. Their effects on the education of children with special needs are equally complex and overlapping, as well as being indirect and often subtle, but the three examples together show how important it is not to consider special needs education in isolation. The first is immigration, as an example of a demographic trend; the second is unemployment, as an example of a socio-economic change; the third is microcomputers, as an example of a technological development.

Immigration: a demographic trend

The influx of immigrants into any country in Europe depends on a number of factors, including historical ones like imperial interests, economic ones like the demand for labour and political ones like freedom of movement. Britain and France, for example, have long traditions of empire that have affected the influx of, say, Asian and Afro-Caribbean families and Algerians respectively. Other countries, like the Federal Republic of Germany, had comparatively little previous experience in coping with their ethnic minorities – in Germany's case a figure of about 1 million, of whom roughly half are Turkish. The balance of nationalities is another important factor here, and again economic considerations tend to ensure that immigrant families cluster in certain parts of the country, to the extent that in some schools the children of indigenous parents may themselves come to represent an 'ethnic minority'.

On the other hand, it is important to recognise that children from minority backgrounds do not automatically have special educational needs. In Britain, for example, the very influential Warnock Report (Department of Education and Science 1978a) deliberately excluded such children from its brief, while recognising that many of them do experience difficulties. Akalin (1985), writing about immigrant children in West Germany, describes a range of educational problems, including those caused by different languages, different social conventions, religious beliefs, social status and general differences between family and school. And what should be the aims of the education they are offered? Should the host country try to assimilate them or encourage them to preserve their own cultural heritage? Overt or covert racism may need to be combated, though its expression will depend on factors such as how apparent the differences in appearance and behaviour are. (Significantly, visibility is also a major factor in attitudes towards children with special educational needs.)

The rights of minority groups have long been officially recognised in the European Community, going back to Article 48 of the Treaty of Rome outlawing any kind of discrimination, but it is clear that problems still arise. Wijnstra (1984), for example, describes the difficulties of referring minority children to special education in Holland. Assessment and diagnosis are difficult because of a lack of adequate, non-discriminatory instruments – true culture-free tests have yet to be designed. On the other hand, children from minority groups are clearly over-represented both in segregated special schools and in special classes in ordinary schools.

Although differences in cultural values can cause problems (for example, the use of corporal punishment, separate education of boys and girls, religious and moral education) this issue is a very sensitive one and innovatory projects have tended to focus more on problems caused by language differences. This is equally the case where ethnic groups may be very well established. In Yugoslavia, for instance, a multi-ethnic society has resulted in the 'language of the environment' movement, where all the different languages spoken in one area can be offered to the pupils. Where Slav and Hungarian children are educated together, for example, each has to learn the language of the other. Moreover, if several languages are spoken in any one school, it needs a request from only 15 pupils for the school to be legally obliged to provide some classes for that group of pupils in their own language. Similarly, in Sweden, the Helsinki Act ended the distinction between ethnic groups and the *Hemspràk* movement has now established that, even if only one pupil in a school requests it, the school must provide some tuition in that pupil's language.

The position for children with learning difficulties, however, may not always be so clear. In Belgium, for example, all children have had to be taught both French and Dutch, but it was possible for those with learning difficulties to be excluded. However, the government is now about to devolve control of education to linguistically determined community authorities, which will presumably emphasise their own language and thus hopefully make the integration of children with learning difficulties more viable. Carrying such ideas even further are several innovations, often controversial, where attempts have been made not only to provide some native language lessons, but to have a large proportion or even the whole of the curriculum taught in the native language of the ethnic minority group. Opinions about such innovations are strongly divided between those who maintain the right to receive such education, preserving cultural traditions and narrowing the gap between home and school, and those who see it as emphasising the segregation of ethnic minority groups. In spite of the controversy, the demand clearly cannot be ignored, and there have now been proposals for a European Charter for regional and minority languages (Council of Europe 1985) which would aim at a general transfer of power to regional and local level, and at bilingualism as a minimum.

A major factor that could cause radical changes in all European educational systems is the legislation that will end most internal barriers by 1992. Some welcome the changes – Spanish Minister of Education Javier Solana, for example, sees an opportunity to improve Spanish education to allow his country to take a full part in the European Community. Others are anxious about large-scale immigration, with all the educational problems discussed above. Most countries are reviewing their language teaching policies – the new French Education Minister Lionel Jospin, for example, wants to introduce foreign languages teaching in all primary schools by 1993, in spite of fears that many teachers will not cope (Follain 1988). It is too early to predict the effects on children with learning difficulties, but there is a danger that the curriculum they receive will become even more restricted in comparison with that of their peers. In particular, they may well be excluded from a growing emphasis on learning a second language – if pupils with special needs are withdrawn from mainstream lessons, it is very common for them to miss foreign language work on the grounds that they cannot even cope with their own language properly (e.g. Clunies-Ross and Wimhurst 1983). If this trend does continue, it means that children with learning difficulties will receive an even more impoverished curriculum, which will in turn make it even harder for them to take their place in a wider, more open European Community.

Unemployment: a socio-economic change

During the 1980s, most European countries have experienced rising unemployment, due to a number of factors like the oil crisis and technological advances. Even with a shift towards service industries, it is clear that, in a declining job market, young people with disabilities are in danger of ending up at the bottom of the pile (see, for example, Beresford *et al.* 1982). This can mean permanent unemployment, or work in a 'protected' workshop or, at very best, badly paid jobs that nobody else is prepared to do, but that can at least bring some feelings of worth as well as a degree of financial independence.

Although this sorry state of affairs has the most obvious implications for school leavers, there are bound to be indirect results affecting the whole of the educational system. Nor is it just the small proportion with the most obvious or severe disabilities who suffer. In the Federal Republic of Germany, for example, more and more parents are trying to keep their children out of the *Hauptschule* because of the low status of its qualifications, and the whole tripartite system is experiencing severe problems (Simon 1986). Children with special needs are in an even worse position, and those who have been to special school have little hope – a leaving report from the *Schule für Lernbehinderte* is worth even less in the job market (Heidegger 1988).

Even if current unemployment figures are viewed more optimistically, as a step on the way to a shift in employment patterns rather than as a permanent loss of work for a substantial minority, the position for young people with learning difficulties is not much better. A shift away from production to service industry means that there must be a radical change in our attitudes towards the disabled if they are to compete for jobs involving 'dealing with people' rather than taking on the relatively simple but repetitive work of the production line. Robots replace factory workers, not managers. Moreover, the factory-floor jobs that do remain in industry will almost certainly demand a higher level of technical skill, which will be seen as being beyond many of those who experienced learning difficulties at school.

Finally, if unemployment is viewed as part of a larger and more general economic decline in Europe, then the direct implications for younger children with special needs can be more clearly seen. Whatever form it takes, differentiated provision for such children is almost always expensive. Even when specialised equipment is not necessary, children with special needs usually enjoy better teacher–pupil ratios or the benefits of ancillary staff. When they are integrated into ordinary schools, such material and human resources have to be spread more thinly, resulting in rising costs. It is a sad fact of life, therefore, that children with special needs may be the first to suffer in times of economic decline.

Interestingly, the logic behind such cuts may not in fact be sound. A UNESCO study carried out in 1978 suggested that, taking all the costs into account, special education costs about two-thirds as much again as ordinary education. The figures are very hard to produce and compare, but it is possible that it is in fact *more* economical to provide special education programmes for children with special needs than not to. The research concluded that 'the contribution to society made by a trained, employable handicapped individual is approximately nine times greater than the costs of educating and training that person, thereby making special education and rehabilitation a sound economic investment for any society' (Fink and Friend 1985).

In reality, however, few of those in charge of educational policy are able to take such a long-term view, and it is still very much the case that, in times of economic decline as reflected in rising unemployment, special educational provision tends to be one of the casualties.

Microcomputers: a technological development

Computers and the advent of the new technology are considered in terms of their impact on primary education generally in Section 3 of this book. However, some particular benefits for children with special needs can be outlined here, beginning with a brief look at how they might help those with different sorts of needs, such as physical disabilities, learning difficulties or emotional and behavioural problems.

1 Children who have previously been unable to communicate because of severe physical disability can have a whole new world opened up to them by a computer and the use of devices like concept keyboards (or even by electric typewriters) and 'unicorn' sticks. The powerful poetry of the Irish boy Christy Nolan, full of startling images, was one of the best-known examples of such writing, which has also served to give us an insight into the world of the severely disabled. At a less severe level, a computer linked to a word processor can enable children with specific writing and spelling problems to create beautifully produced, totally correct work on paper, often for the first time. Drafting and redrafting are made much easier, and the end-product does not depend on complex fine-motor skills.

2 For children with a wide range of learning difficulties a computer can provide concrete, visual examples, often using colour and movement and involving active participation from the learner. Significantly, such benefits are seen as

important across a wide range of different learning theories. A computer can repeat an identical program an infinite number of times, with or without variations, enabling valuable 'over-learning' to take place. A good program will be flexible enough to respond appropriately to errors and is, of course, infinitely more patient than even the best teacher!

3 For children with emotional and behaviour problems, computer time can be used as a valued reward and, to the extent that it can replace many of the more mundane and mechanical tasks of teaching, can free the teacher to work on more 'human' personal and social skills. The very fact that a computer is *not* a teacher can equally be an advantage for children who mistrust adults or who find it hard to relate to them.

In spite of these apparent advantages for children with special needs, as well as those for 'normal' children, the idea of introducing computers into primary schools has been received with different degrees of enthusiasm in different European states. In some countries, such as West Germany and Hungary, computers have not really been accepted as a valid part of the primary curriculum, while in countries like France, Denmark and Britain their use in primary schools has been an important area in innovation and research. One Danish study, for example, found that girls using computers did significantly better in all-girl groups than in mixed groups, where they tended to be overshadowed by the boys. In Britain, central government began a large-scale Microelectronics Education Programme (MEP) in 1980, followed up by a 'Micro in Primary Schools' scheme to provide grants of up to 50 per cent for the purchase of hardware and to encourage in-service courses for teachers.

It is, however, important to distinguish between teaching children *about* computers in their own right, and teaching them to *use* computers as another classroom resource, opening up wider debate about the content and the delivery of the primary curriculum. In fact, attitudes may change as computers become less expensive and teachers become less anxious about them! Teacher anxiety is not in fact a trivial point, and many primary teachers may still feel inadequate when faced with a humming keyboard and a blank screen. It is not enough simply to place computers in primary schools, and there are also important in-service implications for teachers if they are to be used effectively.

Developments are taking place quickly. Some of the early programs for children with learning difficulties offered little more than added motivation for carrying out tasks that could have been done just as well on paper, but more recent software has shown how important it is to have dual expertise in both programming and understanding children's learning difficulties. The development of interactive video and of even more powerful hardware is making this a field that cannot be ignored, but how far it will be allowed to penetrate into the education of children with special needs is a matter, not for computer experts, but for teachers and for those who plan and manage the curriculum.

3. Special needs education in the context of educational systems

Immigration, unemployment and microcomputers are only three examples of wide social changes that are taking place throughout Europe, and their effects on the education of children with special needs tend of necessity to be rather indirect and long term. This part of the chapter therefore looks at the educational systems of Europe as a more direct and immediate context for considering provision for children with special educational needs. This is attempted at three levels. At the most general level, the place of special provision is considered in relation to the organisation of the whole educational system, a key factor being the degree of central as opposed to local or private control. Discussion then turns to the current status of differentiated special provision outside the normal systems, and finally to differentiated provision actually within special education itself, in the form of category systems.

Special needs education and centralised control

The degree of centralised state control is probably the most important single factor to consider when looking at the organisation of educational provision at the national level, and it is immediately apparent that the countries of Europe differ enormously in the extent to which their educational systems are centrally organised. In Greece, France, the USSR and Hungary, for example, as well as in many other countries, individual teachers do have some independence in such matters as teaching methods, but the emphasis is on central organisation and a national curriculum. A system like the Danish one is rather different because, although legislation is passed at national level, responsibility is decentralised to the extent that most laws deliberately allow for local interpretation and deviation. In other countries like Switzerland and the Federal Republic of Germany, educational policy is very much decided at local level, while the United Kingdom currently has an almost entirely decentralised system where the principle of autonomy extends not only to local authorities, but also to a large extent to individual schools and even to individual teachers operating in their own classrooms. The situation, however, is not entirely static. In Belgium, for example, preparations are being made to devolve the control of education from national government to community authorities, while Denmark and Norway have also been moving more towards local control of education. Conversely, Britain is now taking major steps towards central government control, with a national curriculum and national assessment.

The degree of centralisation clearly has important implications for the provision of education for children with special needs. For example, a national curriculum should carry with it the obvious advantage of the same educational opportunity regardless of where a child happens to live. What really matters for children with special needs, however, is not so much the existence of a national curriculum as opposed to local autonomy, but the degree to which their access to such a curriculum is restricted or denied, and the willingness of the administration to provide extra resources to enable them to participate as fully as possible. The issue can clearly become a controversial one that may also reflect different ideological stances at a deeper level. For instance, in some countries individual children with special needs may be legally entitled to a special curriculum designed to meet their needs, resulting in provision like that of the Individual Educational Programs in the United States. Conversely, in other countries the long-term aim may be to get as many children as possible on to the national curriculum, as in the USSR (Sutton 1988).

The issue becomes ever more controversial when the emotive question of assessment is raised. If children with special needs share a common national curriculum with their peers, should they all be assessed in the same way? If assessment does take place, some children will clearly do 'better' than others even if norm-referenced tests are explicitly avoided. And what happens to those who 'fail' in the sense that they are not yet ready to go on to the next stage of the established curriculum? One solution, adopted in several European countries, has been that such children should retake the year's work. This has been quite common in the Federal Republic of Germany, for example, or in Holland, where children who have been held back a grade may then be given a legally compulsory test to see if they need to be transferred to the special educational system. Pijl (1983), however, describes the problems inherent in such a system, including the point that the assessment often does not set goals or tell teachers what help the children need.

Elsewhere, the practice of holding children with learning difficulties back for a year is on the decline. In France, for example, Cullen (1985) reports some interesting findings about *redoublants*. Many had no pre-school education, or entered school relatively late. About 30 per cent need a second repeat year, about 20 per cent go into special education, and about 50 per cent are able to carry on with the national curriculum. Alternatives are being considered, however. In some areas of France, the whole 2–11 age-range is divided into three 'cycles' (2–5, 5–8 and 8–11) where children stay with the same teacher for three years, almost eliminating the need for repeating a grade.

Retaking the year's work is one of the ways in which a nationally controlled education system, with a national curriculum, can attempt to cater for children with special needs. However, it is very clear that some children have traditionally been seen as unable to cope with the normal curriculum at all, and when one turns to special school systems a very different picture emerges. Special education has not evolved as part of state-controlled systems – just the opposite in fact. In all European states, private initiatives played the major part in setting up segregated special provision. Based usually on religious or humanitarian values, they placed an emphasis on care and, where necessary, on medical help rather than on education. In some countries, such private provision has been entirely or almost entirely replaced by the state, either at the local or national level, while elsewhere the 'charitable' status of special education remains as its basis. Once again, there are wide differences between European states. For example, countries like France, Greece, Belgium, Switzerland and the Netherlands retain a considerable number of privately run establishments, while Denmark has very few. In contrast, Ireland's strong tradition of Christian-based education and close Church involvement has resulted in a special school system that is almost entirely private.

There are also major differences in the financing of private special schools. Thus in Switzerland there is heavy reliance on funding from religious and philanthropic sources, while the Irish special schools are subsidised almost entirely by the state. In the Netherlands, about two-thirds of *all* ordinary primary schools are privately run, but the state finances both public and private education on an equal footing. Similarly, the state pays for all private special education, provided it does not exceed the norms fixed by the Ministry of Education. The school board receives local funding for buildings and equipment, and central government funding to cover staff costs. In other countries, private and public special schools run in parallel with different amounts of state subsidies and different degrees of state supervision. In Britain, for example, local education authorities may send children to officially approved establishments, many of which are boarding schools, and pay for accommodation and tuition.

The degree of centralisation has major implications for attempts to establish national policy for children with special needs or, conversely, to set up local experiments to look at innovations such as integrating children with special needs into ordinary schools. In practice, the distribution of responsibility between state, local and private control and funding is highly complex and may tend to emphasise the separatist basis of special educational provision. It is to such separate provision that discussion now turns.

Special segregated provision

Differentiated provision for children with special educational needs developed in very similar ways in most European countries through the nineteenth century and into the twentieth. As has been discussed above, a small minority of children were considered 'ineducable' and provision, where it occurred at all, was on a haphazard basis, usually organised by the Church or by charitable groups, and with an emphasis on care rather than education. Gradually, however, with the growth of universal compulsory education came a recognition of the rights of *all* children to an appropriate education, and the consequent development of separate special educational systems.

These separate special systems have formed the basis for provision in all

European states and it is only comparatively recently that their contribution has been questioned, and then only in some countries. In many countries, the separate special educational systems are well established and are still seen to be meeting the special needs of their pupils. Thus in 1976, Eberhard Mannschatz, describing the educational system of the German Democratic Republic, wrote:

> It is the aim of our national educational policy to develop the personality of each individual child to the full, and in order to do so, it is essential to create specific, appropriate conditions in which children with serious physical handicaps and mental deficiencies can develop their talents and capacities. Such conditions exist in schools for physically handicapped and mentally retarded children.

In West Germany, the overall position seems similar, although there are differences between the individual federal states. Thus the policy of Berlin, for instance, is that

> Special schools and special school facilities serve, to a very great extent, the realisation of the right of handicapped children and young persons to education and teaching in line with their individual talent and individual achievement level. (Akalin 1985)

A similar point was made with regard to the official position in the Netherlands, where the Ministry of Education and Science (1979) maintained support for a separate system on the grounds that

> Handicapped children often have a far better chance of developing their potential here than in ordinary schools, because attention is paid to emotional problems as well as learning difficulties, often with the help of medical or para-medical specialists.

More recent reviews (e.g. Pijl 1983; HM Inspectors of Schools 1987) suggest that the position has not altered very much and that the special school system of the Netherlands is not under threat.

Indeed, in some countries, the trend seems to be towards a separate special educational system that is becoming even more separated and more specialised. Csapo (1984), for example, describes an increase in the number of special schools in the USSR and an increase in the amount of specialisation, with children grouped according to both age and the degree of handicap. In Hungary, Gordosné Szabó (1986) discusses the emergence of a whole science of special education, recognised as an independent discipline and developing new branches like the sociology of special educational institutions and special educational anthropology.

It would be misleading, however, to suggest that the continued existence of special school systems throughout most of Europe implies either a lack of awareness of the problems they can cause or an unwillingness to consider change. Both West Germany and the Netherlands recognise an important long-term aim of closer links between the normal and special systems, with as many children as possible being integrated into ordinary schools. The whole question of integration is a central one, and represents a major controversial issue in special needs education. It will, therefore, be discussed more fully in section 4 of this chapter. For the moment, however, it is clear that, while recognising the problems, many European countries find it best to maintain a segregated special school system. It is equally clear that the special needs of individual children vary enormously. How have special school systems in Europe evolved to try to meet this wide range of individual needs?

Differentiation within special segregated provision

Within the framework of segregated provision for children with special needs, category systems have been employed throughout the European Community almost without exception. Thus children seen as being unable to cope in ordinary schools have been categorised in order to place them in the most appropriate type of special school.

Although they cater for the same range of special needs generally, the category systems vary in a number of ways between countries, an obvious example being the actual number of categories employed. In Belgium, for example, eight types of special education have been created to cater for slight mental backwardness, moderate or severe mental backwardness, emotional disturbance, physical deficiencies, sick children, visual, auditory and language difficulties (Ministère de l'Education Nationale & Ministerie van Onderwijs 1986). The Republic of Ireland also has eight types of special school, though the categories are not identical to the Belgian ones and some of the provision (e.g. for multiple-handicapped children and for those with specific reading difficulties) is only on a very small scale. The Federal Republic of Germany uses 10 categories, and the Netherlands has 15 catering for about 100,000 children in 1,000 schools, with special provision also made for itinerants' children. There have been attempts to bring some sort of conformity, or at least allow comparisons to be made. Jørgensen (1980) for example, while recognising the limitations of category systems, listed parallel terms employed in eight European countries to describe a range of 12 categories, in the hope of improving the exchange of information. However, it is very unlikely that countries will be willing to change their category systems in order to bring them in line with other countries, and the existing ones usually seem well established.

The actual proportion of children categorised as requiring special provision has also varied considerably between European countries. In Britain, for example, about 2 per cent of the school population have been educated in special schools, though the legislation of 1981 abolished the 10 categories that previously existed, and it is difficult to make comparisons with more recent figures. In France, the national figure is more like 4 per cent, while in countries such as West Germany and the Irish Republic about 8 per cent are catered for in special schools. Such discrepancies are hardly surprising, and clearly depend not so much on actual differences between the children of different countries as on differences in policy and provision.

Equally, there may be considerable differences not only between countries, but actually within countries themselves. Again, this is not surprising in systems where educational control is exercised at local rather than national level. In England, for example, with strong traditions of local autonomy, some local educational authorities have maintained levels of provision very different from the national average (e.g. Merry 1986). More surprising, however, is the finding that large local differences may exist in countries that appear to have comparatively strong central control. Csapo (1984) quotes figures to show that in the Soviet Union the percentage of children enrolled in auxiliary classes ranges from 0.6 per cent to 3 per cent across the republics. In France, inspite of strong traditions of central government control, there are equally large variations - special provision is made for about 1 per cent of children in Paris, and for about 7 per cent in Amiens, for example (Cullen 1985). In Poland, while there is a general growth in integrating pupils with special needs into ordinary classes, there are still considerable differences between the regions (Kelly 1988a).

The reasons for such discrepancies are harder to explain. To some extent, they could involve actual differences between the needs of children brought up in one environment rather than another - in an inner city rather than a rural community, for example. It is, however, more likely that local autonomy has been exercised in the face of national control - certainly the separate or integrated education of children with special needs often becomes an emotive issue that can give rise to strong local feelings and demands for action in a way that some other sorts of decisions about education may not.

Although the historical development of segregated provision has followed a similar pattern in most European countries, these figures illustrate the fact that there are major differences both between and within countries in deciding on how many children need special provision and in the way this provision is categorised. However, category systems are being increasingly criticised and, even where the traditional categories have not actually been abolished (as is the case in Britain, for example), there have sometimes been changes in terminology that reflect changing attitudes. Thus in France, '*inadaptés*' have become referred to instead as '*enfants en difficulté*', suggesting that their problems may not necessarily be entirely 'within child'. In fact, the whole notion of segregated special education is beginning to come under fire in many European states, and the integration of children with special needs into ordinary schools is now being at least considered as an alternative. The next part of this chapter, which focuses on some key areas in special needs education, therefore begins by looking at the issue of integration.

4. Some current issues in special needs education

Integration

Of all the current concerns in the field of special educational needs, integration would seem to be the most important and most central. It is an emotive issue that raises questions not only about the relative benefits of segregated and integrated provision, but also about the whole nature and aims of education and indeed even wider moral and philosophical issues. Common themes can be traced across national boundaries, and the policy changes currently taking place in several European countries reflect often radical developments in our attitudes to children with special educational needs.

At the most general level, the movement towards integration can be seen as part of a wider recognition of human rights and equality of opportunity. In its own way, integration is one expression of a growing sense of wider responsibility towards all those who have traditionally been in some sense oppressed, whether on the grounds of race, religion, culture, sex, age, class or disability. It is significant that many of the arguments in favour of integration are based on moral grounds rather than on 'hard' research data, though it is equally true that there is a similar lack of 'hard' data to support segregated provision! (e.g. Fink and Friend 1985).

When the increasing recognition of human rights is translated into policy, integration can again be seen in a wider context, this time a social one. In many European countries, legislation has been enacted that recognises the rights of various sorts of minority groups – of both parents and children, or of hospital patients for example. Indeed, there is a direct parallel with the current British policy of placing mentally handicapped adults in the community rather than in institutions. Similarly, more widespread recognition of the general right to information has its parallel in increased parental involvement in education systems and in more open and accessible school records, both of which could have important effects on the education of children with special needs. The European Community legislation that will end many trade and other barriers by 1992 can also be seen as an important step towards freedom of movement whose implications for children with special needs have already been mentioned.

However, when one looks more closely at educational systems themselves, it becomes clear that the growth of integration has taken at least some of its impetus from dissatisfaction with established segregated provision, as well as from the more general human rights movement. For example, during the 1970s, growing concern was expressed about the usefulness of 'traditional' forms of assessment, and with the validity and reliability of many norm-referenced tests. It has become increasingly clear that children with special educational needs simply do not represent a separate, identifiable minority group for whom segregated provision can be easily and consistently justified.

Similarly, while category systems gave administrative advantages, it has become clear that they cannot always reflect the true complexities of an individual's educational needs. Multiple-handicapped children represented an obvious problem, though some countries avoided this by using 'multiple handicap' as one of their category labels. Even so, category systems carry all the disadvantages of labelling and are difficult to operate flexibly in practice, so that it can, for example, be very hard to move a child once she or he has been categorised. Moreover, the apparent incidence in each category clearly depends to a large extent on finance and the sheer availability of each type of provision, and not just on the child's needs.

Objections to segregation have also been made on more general educational grounds. Truly 'comprehensive' or 'community' education should properly be for *all* the children in the neighbourhood. Moreover, if education is seen as a potent factor in bringing about social change, then integration can serve a long-term social function in changing attitudes towards the disabled. In this case, integration is valuable not only to those with special needs who need to learn to live in 'normal' society, but also to their 'normal' peers who need to develop positive and accepting attitudes. It could also be argued that segregated provision is simply a device to allow an imperfect system to carry on regardless rather than consider changing. This argument carries even more conviction when coupled with growing dissatisfaction with the 'deficit' model in which 'within-child' factors are seen as the major source of difficulties. In contrast, more recent educational theories such as the 'systems' approach or the 'ecological' model (e.g. Hallahan and Kauffman 1986) have encouraged us to view the child's difficulties in the context of educational settings and to realise that the school can actually be a source of educational difficulties rather than simply a stage on which the child's personal inadequacies are played out.

The notion of integration has, therefore, been gaining ground for a variety of philosophical, social and educational reasons throughout many of the countries of Europe and numerous policy statements have proposed that as many children as possible should be educated within the normal school system. However, a few examples will show that, in practice, there is still a wide range of attitudes towards the integration of children with special needs.

Italy is often quoted as being the European country where the most dramatic changes have taken place (e.g. McCleary and Buchanan 1987). The tradition of caring and protecting, based on religious principles, gradually came more into question during the 1960s, resulting in legislation in 1971 in favour of integrating all but the most severely handicapped. Further legislation in 1977 facilitated integration by limiting class size to 20 in integrated classes, including a maximum of two handicapped pupils. This policy proved so successful that, by 1980, only 0.32 per cent of primary-aged children were still being educated in special schools (Cecchini and McCleary 1985), in spite of some objections to what has been called 'wild integration' in which all children are automatically placed in ordinary schools without full consideration of their individual needs.

In other countries, while there is general agreement with the philosophy of integration, its implementation has been less sweeping. In Denmark, for example, integration is encouraged where possible and where judged to be appropriate by special advisers. In the Netherlands, distinctions were drawn between three groups of children:

(i) Those who can succeed, with some individual support, in ordinary schools.
(ii) Those who need some time in special schools, but can eventually return to ordinary ones.
(iii) Those who need to stay in special schools.
(Ministry of Education and Science (Netherlands) 1979)

Some countries, therefore, while recognising the value of integration, maintain that their established special school systems are still the best form of provision for some children.

Most of the West German states, for example, seem to take this view, intending to maintain their special schools while trying to keep them less segregated and distinct from the rest of the system, though major local differences do occur. For example, October 1988 saw the end of a legal battle in the state of Hesse, when two mentally handicapped children were finally integrated into ordinary classes against the wishes of Christean Wagner, the State Education Minister. At the same time, Rosemarie Raab, Hamburg's Education Minister, went on record as saying that her aim was to encourage integration in all primary schools, with 'across the board provision' by the year 2000 (Bendelow 1988). However, it must be remembered that the national secondary school system is itself built on a tripartite division, and it is therefore unlikely that integration on the lines of the Italian model will ever take place (e.g. Heidegger 1988).

Another example would be the Soviet Union, where official policy is that special schools can provide the best education for children with special needs. There has, therefore, been more emphasis on improving diagnosis and differentiation between sub-categories, leading to an expansion of the special school system and its four main categories (Csapo 1984). However, such children are regarded as a distinct minority group of 'oligophrenics' who will never be able to cope with the full range of the national curriculum. Others, who are seen as having the potential to succeed, may be given extra help for a while before returning to mainstream schools. Integration is therefore seen as a long-term goal rather than an immediate solution to the child's current needs (Sutton 1988).

It would be misleading, however, to suggest that the situation is static. All over Europe, small-scale integration projects are being run on an experimental basis. McGee *et al.* (1987), for example, describe one such local experiment in Portugal and note, amongst other things, the benefits to the 'normal' children as well as to those with special needs. Indeed, in some areas, the official policy may be to conduct such experiments to try to assess the advantages and disadvantages of integration before taking the plunge on a large scale. This is probably true in France and the Netherlands, for example, as well as a number of other countries. Moreover, when integration actually does take place, one of the major consequences in terms of policy may well be administrative decentralisation in which local authorities take on more responsibility (Jørgensen 1980). Such experimental projects show that integration *can* work, and offer examples of good practice for developing it on a wider scale. McGee *et al.*'s Portuguese project, for example, showed the value of getting press coverage to raise the awareness of the whole community, while other studies have suggested ways of involving parents and other professionals as well as the importance of preparing the staff and children of the school.

Finally, it is worth noting that the integration–segregation issue need not be a totally divisive one in which special schools will eventually emerge as the 'losers'. Integration is clearly not an 'all-or-nothing' affair and most authorities recognise the need for a continuum of provision to match the continuum of needs, in which special schools can still play a role, albeit a rather different one. For example, Marchesi (1986) describes an integration project in Spain that involved developing new roles for special schools as resource centres offering help to teachers in ordinary schools. Similarly, Kelly (1988b) discusses how special schools in Norway still have important roles to play in a system where integration is on the increase.

Integration is clearly not an easy solution. In many cases, it requires radical restructuring and changing of deep-seated attitudes about the nature of handicap as well as the nature of education. In times of economic difficulties, it is certainly not a cheap solution either, though anxieties have been expressed that authorities may seize upon it for precisely that reason, simply dumping children with special needs into the ordinary school system. Booth (1982) makes this point when discussing integration in Norway, for example, but such fears have been frequently voiced elsewhere. In fact, if integrationist policies are carried out properly, it is likely that they will be more expensive because resources will be spread more widely rather than concentrated in a few special schools. Reluctance to implement integration on a large scale can therefore be traced to a number of factors, ranging from financial considerations to long-established attitudes about disability and education. In spite of these problems, a genuine shift does appear to be beginning to take place in a number of European states, and integration is probably the key issue in current European developments in special needs education.

Young children with special educational needs

The second area chosen for discussion arises from widespread concern about provision for young children with special needs and the place of such provision in the educational system. In most European countries, the pattern is for compulsory education to begin between the ages of 5 and 7, with voluntary provision being available for younger children in the form of nursery school or kindergarten. Not surprisingly, there are wide differences in the content and organisation of this provision, and in the proportion of children for whom it is available. In West Germany, for example, about 75 per cent of the places are provided privately and about 70 per cent of 3–6 year olds actually attend. In Hungary, attendance is even higher at around 90 per cent, and almost all the remaining 10 per cent attend a 192 hour pre-school preparatory training course (Dovala 1985). In contrast, provision for young children in many other European countries, such as Great Britain, tends to be localised and fragmentary, in spite of the now universal recognition of the crucial importance of the early years and their effects on the rest of a child's education.

Against this background, as one would expect, there are considerable differences in the way European countries deal with young children with special educational needs, though some trends do emerge. One such trend is a move towards earlier detection of difficulties and an emphasis on prevention rather than 'cure'. Fink and Friend (1985), for example, discuss the major causes of disability that need to be considered in order to make prevention possible. Improvements in nutrition, medical care and mental health are seen as major goals, but they also recognise the importance of early childhood education.

Most European countries now realise the importance of such early special educational provision. Akalin (1985), for example, describes the 'special pedagogical centres' that have been set up in the Federal Republic of Germany, offering free early diagnosis and practical help for parents. Similarly, in France, although compulsory schooling begins at 6, free provision is available from birth onwards, with well-established programmes for children with special needs, again offering early diagnosis and prevention. In general, it would seem easier to cater for young children with special needs in countries where the official age of entry into the educational system is low. Thus the 1985 Primary Education Act in the Netherlands, which reorganised traditional nursery and primary schools into 'basic schools' for children aged 4–12, is bound to have particularly significant effects on the education of children with special needs. Similarly, there has been a lowering of the school starting age to 6 in the USSR, Bulgaria and Poland, with the establishment of the 'zero class'. The name is deliberately chosen to imply that the first year has not simply been tacked on, but represents a different approach where only part of the time is spent in formal learning.

Other European countries are now also taking steps to improve opportunities for young children with special needs. In Greece, for example, the start of the 1980s saw official recognition of the fact that only about 5–8 per cent of pre-school children who needed special educational provision were in fact receiving it (Ministry of Education (Greece) 1981). The Law of 1981 concerning 'special education, special vocational education, occupation and social care of handicapped children' gave a legal base for reorganising the whole system, with early diagnosis centres and more special *Nipiagogia* (kindergartens) as priorities.

However, earlier formal provision does not necessarily mean that children with special needs will automatically get a better deal. For a start, there can be considerable difficulties in diagnosing the problems of young children. Then there is the widely recognised finding that the age of diagnosis or referral is varied for different 'categories' of handicap. Severe physical and sensory impairment can usually be detected relatively early, while specific and less severe learning problems are often not so apparent, and emotional and behaviour difficulties emerge even later. There are several reasons for this. For example, 'within-child' factors could mean that a handicapping condition may be undetectable at birth and only manifest itself later as the child's condition deteriorates. Difficulties for professionals in making valid and reliable assessments of young children can be compounded at the family level by an understandable reluctance to recognise that there is anything wrong, and fear of the social stigma of having an 'abnormal' child. But there has also been during the 1980s a growing recognition of the school itself as a factor in causing learning difficulties, or at the very least providing the context in which they emerge.

Putnam (1979) proposed a four-stage model in which different groups of children with special needs are catered for as a country's normal education system is first established and then expanded. At the first stage, for example, school attendance is optional and only children with sensory defects are catered for. When schooling becomes compulsory, provision is made for children with severe learning difficulties. Acceptance of the idea that provision can actually *define* need may, however, be understandably slow in coming about, since it implies not only that existing educational provision should be widened to take in younger children, but also that the system itself must be ready to change in order to cater for young children with special educational needs.

This view has received indirect support from changing theoretical notions about the way in which young children learn or fail to learn. For example, the vastly influential work of Piaget began to come under attack during the 1970s as new experimental studies showed that young children *could* acquire concepts earlier than had been thought, provided the context was right (see e.g. Donaldson 1978). At the same time, writers like Feuerstein (1979) were attacking the 'critical period' hypothesis, which had proposed that certain things had to be learned at certain stages of a child's development or they would never be properly learned at all.

The increasingly popular view that young children's learning and development are highly contextual, therefore, has indirect but important implications for the education of all children with special needs because it shifts the focus away from 'within-child' factors in learning failure towards an emphasis on the role of the teacher and the school. Whether the resource implications of such changes for young children will be realised in the current financial climate is a different matter. In spite of both theoretical shifts and numerous reports and recommendations, it does still often seem that those who work with young children with special needs are seen as having doubly low status in European educational systems which emphasise academic attainment.

Working with parents and with other professionals

Widespread recognition of the crucial importance of identifying and helping young children with special needs as early as possible is one reason for increasing co-operation with parents. Such co-operation is considered in depth in Chapter 4.1, and here only a brief discussion of work with parents of children with special needs will be offered.

It is very clear that, from the moment they become aware of their children's special problems, parents themselves, and indeed the whole of the family, need to be seen as having special needs of their own (e.g. Furneaux 1988). Reactions to finding that your child is abnormal in some way can be varied and complex, ranging from disbelief and denial, through a sense of loss and injustice, to depression, anger and guilt. Professionals need to be very sensitive to such reactions and in helping parents to adjust and come to terms with both their children and their own feelings. (See, for example, Cunningham and Davis, 1985.) Support from other parents in a similar situation is also particularly valuable, and there is a wide range of parent support groups, voluntary and state organisations in the various European countries. The ways in which they are funded and organised differ considerably and are obviously affected by the way in which the normal special education systems of each country are run, as discussed in section 3 of this chapter. If such support groups are run on a purely voluntary basis they can offer immense help to parents, but do raise the difficult question of whether they also enable local or national government to avoid some of its responsibilities. On the other hand, independence from the official system does allow the voluntary bodies to act as pressure groups and to question official policies more openly and freely. Conversely, state or local authorities can help parents a lot simply by providing information. Thus the French Ministry of Education has produced a booklet for parents of children with special needs, containing answers to 263 common questions that parents have asked, and using the centralised system to advantage to make the information cheap and easy to obtain (ONISEP 1982). Of course, much more individual help and information needs to be provided at local level – a good example being the Portage system now used in several local authorities in Britain. Here, trained Portage workers make weekly home visits and train parents to help their children with specific skills such as eating and dressing, catering for the particular needs of individual children. In other countries, similar help is frequently provided in the form of clinics or centres such as the

French 'early medico-social activity centres' for children with severe learning difficulties (Zucman 1985) or West Germany's 'special pedagogical centres' described above, where parents take their children for diagnosis and for help.

When children reach school age, co-operation with parents will obviously depend even more on how the ordinary and special school systems are organised, as well as on underlying factors such as those discussed in section 2 of this chapter. In Norway, for example, Stangvik (1978) describes how the scattered population and large distances between settlements have been a factor in developing local rather than centralised provision, with a hearty dislike of bureaucracy. On the other hand, those same demographic factors can cause problems for placing children with special needs, with far-reaching implications for their families. The nearest special school may be many miles away, causing practical problems as well as discouraging close parent–school co-operation. Residential schools are another solution offered in many European countries, but they raise complex issues about the role of the family and the need to balance parents' rights with those of their children.

In general, there has been a trend in most countries to increase the rights of all parents, and not just those of children with special needs. Ultimately, however, the legal rights of parents differ considerably across the different European states. In the Netherlands, for example, parents have the final decision on whether or not their child should receive special education. In most other countries, parents must be consulted and involved in such decisions, but they alone do not have the final say. Thus in France, special education commissions, set up locally, enable groups of experts to consult parents. If agreement cannot be reached, the matter is decided judicially, and it is ultimately possible for parents to be legally obliged to send their child to a special school. Such confrontations are rare, however, and the general trend has been to see parents not only as having the right to information, but as active partners with their own special and equally valid contributions.

Cunningham and Davis (1985) outline three different basic models to describe the ways in which parents and professionals co-operate – the 'expert', 'transplant' and 'consumer' models. In the first, there may be little actual co-operation because the professionals are seen as experts whose only real duty to the parents is to keep them informed. In the 'transplant' model, the professional uses the parents as a source of information to help diagnosis, and then trains them to cope. In the 'consumer' model, this pattern is largely reversed – the parents use the professionals to help them get what they want for their child. In very general terms, the 'expert' model is being replaced by the other two, with perhaps a particular emphasis on the 'consumer' model in countries where parental rights have been particularly extended.

Some of the implications for various professionals working with special needs children and their parents are immediately apparent, and another trend in many European countries has been to recognise changing roles for professionals such as psychologists, social workers and medical experts. The growing emphasis on assessing individual children's needs rather than simply categorising them, for example, means that professionals have to co-operate more closely not only with parents, but also with each other. Several countries have, therefore, set up systems for improving 'multi-professional' assessment. The Danish system, for instance, requires close co-operation between professionals working for the health authority, the social authority and the educational authority (Elvin 1981), and the development of similar multi-disciplinary teams from medical, social and educational services is happening in West Germany (McCleary and Buchanan 1987).

Of course, problems do arise! McCleary and Buchanan also describe some of the difficulties inherent in the French system, for example, where the Social Affairs Ministry is responsible for the severely handicapped while the Health Ministry is responsible for physically handicapped and psychiatric cases. Since 1976, however, 'special education commissions' have been attempting to provide multi-professional assessment of individual children, and to overcome some of the difficulties in liaison. Similar attempts have been made in Switzerland through 'medico-psycho-pedagogic clinics' or in the 'psychological -medical-social centres' set up by the Belgian Ministry of Special Education (Hayes 1978). The official status of such organisations may differ from country to country, of course. In the Swiss example, the centres tend to have little actual legal underpinning, while in Norway there was actual legislation in 1975 to set up 'Educational psychology centres' to co-ordinate the work of psychologists, counsellors, social workers, physiotherapists and teachers. Legislation may also be used to encourage liaison at the highest national level. In Greece, for example, a law passed in 1981 provided the basis for multi-professional liaison through the setting up of a Co-ordination Council with members from the ministries of Education, Social Services, Labour and Justice. As has already been noted, the way in which different countries organise such multi-professional groups will depend on a number of factors like the degree of centralisation, or even the size of the country. Thus in Luxembourg, individual referrals are decided by a board which includes the ministry's Chief Inspector of Primary Schools, the Director of Special Education and representatives from the ministries of Health and Family Affairs - a level of government involvement that would be impractical in a larger country.

In practice, co-operation may be difficult to achieve, and it could even be argued that many professionals find it difficult to change deep-seated attitudes about their work and their roles as experts. However, in spite of the difficulties and the different ways in which various European countries have tried to overcome them, organised professional co-operation does emerge as an important and growing trend.

Finally, changes are also beginning to take place in the ways in which special needs teachers work, not just with parents and with other professionals, but also with their colleagues within the schools. In general, new ideas about special needs education imply closer co-operation between teachers themselves as well as between professionals outside schools. If children with special needs are no longer to be seen as a tiny, clearly identifiable minority group, and if many of those who would previously have been seen in that way are now being integrated into ordinary school, it follows that *all* teachers will need to become 'special needs teachers'. This shift has important implications both for 'ordinary' class teachers and for those who have been regarded as the experts. In the past, it was acceptable for class teachers to leave it to the experts, while specialist remedial teachers, who would otherwise have probably had low status, were at least recognised as having some sort of mystique of their own. More recent ideas are beginning to force both sides to re-examine their positions. Like their counterparts in special schools, remedial teachers will be more and more expected to advise other staff and to work with children and class teachers in ordinary classrooms in a 'support' role. Such 'whole school' approaches to special needs will clearly require new skills if teachers are to work successfully together, and many issues will be raised at school level that have parallels in the wider implementation of integrationist policies in the educational systems themselves.

For example, such changing roles will clearly carry implications for training both class teachers and specialist teachers at both initial and in-service levels. In most European countries, while initial training may now contain an element of special needs awareness, most actual training is done at the in-service level. In Denmark, for example, teachers need two years' experience before they can be considered for an 18 month course to become special needs teachers. Similar normal teaching experience is expected in a number of other countries such as France and Northern Ireland, although, in practice, teachers in some countries can move into special schools without any extra formal training whatsoever. Elsewhere, special training may be offered at both the initial and the in-service level, as is the case in the Federal Republic of Germany, while in other countries, such as the German Democratic Republic, considerable use is made of successful, experienced teachers who are given advisory status and reduced timetables in order to help their colleagues. In spite of all these efforts, however, authorities in most countries recognise that there is still not enough training either for raising the awareness and improving the skills of ordinary class teachers, or for enabling special needs teachers to take on the new roles that will be expected of them because of changing views about the whole nature of special needs education.

5. Summary and conclusions

This chapter has deliberately avoided the use of separate sections on particular areas of special need such as physical handicap or emotional and behaviour problems, largely because such categorisation would be contrary to current notions about special needs education in many European countries. Instead it has tried to present a general overview of some important issues, both in the context of the different educational systems of the various states and in the wider context of a Europe that is undergoing major social, cultural and technological changes. Such an approach is of necessity selective, so that no mention has been made of some areas such as the transfer to secondary school or the particular needs of gifted children, for example. However, some important trends do emerge, showing changing ideas about the nature of special needs education, even though there are widespread differences in the practical effects of such trends because of different social, cultural, political and educational traditions in the different countries of Europe. The trends are related to each other in complex ways, but some of the main ones could be summarised as follows:

(1) Although some European states retain the original voluntary or religious basis that characterised earlier attempts to cater for children with special needs, provision in many other countries has now come under the control of local or central government. Equally important has been a shift away from caring for and protecting children, often selected on the basis of a medical model, towards a recognition of their right to education, interpreted in the widest sense to include social and emotional needs as well as intellectual ones.

(2) There appears to be a growing recognition that children with special educational needs should not be seen as a small minority who can be reliably identified by norm-referenced tests and placed into appropriate categories. Instead, the educational needs of individual children should be considered as far as possible. For such individual assessment to be successful, different professionals need to work together closely and with parents.

(3) From such a view, it follows that segregated special provision is not the only answer, and that there should be a flexible continuum of provision, with children integrated into the ordinary system as far as possible. Integration as an ideal seems to have support even in countries where special provision is maintained as meeting the needs of a small minority. It is also an important notion whether the practice is to set up individual educational programmes or to use special provision to get as many children as possible on to the same national curriculum eventually. Integrationist views stem partly from growing dissatisfaction with traditional segregated provision, and partly from wider changes such as the human rights movement.

(4) Integration issues have parallels with the ways in which provision is organised within ordinary schools themselves. In particular, new roles and skills are being expected of both ordinary class teachers and special needs specialists, with a growing emphasis on co-operation, on in-class support rather than withdrawal, and on a general 'whole school' approach involving *all* teachers.

(5) The focus on 'within-child' factors as the main source of difficulties has shifted towards a recognition of the school's role, at the very least as a context, if not an actual causal factor, in creating special educational needs. This implies a need for schools themselves to consider changing to meet the needs of a wider range of children, in the sorts of ways mentioned in the previous paragraph.

(6) Consideration of the contexts of learning, again coupled with a growing recognition of human rights generally, has resulted in an increased willingness to see parents as active partners in meeting children's needs. In turn, this has given added impetus to the importance of working with young children in an attempt to prevent some of the problems arising in the first place.

General trends such as these suggest that it is not simply the classroom experiences of a small minority of children that are changing, but our whole concept of the nature of special educational needs. It will take time to change deep-seated attitudes and to modify current provision to meet these needs, but these changes will have far-reaching effects on both 'ordinary' and 'special' children and their families, on all teachers and other professionals, and ultimately on the actual educational systems of Europe themselves.

SECTION 5

ROLE, STATUS AND PROFESSIONALISM IN EUROPEAN PRIMARY TEACHERS

Introduction

Eric Hoyle

In this Section we address the problems of the status of primary teachers, their roles and relationships and processes of induction into the profession. The concept of the primary school teacher as a professional is explored by Professor Hoyle in the opening chapter. Hoyle uses his now well-established distinction between restricted and extended professionality to explore, in particular, the contrasts in perceptions of primary teachers in England and France and to stress the links between professionality and autonomy. He notes the developing trend in most countries to give parents a greater say in the management of primary schooling and concludes that in the next decade primary teachers will experience greater role uncertainty, in contrast to secondary colleagues. This is because they will need to strive towards greater academic status while at the same time learning to cope with a wider range of responsibilities in response to social change.

This emphasis on school-focused development, which Hoyle suggests is one of the major characteristics of the modern primary school, is taken up by Mats Ekholm. Ekholm notes that the school leader, besides having the traditional responsibility for routine matters such as timetabling, assigning teachers to particular teaching responsibilities and ensuring that local authority policies are implemented, has increasingly become the central figure in the process of schools' improvement. He notes that efforts to induct teachers into leadership roles within the primary school vary considerably between different European countries. This is often related to the way in which school leaders are chosen. In some countries, for example, there is strong 'in-breeding' of school leaders. Ekholm sees the role of the leader changing with less hierarchical management and greater emphasis on trust, learning and collaboration.

Finally, David Winkley examines the training needs of teachers within the context of these wider responsibilities and the demands for greater accountability. While Winkley finds many common characteristics across the different European countries, there are also important differences in the length of training courses and the relationships between schools and the training institutions.

Winkley traces out an agenda for the future that envisages greater co-operation between institutions of higher education, local authorities and the schools. Among the outstanding issues is the need to develop a more effective pedagogy and the need to build into the system regular periods of retraining for updating the teachers' knowledge. For Winkley the issue of pedagogy is all important. He implies that, without a wider recognition that primary teaching is in itself a challenging, intellectual task, on a par with the secondary teachers' subject expertise, the professional status of the primary teacher will never be raised to the level it deserves.

CHAPTER 5.1

The Primary School Teacher as Professional

Eric Hoyle

The purpose of this chapter is to explore changing patterns of professionality amongst primary school teachers in Europe. We can define *professionality* at this point as the set of professional knowledge, skills and values entailed in professional practice. One is thus concerned with exploring the degree to which primary school teachers have, over recent years, been upgrading their knowledge, enhancing their skills and developing the values that are inherent in truly professional work. However, this is not a simple descriptive task. In the first place, although the study of teachers and teaching in Europe has in recent years developed to the degree that makes a volume such as this possible, there are not yet sufficient comparative data to enable detailed comparisons to be made across systems and over time. But more important is the fact that professionality remains a contested concept. In so far as *professionality* is a quality that is possessed by members of a *profession*, the degree to which teaching in general and primary school teaching in particular are regarded as a profession, with all that the term implies for status, remuneration, work conditions and autonomy, is a matter of dispute. Moreover, in so far as we seek to detach the notion of *professionality* from the concept of *profession* in the sense that it is applied to levels of skill in *any* occupation, notions of what constitutes professionality vary considerably between societies and, within those societies, between teachers and laymen and amongst teachers themselves.

1. The concept of a profession

All European languages have an equivalent term to *profession* to refer to certain prestigious occupations such as medicine, law and architecture. It is thus a descriptive term that may also have the nuance of a 'calling' or 'vocation', which implies a particular kind of commitment over and above skill. Teaching is invariably included within the category of professions.

However, sociological analysis takes one beyond the broad usage to 'unpack' the concept. One approach seeks to identify the characteristics that distinguish a profession from other kinds of occupation. Numerous lists of such criteria have been generated over the past 70 years and, although there are variations, a surprising degree of correlation exists between the different lists. The outcome of this approach is an 'ideal type' of profession, which I have summarised elsewhere (Hoyle 1980) as follows:

1. A profession is an occupation that performs a crucial social function.
2. The exercise of this function requires a considerable degree of skill.
3. This skill is exercised in situations that are not wholly routine but in which new problems and situations have to be handled.
4. Thus, although knowledge gained through experience is important, this recipe-type knowledge is insufficient to meet professional demands and the practitioner has to draw on a body of systematic knowledge.
5. The acquisition of this body of knowledge and the development of specific skills require a lengthy period of higher education.
6. This period of education and training also involves the process of socialisation into professional values.
7. These values tend to centre on the pre-eminence of clients' interests and to some degree they are made explicit in a code of ethics.
8. Because knowledge-based skills are exercised in non-routine situations, it is essential for the professional to have the freedom to make his/her own judgements with regard to appropriate practice.
9. Because professional practice is so specialised, the organised profession should have a strong voice in the shaping of relevant public policy, a large degree of control over the exercise of professional responsibilities, and a high degree of autonomy in relation to the state.
10. Lengthy training, responsibility and client-centredness are necessarily rewarded by high prestige and a high level of remuneration.

Conventionally this model is used as the source for the distinctive criteria of a profession, and existing or aspiring professions are matched against these criteria thus yielding a continuum of occupations some of which, such as law and medicine, meet all the criteria to their fullest extent whilst others, such as teaching, fall short of the ideal type and are variously referred to as semi- or quasi-professions.

This approach has been widely criticised on two major grounds. One is that the model imputes to the professions qualities that are not always in evidence in practice. Thus the claim that professions deploy an esoteric body of knowledge is questioned. It is suggested, for example, that a large element in medical and legal practice is, in fact, routine. It thus follows that the training undergone by the professions is unnecessarily long, its length being more concerned with exclusivity, status and remuneration than with the acquisition of essential knowledge and skill. Likewise, the notion of autonomy is questioned in terms of its function as a defence against public accountability rather than the necessary freedom to exercise one's professional judgement. A second ground of radical criticism is that the model entails a circular argument in that, since the criteria have been derived from the pre-eminent occupations themselves, taking them at their own evaluation as expressed by occupational elites rather than from practice, it is thus unsurprising that they meet these criteria. On this view it is conceivable that other criteria could be derived either by a study of practice or by hypothesising the public good.

An alternative view of the concept of profession is that is is less a descriptive than a prescriptive or even ideological category. In short, when the term *profession* is used its purpose is to *persuade*. When used by professional elites its purpose is to enhance claims to status, remuneration or autonomy. When used by government its purpose is often political, for example to inhibit industrial action by appealing to the service ethic of the profession, or to gain acceptance of a decision on pay and conditions by appealing to the altruism that is inherent in the notion of calling. On this view the professions are seen as having used their growing control of the market as a source of power and status (Larson 1977).

This chapter utilises both perspectives. Although many of the criticisms of the ideal type are valid, it will be used in this discussion for heuristic purposes by taking the alleged characteristics of a profession as a means of entering into a discussion of many of the substantive aspects of primary school teaching as a profession, particularly issues of skill, knowledge, autonomy, relationship with clients and status. Despite their different intellectual and ideological origins, the ideal-type approach and the concept-in-use approach are not incompatible in the context of this chapter, since professional associations in teaching deploy the characteristics of the ideal-type model in their quest for an improvement in status, pay and conditions. For example, the teaching profession, through its organisations, emphasises the importance of theoretical knowledge, the need for lengthy training, the benefits of teacher autonomy, and so forth.

The term *professionalisation* refers to the process whereby an occupation progressively meets more of the criteria of a profession or meets the criteria to a greater degree. In most European countries, teaching, including primary school teaching, has been in the process of professionalisation throughout much of the present century, with an acceleration, especially in the case of primary school teaching, in recent years. The most general developments in the professionalisation process include the strengthening of the boundary between the qualified and the unqualified, the extension of the period of initial training and the increase in the body of theoretical knowledge that teachers are expected to acquire during initial training, plus a greater degree of specialisation – more so at the secondary than the primary level.

Professionalisation is usually considered to be a unitary process, but it is perhaps necessary to differentiate between two elements that, although they are probably closely inter-related, can be conceptually distinguished for the purpose of analysis. The two elements are: meeting the criteria of a profession and increasing the *professionality* of teachers. In other words, although the formal fulfilment of the usual criteria of a profession will normally entail an improvement in the professionality of teachers, and hence the quality of education, it is at least conceivable that they will not invariably proceed *pari passu*. It should be remembered that it is often the teacher associations that press for measures whereby the criteria of a profession are increasingly met. The argument for such measures is almost invariably presented in terms of improvements in the professionality of teachers but intertwined with a concern for the improvement of status, pay and conditions. Similarly, governments adopt policies whereby teachers increasingly meet the criteria of a profession. One must repeat, however, that while such trends will normally lead to the enhancement of the professionality of teachers they cannot be axiomatically assumed to do so. The extension of the course of initial training entails professionalisation and will almost certainly enhance the professionality of teachers. However, it is conceivable that if the extension of the course entails the introduction of a high degree of theoretical knowledge - itself a mark of professionalisation - professionality may not be improved. If the theoretical knowledge is transmitted in a way that is inert, has little impact on practice, professionality may not be enhanced. Similarly, such elements in professionalisation as the self-government of the teaching profession and the introduction of a code of professional ethics may meet the conventional requirements of professional status, will most likely enhance the quality of education, but cannot axiomatically be assumed to do so. In short, professionalisation cannot be accepted uncritically as constituting an enhancement in the quality of education.

Professionality was defined earlier as the quality of the professional knowledge, skills and values entailed in professional practice. Although this simplistic definition would probably enjoy wide support, any elaboration of what would constitute professionality in educational settings would soon generate disputes. These disputes would take a number of forms. Since professionality assumes effectiveness, one form of the dispute would take one into the whole debate surrounding teacher effectiveness. At another level, disputes would arise about the appropriate professional role of the teacher in relation to pupils, their parents and the state. Ultimately these disputes are interconnected. However, the remainder of this chapter will focus on the professional role of the teacher, its scope and responsibilities and, in broad terms, the skills, knowledge and values entailed, but not with detailed matters of teaching methods and styles. The discussion will aim to bring out national differences and current convergencies by addressing various themes.

Restricted and extended professionality

Before proceeding to address a number of themes relating to the professionality of the primary school teacher it would be useful to consider two concepts that underpin much of the discussion below. I initially drew a distinction between *restricted* and *extended professionality* in the early 1970s and, although the social, political and educational climate has changed in many countries since the late 1960s and early 1970s, the distinction remains a useful one. As originally formulated, the distinctions made between the two forms of professionality are as follows (Hoyle 1974):

Restricted professionality	*Extended professionality*
Skills derived from experience	Skills derived from a mediation between experience and theory
Perspective limited to the immediate in time and place	Perspective embracing the broader social context of education
Classroom events perceived in isolation	Classroom events perceived in relation to school policies and goals
Introspective with regard to methods	Methods compared with those of colleagues and with reports of practice
Value placed on autonomy	Value placed on professional collaboration
Limited involvement in non-teaching professional activities	High involvement in non-teaching professional activities (esp. teachers' centres, subject associations, research)
Infrequent reading of professional literature	Regular reading of professional literature
Involvement in in-service work limited and confined to practical courses	Involvement in in-service work considerable and includes courses of a theoretical nature
Teaching seen as an intuitive activity	Teaching seen as a rational activity

This somewhat oversimplified distinction requires greater elaboration. Essentially the two categories imply a different individual perspective on the task of teaching. Restricted professionals perceive their work in terms of their classroom activities, which are based largely on experience and intuition. The term *restricted* refers to their perspective and not their competence. Restricted professionals will vary in competence but the very best are excellent teachers within this mode, demonstrating a very high order of classroom skills. The distinction also suggests differences in activity as well as orientation, and extended professionals engage in a wider range of professional activities outside the classroom. The unresolved question implicit in the distinction is whether it is to be considered a continuum or whether it indicates two relatively distinct orientations to the teacher's professional tasks. A concomitant question is whether engagement in professional activities of an extended kind – perhaps through programmes of professional development – can in themselves lead to the adoption of a more extended orientation. A further question is whether extended professionality, as an orientation and as an involvement in associated forms of professional development, is inimical to the level of classroom competence implied at the highest level of restricted professionality. Although this question remains unresolved and, in any case, somewhat difficult to establish empirically, it is nevertheless an important issue for the strategies of professional development.

It can be hypothesised that, both as an occupation and as a set of related activities, the distribution of restricted and extended professionality within a teaching force will be patterned. The patterning may be, to some extent, by personality characteristics but it has often been suggested that it may be patterned by categories, e.g. male/female, primary/secondary, young/old. But the more significant question in the context of this chapter is whether there are variations in the professional orientations of teachers as a group in different European systems that are due to different expectations of the role of the teacher and whether their expectations, and teachers' responses to them, are changing as a result of wider changes in those societies.

2. The professionality of the European primary school teacher

The above distinction between restricted and extended professionality was developed with the teaching profession in Britain and North America in mind. The concept needs further elaboration in relation to European primary school teachers, particularly those in centralised systems where the function of primary education is seen as transmitting a common curriculum. In such countries teaching entails the effective transmission of this common curriculum. In terms of the distinction made above this can be construed as *restricted* professionality. However, the category must be further developed in order to take account of different patterns of educational control. In a situation where the primary teacher enjoys a relatively high degree of autonomy, restricted professionality is a matter of individual beliefs about the function of education and the teacher's role. In centralised systems, where teacher autonomy is limited, the restrictiveness of the teacher's professionality is inherent in the system and thus what constitutes professionality is perceived differently by those who control education and by the teachers themselves. It is professional in the general sense in which this term is used – that of bringing maximum skill to a particular task.

Although there are certain fundamental expectations that primary school teachers as professionals must fulfil, notions of professional responsibility vary across systems. In particular, variations occur in relation to the *scope* of the professional role. This is well illustrated in one of the few systematic comparative studies of the primary school teacher's professional role (Broadfoot *et al.* 1987), in which 360 teachers in England and in France were questioned on the views of their professional responsibility. The results indicated a significant difference in the perceptions of the two groups of teachers. Some of the major differences found were as follows:

1. French primary school teachers were more concerned than their English counterparts with the transmission of a body of curriculum knowledge. In contrast, the latter were more child-centred and concerned with orienting their teaching towards the personal needs and interests of their pupils and encouraging pupils to acquire the skills that would allow them to direct their own learning.
2. A much wider range of teaching styles was reported by English teachers, who also expressed the view that this was a problematic issue for them since they perceived many sources of different expectations regarding teaching style. On the other hand, this was not a contentious area for French teachers who accepted a traditional didactic style without question.
3. English teachers were far less certain about their roles than their French counterparts. In the absence of strong central direction they, to a degree, made their own roles in conditions of uncertainty.
4. English teachers saw their role as encouraging a wide range of learning outcomes entailing personal and social as well as cognitive developments. On the other hand, French teachers were almost exclusively concerned with the academic achievements of the pupils.
5. French teachers do not look to their colleagues for support in their professional work, nor are they particularly concerned about their personal relationships with their pupils. They are clear about their professional role and perform it without fear or favour. On the other hand, the English teacher laid much greater store by personal relationships with pupils and consensual professional relationships with colleagues.
6. French teachers assess their pupils via regular tests and the appropriate standards must be met if the pupil is to make upward progress and enter the secondary college. Since the abolition of the 11+ in Britain, the English primary school teacher has been relatively free from the task of overt evaluation, although the authors suggest that covert evaluation occurs.

This piece of research confirms widely held views on differences between the structure and functions of education in the two countries and the roles of teachers.

The first and most obvious point to be made is that teachers' conceptions of their responsibility are relative to the nature of their different educational systems and underpinning assumptions. The French primary school teacher's conceptions are closely related to the clear expectations of a centralised system which has, since Napoleonic times, emphasised the inculcation of an agreed body of knowledge, a set of conceptions that – though we haven't the same degree of comparative data to support the position – would appear to be shared by primary school teachers in those European countries that have been influenced by the Napoleonic code. It is perhaps tempting to see the primary teacher's role in England and Wales as in some sense more 'professional' in being oriented to the immediate client, the pupil, rather than to the state-as-client. But this would be unwarranted. One reason is that the role of the English primary teacher is itself shaped by cultural, political and administrative factors that bear the legacy of a history of elementary education in which a variety of forces led to a highly decentralised system. This yielded great opportunities for school and teacher autonomy, which has been advanced by the actions of the teacher unions. Thus the historical influences on the teacher's professional role in England and Wales exist but are less easily identified than in the French case. The issue therefore is the capacity of primary school teachers to develop their professional responsibilities in the light of changes within their own systems. This capacity may well be enhanced through the adoption of a comparative perspective.

Broadfoot *et al.* (1987) present the problems confronting French and English primary school teachers as follows:

> As social and policy changes provide a different context within which the primary teacher has to work we need to examine the relative adaptability of these two different approaches to teaching. Who has the greatest crisis in morale – the French *instituteur* who, tied to a traditional curriculum which may have little relevance or appeal for many pupils, has neither the right nor the skill to change it, or the English primary teacher who sets herself the unachievable goal of an individualised pedagogy in a class of over 30 pupils and who has no clear idea of the limits of her responsibility? For pupils, what is the respective impact of coping, as in France, with an impersonal, often harsh, pedagogy and an often arid curriculum as compared to a typically more liberal, but highly varying, set of teacher expectations as in England?

In fact, since the research was undertaken, legislative changes in Britain have occurred that would appear to be predicated upon a shift in the role of the English primary school teacher in the direction of that of their French counterpart, particularly through the implementation of a national curriculum and the systematic assessment of pupils. To what extent this shift will occur remains to be seen. However, until such changes occur, we can use the evidence of Broadfoot and colleagues as the basis of a discussion of the extent to which differences in the scope of the teaching role in France and England meet the conventional criteria of a profession.

There is little doubt that the scope of the role of the French primary school teacher is more limited than that of his/her English counterpart. Content is prescribed and pedagogy is straightforwardly didactic. There is thus less scope for individual judgement and the role is more routinised. One must not, however, draw too strong a contrast between the two roles. There is certainly much routine in the role of the English primary school teacher, but the pupil orientation and the greater pervasiveness of the role are likely to yield opportunities for the exercise of professional judgement. The situation confronting the English teacher is less certain and one characteristic of a profession is alleged to be the capacity to function effectively in 'uncertain situations' (Merton *et al.* 1957). However, English teachers are only effectively more professional in this respect if they have the professional capacity and commitment to fulfil the role. Doubts about this capacity have presumably lain beneath the accelerating movement towards accountability over the past ten years. It may be that the French primary school teacher is, in a sense, more 'professional' in the sense of performing skilfully in a more restricted role. Needless to say, no data exist that allow us to make these comparisons.

A high degree of client-orientation is held to be a *sine qua non* of professional standing. However, comparison of the professionality of English and French teachers is complicated by the fact that they are oriented to different clienteles. For the English teacher, the client is the pupil and the professional skill arises from the interpretation and fulfilment of pupil needs. For the French teacher, professionality lies in the detached and effective transmission of a national curriculum in the interests of equality and national unity. As Broadfoot *et al.* (1987) express it: '. . . French teachers seem far less bothered with concerns about damaging pupil self-esteem and favouritism. Their approach is typically strict on evaluation, often harsh and punitive . . . .' This approach appears to have affinities with the detachment of bureaucracy – a principle of organisation that is frequently juxtaposed to professionality. Yet Parsons (1968), one of the key sociological analysts of the professions, took the view that it was functional for the professions to adopt the detached stance of *affective neutrality* in order better to make judgements about the needs of clients.

Thus the question of whether primary school teachers in France and similar centralised European systems are more or less professional than their English counterparts cannot be answered unequivocally. However, the English teacher appears to have the more professional role if the pupil is seen as the immediate client and if s/he has the extended professionality that allows him/her to fulfil these expectations. We can return to the question of professionality in a later section. In the meantime, we can consider separately one key criterion of a profession: autonomy.

3. Professional autonomy and the teacher

The conventional model of a profession, as we have seen, puts a high premium on practitioner autonomy. However, the issue of autonomy is far from clear cut and a number of issues need to be explored.

The primary school teacher in a centralised European system appears to have less autonomy than his/her counterpart in, say, the English system. A national curriculum leaves only limited scope for the exercise of autonomy in relation to content and teachers interpret their teaching style as being essentially didactic. However, within the constraints inherent in a national curriculum, the teacher in the centralised system appears to enjoy a relatively high degree of autonomy in relation to colleagues, head teachers and parents. Inspectors are seen as agents of the national system and therefore part of the constraining process. Primary school teachers in England, on the other hand, have enjoyed a high degree of autonomy in relation to national curricular aims. They have also hitherto enjoyed a high degree of autonomy *vis-à-vis* parents. The major constraints on autonomy are to be found within the school itself. Although the head teacher has a high degree of legal authority, in practice the leadership styles of head teachers are rarely based on the overt exercise of legal authority. The teacher's autonomy is ultimately the outcome of an implicit negotiation with the head teacher. Yet, despite the degree of autonomy that the English primary school teacher enjoys, Broadfoot *et al.* (1988) show that English primary teachers to a greater degree than French primary school teachers feel accountable to other groups, as Table 5.1.1 shows. Of course, one must recognise that these are reported perceptions of responsibility rather than its enactment. However, if one accepts a relationship between perceptions and behaviour, the traditional connection between high professional status and high practitioner autonomy must be questioned.

The conventional model of a profession was generated in an era in which the professions had established a high degree of autonomy by means of a variety of rhetorics and strategies (Larson 1977). However, changing concepts of professional responsibility include a growing emphasis on greater account-

Table 5.1.1 Accountability to whom: percentage of teachers mentioning each of the following categories

Responsible to:	*England* %	*France* %
Children	91.0	93.9
Colleagues	29.3	3.8
Parents	25.4	8.0
Employers	12.7	8.6
Head teacher	11.5	0.4
The school	9.4	2.3
Myself	7.6	3.1
Society	6.8	3.0
Governors	1.9	0.4
Other professionals	1.7	0.4
Senior staff	1.3	0.4
Other	0	2.2
Total no. of teachers responding	360	360

ability to parents. Accountability can be seen as inimical to the authority on which the professions have placed such stress. On the other hand, responsiveness to clients - itself an important element in the ethic of professionality - can be seen as, perhaps, the higher professional good. However, two problems are entailed. One is that teachers have a multiplicity of clients whose expectations may well be in conflict. The other is that the optimum balance between professional expertise and public accountability is difficult to conceptualise and, even more so, to institutionalise. The European primary school teacher has been caught up in these uncertainties over recent years, particularly in relation to their relationship with parents.

There is substantial and unequivocal evidence that pupil progress is associated with parental support and interest in their schooling. One of the most substantial pieces of research on this issue was reported in *Children and their Primary Schools* (Plowden Report: Department of Education and Science 1967). The report advocated stronger links between the parents of primary school children and their schools. However, the issue as far as the professional status and the professionality of the primary school teacher is concerned is the nature of that relationship, in particular whether a closer relationship enhances the status of the teacher by allowing a wider scope for professional expertise wherein parents constitute a wider clientele or detracts from it when parents, particularly if they are organised and their participation is legitimated, constitute a threat to the professional autonomy of the teacher.

The relationship between parents and schools has been systematically studied on a comparative basis by Beattie (1985) who took France, Italy, the German Federal Republic and England and Wales as his case systems. Although the study is not directly concerned with the relationship between parental participation and teacher professionality, the manner in which the issue is conceptualised and the rich data provided constitute a useful basis to a discussion of professionality.

Beattie links the following as a set of commonsense perceptions of those areas of schooling that parents might seek to influence:

- (i) progress of individual pupils: e.g. promotion from one class to another, allocation to secondary school, discipline;
- (ii) curriculum, internal organization of the school and school-related extra-curricular activity: e.g. subjects or other facilities available within school time: grouping (mixed-ability or otherwise); peripheral activities of the curriculum such as outings, extra sports clubs, or sex education out of school time;
- (iii) appointment and control of personnel;
- (iv) resourcing: decisions about whatever funds are available;
- (v) planning of school provision (local, regional, national), including decisions about going comprehensive;
- (vi) improvements of school–community relations.

His interest lies in the types of parental participation and with exploring the strengths of the two competing socio-political interpretations, which, though ultimately relevant to this section, cannot be considered in detail. However, two points can be noted. One is that, in all four countries studied, parental participation has been a long-term development, often given a considerable impetus by the socio-political changes of the late 1960s and becoming a matter of legislation in these years: France (1968), Italy (1973), Germany (mainly 1964–9) and England and Wales (1980). A second point is that he found that, broadly speaking, the movement towards greater parental participation had two major sources. One was the state, which saw the creation of structures for participation as a means of handling the 'legitimation crisis' noted by Habermas (1976). The other was the grassroots social movement whereby parents – mainly middle-class parents – sought a degree of participation in determining the internal activities of the schools that their children attended. Beattie sees the first approach as essentially conservative and the latter as essentially reformist or even revolutionary. The pattern of participation in the four case countries varies – and it is beyond the scope of this chapter even to summarise Beattie's complex data – but in all cases there is a real threat to teacher autonomy, although this takes different forms in the centralised and decentralised systems.

Beattie does not specifically deal with the question of the professional autonomy of the teacher since this is not part of his argument. It is mentioned at one point as one of the barriers to parental influence on schools. At other points, autonomy is discussed as a characteristic of the school, with no differentiation made between the relative roles and powers of parents and teachers. And, yet again, parents are seen, in systems such as England and Wales where schools enjoy a relative degree of autonomy, as potentially imposing a degree of similarity on schools as they 'curb the eccentricities of individual headteachers' (p. 233). What the study does show is that, in both centralised and decentralised systems, teachers are having to come to terms with various patterns of parent participation, the forms of which are often unclear. One can assume that they have a number of differing aims, which can be grouped into two categories, one of which is *conservative* and is concerned with legitimating the purposes of the state and the other is *reformist* or even *revolutionary* and springs from a feeling of powerlessness against the state.

Beattie's work illustrates the fact that parental influence is growing but that its patterning differs. His analysis does not, because it was not intended to, illuminate the impact of any of the forms of participation on the professional role of the teacher. It is difficult to say, in the absence of adequate comparative evidence, the likely effect upon teacher autonomy. *Prima facie* it might appear that, where teacher autonomy has been high, increased parental involvement may involve a reduction in the degree of autonomy. Where autonomy has been low and where parental involvement entails a legitimation of the purposes of the state, autonomy seems destined to remain severely limited. Where teacher autonomy has been low and parental involvement is reformist in character, the teachers will be cross-pressured with unpredictable consequences. Professionality may be construed as implementing the curriculum as effectively as possible by whomsoever the curriculum is determined. However, a situation of increasing parental influence perhaps paradoxically affords the teacher at least the opportunity of influencing curriculum and method through professional assertiveness. But professional assertiveness is likely to be effective only in so far as the professional status of the primary teacher, based on a body of knowledge that is accepted as authoritative by the layman, is enhanced. We can, therefore, turn to the question of status.

4. The status of primary school teacher

The status of the teacher is a policy issue, not least for the primary education sector. Enhanced status is important to the teachers themselves in so far as it is an indicator of the worthwhileness of their work in the eyes of society at large and, therefore, enhances the intrinsic satisfaction of teaching - and perhaps also extrinsic rewards - but it is also important in that the higher the status of teachers the more influential is their profession likely to be.

Occupational status is the standing of an occupation in relation to others within and across societies. The empirical approach to this standing rests on the use of ratings of occupational prestige. However, such ratings do not capture the pervasive and diffuse feelings that the public has towards members of a particular occupation or a section of it, or the subtle differences in social status between teachers in the many European single-teacher village schools and those in urban areas. Moreover, occupational status is also closely linked with social class since, in so far as class has an economic basis, occupation is a particularly salient indication of social status. To pursue this line would be to raise issues of the class position of teachers in the division of labour. Since a full explanation of the status of teaching is beyond the scope of this chapter, attention will focus on occupational prestige and the possible determinants of the status of teaching as an occupation.

The measurement of occupational prestige entails subjects placing a given set of occupations in rank order. Because of the very different methods used, international comparisons are difficult. Despite these difficulties, one can generalise that teaching, treated as an undifferentiated category, is to be located at the lower end of the highest quartile of the distribution of occupations and that this position has changed relatively little over the past 50 years (Hodge *et al.* 1966; Hoyle 1985; Bolte 1955, quoted Kob 1961). However, this broad generalisation has to be hedged by many qualifications, not the least of which, and the most important as far as this chapter is concerned, is that there occur *intra*-occupational differences in the prestige ratings of teachers within the secondary sector but most clearly between the secondary and primary sectors (Halls 1976; Bernbaum *et al.* 1969; Hearnden 1976; Boucher 1982).

This difference in occupational prestige between secondary and primary school teachers is universal. However, the *degree* of difference varies in a number of ways. Teachers of all kinds tend to perceive a lesser degree of difference in prestige between primary and secondary colleagues and females record less difference than males. There are also indications of differences in the relative ranking of secondary and primary level teachers across countries. Although existing data do not permit unequivocal statements on this issue, it can be tentatively suggested that difference in prestige is greater in continental Western Europe than in the United States, Britain, and possibly Eastern Europe. It should also be added that, despite the notorious problem of international salary comparisons, the secondary–primary difference in prestige in Western Europe is reflected in salary differentials.

The data on the relative prestige of secondary and primary school teachers confirm a widely held view but, in order to explore the sources of this difference, we must address the broader issue of status.

That teaching lacks the status of the major professions has been attributed to a variety of factors. These can be grouped as follows:

- *Knowledge and skill*: Teachers are regarded as needing a lower level of expertise than major professionals.
- *Autonomy*: Teachers are seen as being more bureaucratically constrained than professionals in private practice and even professionals employed in organisations.
- *Characteristics of teachers*: The social class background and educational achievements are lower than those of the major professions and their personality characteristics are believed to be 'unenterprising'.
- *Client and client relations*: The teacher's clients are young, captive and confronted in groups over a lengthy period of time and potentially prone to indiscipline.
- *Intermediacy*: The teacher stands in an intermediate relationship with the wider world into which their charges will eventually pass. They are intermediate between the world of the child and the world of the adult, the world of work and the world of non-work, the moral world of the school (the 'museum of virtue') and the less fastidious world outside, and the world in which knowledge is created (the academy) and the world in which knowledge is used.
- *Size*: Teaching is by far the largest of the professions.
- *Careers*: The circumstances of appointment, lack of career opportunities, the lack of clear criteria of success and, we can add here, the relatively low salaries of the majority of teachers compared with salaries in other professions.

Of course, this list touches on only some of the determinants of status. The patterning will vary by country and by stages of schooling within each country, yielding different status levels for primary and secondary teachers. Moreover, the factors listed above are interactive and we have no research findings that enable us to identify the key causal factors or the influential patterns of interaction. My best guess is that a key factor in determining the status of teachers is the fact that their clients are *young*, closely followed by the fact that teaching is by far the largest profession, which perforce determines a salary level that is not competitive with the major professions, with consequent implications for recruitment and the collective quality of teachers. A related factor is that in most societies the majority of teachers are women - partly because of the conventional assumptions about the appropriateness of the role of the female teacher in the early years of schooling and partly because of career opportunities - and that in most societies patriarchal attitudes continue to prevail and thus influence the status of teaching. The hypothesised key determinant on the status of teachers of the youth of their clientele is perhaps partly offset by the academic standing in some European countries of teachers at the highest levels of an elite secondary system of schools, a pattern that serves to depress the status of the primary school teacher relative to the secondary school teacher.

Measures of *occupational prestige* necessarily oversimplify the subtleties of status but nevertheless have value in allowing the perceived status of teachers to be compared with that of other professions, of teachers in different systems and of different types of teachers within a single teacher. The status differential between primary and secondary level teachers is reflected in the different forms of training received. The general pattern in Europe before the Second World War was for secondary teachers to be products of the universities and to have undergone their pedagogical training there or to have entered teaching directly without formal training, whereas primary school teachers tended to have entered teaching via special secondary schools that provided them with a secondary education and also with educational and professional studies including practical teaching. After the war, there was a movement in most systems to move the training of primary teachers into the tertiary education sphere, in some instances with close links with the universities, though the rate of change varies between different systems (see Organisation for Economic Co-operation and Development 1985, 1986, 1987). This movement to the greater professionalisation of the primary school teacher has *formally* reduced one source of status differential between primary and secondary school teachers, but the evidence for a *perceived* equalisation of status - within the teaching profession and amongst the population at large - is not such as to permit generalisation. Few European countries have gone as far as England and Wales in creating a system whereby the two modes of entry to teaching - the four-year concurrent course and the three-plus-one consecutive course - are available to entrants to primary and secondary education, all of whom are graduates and on a common secondary scale. This is slowly creating a population of primary school teachers containing many more confident, extended professionals, though no data are available to establish whether this has enhanced their status relative to secondary school teachers.

5. Professional development and careers

It is a truism to note that social change increasingly impinges on the schools. It is also the case that, in responding to these pressures, the teacher's role in most societies has been undergoing considerable expansion. This role expansion has perhaps occurred most clearly at the secondary level, but the primary school teacher is also beset by increasing expectations, not only in terms of subject matter knowledge. The areas in which the teacher's role has been under pressure to expand include the following: responsiveness to parental expectations, social education, pastoral care, curriculum development, school management, technological development, assessment, links with other professionals in the social and welfare fields, combating discrimination, and professional development. This last aspect of role expansion - professional development - underpins the others since all require the acquisition of new knowledge, skills and attitudes.

In common with teachers in Great Britain and North America, primary school teachers in Europe are responding to the expectation that they will develop their skills over a professional career. However, emerging models of professional development, strongly supported and sponsored by the OECD and other agencies, are somewhat out of kilter with the roles of primary school teachers and the training they have received. The currently favoured model of professional development is focused on school improvement. In essence, the school is perceived as a problem-solving organisation responsive to changing situations, locally and nationally, with staff undertaking professional development activities of a variety of kings (Bolam 1978) in order to acquire the knowledge and skills required to respond to change. However, this model runs counter to traditional teacher roles. It is predicated on a higher degree of autonomy than is available to teachers in highly centralised systems. Moreover, it runs counter to efforts to upgrade the professional status of primary school teachers. In seeking to upgrade status, many countries have sought to associate primary teaching much more closely with the universities via various institutional patterns. The result has been an increasing emphasis on the academic aspect of pedagogical studies, which gives priority to theory. However, school-focused patterns of professional development give priority to problems-to-be-solved. The relationship between theory and practice in this case is more subtle and complex - and also problematic. Support for professional development may be given by universities but it is increasingly given by other kinds of institutions through a variety of forms of delivery systems.

If one accepts the validity of the model of professional-development-for-school-improvement one can foresee a continuing uncertainty in the relationship between professionality, status and career. Professionality can be seen as having three major components: subject matter knowledge, educational theory and pedagogical and associated skills. Needless to say, the relationship between these in the teacher's formation and throughout a teaching career is permanently contested and presents an apparently intractable problem. The dilemmas are particularly acute for European primary school teachers. It is generally held that their status will be enhanced with a greater emphasis on academic subject content and, in a genuine attempt to enhance the status of the primary school teacher, many governments have placed an emphasis on this aspect. There is no doubt that primary school teachers need a sound academic education, but an overemphasis on a single academic subject - taught at the expense of professional needs - could be a disadvantage. It is even doubtful whether such an emphasis does, in fact, greatly enhance status if, as was argued above, the key determinant of status is that the teacher's clients are young. Similarly, an emphasis on the academic aspects of pedagogy may add little to the status of the primary school teacher and detract from more relevant aspects of pedagogy unless the university or training institution has achieved a successful integration.

European countries tend to have flat career structures for primary school teachers. In some systems, career achievement is seen in terms of a move from primary school teaching into teaching in the lower secondary school, a move that is related to achievement in an academic subject. Although it is a contentious matter, there is perhaps a case for increasing the career opportunities of teachers within the primary system, so long as - and this is the practical difficulty - progression is associated with increased professionality achieved through professional development.

It would appear that most European countries are seeking to develop school-focused patterns of professional development but that traditional concepts of academic status remain a barrier. The paradox of the situation, in Europe as well as in Britain, is that increased professionality is unlikely to increase the social status of the teacher and the primary school teacher in particular (Hoyle 1982). Professional development, undertaken in the interests of pupils, does not entail activities that easily meet traditional academic criteria. The emphasis is on practice rather than theory, action research rather than basic research, interdisciplinary rather than monodisciplinary approaches, curriculum development rather than subject content knowledge, and so forth. The process of professional development is intellectually demanding but not in conventional academic, status-enhancing ways. Since, if the earlier argument is correct, European primary school teachers are unlikely to enhance their status by academic achievements alone - they will still fall short of the major profession and even (in the short term) the secondary teaching profession - the alternative path of school-focused professional development would cost them little but would enhance the quality of schooling.

An important issue, but one that must remain unexamined in any detail in this chapter, is that of the work satisfaction of primary school teachers. The well-known two-factor theory of Herzberg (1966) appears, with some modifications (Nias 1981), to apply to primary school teachers. This theory, brieflly stated, holds that work itself is the major source of satisfaction, whilst other – 'hygiene' – factors, such as salary, working conditions, relationships with management, are sources of dissatisfaction. One might tentatively hypothesise that the major source of job satisfaction for European primary school teachers lies in having a sense of achievement at having effectively transmitted the prescribed curriculum. This raises the question of whether they are likely to derive job satisfaction from an increasingly extended role, perhaps with greater autonomy. There are certainly dangers here that only well-conceived patterns of professional development could overcome.

6. Conclusion

The situation of the teacher in European societies challenges widely accepted notions of what constitutes a professional person. The two basic criteria of professional status are specialised knowledge and autonomy. Secondary school teachers in Europe enjoy a comparatively high status because of their possession of academic expertise in the form of subject matter knowledge. This would not appear to affect the relative lack of autonomy. Primary school teachers have a considerably lower status than their secondary counterparts. They have, hitherto, had a less academic higher education than their secondary counterparts, but have been subject to the same limitation of autonomy. Their *professionality* is seen largely in terms of the effective transmission of an agreed curriculum within a limited conception of the scope of the teacher's role.

In many European societies two convergent processes are affecting the role of the primary school teacher. One is the attempt to upgrade their status by associating their formation most closely with the universities. The other is the emphasis on professional development designed to enable them to meet the growing obligations of the role in response to social change. The prevalent model of professional development is school focused and problem oriented. This requires the acquisition and utilisation of knowledge and skills that are, to some degree, outside the conventions accepted by the academy and may serve to generate some of the role uncertainties experienced by the primary school teacher in England and Wales.

To the extent that the status of teaching as a profession is probably determined by the fact that their clients are young, there would appear to be an inherent barrier to a *considerable* enhancement of status, which the increasing academic levels achieved by primary school teachers, though perhaps contributing to a status closer to that of secondary school teachers, will not greatly change. In so far as European primary school teachers enhance their skills through professional development they may well be in the position of enhancing their professionality but not – at least in the short term – their status.

CHAPTER 5.2

Structures of School Management in Europe

Mats Ekholm

Primary schools in most parts of Europe currently have some form of school management structure. This was not the case when popular education was first introduced and, in order to understand the contemporary primary school and its organisational structure, it is useful to establish when and why specific parts of the organisational structure, like the managerial element, were implemented. As a social institution the school is based on some very simple ideas, the most basic being that interactions between people with different levels of knowledge and skill are a profitable means of educative exchange. Strongly linked to this idea are two other basic assumptions: that the outcome of the educational process that occurs in these interactions depends on the quality of work of the student as well as on the quality of the work of the teacher.

Early roots

In the early days of western society, school activities took place where the teacher could find space to meet his students. There were no specific institutions called schools. Elementary classes held in Rome more than 2,000 years ago were held in an open porch (*pergula*) in the public square, protected from the passing traffic only by a sheet of tent-cloth stretched from pillar to pillar. Pupils sat on benches and wrote on wax tablets across their knees; the master sat on a raised platform (Castle 1961). Elementary education was not for all and only those who could afford to pay for the work of the teacher could send their boys to the school.

This kind of interaction between teachers and students was maintained in many of the European countries in its original form for a long time. The effectiveness of the pattern was recognised and utilised by the church. Churches can thus be seen as constituting an extensive form of adult education. Closely linked to this large-scale adult education effort, the church contributed in most European countries to the development of elementary education. Rooms in churches or in monasteries were used as meeting places for the teacher and the pupils, but for a substantial period in the history of most countries only a small proportion of the children attended such schools.

During this period, no specific form of school management, in the modern sense, existed. When the primary school was linked to another institution, e.g. a church, the leadership was exercised by the mother institution. A strong tradition thus developed that allowed teachers to function relatively autonomously.

The birth of modern schools

In the early years of the nineteenth century it became common in most nations to believe that all young citizens should have their share of elementary education. School houses were built and teachers were educated in systematic ways. In several of the European countries the new school houses were small places where only a couple of classes were held. They were built as close as possible to where people lived and, as most countries had a low degree of industrialisation, this meant scattered villages. At that time teachers worked as cultural partisans, seeking to enlighten people in ways other than that of the church. Although they maintained religious and moral education, many of them introduced young people to ideas other than those found in the Bible, e.g. about the natural world. But, as cultural partisans, teachers were also in some countries controlled by the state. Systems of inspection were developed and these functioned as agencies of control. In countries where inspectors were introduced they fulfilled some of the functions of contemporary school management. The inspectors not only checked what the teachers were doing, but they were also responsible for informing teachers about educational innovations and guidelines for the teaching process.

During the latter part of the nineteenth century and the first half of the twentieth century patterns of production changed in most European countries. The number of people involved in farming decreased in most countries in dramatic ways as industrialisation and urbanisation occurred. At the same time, large-scale changes took place; the idea of common comprehensive education for all children became accepted and schools were established for urban children. These schools grew so large that in most countries some kind of school management function was introduced and one the teachers of the school became the first among colleagues – *primus inter pares*. However, although the management of the primary school is similar in many European countries, there are also many differences. In broad terms there are three main solutions to the problem of school management in European countries today.

The teacher-managed school

This first solution can be described as the school *without* one evident school leader[1] as in some of the cantons of Switzerland. The original village schools have come together into larger buildings, but inside each of the classrooms the teacher is autonomous and, as was the case when more common schools were created, trusted by the community to do the job in an acceptable way. The elementary school in Switzerland does not, however, totally lack school management. It is responsible to the communal school board, as is the case in many other European countries (e.g. the Nordic countries), and the school directorate at the canton level. The communal school board - on which everyone who has the right to vote and who is not working as a teacher in the commune can have a seat - appoints new teachers and deals mainly with certain administrative questions. In theory the commune school board ought to deal with educational matters but seldom has the time to do so.

In this form of school management, tasks that school leaders elsewhere undertake are divided among all the teachers in the school. However, sometimes no division of tasks is made and each teacher undertakes his or her own administrative duties.

The subdivision of tasks among teachers in Swiss schools is exemplified by Frehner (1986). He describes an elementary school of the Swiss system in which there is a teacher who has a specific responsibility for materials - ensuring that school materials are permanently available in sufficient quantities. Another teacher at the same school may have the task of being the school building chairman and is responsible for order within the school building. Other teachers may be responsible for tasks like timetabling, custodians of learning and teaching aids, apparatus, the garden or the gymnasium. There may also be one teacher who has responsibility, with the agreement of the school board, for allocating newly arrived students to classes according to age. The training of teachers to engage in school management tasks in a Swiss school depends on the size of the school. The larger the school, the more common it is to find one teacher undertaking each of the tasks. In Swiss schools, teachers do not give instructions to colleagues or act as change agents.

One school - one leader

The second solution is common throughout much of Europe. It can be described as 'one school, one leader'. This principle of school management structure is predominant in Austria, Belgium, Denmark, Finland, France, Germany, Hungary, Ireland, Italy, the Netherlands, Norway, Poland, Spain, Czechoslovakia and the United Kingdom. Sometimes in sparsely populated areas there are so few students and teachers that there is no perceived need for one of the teachers to be the school leader. But in some countries, e.g. Finland, each school is obliged to have a formal school leader however few students or teachers there are. In most European elementary schools there are, however, larger groups of students and teachers and there is also a school leader.

The school leader in the elementary school often functions without assistant principals and with limited clerical help. She will also have teaching responsibilities of her own. Sometimes in smaller schools these responsibilities are such that the school leader is much more a teacher than a school leader. In some sparsely populated areas of the nations mentioned above, the closeness to the Swiss system is clear. The difference between the work of the school leader in an elementary school in far north Finland or on an island along the Norwegian coast lies only in the fact that in the Norwegian or Finnish school one of the teachers holds the formal position of school leader.

In larger elementary schools in towns and cities the school leader has more time allocated for dealing with specific school management tasks but still retains teaching responsibilities. The main task of the school leader of the elementary school seems to be to *maintain* the quality of the school, not to *develop* or *improve* it. The school leader is engaged in time-scheduling, assigning teachers their particular teaching responsibilities, seeing that the curriculum is taught, and that rules and policies are respected. Although there may be minor differences in the structuring of school management among the different countries, the school leaders seem in general to be occupied with the conditions of learning.

The school leader of the elementary school seems to function very much as a resource facilitator for other teachers in the school. She makes overall plans for the school, collects judgements about the need for new materials and orders them, negotiates with the central authorities about the budget, and takes care of the planning of student numbers. Usually she makes sure that relevant information about the students is stored in the school registers. The school leader is also used by other teachers when there are conflicts between the teacher and student or parents. The school leader is expected to take responsibility for resolving these conflicts. Elementary school leaders chair meetings within their school and represent the school at meetings.

In most school systems where the idea of 'one school – one school leader' is practised, the elementary level of the school system itself is easily identified because students who belong to the elementary level are housed in separate school buildings. However, there are systems in which the elementary level of schooling is less evidently identified, e.g. in the Danish system where the elementary level is just the first six years of the 10-year compulsory *folkskolen*, but the same system of one school – one leader is used. The idea of keeping one obviously responsible position on a school site seems to have been widely used in order to establish a focus for communications with the school.

School leader of a school management area

The third structural solution to the school management of elementary schools is fully practised only in Sweden, although in some other countries, e.g. in parts of Portugal, this solution is used in sparsely populated areas. This solution is based on the assumption that the school may have more than one site. The school leader is thus responsible for a geographical area or district.

In Sweden, the first nine school years are seen as an administrative unit. The students pass through three different stages - lower, middle and higher stages of the *grundskola* - where they meet new teachers in each stage of the school. But all three stages are kept together and are looked upon as one local organisation. This local organisation within the Swedish *kommun* is administratively part of the *kommun*'s geographical area. Within such a school management area ('*rektorsområde*') one will usually find about 500–600 students and about 70–80 teachers, two or three school leaders and about 30 people working with food services, student care, counselling, maintenance services, and as clerks, etc. Within each school management area there are three or four school sites. In larger cities, a school management area may have only one site. In rural and sparsely populated areas, one may find as many as seven–ten smaller schools within the school management area.

School leaders in Sweden with responsibility for elementary education have a somewhat different task from that of some of their colleagues in other countries. Here the school leader is in charge of a local organisation that covers more than elementary schools usually do in other countries. This means that the school leader also has management responsibilities for the early stage of the secondary level of the school system and for the non-teaching staff of the school. Although Swedish school leaders therefore have a somewhat more distant relationship with the elementary part of the school, they fulfil the same functions with regard to the elementary school and its teachers as do other school leaders in other European countries. In Sweden, neither the school leader of a school management area nor her assistant school leaders necessarily teaches at elementary level. It may very well be a former subject teacher for the later stages of the *grundskola* who has been appointed as school leader.

The Swedish school leader can rely on a somewhat different substructure of her school management area from that of her European colleagues. Where many other countries lack subsystems of leadership at the elementary level, the Swedish school management area is divided into several working units and in each of these a teacher has responsibility as the unit leader. In most Swedish elementary schools the school leader and her assistants use these teachers as sub-managers. The school leader, her deputies and the unit leaders meet regularly to decide on important local topics, such as how the local working plan is to be developed, in what way the in-service training of teachers is to be organised during the year, or what money is needed in the next year, etc. The school leader in the Swedish system uses unit leaders to direct the teachers' work and to participate both in important policy decisions of the school and in the day-to-day work of the teachers. The school leader and her deputies in the Swedish school have only a small amount of teaching responsibility to share within the group, which may mean that one of the group does not teach at all. Sometimes the school leaders divide the teaching responsibility in such a way that all of them teach.

Comparisons between the three patterns

Although there exist at least three different management structures in European elementary schools, it is striking that the main functions of the school leaders are rather similar in each. They are there to run the school and to check that the children receive proper education. They are expected to do so in a non-demanding way. Teachers want their school leaders to be supportive, not controlling or demanding (Ekholm and Sandström 1982). The most powerful instruments of management that the school leader has are the timetable and teacher distribution within the school. Most school leaders undertake very few experiments with these two managerial tools. Many schools seem to be managed more for today and sometimes for yesterday than with the future in sight (Buckley 1985).

For a long time school leaders at elementary level have spent a high proportion of their time on administrative work. In some countries this is because there has been a lack of administrative support: clerks working in elementary schools are seldom employed full time; deputies have only small proportions of their time assigned for school leader duties – they remain more as teachers than school leaders. In other countries, the preoccupation with administrative duties occurs because of other reasons. In centralised systems like France, Sweden or in several *Länder* of West Germany, the central authorities expect school leaders closely to follow work schemes that the central authorities produce. The authorities have long expected school leaders in these countries to be to some extent the 'long arm' of the authorities themselves. School leaders are also expected to answer all the questions that these central bodies ask.

In small primary schools the school leader is much more of a class teacher, whose heart is with the children in her class and not in the management of the school. When this school leader, with almost full-time teaching assignments, solves her school leader problems, it will be by repeating solutions that cost little energy and time. School leaders at the elementary level give high priority to working with the curriculum. They also want contact with other teachers. The leadership style in most primary schools is informal since the place of work is small and people within the school get to know each other quite well. The time that the elementary school leader has to spend on these issues is, however, somewhat restricted, as consultations with parents, governors, administrators, advisers, inspectors, salesmen, and others, detract from curriculum work and teacher contacts.

There are several things that the manager of a non-educational organisation can do that school leaders of elementary school cannot. School leaders do not distribute different rewards to the teachers, nor can they use systems of control in the working process in the school in the same way as leaders in other forms of organisation. Managerial evaluation of work performance is not an accepted pattern for schools in most European countries. In non-educational organisations, the manager makes clear demands on the participant. In European elementary schools it is rare that the school leader is the one who communicates the demands of the single teacher or of the teachers as a group. Instructions are passed down the hierarchy. The local school leader in many European countries simply informs the teacher of the local school of these instructions.

School management and school structure

Elementary schools can scarcely be seen as hierarchies or bureaucracies. As Miles and Ekholm (1985) have reminded us, there are many other ways to perceive the organisational structure of the local school. Some nations seem to have seen elementary schools as a kind of a professionalised and collegial organisation, in which teaching and learning are seen as something rather complex and therefore requiring effective training. The school's mission is to apply professional competence to the needs of the students who lack knowledge and skills. The professional/collegial school serves the old basic idea of getting the knowledgeable person to interact with the person with less knowledge. In such a school, working procedures have a flavour of 'professional discretion', mutual trust and feedback by peers. Such feedback relates to professional standards rather than to regulations or a nationwide curriculum. The role of the school leader is restricted to dealing with necessary administration and, although she is welcome to support teaching, if she comes into a classroom she is expected to play her part in the teaching process and not merely to observe and give feedback.

Although those who plan national school systems may perceive elementary schools as professional/collegial organisations, many elementary schools appear to function more like 'natural systems' or 'spontaneous' local organisations. In such schools goals are not seen as clear, neither are the methods used. In this model the school seems to follow the basic principle that 'things will work themselves out'. The working procedures in such an organisation are decentralised and non-standardised and will have emerged organically as the demands of the situation developed. Goals emerge through actions rather than through prior definition. 'What works is good' might be the motto in such a school. Teaching in this kind of organisation is sometimes seen more as an art than a craft or profession. For the school leader, the work of management in a school that functions as a natural system consists, essentially, of day-to-day coping with streams of problems requiring immediate solutions. The school leader in such a primary school 'has no tradition of delegation, and the flat, class-based structure of most of the schools encourages teacher independence rather than teacher interdependence' (Coulson 1980, p. 282).

Transition of teachers to school leaders

To be a school leader in an elementary school is, in most European countries, much more like having a profession other than that of a teacher. Their teaching responsibilities are, in many countries, so low that the school leader and others understand that teaching is only a minor part of the total job. In other countries this is not the case. When a teacher is appointed to a position as a school leader, she has, in a sense, left her old profession. However, many teachers going into the new job refuse to accept that they have left the old one. They fight to keep continued contact with children and they are more than willing to replace other teachers in class. However, soon enough the administrative part of the school leader job usually swallows the newcomer and draws them away from the teacher's tasks that they had.

Becoming a school leader seems, in several countries, to be a smooth socialisation process. In Norway and Denmark, for example, it is not uncommon to do the job on an acting basis before being accepted. During these periods teachers have the chance to experience the school leader position, but they are usually occupied with limited administrative tasks or working on time-scheduling. More complicated tasks, like managing negotiations, are often kept from the acting leader.

Most European countries have not had any preparatory education for teachers who aspire to become school leaders. However, there now exist possibilities of study at university level or at polytechnic institutes in Great Britain in order to gain an academic understanding of school management perspectives. In France, new school leaders have three months of preparatory training. In Hungary there is also a three-month training programme for teachers who want to become school leaders in Budapest (Kozma 1984).

In several countries there are evident signs that the work of school leaders has become a profession of its own, out of the teacher sphere. Specific trade unions for school leaders have evolved and different nations offer new school leaders extended educational programmes when they have accepted a position. In Norway, a large-scale in-service programme for school leaders has been introduced recently (LIS 1988), and in Sweden a 12-year experiment with a compulsory two-year in-service training programme for school leaders has led to an institutionalisation of a five-year basic education (based on on-the-job training principles) for new school leaders and a continuous compulsory in-service training programme for all school leaders. In the Netherlands, school leaders are offered different training programmes when they have accepted a position. In Spain, the Polytechnic University of Madrid offers courses to school leaders in school management (Gonzales-Tirados 1983). Training programmes of different length and kind are offered for school leaders in various *Bundesländer* of West Germany. In Czechoslovakia, all new school leaders participate in introductory training programmes together with leaders from non-educational organisations.

All these efforts to help school leaders into their new jobs or to stimulate them to do other things in their jobs through educational programmes may be interpreted as signs of the determination of different countries to invest in the leadership of their schools. In many countries this investment is obvious. In others, school improvement has been shown to be going rather slowly and cautiously (see Ekholm, 1987, for a report on a five-year review of improvement work in 35 Swedish schools).

When a teacher has accepted a job as a school leader and starts to get involved in the new tasks, she is sometimes perceived as something of a traitor. In a report on the situation of school leaders in France, Caré and Lafond (1986) make some remarks about this phenomenon:

> For the teaching staff, the Head is someone who has betrayed the noble profession of teaching. They forget that he was a teacher first, like them, and see him only as the person in authority. Teachers are hardly aware of having real collegiate power and an equally real and particularly decisive influence on their pupils. They can see only this power confronting them and seeming always to be threatening their independence. (p. 146)

When Caré and Lafond describe the situation of school leaders they use the pronoun 'he' for the school leader. I have tried throughout this text to use the pronoun 'she', mainly to accustom the reader to the notion of female school leaders. In European elementary schools the overwhelming proportion of teachers are female, but school leaders are, in some countries to a dramatically large extent, male. Statistics collected some years ago (SOU 1980) showed that 52 per cent of the school leaders of French primary schools were women, with 43 per cent in England, 28 per cent in Poland, 25 per cent in the Soviet Union and in the German Democratic Republic, 16 per cent in Finland, 12 per cent in Sweden, 10 per cent in Norway, 8 per cent in Denmark, and 4 per cent in the Netherlands. However, some recent figures show that the proportions of women in school leader positions are moving in different directions. In the Netherlands, there was a decrease from 4 per cent in 1978 down to 3 per cent in 1982, as the proportion of women teachers fell from 44 per cent to 42 per cent, whereas in Sweden, the rate of women working as school leaders in the *grundskola* increased between 1978 and 1988 from 12 per cent to 24 per cent.

The Swedes have also found that there is very little mobility in their schools amongst school leaders. In two cases out of three, leaders are appointed from existing staff (Ekholm 1988). This strong 'in-breeding' has worried the authorities in Sweden. In some school systems there is even greater 'in-breeding', especially where, as in Spain, the teachers of the local school are the real selectors of their own leaders. In other countries the school system has chosen to avoid this effect by regulation – for example, in the *Länder* of the Federal Republic of Germany schools are not allowed to choose a new school leader from among the teachers of the school.

The procedures for selecting school leaders differ between the European countries. In Italy, candidates take written exams that are arranged centrally during a three-day period each year. A panel of professors of education makes judgements about the qualities of the applicants. In the Scandinavian countries the local boards of education, on which local politicians sit, are responsible for the selection of school leaders. In England, the local education authority as well as the governing body of the school have a say. In Hungary and Czechoslovakia it is the Department of Education that appoints the school leader. In the Federal Republic of Germany a temporary committee, composed of teachers from the school, parents, a *Schulrat* and people of the board of the commune, selects the school leader of the elementary school. Whoever has the power to appoint a new school leader in the different countries, the same rule always applies – school leaders need to have been teachers.

Tomorrow's school leaders today

Some of the conditions that regulate the work of school leaders are slowly changing. First, somewhat more administrative support is now given to school leaders in some countries. During the last few decades new expectations of school leaders have arisen. They are often encouraged to act independently but, at the same time, to be accountable within the decentralised power structure that has been developed in many countries (see Van Velzen, 1979, for the Netherlands; Vandenberghe, 1988, for Belgium; and Caré and Lafond, 1986, for France). The demand for a more autonomous local school leader in countries with very different basic structures of school system – from decentralised systems like the British to highly centralised systems like the French and the Swedish – seems to be connected with the existence of economies that have been characterised by austerity. When money is short it is seen as important that local levels of the school system create new solutions that cost less than the old ones. Among other new expectations that have been put on school leaders in the elementary parts of the school systems during recent years are that they ought to take a lead in improvement work in schools (Hämäläinen 1986; Stegö *et al.* 1987). Politicians in most European countries have put their faith in political management strategies, like the goal-based accountability model, instead of trusting implementation models of school improvement (see Seashore-Louis and Van Velzen 1986) and thereby putting their faith also in the power of the local school leaders to improve practice.

Methods of school self-review are being developed and these can be used as a starting point for the improvement process. When school-based reviews are undertaken it sometimes becomes necessary for the staff to change their teaching styles and classroom organisation, which often leads to negotiations and conflict-solving. At such times, it is obvious that the school leader will be the focus of attention both within and from beyond the school, and will need to be prepared to speak out and react on behalf of the school as a whole. As Lloyd (1985, p. 294) concludes in a discussion of the role of the school leader in British schools under improvement pressure, 'there is little scope for delegation in these circumstances, which emphasises perhaps most acutely the head's exposed and sometimes rather lonely position.' School leaders are also expected to involve themselves in the in-service training of teachers and there has been a growing emphasis on patterns of school-based in-service training since the late 1970s.

These expectations that school leaders will take a lead in the improvement work have emerged in different cultures at different times. In Great Britain, the campaign started with proposals for school-based in-service training in the late 1970s, and during the 1980s proposals have also been made for school-based reviews. In the Netherlands, proposals were made in the early 1980s when a new law on basic education was passed where the duties of the local school leader (*Director*) were defined. This school leader is required to be the educational, administrative and building leader of the school and to be responsible for the school's work plan. The improvement expectations put on the shoulders of local school leaders are also very evident in Swedish society since the mid-1970s, when all school leaders were obliged to participate in school leader education programmes. In Belgium, the reform of the primary school started in the mid-1970s, when the work of the local leader in organising the change was seen as very important.

In several of the countries where there are new definitions of the school leader's work, there are also discussions of what kind of basic organisation there should be in elementary schools. I will use the Dutch, the Norwegian and the Swedish systems as examples here. In all three systems the central government has required local schools to establish working plans. The idea of a shared working plan for the local school that would give each school an evident profile is reminiscent of the local curriculum of British schools but has a somewhat different flavour. Behind this request there seems to be a vision of the organisational structure of the elementary school that is not the one usually perceived today. Central governments want to replace the images of professional/collegial and natural/spontaneous local school organisations with an image of a responsible group-based organisation. This form of school organisation assumes that the goals of education are reasonably clear but that the teaching is a somewhat ambiguous process. The ambiguity is resolved by seeing the organisation as an interdependent collection of parts, guided by feedback from each other and from the environment. Key words in such an organisation are trust, learning and collaboration. The responsible, group-based school stresses the social aspects of communication, good problem-solving, a positive climate, and the technical aspects of teaching.

In this kind of school the local policy of the school is determined by all the members of staff. The policy is expressed in a working plan, which emerges from the interaction and joint efforts of the people involved. This entails the local schools examining what is behind central guidelines for the school and translating these ideas into local needs. Thus, local policy changes and develops through the shared experience of learning and adapting to environmental pressures by the members of the school. The school leaders in such schools concentrate on leading, helping and engaging all members of the school in thoughtful joint work and improvement. As the teaching in such a school is seen as active involvement by the students, which means that learning often takes place through enquiry methods and problem-solving, the manager's traditional time-scheduling tasks run into trouble.

Whether or not group schools become more common in the future remains to be seen. However, it seems to be important for this organisational structure of the local school to replace the more common images of professional/collegial and natural/spontaneous schools. If alternative organisational images of local schools continue to develop in the minds of politicians as well as of teachers there may develop a wider use of school leaders than at present. School leaders' presently rather restricted spheres of action – to administer, to chair teacher meetings, to deal with delinquent children, to meet parents and governors – could be broadened. Research on effective behaviour among school leaders has shown that they need to do other things if they are to give more to the school (see Cohen 1982; Leithwood and Montgomery 1982; Mortimore *et al.* 1988; and Purkey and Smith 1983). Among these are: clarifying the goals of the school, developing staff commitment to these goals, co-ordinating both decisions and actions so that many members of the school really share responsibility for the 'production', co-ordinating the evaluation of the work of the adults of the school, co-ordinating improvement work in the teaching and learning processes, and also enabling students to express their views on the life of the school.

Note

1. In the following I will use the term 'school leader' to describe the person who has such a role at the local school and is expected to conduct the managerial tasks there. As the term to describe the role is different in different European countries – head teacher, principal, *Rektor*, *Dirretore*, *Director*, *Skolforeståndare*, etc. – I am thus using a term that is not used in any national system. The problem with this term, when using it in descriptions of school systems for people with English as a basic language, is clearly discussed in Hopes (1986), pp. 15–17.

CHAPTER 5.3

Primary Teacher Training in Europe

David Winkley

1. The current state of teacher training

Throughout Europe, the early 1970s was a period marked by educational expansion in a context of political and financial stability and of public consensus concerning what the schools were delivering. 'Progressiveness' was in the air, even if there was evidence that teachers in practice were constitutionally conservative and cautious of change. This expansion reached its apogee in 1975, the year the highest proportion of gross domestic product was invested in education. Whilst there were still differences in quality of teacher training everywhere - most obviously determined by differences in length of pre-qualifying courses - there was a steady expansion of the numbers of student teachers. Whilst some institutions of higher education maintained a conservative approach to teaching methods, others were in the forefront of reform. Courses were reassessed in terms of length and content as institutions grew in number and size. There was everywhere a sense of an improving and consolidating service.

The later 1970s and the 1980s broke the pattern of this evolution in important ways. Between 1975 and 1985 the whole of Europe, with the exceptions of Ireland and Greece, witnessed a major demographic population change. The scale varied from place to place, but the trend was unmistakeably similar: a decline in the birth rate caused pupil numbers steadily to drop, whilst a new cold wind of economic competition and a rise in general unemployment raised questions about the ability of schools to fulfil their obligations. Teacher educators, as the *prima mobile* responsible, were caught up in the backlash of a scrutiny of school standards and the strategic problem (most striking in Austria and the Federal Republic of Germany, but seen widely across Europe) of too many teachers trained for too few jobs.

This generated a new political interest in education. A plethora of education bills came onto the statute books during the decade beginning in 1975, accompanied by declining resources. As Otto Minaly (1986) has put it, budget cutbacks were to some extent legitimised by casting doubts on the efficiency of the educational enterprise.

Statistical data were amassed, not always convincingly, to show that standards had been falling (Lundgren 1987). Teachers and those ultimately responsible, teacher-trainers, were attacked from all sides, for a variety of reasons - sometimes urged to reinstate traditional teaching methods, which there is no strong evidence teachers ever abandoned (Wittrock 1986), sometimes pressed to be less conservative and to respond more rapidly to change. Teachers in different countries were seen, depending on the perspective taken, as under-trained in subject knowledge, in technical classroom skills, and in theoretical knowledge of children. The ever-complicating evolution of curriculum and classroom life during the previous decade led to the view that teachers needed greater subject knowledge and more clearly defined specialist skills and clearer objectives, but equally must respond as best they may to multiplying demands of school and community life. An ever-increasing pressure to take on more has led schools and teacher-trainers everywhere to suffer from curriculum overload.

The fact that, with the exception of Greece, teachers are increasingly predominantly women and most educational managers and administrators are men has added another sharp element to the debate.

These developments have impacted upon higher educational institutions in different ways. All governments have set out to rationalise teacher recruitment and employment by limiting numbers of student teachers, with some countries culling whole departments or even whole institutions. Most countries have paid close attention to control of teacher supply, scrutinising entry qualifications and analysing prospective national requirements.

Paradoxically this intensification of political scrutiny has accelerated a historical trend towards improving the qualifications of teachers - an important continuity with earlier decades. There has been growing recognition of the need to match primary training with established traditions of graduate training for secondary teachers. There is strong evidence of a general lengthening of courses for primary teachers, with their qualifications increasingly matching those of secondary colleagues. At its most advanced, primary training is based on a four-year specialist degree in education, or a full one-year education qualification following a three-year subject degree course. Many countries are striving to match those models. In Belgium and Finland, for example, courses have extended from two to three years. Norway has extended training for all primary and secondary teachers to full graduate status and a four-year training.

Extended length of training has been accompanied by a closer relationship between teacher-training institutions of all kinds and universities. Ireland, for example, extended training to three years in 1975, simultaneously affiliating colleges of education to universities. Since 1986, primary student teachers in France have received three years training (up from two) and will need to complete a two-year university course to be admitted to training college. In Iceland since 1978 all teachers have a university training for a minimum of three years. Spain (Neave 1987, p. 173) has the long-term aim of firmly locating teacher training in a university context, and the Spanish University Reform Act has encouraged the setting up of departments in universities to help co-ordinate and develop a unifying philosophy for the whole of the teacher-training process. Italy has recently brought a bill to parliament based on a 1974 presidential decree that all categories of teacher must have 'a complete university-level education to be obtained at a university or other institution of higher education'. Malta already has a fully integrated university-based five-year teacher-training programme, though teachers may take a specialist option in the primary phase.

Some countries historically have a two- (or even three-) tier system for primary education, separating pre-primary from primary and lower secondary, with corresponding varying lengths of training. In some places (e.g. Austria, Germany and Italy), pre-primary training is still largely an apprenticeship model, with training at higher secondary school level. The trend, however, is to bring pre-primary together with primary teacher training under the aegis of the universities (or other accredited higher education institutions). In Law 1268/82, for instance, Greece shifted pre-primary education from two-year colleges to university-based education departments. Training for pre-primary and primary alike will now last four years.

It is likely that in time, with the increasingly closer matching of the teacher-training programmes across Europe, we shall see pre-primary courses dovetailing with and even integrating fully with primary programmes, though primary programmes may well contain specialist course elements focusing on early, middle and later primary years.

These Europe-wide pressures on institutions to improve training quality are mirrored by signs that the central dilemma in designing courses requires compromises between (i) the need for students to have recognised graduate academic status, (ii) the requirement that student teachers should also develop effective command of the practical skills demanded in the complex world of the modern classroom, and (iii) the need to have some theoretical knowledge of both educational practice and research, and of child development. The pressure to increase the subject-specific orientation in the primary school is the product partly of an increasing sense that knowledge in depth improves teaching delivery of a subject area even in the earlier years of education, and partly of a concern to match the content of training for an education degree with other subject degree courses.

Government interest in this debate has led to different outcomes in different countries. Most striking has been the shift to a focus on improving the primary teacher's subject specialist expertise. In French-speaking Belgium, for example, there has been a call for an increase in the academic content in subjects taught at primary level, and in the UK there is now a mandatory two-year minimum main subject requirement for all students choosing the four-year education-degree route into teaching.

There seems to be an increasing likelihood of other countries following suit with the recognition of the increased demands subject teaching is making in the primary classroom. Currently only the Netherlands has held out against this trend, coming out on the side of generalist class teaching by integrating pre-primary and primary teacher training, with all students teaching a full curriculum including music, drawing and PE – though even on these courses some subject specialism is encouraged.

The concern to improve subject knowledge has been balanced by an equally sharp recognition of the importance of relating theory to practice. There has been increasing pressure at both primary and secondary levels of teacher training for closer integration of theory and practice – placing training firmly in a practical school context, aiming to produce teachers with good classroom management skills and the technical know-how to interpret their subject training. This has led to closer scrutiny of the pedagogical elements in courses, calls for more imaginative and flexible relationships with schools, and (as in the UK) requirements that teachers of pedagogy maintain close connections with classroom experience. The WCOTP Conference of the Committee of Senior Officials in Strasbourg in 1986, for example, strongly reiterated the need for attention to the issue of closely linking academic with pedagogical and practical classroom delivery. The first general principle in its summary of recommendations was that knowledge and research skills 'should be carried through as far as possible into the practical work in the real setting of the school and social milieu in which it operates' (WCOTP 1986). Similar concerns dominated discussions at the 1986 Conference of Directors of Education Research Institutions in Hungary <DECS/Rech [86] 75>. The problem has been pressure on teacher-training courses to develop school-oriented components in course design against the background of a steady increase in academic content. Some countries have shown particular concerns about resulting imbalances in course design. Italy, for example, has had no tradition of professional technical training at higher education level. Liechtenstein similarly considers that the sound theoretical foundation in teacher training currently on offer is not matched by practical training.

Adjustment towards either increased subject specialism and/or more attention to practical methodology has, however, in many cases blurred the line between the traditional practice-oriented primary and the more subject-oriented secondary training courses. Signs are evident in Austria, Belgium, Denmark, Sweden and Switzerland, and affect secondary as much as primary teacher training. In Sweden, for instance, the 1985 education reforms (which came into effect in 1988) eliminated distinctions between junior, intermediate and senior teachers, replacing them with two phases (grades 1–7 and grades 4–9). This has had the effect of reinforcing subject-based training at the primary levels, counterbalanced by a broader approach to subject discipline based teaching after 12 years of age.

It is worth adding that in some countries there has been an additional concern about the need to reinforce both research skills and the theoretical knowledge of student teachers in theoretical aspects of child development. In France, for instance, there is currently concern about a lack of a tradition of theoretical background in the understanding of children, and the inability of teachers to interpret current research. This compares with somewhat utilitarian pressures in the UK to trim 'educational theory' courses, which have never been especially popular, while strengthening the emphasis on 'methodology' – the interpreting of subject knowledge into effective classroom delivery.

There have inevitably been consequences for course design in teacher training as a knock-on effect of this general debate and governments' tightening of expectations of schools. One has been constraint on choice of *content* of curriculum, with governments sometimes specifying in detail what subject matter ought to be taught, for how long, and how, generally, courses ought to be constructed. The 'rationalisation' of curriculum in schools (Lundgren 1987) has also been a process of strengthening accountability through assessment. Here we see the setting up of centrally defined criteria and objectives designed to restore confidence in the school and teacher-training system.

These intrusions have taken very different forms. The UK, for example, has seen the advent of the Council for the Accreditation of Teacher Education (CATE) laying down for the first time criteria for course accreditation in initial teacher training. Very different kinds of reforms in the Netherlands have emphasised the importance of close relationships between teacher education and schools, with current plans attaching high importance to on-the-job training (Neave 1987, p.14).

Some of the criteria identified by the UK link with developments in other countries. There has been increased attention, for example, to such matters as special needs and the multicultural curriculum.

The introduction of special education as an integral part of initial training at all levels has been endorsed by Denmark, Finland, Greece, Norway and Sweden: the emphasis is overwhelmingly on the integration of special needs children into mainstream schooling wherever possible. In some cases (e.g. Ireland) courses within initial training lead to specialist qualifications. In Cyprus and Turkey, there are special options for graduates lasting for one year. In Switzerland, training in special needs follows on directly from basic teacher graduation for between two and three years.

There have been similar concerns in many countries for attention in teacher training to the multicultural needs of minority cultures – recognising that Europe is increasingly multi-ethnic in its racial constitution, and that pluralism of cultures and religions is a major political issue. Both special needs and multicultural issues have moved up the agenda of the compulsory training programme in a number of European countries (Rey 1986).

Other countries do not encourage a permeation model for special needs on basic training courses; instead they see special education largely in the context of in-service training (INSET) or through post-graduate qualifications for teachers who subsequently wish to specialise.

Here, however, we often see a blurring of initial training and INSET, with 'full training' being a combination of elements of both. The question here, with the considerable increase in in-service provision across Europe, is how the two modes of training might be best interpreted and balanced. For governments eager to introduce curriculum reforms and to respond rapidly to what they see as the needs of industrial and social transformation, the focus on in-service training to implement rapid delivery of change seems particularly important. As Neave puts it: 'From being an ancillary activity designed to support what might be termed incremental change, it [INSET] has assumed a status central to the acceleration of adjustment and the fine tuning of education's response to industrial, occupational and social transformation' (Neave 1987, p. 19).

Schools throughout Europe contain a majority of teachers trained during the expansion periods of the 1960s and 1970s, who are likely to remain in post for some years to come. And yet it is these teachers who have to face curriculum change and adjustment to a more demanding and rapidly developing curriculum world. The political response has been to pay much closer attention to the expansion of the INSET programmes.

The problem is that with this expansion INSET is everywhere impeded by the need to support programmes and courses adequately with supply or relief teachers who are often not available and are, in any event, expensive. There is also the underlying question of the adequacy of the 'short course' principle in training teachers for what are often difficult and complex tasks calling for sustained and highly developed skills. The clear trend, however, is towards a prolonging of training both at initial and continuous post-qualification levels in response to growing demands (and implicit recognition of the need for a highly trained cohort of teachers receiving sustained professional support), though in the 1990s this is likely to be balanced against countermanding instincts of governments faced with recruiting problems to make entry into teaching easier, particularly for mature entrants.

All this throws up the issue of institutional autonomy, and questions about accountability of course designers and tutors to governments or their agencies. Again, different countries have come to different arrangements in the delicate balance between central mechanisms of control and local institutional autonomy. In some cases this has led to increased government control of curriculum accountability at all levels. In Britain, the Education Reform Bill of 1987 is highly centralist in orientation, insisting on compulsory testing of all children at ages 7, 11 and 14 on a centrally prescribed curriculum. This seems likely in the 1990s to have an effect on the (already limited) freedom of higher education institutions to determine their own curriculum. The UK is out of step here with most of the rest of Europe, which, whilst starting in many cases from a more centralised structure, has moved towards increased decentralisation. Other countries have also formalised new courses - such as those integrating pre-primary with primary programmes. These often 'prioritise' particular areas of the curriculum, as in Denmark, which attaches particular importance to natural sciences and remedial education, or in Belgium, stressing maths, with both countries focusing on mother-tongue teaching. The Netherlands has gone furthest in a decentralist direction: although the report of the discussion paper of 1986 *Higher Education, Autonomy and Quality* (Neave 1987) bears some relation to the UK government paper *Teaching Quality* (Department of Education and Science 1988b), the outcomes are the reverse. The UK centralisation of curriculum combines with financial decentralisation of schools; the Netherlands looks for greater autonomy in practice to enable educational institutions to adapt their programmes more quickly and effectively to meet changing needs. Where the UK is introducing standardised study programmes, in the Netherlands they have virtually ceased to exist (Neave 1987, p. 143).

We may note, in conclusion, that there are many features that teacher training across Europe has in common - not least vulnerability to the swings of general economic and political trends. There are important continuities and correspondencies between issues concerning course designers (particularly in trying to resolve the tension between academic knowledge and practical teaching skills) and in the professional development of primary teachers to full graduate status, equivalent to other professional groups. The length of training is increasing with a growing sense of the importance of the early childhood years for personal and educational progress. Life is growing more complicated everywhere, too, and countries and institutions are struggling to resolve the dilemma of mushrooming demands on teachers, as against the instinct to impose, rationalise, order and even simplify the training process.

On the other hand, there remain striking differences between countries, particularly in the length and substance of training courses. There are still in many countries considerable differences between the modes of training for primary and secondary teachers. There are, if anything, recent tendencies in most countries to look to decentralising issues such as curriculum design.

Overall, the impression is of common underlying trends that seem part of a long historical continuity both to improve the quality of primary teaching and to come in the long run to common cross-European perspectives in course design and teaching practice.

2. Challenges for the future

Schools exist in a political and technological context: they may lead (or, more commonly perhaps, follow) the momentum of social events (1985 Council of Europe Teachers' Seminar on *The role of the teachers in innovation*

<DECS/EGT [85] 45>) and the teacher training of the future will, as in the past, inevitably be shaped in part by the requirements of schools and the expectations of communities, highly influenced at central level by the values and complexions of governments.

Some of these requirements are predictable: the rapidly developing technological revolution will inevitably force major changes on patterns of classroom instruction. We can anticipate a time when children have extensive hands-on access to computers, which will require a new rationalisation of information software and teachers able to overview the transmissional process. Training will need to give close attention to the organisational skills required to manage the learning requirements of individuals in ever more sophisticated ways.

It seems likely that, in response to the growing opportunities offered by access to new technology, teaching will become (even more than at present) a highly skilled organisational and managerial task. The pinpointing of children's abilities and the tailor-made ordering of the most effective ways of supporting their progress will lead to a tension between central definition and rationalisation of curriculum (closely involving publishing and software production) and the very complex requirements of decision making at local school and classroom level. On the one hand, there will be the need to think about individuals, their families and communities; on the other, there will be the increasing tendency for nations and, beyond nations, Europe as a whole to control and define the parameters of curriculum and assessment. There may be pressure to link curriculum packages with computer, audio, tele-visual and print-based media (WCOTP 1986). <CDCC [86] 28>. Considerable advantages will be seen in the large-scale rationalisation of some aspects of learning programmes. But there will be dangers too. There may be a clash between requirements to rationalise curriculum and assessment programmes at the centre and the need for teachers to retain a sense of personal values that will not lose sight of individuals in a pluralistic, multicultural society.

This leads to another critical area likely to receive reappraisal: the role of the school in supporting the social and emotional needs of children. The counselling of pupils must be recognised as a function that all teachers perform (WCOTP 1986). Children will need to be helped through the forest of ethical, cultural and value-laden choices open to them as citizens of the future. The stability and confidence coming from a secure sense of personal and cultural identity will be the foundation of people who can cope best with a changing environment. As the Council of Europe Teachers' Seminar in 1985 put it: 'There is very strong feeling that, over and above changes to structures, methods and content, the aim is the general development of the child's personality' <DECS/EGT [85] 45, p. 44>.

Some countries have already set up educational initiatives to develop these aspects of teaching further. A striking example of a project pressing in this direction has been Belgium's Project VLO, which came into operation in 1983, with a focus on promoting the all-round balanced and steady development of the child's personality with 'integration, development of artistic creativity and flexible organisation of activities' <DECS/EGT [85] 45, p. 14>.

The understanding of democratic values will begin in the classroom, and one task of the teacher will be to encourage independent-mindedness in a disciplined and stable school world. Teacher training will need to mirror here the model of education teachers will offer their future pupils (Fox 1985). This has been noted in Portugal where, as part of the democratisation process post-1974, liberal ideas have swept through schools, pressing them to concentrate more on the all-round development of children. With two-thirds of the world's democracies to be found in Europe, the consciousness of the importance of the school and the training of teachers as a key factor in support of the democratic process is likely to become more, rather than less, significant (Fox 1985, p. 4).

A consistent part of 'personal' awareness of pupil need will be the role of the school in relation to the 20–25 per cent of children at risk of educational failure, and the overlapping 10 per cent with emotional or behavioural difficulties. Failing groups have persistently been identified as a cause for concern, as illustrated by the recent debate in France about failing youngsters <DECS/EGT [85] 45, p. 6>. Some countries have already launched major initiatives to tackle these problems. Switzerland, for example, set up its Rhapsody project in Geneva, with a view to accelerating the progress of slow learners <DECS/EGT [85] 45, pp. 18–21> and France set up the ZEP scheme to combat educational inequalities <DECS/EGT [85] 45, pp. 25–19>. Paradoxically, solutions in the long run may lie in generalisable and non-discriminatory approaches, such as counselling available to all students, adequate diagnosis for all, and more caution in categorising pupils – generally seeing students more as *persons*.

Teacher-training institutions will be in the vanguard of developments thrown up by these challenges and will need to tackle, as independently as they can, the considerable task of training a teacher to a high intellectual level, with an appropriate knowledge-base and requisite technical skills, without losing sight of the need for personal and ethical strengths in a world that will require:

- highly developed skills in diagnosing the needs of individuals,
- an element of specialist knowledge in depth,
- highly developed organisational and managerial skills,
- a sensitive understanding of the social and emotional needs of children,
- knowledge of the range of technical programmes on offer with the skill to manage and interact with pupils in appropriate ways,
- a sense of democratic values, and a balanced, independent personal stance,
- an ability to work in groups or as part of a professional team,
- an ability to understand and relate to the cultures and values of other communities and families,
- the ability to work with parents and communities.

The teacher of the future is likely to become an arbiter between complex - and not always necessarily compatible - forces, and will need to uphold the integrity of the child and the child's learning, which is at the heart of the educational process. No centralised programme of instruction or curriculum is likely to be adequate and complete for any one individual. In the classroom or 'instructional base', the teacher will need to interact with pupils in ways that

- are appropriate for individual learners,
- have a wide sense of 'learning' as a process that goes beyond school; and needs to be carefully shaped between one age phase and the next,
- help the student appreciate the importance of active learning, in which the pupils themselves make decisions about their own learning, and themselves develop the skills of co-operative learning and enterprise. (Helliwell 1986, p.15)

The challenge for teachers will be to provide a stable learning environment in which, as Lundgren (1987, p. 37) puts it, 'rules are visible and life predictable', whilst adapting sensitively in a structured but rapidly responsive improvisatory way - like a skilled jazz musician - at a personal level to pupils who take learning on for themselves in unexpected ways, and, at a social level, to the vagaries of rapid system change. The corresponding challenge for teacher-trainers will be to accommodate the demands of curriculum rationalisation and technological advance with the personal development of individual students: pressure will be on institutions to design courses to respond to these diverse needs and it is likely that the sheer demands made in the future, and the need to command specialist skills, will increasingly locate initial teacher training as one major component in a long-term planned programme of professional development.

3. Meeting the challenge

How well will teacher-trainers be able to respond, given the present trends and the constraints on what is possible? The logic of continuity suggests that the current historical progress of the teacher towards full graduate and professional status (even given the current cross-European low morale amongst teachers) is likely to continue. Evidence of what Lundgren (1987) calls 'visible teacher knowledge' will support growing professionalism. The teaching process will certainly not become simpler, intellectually less demanding or less stressful.

There may, however, be serious constraints on progress, at least in the short term (quite apart from familiar but unpredictable problems with resourcing for innovation). The 1990s are likely to see new problems in recruitment of the highly trained graduate personnel required, as the demography of the falling population in the 1970s comes home to roost. Recruitment problems in some countries may force governments to look to ways of short-circuiting teacher training, even, as the UK is currently doing, looking to the possibility of a largely school-based apprenticeship model (e.g. for late entrants with previous professional experience in other fields). Maverick and emergency developments of this kind will be inhibited to some extent by increasing pressures to standardise the teacher-qualifying requirements at a European level, probably at graduate status, with the breaking down of employment boundaries in the EEC after 1992.

Most rapid progress will be made when institutional and governmental interests coincide (Lanier 1984). Closer relationships between schools and institutions, for instance, are very likely, and one outcome of this increasingly close link will be an improved dovetailing of initial teaching with INSET and professional post-qualification training. The concept of 'training and retraining' through one's professional career is likely to develop rapidly – which will be to the advantage of teachers, who will be able to pursue more satisfactorily a career based in the classroom. It will also help support schools and school systems requiring effective responses to changing circumstances. When it comes to course design, tensions between the requirements to study at a specialist academic level and the need to acquire technical classroom practice skills will need resolution – which is likely to lie in an increased sophistication of course design, a lengthening of courses at pre-graduate level, and a greatly improved pattern of postgraduate development through INSET, perhaps along the medical model, with access to further qualifications suitable to the needs of classroom practitioners.

The pressure to change may force even closer scrutiny of the nature of effective classroom teaching, set against more sophisticated criteria than we have at present: the instruction process itself will be under review (Lundgren 1987, p. 41). One question here will be how far we can trust teacher-trainers (and beyond them teachers) in the important task of managing changes in pedagogical theory and practice. Governments will have to accept that teachers of the future will inevitably require flexibility of mind and a highly trained and adaptable intelligence, as well as a personable manner and emotional and social balance. Technical skills will need to be accompanied by the requirement to be mentors for parents. Trust will accompany growing professional status but will not be easy and inevitable for governments, who will have a continuing concern for the rationalisation of curriculum at a central level – increasingly developing accountability indicators for the service as a whole.

Many detailed questions remain unresolved. What, in the face of a rapidly changing world leading up to the turn of the century, will *be* the appropriate balances between subject and methodological expertise? What elements of specialist training will be required? What will be the appropriate balance between theory and practice? What elements will require principal emphasis in initial training, and what should be programmed later through INSET? How shall we fit it all in? Certainly schools and higher education institutions will be required to work out solutions together: we are likely to see a growing integration of the various educational sections, in which increased specialism (both of subject and phase) will be offset by joint planning and working teams, exchanges between sectors, and a greatly improved dissemination process. Teacher research will be important in all this, as Spain has recognised (Conference of Directors of Education Research Institutions <DECS/Rech [86] 75>. Higher education institutions will be the nerve centre of developments here, supporting work in schools and taking an extended role in evaluating progress.

We shall need to consider the kinds of assessment process required to deal with the wide range of evidence of progress that will be expected by parents and governments. Problems here will not be easily resolved, and there will inevitably be political overtones. As now, there will be significant national differences. Governments may tend to the view of the Netherlands or Spain, which see teacher-educators at a high level determining and defining the philosophy and development in depth of the teacher education service. At the other end of the spectrum, somewhat out of phase with the rest of Europe, is the UK's imposition of the centralised assessment and curriculum structure on schools and teacher-training institutions. These differences are undoubtedly underpinned by political values. It will be interesting to see how the evolution of Europe as a whole draws together common principles of value in ways that influence practice internationally – or the degree to which states shape their own distinctive politically coloured educational practices.

Politics of any colour, however, can have only a limited impact on the transmissional aspects of teaching. There will be the key question of whether current pedagogical understanding of the learning process will be up to the demands that the future will make. Again, research will be important here, and there will be any number of key issues to consider. Do we know enough about effective teaching and learning? Teachers at all levels will increasingly be required to make judgements *between* options: to ask *why* to choose one approach rather than another. As Edward Bond puts it, poetically,

> But your mind is full of modern knowledge
> How is it used
> In our modern world?

They will need to account for the patterns of decisions they make over the use of the limited time any teacher has available – to be able, for example, to advise parents on educationally effective use of time outside school hours, or how best to use the school as a resource for educational advantage outside school hours. We still know far too little about the most equitable balances between, say, leisure, creative play and activity, and programmed informational and skill learning. We need to know more about the role of motivation, of parents in supporting children's learning, of the value of subject content in relation to personal adaptation and learning skills, of the virtues of subject integration, and of the long-term importance of planned balances between phases and course subjects. Evidence from classroom research on all these issues will filter into curriculum design in higher education courses.

Teacher training will have a key role in helping to advance our understanding of these issues, but will be unable to do so without helping teachers to develop the intellectual weaponry to justify and have confidence in their own practices. Confident justification will have the effect of stabilising the relationships between governments and educational services.

The future need will be to create stability through well-balanced curriculum programmes whilst recognising that learning also has a curious liquidity (Dewey 1967), an elusiveness and diversity – requiring teachers who combine personal confidence with understanding of others, clear thinking with imagination, and an intellectually entrepreneurial ingenuity in their professional practice. This confidence will encourage a corresponding recognition of the enormous importance of the foundations of learning and motivation in the early years – which itself in the long run will lead to a heightened valuing of the work of those who dedicate their lives to young children.

SECTION 6

IMPLEMENTING CHANGE: INNOVATION IN EUROPEAN PRIMARY EDUCATION

Introduction

Maurice Galton

The two chapters in this Section are concerned with the processes and practicalities of innovation in primary education within the countries that constitute the membership of the Council of Europe. The first chapter reviews changes in thinking about the innovation process that have occurred during the last two decades as a result of the failure of the large-scale curriculum development projects of the late 1960s to have a dramatic influence on what happens in the classroom. Alternative strategies based upon innovation at school level have also been shown to have certain weaknesses, particularly the difficulty of co-ordinating the different programmes in different schools so that a coherent philosophy of primary education can be pursued. Following the economic crisis of the 1970s, European governments of all complexions began to look for ways in which national policy might be implemented within the primary school without at the same time replicating the weaknesses of the earlier curriculum development programmes. Increasingly, member states have come to see innovation as an interactive process that requires links to be developed between those responsible for policy and those who have to put that policy into practice. The notion of backward mapping, whereby the implications of policy at classroom level are first investigated before policy is finally developed, can be seen to operate in different ways in the various member states of the Council. These differences are discussed and analysed.

In Chapter 6.2 the factors governing successful implementation of such policies in school are thoroughly discussed. Dr Kopmels describes the work of the contact schools, which were all chosen by the various governments of Project No. 8 to illustrate aspects of successful innovation, and he attempts a synthesis of the factors that contributed to this success. In particular, he stresses the need for appropriate management structures that allow all participants in the process to be informed about what decisions need to be taken and how such conclusions will be arrived at. He emphasises the need for close co-operation with outside agencies, which include both parents and consultants, and describes various ways of advancing these activities. He singles out for particular attention those schools that seriously consider the emotional needs of children as well as their cognitive development. Kopmels argues that, if children are to become autonomous in their learning, then they need to project a satisfactory self-image both with their teacher and with their peers. Thus it is important for children to understand how their behaviour influences the attitudes of other children and teachers within the school; Kopmels describes several programmes where this kind of development is fostered.

Despite the differences of context in each of the contact schools, common themes emerge. All of them strive to develop commitment in the staff by means of co-operative working between teachers and pupils. All of the innovations described gave rise at some time or other to conflict among staff as ideas, beliefs and values were challenged during the innovation process. Kopmels shows how, with careful planning and wise leadership, such difficulties can be overcome and thus lead to a more effective school.

CHAPTER 6.1

Research and innovation

Maurice Galton

The 1960s were the period of the large-scale curriculum development project, particularly in the United States. As a consequence it was also followed by a period where thinking about the processes of educational change and innovation became something of a growth industry. In many European countries, notably in the United Kingdom and in the Scandinavian region, much of this curriculum development centred around the growth of secondary education and, in particular, the development of a comprehensive system. By the time that European countries began to look at the needs of primary schools, in the wake of the oil crisis of the 1970s, thinking about educational change had become somewhat diffuse. Educators meeting at Vaduz in Liechtenstein in November 1982 had little difficulty in agreeing a set of common aims and charting important future developments. It was more difficult, however, to suggest a strategy for carrying out such developments within the different countries forming the membership of the Council of Europe. While the influence of researchers in the United States has remained strong because certain key figures within the European movement had maintained strong contacts with American researchers such as Michael Fullan (1982) and Bruce Joyce (Joyce and Showers 1980) European thinking had also been heavily influenced by the action research approach developed within the United Kingdom by the late Lawrence Stenhouse and his associates at the Centre for Applied Research in Education (CARE), at the University of East Anglia. In particular, the tension between the large-scale American change strategies and those arising out of the 'action research' model has been a constant theme in the search for an effective strategy of innovation – one that maintained the advantages of the different approaches while limiting the problems associated with each of them.

1. Approaches to innovation in the 1970s

During the last two decades the definition of the 'innovation' process has undergone various modifications. In the 1960s, innovation was largely defined as the *take up*. Thus agencies concerned to bring about changes in the educational system, whether such changes concerned new curriculum projects or government-initiated activity, thought of innovation largely in terms of the success achieved in persuading schools or local authorities to adopt the new scheme. Information about adoption was largely collected through self-report, but might also include other quantifiable indicators such as the purchase of relevant books and equipment. However, the evaluations of these early projects tended to show that a basic weakness in this approach was the assumption that the new innovating package was 'teacher proof'. In many cases schools appeared to adapt the new programme to existing methods of working, which were often contrary to the intentions of the curriculum developer.

Thus in the early 1970s the focus on the innovation process turned to *diffusion*, the study of the take-up process itself. Information from these studies suggested the need for organised planned programmes to control this diffusion process so that innovation came to be studied more in terms of its *dissemination*.

Every one of these approaches to innovation was characterised by a notion of rationality. All assumed that, provided the need for change could be presented in a logical and coherent manner, those who were asked to adopt new practices would do so if they could be persuaded of this inherent logic. Chin and Benne (1969), for example, argued that since people are generally keen to exercise their responsibilities in the most efficient manner they would adopt any proposed change if it appeared rational and seemed to offer a better way of doing things. Change therefore occurred as a result of an internal intellectual process based either upon philosophical underpinning or empirical demonstration. The most thorough explication of this model was that of Havelock (1971) in the research, development, dissemination (RD and D) approach. In its purist form, this model could be said to have guided many of the major curriculum development projects in the United States during the 1960s, and in the United Kingdom it was the basis for the Nuffield Science Projects in the late 1960s and early 1970s. The RD and D model assumed a diffusion of a well-researched and developed innovation by a small, expert and well-resourced central team. Using Schon's (1971) terminology, it was a centre-to-periphery approach.

In retrospect, as House (1981) has demonstrated, such models achieved less than expected because of deficiencies in their main assumptions. First, there was a general lack of psychological insight, particularly the failure to understand that change calls for an emotional as well as a rational commitment on the part of the participant. Second, the role of the facilitator was poorly defined and often exaggerated. As MacDonald and Walker (1976) have argued when commenting on the Keele Integrated Studies Project, the team consisting of two people and a secretary 'commanded no-one' and 'could afford to offend very few'. They depended 'entirely upon the voluntary co-operation of system personnel' and had 'only a short time in which to ensure the survival of their work in schools and to secure their own personal futures' (MacDonald and Walker 1976, p. 48). Third, the model took no account of the social and cultural impact of new innovatory programmes, particularly in such contentious areas as race, where there was likely to be a plurality of values among those being asked to adopt the innovation.

The partial failure of these rationally planned approaches led, in turn, to a greater concentration on the process of change within the system. System-centred approaches included those defined by Chin and Benne (1969) as normative re-educative and by Havelock (1973) as problem-solving. These models were more concerned to analyse values and attitudes, the participants' conceptions of their roles and the relationships within the groups of people concerned with the innovation process within the institution. Suggested strategies all stressed the need to change crucial values and attitudes so that the practitioner, rather than simply accepting change in the interests of efficiency, now co-operated because of improved motivation. In Havelock's problem-solving approach, the external change agent who was responsible for the curriculum innovation acted mainly as a resource or as a consultant. This allowed the consultant's clients, who had the task of bringing about the change in each institution, to feel both responsibility for and ownership of any new practice that was developed as a result of the innovation. The main advantage claimed for these approaches, therefore, was that they brought about a strong commitment to the implementation of change and that in the process the curriculum was likely to be modified in a way that made it suitable and relevant to the particular needs of the institution.

Consultants could either respond to the clients' demands in a relatively pragmatic manner or, as in Schmuck and Miles' (1971) organisational development model, provide a structured programme that enabled the clients to speed up the problem-solving process, which in its more pragmatic form tended to be very time consuming. Thus Schmuck and Miles' (1971) programme included practical sessions that helped clients, amongst other things, to improve the running of group meetings, as well as to uncover and work with conflict. Apart from the length of time involved when using these approaches, there were also obvious limitations in terms of their efficiency. The consultant can work with only very few institutions at any one time. More importantly, there is a tendency for consultants to be acceptable only if they share the prevailing ideology of the institution that has determined the need for the innovation. Those individuals or groups within the institution whose value systems are opposed to the prevailing ideology are not likely to be attracted into or to be accepted as part of the innovation group.

Greater cohesion can sometimes be obtained by defining goals in such a way as to ensure ambiguity in the form of language used. This solution is not unlike a meeting of EEC ministers who can draw up an agreement and then depart to their respective countries to interpret the document in ways that allow each country to continue as before. Furthermore, although such solutions may have the advantage of reflecting the needs of an individual institution, there is no guarantee that what has been decided is a 'best buy' or that a better solution could not have been obtained with the help of experts or collaboration between different institutions.

For this reason other models, which recognise these conflict processes during social interaction but which attempt to manipulate them, have also been advocated by Havelock (1973). Havelock argued that acceptance by key individuals within the institution is likely to influence others. If, therefore, a certain proportion of individuals can be persuaded to support the innovation, others will then follow. Thus the process attempts to seek out key individuals and set them up as models. The main weakness of this approach, however, is that it plays down the distinction between *acceptance* and *commitment*, so that some individuals simply adopt the innovation because it is to their personal advantage. Once they have been rewarded, such individuals are unlikely to seek further support for innovation unless they have come to value the process for its own ends. Thus the need for a genuine change in values and attitudes and a determination on the part of the consultants to bring latent conflict among clients out into the open remain dominant themes within the innovation debate.

2. Innovation in the 1980s

By the 1980s, therefore, there was something of an impasse between those who, for efficiency's sake, continued to try and adapt the centre-to-periphery model, while others argued for consultative approaches in which decision making was highly localised within each individual institution participating within the innovation. Elliott (1985), in arguing forcibly for the latter approach, showed that the project team's intentions were not always seen in the same way by teachers. Whereas the developers tended to stress the value of certain activities and educational purposes, most of the teachers were primarily concerned about the practicality of the innovation. During an innovation of this kind, various participants in the process – the developers, the local authority and the schools – will by means of their interactions attempt to negotiate and bargain to achieve their own ends. In the process, the purposes and principles that constitute the value system upon which the project has been developed are gradually tempered by the need to produce schemes that are capable of realisation in practice. Thus, in essence, the role of the school is to adapt and develop the framework provided by the development agency. In the early action-research programme this negotiation was largely left to questions of value, but more recent studies now suggest that the bargaining is more extensive because teachers and other actors involved in the educational process may also have different perspectives in other areas such as pedagogy, evaluation and the factors that both inhibit and enhance children's learning.

A logical step in extending this negotiated model while retaining an overall framework has been the introduction of networking, whereby different institutions, although adapting the innovation to meet their particular needs, nevertheless come together on a regular basis to exchange ideas. This is said to reduce the possibility that each school duplicates work already carried out at another institution. Pritchard (1980), however, has argued that, to be effective, networks should be temporary. The process involving individual innovators contributing to informal contact with other groups can become institutionalised and turn into a more formal system. Moreover, after the initial surge of energy associated with production of the first concrete products of this collaboration, there is likely to be a gradual reduction in interest by individual institutions as they concentrate on making the new development work within their own establishments. Gradually, therefore, the co-operative spirit is dissipated, unless fresh networks emerge that lead to further innovation. One major issue concerns the role of institutions within these temporary networks. Outside funding, it is argued, carries with it the danger that only those innovations that are approved of by the funding agency will be supported. At the other extreme, where networks choose to remain outside the main system, they are likely to be resourced at very low levels and will be unable to disseminate their results effectively.

3. Research and Innovation

During the period when these ideas were being developed, contacts between American and European researchers began to grow. These joint studies explored the gradual adoption of new innovation within different institutional settings by means of detailed case studies. Researchers such as Huberman and Miles (1984) attempted to construct models of effective innovation appropriate to different institutional settings, while Miles (1983) and Fullan (1982, 1985) have applied a social constructivist approach to the understanding of innovation.

Studies of attribution theory in educational settings have also contributed a better understanding of what earlier Doyle and Ponder (1976) termed the 'practicality ethic' in teachers' decision making. Faced with difficulties and unsure of success, participants in the innovation tend to look for factors that lie outside their personal control and for which, therefore, they have no responsibility. Thus, for most teachers, innovation failed because of lack of resources, difficulties with parents or the social and intellectual deficiencies of pupils. The observer or consultant, on the other hand, too readily tended to describe such reasoning as 'excuses' and saw the failure of innovation in terms of the teachers' reluctance to change from safe forms of didactic practice to more open-ended teaching strategies in which they were less certain of retaining control of the situation.

Two main strategies were developed to overcome this attribution gap between the observer and the participant within the innovation process. The first response was to institute programmes within in-service training that based pedagogy upon sound pyschological principles and that developed coaching procedures to ensure that new skills were learned in small steps so that the majority of participants were guaranteed success at each stage (Joyce and Showers 1980). These methods do not appear to have enjoyed a great deal of success within Europe where there has been greater resistance to the 'direct instruction' paradigm and increasing emphasis on greater differentiation of the learning process but by means of suitable forms of assessment (Cardinet 1986).

The second approach has initially accepted, at face value, teachers' attributions of failure to innovate to a failure to resource schools adequately. Such views went unchallenged until the teachers became committed to the particular innovation. One outstanding example of this approach can be found in the primary reform movement in the Netherlands. Here, in the first instance, schools volunteering to take part in the innovation were given extra resources, including additional staffing, on the clear understanding that, once the innovation had been successfully implemented, levels of resourcing would gradually return to normal. The initial question posed to the schools involved was, therefore, how much of the change can be preserved under normal funding arrangements. The Dutch experience showed that, once schools were committed to the innovation and could see its positive effects on the pupils, they became reluctant to abandon what had been achieved even when resources were reduced to the original level. Therefore schools found imaginative ways of improvising so that innovatory practices could be preserved. The conclusion of those who assessed the impact of the changes was that little was lost as a result of these reductions in resources. An additional gain from the process arose because, initially, curriculum development in schools was associated with additional resourcing so there was general professional support for curriculum innovation and fewer negative attitudes amongst the profession (Noordwijk Symposium <DECS/EGT [85] 16>).

Another large-scale experiment in innovation concerned the primary school reform programme in Belgium (Han-sur-Lesse Symposium <DECS/EGT [84] 24>). Arising out of this experience, Vandenberghe (1988) argues that school-based innovation, of the kind proposed by Elliott (1973), including networking systems operating outside of a national framework, is no longer practicable in the current context. Although the key characteristics identified in studies relating to school improvement are still valid, there is a need to rethink how such changes can be promoted in schools within the context of slow economic growth and increased opportunities for servicing coupled with the rapid transformation of the present value system within most European societies. Vandenberghe supports Van Velzen *et al.*'s (1985) argument that the demand for change within the school system comes from three basic sources. The first concerns the process of decentralisation, the accountability movement and the preoccupation with school effectiveness. The second source concerns the social processes involving the change in the family's role, with increasing emphasis on individual participation. This can be seen within the school system by the growing involvement of parents and others in the management of school. The third source concerns the growth in knowledge, not only in the traditional psychological areas to do with pupils' learning and with pedagogy, but also in those relating to the whole school and its organisational functioning. Thus, within this climate it is no longer feasible for curriculum specialists to urge reform on schools. Instead, Vandenberghe (1988, p. 154) argues that:

> rather than impose a decision, the objective is to actively involve the school partners (teachers, administrators, parents, consultants, pupils) in the main decisions affecting the school. The new strategy for school improvement will be an amalgamation of approaches from the previous periods. Primary schools (and the teachers) will have to cope with curriculum development projects, changes in the teaching–learning processes, school organisation and pedagogical–didactical issues. The work will be more classroom and school orientated: less structural and more content and process orientated. The teacher will get more priority in the change process, without neglecting the school leader and the remedial teacher and other specialists in the team. More attention will be paid to the processes of strengthening the school's capacity to deal with change.

This view sees change as a continuing process in which schools at any one time will not all be at the same stage of development. School diversity is therefore one of the biggest obstacles for policy makers during innovation. Because of this, Vandenberghe (1988) rejects reliance on what he terms 'forward mapping strategies whereby the policy makers spell out the steps and processes which are necessary from a logical point of view in order to implement a school improvement policy'. This is because forward mapping is usually done from the policy makers' perspective (Van Velzen *et al.* 1985, p. 254). In its place, Vandenberghe suggests a process of backward mapping, which 'emphasises the importance of including the perspectives of local level decision makers in the development of policy'. According to Vandenberghe (1988, p. 152),

> Instead of starting from the central or local policy maker's view and describing steps to take and problems to overcome, this approach starts at the level where policy is actually implemented, in this case the classroom and school levels. Problems schools are likely to have with implementation of policy are identified and enfactored into the setting of policy. The purpose is to reduce the unanticipated consequences that always accompany any innovation.

At the beginning of Project No. 8's study of *Innovation in the Primary School* similar concern was expressed that policy makers in different countries tended to pay more attention to those aspects of the innovation process that were easily identifiable in terms of outcomes. Thus, for example, the introduction of information technology into the primary school was seen by some administrators simply in terms of providing more computers for children. The introduction of a computer into a school, however, brings with it a whole range of problems concerning the way that pupils work together, and this in turn requires consideration of both cognitive and affective processes. In view of this, Vandenberghe (1988, p. 155) argues that innovations should be characterised in terms of either *additive* or *long-term* policies. Additive policies consist of various initiatives that are developed independently of each other. Schools receive numerous requests from both national and local policy makers to promote a variety of changes. Vandenberghe concludes that in many instances this kind of policy change leads to 'non-implementation'.

Priorities for *long-term* policy making should be formulated as clearly as possible. Vandenberghe describes this as a 'meta-policy' and such large-scale plan change needs explicit policy at different levels – national, regional and local. This leads Vandenberghe to conclude that the various groups operating at various decision levels need 'to trace out a concrete policy in a more or less co-ordinated way' (Vandenberghe 1988, p. 155). In suggesting how such a policy might be formulated, Vandenberghe adopts the rules previously set out by Schon (1981):

> Those 'above' must learn to name the 'themes' of policy change and to create conditions conducive to initiatives for those 'below'. A 'theme of policy' names the domain in which initiatives are called for, but leaves the specification by which performance is to be judged upon.
>
> Those 'below' must learn to take initiatives in a thoughtful way, that is reflecting on the conditions and content of their own practice.
>
> Those 'above' must learn to describe, appreciate and evaluate the initiatives in practice undertaken by those 'below' especially when evaluation cannot be done in relation to an established policy but only in relation to a 'theme of policy'.

To this Vandenberghe adds a fourth rule, namely that those 'above' must learn to play the roles of broker, facilitator and disseminator of local learning (Vandenberghe 1988, pp. 156–7).

Within the Council of Europe, several countries besides Belgium have attempted to put these or similar principles into practice. In Sweden, for example, within the primary reform scheme, the government sets out various policy themes. Money to facilitate innovation in these areas is then dispersed to regions. Within regions, schools are able to bid for a portion of this money in order to promote innovation in a way that meets the demands of the particular institution. Local authority inspectors are used to evaluate the programmes (Stockholm Symposium <DECS/EGT [87] 33>).

A further example of backward mapping can be seen in the curriculum programme described at the same Stockholm conference by the representative from Denmark. Here again, policy themes are suggested to schools, which then plan and execute programmes of innovation. At the end of the programme, schools have a responsibility to write up their findings, for which the teachers concerned are paid a small additional sum of money. The reports from different schools are then summarised by a curriculum implementation group, which forwards this summary to the Ministry of Education as a basis for policy making. The scheme is said to have an advantage in that very few schools oppose subsequent policy. Each policy is based upon recommendations emanating from the same schools that subsequently have to implement the changes. A further benefit concerns the attributions referred to earlier whereby teachers often account for their failure to implement policy changes. With the system developed by Denmark, because different schools are likely to put forward different attributions, it is possible for those whose task it is to summarise the various documents to identify which attributions were common to the majority of schools and which might be an attempt by teachers to relieve themselves of the responsibility for personal failings.

In the United Kingdom during the last decade, the role of the national inspectorate has had a profound effect at primary level leading to a series of documents with the title *Curriculum Matters* (Department of Education and Science 1985). In contrast to some of the other European countries, the major concern has been with the extent of the diversity at present reflected in the system. Aspects of this diversity concern curriculum provision where the amount of time pupils, within the same classroom, devote to a particular subject can vary enormously. Diversity between schools is also reflected by the length of the school day.

In one recent study (Galton *et al.* 1985) it was shown that within one local authority there was a difference in time allocation of one hour a day, adding up to nearly one day per week. Recent research at junior level (Mortimore *et al.* 1988) and at infant level (Tizard *et al.* 1988) demonstrates that the patterns of organisation and teaching within the primary classroom remain much the same as those observed nearly a decade earlier by Galton *et al.* (1980) and by HM Inspectors (Department of Education and Science 1978b). In Tizard's study, for example, a large proportion of the time in the reception classes was given over to routine and management activities. The response by central government is to set out a curriculum framework and to couple it with a series of assessment targets at the ages of 7 and 11. The assessments, as proposed by the Black Committee (Task Group on Assessment and Testing 1988), are criterion related and are graded over a number of levels. Thus the curriculum will, in part, be assessment driven, since teachers will need to incorporate the various types of graded assessment task into their teaching in order to prepare children adequately. These changes are accompanied by a degree of external accountability in that the powers of parents on management committees are increased and the assessments of children at 11 will be published.

The innovation model adopted is essentially a 'top-down' approach involving the formation of a National Curriculum Council. Although membership of the Council and its advisory committees contains a significant proportion of practitioners, their task is essentially to formulate a 'blue print' that will then be handed down to local authorities whose task it will be to arrange programmes of in-service activities for local teachers. Each local authority proposal will be submitted to the Department of Education for approval. Such an approach is not totally consistent with recent research on the implementation of new innovation. It remains to be seen, therefore, how successful the programme will be in fulfilling the government's objective of allowing teachers to continue to exercise freedom as to how they teach within an agreed framework. Critics argue that the stress of assessment, and the fear that if a school does not produce successful results it will lose custom and hence resources, will lead to a severe restriction on the range of teaching strategies adopted as schools and teachers gradually concentrate on only those aspects of the curriculum that are subject to public assessment.

4. Innovation and Project No. 8

As part of its activities, Project No. 8 commissioned a series of short case studies. In submitting cases for consideration each country was asked to choose an example of a successful innovation. Some of the innovations are summarised within the project's Final Report (<DECS/EGT [87] 23>, Appendix 3, pp. 127–50). In the Final Report an analysis of the procedures adopted by those responsible for carrying out the innovations described in the case studies led to identification of five major styles of innovation. Most of these were variants on the traditional 'centre-to-periphery' model of curriculum change described earlier.

Nearly one-third of all the case studies involved a *course development approach*. For the most part, teachers attended courses held under the auspices of the local education authorities during which the objectives and methods of the desired innovations were presented. These teachers were then required to go back to schools and act as 'change agents'. One example concerned the improvement of creative and aesthetic skills of children through art and drama in the city of Athens <DECS/EGT [85] 56>.

A variation of this approach was termed the *training team approach*. This attempted to overcome the weaknesses of course-based in-service training where the teachers who are required to return to schools as change agents do not feel sufficiently confident to take on the work of trainer and in the absence of external support are unable to achieve the desired changes in classroom practice. In the training team approach, which was used in approximately 12 per cent of all case studies, the local education authority selects a group of experienced teachers to help plan the in-service programme and then to run it. These teachers then follow up the programme by travelling round schools that are taking part in the innovation to support the attempts of teachers in implementing changes in their own classrooms. The team of teachers helps to diagnose difficulties and provide additional training where necessary. A programme run along these lines was used to introduce microcomputers in the primary classroom in the city of Leeds in the United Kingdom <DECS/EGT [85] 24>.

At the other extreme were the *school-based approaches* involving the attempt by a single school to implement changes in response to problems that have been identified by the whole educational community. One-fifth of all school-based approaches involve no outside help but involve a school attempting to use a 'problem-solving' approach. One example concerned the attempt by schools in France <DECS/EGT [86] 55> to alter their timetable so that school work could be more closely integrated with other activities run by parents and the 'Youth and Sport' Department of the City Council. In each case the individual school set up a local support committee comprised of parents, city council officials and voluntary organisations to monitor the progress of the local experiment. A further 20 per cent of school-based approaches involve the use of a consultant, usually from an institution of higher education or in the form of local authority advisers or inspectors. A very successful example of this approach is described in the case study of Icelandic schools <DECS/EGT [86] 36>.

A further 25 per cent of the innovations adopted some form of networking in association with consultancy using a *clustering approach* in which schools identified similar problems and then worked together to solve them. This style of innovation was tried in France, where a group of schools in priority education areas attempted to solve the problems of students who 'dropped out' of the system <DECS/EGT [86] 17>.

One style, notable by its absence, has been termed the *cascade approach*, an approach currently being advocated in the implementation of the new national curriculum proposals within the United Kingdom. At the first stage of the cascade a small group of experts receive training. They then break into teams and train other groups. For example, it was suggested that the 40 individuals in the team then form ten teams of four, each training another 40 people, giving a total of 400 trainers. This allows 100 courses to proceed simultaneously involving two teachers from 20 schools. Taking two teachers from each school avoids one of the main weaknesses of the course-based approach, where teachers who attend such courses often complain of feelings of isolation when returning to schools because they have no colleague with whom to share the new ideas that they have been introduced to in the course of the in-service programme. Cascade approaches, however, have yet to be fully evaluated and there are concerns about the extent to which the principles of the innovation can be communicated effectively at the various levels without considerable training of the training teams.

5. Obstacles to innovation

In evaluating the various case studies, a number of common problems emerged across the different countries. Over 90 per cent of the evaluators cited insufficient resources as the reason why most of the innovations failed to develop fully according to plan. Only a small proportion of the schools tried to overcome this problem by redeploying existing resources or by looking for some other local supplementary support - some schools, for example, made use of students from training colleges, while others involved parents. In almost all of the studies no special time was allowed for teachers to reflect critically on their practice during the innovation period. Teachers complained, in particular, that there was not enough time during the preliminary phase when situations were being analysed and plans worked out. In nearly every country within the Council of Europe, local authorities seem to regard the teachers' 'out of class' time (vacations and after-school hours) as the appropriate time for this reflective activity. Most teachers involved in the case studies, however, regarded this time as their own and argued that if the innovation was sufficiently important for the authorities then they should be provided with free time during working hours for discussion and reflection. Where time was not made available, then small additional payments, as in the Danish system, helped to overcome this problem because teachers then felt that their efforts were being formally acknowledged. There was some evidence, as in the Icelandic case study for example, that when a local authority did make time for reflection during school hours then the staff concerned were more likely to work on during the vacation or after school hours on the innovation programme.

There was little evidence in any of the case studies of local authorities using the principle of 'backward mapping' suggested by Vandenberghe (1988). Neither did local authorities appear to place much emphasis on keeping 'channels of communication' open between those responsible for national policy and those responsible for carrying out that policy at local and school level. For the most part this was done by forming representative committees on which both teachers and policy makers sat or by assuming that this role could be carried out by the advisers or inspectors. Very little consideration was given to the problematic role of the latter group who were required to combine both a consultant's and an inspectorial role. In only 20 per cent of the innovations reported during the case studies did any formal channel of communication between different levels appear to have been established.

A constantly recurring theme within the case studies was the breakdown of communication within the school itself as a factor inhibiting innovation and change. Nearly 75 per cent of all the cases mentioned this effect, reporting that there were many problems in human relationships between staff within institutions and between the school staff and the local authority advisers and inspectors. Few heads or advisers seemed to appreciate that conflict and change go hand in hand because innovation will inevitably challenge existing values. Many head teachers in the studies appeared to back away from the consequences of these potential confrontations. As some staff became strongly committed to the innovation they would tend to challenge the position of colleagues who were slower to accept the new ideas. In order to reduce tensions between the staff, head teachers would often try to redirect the energies of the committed staff into 'safer' forms of activity such as the development of new reading schemes or a fund-raising project.

Interestingly there was no strong association between the different styles of innovation and the various countries where the innovations were carried out. Thus countries with highly centralised educational systems did not always adopt 'top-down' models of innovation. Neither was there a tendency in decentralised systems to engage in more 'problem-solving' localised school-based innovations.

The findings to emerge from Project No. 8 are in general in agreement with those from research that has been undertaken in the United States during the past decade, where one writer has argued that 'whether we looked at local problem solving, research transformed into practice, action research or networking (i.e. cascade approaches) we were drawn to teachers, their world and their work as starting points for improving schools' (Passon 1986). During the 1980s many countries moved away from attempts to compel all schools to change policies to situations where perhaps too much emphasis has been placed on small-scale localised initiatives. Most countries now face the challenge of using the impetus of nationally agreed aims concerning the primary school to stimulate changes in school that, 'nevertheless, take into account the organisational relationship of the school, the climate and the environment of the school and the transactions between teachers and learners' (Passon 1986). Innovation as it is now understood involves three basic characteristics of *conflict*, *commitment* and *collaboration*. While the study of schools and classrooms has reached a stage where there is now a better understanding of the factors that inhibit innovation by teachers, considerable research is still needed on the ways in which those with responsibility to promote change in schools, such as the advisory and inspectorial service and the principal and head teacher, can develop adequate models of leadership and so act as catalysts for change.

This theme of management for change is now a central feature of most in-service programmes within the member states of the Council of Europe. Many management activities in the past have, however, been highly functional in their approach and have tended to avoid the more detailed discussion of human relationship problems. Thus many schools are encouraged to promote innovation by writing general guidelines for practice and these are often so vague and general that every teacher can subscribe to them without experiencing any internal crisis or any disturbance of their personal value system. The project therefore concluded that two things were necessary to promote real change within the primary schools of Europe.

First, there needs to be a far greater recognition by those in authority of the problems that head teachers and their staff are likely to face when attempting to innovate. This includes a need for support against more cautious elements among parents and teachers who resist change. Better training for head teachers is essential so that they can respond creatively to opposition among the staff and manage the tensions that this opposition causes more effectively. The second recommendation was that education authorities should watch carefully for heads and principals who appear to promote and implement innovation more successfully than others and use these as trainers for their colleagues. At the moment there is too little long-term planning in career development among teachers in most European countries. In many instances innovation programmes have come to an abrupt end because key staff have left school to seek promotion before their colleagues have developed a genuine commitment to the new changes.

Thus in the next few years most member countries of the Council of Europe will concentrate on developing more effective training of teachers, head teachers and advisers, while attempting to promote greater continuity between the initial and in-service programmes of training. In this way it is hoped that more primary schools will be equipped to face the twin challenges presented by the rapidly changing nature of society and the increase in knowledge about the way in which children learn most effectively.

CHAPTER 6.2

Innovation in Practice

Dook Kopmels

The Contact School Plan

The Contact School Plan was a network of 12 contact schools providing liaison between primary schools engaged in innovation. It was a part of Project No. 8 'Innovation in primary education' of the Council for Cultural Co-operation of the Council of Europe during the period 1982–7.

The Contact School Plan (Kopmels 1987; <DECS/EGT [87] 34>) was added to Project No. 8 in order to allow the people who were actively involved in innovation in primary schools in Europe to have a direct and concrete input in the project. Project No. 8 was never meant just to produce rhetoric about innovation: it hoped to pass on, systematise and generalise successful experiences and set-backs in the reality of the innovation within the various member states of the Council of Europe.

Twelve schools took part in the Contact School Plan. These were:

Austria:	Volkschule 15, Vienna
Cyprus:	Kornesios Primary School, Nicosia
Denmark:	Bankagerskolan, Horsens
Finland:	Linnala School, Imatra
Germany:	Albert Schweitzer Grundschule, Freiburg
Greece:	128th Primary School, Athens
Italy:	C. Laurenti School, Civitavecchia
Netherlands:	H.K. Van Duyvenvoorde Primary School, Oost-Souburg
Norway:	Vardåsen Primary School, Kristiansand
Sweden:	Fajanskolan, Falkenberg
Switzerland:	Guthirt Primary School, Zug
United Kingdom:	St Aidan's Primary School, London

The following descriptions illustrate the style of the innovation programmes attempted in three of the contact schools, representing the northern, central and southern European membership of the CDCC.

Italy: C. Laurenti, Civitavecchia

Civitavecchia is a seaside town with a port which is quite important and an industrial area. The primary school 'Cesare Laurenti' is a school for children from 6 to 11 years old. At the time of the innovation it had 400 children in 20 classes with 30 teachers, some of whom worked part time. School lasted for 35 hours a week with a 7-hour day. One class was devoted entirely to 5-year-old children. The school innovation concerned four full-time classes shared by eight teachers.

The aim of the innovation in the school was to integrate two types of schools that are separated in Italy – the nursery school (3–5-year-old children) and the primary school (6–11-year-old children) – into a new type of school. Italian primary schools usually start the year in mid-September and close at the end of the second week of June. There are 205 days in a school year and in most of the schools lessons are given six days a week. Children attend lessons for 4 hours a day. Usually there is a maximum of 25 children in each form. However, in some cases, children with learning difficulties are mixed with other children and these classes are generally grouped by age. In such 'mixed' classes, the maximum number of pupils is reduced to 20.

In Civitavecchia Experimental School, however, children attended for five school days a week. The school remained closed on Saturdays and each day lasted from 8.30 a.m. to 3.00 p.m. with a lunch break from 12.30 p.m. to 1.00 p.m. included within the school timetable. Another aim of the innovation was the introduction of new programmes of study with new subjects such as statistics, probability, computer studies, education of sound, and music. School activities for the children were organised either as games or tasks. The organisation of these activities was in terms of either individual work, small group activities or collective activities involving the whole class.

The teachers were also deeply committed to the innovation. Team work was encouraged outside the classroom as well as inside. Team members taught partly together and partly on a rota basis. Teachers did not specialise completely but all had a main responsibility for teaching a particular curriculum area. Weekly meetings of the head teacher and staff took place to review the progress of the innovation plan and to study the use of new pedagogic methods.

Finland: Linnala School, Imatra

Linnala Comprehensive School is situated in the centre of the town of Imatra. The school's catchment area covers a wide range of social strata with a large number of single-parent families. The pupils in the school were aged between 7 and 12 years, making up school grades 1–6. There were 12 teachers for a total of 228 pupils.

The innovations carried out in the school were twofold: experimentation, prior to full implementation of the now generally accepted school timetable introduced by the ministry, and development of co-operation between the school and parents.

The introduction of the recommended school timetable by the ministry involved the forming of teaching groups for pedagogical rather than administrative reasons, using teachers as effectively as possible to reach the general educational goals set for the comprehensive school. In the new school legislation, permanent and temporary co-operation between teachers within the actual teaching situation was required. In addition, co-operation between the school and pupils' homes was also developed:

- by introducing more direct contacts with parents, with teachers visiting the home of each pupil;
- by introducing monthly teacher/parent meetings in certain school grades;
- by introducing a specially designed pupils' reminder book used by pupils as a general notebook and by the teachers as a medium for notifying parents;
- by launching a visual media project with the aim of establishing co-operation between parents and the school to check the detrimental effects of indiscriminate TV and video viewing by pupils at home.

Federal Republic of Germany: A. Schweitzer-Schule Freiburg

The Albert Schweitzer School is a school for 6–10-year-old children. At the time of the case study there were 11 classes (230 children who were taught by 16 teachers of whom only 6 were full time). Freiburg-Landwasser is a new satellite town and part of the town of Freiburg, which is close to the French border and has approximately 180,000 inhabitants.

Landwasser itself has 9,000 inhabitants who work either in the town or in the neighbourhood. The aim of the innovation in this school was to teach French as a second language to pupils of classes 3 and 4 (9 and 10 year olds). The aim was to encourge pupils to learn about their French neighbours, their art, their mentality and their culture.

It was considered essential that children should be provided with the kinds of experience that would lead them to see the importance of language as a means of making oneself understood in meetings with people across the border. The 'play' approach was used in order to achieve this aim. French lessons, integrated within the morning curriculum, were presented as a supplementary programme in addition to the normal curriculum. The nearness of the border required that all pupils, and not only those with the greatest ability, should be provided with appropriate experiences that helped them to understand that language is not something merely to be learnt but provides the only means whereby one can express oneself and develop closer contact between different peoples.

In addition to the three special hour supplementary programme, teachers and pupils were encouraged to introduce the same themes into the normal school work involving singing, dancing and painting. This was particularly important for the less able pupils and, in particular, for children with language difficulties including children of foreign employees and refugees. This special language programme, involving teachers, children and parents, was co-ordinated and developed by the College of Education in Freiburg. The contact school was just one of the 300 primary schools that took part in this project. Overall some 6,000 pupils were involved.

These examples illustrate three different approaches to innovation. In the German case the school was drawn into a larger-scale programme of innovation developed and co-ordinated from outside. This was also true in the Finnish case study with respect to the new curriculum guidelines, but the school had then taken the opportunity of extending the legally required programme of innovation to include specific objectives that the school itself considered of importance. In the Italian case study, the programme was experimental in that the teachers were attempting to reconstruct their way of working in a manner that differed appreciably from accepted practice. In addition to these differences in the style of innovation, the context of innovation in each of the 12 contact schools also differed appreciably. There were differences in the systems of education, in national policies of innovation and in language.

All these things added to the difficulties of the representatives from each school when discussing together in order to strengthen common themes. A further difficulty was that, although school improvement was a daily occupation for all the teachers, identifying the essential characteristics of the processes proved for all involved a very difficult task. However, all participants in the discussion were agreed that, wherever the initiative for the project came from or however much external influences were brought to bear upon the progress of change in school, it was the teachers (whether as a school team or as an influential group within the school) who were the ones who made the changes. The teachers therefore took the crucial decisions and were, in the last analysis, responsible for deciding whether to accept or reject external assistance.

During the contact school meetings and visits, therefore, a recurring theme concerned the communalities between each of the schools as they strove for school improvement. By the end of the programme all participants were agreed that certain characteristics could be identified as important in working towards innovation in primary education. The remainder of this chapter discusses these characteristics and provides, it is hoped, helpful information for those who seek school improvement from within.

2. The five-zones model

From the case studies that were carried out during the period of the project, a number of different styles of innovation were identified (see Chapter 6.1). Most of these were variants on the traditional 'centre-to-periphery' model of curriculum change. The traditional model, although extremely cost-effective, has been criticised because of the failure to understand fully the concerns of those who have to implement the innovation. It has been argued, however, that the alternative, school-focused innovation risks being too one-sided, promoting only one aspect of education and paying too little attention to other important concerns, thus failing to provide sufficient continuity between schools.

The 'five-zones model' (Figure 6.2.1), which has been developed on the basis of the contact school experiences, proved a very helpful instrument for teachers, consultants and authorities. It draws attention to the specific zones of education that must not be neglected if real change is to take place.

Zone 1 is concerned with the aims and principles guiding the work of the teaching staff (not only the didactic approach and organisation, but also pedagogy). Zone 2 covers the circumstances under which the teaching staff can work (group division, the moving of children from one group to another, the reporting system, organisation within the groups, the work done with groups of mixed abilities, the use of space in school). Zone 3 is the subject matter, the aspect devoted to development of the didactic approach, choice of activities, observations, evaluation and so on. Zones 4 and 5 indicate how good organisation and good external contacts can enhance the success of the programme.

The five zones delineate areas within which school improvement can take place. They also indicate coherence: changes in one zone have consequences in another so that changes must be planned in all five areas.

For example, the introduction of working with mixed age-groups instead of working with a single age-group or year groups based upon equivalent grades would constitute an improvement under zone 2, the 'Organisation of education'. Teachers who worked on this aspect of innovation, however, came to realise that the more important effect was the possibility of having a greater influence on the social and emotional development of the children involved. They came to recognise the need for each child to develop a realistic, satisfactory self-image. Discussions among staff of ways of enhancing the children's self-image directed attention to zone 4, concerning co-operation between teams of teachers. These discussions then led teachers to identify the development of children's self-image as an important principle within zone 1, concerning the educational goals of the school. As a result a programme of special lessons was prepared for older children that set out to help them cope with emotions and, in particular, to provide them with a greater awareness of how their own behaviour influenced the way in which others (both teachers and peers) judged them. This moved the discussions into zone 3. After the

Figure 6.2.1 The five-zones model of school improvement

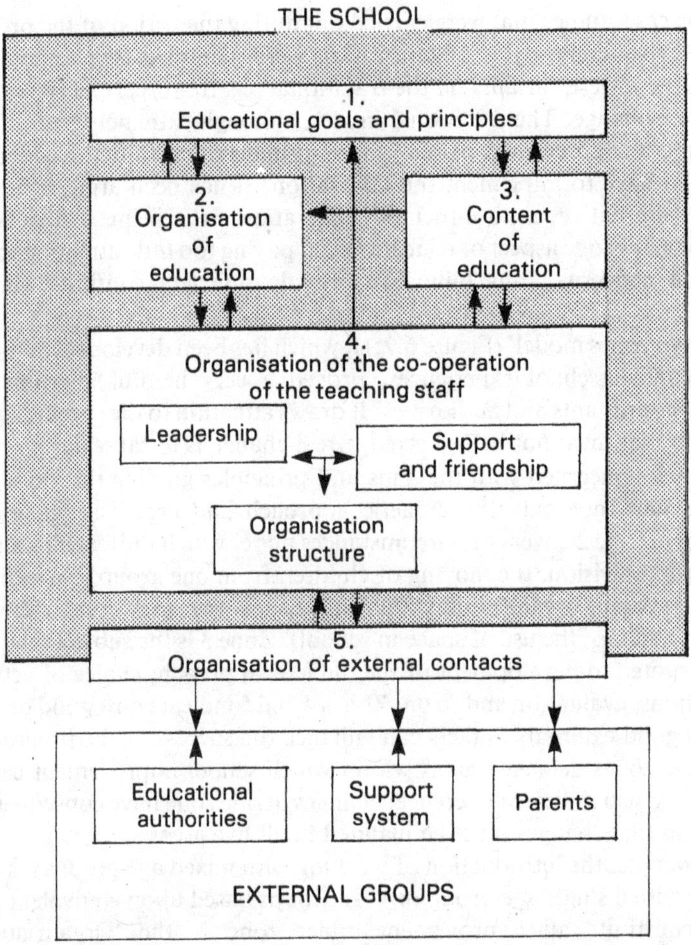

programme had been tried out on a small number of children, it was extended to the whole school and at the same time, in preparation for this major development, a number of evening meetings for interested parents was held so that discussion then shifted into zone 5.

This five-zones model has been used here to analyse the progress reports of the 12 contact schools in Project No. 8.

Educational goals and principles

In zone 1 all the contact schools identified three important principles governing their approach to school improvement: the first of these was active individualisation of the learning process; the second concerned the recognition of the importance of pupil autonomy and co-operation; and the third area concerned the nature of the relationship between the child and the teacher, which could promote learning.

Active individualisation

All the contact schools endeavoured to encourage children not only to learn more but also to learn more useful things. This approach was not simply to do with offering more subject matter but also required each child to utilise all their abilities so that they achieved a greater command and control of their own environment. This approach was based on a particular view about learning and development, which can be summarised as follows. In the age-range 4–12, children learn most from working with concrete objects until they arrive at a stage of working consciously. This learning process is stimulated by verbal activity – by putting ideas into words either to other children or to the teacher.

This approach implies pedagogical choices that have a number of far-reaching implications. If, for example, one allows the children to engage in activities that stimulate their development on a very broad base, where they work with building and construction materials or tell or write their own story, then the teacher needs to observe how children accomplish these tasks so that they can suggest complementary activities for each child that take the learning a stage further. For this the teacher needs many resources, such as ways to observe children and to record their progress, materials to occupy children actively, and additional resources to advance children's learning further. Such activities are based not only upon the three Rs (reading, writing and arithmetic), on which naturally much time is spent, but also upon other matters of importance such as knowing the world and what happens in the world, developing various ways of expressing thoughts and feelings, and creating a sense of enjoyment while doing these things.

During this process, which requires active individualisation of learning, children should be confronted with things that they are only to some degree ready for but that require them to take an active part in education both mentally and physically and where during the work children can have direct feedback from the teacher (correction, explanation, encouragement, confirmation and help). For this to happen both the teacher and child need to 'activate' each other in the teaching/learning process. This 'active' aspect of individualisation therefore includes the concept of 'interactive learning', which emphasises the immediate exchange of information requiring the development of open-ended investigative styles of working in schools designed to stimulate the development of children's problem-solving strategies.

An example of this approach can be found in the Swedish contact school, Fajanskolan. This school is situated on a new housing estate in Falkenberg, which is on the west coast of Sweden. There is a day-care centre for children from 9 months to 13 years and the elementary school is housed in the same premises so that it is possible for a family with several children to have them all taught under one roof. The school is divided into three colour units, with each unit containing children from the full age-range. Each colour unit consists not only of teaching staff but also of some cleaning and kitchen personnel. Children in the respective units therefore meet the same group of adults throughout their stay at Fajanskolan and this creates a feeling of security, which is also essential for effective learning. The school's motto is 'All children are everyone's children'. This principle influences the way that teachers work together – the nursery school's creative working methods have influenced the work of the elementary school, while the language development and practical application of mathematics programmes have been incorporated into the curriculum activities in the nursery section. This provides greater continuity for the children.

Autonomy and co-operation

An important object of Fajanskolan is to create pupils who can take responsibility for themselves not only now but later as adults. Children are trained from the very start to plan and be responsible for their own work. In their final three years at Fajanskolan pupils are expected to plan and carry out each week's work in most subjects. Another important principle for this contact school is to develop 'autonomy' and co-operation among pupils. The school aims to stress the importance for each child of being a person, somebody with their own thoughts, feelings and desires who is not just in school to do what grown-ups say. From a very early age children do make decisions for themselves and teachers at Fajanskolan try to reinforce this natural striving for autonomy.

At the beginning, the children's choices are relatively simple and centre on what to do ('Shall I go and play with sand or with dolls?'). Gradually they are encouraged to work out for themselves how to tackle problems ('Shall I do my sums using blocks or a calculator?') and later they are encouraged to plan their own work and divide their own time ('Shall I do something I like first or shall I finish what I find hard to do? Do I need somebody to help me decide?'). Thus, by learning to do things for themselves, children are automatically confronted with other people within the classroom. There are other children with whom they join to work or play and of course the teacher who makes so many demands upon them. To be able to exercise criticism and to choose individually, an individual needs a good deal of specific knowledge and moral courage. A conformist education does not encourage such independent thinking.

Many contact schools therefore thought it necessary to encourage autonomy right from the start because they wished to succeed in helping children reach the highest possible levels of emotional and cognitive development. At the same time, however, this principle of 'autonomy' does not mean that children should be trained to be individualists or egoists. On the contrary, in the pursuit of autonomy there is the implication that each child needs to respect others' freedom. In the contact schools, children were taught this by explicitly bringing them into situations where co-operation was necessary both for the learning process and for deliberation about rules that hold good in a particular group, including matters concerning the running of the whole school. Co-operation, therefore, is working together and living together on the basis of equivalence and respect for everybody's autonomy and forms a logical and psychological counterpart of autonomy itself.

In many of the contact schools, co-operation was the central principle in the composition of work programmes. This included co-operation of children in relatively open learning situations, working towards reduction in the use of power when solving problems between the teacher and the child, reducing the risks that children become stereotyped in a particular class by organising flexible age-groups, and providing many opportunities for children to exercise their own initiative in making contributions to activities.

Relationships between the child and the teacher

Good relationships with every child are necessary if teaching is to be organised smoothly and conveniently. Working in small groups requires skilful organisation by teachers, and this task is managed more easily when they are not required to spend too much time on matters of classroom management. The nature of the relationship between teachers and children therefore determines the success of the innovation. Further, once the relationship between children and teachers is well established, relations between parents and teachers can be developed. The contact schools agreed that in each of their countries there was an increasing problem in establishing satisfying social relationships between children and adults. They agreed that it was an explicit task for the school to provide children with certain models with which they could identify. Thus the principles governing the relationships between staff in the schools needed to be the same as those governing the relationships between the staff and the children.

At some schools this principle has led to explicit educational activities in the field of 'Learning to work together' and of 'Self-control and learning to be myself' for the older children. Such an approach demands very open contacts with parents about the child and many schools have recognised both the necessity and the difficulty of developing this kind of home–school relationship. In developing these approaches towards school improvement it is first necessary to spend time talking about the pedagogical aspects of education and to help teachers improve their skills, insights and attitudes in this area. In the Dutch contact school, and in other schools in the Netherlands, a special 35 hour workshop has been used for this purpose. The same kind of workshop has also been organised for Greek teachers, including those of the contact school in Athens. The programme is based upon the teacher effectiveness training workshop and materials developed and evaluated in the United States by Thomas Gordon (1974). The programmes, which have been translated into several languages, now operate in Belgium, Finland, France, the Netherlands and Switzerland. In this context, effectiveness is defined as 'to have a positive influence on another'. This, rather than the financial rewards, is why most teachers wish to teach. Indeed, the general dissatisfaction and 'burn-out' among teachers usually come from the painful conclusion that they are not able to have this positive influence.

In the Netherlands, one sample of 209 teachers who had participated in teacher effectiveness training produced the evaluation in Table 6.2.1 when asked whether the course had improved their effectiveness on each of the 12 central themes. The table shows that at least 70 per cent of the participants concluded that they had improved in every case.

Table 6.2.1 Evaluation of Teacher Effectiveness Training Programme

Goal	*Improvement* (% of teachers)
Effective listening	91.5
Being clear (clear sending)	92.0
Discrimination between 'behaviour' and 'interpretation'	81.5
Noticing the difference between 'problems of the child', 'problem of the teacher' (problem ownership)	95.5
Solving problem between child and teacher without remaining resentful	78.5
Avoiding 'roadblocks' in communication (threatening, calling names, sarcasm, questioning, etc.)	69.5
Discrimination between 'need conflicts' and 'value collisions'	73.5
Willingness to change one's view of children's behaviour	80.0
Modelling important values in one's own behaviour	69.5
Giving advice	75.5
Handling children's deviant behaviour	90.0
Helping children to solve their own problems	90.5

Organisation of education

In the second zone, ways of organising teaching are considered. Among the issues considered are how children are divided among teaching staff, whether groups are formed according to an age standard or a performance grade, the length of time that children stay in a particular group, the forms of reporting and the relationship of a particular teacher to their register group. In the contact schools, questions were continually raised about three particular issues: first, the methods used for monitoring progress and development; second, the arrangement of time and the choice of didactic working methods; and, third, the problem associated with mixed age-groups.

In all the contact schools the organisation of the learning process was complicated, unlike classes where all children were busy working at the same thing at the same time. Within this complex situation the teacher is not always automatically aware of the children's progress and development, and without special measures there is an increased risk of a child slackening or stagnating in their learning. Considerable attention was therefore paid to the formative evaluation process and the ways in which this could be built into the active learning. In the contact schools many forms of systematic observation and reporting have been developed by teachers, aided by consultants. In the Netherlands contact school, for example, children's mathematical progress was monitored by regular tests after each set of assignments. These tests were all computerised, with each child having their own password. The pupils would bring the summary print-out of their performance to the teacher so they could quickly identify any particular problem. Use was also made of tape-recordings for language work. Again, pupils were encouraged to summarise their progress and note any difficulty as a way of cutting down the time typically used by teachers to check details of the individual pupil's working methods. Most of the contact schools also shared didactic working methods and the arrangement of time.

Frequently individual activities within groups was the main form of organisation, but a considerable amount of whole classwork still took place where children were encouraged to express themselves, celebrate each other's successes, discuss arrangements for future activities and evaluate their progress. In several of the schools, a regular number of successive activities was found necessary for children up to about 8 years of age. A fixed rhythm during the day was considered conducive to clarity and feelings of security of such children. In diversifying various didactic working methods, the contact schools also took into account a division of what might be called three kinds of time: diffused time, individual time and optimum time.

Diffused time

In the contact schools, classrooms were active places. Both teachers and children were continually being bombarded with incoming stimuli. There could be four children playing a game in a group, three children discussing questions about the text they had read, two children working with construction material and so on, while the teacher instructed other children how to read with expression. In such circumstances, individuals learn how to screen incoming stimuli – paying attention to certain noises, feelings and sights, but ignoring others. This process requires concentration on the part of the child and uses up energy in order to suppress awareness of all the incoming stimuli that are to be ignored. Ultimately both the teacher's and the child's supply of energy is limited. Neither children nor teachers can stand diffusion (and confusion) all the time.

Individual time

Individual time, however, has the quality of decreased sensory input. Each person in a learning environment must be able to have some time alone away from the crowd in which to think, reorganise work or even play on their own. In order to create this space, contact schools have developed a range of solutions, including quiet corners in the classroom, individual study cabins, special 'solo places' outside the classroom, more use of library space and stockrooms, and the use of screens to divide the classroom into several spaces. One of the reasons why the Netherlands contact school put a proportion of its programme on audio tape was to give the children an opportunity to wear headphones and thus shut out the other sounds in the classroom.

Optimum time

Optimum time is the interpersonal time that occurs between the teacher and the child, during which good relationships are built. This optimum time period was often used to provide direct feedback. The contact schools found that this time must be organised rather than left to chance.

Most of the contact schools had classes that were organised in mixed age-groups. In such classes the curriculum cannot be organised on a subject matter basis, particularly in countries such as Norway where the law makes integration of handicapped children into the local school a parental right. Under such an arrangement, individualisation of the learning process is essential. Within the mixed age classes all teachers in the contact school often made use of homogeneous groups related to the cognitive development of the participants. Teachers in the contact schools offered the following reasons for preferring to work with this kind of mixed age arrangement:

1. Mixed age-groups offered more opportunities for developing social and emotional behaviour. Children were able to gain experience from changing social positions within a group. In most cases the children were with the same teacher for about two years so that they were able to learn how to support 'beginners' as they moved up the age-range.
2. Within mixed age-groups it was possible to offer children more opportunity to learn from each other. In countries where previously only children who passed the end-of-year examination could move up to the next year, it was felt that working in mixed groups offered better opportunities for continuous development of all individuals. In these countries it was usual to consider moves from the existing group three times a year. The system also offered much greater flexibility in the presentation of subject matter, which was not, as in the past, linked closely to the 'class year'. All these advantages could also be realised in age groups, but it was the additional freedom relating to the presentation of subject matter at appropriate times for individual children that was considered by teachers in the contact schools to be the greatest advantage of working in mixed age-groups.

Content of education

Even granting the diversity of different national traditions, there were still a number of similarities between the contact schools in their approach to the presentation of the content of the curriculum. First, most of the schools attempted to cover the areas of knowledge and the areas of expression by presenting the subject matter in ways that linked it to daily life. In order to cover the range of curriculum areas some contact schools broke with the tradition of one teacher for each class towards the top end of the school so that colleagues with different expertise could inspire and stimulate pupils in their subject specialism. Generally, however, the activities were chosen with the aim of stimulating broad development rather than coverage of a particular subject area. Thus in a discussion children learned not only something of the subjects studied but also about language, their powers of concentration and their specific skills of listening. Such activities were common to all subject areas and teachers in the contact schools were encouraged to plan their work with these in mind. The importance of such activities also arose because many contact schools were looking for a synthesis between what could be defined as 'playing' and learning. Younger children, in particular, require numerous opportunities for activities such as sand and water play, block-building and other motor development, while at the same time learning to read, do arithmetic and to write. To organise the content of the curriculum in this way teachers had to understand the different applications that could arise from the performance of a given task. Tasks were therefore analysed in terms of process skills rather than simply of subject matter.

Co-operation between teachers

This zone deals with how the school is managed and concerns such issues as the organisational structure, the leadership style and the support and friendship between colleagues. In most of the contact schools this zone of improvement concerns just the teaching staff. In only a few of the contact schools has co-operation been extended to the ancillary staff and other adults involved in the school.

Organisational structure

In most European schools, the organisational structure is unclear. The experiences of the contact schools suggest that, as long as things run smoothly, this situation does not matter. But without a clear organisational structure a school is unable to cope when a conflict arises. A sound organisational structure clarifies the decision-making process within the school, making explicit the financial control arrangements and who decides what takes place in a particular class. Satisfactory agreements must be made about these matters so that a well-ordered outline of procedures is available for all staff.

In a number of contact schools, developments have taken place in which the organisational structure, consisting of a collection of practices (some new and some carried over from previous administrations), has been consciously worked out to provide well set out organisational structures that have been explicitly agreed by all the teachers. In most cases, the establishment of this consensus has taken place despite the presence of teachers who were ineffective or reluctant to change, despite unexpected events that occurred during the process of school improvement and despite negative reactions from the local community. In order for the school to be able to cope with such difficulties, which can lead to internal conflicts among the teaching staff, three conditions were found to be necessary. First, there must be clarity, in that the structure of organisation must be concrete and clear for all concerned so that everybody is aware of the tasks that are expected of them. Second, there must be perception among the participants of what is taking place within the organisational structure. It is not necessary for teachers to do everything together, but, where something is done by a sub-group or by an individual, those who are not directly involved must be aware of what is taking place. Third, there must be consistency. The organisational structure must not become an aim in itself but must provide a model for all other activities leading to school improvement.

Leadership style

In addressing the problems of school management, two different procedures may be recognised. In the first procedure, teachers in the school are responsible for their own class and the principal has responsibility for ensuring coherence between the different teaching programmes and for taking care of financial and administrative provision. The principal will also be responsible for external contacts within the community. Within this system, the principal decides when internal consultation is necessary and on what matters s/he takes direct action. In the last analysis, the principal's decision is final.

In the second case, however, the main focus in the school is on the degree of coherence in the work of the various classes. This means there is more consultation about matters of education between the staff, and this consultation is designed to ensure that each teacher receives mutual support from colleagues in the development of educational policy within the school. In determining this policy, external contacts such as the local authority and parents are allowed to play a role. Decisions on educational policy are taken when everyone whose duty it is to carry them out agrees. The management can still be arranged in various ways, with many tasks delegated or else remaining with the principal. Financial and administrative matters come up for discussion only when they have a direct effect upon the teaching programme.

These two forms of organisation are well-known variants of organisational theory. The first strategy is appropriate for companies where the relationship between various departments is of little importance or can be guaranteed because each department uses similar procedures when relating to other departments. The second strategy is more appropriate for companies where decisions taken in one department have important consequences for other departments so that different departments must develop in the same direction. For the typical situation as it exists in most European primary schools, the second strategy is more appropriate because primary education must provide a degree of coherence so that students can go from one class to another in an uninterrupted process of development. Problems can, however, exist when schools try to adopt this strategy.

In most contact schools the more obvious forms of co-operation were between sub-teams of teachers working with the same age-group of children. In order to provide greater coherence, some contact schools found it necessary either to make some teachers members of more than one sub-group or to set up a formal system of representation to ensure that each sub-team consulted with the others to retain an overview and to ensure continuity. The contact schools also operated a system of full staff meetings in which the various year group teams came together, but this was found to be exceedingly time consuming for all the parties involved and it was often found difficult to obtain general solutions that appealed to all sub-groups. Generally it was agreed that the best system involved three sub-groups – an early years, middle and upper primary school group. Coherence was maintained by having overlap of sub-teams and by a Management Council composed of the chairpeople of the various sub-groups. The head teacher was involved as both the formal leader of the central group and as a member of a sub-team.

The main responsibility of the sub-groups was to promote the quality of education in every class and to ensure continuity between the different levels. Much of the sub-group meetings consisted of consulting about work. The meetings were an opportunity not only to bring up problems but also to keep others informed of what was happening and to prepare future activities together. Sometimes a sub-group needed to approach individuals outside school, but it was felt that this should always be arranged through the central group. All meetings of the sub-group should have an agenda.

The central group's main purpose was to provide conditions and procedures that ensure internal co-operation between staff, stimulating teaching and learning and co-ordinating various activities. Besides keeping track of the total functioning of the school, the central group promoted external contacts and initiated policy. To discuss all these things with everybody, as is the practice in many schools, has been found by the contact members to lead generally to bad decision making and fuzzy arrangements. All agreed that some form of decision-making procedure was necessary. Central group meetings should have both an agenda and a list of resolutions. They should always discuss the implementation of any decisions taken at the previous meeting, any resolutions from the sub-group meeting and any correspondence dealing with pupils who are either entering or leaving the school. All resolutions should be distributed to the staff so that they have an opportunity to comment before these meetings.

Support and friendship

The contact schools gave a great deal of attention to ways of developing team work among teachers. Most teachers do not do their work just to earn a living. They require also recognition, respect and appreciation from colleagues. Teachers need to achieve success in order to prove their capabilities and they also need to have opportunities to develop their talents. The role of the head teacher was found to be very important in all the contact schools in facilitating this kind of team work. At the contact schools there appeared to be three sorts of tasks associated with leadership. All the schools had head teachers who attempted to share their authority and power of decision making with others. They appeared to have the ability to associate with people and to be clear about their aims without seeking to impose these unilaterally on the rest of the staff. Head teachers and principals were not always in the limelight, were seen by their colleagues to be honest in their dealings with other people and prepared to take responsibility for difficult decisions. Head teachers were also concerned with content. Teachers in the contact schools expected them to have some expertise in one or more aspects of primary education and to have concern for the well-being of all children in the school.

External contacts

The notion of external contact differed across the contact schools. Some schools considered this to refer only to parents while others extended it to include contact with the school board or with governors and contact with other establishments outside the school. Included in the latter were links with professional expertise outside the school.

Contacts with parents

All contact schools gave this priority, emphasising that both the motivation and involvement of the children are increased when parents become a part of school life. Many contacts with parents concerned their child's progress and welfare. The contact schools used a variety of ways in which to share information on these matters – ranging from discussion with individual parents, written statements in the forms of reports and letters, class parent evenings and, in some cases, discussion groups on educational topics. Not all these contacts took place in the school. Often, particularly in the early years, teachers would visit parents in the home.

Many contact schools also established relationships with parents to do with many matters concerning the school. Parents and teachers worked together to improve the general quality of provision or to raise funds. Examples among the contact schools included running the school newspaper, establishing a gardening committee or a carpenters' working group, and helping to cover books. In the contact schools, unlike in many primary schools in Europe outside the United Kingdom, there was a deliberate effort to involve parents in the classroom, either helping children to read or working in the handicraft area. Some schools also did a great deal to develop general contact outside school by organising walking trips, bicycle rallies, intercultural events and other social activities such as barbeques and dances. Some schools also organised opportunities for parents and teachers to discuss ways of improving both school effectiveness and parent–teacher relationships. Advisory councils (parent–teacher associations) were used for this purpose, but in some cases parents were invited to take an active part in the working out of the school's programme of work.

Professional aid

In discussions between representatives of the contact schools a recurring theme concerned the value of expert support for teachers. Practices, however, varied enormously across the contact schools. Some schools were unable to avail themselves of outside consultants, while for others the availability of expert help was a permanent feature of their working method. The clearest examples of the latter case were the Cyprus contact school, which was associated with the Nicosia College of Education, and the Dutch contact school, which has the permanent support of a regional pedagogic centre. Those contact schools that enjoyed the greatest amount of external help considered that this support was indispensable for developing appropriate in-service training courses, for helping to develop a systematic programme for implementing changes, for providing advice about children who were either behind or advanced in their development (both academic and social), and for advising and supporting the head teachers in their attempt to develop working methods for 'active individualisation'.

By way of an example the Regional Pedagogic Centre of Zeeland (RPCZ) may be cited. The purpose of the RPCZ is to render aid and assistance to primary schools, and this is available for all parties involved – teachers, children, parents and authorities. The RPCZ helps schools in a number of ways. It is involved in activities with teaching teams, assessment of individual children, counselling and discussion with one or more teachers about a particular child, observing in class, offering specific child guidance, conducting tests in order to diagnose problems, discussions with parents and providing in-service programmes for the general training of teachers within schools. The pedagogic centre has a staff of 70 and is divided into area teams, which include educational psychologists as well as advisers in specific subject areas. The centre offers planned guidance and occasional guidance in any area of work in which a school requires help. Planned guidance is given to schools prepared to work on a systematic programme of change or innovation. The centre is committed to continuing to work with a school and with the class teachers in helping to put its solutions into practice. Finally, the centre offers open programmes in the form of workshop seminars and different forms of training. Each year these programmes are composed in consultation with teachers and their representatives and can involve co-operation with other institutions such as the teacher-training college. All RPCZ aid is intended for schools that want to improve something in a systematic way. Currently, for example, the centre is working with a group of small schools to improve curriculum provision and to look for ways in which they can give each other mutual support.

3. Characteristics of school improvement

In this chapter, a number of characteristics relating to the five zones have formed specific features of school improvement within the contact schools. However, not all these characteristics are found in each school. From the reports of staff in the contact schools it is claimed that greatest improvement has already taken place in the arrangements of time and didactic working methods and in relationships with parents. Most schools felt that further development work was needed, especially in the areas of greater co-operation, monitoring progress and development and the organisational structure of the school. Indeed, although initially there was less interest in aspects of organisational structure by the last year of Project No. 8 this area was the subject of school improvement in all contact schools, the only one of the characteristics to have been adopted universally. It would seem, therefore, that, as a result of the processes already described earlier and the problems that can be experienced during innovation (such as conflict among teachers, the need to involve parents, and the pressures of work that are felt by teachers), the head teachers and staff felt a clear need to establish more effective consultation and decision-making procedures that could delegate tasks to different groups of people rather than having all members of staff involved in everything. The desired outcome of these efforts is to establish a clear, efficiently functioning organised structure.

4. Epilogue

I became a teacher because it seemed an interesting occupation. Gradually I became an enthusiastic teacher and then an enthusiastic head teacher because I felt seized by the possibilities that the profession offered, particularly the significance of helping growing children develop not only their capacity to learn but also their emotions and personal relationships. Later as a consultant, and even more now as director of a school support centre, I am driven by the same aim – to work for a better future or rather a better present for children. Those of us involved in this work, which embodies so many complex, important and exciting things like school improvement, zones and characteristics, would do well to pause from time to time and to ponder that all these complexities are supposed to have their effect on the ordinary, everyday life of a child and of a teacher.

APPENDIX 1

Publications on Primary Education Reported by the National Authorities in the Member States

These publications were recommended, with comments, by certain of the member states. They are reproduced in alphabetical order, almost exactly as they were submitted by the national authorities concerned, but many of the comments have been abbreviated. It should, however, be emphasised that these lists are only selections from the material available in the different countries. In one or two cases, brief journal articles included in the original lists have been omitted here.

Austria

1. Antoni, D. and Wolf, W. (eds). *Maßnahmen im Schuleingangbereich*. Federal Ministry of Education, Arts and Sports, Vienna, 1986.

   This brochure gives recommendations on the basis of the new primary school curriculum, e.g. how to start schooling, and how to change assessment, for pilot projects in the school entrance phase, for initial and in-service training, and for the more effective information of parents and guardians.

2. Boyer, L. *Kommentar zur Ausgangsschrift*. Federal Ministry of Education, Arts and Sports, Vienna, 1986.

   This booklet gives a short summary of the history of handwriting in Austria and the reasons for a reform. It compares international developments in this field and gives concise background information about the new alphabet.

3. Buchberger, F. and Satzke, K. (eds). *Förderunterricht: Grundlagen; Verfahren; Ergebnisse*. 237pp. Jugend & Volk, Wien-München, 1980. ISBN 3-71441-5326-2.

   The first part outlines the theoretical basis of remedial instruction; the second deals with didactical problems such as introductory reading, going beyond the number 10, doing arithmetic in set form, etc.; the third presents the results of pilot studies designed to implement remedial instruction in relation to the teaching schedule. It also contains the legal basis of remedial instruction.

4. Burgstaller, F. and Leitner, L. *Pädagogische Markierung: Probleme: Prozesse: Perspektiven: 25 Jahre österreichische Schulgeschichte (1962–1987).* 299pp. Österreichischer Bundesverlag, Vienna, 1987.

   This book deals with the history of schools in Austria since 1962, and mentions the problems, processes, perspectives and trends in pre-school and in primary education as well as in the other types of schools and in initial teacher education. It is also very helpful as a source of further references.

5. Federal Ministry of Education, Arts and Sports, in co-operation with Federal Ministry of Science and Research. *Austria: Organization of Education 1984–86*, Vienna, 1986.

   This booklet gives a brief summary of the organisation and structure of the whole Austrian education system, its principles, aims, and objectives, and material on curricula, pilot projects, educational statistics and documentary references.

6. Haberl, H. (ed.). *Selbsttätiges und individuelles Lernen in freien Arbeitsphasen: Schriftenreihe zur pädagogischen Tatsachenforschung.* 56pp. Pädagogisches Institut des Bundes, Salzburg, 1986.

   This brochure gives a brief introduction to Project No. 8's case study *Spontaneous and individual learning in free choice periods (Montessori) in Salzburg*. (See also <DECS/EGT [85] 62>)

A number of articles relevant to Austrian primary education are also to be found in journals such as *Erziehung und Unterricht*.

Belgium

A. Flemish-speaking system

Evaluation of the 'Project-VLO' has given rise to two publications covering a number of relevant aspects:

1. Four reports commissioned by the Ministry and the Commission for the Reform of Basic Education and produced by De Block and Martens of the University of Ghent and by Vandenberghe and Janssens of the University of Louvain.

2. A synthesis of these reports published by the Ministry of Education (Flemish-speaking sector) under the title *Informatieblad*, special issue, Brussels, October 1981 (Ref: D/1981/2771/2).

B. French system

Several reports have been produced since 1976–7 by the Inspectorate, *animateurs*, parent associations and the federations of organising authorities on the launching of the 'Cycle 5–8' scheme and its results from the points of view of the teaching team and pupils' achievement. The following may be mentioned as of particular interest:

1. Piron and Pirlet. *Rapport sur la mise en place du 'Cycle 5–8'*. 220pp. Ministry of Education, Brussels, 1980 (February).
2. *Animation et inspection – rapport sur l'évaluation des élèves et des équipes.* 80pp. Ministry of Education, Brussels, 1981 (June).
3. Blondin and Massoz. *Recherches sur les compétences minimales à atteindre en fin de cycle 5–8.* 400pp. University of Liège, Liège, 1981.
4. Cref. *Le cycle 5–8: où est-on?* 40pp. Ministry of Education, Brussels, 1981.

Cyprus

1. Department of Primary Education. *Curriculum for the primary schools.* 326pp. Ministry of Education, 1981.

   After a short foreword and a brief reference to the main characteristics of pre-primary and primary school children, suggestions are made for the aims, objectives, content, methodology and evaluation of each subject taught in pre-primary and primary school.

2. Papadopoulos, A. *Leadership qualities needed by principals and inspectors – opinions of teachers in Cyprus.* 26 pp. A. Papadopoulos, 1980.

   The opinions of teachers are investigated, by means of a questionnaire, regarding the qualities needed by principals and inspectors. A certain set of qualities is finally identified.

Germany (West)

1. Hopf, D., Krappmann, L. and Scheerer, H. 'Aktuelle Probleme der Grundschule' [Current problems in primary education] in *Bildung in der Bundesrepublik Deutschland* [Education in the Federal Republic of Germany]. 2 vols. Klett-Cotta, Stuttgart, 1980. ISBN 3-12-930-650-4.

   This report is based on interviews with educational experts, politicians, representatives of school administrations and 12 case studies carried out at schools in northern and southern Germany, Berlin and the Ruhr region. Although the report does not describe the 'ideal' primary school, it does give a realistic description of 'practice' in primary schools and, as such, uncovers fundamental weaknesses. Trends and shortcomings in the theory and practice of primary school teaching are identified.

2. Lichtenstein-Rother, Ilse. *Jedem Kind seine Chance: individuelle Förderung in der Schule* [Every child should have a chance: individual attention in schools]. Herder, Freiburg, 1980.

   This book adopts a partisan educational and political stance, but is also based on systematic observation and is aimed at supporting everyday practice. The introductory chapter provides a cohesive framework for the rest of the book. Emphasis is laid on the importance of moving forward from reforms already initiated to a more egalitarian system within which individual attention should be given to all children in primary education if the truly educational functions of primary schools are to be realised.

3. The most important journal for people, particularly teachers, working in primary education is *Grundschule: Zeitschrift für die Grundschule des Schulwesens* [Primary School: Journal for Primary Education], edited by Erwin Schwarz and published by Georg Westerman Verlag, Braunschweig. It offers practical suggestions, academic discussion of various curricular areas, regular comparisons with primary education in other countries, and relevant book reviews.

Ireland

1. Publications from the Department of Education (Dublin): *English in the primary school*, 1982; *Daoneolas agus Eolas Imshaoíl*, 1983; *Tuairisc ar na Seimineair do Phriomhóidí Bunscoileanna*, Samhain/Nollaig, 1984; *Report of the Working Party on the Primary School Curriculum and the Disadvantaged Child*, 1985; *An Ghaelige: Tuairisc ar Fheidhmiu an Churaclaim sna Bunscoileanna,* 1985; *Guidelines on remedial education*, 1988.

2. Publications from the Curriculum and Examinations Board (Dublin): *Issues and structures in education*, 1984; *The arts in education: a discussion paper,* 1985; *Assessment and certification: a consultative document,* 1985; *Primary education: a discussion paper,* 1985; *Planning, introducing and developing transition year programmes*, 1986; *In our schools: a framework for curriculum and assessment*, 1986.

3. Coolahan, J. *Irish education: history and structure*. 329pp. Institute of Public Administration, Dublin, 1981. ISBN 0-906980-03-8.

4. Greanedy, V. and Kellaghan, T. *Equality of opportunity in Irish schools: a longitudinal study of 500 students*. Educational Company, Dublin, 1984.

5. Harris, J. *Spoken Irish in primary schools: an analysis of achievement*. Instituid Teangeolaíochta Éireann, Dublin, 1984.
6. Irish National Teachers' Organisation. *Educational administration in Ireland: proposals for reform*. INTA, Dublin, 1984.
7. O Suílleabháin, Gearóid (Chairman). *Report of the Committee on In-service Education*. Stationery Office, Dublin, 1984.

Luxembourg

1. Collected educational legislation, published by the Ministry of National Education.
2. *Courrier de l'Education Nationale*, published by the Ministry of National Education.
3. Publications of the *Service d'Innovation et de Recherches Pédagogiques* (SIRP) of the Ministry of National Education.

Spain

Books of reference on basic general education (BGE; EGB = educación general básica).

1. Asensi, J. *et al. The initial basic education course*. 490pp. Santillana, Madrid, 1981. ISBN 84-294-1814-8.

   Specialists from different educational fields review the programming, organisation, teaching techniques, assessment, resource materials, etc. of the initial stage in the light of the implementation of revised syllabuses for this stage.

2. Arribas, C. *et al. The middle basic education course*. 360pp. Santillana, Madrid, 1982. ISBN 84-294-1952-7.

   A collection of articles by different specialists dealing with the most significant aspects of programming, assessment, organisation, teaching techniques and material, teacher training, etc. in line with the new approach in the revised syllabuses for the middle course.

3. Ministry of Education and Science. *New regulations on basic education*. General Directorate of Basic Education, Ministry of Education and Science (Legislative Collection No.4). 109pp. Madrid, 1981. ISBN 84-369-0873-2.
4. Further information about the revised syllabuses and their implementation can be found in reprints from the journal *Vida escolar*, issued by the Publications Department of the Ministry of Education and Science,

especially *Basic document on revised syllabuses*, No. 206, March–April 1980; *Revised syllabuses for pre-school education and the initial course*, No. 208, September–October 1980; and *Revised syllabuses for the middle course*, Nos 216–217, March–June 1982.

United Kingdom

A. England and Wales

1. Assessment of Performance Unit. *Science: Assessment Framework, Age 11*. 44pp. Department of Education and Science, London, 1984. ISBN 0-86357-012-7.

   This report concentrates on the Unit's purpose and methods, which are discussed and illustrated in detail through examples of children's work. Similar materials have been produced for English language and for mathematics.

2. Bennett, N. *et al. The quality of pupil learning experiences*. 262pp. Lawrence Erlbaum Associates, London, 1984. ISBN 0-86377-011-8.

   Report on a research project that paid particular attention to the tasks assigned to children, to the degree of match between those tasks and pupil attainment, to detailed observation of children at work, to the breadth, structure and coherence of the language and mathematics curriculum, to the experience of working in groups, and to the relationship between curriculum structure and pupil attainment. The complexity of classroom life is emphasised.

3. Education, Science and Arts Committee of the House of Commons. *Achievement in primary schools*. Vol. 1 of Report. 297pp. HMSO, London, 1986. ISBN 0-10-011165-3.

   This report, relating to England, attempted to identify the factors that encourage and those that inhibit a child's achievement at primary school, taking particular note of: pre-school education and its links with primary schools; the effects of falling rolls; the viability of small schools; methods of teaching, including remedial teaching; the curriculum, including the role of specialist teaching; the role of parents; the role of school governors; and comparisons with primary education in certain other countries.

4. HM Inspectors of Schools. *Education observed*. A series of booklets written by HMI. Department of Science, London, 1984 and subsequently. ISBN 0-85522-141-0.

   These booklets, based on formal inspections, provide periodic reviews couched in a manner that enables general messages and trends to reach a wider audience more readily.

5. HM Inspectors of Schools (Wales). *Curriculum and organisation of primary schools in Wales*. 43pp. Welsh Office, Cardiff, 1984. ISBN 0-86348-058-6.

   This is a general account based on recent inspections, with particular emphasis on curriculum and on factors that affect the quality of provision of primary education, such as organisation, balance and breadth of learning, staffing, and policies in assessment and record keeping. The problems faced by small rural schools are discussed.

B. Scotland

1. Consultative Committee on the Curriculum. *Education 10–14 in Scotland: a discussion paper*. 215pp. Edinburgh, 1986. ISBN 0-947985-06-9.

   This report brings out the mismatch between coherent, continuous, progressive and wide-ranging development and the discontinuities found within and between schools in Scotland, and seeks to construct a suitable rationale for schooling in its age-range and especially 12–14.

2. Committee on Primary Education. *Primary education in the eighties*. 84pp. Edinburgh, 1984. ISBN 0-947942-15-7.

   This paper makes many recommendations about the form and content of Scottish primary education in five main areas: the curriculum; the responsibilities of teachers; the school community; the school, the teacher and the wider curriculum; and staff development.

APPENDIX 2

Some Activities Organised by the CDCC Relevant to the Theme of Project No. 8

These activities are frequently referred to elsewhere in the Handbook, especially in Sections 2 and 6. References noted here are not repeated in the second part of the Bibliography.

A. Conferences and seminars

The following list includes the events organised by the Council that seem most relevant to Project No. 8. Other related events are listed in the Project's *Final Report*. <DECS/EGT [87] 23, Appendix 1>.

1982.

Vaduz (Liechtenstein). *Primary education in Western Europe: Aims, problems and trends* <DECS/EGT [83] 64>.

1983

Varese (Italy). Teachers' Seminar on *Europe in primary schools* <DECS/EGT [83] 87>.

Donaueschingen (Federal Republic of Germany). 19th Council of Europe Teachers' Seminar on *The teaching of history in primary schools: objectives, methods and problems* <DECS/EGT [84] 1>.

Donaueschingen (Federal Republic of Germany). 20th Council of Europe Teachers' Seminar on *The training of teachers of gypsy children* <DECS/EGT [83] 63>.

Han-sur-Lesse (Belgium). Symposium on *Innovation in primary education in Western Europe* <DECS/EGT [84] 24>.

Donaueschingen (Federal Republic of Germany). 21st Council of Europe Teachers' Seminar on *Development education in primary schools* <DECS/EGT [84] 40>.

1984

Donaueschingen (Federal Republic of Germany). 24th Council of Europe Teachers' Seminar on *Urban environmental education in primary schools*<DECS/EGT [84] 42>.

Noordwijk (Netherlands). Symposium on *The management of innovation in primary education* <DECS/EGT [85] 16>.

1985

Donaueschingen (Federal Republic of Germany). 27th Council of Europe Teachers' Seminar on *The role of the teachers in innovation* <DECS/EGT [85] 45>.

Donaueschingen (Federal Republic of Germany). 28th Council of Europe Teachers' Seminar on *Human rights education in primary schools* <DECS/EGT [85] 46>.

Rome (Italy). Symposium on *Children with special needs in the primary school* <DECS/EGT [86] 16>.

Donaueschingen (Federal Republic of Germany). 29th Council of Europe Teachers' Seminar on *Geography for international understanding in primary schools.* <DECS/EGT [85] 47-E>.

1986

Cambridge (United Kingdom). Symposium on *Science and technology in the primary school.* <DECS/EGT [86] 59>.

Donaueschingen (Federal Republic of Germany). Council of Europe Teachers' Seminar on *The role of the headteacher in innovation in primary schools* <DECS/EGT [86] 72>.

Donaueschingen (Federal Republic of Germany). 33rd Council of Europe Teachers' Seminar on *Mass media education in primary schools* <DECS/EGT [86] 73-E>.

Lyngby (Denmark). Symposium on *The new technologies and the primary school* <DECS/EGT [87] 48>.

1987

Stockholm (Sweden). Symposium on *The implementation of innovation in primary education at the local level* <DECS/EGT [87] 33>.

Donaueschingen (Federal Republic of Germany). 36th Council of Europe Teachers' Seminar on *Equal opportunities for girls: the role of the primary school* <DECS/EGT [87] 37-E>.

B. Contact school plan

This plan, discussed in Chapter 6.2 of the Handbook, involved a network of 12 schools engaged in innovation sharing experiences under the direction of a Working Group. The areas of innovation were: educational goals and principles; organisation of education; content of education; organisation of the co-operation of the teaching staff; organisation of external contacts. The participating schools were:

Volksschule 15, Vienna, Austria
Kornesios Primary School, Nicosia, Cyprus
Bankagerskolan, Horsens, Denmark
Linnala School, Imatra, Finland
Schweitzer Grundschule, Freiburg, Germany (West)
128th Primary School, Athens, Greece
C. Laurenti School, Civitavecchia, Italy
H.K. Van Duyvenvoorde Primary School, Oost-Souburg, Netherlands
Vardåsen Primary School, Kristiansand, Norway
Fajanskolan, Falkenberg, Sweden
Guthirt Primary School, Zug, Switzerland
St. Aidan's Primary School, London, England.

C. Case studies of innovation

Fourteen case studies in ten member states were published in connection with Project No. 8. Each was monitored by one or more experts from elsewhere in the CDCC. The reports were submitted as follows:

1. *Spontaneous and individual learning in free choice periods (Montessori) in Salzburg*. Volkschule Liefering II, Salzburg, Austria. Report by Angela Anning (United Kingdom). <DECS/EGT [85] 62>

2. *School-based review as an introduction strategy for the new-style primary education (VLO) project in Belgium*. Flemish primary schools in Belgium. Report by Pieter Schuurman and others (Netherlands). <DECS/EGT [86] 65>

3. *Modified timetable arrangements in French-speaking Belgium*. Châtelet Athénée Royal Primary School. Report by Jean Rioult (France). <DECS/EGT [86] 56>

4. *The use of microcomputers in the primary schools of the city of Leeds*. Leeds, England. Report by A. A. Hermans (Netherlands). <DECS/EGT [85] 24>

5. *Delegation of decision making from State level to local authorities*. Vantaa Hiekkaharju, Finland. Report by Hrólfur Kjartansson (Iceland). <DECS/EGT [86] 54>

6. *The use of microcomputers in primary schools in Bar-le-Duc*. Bar-le-Duc, France. Report by Robert Dieschbourg (Luxembourg). <DECS/EGT [85] 44>

7. *Relations between school establishments and relations between the school and its social environment – ZEP (Zone d'éducation prioritaire – priority*

education area). Grigny-la-Grande-Borne, France. Report by Angel Logaro Martiny (Spain). <DECS/EGT [86] 17>

8. *The improvement of creative and aesthetic skills of children through art and drama in the city of Athens.* Maraslios Elementary Schools, Athens, Greece. Report by Stig Eriksson (Norway). <DECS/EGT [85] 56>
9. *Co-ordinated school work in Iceland.* Icelandic primary schools. Report by Maurice Galton (United Kingdom). <DECS/EGT [86] 36>
10. *Teaching through mass media for the acquisition of basic language skills.* Ceccherelli School, Modena, Italy. Report by J. Purtois and A. Forgione (Belgium). <DECS/EGT [86] 10>
11. *Parent–school relationship at the primary level of the basic school in Norway.* Vest-Agder County, Norway. Report by Leopold Kratochwil (Austria). <DECS/EGT [85] 65>
12. *Assistance to isolated schools in mountain regions in France.* EMALA Team Project, Département des Hautes-Alpes. Report by Paolo Orefice (Italy). <DECS/EGT [86] 56>
13. *School timetable reform in France.* Pierre et Marie Curie School, Pau, and primary schools at Le Teil, France. Report by Y. Tournier and P. Beumier (Belgium). <DECS/EGT [86] 55>
14. *School development in practice.* Discussion of 'Education Centres' as a means of introducing innovations in primary education in the Netherlands. Report by Anton Strittmatter (Switzerland). <DECS/EGT [87] 18>

D. Research workshops

1983

Neusiedl-am-See (Austria). Third all-European Conference of Directors of Educational Reseach Institutions on research devoted to primary education 5–10. <DECS/Rech [83] 56; DECS/EGT [84] Misc.7>

1984

Puidoux-Chexbres (Switzerland). Teaching research workshop on the renewal of mathematics teaching in the primary school. <DECS/Rech [84] 78; DECS/EGT [84] 78>

Edinburgh (Scotland). Research workshop on *Science and microcomputers in the primary school.* <DECS/Rech [84] 58; DECS/EGT [84] Misc.34>

1985

Madrid (Spain). Teaching research workshop on the development of the child in primary schools. <DECS/Rech [85] 61>

1986

Tilburg (Netherlands). Research workshop on *The learning of reading and writing*. <DECS/Rech [86] 80; DECS/EGT [87] Misc. 19>

Bibliography

General references to the Handbook as a whole are given in alphabetical order. Where exact page references are given in respect of particular chapters, those are specified in brackets. References to CDCC documentation are for the most part included in Appendix 2, but some additional CDCC citations are to be found in a separate list at the end of the Bibliography. These lists of CDCC documents should be examined in order to locate citations not included among the general references in the main list.

General

Akalin, O. (ed.) *The special school system in the Federal Republic of Germany.* Inter Nationes, Bonn, 1985.

Arbeitsgruppe Elternarbeit (ed.) *Elterninitiative: Reihe Materialen für die Elternarbeit.* Vol. 6. Deutsches Jugendinstitut, München, 1981, pp. 185ff, 193.

Ashford, S. H. 'Family matters', in R. Jowell, S. H. Witherspoon and L. Brook (eds) *British social attitudes. The 1987 Report.* Gower, Aldershot (England), 1987, p. 124.

Balacheff, N. *Recherches en didactique des mathématiques.* Editions La Pensée Sauvage, Grenoble, 1987.

Ball, D., Higgo, J., Oldnow, A., Straker, A. and Wood, J. *Will mathematics count?* AUCBE Publication, Endymion Road, Hatfield, Herts AL10 8AU, England, 1987.

Bassey, M. *Nine hundred primary school teachers.* NFER, Slough (England), 1978, pp. 68ff, 108.

Bastide, H. *Les enfants d'immigrés et l'enseignement français.* Presses Universitaires de France, Paris, 1982.

Beattie, N. M. *Professional parents: parent participation in four Western European countries.* Falmer Press, Lewes (UK), 1985 (for Chapter 4.1, pp. 27–63).

Benattig, R. *Les Migrants en Europe: quel avenir éducatif et culturel?* L'Harmattan, Paris, 1988.

Bendelow, P. 'Parent pressure forces admission of handicapped', *Times educational supplement*, 28 October 1988.

Beresford, P. *et al.* 'An ESN(s) school and the labour market', in I. Booth and J. Stratham (eds) *The nature of special education.* Croom Helm, London, 1982.

Bernbaum, G., Noble, G. and Whiteside, T. 'Intra-occupational prestige differentiation in teaching', in S. J. Eggleston (ed.), *Pedagogica Europaea*, 5, W. & R. Chambers, London, 1969, pp. 1–59.

Betænkning vedrørende folkeskolens specialundervising. Afgivet af det af Undervisningsministeriet den 22 februar 1984 nedsatte udvalg. Betænkning nr. 1092. Undervisningsministeriet, København, 1987.

Birch, H. G. and Gussow, J. D. *Disadvantaged children: health, nutrition and school failure*. New York, 1970, pp. 266f.

Birkelbach, B. U. 'Ausländische Eltern verändern unsere Elternarbeit', in *Theorie und Praxis der Sozialpädagogik*, 3, 1982, pp. 148ff.

Black, P. See Task Group on Assessment and Testing.

Blyth, W. A. L. *Development, experience and curriculum in primary education*. Croom Helm, London, 1984.

Bolam, R. *Innovation in in-service education and the training of teachers: practice and theory*. OECD/CERI, Paris, 1978.

Bolte, K. M. *Wandlungen und Strukturen in unserer Gesellschaft: Untersuchungsbericht des soziologischen Seminars der Universität Kiel*. University of Kiel, Kiel (Federal Republic of Germany), 1955.

Boocock, S. S. 'The social context of childhood', in *Proceedings of the American Philosophical Society: ecology of child development 6*, 119, 1975, p. 423.

Booth, T. *National perspectives*. Open University Press, Milton Keynes (England), 1982.

Boppel, W. and Kollenberg, U. *Mitbestimmung in der Schule*. Köln, 1981, pp. 35f.

Borgmeier, C. M., Foellingalbers, M. and Nilshon, J. *Situation Schulanfang: Analysen: Anregungen*. Stuttgart/Berlin, 1980.

Boucher, L. *Tradition and change in Swedish education*. Pergamon, Oxford (England), 1982.

Brembeck, C. S. 'Education for self-renewal', in J. W. Hansen and C. S. Brembeck (eds) *Education and the development of nations*. Holt, Rinehart and Winston, New York, 1966.

Broadfoot, P. *et al.* 'Teachers' conceptions of their professional responsibility: some international comparisons', *Comparative education*, 23, 3, 1987, pp. 287–301.

Broadfoot, P., Osborn, M., Gilly, M. and Paillet, A. 'What responsibility means to teachers: national contexts and classroom constants', *British journal of sociology of education*, 9, 3, 1988, pp. 265–87.

Brown, J. S. and Burton, R. R. 'Diagnostic models for procedural bugs in basic mathematical skills', *Cognitive science*, 2, 1978, pp. 155–91.

Brown, J. S. and van Lehn, K. 'Repair theory: a generative theory of bugs in procedural skills', *Cognitive science*, 4, 1980, pp. 379–426.

Bruner, J. S. *The process of education*. Harvard University Press, Cambridge, Mass., 1966.

Buchan, L., Clemerson, J. and Davis, H. 'Working with families of children with special needs: the parent-adviser scheme', in *Child care, health and development*, 2, 1988, pp. 81–91.

Buckley, J. *The training of secondary school heads in western Europe*. NFER–Nelson, Windsor (UK), 1985.

Bürgerschaft der Freien und Hansestadt Hamburg. *Mitteilung des Senats an die Bürgerschaft. Bericht über die Schulversuche Vorschulklasse und Eingangsstufe*. Drucksache 9/4384 vom 30.3. 1982.

Burns, J. *The study of parental involvement in four federal education programs; executive summary*. Department of Education Office of Planning, Budget and Evaluation, Washington, DC, 1982

Burstall, Clare. *Primary French in the balance*. NFER, Slough (UK), 1974.

Burton, R. R. 'Diagnosing bugs in a simple procedural skill', in D. H. Sleeman and J. S. Brown (eds) *Intelligent tutoring systems*. Academic Press, London, 1982.

Busch, Fr. W. 'Elternhaus und Schule in der DDR', K. Schleicher (ed.) *Elternhaus und Schule: Kooperation ohne Erfolg*. Schwann, Düsseldorf, 1972.

Caré, C. and Lafond, A. 'France', in C. Hopes (ed.) *The school leader and school improvement: case studies from ten OECD countries*. Technical Report No. 2 of the ISIP Project. OECD, ACCO, Leuven (Belgium), 1986.

Cardinet, J. *Les Modèles de l'évaluation scolaire et pratique*. De Boeck, Brussels, 1986.

Carrel, A. *Mennesket, det ukendte*. Gyldendal, København, 1936.

Castle, E. B. *Ancient education and today*. Penguin Books, Harmondsworth, 1961.

Cecchini, M. and McCleary, I. 'Pre-school handicapped in Italy: a research-based developmental model', in *Journal of the division for early childhood*, 9, 31, 1985, pp. 254–65.

Centraal Bureau voor het Katholiek Onderwijs *et al*. *Medezeggenschap in het onderwijs*, deel 1–2, Gravenhage, 1982.

Centre for Educational Research and Innovation (CERI). *Creativity of the school*. OECD, Paris, 1978.

Chall, J. S. *Learning to read: the great debate*. 2nd edn, revised. McGraw Hill, New York, 1983a.

Chall, J. S. *Stages of reading development*. McGraw Hill, New York, 1983b.

Chapman, L. J. *Reading: from 5–11 years*. Open University Press, Milton Keynes (England), 1987.

Chin, R. and Benne, K. D. 'General strategies for effecting changes in human systems', in W. G. Bennis, K. D. Benne and R. Chin (eds) *The planning of change*. 2nd edn. Holt, Rinehart & Winston, New York, 1969.

Christiansen, P. E. *et al*. *Det synlige sprog*. Bibliotekscentralen, Ballerup (Denmark), 1987.

Clark, M. M. *Young fluent readers: what can they teach us?* Heinemann Educational, London, 1976.

Clay, M. M. 'Early childhood and cultural diversity in New Zealand', *Reading teacher*, 29, 1976, pp. 333–42.

Clunies-Ross, L. and Wimhurst, S. *The right balance: provision for slow learners in secondary schools*. NFER-Nelson, Windsor, 1983.

Cohen, M. 'Effective schools: what research tells us', *State education leader*, Summer 1982.

Coulson, A. A. 'The role of the primary head', in T. Bush *et al.* (eds) *Approaches to school management*. Harper & Row, London, 1980.

Council of Europe. 'A European charter for the regional and minority languages of Europe', *Western European education*, 17, 1, 1985, pp. 16–18.

Csapo, M. 'Special education in the USSR: trends and accomplishments', *Remedial and special education*, 5, 2, 1984, pp. 5–15.

Cullen, H. 'SEN provision in France', *Support for learning*, 1, 1, 1985, pp. 27–8.

Cunningham, C. and Davis, H. *Working with parents: framework for collaboration*. Open University Press, Milton Keynes (England), 1985.

Cyster, R., Clift, P. S. and Battle, S. 'Parental involvement in primary schools', in *A report of the National Foundation for Educational Research in England and Wales*. NFER, Windsor (England), 1979, pp. 31ff, 53, 60, 70, 199.

Dalby, M. A. *et al. Bogen om læsning I – forudsætninger og status*. Munksgaard/Danmarks pædagogiske Institut, København, 1983.

Dalby, M. A. *et al. Bogen om læsning II – en fædighed i udvikling*. Munksgaard/Danmarks pædagogiske Institut, København, 1989.

Davies, D. 'Parental involvement in the public schools: opportunities for administrators', *Education and urban society*, 2, 1987, pp. 158f.

Davies, J. and Davies, P. A. 'Parents, teachers and children with special needs', in C. Cullingford (ed.) *Parents, teachers and schools*. Royce Ltd, London, 1985, p. 119.

Department of Education and Science (Ministry of Education). *Parent-teacher relations in schools*. Education Survey 5. HMSO, London, 1962, p. 2.

Department of Education and Science (for Central Advisory Council for Education [England]). *Children and their primary schools* (Plowden Report). HMSO, London, 1967 (for Chapter 4.1, pp. 32ff).

Department of Education and Science. *A new partnership for our schools* (Taylor Report). Report of Committee of Enquiry appointed by the Secretaries of State for Education and Science. HMSO, London, 1977.

Department of Education and Science. *Special educational needs* (Warnock Report). Report of the Committee of Enquiry into handicapped children and young people. HMSO, London, 1978a (for Chapter 4.1, p. 155).

Department of Education and Science. *Primary education in England: a survey by H.M. Inspectors of Schools.* HMSO, London, 1978b, p. 26.

Department of Education and Science. *Circulars and administrative memoranda issued in 1981.* HMSO, London, 1982, p. 32.

Department of Education and Science. *Parental influence at school: a new framework for school government in England and Wales.* 'Green Paper' presented to Parliament. HMSO, London, 1984, pp. 1, 11, 12–19, 29.

Department of Education and Science. 'The curriculum from 5–16', *Curriculum Matters No. 2.* HMSO, London, 1985.

Department of Education and Science. *Mathematics for ages 5 to 16.* DES and Welsh Office, London and Cardiff, 1988a.

Department of Education and Science. *Teaching quality.* HMSO, London, 1988b.

Department of Education for Northern Ireland. *Report of the working party on educational welfare.* HMSO, Belfast, 1976.

Dewey, J. 'Knowledge is no longer an immobile soil; it has been liquified'; from 'The school and society', in M. S. Dworkin, *Dewey on education.* Teachers College Press, Columbia University, New York, 1967.

Dolch, J. *Das Elternrecht in der Erziehung.* Langensalza (Republic of Germany), 1928.

Donaldson, M. *Children's minds.* Fontana, London, 1978.

Dottrens, R. *The primary school curriculum.* UNESCO, Paris, 1962.

Douglas, J. W. B. *The home and the school.* National Children's Bureau, London, 1969.

Douglas, J. W. B., Ross, J. H. and Simpson, H. R. *All our future: a longitudinal study of secondary education.* London, 1968, pp. 83ff.

Dovala, M. *Experiments and innovations in the primary level curriculum in Hungary.* UNESCO, Institute for Education, Hamburg, 1985.

Downing, J. *Comparative reading: cross-national study of behavior and processes in reading and writing.* Macmillan, New York, 1973.

Doyle, W. and Ponder, C. 'The practicality ethic in teacher decision making' (mimeo). North State University of Texas, 1976.

Ekholm, M. 'School reforms and local response: an evaluation of school reviews in 35 school management areas in Sweden 1980–1985', *Compare*, 17, 2, 1987.

Ekholm, M. '"Inavel" bland skolledarna försvagar ledarskapet', *Skolledaren*, 4, 1988.

Ekholm, M. and Sandström, B. *Skolledarskap och skolledarroll. En enkätundersökning.* Skolledarutbildningens skriftserie, Linköping, 1982.

Elliott, J. 'Supporting teachers' research in the classroom', *New Era*, 54, 1973.

Elliott, J. 'Facilitating action research in schools: some dilemmas', in R. Burgess (ed.) *Field methods in the study of education.* Falmer Press, Lewes (England), 1985, pp. 235–62.

Elstgeest, J. 'Encounter, interaction, dialogue', in W. Harlen (ed.) *Primary science: taking the plunge*. Heinemann, London, 1985.

Elstgeest, J. 'Children, mirrors and reflections: Children and the science of water, Children do science in their environment: Soap films and bubbles'. Regional Pedagogic Centre of Zeeland (RPCZ) (mimeo), Middelburg (Neths), 1987.

Elvin, H. L. (ed.) *The educational systems in the European community: a guide*. NFER-Nelson, Windsor (UK), 1981.

Ennever, L. and Harlen, W. *With objectives in mind*. Schools Council Science 5/13 Project. Macdonald Educational, London, 1972.

Epstein, J. L. 'Parent involvement. What research says to administrators', *Education and Urban Society*, 2, 1987, pp. 123f.

Epstein, J. L. and Becker, H. J. 'Teachers' reported practices of parent involvement: problems and possibilities', *Elementary school record*, 2, 83, 1982, pp. 80, 95.

Federal Republic of Germany. *The state of the handicapped*. Government Report, 1984.

Fehrmann, P. G., Keith, T. A. and Reimers, T. H. M. 'Home influence on school learning: direct and indirect effects of parental involvement on high school grades', *Journal of educational research*, 6, 1987, pp. 330–7.

Feilitzen, D. V. 'Ergebnisse skandinavischer Forschungen zum Thema: Kind und Fernsehen im Sozialisationsprozeß', *Fernsehen und Bildung*, 2–3, 1975, pp. 143ff.

Feuerstein, R. *The dynamic assessment of retarded performers*. University Park Press, Baltimore, Md, 1979.

Feyler, J. and Hutin, R. 'L'Expérience "Fluidité" (canton de Genève)', in J.-P. Meylan (ed.) *Evaluation d'innovations dans l'école primaire*. Haupt, Berne, 1981.

Fink, A. H. and Friend, M. 'Special education', in T. Husén and N. Postlethwaite (eds) *International encylopaedia of education; researches and studies*. Vol. 8. Pergamon Press, Oxford (England), 1985.

Flesza, G. 'Elternarbeit als wichtige Komponente für Unterricht und Erziehung ausländischer Schüler', *Blätter für Lehrerfortbildung*, 6, 1982, pp. 260ff.

Follain, M. 'Change under way despite doubts over interference', *Times educational supplement*, 16 September 1988, p. 21.

Fowler, G. 'Falling school rolls and home-school links', in M. Craft, J. Raynor and L. Cohen (eds). *Linking home and school: a new review*. Longman, London, 1983, pp. 21, 35.

Frehner, H. 'Switzerland', in C. Hopes (ed.) *The school leader and school improvement: case studies from ten OECD countries*. Technical Report No. 2 of the ISIP Project. OECD, ACCO, Leuven (Belgium), 1986.

Freie und Hansestadt Hamburg. *Behörde für Schule und Berufsbilding: Amt für Schule, Referat vorschülische Erziehung und Grundschule, Handreich-*

ung; Mitarbeit von Eltern im Unterricht der Grundschule. Hamburg, 1981, p. 2.

Friend, J.E. and Burton, R.R. 'Teacher's guide for diagnostic testing in arithmetic: subtraction' (xerox). Palo Alto Research Center, Palo Alto, California, 1980.

Frith, U. 'Reading by eye and ear', in P.A. Kolers *et al.* (eds) *Processing of visible language. I*. Plenum, New York, 1979.

Frith, U. 'Beneath the surface of developmental dyslexia', in K.E. Patterson *et al. Surface dyslexia: neuropsychological and cognitive studies of phonological reading*. Lawrence Erlbaum Associates, London, 1985, pp. 301–30.

Fullan, M. *The meaning of educational change*. Teachers College Press, Columbia University, New York, 1982.

Fullan, M. 'Change processes and strategies at the local level', *Elementary school journal*, 85, 3, 1985, pp. 391–421.

Furneaux, B. *Special parents*. Open University Press, Milton Keynes (England), 1988.

Gallup, G.H. 'The 12th annual Gallup Poll of the public's attitudes toward the public schools', *Phi Delta Kappan*, 62, 1, 1980, pp. 36ff.

Galton, M., Simon, B. and Croll, P. *Inside the primary classroom*. Routledge & Kegan Paul, London, 1980.

Galton, M., Bernbaum, G., Patrick, H. and Appleyard, R. *Curriculum provision in small primary schools*. A report to the Department of Education and Science. University of Leicester School of Education, 1985.

Gather Thurler, M. and Kopmels, D. *Innovation dans l'enseignement primaire*. CDIP, Berne, 1988.

Gather Thurler, M. and Perrenoud, P. (eds) *Savoir évaluer pour mieux enseigner – quelle formation des maîtres?* Cahier No. 26. SRS, Genève, 1988.

Ghilardi, F. 'Dynamics of curriculum reform in primary education in Italy'. Unpublished paper, 1988.

Gonzales-Tirados, R.M. 'Programme for the training of school directors in Spain', in S. Hegarty (ed.) *Training for management in schools*. Council of Europe. NFER-Nelson, Windsor (England), 1983.

Gordon, I.J. *Parent involvement in compensatory education*. Urbana, Illinois, 1970.

Gordon, T. *T.E.T.: teacher effectiveness training*. Peter Wyden, New York, 1974.

Gordosné Szabó, A. 'The science of special education in Hungary', *International journal of special education*, 1, 1, 1986, pp. 93–102.

Grabbe, B. *Chancen und Elternmitarbeit im Unterricht der Grundschule*. Frankfurt-am-Main, 1983, pp. 34ff.

Gray, W.S. *The teaching of reading and writing*. UNESCO, Paris, 1956.

Grothloh-Amberg, H. 'Beeinflussung des Verhaltens durch den Schuleintritt', *Beiheft zur schweizische Zeitschrift für Psychologie und ihre Anwendung*, 52, 1971, p. 55.

Günther, M. and Heitmeyer, W. 'Eltern und Schule-Einstellung und Voraussetzungen', in *Arbeitsgemeinschaft demokratischer Bildungswerke/Heimvolkshochschule.* Schulmitwirkung und Schulalltag, Teil II, Bielefeld (Federal Republic of Germany), 1981, p. 171.

Habermas, J. *Legitimation crisis.* Heinemann, London, 1976.

Hagen, P. *Hoe wij leren lezen.* Zwijsen, Tilburg (Neths), 1984.

Hall, E. T. *Beyond culture.* Doubleday, New York, 1976.

Hallahan, D. P. and Kauffman, J. M. *Exceptional children.* 3rd edn. Prentice-Hall, Englewood Cliffs, 1986.

Halls, W. D. *Education, culture and politics in modern France.* Pergamon, Oxford (England), 1976.

Halsey, A. H., Floud, J. E. and Anderson, C. A. (eds) *Education, economy and society.* Free Press, New York, 1967, p. 3.

Hämäläinen, K. *Skolans föreståndare och skolans utveckling.* Finlands Stadsförbund, Karis (Finland), 1986.

Hannon, P. and Jackson, A. 'Educational home-visiting and the teaching of reading', in J. Bastiani (ed.) *Perspectives on home-school relations.* NFER-Nelson, Windsor (England), 1987, pp. 248ff.

Hansen, D. A. 'Family-school articulations: the effects of interaction rule mismatch', *American educational research journal,* 4, 1986, pp. 643–59.

Harland, J. and Lawton, D. 'The development of comprehensive education for the 11–16 age-group in England', *International journal of educational research,* 12, 15, 1988, pp. 461–70.

Harlen, W. *Teaching and learning primary science.* Harper & Row, London, 1985.

Harlen, W. and Tanuputra, G. *Education, industry and technology in the primary school.* Proceedings of International Conference on Science, Technology and Human Needs, Bangalore, India. ICSU/CTS, Paris, 1985.

Harris T. L. and Hodges, R. E. (eds) *A dictionary of reading and related terms.* International Reading Association, Newark, Del, 1981.

Havelock, R. G. *Planning for innovation through dissemination and utilization of knowledge.* Institute for Social Research, University of Michigan, Ann Arbor, Mich, 1971.

Havelock, R. G. *The change agent's guide to innovation in education.* Prentice-Hall, Englewood Cliffs, NJ, 1973.

Havlicek, D. and Steinmann, M. *Radio, Fernsehen und Kinder.* SRG-Forschungsdienst, Bern, 1980.

Hawkins, D. 'I, thou and it', *Daedalus: Journal Academy of Arts and Science,* 94, 2, 1965.

Hawkins, D. *The informed vision: essays on learning and human nature.* Agathon Press, New York, 1974.

Hayes, C. W. 'A Belgian approach to learning disabilities' (mimeo). Paper presented to the World Congress on Future Special Education, Stirling (Scotland), 1978.

Hearnden, A. *Education, culture and politics in West Germany*. Pergamon, London, 1976.

Heiberg, K. and Crogh, T. *Læsemetoder og læseaktiviteter: en kommenteret oversigt*. Danmarks pædagogiske Institut, København, 1983.

Heidegger, B. 'The German school system – and integration', *Support for learning*, 3, 1, 1988, pp. 41–3.

Heller, W. (ed.) *Ecole primaire suisse: une école pour apprendre: 22 thèses pour le développement de l'école primaire*. CDIP, Berne, 1986.

Helliwell, D. (ed.) *New challenges for teachers and their education*. Committee of Senior Officials, a Report prepared by ATEE, 1986.

Henderson, A. *Parent participation: student achievement; the evidence grows*. National Committee for Citizens' Education, Columbia, Md, 1981.

Hennessy, S., Evertsz, R., Ellis, D., Black, P., O'Shea, T. and Floyd, A. *Design specification for 'Shopping on Mars', a computer-based educational activity*. Technical Report No. 29. Centre for Information Technology, Open University, Milton Keynes (England), 1988.

Herzberg, F. *Work and the nature of man*. World Publishing Co., Pittsburgh (USA), 1966.

Hildbrand, J. *Versuchsmodelle im Sonderklassenwesen*. Pädagogische Abteilung der Erziehungsdirektion, Zürich, 1987.

Hill, C. Report of a Parliamentary Group Video Enquiry (Guildford Report). *Video, violence and children: children's viewing patterns in England and Wales*. Part I. HMSO, London, 1983.

HM Inspectors of Schools (England and Wales). *Education in the Federal Republic of Germany: aspects of curriculum and assessment*. HMSO, London, 1986.

HM Inspectors of Schools (England and Wales). *Aspects of primary education in the Netherlands*. HMSO, London, 1987.

Hobbs, N., Dokecki, P. P. *et al. Strengthening families*. Jossey-Bass, San Francisco, 1984.

Hodge, R. W., Treiman, D. J. and Rossi, P. 'A comparative study of occupational prestige', in R. Bendix and S. M. Lipset (eds) *Class, status and power: social comparative perspective*. 2nd edn. Free Press, New York, 1966.

Hopes, C. (ed.) *The school leader and school improvement: case studies from ten OECD countries*. Technical Report No. 2 of the ISIP Project. OECD, ACCO, Leuven (Belgium), 1986.

Hornby, G., Murray, R. and Jones, R. 'Establishing a parent-to-parent service', *Child care, health and development*, 4, 1987, pp. 277–86.

House, E. R. 'Three perspectives of innovations: technological, political and cultural', in R. Lehming and M. Kane (eds) *Improving schools: using what we know*. Sage Publications, Beverly Hills, Calif, 1981.

House of Commons Education, Science and Arts Committee. *Achievement in primary schools*. Vols 1 and 2. HMSO, London, 1986. (See also Appendix 1 of this Handbook.)

Hoyle, E. 'Professionality, professionalism and control in teaching', *London educational review*, 3, 2, 1974, pp. 13–19.

Hoyle, E. 'Professionalization and deprofessionalization in education', in E. Hoyle and J. Megarry (eds) *World yearbook of education 1980: the professional development of teachers*. Kogan Page, London, 1980.

Hoyle, E. 'The professionalization of teachers: a paradox', *British journal of educational studies*, 3, 2, 1982, pp. 161–71.

Hoyle, E. 'The social background of teachers', in *International encyclopaedia of education*. Pergamon, London, 1985, pp. 5073–85.

Hoyle, E. 'Teachers' roles and careers', in *Managing schools*, Open University Course E325. Open University Press, Milton Keynes (England), 1988, pp. 7–20.

Hoyles, C. 'Scaling a mountain – a study of the use, discrimination and generalisation of some mathematical concepts in a LOGO environment', *European journal of psychology of education*, 1, 2, 1986, pp. 111–26.

Hoyles, C. and Noss, R. 'Children working in a structured LOGO environment: from doing to understanding', in N. Balacheff (ed.) *Recherches en didactique des mathématiques*. Editions La Pensée Sauvage, Grenoble, 1987.

Huberman, M. (ed.) *Assurer la réussite des apprentissages scolaires? Les propositions de la pédagogie de maîtrise*. Delachaux & Niestlé, Paris, 1988.

Huberman, M. and Miles, M. *Innovation up close: how school improvement works*, 1984.

Huelshoff, R., Gille, R. *et al. Eltern und Lehrer: Theorie und Praxis schülischer Elternarbeit*. Paderborn (Federal Republic of Germany), 1979, p. 14.

Huettenmoser, M. 'Probleme des Uebergangs vom Kindergarten in die Grundschule', in J.P. Meylan (ed.) *Evaluation d'innovations dans l'école primaire*. Haupt, Berne, 1981.

Jackson, A.C., Fletcher, C. and Messer, D. 'Effects of experience on microcomputer use in primary schools: results of a second survey', *Journal of computer-assisted learning*, 4, 1988, pp. 214–26.

Jacquet, F. 'Evaluation d'un nouveau programme de mathématique dans les écoles primaires de Suisse romande', in *Bulletin CDIP 23(b)*, Conférence Suisse des Directeurs Cantonaux de l'Instruction Publique, Genève, 1980, pp. 33–43.

Jansen, M. *Danskmetodik*, Gjellerup, København, 1959.

Jansen, M. *How long will we go on waiting for 'the great pumpkin'?* Paper read at Second World Congress on Reading. Danish Institute for Educational Research, København, 1968.

Jansen, M. *Danske læsebøger 1–7, skoleår. I. del. Registrering stering og analyse. II de. Forfatter- og titelregister.* Danmarks pædagogiske Institut, 1969, nr. 70.

Jansen, M. 'A country with no illiterates – but a threatening situation for severely disabled readers', *Journal of reading*, 30, 7, 1987, p. 601.

Jansen, M. *Readers - and reading development - with emphasis on the importance of children's reading and children's literature now and in the future society.* Danish Institute for Educational Research, København, 1988.

Jansen, M., Jacobsen, B. and Jensen, P.E. *The teaching of reading - without really any method: an analysis of reading instruction in Denmark.* Munksgaard, København and Humanities Press, NJ (USA), 1978.

Jansen, M., Kreiner, S., Krogh, T. and Nielsen, H.W. *Sproglige forudsætninger og senere skolegangsresultater.* Søllerød kommune/Forlaget Skolepsykologi/Danmarks pædagogiske Institut, København, 1987. Den blå serie nr. 10.

Jónsdóttir, S. 'Human being and environment: innovation project in the canton of Lucerne (Switzerland) compared to the Social Science Curriculum Project in Iceland'. Lecture given in Montreux, Switzerland, 1988.

Jönsson, A. *TV ett hot eller en resours för barn. En longitudinell studie av relationarena mellan TV och skola.* Disputats. CWK Gleerup, Malmö (Sweden), 1985.

Jørgensen, S. *Special education in the European community.* ECSC, 1980.

Jowett, S. and Baginsky, M. 'Parents and education: a survey of their involvement and a discussion of some issues', *Educational research journal*, 1, 1988, pp. 36ff.

Joyce, B. and Showers, B. 'Improving in-service training: the messages of research', *Educational leadership*, 37, 1980, pp. 379–85.

Karplus, R. 'The science curriculum improvement study', *Journal of research in science teaching*, 2, 1964, pp. 293–303.

Kelly, C. 'The Polish road', *Special children*, April 1988a, pp. 10–12.

Kelly, C. 'Defending choice in Norway', *Special children*, 1988b (OU), pp. 8–9.

Keyes, C. *Ethnic change.* University of Washington Press, Seattle, 1981.

Kifer, E. 'Home environment and the IEA surveys' (mimeo). University of Kentucky, Lexington, 1975.

King, E.J. *Other schools and ours: comparative studies for today.* 5th edn. Holt, Rinehart & Winston, London, 1979.

Kob, J. *Das soziale Berufsbewusstsein des Lehrers der höheren Schule: eine soziologische Lehrtstudie.* Werkbund, Würzburg (Federal Republic of Germany), 1958: also 'Definition of the teacher's role', in A.H. Halsey, J. Floud and C.A. Anderson (eds) *Education, economy and society.* Free Press, New York, 1961.

Kogan, M. 'Parents and school governing bodies', in C. Cullingford (ed.) *Parents, teachers and schools.* Royce Ltd, London, 1985, pp. 64ff.

Koivumäki, S., Korpinen, E. and Pekkala, E. 'Parent–teacher conferences as a form of home-school cooperation', *Institute for Educational Research Bulletin*, 152, 1980.

Kopmels, D. *The Zeeland Small Schools Project*. RPCZ, Middelburg (Neths), 1987.

Korpinen, E., Husso, M. L. and Korpinen, R. *Collaboration between home and school*. Parts II and III. Finnish Institute for Educational Research, 1980.

Korpinen, E. and Lang, A. 'Experiment on verbal school reports and collaboration between home and school II. Parents' views of the experiment and the effects of the experiment', *Institute for Educational Research Bulletin*, 132, 1979.

Kozma, T. *An evaluation of the leadership training courses and recommendations for their improvement*. Information Report. Hungarian Institute for Educational Research, Budapest, 1984.

Krustup, E. V. 'Chokerende bibliotekstal', *Det danske Bogmarked*, 133, 50, 1987a, pp. 1687–92.

Krustup, E. V. 'Nærbilleder af bogsalget 1987', *Det danske Bogmarked*, 134, 39, 1987b, pp. 1245–53.

Kulkarni, D. and Simon, H. A. 'The processes of scientific discovery: the strategy of experimentation', *Cognitive psychology*, 12, 1988, pp. 139–73.

Lanier, J. E. *Research on teacher education*. Occasional Paper No. 80. Institute for Research on Teaching. Michigan State University, East Lansing, Mich., 1984, pp. 132–3.

Larson, M. S. *The rise of professionalism*. University of California Press, Berkeley (USA), 1977.

Leger, Alain. 'Les Déterminants des carrières enseignantes', *Revue française de sociologie*, 22, 1981, pp. 549–74.

Leggatt, T. 'Teaching as a profession', in J. A. Jackson (ed.) *Professions and professionalisation*. Cambridge University Press, Cambridge (England), 1970, pp. 157–77.

Leithwood, K. and Montgomery, D. J. 'The role of the elementary school principal in program improvement', *Review of educational research*, 52, 1982, pp. 309–39.

Lesourne, J. *Education et société demain*. Rapport au Ministre de l'Education nationale. La Découverte. Le Monde de l'Education, Paris, 1987.

Levine, K. 'Functional literacy: fond illusions and false economies', *Harvard educational review*, 52, 1982, pp. 249–66.

Lewis, H. D. *The French education system*. Croom Helm, London, 1985.

Lewis, R. *Learning through microworlds*. Occasional Paper ITW/26/28. Department of Psychology, University of Lancaster (England), 1988.

Liegle, L. *Familienerziehung und sozialer Wandel in der Sowjetunion*. Berlin, 1970, pp. 8ff, 14.

Liell, P. and Saunders, J. B. (eds) *The law of education*. 9th edn. Butterworth, London, 1986, pp. B 384ff.

Lindell, E. 'Vent lidt med revolutionen!', in A. W. Edfeldt, E. Lindell *et al. LTG, for og imod – og hvad siger svensk forskning Læserapport*, 5, Landsforeningen af Læsepædagoger, København, 1982, pp. 13–20.

LIS (Ledelse i skolen). *Rammeplan for ledelseutvikling i grunnskolen*. Grunnskolerådet, Oslo, 1988.

Lloyd, K. 'Management and leadership in the primary school', in M. Hughes, P. Ribbins and H. Thomas (eds) *Managing education: the system and the institution*. Holt, Rinehart & Winston, London, 1985.

Louis, K. S. 'Dissemination systems: some lessons from programs of the past', in W. J. Paisley and M. Butler (eds) *Knowledge utilisation: systems in education: dissemination, technical assistance, networking*. Sage Publications, Beverly Hills/London, 1983, pp. 65–88.

Lundberg, I. *Språk och läsning*. Liber, Stockholm, 1984.

Lundberg, I., Frost, J. and Petersen, O.-P. 'Effects of an extensive program for stimulating phonological awareness in preschool children', *Reading research quarterly*, XXIII, 3, 1988, pp. 263–84.

Lundgren, U. P. 'The development of the Middle School in Sweden: research and evaluation', *International journal of educational research*, 12, 5, 1988, pp. 481–94.

Lynch, E. W. and Stein, R. C. 'Parent participation by ethnicity: a comparison of hispanic, black and Anglo families', *Exceptional children*, 54, 2, 1987, pp. 105–11.

Lynch, J. and Pinlott, J. *Parents and teachers*. Schools Council Research Studies, London, 1976, p. 7.

MacBeth, A. *Das Kind dazwischen; ein Bericht über die Beziehung zwischen Schule und Familie in den Mitgliedsstaaten der Europäischen Gemeinschaft*. Kommission der europäischen Gemeinschaften, Bildungsreihe No. 13, Luxembourg, 1984, pp. 32f, 124f.

MacBeth, A., Mackenzie, M. and Breckenridge, I. (Scottish School Councils). *Policy-making: participation or irrelevance?* HMSO, Edinburgh, 1980, pp. 30f, 34ff, 43.

McCleary, I. D. and Buchanan, M. 'Current trends and issues in special education in selected European countries', *International journal of special education*, 2, 1, 1987, pp. 25–39.

MacDonald, B. and Walker, R. *Changing the curriculum*. Open Books, London, 1976.

McGee, J. J., Madeira, R. and Mendlascino, F. 'Integration in Portugal', *Teaching exceptional children*, 20, 1, 1987, pp. 26–7.

McLean, M. 'The Conservative education policy in comparative perspective', *British journal of educational studies*, 36, 3, 1988, pp. 200–17.

Maddaford, C. A. 'International parent–teacher relations', in T. M. Cluderay, *Home and school relations. Aspects of education*, 18, University of Hull, Hull (England), 1972, p. 68.

Maguire, M. Article in OECD *Observer*, 148, October/November 1987.

Mallinson, V. *The Western European idea in education*. Pergamon Press, Oxford (UK), 1980.

Mannschatz, E. 'Special education in the German Democratic Republic', *Prospects*, 6, 4, 1976, pp. 637–40.

Marchesi, A. 'Project for integration of pupils with special needs in Spain', *European journal of special needs education*, 1, 2, 1986, pp. 125–33.

Marjoribanks, K. 'Evaluation studies: schools, families and children's achievements', *Studies in educational evaluation*, 3, 1980, pp. 253–64.

Mayer, E. G. *'Tat'-sachen: Beiträge zur Erstellung des Schulprograms für den Sachunterricht in der Grundschule* (Nordrhein-Westfalen). Agentur Dieck, Heinsburg (Federal Republic of Germany), 1985.

Mendras, H. 'Fluctuations et tendances longues des valeurs et des idéologies', in J. Lesourne, *Education et société demain*. Rapport au Ministre de l'Education nationale. La Découverte. Le Monde de l'Education, Paris, 1987.

Merry, R. 'The education of children with special educational needs in England', *International review of education*, 32, 1986, pp. 23–32.

Merton, R. K. *et al. The student physician*. Harvard University Press, Cambridge, Mass., 1957.

Miles, M. 'Unravelling the mystery of institutionalization', *Educational leadership*, 41, 3, 1983.

Miles, M. B. and Ekholm, M. 'School improvement at the school level', in W. van Velzen, M. B. Miles, M. Ekholm, U. Hameyer and D. Robin. *Making school improvement work: a conceptual guide to practice*. ISIP-OECD. ACCO, Leuven (Belgium), 1985.

Ministère de l'Education nationale and Ministerie van Onderwijs. *Educational developments in Belgium*. Brussels, 1986.

Ministry of Education (Denmark). *The school, the pupil and the parents: a guide to cooperation between the home and the school*. København, 1979, p. 5.

Ministry of Education (Greece). 'Greece: special education: an overview', *Western European education*, 16, 2, 1981, pp. 85–7.

Ministry of Education and Science (Netherlands). *Special education in the Netherlands*. The Hague, 1979.

Mitter, W. 'Elternhaus und Schule in der Sowjetunion', in K. Schleicher (ed.) *Elternhaus und Schule. Kooperation ohne Erfolg*. Schwann, Düsseldorf, 1972.

Moles, A. *Sociodynamique de la culture*. Mouton, Paris-la-Haye, 1968.

Moles, O. C. 'Synthesis of recent research on parent participation in children's education', *Education leadership*, 2, 1982, pp. 44ff.

Montagner, H. *Les Rythmes de l'enfant et de l'adolescent*. Stock, Paris, 1983.

Morin, E. *Pour sortir du vingtième siècle*. Nathan, Paris, 1981.

Mortimore, P., Sammons, P. *et al. School matters: the junior years*. Open Books, London, 1988.

National Education Association (NEA). 'Nationwide teacher opinion poll' (mimeo). Washington, DC, 1981.

Neave, G. *The EEC and education*. Trentham Books, Stoke-on-Trent (England), 1984.

Nias, J. 'Teacher satisfaction and dissatisfaction: Herzberg's "two-factor" hypothesis re-visited', *British journal of sociology of education*, 2, 3, 1981, pp. 235–44.

Norwegian Ministry of Church and Education. Act of 13 June 1969, No. 24, concerning the basic school, and supplementary Act of 13 June 1975. Oslo, n.d., pp. 5, 23.

Norwegian Ministry of Church and Education. *Education in Norway*. Oslo, 1982, pp. 44f.

Oertel, L., Rosenberg, S. and Aeberli, Ch. 'Abteilungsübergreifende Versuche an der Oberstufe im Kanton Zürich', *Education et recherche*, 3, 1986, pp. 73–114.

ONISEP. *Guide pratique de la scolarité*. ONISEP, Paris, 1982.

Organization for Economic Cooperation and Development. *Reviews of national policies for education: Italy*. OECD, Paris, 1985.

Organization for Economic Cooperation and Development. *Reviews of national policies for education: Spain*. OECD, Paris, 1986.

Organization for Economic Cooperation and Development. *Reviews of national policies for education: Iceland*. OECD, Paris, 1987.

O'Shea, T. and Self, J. A. *Learning and teaching with computers*. Prentice Hall, New York, 1983.

O'Shea, T., Evertsz, R., Hennessy, S., Floyd, A., Fox, M. and Elsomcook, M. *Artificial intelligence and education: intelligent computer-assisted instructions*. Chapman & Hall, London, 1988.

Papert, S. *Mindstorms: children, computers and powerful ideas*. Harvester Press, Brighton (England), 1980.

Parsons, T. *The social system*. Free Press, Glencoe, Ill., 1951.

Parsons, T. 'Professions', in *International encylopaedia of the social sciences*. Collier-Macmillan, New York, 1968.

Passon, M. 'Beyond Commission reports: towards meaningful school improvement', in A. Liberman (ed.) *Rethinking school improvement: research, craft, concept*. Teachers College Press, Columbia University, New York, 1986.

Paulig, P. 'Family and school from the point of view of parents and pupils' (mimeo). Paper presented at meeting of International Union of Family Organisations Commission on Education. München, 6–8 October 1983.

Peaker, G. F. *The Plowden children four years later*. NFER, Slough (England), 1971.

Pekkala, E. and Koivumäki, S. 'Personal discussion as one form of collaboration between home and school. Part II', *Institute for Educational*

Research Bulletin, 196, 1982.

Perrenoud, P. 'De quoi la réussite scolaire est-elle faite?' *Education et recherche*, 1, 1985, pp. 133–60.

Perrenoud, P. and Montandon, C. *Entre parents et enseignants: un dialogue impossible?* Lang, Berne, 1987.

Perret-Clermont, A.-N. *La Construction de l'intelligence dans l'interaction sociale*. Lang, Berne, 1979.

Pijl, S. J. 'Individual educational plans in Dutch special education: so far, so good?' (mimeo). Paper presented at the 5th International Conference on Learning Disabilities. San Francisco, October 1983.

Plomp, T., van Deursen, K., and Moonen, K. (eds). *CAL for Europe*. North-Holland, Amsterdam, 1987.

Plowden Report: see Department of Education and Science, 1967.

Plowden, J.B. Presidential address at annual conference of Pre-school Playgroups Association (mimeo), 8 April 1973.

Postlethwaite, N. A selection from the overall findings of the IEA study in science, reading, comprehension, literature, French as a foreign language, English as a foreign language, and civic education. IIEP *Occasional papers* No. 30, Paris, 1974.

Postlethwaite, N. (ed.) *Encyclopedia of comparative education and national systems of education*. Pergamon Press, Oxford, 1988.

Pritchard, R. M. O. 'An analytical bibliography on the theory and practice of educational information networks', in G. Psacharadopoulos (ed.) *Information: an essential factor in educational planning and policy*. UNESCO, Paris, 1980.

Pritchard, R.M.O. 'Pupil and parent representation in Ireland and Germany', *Comparative education*, 3, 1981, p. 283.

Purkey, S.C. and Smith, M.S. 'Effective schools: a review', *Elementary school journal*, 83, 4, 1983.

Putnam, R.W. 'Special education: some cross-national comparisons', *Comparative education*, 15, 1979, pp. 83–98.

Raven, J. *Parents, teachers and children: a study of an educational home visiting scheme*. Scottish Council for Research in Education, Edinburgh, 1980, pp. 89f, 163f.

Richmond, P.E. (ed.) *New trends in integrated science. Vol. 1. 1969–70*. UNESCO, Paris, 1971.

Roberts, J.M. *Skabelsen af én verden ca. 1500 - ca. 1800*. Forums Verdenshistorie, Forum, København, 1982.

Roebbelen, J. *Zum Problem des Elternrechts*. Heidelberg, 1966.

Rupp, J.C.C. 'Niederlande', in K. Schleicher (ed.) *Elternhaus und Schule: Kooperation ohne Erfolg*. Schwann, Düsseldorf, 1972.

Sanger, C. 'Review of software package WEST', *The computing teacher*, 15, 8, 1988, pp. 53–5.

Sass, J. and Holzmueller, H. 'Bildungsverhalten und Belastungen in Familien mit schulpflichtigen Kindern: Ergebnisse einer empirischen Befragung "Familie und Plazierung"'. DJI, München, 1977.

Schleicher, K. 'Elternhaus und Schule in England' and 'Elternhaus und Schule in den vereinigten Staaten von Amerika', in K. Schleicher (ed.) *Elternhaus und Schule: Kooperation ohne Erfolg*. Schwann, Düsseldorf, 1972, pp. 85ff, 195ff, 207f.

Schleicher, K. 'Elternmitwirkung in der Eingangsstufe des Primarbereichs', in *Deutscher Bildungsrat: Gutachten und Studien der Bildungskommission: die Eingangsstufe des Primarbereichs*. Vol. 3. Stuttgart, 1975, p. 231.

Schmuck, R. A. and Miles, M. B. *Organizational development in schools*. University Associates, La Jolla, Calif., 1971.

Schon, D. *Beyond the stable state*. Temple Smith, London, 1971.

Schon, A. D. 'A review of "the federal role in curriculum development"', *Educational policy and analysis*, 3, 5, 1981, pp. 55–61.

Schools Council. *Young school leavers*. Enquiry I. HMSO, London, 1968, p. 43.

Schools Council. *Science 5/13 Publication Series*. Macdonald Educational, London, 1975.

Schultze, W. *Schools in Europe* (revised edition). Verlag Julius Beltz, Weinheim/Berlin, 1968.

Schweizerische Studiengruppe. 'Zusammenarbeit Eltern–Lehrer–Schulbehörden; die Situation der Elternvereine in der Schweiz' (mimeo). Ergebnisse einer Unfrage, durchgeführt in Jan. 1979. 1980, pp. 27, 45ff, 72.

Schweizerische Studiengruppe. 'Zusammenarbeit Eltern–Lehrer–Schulbehörden: Modelle und Modellelemente der Zusammenarbeit zwischen Lehrern, Schulbehörden und der Elterngruppe' (mimeo). Dokumentation der Tagung vom 13–14 Nov. 1982. 1982.

Seashore-Louis, K. and Van Velzen, W. 'Politics for school improvement: a comparative analysis of four policy issues'. Paper presented at the meeting of the International School Improvement Project. OECD, Toronto, 19–25 October 1986.

Seiber, S. D. 'Images of the practitioner and strategies for educational change', *Sociology of education*, 45, 1972, pp. 45–8.

Seipp, P. and Haugg, W. (eds). *Schulrecht: ergänzbare Sammlung der Vorschritten für Schule und Schulverwaltung in Hessen*. Loseblattsammlung, Berlin, 1954, pp. 29ff.

Sexton, P. C. *Education and income: inequalities of opportunity in our public schools*. New York, 1961.

Sharrock, A. N. *Home and school relations*. London, 1970.

Shorter, E. *The making of the modern family*. Basic Books, New York, 1975.

Shuck, A., Ulsh, F. L. and Platt, J. S. 'Parents encourage pupils (PEP): an inner-city parent involvement reading project', *Reading teacher*, 6, 1983, pp. 524ff.

Simon, J. 'Who's failing the failures?' *Special children*, November 1986, pp. 10–12.

SIPRI (ed.) *Die Vorbereitung der Lehrer auf die Pflege der Elternkontakte in Lehrerausbildung, Lehrerfortbildung und Junglehrerbetreuung; Resultate einer Erhebung bei den Institutionen der Primarlehrerausbildung, der Junglehrerbetreuung und der Lehrerfortbildung in der Schweiz.* Werkstattbericht 2, Genf (Switzerland), 1983, pp. 9ff, 13, 16, 20, 29ff.

SIPRI IV. *Famille-école. Compte-rendu d'experiences vécues.* CDIP, Genève, 1986.

SLO. 'Natuuronderwijs in Grote Lijnen' (mimeo). Enschede (Neths), 1988.

Söderbergh, R. *Reading in early childhood: a linguistic study of a preschool child's gradual acquisition of reading ability.* Georgetown University Press, Washington, DC, 1977.

Söderbergh, R. *Barnets tidiga språkutveckling.* Liber Förlag, Stockholm, 1979.

Söderbergh, R. *Barnspråksnytt - en presentation.* Report from the Second International Congress for the Study of Child Language, Vancouver, BC, 9–14 August 1981. Stockholm University, Institutionen för nordiska språk, Avdelningen för barnspråksforskning. Paper No. 9, 1982.

Söderbergh, R. 'Acquisition of spoken and written language in early childhood', in I. Kurcz, G. W. Shugar and J. H. Danks (eds) *Knowledge and language.* North-Holland, Amsterdam, 1986, pp. 629–66.

Sonesson, I. 'TV - en trussel eller en hjælp for børn?' *Læsepædagogen*, 35, 5, 1987, pp. 217–22.

SOU. Statens Offentliga Utredningar. *Fler kvinnor som skolledare*, 1980: 19. Utbildningsdepartementet, Stockholm, 1980.

Stangvik, Q. 'Learning disabilities in Norway', *Remedial education*, 13, 1, 1978, pp. 26–38.

Stanovich, K. E. 'Matthew effects in reading: some consequences of individual differences in the acquisition of literacy', *Reading research quarterly*, XXI, 4, 1986, pp. 360–407.

Stanovich, K.E. '"Matthæus-tendensen" - hvorfor? - og hvad kan der gøres?' *Læserapport*, 16–17, Landsforeningen af Læsepædagoger, København, 1988.

Stegö, N. E., Gielen, K., Glatter, R. and Hord, S. M. (eds). *The role of school leaders in school improvement.* ISIP–OECD. ACCO, Leuven (Belgium), 1987.

Suessmuth, R. 'Partizipation in westeuropäischen Schulsystemen', *Bildung und Erziehung*, 4, 1973, pp. 245ff.

Sundblad, B. Dominkovic, K. and Allard, B. *LUS - en bok om läsutveckling.* Liber Utbildningsförlaget, Stockholm, 1981.

Sutherland, R. 'What are the links between variable in LOGO and variable in Algebra?', in N. Balacheff (ed.) *Recherches en didactique des mathématiques.* Editions La Pensée Sauvage, Grenoble, 1987.

Sutton, A. 'Thoroughly perfectible pupils', *Times educational supplement*, 14 October 1988.

Sweller, J. 'Cognitive load during problem solving: effects of learning', *Cognitive science*, 12, 1988, pp. 257–85.

Task Group on Assessment and Testing (TGAT). *The national curriculum: Report* and *Three supplementary reports*. Department of Education and Science, London, 1988.

Taylor, K. W. 'How parents contribute to curriculum-making in the United States', in *Yearbook of Education*. Evans, London, 1958, pp. 430ff.

Taylor Report: see Department of Education and Science, 1977.

Tingsten, H. *Gud och fosterlandet. Studier i hundra års skolpropaganda*. P. A. Norstedt & Söners Förlag, Stockholm, 1969.

Tite, H. C. 'Play with literacy: a home–school liaison project to support school beginners', in P. Smith (ed.) *Parents and teachers together*. Macmillan, London, 1987, pp. 122ff.

Tizard, B., Mortimore, J. and Burchell, B. *Involving parents in nursery and infant schools: a source book for teachers*. London, 1981.

Tizard, B., Blatchford, D., Burke, J., Farquhar, C. and Plewis, I. *Young children at school in the inner city*. Lawrence Erlbaum Associates, Hove (England) and London, 1988.

Touraine, A. 'Les Jeunes et l'école', in Rectorat de Grenoble, *Les Jeunes, l'école, la société*. CNDP/CRDP, Grenoble (France), 1986.

UNESCO. *World illiteracy at mid-century*. UNESCO, Paris, 1957.

UNESCO. *New trends in integrated science education*. Vols 1–5. UNESCO, Paris, 1971–8.

UNESCO. *Economic aspects of special education: Czechoslovakia; New Zealand; USA*. UNESCO, Paris, 1978.

UNESCO. *New trends in primary school science education*. UNESCO, Paris, 1983.

UNESCO. *The training of primary science educators: a workshop approach*. Document No. 13. UNESCO, Paris, 1985.

UNESCO. *Primary education in Cyprus*. Consultancy Report, Ed. 154.722.1. UNESCO, Paris, 1988a.

UNESCO. *Primary science teacher training for process-based learning*. Report of Workshop held in Barbados, 31 August–9 September. Commonwealth Secretariat/UNESCO, 1988b.

Van de Kaa, D. 'Demographic change and social policy: a European perspective', in M. Buxton and E. Craven (eds) *The uncertain future: demographic change and social policy*. 1976, pp. 62f.

Vandenberghe, R. 'Teacher's role in educational change', *British journal of inservice education*, 11, 1, 1984, pp. 14–25.

Vandenberghe, R. 'School improvement: a European perspective', in F. W. Parkay (ed.) *Improving schools for the 21st century: implications from research and development*. Research and Development Center on School Improvement, University of Florida, Gainsville, Florida, 1988.

Van der Eyken, W. *The education of three-to-eight year olds in Europe in the Eighties*. NFER-Nelson, Slough (UK), 1982 (for Chapter 4.1, p. 158).

Van Ham, P. 'De wet medezeggenschap onderwijs en de plaats van de ouder', *Kontakt*, 3, 1983, pp. 9f.

van Lehn, K. 'Bugs are not enough: empirical studies of bugs, impasses and repairs in procedural skills', *Journal of mathematical behaviour*, 3, 1982, pp. 3–72.

Van Velzen, W. *Developing an autonomous school*. Dutch Council for Catholic Education, The Hague, 1979.

Van Velzen, W. G., Miles, M. B., Ekholm, M., Hameyer, U. and Robin, D. *Making school improvement work: a conceptual guide to practice*. (ISIP Book, 1). ACCO, Leuven (Belgium), 1985.

Vellutino, F. R. 'Dyslexia', *Scientific American*, 256, 3, 1987, pp. 20–7.

Vogel, W. *Die Beziehungen zwischen Elternhaus und Schule in Industrielländern*. Zürich, 1980.

von Hentig, H. 'Eine Bildungspolitik ohne Experimentalaufträge ist tot', *Pädagogik heute*, 1987.

Warnock Report: see Department of Education and Science, 1978a.

Wijnstra, J. M. 'Referral of minority children to special education in Holland' (mimeo). Paper presented to the 7th World Congress of Applied Linguistics. Brussels, 1984.

Wittrock, M. (ed.) *Third handbook of research on teaching*. Macmillan, New York and London, 1986.

Wolfendale, S. *Parental participation in children's development and education*. London, 1983, pp. 1, 72ff.

Woodhead, M. *Pre-school education in Western Europe: issues, policies and trends. A Report of the Council of Europe's project on pre-school education*. Longman, for Council of Europe, London and New York, 1979.

Woodhead, M. *Pre-school education*. Council for Cultural Co-operation. Council of Europe, Strasbourg, 1981.

Zubke, F. R. *Eltern und politische Arbeit. Zur politischen Funktion elterlicher Beteiligung in der Institution Schule*. Stuttgart, 1980, pp. 54f.

Zucman, E. 'Early childhood programme for the handicapped in France', *Journal of the division for early childhood*, 9, 3, 1985, pp. 237–45.

CDCC, etc., documentation additional to items included in Appendix 2

Adams, F. *General report: workshop on computers and science in primary education* <DECS/Rech [84] 58>. (See also Appendix 2, D)

AVT (Netherlands) *Lessons from practice: The Primary Education Act reviewed*. Working document distributed to participants to Project No. 8 Symposium in Noordwijkerhout, The Netherlands, 1988.

ATD Quart-Monde International Movement. *The relationship between the primary school and underprivileged families*. Report submitted to Project No. 8, 1985 <DECS/EGT [85] 21>.

Baio, V. Report in M. Leurin, *Querying the intercultural approach* <DECS/EGT [85] 34> pp. 10–14.

Beeler, A. *The natural scientific aspects of man and environment in the curriculum of primary schools* <DECS/Rech [84] 31>.

Blanc, E. *General report: workshop on the renewal of mathematics teaching in primary education* <DECS/Rech [84] 30>.

Cardinet, J. *Evaluation of mathematics teaching in primary schools in French-speaking Switzerland* <DECS/Rech [84] 10>.

Cetinsoy, M. 'Case study on Hajitkoum migrant cultural action group Brussels'. CDCC Project No. 7. *The education and cultural development of migrants* <DECS/EGT [83]>.

Commission of the European Communities. 'The school and the family in the European community' (mimeo). Report on the proceedings of the EEC School and Family Conference, Luxembourg, 23–25 March 1983, pp. 5f.

Compagnoni, E. 'Case study on relations between Italian parents' organisations and schools in the canton of Zürich'. CDCC Project No. 7. *The education and cultural development of migrants* <DECS/EGT [82]>.

Conference of Directors of Education Research Institutions. *Report*. Council of Europe, Eger (Hungary), 1986 <MED 15 HF 52>. (See also <DECS/Rech [86] 75>.)

Council for Cultural Co-operation (ed.) *Towards closer collaboration between the home and the school: a pilot project in Norwegian compulsory basic school* <DECS/EGT [83] 51>.

Council for Cultural Co-operation. *Compendium of information on intercultural education schemes in Europe* <DECS/EGT [83] 62>.

Council for Cultural Co-operation (ed.) *European teachers' seminar on 'Bullying in schools'* <DECS/EGT [88] 5-E>.

Council of Europe Memorandum. *Innovation in primary education* <CDCC [87] 53>.

Dieschbourg, R. *The use of microcomputers in primary schools in Bar-le-Duc, France* <DECS/EGT [84] 10>. (See also Appendix 2, C6.)

Duval, J. *Pupils' spontaneous ideas in learning of science: the case of light*. Paper presented to Educational Research Workshop on *Child development in the primary school*. Madrid, 1985 <DECS/Rech [85] 60>. (See also Appendix 2, D.)

Educational Research Workshops: see Duval, J., Gordon, A.

Eriksson, S. *The improvement of creative and aesthetic skills of children through art and drama in the city of Athens*. Report on Case-Study in Maraslios Elementary Schools. 1985 <DECS/EGT [85] 56>. (See also Appendix 2, C8.)

European Teachers' Seminar. *The role of the head teacher in innovation*. CDCC, Strasbourg, 1986 <DECS/EGT [86] 72>. (See also Appendix 2, A.)

Fox, G. T. *Challenging how teachers are educated: a source for dialogue and action*. Committee of Senior Officials, Council of Europe, 1985 <MED 15 HF 28>.

Fyfe, A. J. *Possible uses of computers in primary education: the United Kingdom example* <DECS/Rech [84] 34>.

Gjone, G. *New mathematics for the primary school* <DECS/Rech [84] 12>.

Goffree, G. *The teaching of mathematics in primary schools from the perspective of the initial training of teachers in the Netherlands* <DECS/Rech [84] 16>.

Gordon, A. *Learning processes (and obstacles) of science pupils aged 6–14*. Paper presented to Educational Research Workshop on *Science and computers in primary education*, Edinburgh, 1984 <DECS/DECM [84] 33>. (See also Appendix 2, D: <DECS/Rech [84] 58; DECS/EGT [84] Misc. 34>.)

Habran, L. *Renewal of mathematics teaching in primary schools in French-speaking Belgium* <DECS/Rech [84] 16>.

Huart, M. *Case study on cooperation between Portuguese-speaking community, school and the Dutch authorities in Rotterdam and Amsterdam*. CDCC Project No. 7. *The education and cultural development of migrants* <DECS/EGT [82] 10>.

Ingeborgrued, A. O. *Reflections on home-school links in the future*. Paper presented at European Teachers' Course of the CDCC's Teacher Bursaries Scheme, Kristiansand, 11 August 1984, p. 13.

Jensen, J. C. *The renewal of mathematics teaching in primary education in Denmark* <DECS/Rech [84] 28>.

Jensen, J. C. *The new technologies and the primary school* <DECS/EGT [86] 48>.

Kananoja, T. *The school and home collaboration in Finland*. Paper prepared for the European Teachers' Course of the CDCC's Teacher Bursaries Scheme, Kristiansand, 12 August 1984.

Kopmels, D. 'School improvement from within', in *Final Report* of Project No. 8, 1987 <DECS/EGT [87] 34 = CDCC (88) 15>.

Kratochwil, L. *Parent-school relationship at the primary level of the basic school in Norway*. Report on Vest-Agder county, Norway, 1985 <DECS/EGT [85] 65>. (See also Appendix 2, C11.)

Kriszten, A. *Procedures for writing primary school textbooks in the Canton of Zürich* <DECS/Rech [84] 13>.

Lauter, J. *Developments in the field of mathematics teaching in primary schools* <DECS/Rech [84] 20>.

Le Bras, H. *Child and family: demographic developments in the OECD countries*. OECD, CERI, Paris, 1979, p. 159.

Leurin, M. *Querying the intercultural approach?* CDCC, Strasbourg, 1985 <DECS/EGT [85] 34>.

Lithman, Y. G. *For better or worse*. Report submitted to Project No. 7 on *The education and cultural development of migrants*, 1985 <DECS/EGT [85] 13>.

Lundgren, U. P. *New challenges for teachers and their schools*. Report prepared for 15th session of CDCC, 1987 <MED 15 NF 39>, p. 9.

Minaly, O. *New challenges for the school and for teachers: an attempt for interpretation of problems* <DECS/Rech [86] 61>.

Neave, G. *New challenges for teachers and their education: national reports of education*. Standing Conference of European Ministers of Education, 1987 <MED 15–4>.

Olmos, A. 'Case study of Swiss migrant joint associations'. CDCC Project No. 7. *Education and cultural development of migrants* <DECS/EGT [83] 5>.

Petite, J. *Expectations at secondary level and trends in primary education in Europe*. Report submitted on behalf of FIPESO to Project No. 8, 1985 <DECS/EGT [85] 64>.

Project No. 8. *Final Report* 1987 <DECS/EGT [87] 23>.

Rey, M. *Training teachers in intercultural education?* CDCC, Strasbourg, 1986.

Robert, F. *Possible use of computers in primary education – the example of France* <DECS/Rech [84] 32>.

Sannes, M. *The needs of school children at home and at school*. Paper presented at European Teachers' Course of the CDCC's Teacher Bursaries Scheme, Kristiansand, 7 August 1984.

Schleicher, K. *Preparation for family life*. CDCC Project No. 1. *Preparation for family life*. Council of Europe, Strasbourg, 1982, p. 6.

Schleicher, K. *Co-operation between school and family: prerequisites; implementations; problems*. Document submitted to Project No. 8, 1985 <DECS/EGT [85] 58>.

Symposium on *The intercultural training of teachers* (L'Aquila). Strasbourg, 1982 <DECS/EGT [82] 61>.

Symposium on *Science and technology in the primary school*. Cambridge (England), 1986 <DECS/EGT [86] 59>. (See also Appendix 2, A.)

Vandenberghe, R. 'The process of innovation: an exploratory analysis', in *Final Report* of Project No. 8 <DECS/EGT [87] 23 = CDCC (88) 13>.

van der Hoven, G. and Kopmels, D. 'Main curriculum conclusions to Project No. 8: Innovation in primary education'. Addendum to Appendix IV in *Final Report* of Project No. 8 <DECS/DECM [84] 33>. (See also <DECS/EGT [87] 23>.)

van der Klauw, C. F. *Final report: interactive learning and the new technologies* <DECS/Rech [87] 31>.

Verhagen, P. W. *Interactive learning with the new technologies; when will it be successful?* <DECS/Rech [87] 26>.

WCOTP. Conference of Senior Officials, World Confederation of Organisations of the Teaching Profession, *Recommendations on new challenges for teachers and teacher education.* Council of Europe, Strasbourg, 1986 <MED 15 HF 52>.

WCOTP (World Confederation of Organisations of the Teaching Profession). Report: *New technologies and the training of teachers.* Council for Cultural Co-operation, Strasbourg, 1986 <CDCC [86] 28>.

Vandenberghe, R. 'The process of innovation: an exploratory analysis', in *Final Report of Project No. 8* <DECS/EGT (88) 12> <DECS (88) [illegible]>

van der Hoven, G. and Koning, [illegible] Mate curriculum [illegible] innovation in primary education [illegible] in *Final Report of Project No. 8* <DECS/EGT/M (8[illegible]) 23> (see also <DECS/EGT (8[illegible]) 23 [illegible]>)

van der Klauw, J. F. [illegible] *Toward interactive learning and the new technology?* <DECS/Rech (87) 21>

Verheijen, P. N. *Interactive learning with the new technology: when will it be successful?* <DECS/Rech (87) [illegible]>

WCOTP Conference of Senior Officials, World Confederation of Organisations of the Teaching Profession, *Recommendations on new challenges for teachers and teacher education*, Council of Europe, Strasbourg, 1986, <MED-15-HF 52>

WCOTP (World Confederation of Organisations of the Teaching Profession) Report: *New technologies and the training of teachers*, Council for Cultural Co-operation, Strasbourg, 1986 <DECS (86) [illegible]>